STREET ATLAS

Glasgow

& West Central Scotland

Contents

IV *Key to maps*

VI *Administrative boundaries*

1 *Street maps*

240 *Index explanation and abbreviations*

241 *Index of towns, villages and rural localities*

242 *Index of street names*

PHILIP'S

First edition published 1995
Reprinted 1996 by

Ordnance Survey   and   George Philip Ltd.
Romsey Road   an imprint of Reed Books
Maybush   Michelin House, 81 Fulham Road, London, SW3 6RB
Southampton SO16 4GU   and Auckland, Melbourne, Singapore and Toronto

ISBN 0-540-06185-9 (pocket)

© Crown copyright 1995

All rights reserved. No part of this publication may be reproduced, stored in a retrieval
system or transmitted, in any form or by any means, electronic, mechanical,
photocopying, recording or otherwise, without the permission of the Publishers and the
copyright owner.

To the best of the Publishers' knowledge, the information in this atlas was correct at
the time of going to press. No responsibility can be accepted for any errors or their
consequences.

The representation in this atlas of a road, track or path is no evidence of the existence
of a right of way.

**The mapping between pages 1 and 239 (inclusive) in this atlas is derived from
Ordnance Survey® OSCAR® Land-Line® data, and Landranger® mapping.**

Ordnance Survey, OSCAR, Land-Line and Landranger are registered trade marks of
Ordnance Survey, the National Mapping Agency of Great Britain.

Printed in England by Cox and Wyman Ltd., Reading, Berkshire

Key to map symbols

⊜	**British Rail station**
⊖	**Underground station**
(ⓡ)	**Private railway station**
⬤	**Bus or coach station**
(H)	**Heliport**
◆	**Police station** (may not be open 24 hours)
✚	**Hospital with casualty facilities** (may not be open 24 hours)
☐	**Post office**
✛	**Place of worship**
◣	**Important building**
P	**Parking**
174	**Adjoining page indicator**
✕	**No adjoining page**
▬▬	**Motorway**
▬▬	**Dual carriageway**
══	**Main or through road**
A27	**Road numbers** (Department of Transport)
⊤	**Gate or obstruction to traffic** (restrictions may not apply at all times or to all vehicles)
- - - -	**All paths, bridleways, BOAT's, RUPP's, dismantled railways, etc.**
══	**Track**

The representation in this atlas of a road, track or path is no evidence of the existence of a right of way

Amb Sta	**Ambulance Station**	LC	**Level crossing**
Amb Dpo	**Ambulance Depot**	Liby	**Library**
Coll	**College**	Mus	**Museum**
FB	**Footbridge**	Acad	**Academy**
F Sta	**Fire Station**	Sch	**School**
Hospl	**Hospital**	TH	**Town Hall or Town House**

0	¼	½	¾	1 mile
0	250m 500m	250m	1 Kilometre	

The scale of the maps is approximately 2¹/₂ inches to 1 mile (1:25497)

The small numbers around the edges of the maps identify the 1 kilometre National Grid lines

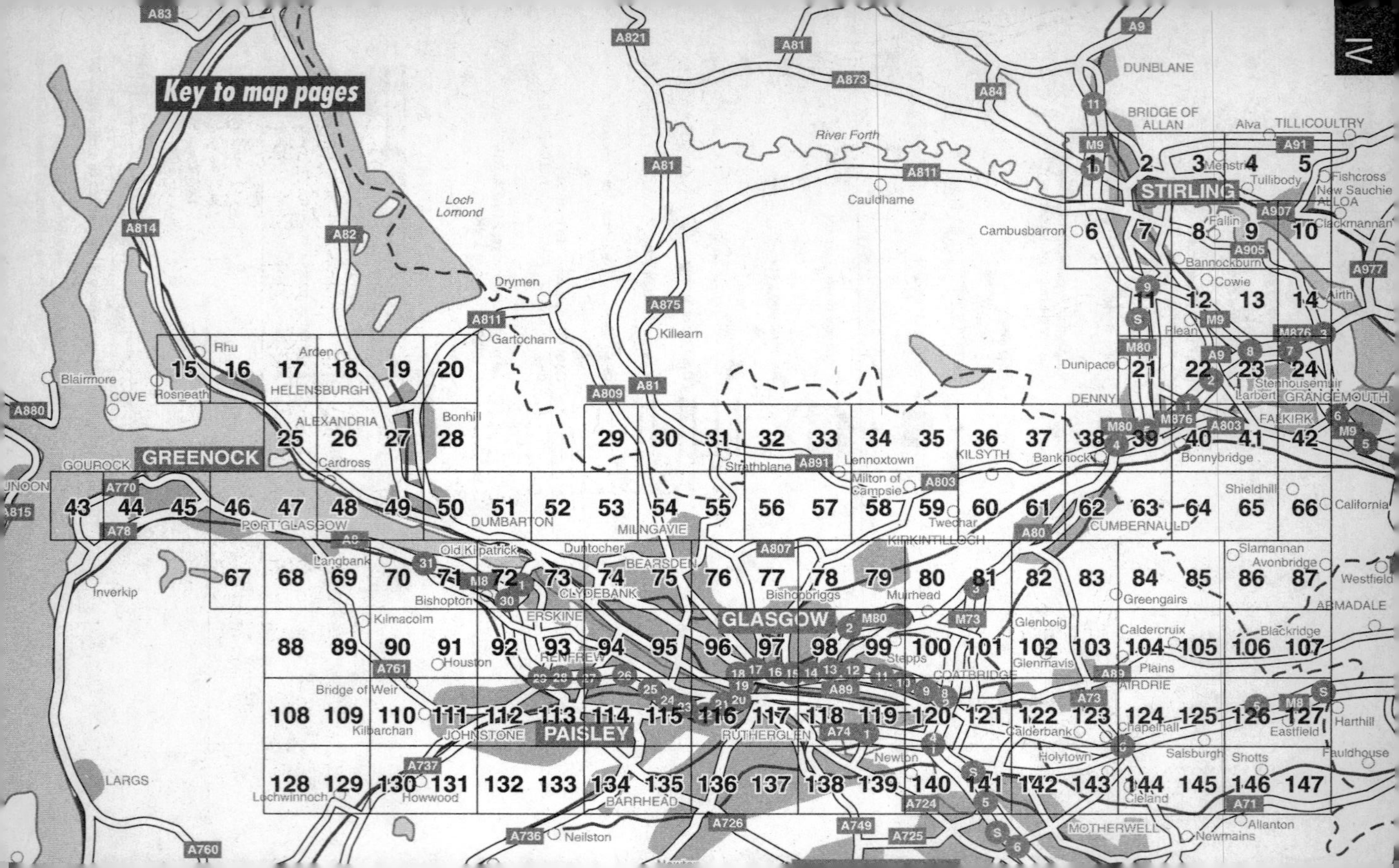

Key to map pages

STIRLING

DUNBLANE

BRIDGE OF ALLAN

TILLICOULTRY

GRANGEMOUTH

FALKIRK

ARMADALE

CUMBERNAULD

KILSYTH

AIRDRIE

MOTHERWELL

GLASGOW

PAISLEY

RUTHERGLEN

BARRHEAD

JOHNSTONE

DUMBARTON

CLYDEBANK

BEARSDEN

MILNGAVIE

ALEXANDRIA

HELENSBURGH

PORT GLASGOW

GREENOCK

GOUROCK

LARGS

Loch Lomond

River Forth

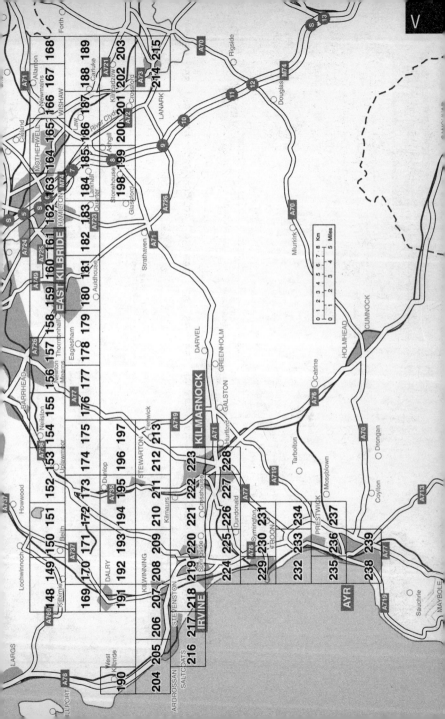

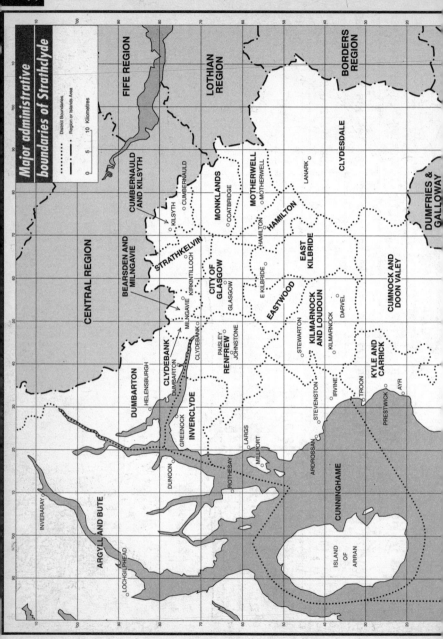

Major administrative boundaries of Strathclyde

District Boundaries
Region or Islands Area

0   5   10 Kilometres

FIFE REGION

LOTHIAN REGION

BORDERS REGION

CENTRAL REGION

CUMBERNAULD AND KILSYTH
○ KILSYTH
○ CUMBERNAULD

BEARSDEN AND MILNGAVIE

STRATHKELVIN
○ KIRKINTILLOCH
○ MILNGAVIE

MONKLANDS
○ COATBRIDGE

MOTHERWELL
○ MOTHERWELL

CLYDESDALE
LANARK ○

CITY OF GLASGOW
○ GLASGOW

HAMILTON
○ HAMILTON

CLYDEBANK
○ CLYDEBANK

RENFREW
○ PAISLEY
○ JOHNSTONE

E KILBRIDE ○

EAST KILBRIDE

EASTWOOD

DUMBARTON
○ HELENSBURGH
○ DUMBARTON

INVERCLYDE
○ GREENOCK

○ LARGS
○ MILLPORT

○ ROTHESAY

DUNOON ○

ARGYLL AND BUTE
○ LOCHGILPHEAD
○ INVERARAY

KILMARNOCK AND LOUDOUN
○ STEWARTON
○ KILMARNOCK
○ DARVEL

CUMNOCK AND DOON VALEY

KYLE AND CARRICK
○ IRVINE
○ TROON
○ PRESTWICK
○ AYR

○ STEVENSTON

○ ARDROSSAN

CUNNINGHAME

ISLAND OF ARRAN

DUMFRIES & GALLOWAY

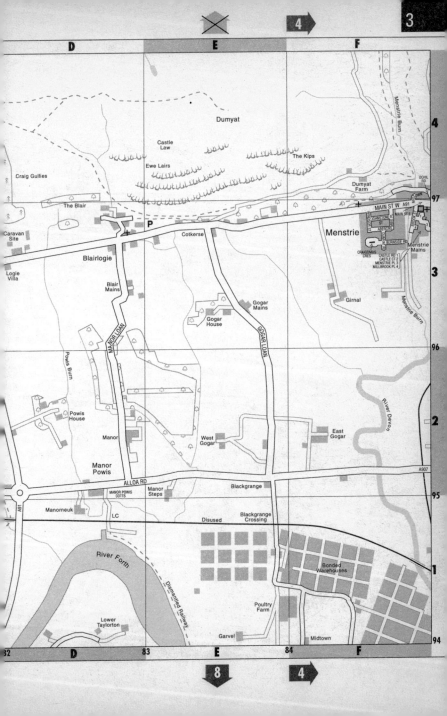

D **E** **F**

Dumyat

Castle
Law

Ewe Lairs

The Kips

Craig Gullies

Dumyat
Farm

OCHIL
RD

The Blair

97

P

MAIN ST W A91

Caravan
Site

Cotkerse

Menstrie

Blairlogie

JOHNSTONE
ST

MAIN ST E

BURNSIDE RD

ARTHUR'S

CRAIGOMUS
CRES

CASTLE RD 1
CASTLE CT 2
MENSTRIE PL 3
MILLBROOK PL 4

Logie
Villa

Blair
Mains

Menstrie
Mains

Girnal

Gogar Mains

Gogar
House

Powis Burn

3

Menstrie Burn

MANOR LOAN

GOGAR LOAN

96

River Devon

Powis
House

Manor

West
Gogar

East
Gogar

2

Manor
Powis

ALLOA RD

A907

Manor Powis
COTTS

Manor
Steps

Blackgrange

95

Manorneuk

LC

Disused

Blackgrange
Crossing

River Forth

Bonded
Warehouses

1

Dismantled Railway

Poultry
Farm

Lower
Taylorton

Garvel

Midtown

94

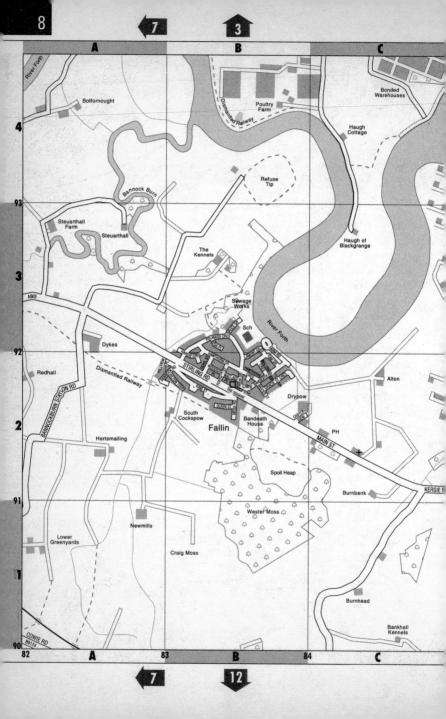

A B C

4

River Forth

Bolfornought

Dismantled Railway

Poultry Farm

Bonded Warehouses

Haugh Cottage

93

Bannock Burn

Steuarthall Farm

Steuarthall

The Kennels

Refuse Tip

Haugh of Blackgrange

3

A905

Sewage Works

River Forth

92

Dykes

Sch

Redhall

Dismantled Railway

STIRLING RD

Alton

BANNOCKBURN STATION RD

THE SQUARE

P.O.

Drypow

2

South Cockspow

Bandeath House

PH

Hartsmailing

Fallin

MAIN ST

91

Burnbank

KERSIE R

Spoil Heap

Newmills

Wester Moss

1

Lower Greenyards

Craig Moss

Burnhead

Bankhall Kennels

90

COWIE RD
B9124

82 A 83 B 84 C

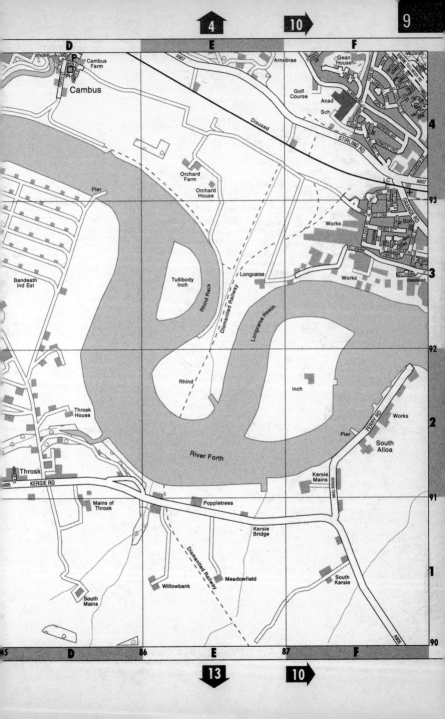

9
5

ALLOA

Clackmannan

River Forth

Dunmore Home Farm

Greenyards

Bannock Burn

Ford

Croftside

Cat Craig

Muiralehouse

MAITLAND AVE

Foot o' Green

The Pirnhall (PH)

Hillhead

Pirnhall

PIRNHALL RD

Back o' Muir

Hospl

4

Rogerhead

Junction 9

A91

Bannockburn House

Gartclush

89

Service Area

Small Burn

3

Cauldbarns

Corse Hill

Croftside Park

88

Kingsburgh

Caravan Site

Auchenbowie

Moss-side

Auchenbowie Wood

Avenue Wood

West Plean

2

Barr Wood

Auchenbowie House

Auchenbowie Burn

Avenuehead Cottage

Muir Wood

Sch

ROMAN ROAD

87

North Durieshill

Greenhill

1

Easterton

Craw Hill

Tip

86

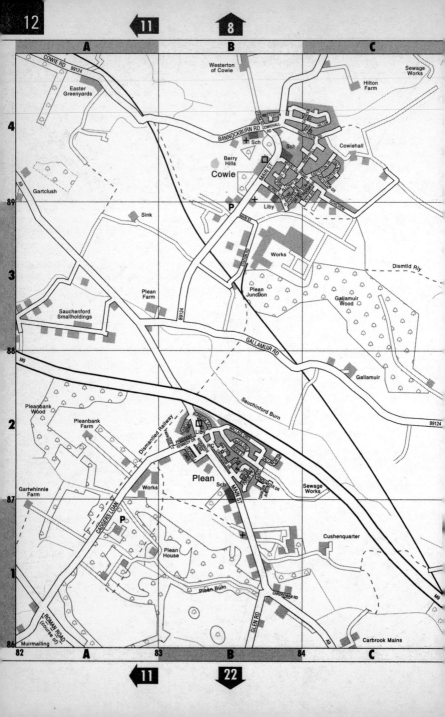

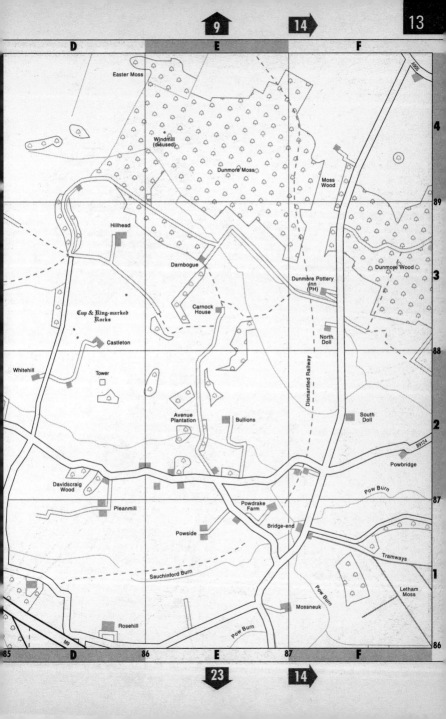

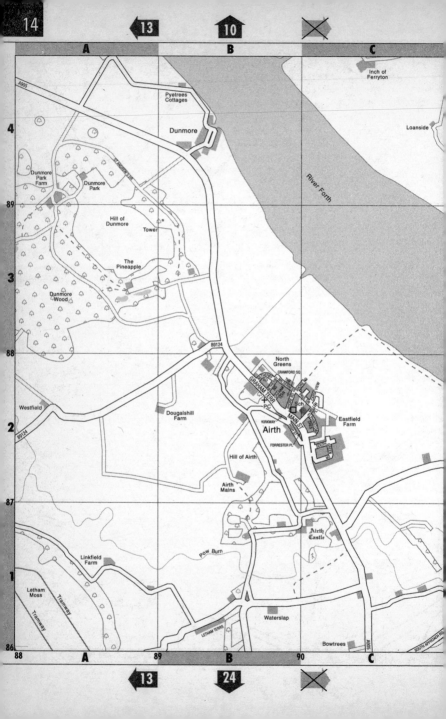

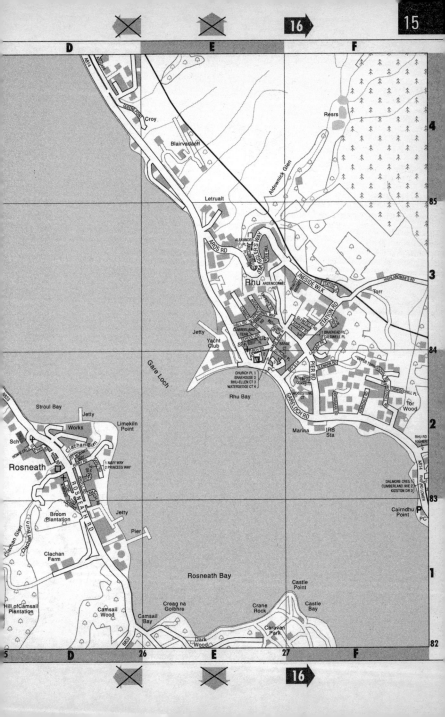

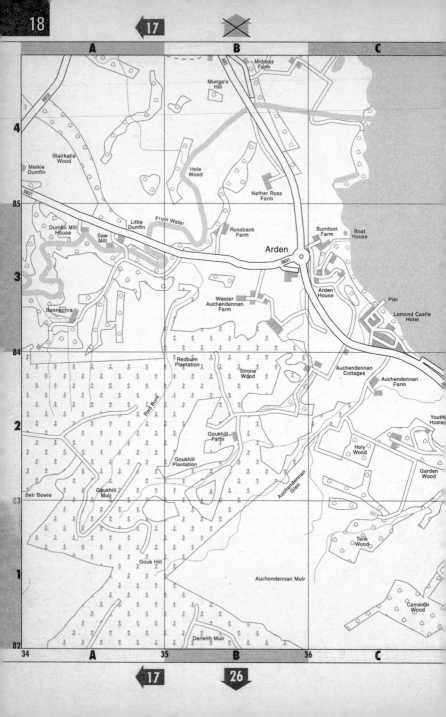

D   E   F

4

Knockour
Wood

Lorn

Knockour
Hill

Black
Roundel

85

Boat
Houses

Boturich
Castle

3

Loch Lomond

Meikle
Boturich

Whinny Hill

84

Ledrishmore
Wood

Burn of Balloch

Over
Balloch

2

Horsehouse
Wood

Stable
Wood

P

P
PCs

83

Cameron
Bay

Cameron
House

PCs

Balloch Castle
Country Park

Ledrishbeg

Cameron House
Farm

Cameron
Wildlife Park

CREINCH
DR

1 McLEAN CRES
2 HARAN RD
3 SHANDON CRES
4 SHANDON BRAE
5 DUMBAIN RD
6 HALDANE TERR

1

MOLLANBOWIE RD

Balloch
Pier

P

River Leven

P

Moss o' Balloch
Plantations

Balloch

DRYMEN RD

CARROCHAN
RD

BALLOCH RD

P

82

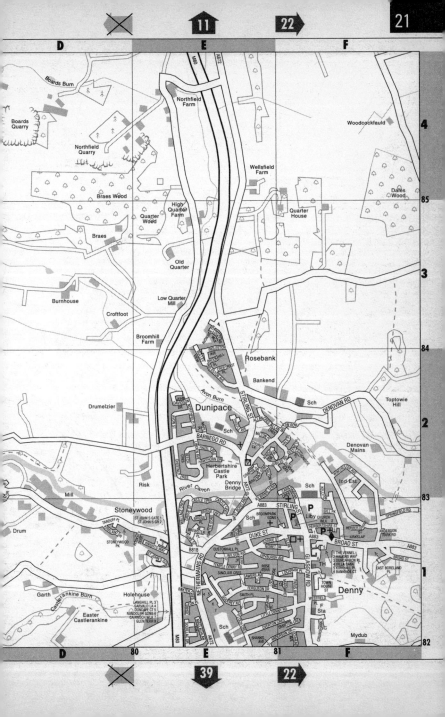

D   E   F

11   22

Boards Burn

Boards
Quarry

Northfield
Farm

Woodcockfauld

4

Northfield
Quarry

Wellsfield
Farm

Braes Wood

High
Quarter
Farm

Quarter
Wood

Quarter
House

Dales
Wood

85

Braes

Old
Quarter

3

Burnhouse

Low Quarter
Mill

Croftfoot

Broomhill
Farm

Rosebank

84

Bankend

Avon Burn

Drumelzier

Denovan Rd

Toptowie
Hill

Dunipace

Sch

2

Barnego Rd

Denovan
Mains

Herbertshire
Castle
Park

Risk

River Carron

Denny
Bridge

Sch

Ind Est

83

Mill

Stoneywood

Sch

A883   Stirling

P

Liby
Church

St John's Gate 1
St John's Gr 2

Drum

Tarduff Pl

Duke St

A883

P

Herbertshire
St

Kirkslaf

Broad St

Anderson
Park Rd

A883

Stoneywood
Pk

1 The Vennel
2 Haigers Way
3 Duncarron Pl
4 Villa Bank
5 Kirkhall Pl
6 Bankside Ct

East Boreland
Pl

Broad St

Garth

Holehouse

Castlerankine Burn

Smith Pl

Denny

Easter
Castlerankine

Langhill Pl 3
Garvald La 4
Duncard Ct 5
Randolph Gdns 6
Cairnoch Wlk 7
Glen Terr 8

Sch

F
Sta

Mydub

82

D   80   E   81   F

39   22

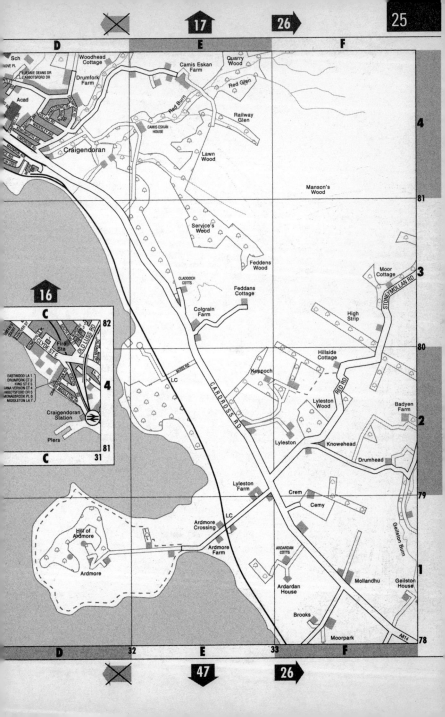

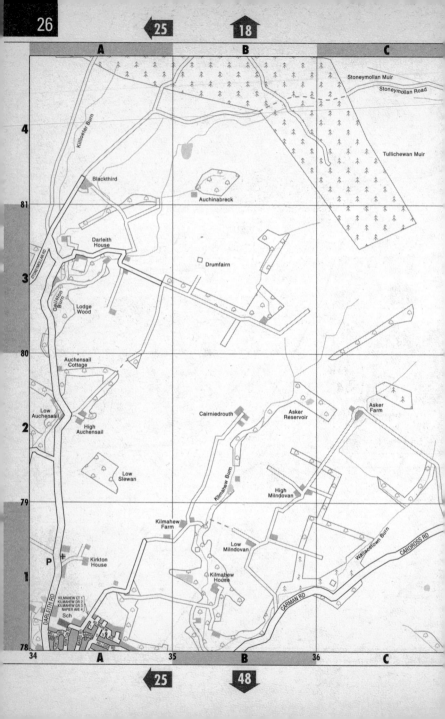

A   B   C

4

81

Stoneymollan Muir

Stoneymollan Road

Tullichewan Muir

Blackthird

Auchinabreck

Darleith House

Drumfairn

3

Gallston Burn

Lodge Wood

80

Auchensail Cottage

Low Auchensail

High Auchensail

2

Cairniedrouth

Asker Reservoir

Asker Farm

Low Slewan

Kilmahew Burn

High Milndovan

79

Kilmahew Farm

Low Milndovan

Wallacetown Burn

CARDROSS RD

P ⊞

Kirkton House

Kilmahew House

1

KILMAHEW CT 1
KILMAHEW GR 2
KILMAHEW GR 3
NAPER AVE 4

Sch

DARLEITH RD

CARMAN RD

78

34   A   35   B   36   C

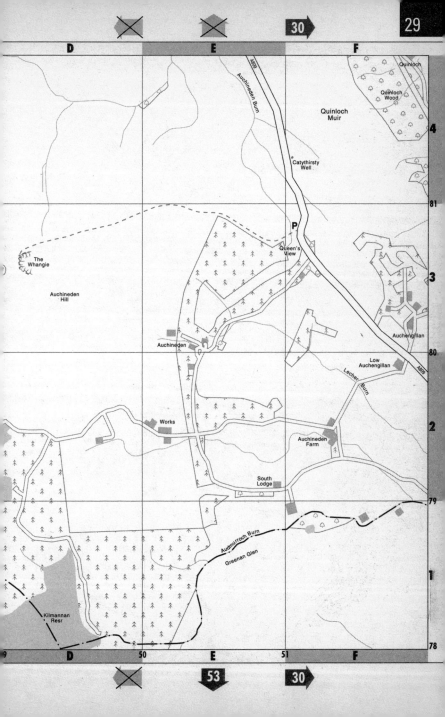

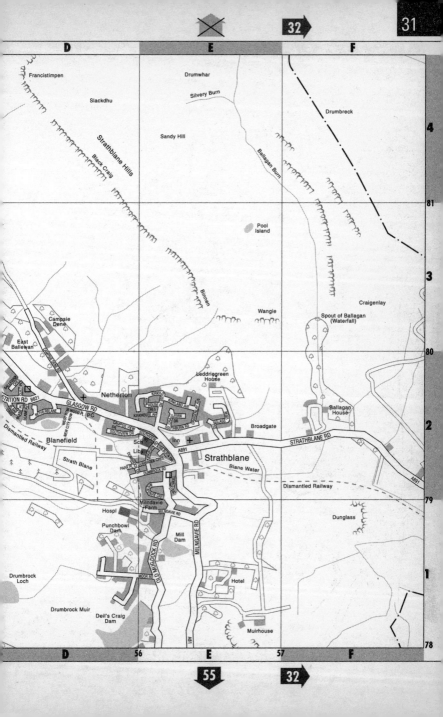

D   E   F

Francistimpen

Drumwhar

Silvery Burn

Slackdhu

Drumbreck

4

Sandy Hill

Strathblane Hills

Ballagan Burn

Black Craig

81

Pool Island

3

Binnein

Wangie

Craigenlay

Campsie Dene

Spout of Ballagan (Waterfall)

East Ballewan

80

Leddriegreen House

Netherton

Ballagan House

GLASGOW RD

KIRKHOUSE RD

Broadgate

STRATHBLANE RD

2

Dismantled Railway

Blanefield

A891

Sch

Inn

Strathblane

Strath Blane

Liby

Blane Water

A891

Dismantled Railway

79

MILNGAVIE RD

Milndavie Farm

Hospl

Dunglass

OLD MUGDOCK RD

Punchbowl Dam

Mill Dam

MILNGAVIE RD

Drumbrock Loch

1

Hotel

Drumbrock Muir

Deil's Craig Dam

A81

Muirhouse

78

D   56   E   57   F

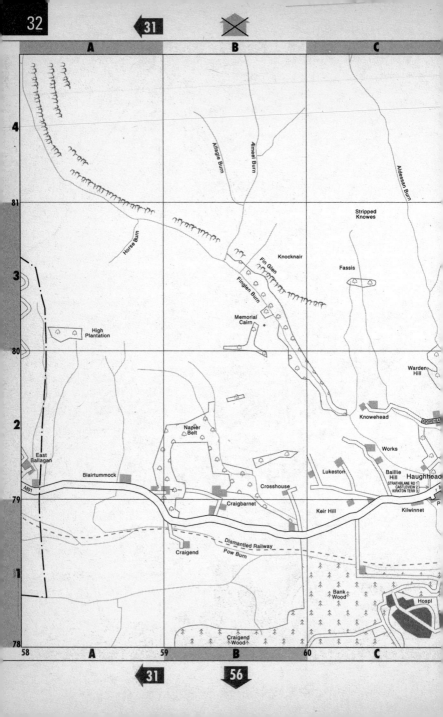

4

31

3

Allagie Burn

Almeel Burn

Aldessan Burn

Horse Burn

Stripped
Knowes

Knocknair

Fin Glen

Fassis

Finglen Burn

Memorial
Cairn

80

High
Plantation

Warden
Hill

2

Napier
Belt

Knowehead

East
Ballagan

Works

Blairtummock

Lukeston

Baillie
Hill

Haughhead

Crosshouse

STRATHBLANE RD 1
CASTLEVIEW 2
KIRKTON TERR 3

79

Craigbarnet

Keir Hill

Kilwinnet

Dismantled Railway

Craigend

Pow Burn

1

Bank
Wood

Hospl

Craigend
Wood

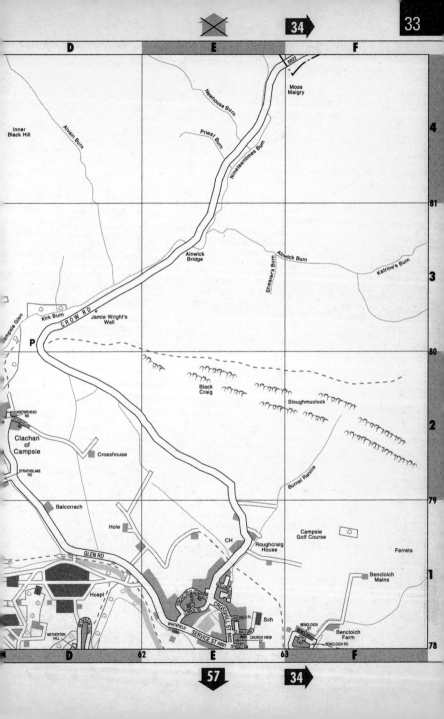

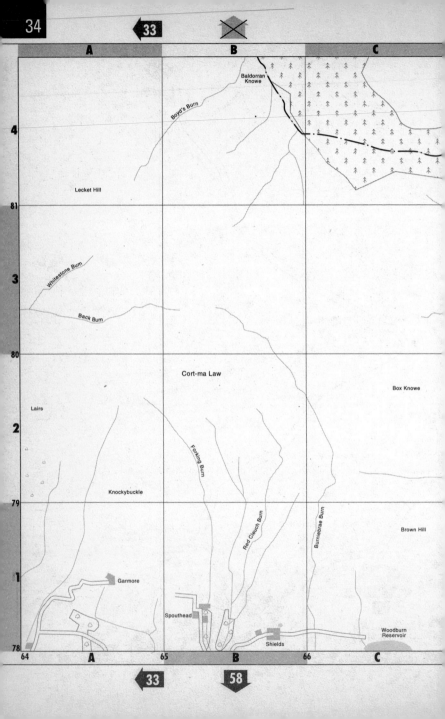

Baldorran Knowe

Boyd's Burn

Lecket Hill

Whitestone Burn

Back Burn

Cort-ma Law

Box Knowe

Lairs

Folking Burn

Knockybuckle

Red Cleuch Burn

Burniebrae Burn

Brown Hill

Garmore

Spouthead

Shields

Woodburn
Reservoir

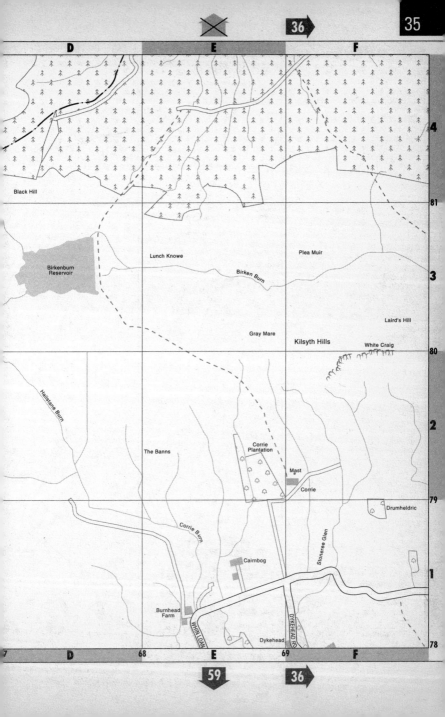

A   B   C

Tappetknowe
Leysbent
Leys
Castlerankine
Linns
4
Rashiehill
Castlerankine Burn
Glenhead
Drumbowie
Reservoir
81
Bottomhead
Bottomhead
Reservoir
Bowridge
3
Whitehill
Easter
Wairds
Craigs
Plantation
Braeface
80
Cowden
Hill
Tomfyne
Wester
Thomaston
Junction
A80
2
Cloybank
Hotel
Banknock
Doups Burn
HOLLANDBUSH AVE
Brick
Works
Dismantled Railway
KILSYTH RD   Sch
Bog
CASTLEVIEW
TERR.
79
Orchard
Farm
West
Auchincloch
Bonny Water
Wyndford
Lock
Auchincloch
Forth and Clyde Canal
A803
Netherwood
1
WYNDFORD RD
Red Burn
B816
Works
Hirst
House
Hotel
B816
CASTLECARY RD
A80
Hirst
78
76   A   77   B   78   C

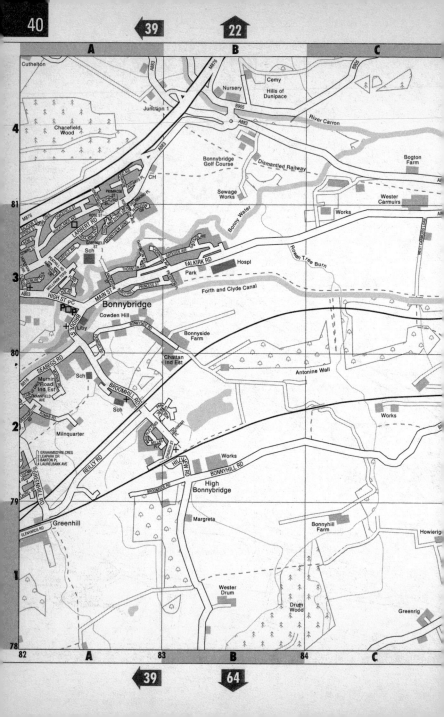

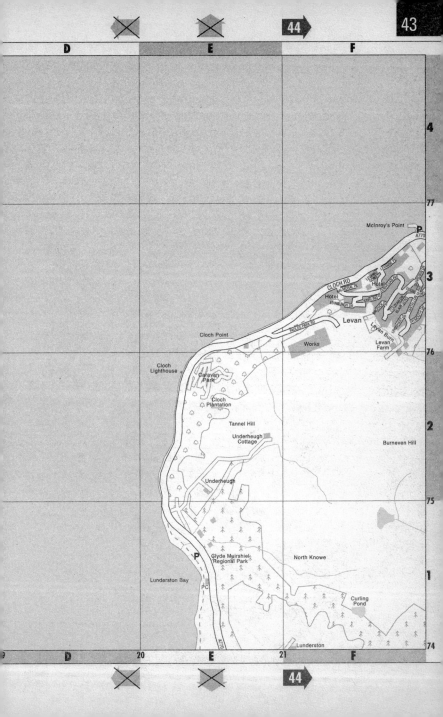

D   E   F

4

77

McInroy's Point   P

A770

CLOCH RD   Hotel

3

Hotel

Levan

Levan Burn

Cloch Point

Works

Levan Farm

76

Cloch Lighthouse

Caravan Park

Cloch Plantation

Tannel Hill

Underheugh Cottage

Burneven Hill

2

Underheugh

75

P

Glyde Muirshiel Regional Park

North Knowe

Lunderston Bay

PC

1

Curling Pond

A770

Lunderston

74

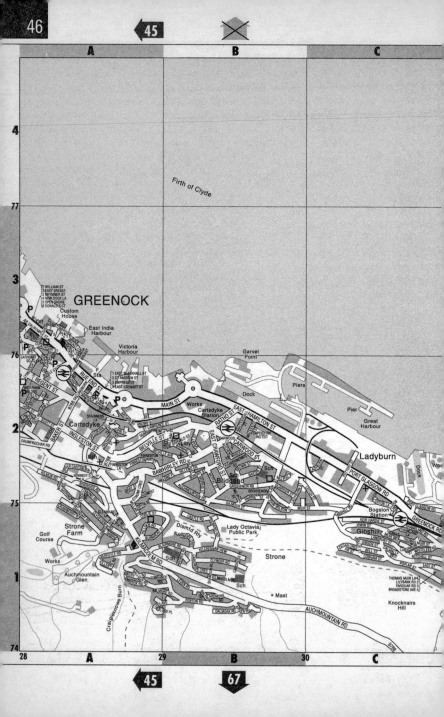

45

A · B · C

4

77

Firth of Clyde

3

1 WILLIAM ST
2 EAST BREAST
3 NEWMBER ST
4 NEW DOCK LA
5 OPEN SHORE
6 DONALD'S CT

GREENOCK

Custom House

East India Harbour

Victoria Harbour

Garvel Point

Off

P

P

P

P

CATHCART

Ry Sta

2

RUE END ST

1 EAST BLACKHALL ST
2 ST ANDREW ST
3 IMPRESS ST
4 EAST STEWART ST

REGENT ST

WELLPARK

Dock

Piers

Pier

Great Harbour

Cartsdyke

MAIN ST

Works

Cartsdyke Station

EAST HAMILTON ST

RATHO ST

CAPELDALE IND EST

STAINNERS

BELVILLE ST

ST LAWRENCE ST

2

BAKER ST

INGLESTON ST

Sch

BAWHIRLEY RD

FINNESTON

BELVILLE ST

EAST CRAWFORD ST

Lby

CARWOOD ST

CARWOOD ST

Sch

Ladyburn

Dock

Wo

DRUMFROCHAR RD

ST CATHERINE

KENNEDY'S

RIVERSIDE

Bridgend

GROSVENOR RD

ASPIRE

WEIR ST

WEIR DON

PORT GLASGOW RD

Bogston Station

GREENOCK RD

Dock

75

Golf Course

Strone Farm

GLENDRA

DUFF ST

CASTLE RD

Dismld Fly

KIRK

Lady Octavia Public Park

Strone

NEW HARBINE ST

IRWIN ST

LANGHOUSE

Gibshill

POPLAR ST

EAST S

Works

1

Auchmountain Glen

KILMACOLM RD

TORRANCE RD

KIRKBRIDGE VIEW

KILCREGGAN

MAXWELL RD

OLD MADELMIAN

KEYHOOR RD

Sch

WILLIAN

GLASS PL

BENTON RD

DALMOAK RD

Mast

MITCHELL ST

GOODMAN ST

THOMAS MUIR LA 1
LILYBANK RD 2
FARQUAR RD 3
BROADSTONE AVE 4

Knocknairs Hill

AUCHMOUNTAIN RD

Craigieknowe Burn

74

28 · A · 29 · B · 30 · C

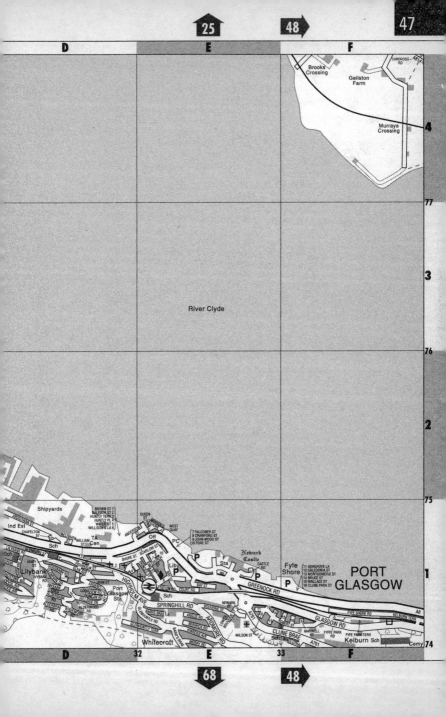

D   E   F

Brooks Crossing

Geilston Farm

CARDROSS RD

A814

Murrays Crossing

4

77

River Clyde

3

76

2

75

Shipyards

Ind Est

BROWN ST 1
BALFOUR ST 2
HUNTLY TERR 3
HUNTLY PL 4
WATER ST 5
WILLISON'S LA 6

CHAPELTON ST

Sch

WILLIAM ST

TA Cen

QUEEN ST

WEST QUAY

Off

PC

7 FALCONER ST
8 CRAWFORD ST
9 JOHN WOOD ST
10 FORE ST

SHORE ST

GLASGOW RD

Lilybank

MARY ST

Sch

LOCHVIEW RD

ALDERWOOD RD

DEAN ST

Port Glasgow Sta

Sch

SPRINGHILL RD

Liby

Sch

Sta

Newark Castle

CASTLE RD

P

Fyfe Shore

P

11 ASHGROVE LA
12 CALEDONIA ST
13 MONTGOMERIE ST
14 BRUCE ST
15 WALLACE ST
16 CLUNE PARK ST

PORT GLASGOW

1

GREENOCK RD

NEWARK

BOGLE ST

BOUVERIE ST

WILSON ST

CLUNE BRAE

A761

MAXWELL ST

Sch

FYFE PARK RD

GLASGOW RD

FYFE SHORE RD

KELBURN TERR

A8

FYFE PARK TERR

Kelburn Sch

Cemy

Whitecroft

MURDAY RD

74

D   32   E   33   F

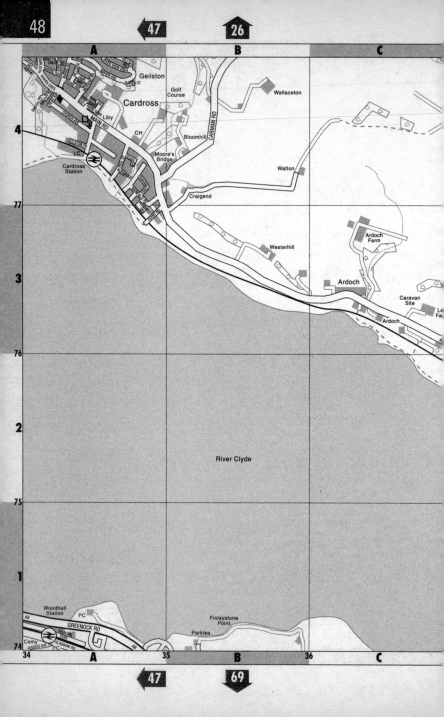

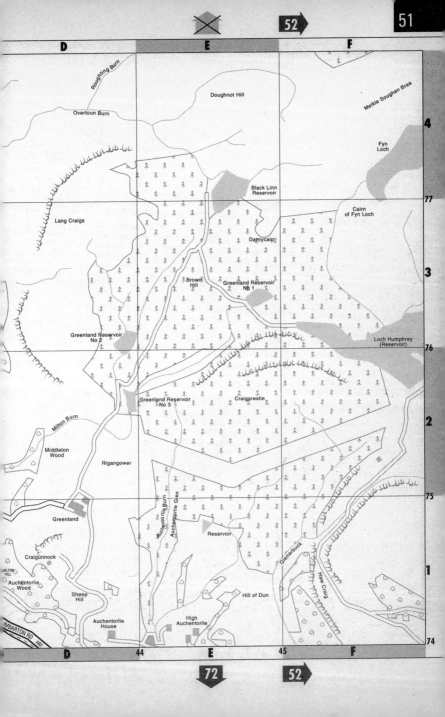

Roughting Burn

Overtoun Burn

Doughnot Hill

Meikle Soughen Brae

Fyn Loch

Black Linn Reservoir

Cairn of Fyn Loch

Lang Craigs

Darnycaip

Brown Hill

Greenland Reservoir No 1

Loch Humphrey (Reservoir)

Greenland Reservoir No 2

Greenland Reservoir No 3

Craigarestie

Milton Burn

Middleton Wood

Rigangower

Auchentorlie Burn

Auchentorlie Glen

Greenland

Reservoir

Glenarbuck

Craigunnock

MILTON HILL

Auchentorlie Wood

Sheep Hill

Hill of Dun

Haw Craig

DUMBARTON RD A82

Auchentorlie House

High Auchentorlie

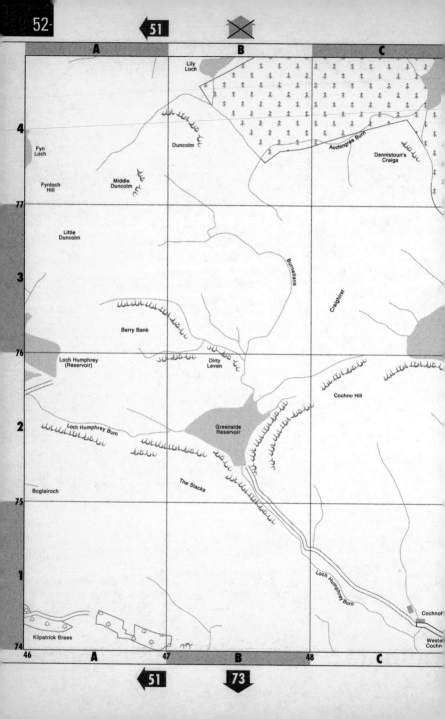

51

A   B   C

Lily
Loch

4

Fyn
Loch

Duncolm

Auchingree Burn

Dennistoun's
Craigs

Fynloch
Hill

Middle
Duncolm

77

Little
Duncolm

Burnellans

3

Craighirst

Berry Bank

76

Loch Humphrey
(Reservoir)

Dirty
Leven

Cochno Hill

2

Loch Humphrey Burn

Greenside
Reservoir

Boglairoch

The Slacks

75

1

Loch Humphrey Burn

Cochno

Kilpatrick Braes

Weste
Cochn

46   A   47   B   48   C

51
73

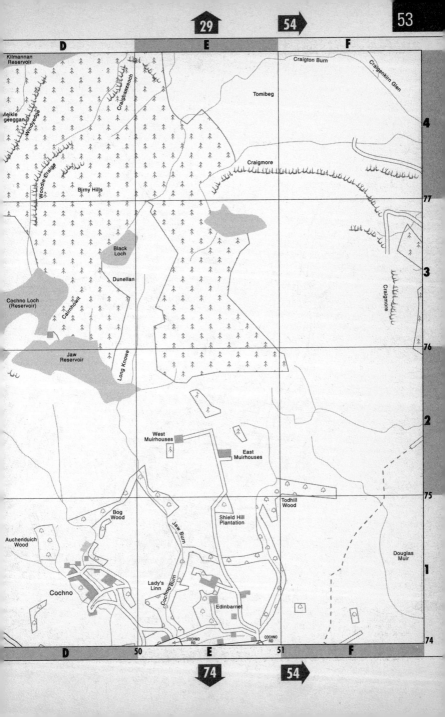

D E F

4

77

Loch Ardinning

Muirhouse Muir

Black Linn

gdock Loch

Caigmaddie Plantation

ugdock Country Park

THE STABLES

Mugdock

Middleton of Mugdock

Caigmaddie Loch

Caigmaddie House

Easterton Farm

Easterton House

A81

3

Bankend

Craigash

Barrachan

76

P

Mugdock Reservoir

Craigmaddie Reservoir

Bankell House

Bankell Farm

2

PC

Tannoch Loch

MILNGAVIE

STRATHBLANE RD

CH

+

Baldernock House

75

MUGDOCK RD

Sch

Back Wood

BALDERNOCK RD

Ford

Dowan

DOWAN RD

Kettlehill Farm

CRAIGMADDIE RD

Off

STATION

B8030

Golf Course

Stable Wood

Craigmaddie Burn

1

Boghail

Milngavie Station

VIEWPARK

Ind Est

WOODBURN WAY

ABP GLASGOW RD

1 NORTH CLAREMONT ST
2 CLAREMONT GDNS
3 SOUTH CLAREMONT LA

Lennox Park

AUCHENHOWIE

Lawn Park

FINLAY RISE

74

D 56 E 57 F

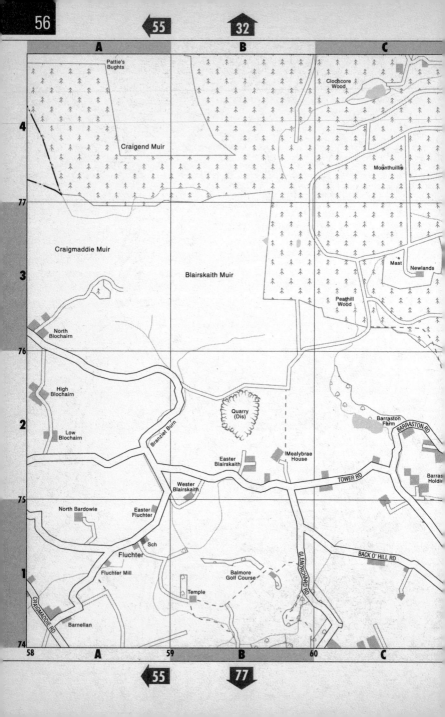

55
32

Pattie's Bughts

Clochcore Wood

4

Craigend Muir

Mounthuillie

77

Craigmaddie Muir

Blairskaith Muir

Mast
Newlands

3

Peathill Wood

North Blochairn

76

High Blochairn

Quarry (Dis)

Barraston Farm

BARRASTON RD

2

Low Blochairn

Branziet Burn

Mealybrae House

Easter Blairskaith

TOWER RD

Barras Holdir

75

North Bardowie

Wester Blairskaith

Easter Fluchter

Sch

BACK O' HILL RD

Fluchter

1

Fluchter Mill

Balmore Golf Course

GLENORCHARD RD

Temple

CRAIGMADDIE RD

Barnellan

74

D
E
F

NETHERTON OVAL
Balglass Farm
Works
Liby
BENCLOICH CRES
Sch
P
P
Off
Southfield
Dismantled Railway
HILLVIEW AVE
Lennoxtown
Westerton
4
Glazert Water
MILTON RD
A891
77
Finniescroft Wood
Dam
Finniescroft
Cherry Tree Cottage
Gallow Hill
Muirhead
Boyd's Burn
Lennoxlea Farm
3
Glenwhapple
Barrhill
Upper Carlestoun
76
Kinkell Farm
Langshot Farm
Whitehill
2
Acre Valley House
Leitchbank
Drumbayne
East Balgrochan Farm
Castle Hill
Balquharrage
75
BARRASTON RD
Red Burn
East Balgrochan
CAMPSIE RD
Cariston
KIRKINTILLOCH RD
Dismantled Railway
West Balgrochan Farm
Balgrochan
West Carlestoun
West Balgrochan
Golf Course
1
Tower
Sch
Torrance
Meadowbank Farm
River Kelvin
MICHAEL McPARLAND DR
74

side

D
62
E
63
F

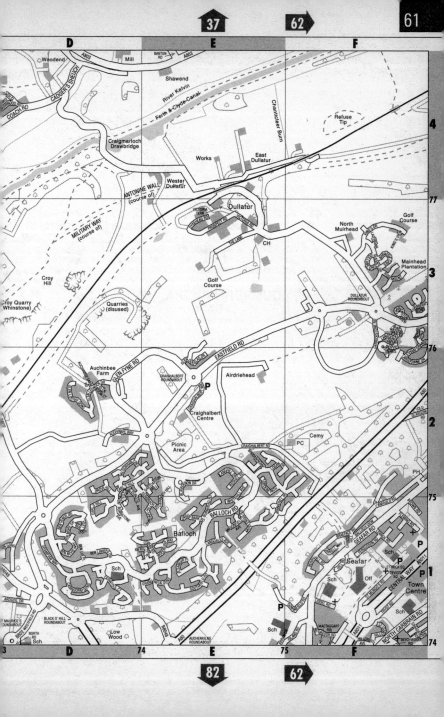

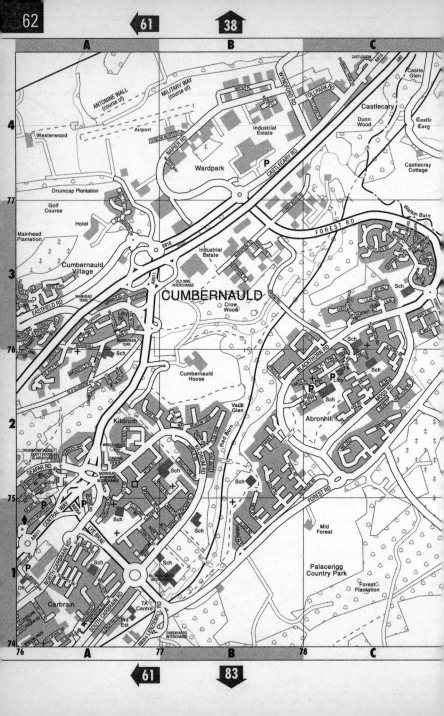

D
E
F

Burnhouse

Wester
Lochdrum

Castlecary
Low Wood

Blackhill

Wester
Lochgreen

Loch
Green

4

Skipperton Burn

Lochgreen

Walton

Bandominie

77

Castlecary
High Wood

3

Kilt
Farm

Kilt Bridge

76

Walton Burn

Graystone Knowe

Crowbank

Arns

Glenhead

Old
Shields

Garbethill
House

2

75

Garbet

Garbethill

1

Fannyside Muir

Easter
Fannyside

74

D
80
E
81
F

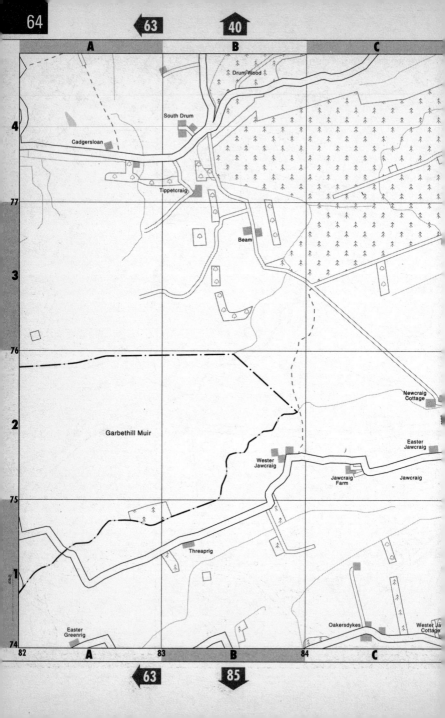

A

B

C

4

Drum Wood

South Drum

Cadgersloan

Tippetcraig

77

Beam

3

76

Newcraig
Cottage

2

Garbethill Muir

Easter
Jawcraig

Wester
Jawcraig

Jawcraig
Farm

Jawcraig

75

Threaprig

1

Easter
Greenrig

Oakersdykes

Wester Ja
Cottage

74

82

A

83

B

84

C

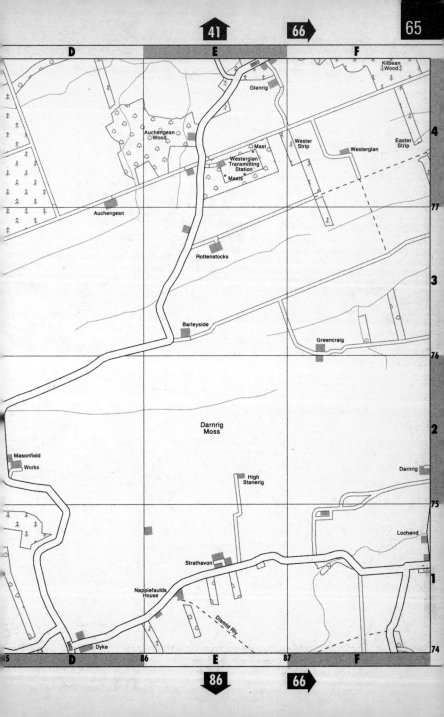

D
E
F

Kilbean Wood

B803

Glenrig

Auchengean Wood

Mast

Wester Strip

Westerglen

Easter Strip

4

Westerglen Transmitting Station

Maets

Auchengean

77

Rottenstocks

3

Barleyside

Greencraig

76

Darnrig Moss

2

Masonfield

Works

High Stanerig

Darnrig

75

Lochend

Strathavon

1

Nappiefaulds House

Dismtd Rly

B803

Dyke

5
D
86
E
87
F
74

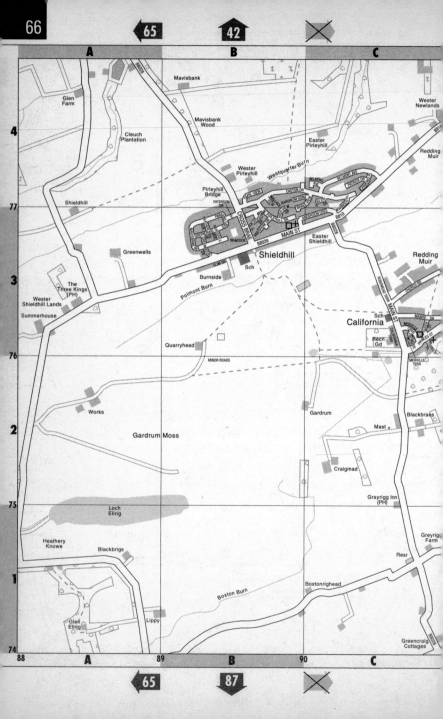

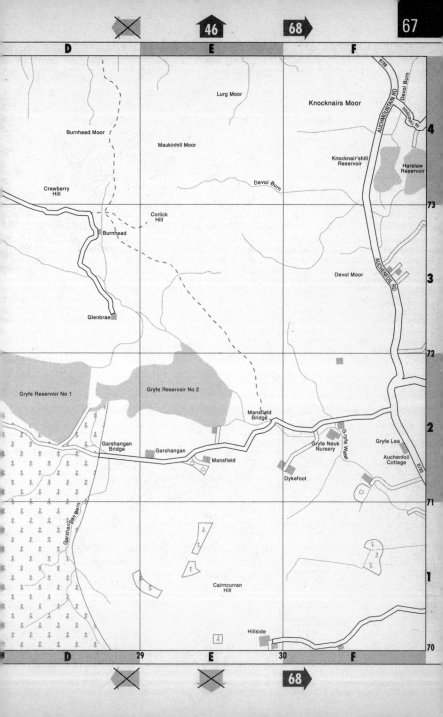

D   E   F

Lurg Moor

Knocknairs Moor

Burnhead Moor

Maukinhill Moor

4

Knocknair'shill
Reservoir

Harelaw
Reservoir

Crawberry
Hill

Devol Burn

73

Corlick
Hill

Burnhead

Devol Moor

3

Glenbrae

72

Gryfe Reservoir No 1

Gryfe Reservoir No 2

Mansfield
Bridge

Garshangan
Bridge

Garshangan

Mansfield

Gryfe Neuk
Nursery

Gryfe Lea

Auchenfoil
Cottage

2

Dykefoot

Garshangan Burn

71

Cairncurran
Hill

1

Hillside

70

D   29   E   30   F

AUCHENFOIL RD

AUCHMOUNTAIN RD

Devol Burn

B788

D E F

4

River Clyde

Milton Island

Longhaugh
Point

73

M8

Fornet Cottage

A8

Ferryhill
Plantation

High Hatton

Laigh
Hatton
Lodge

Convent

3

GREENOCK RD

OLD GREENOCK RD

Slateford

M8

CRESCENT AVE

Lodge

Whitemoss Dam

Bishopton Tunnels

72

WRAISLAND CRES

B789

Drums

Whitemoss

Ingliston
House

Inn

A8

Castlehill
Cottage

Cemy

1 WEST PORTON PL
2 CROSSGATES

2

NEWTON RD

Barbeg Hill

Easter Newton

Ingliston

71

Barmore Hill

Formakin

Paddockcraig

Gatehead

Parkglen Wood

1

Nether Mill

West
Glenshinnoch

Dargavel Burn

BAROCHAN RD

Meiklefield

B789 REILLY RD

70

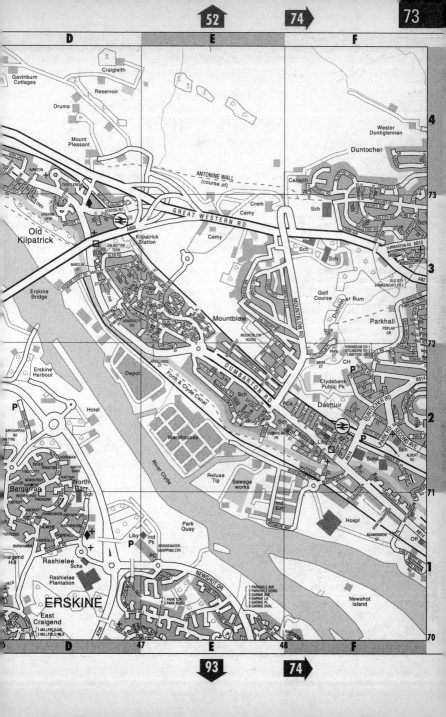

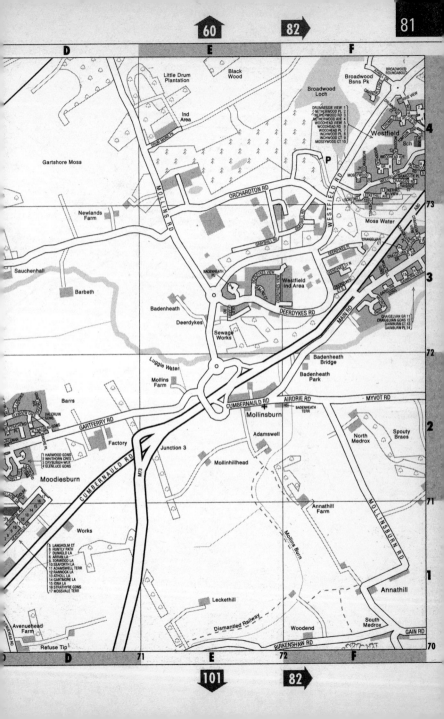

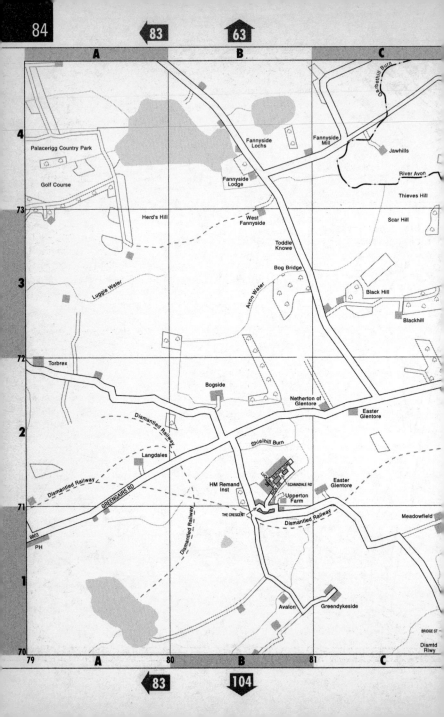

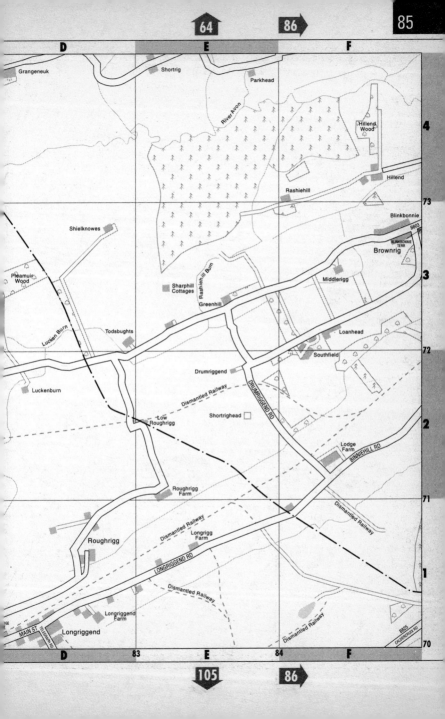

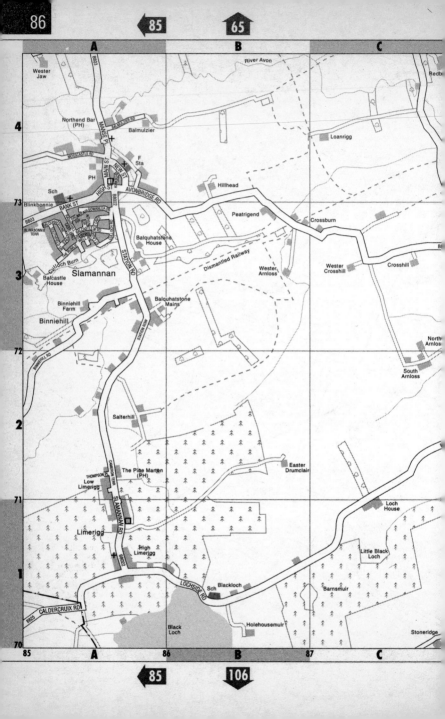

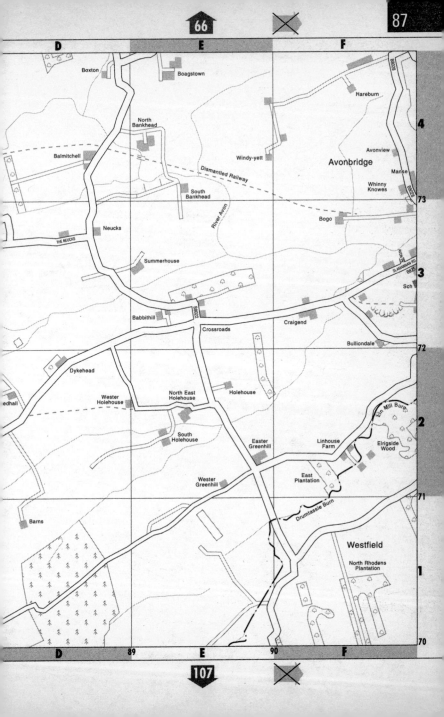

D | E | F

Boxton

Boagstown

Hareburn

North Bankhead

4

Balmitchell

Windy-yett

Avonview

Avonbridge

Manse

South Bankhead

Dismantled Railway

Whinny Knowes

73

Neucks

THE NEUCKS

River Avon

Bogo

Summerhouse

SLAMANNAN RD

Sch

3

Babbithill

Crossroads

Craigend

Bulliondale

72

Dykehead

edhall

Wester Holehouse

North East Holehouse

Holehouse

Lin Mill Burn

2

South Holehouse

Easter Greenhill

Linhouse Farm

Elrigside Wood

Wester Greenhill

East Plantation

71

Barns

Drumtassie Burn

Westfield

North Rhodens Plantation

1

70

D | 89 | E | 90 | F

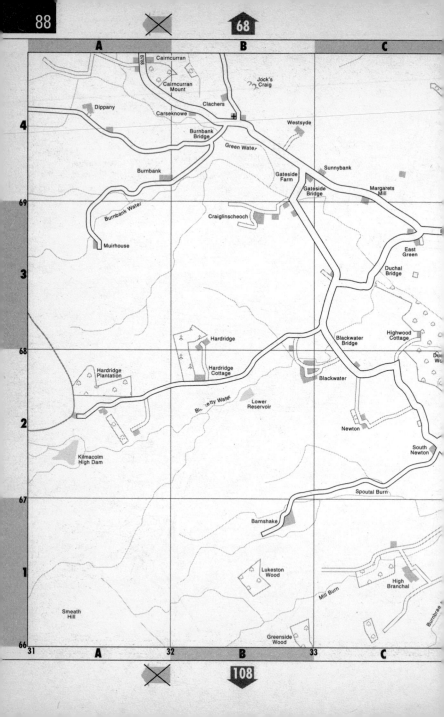

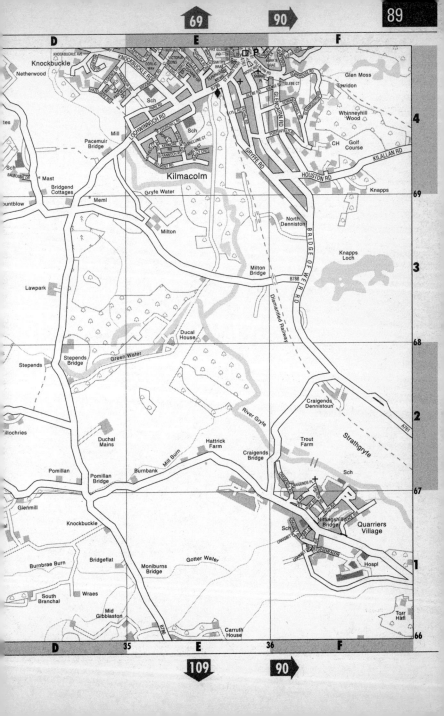

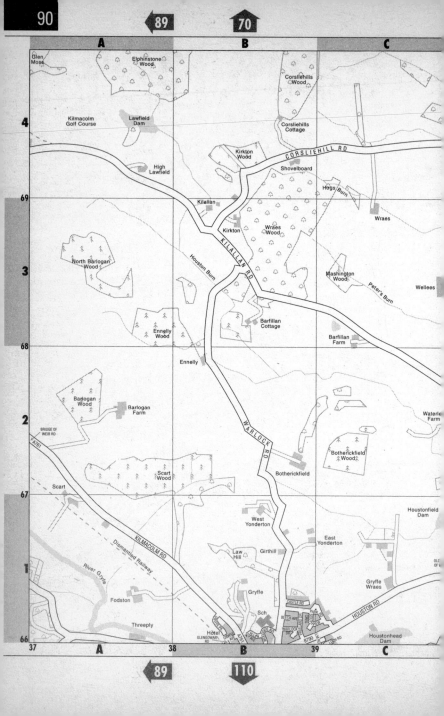

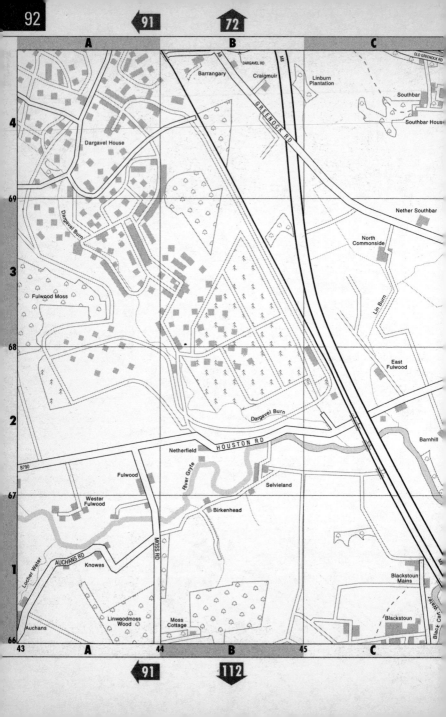

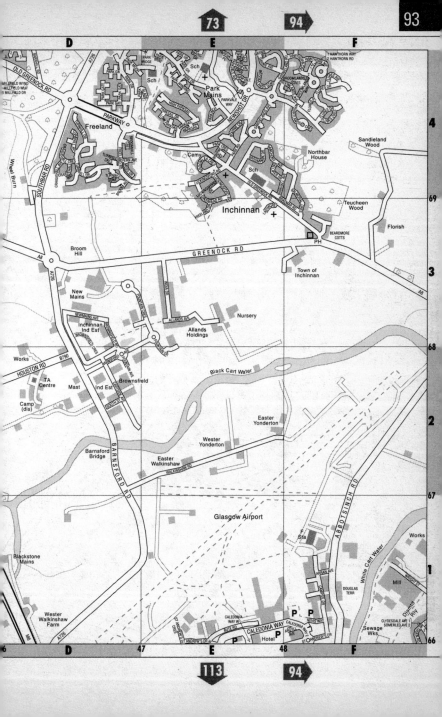

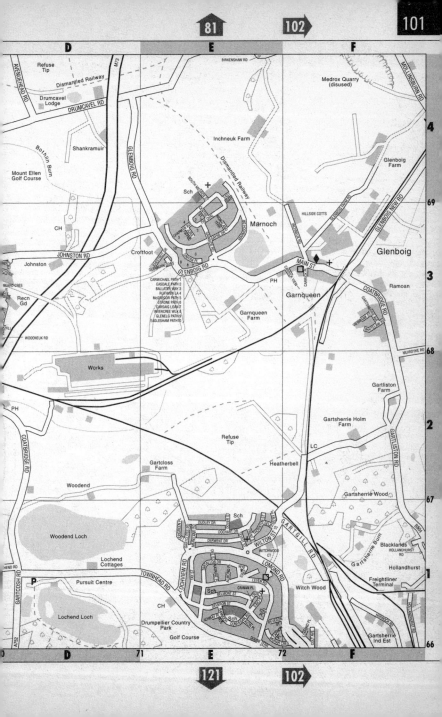

101
82

A   B   C

Callochrig

CALLOCHRIG RD

Gaindykehead

East Lodge
Wood

4

LC

Foot o' Loan
Wood

East
Gartmillan

Shank Burn

Glenmill
Wood

Drumbowie
Farm

Greenfoot

West
Gartmillan

MOLLINSBURN RD

Ardaryth

Dismtd Rly

69

BRACKENHIRST RD

Refuse Tip

Haggmuir

MOLLINSBURN RD

CONDORRAT RD

3

Brackenhirst

Gas Storage
Depot

MUIRDYKE RD

YETT'S HOLE RD

Gartverne Burn

Ryden
Mains

New Monkland

68

Cemy

PC Sch

RAEBOG RD

HAWKWOOD RD

Palace
Farm

BURNLIP RD

Rochsales

PH

Gartverrie
Farm

Copse Wood

Glenmavis

Blackwc
Plantati

2

Cromlet

Braidenhill

Dryflat

COATBRIDGE RD

Golf Course

STRATHMUNGO CRES 1
STAINEYBRAES PL 2

67

CH

DYKEHEAD
CRES

Virtuewell Glen

Sch

DYKEHEAD RD

BALLOCHNEY LA

Kippsbyre

GLENMAVIS RD

Burnfoot

1

SOUTH
COMMONHEAD
AVE

Acad

Kipps

Laggan Qua
LAIDON RD

North Burn

Works

Coatbridge
Ind Est

Greenhill

BALLOCHNEY

WHINHALL RD

COMMONHEAD AV

Sch

COATSWOOD RD BRAE

WAVERLEY ST

CHASSEL ST 1
BRUDE ST 2

B803

CAMERON ST

66

73   A   74   B   75   C

101
122

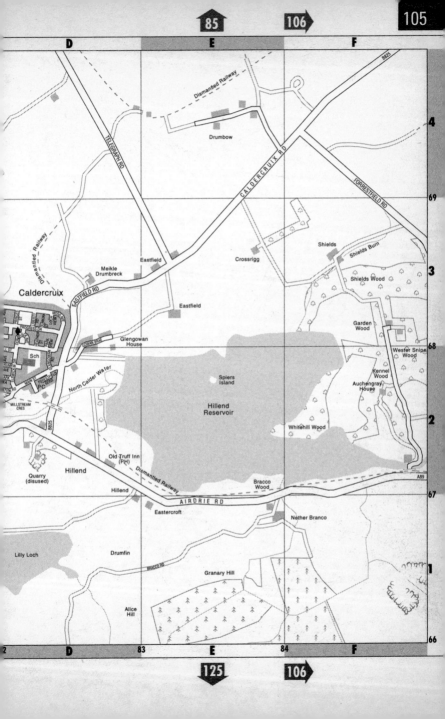

Dismantled Railway

Drumbow

B825

CALDERCRUIX RD

FORRESTFIELD RD

69

Shields

Shields Burn

Dismantled Railway

Eastfield

Crossrigg

Shields Wood

Meikle
Drumbreck

TELEGRAPH RD

EASTFIELD RD

Eastfield

3

Garden
Wood

Wester Snipe
Wood

Caldercruix

Eastfield

68

Glengowan
House

Kennel
Wood

Sch

Spiers
Island

Auchengray
House

North Calder Water

Hillend
Reservoir

MILLSTREAM
CRES

Whitehill Wood

2

B825

Old Truff Inn
(PH)

Dismantled Railway

A89

Quarry
(disused)

Hillend

Bracco
Wood

67

Hillend

Eastercroft

AIRDRIE RD

Nether Branco

Lilly Loch

Drumfin

BRACCO RD

Granary Hill

1

Alice
Hill

66

D   E   F

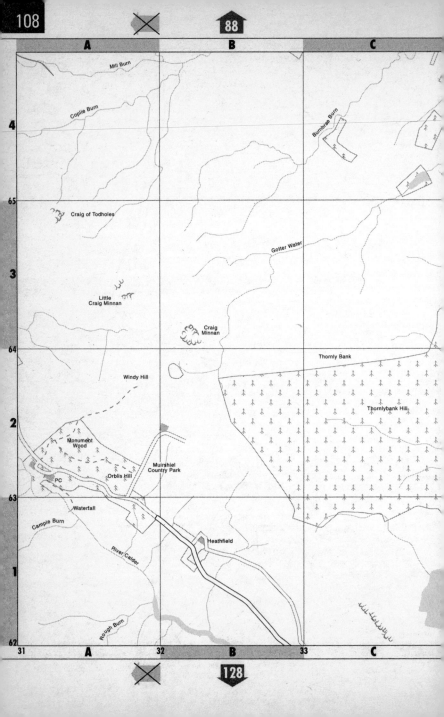

A   B   C

Mill Burn

Coplie Burn

Burnbrae Burn

4

65

Craig of Todholes

Gotter Water

3

Little
Craig Minnan

Craig
Minnan

64

Thornly Bank

Windy Hill

Thornlybank Hill

2

Monument
Wood

Muirshiel
Country Park

Orblis Hill

PC

63

Waterfall

Cample Burn

River Calder

Heathfield

1

Rough Burn

62

31   A   32   B   33   C

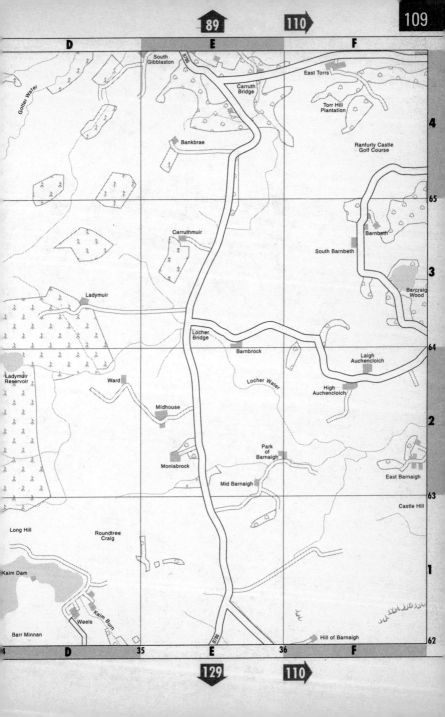

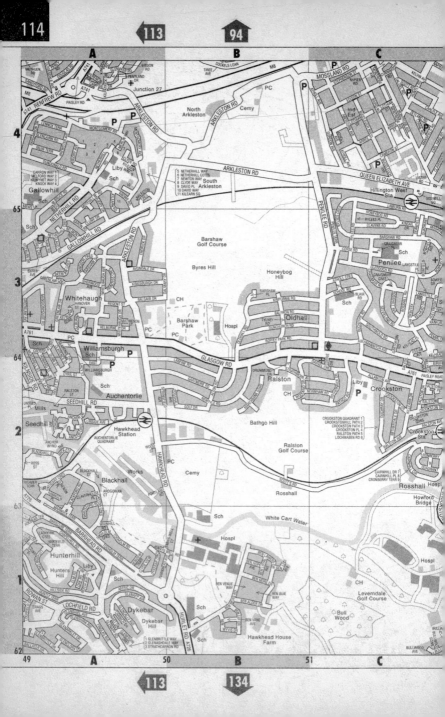

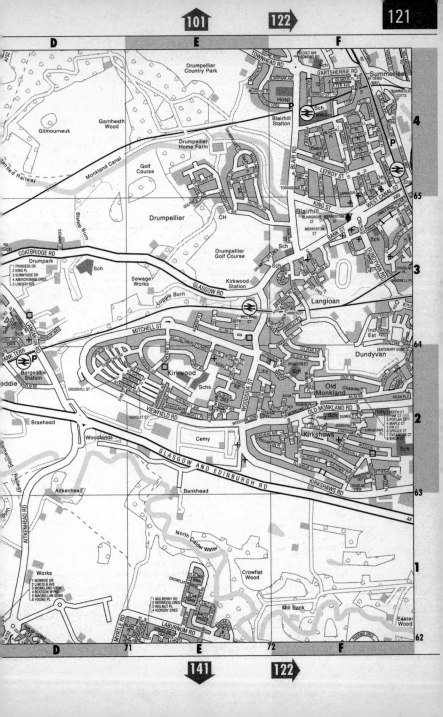

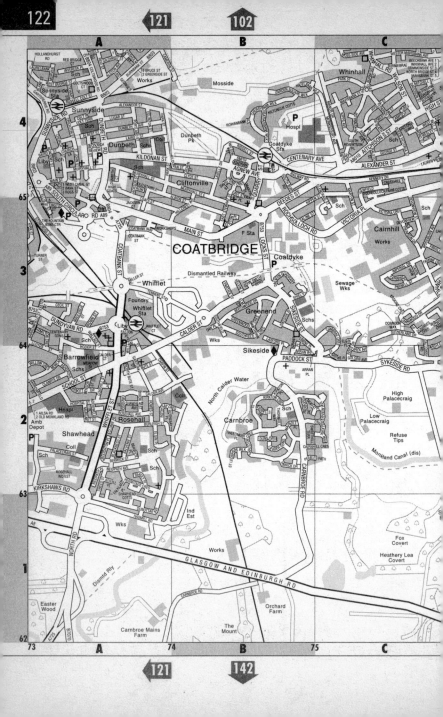

105
126

D   E   F

BLACKHILL

Watch Moss

Black Hill

perdavie

4

Torrance

65

Television
Station   Mast

Dun Daugh

Tod Holes

Forrestburn Water

Mountcow

3

Well Knowe

DUNTILLAND RD

Duntilland Hill

64

Duntilland Farm

Dismantled Railway

Duntilland Quarry

M8

2

Dismantled Railway

Sewage
Works

Shotts Burn

Sch

HIRST RD

B7066

63

Kirk of
Shotts

CROSSART
ST

MAIN ST

MARSHALL TERR

Salsburgh

Threeprig

NEWMILL AND CANTHILL RD

RINGFIELD RD

LORNE
GDNS

Manse

Glebe
Farm

MANSE RD

1

Canthills
Plantation

MARGARET AVE 1
SIGHTHILL TERR 2
BERTRAM DR 3

Riven Loch

Roundknowe
Wood

Spoil
Tip

62

D   83   E   84   F

145
126

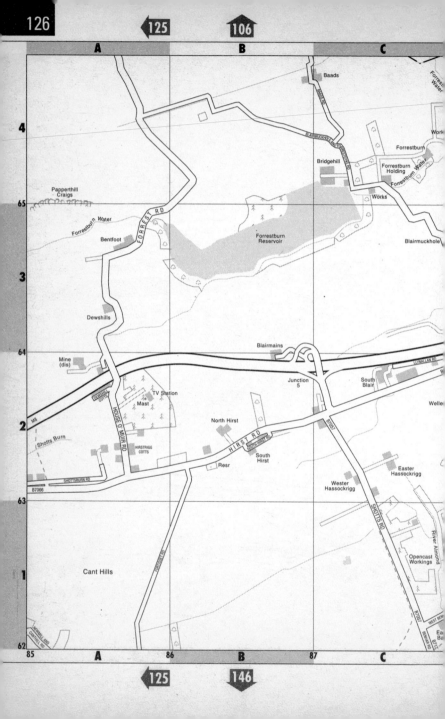

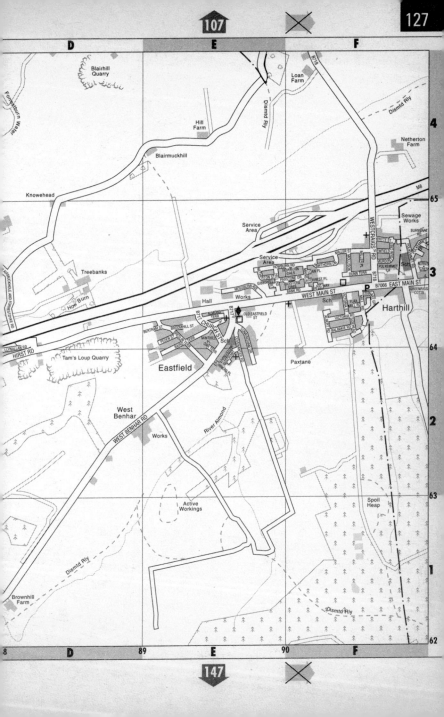

D E F

Blairhill Quarry

Forresburn Water

Loan Farm

B718

Dismtd Rly

Hill Farm

4

Blairmuckhill

Netherton Farm

M8

Knowehead

65

Service Area

Sewage Works

WESTCRAIGS RD

BURNSIDE TERR

WHITEBURN

Treebanks

Service Area

HOWDENHEAD RD

THORNBANK

Works

THORNHILL RD

VICTORIA RD

MILLER ST

MURDOCH TERR

POLKEMMET RD

NORTH CREEK

Sch

3

How Burn

KINGMOORHILL AND FORRESTBURN RD

MUNCIE RD

GIRDSTANE RD

PAXSTONE CRE

BANK RD

WILSON CRE

NORTHORN RD

FORREST PL

DUNN TERR

B718

B7066 EAST MAIN ST

GREENRIGG COTTS

CHURCHILL

Hall

MOSSROGGHILL

WEST MAIN ST

Sch

Harthill

+

OLD EASTFIELD ST

Paxtane

FURM

VICTORIA

2

BERTRAM ST

BROOMHILL ST

B711 CHURCH ST

MINTHILL ST

RAILWAY DR

Sch

RAE HAGE RD

Eastfield

ALMOND TERR

RAILWAY DR

Paxtane

64

HIRST RD

LYNDALE RD

Tam's Loup Quarry

West Benhar

WEST BENHAR RD

Works

River Almond

2

Active Workings

63

Spoil Heap

Dismtd Rly

1

Brownhill Farm

Dismtd Rly

62

8 D 89 E 90 F

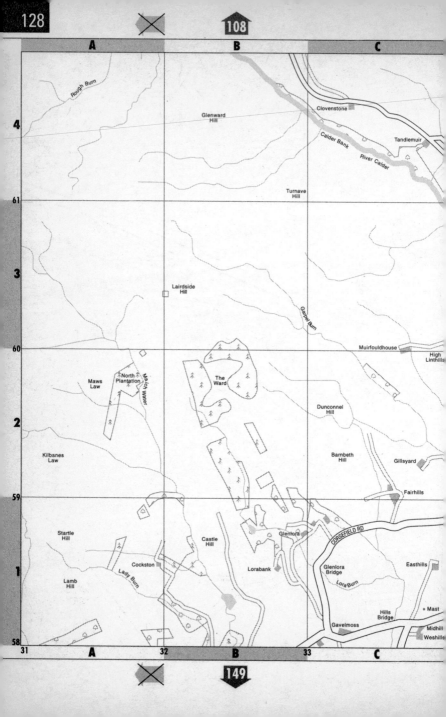

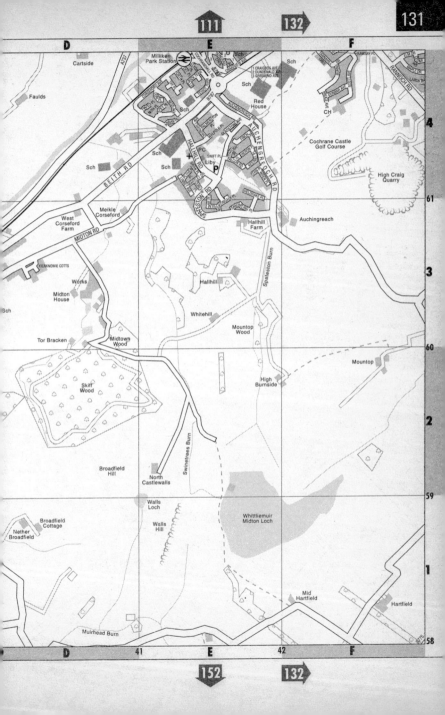

D   E   F

Cartside

Faulds

Milliken Park Station

Sch
1 CRAIGBON AVE
2 DUNDONALD
3 GREENEND AVE
Sch
Red House
Sch
CH

Cochrane Castle Golf Course

High Craig Quarry

4

61

BEITH RD

HALLHILL RD

AUCHENGREOCH RD

SOMERSTON RD

PC
Liby
P
SWIFT PL

Sch
Sch
Sch
Sch
Sch

West Corseford Farm

Meikle Corseford

MIDTON RD

Hallhill Farm

Auchingreach

Fenknowie Cotts

Works

Midton House

Sch

Hallhill

Whitehill

Mountop Wood

Spateston Burn

3

Tor Bracken

Midtown Wood

Skiff Wood

High Burnside

Mountop

60

2

Broadfield Hill

North Castlewalls

Swinetrees Burn

59

Broadfield Cottage

Nether Broadfield

Walls Loch

Walls Hill

Whittliemuir Midton Loch

1

Mid Hartfield

Hartfield

Muirhead Burn

58

D   E   F

41   42

RAMSAY PL
RANNOCH RD
LARCH RD

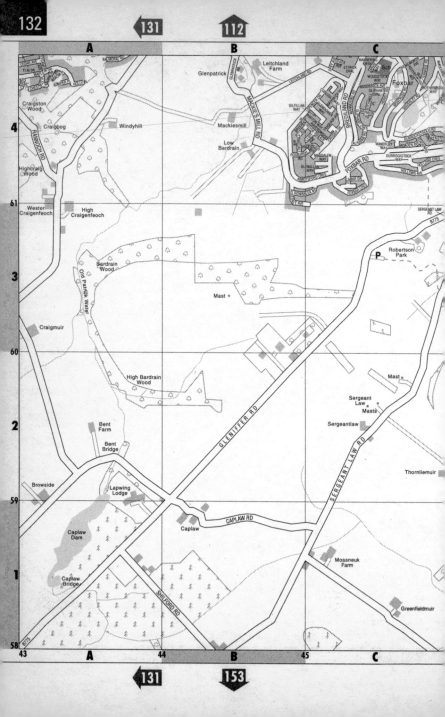

A B C

4

Balmoral

Craigston Wood

Craigbog

Windyhill

Glenpatrick

Leitchland Farm

Mackiesmill

Low Bardrain

Foxbar

Highcraig Wood

RANNOCH RD

MACKIE'S MILL RD

BREDILAND RD

FOXBAR RD

61

Wester Craigenfeoch

High Craigenfeoch

SERGEANT LAW RD
B775

3

Bardrain Wood

Old Patrick Water

Mast

P Robertson Park

Craigmuir

60

High Bardrain Wood

Mast

Sergeant Law

Masts

2

Bent Farm

Bent Bridge

GLENIFFER RD

Sergeantlaw

SERGEANT LAW RD

Thornliemuir

Browside

Lapwing Lodge

59

CAPLAW RD

Caplaw

Caplaw Dam

1

Caplaw Bridge

SHILFORD RD

Mossneuk Farm

Greenfieldmuir

58

B775

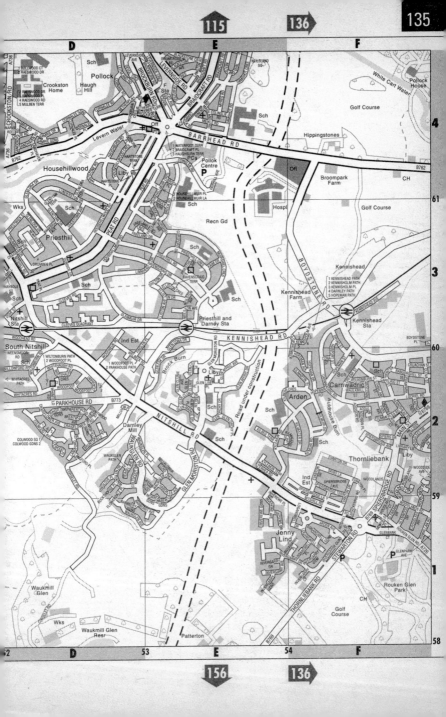

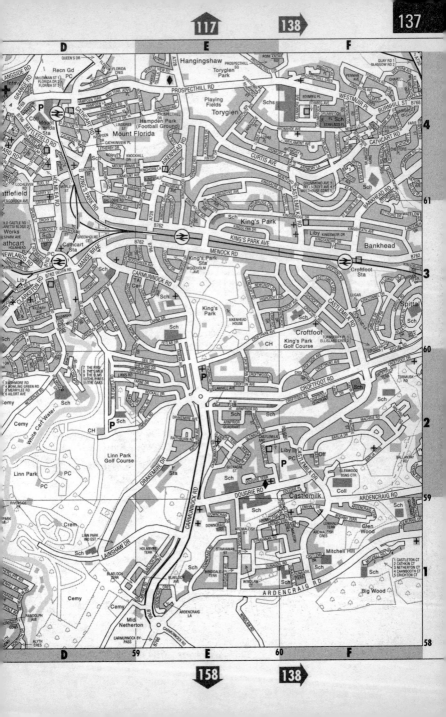

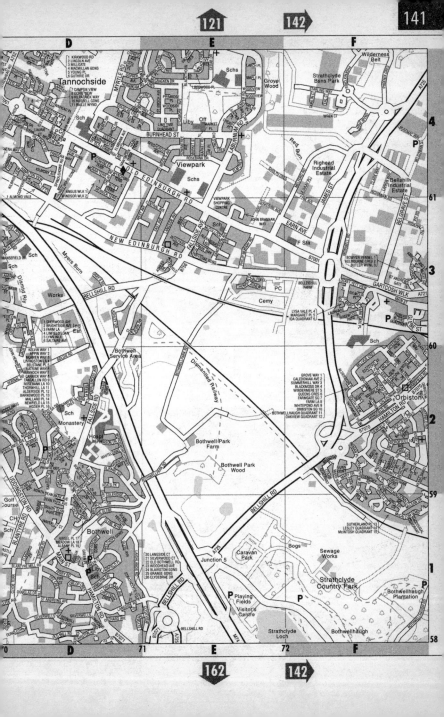

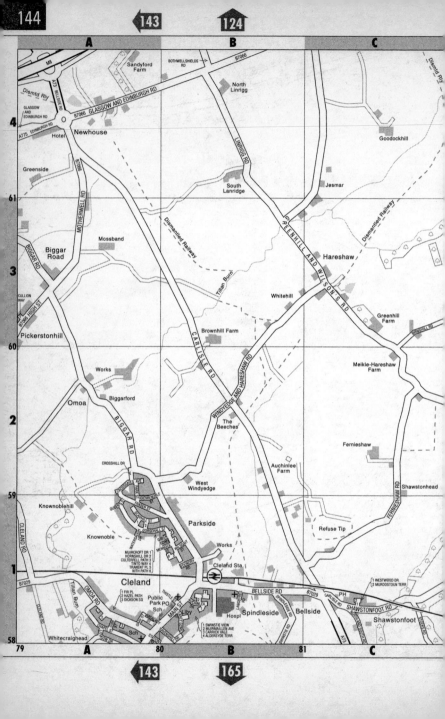

A
B
C

M8
A73 BILLSIDE RD
Sandyford Farm
BOTHWELLSHIELDS RD
B7066
North Linrigg
Dismtd Rly
Dismtd Rly
Glasgow and Edinburgh Rd
A775 EDINBURGH RD
B7066 GLASGOW AND EDINBURGH RD
Goodockhill
4
Hotel
Newhouse
B7066
Greenside
LINRIGG RD
South Lanridge
Jesmar
Dismantled Railway
61
Mossband
GREENHILL AND WILSON'S RD
Dismantled Railway
Hareshaw
Biggar Road
Dismantled Railway
Tillan Burn
Whitehill
Greenhill Farm
3
CULLION WAY
B7066 HIGH ST
BIGGAR RD
MOTHERWELL RD
Brownhill Farm
Meikle-Hareshaw Farm
GREENHILL RD
Pickerstonhill
CARLISLE RD
60
Works
Omoa
Biggarford
BIGGAR RD
WINDYEDGE AND HARESHAW RD
The Beeches
Fernieshaw
2
Auchinlee Farm
FERNIESHAW RD
Shawstonhead
CROSSHILL DR
West Windyedge
Parkside
Refuse Tip
59
Knownoblehill
QUEEN ST
Knownoble
Works
CLELAND RD
MUIRCROFT DR 1
HORNSHILL PATH 2
CULTERFELL PATH 3
TINTO WAY 4
TRAMENT PL 5
NITH PATH 6
Cleland Sta
B7029
OMOA RD
Tillan Burn
Cleland
THISTLE ST
Public Park PO
MAIN ST
BELLSIDE RD
B7029
CARLISLE RD
1 WESTWOOD DR
2 MURDOSTOUN TERR
PH
1
1 FIR PL
2 HAZEL PATH
3 DICKSON SQ
Sch
Liby
Hospl
Spindleside
Bellside
SHAWSTONFOOT RD
Shawstonfoot
A73
Whitecraighead
Sch
1 SWINSTIE VIEW
2 MUIRMAILEN AVE
3 CARRICK VALE
4 ALDERSYDE TERR
58

79
A
80
B
81
C

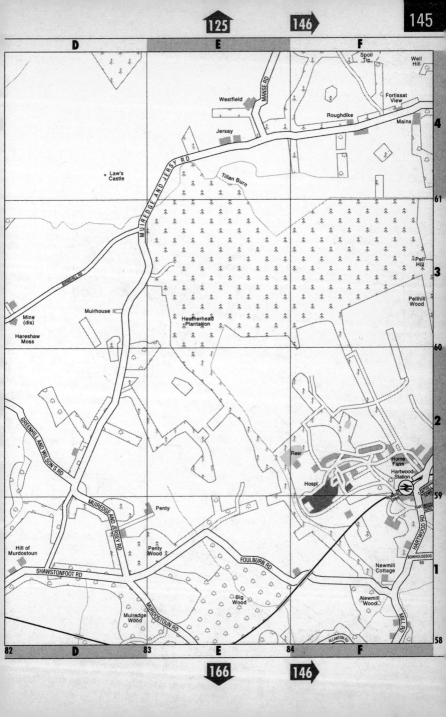

Fauldhouse

4

61

CH
Golf
Course

Amb
Sta

BENHAR RD

Starryshaw
Farm

South Calder Water

Spoil
Heap

Stanebent

3

Cairneyhead

Stane

Torbothie

60

DONALD RD
LINDSAY RD
HILL RD

CONDIE RD

NORTHWELL RD

Torbothie

JLG WAY
AIR WYND

Sch

PC

CORRIERY RD

Cemy

1 ETIVE WAY
2 JLG WAY
3 GAIR WYND
4 BOWMORE WLK.
5 TORRIN LOAN
6 DORINE WYND
7 MORAR WAY
8 CORE LOAN
9 SUNA PATH
10 SALEN LOAN

2

MAIN ST

CHARLOTTE ST

MARCH RD

LOCHEND RD

TULLOCH RD

APPIN TER.

LANGSIDE AVE.

Stane

LINNY CT 1
RAX PATH 2

B7010

SPRINGHILL RD

Springhill

59

STANE RD

SCHOOL RD

MOUNT RD

ELMWOOD RD

LARCHFIELD LA.

NORTHFIELD AVE.

Works

Springhill

SPRINGHILL AND LEADLOCH RD

B7010

B7115 HEADLESSCROSS RD

B7115

Knowton
Farm

Dismantled Railway

Lingore Linn

A71

Works

1

Dismld Rly

58

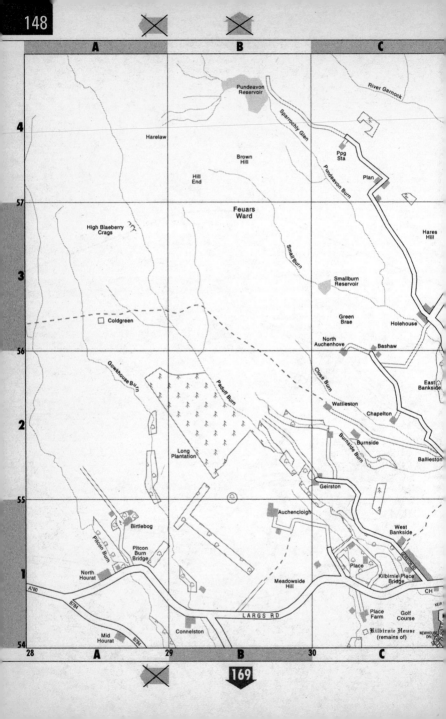

River Garnock

Pundeavon
Reservoir

Sparrochly Glen

Harelaw

Brown
Hill

Ppg
Sta

Plan

Hill
End

Pundeavon Burn

Feuars
Ward

Hares
Hill

High Blaeberry
Crags

Smallburn

Smallburn
Reservoir

Green
Brae

Holehouse

Coldgreen

North
Auchenhove

Bashaw

Gowkhouse Burn

Close Burn

East
Bankside

Padruff Burn

Wattieston

Chapelton

Long
Plantation

Burnetts Burn

Burnside

Ballieston

Geirston

Birtlebog

Auchencloigh

West
Bankside

Pitcon Burn

Pitcon
Burn
Bridge

Place

Kilbirnie Place
Bridge

North
Hourat

CH

A760

B784

Meadowside
Hill

LARGS RD

Place
Farm

Golf
Course

KEIR

Connelston

Kilbirnie House
(remains of)

NEWHOUSE
DRI

Mid
Hourat

B784

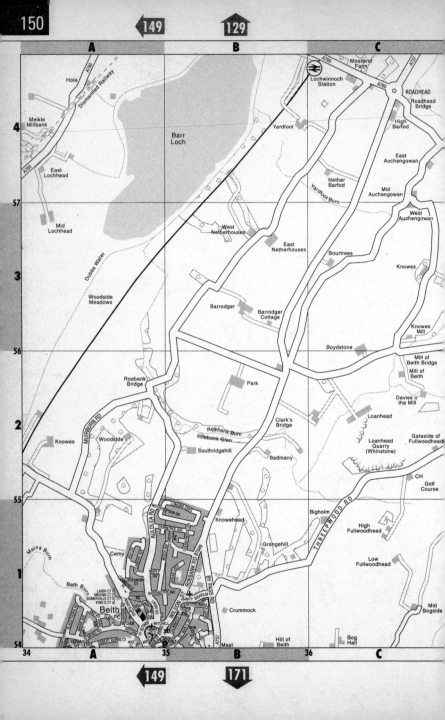

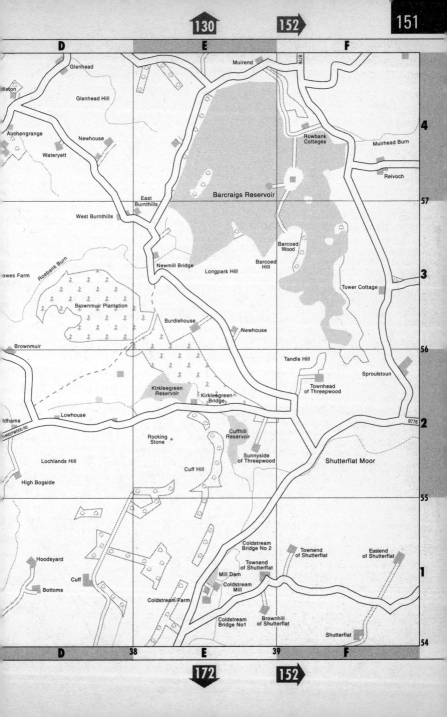

D
E
F

4

Glenhead

illeton

Glenhead Hill

Muirend

B776

Auchengrange

Newhouse

Rowbank
Cottages

Muirhead Burn

Wateryett

Reivoch

East
Burnthills

Barcraigs Reservoir

57

West Burnthills

owes Farm

Roebank Burn

Newmill Bridge

Longpark Hill

Barcoed
Wood

Barcoed
Hill

3

Brownmuir Plantation

Burdiehouse

Newhouse

Tower Cottage

Brownmuir

56

Tandle Hill

Sproulstoun

Kirkleegreen
Reservoir

Kirkleegreen
Bridge

Townhead
of Threepwood

Idhame

THREEPWOOD RD

Lowhouse

Rocking
Stone

Cuffhill
Reservoir

Sunnyside
of Threepwood

B776

2

Lochlands Hill

Cuff Hill

Shutterflat Moor

High Bogside

55

Hoodsyard

Coldstream
Bridge No 2

Townend
of Shutterflat

Eastend
of Shutterflat

Cuff

Townend
of Shutterflat

Bottoms

Mill Dam

Coldstream
Mill

Coldstream Farm

1

Coldstream
Bridge No1

Brownhill
of Shutterflat

Shutterflat

54

D
E
F

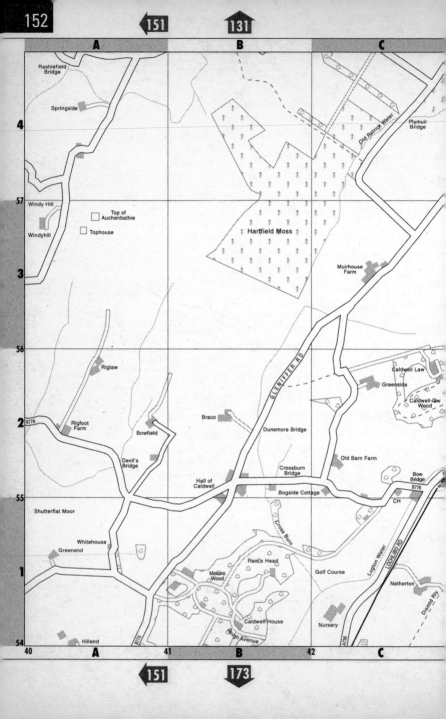

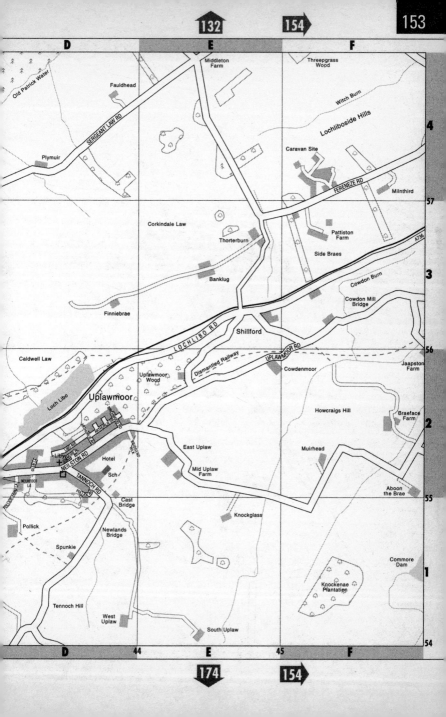

D   E   F

Old Patrick Water

Fauldhead

SERGEANT LAW RD

Plymuir

Middleton Farm

Threepgrass Wood

Witch Burn

Lochliboside Hills

Caravan Site

FERENEZE RD

Milnthird

4

57

Corkindale Law

Thorterburn

Pattiston Farm

Side Braes

A736

Banklug

Cowdon Burn

Cowdon Mill Bridge

3

Finniebrae

LOCHLIBO RD

Shillford

Jaapston Farm

Caldwell Law

Diamantled Railway

UPLAWMOOR RD

Cowdenmoor

56

Uplawmoor Wood

Loch Libo

Uplawmoor

Howcraigs Hill

Braeface Farm

Muirhead

Libr   NEIL RD   ARTHURLIE RD

Hotel

East Uplaw

2

NEILSTON RD

Sch

Mid Uplaw Farm

Aboon the Brae

TANNOCH RD

NEWFOOD La

POLOC La

Cast Bridge

Knockglass

55

Pollick

Newlands Bridge

Spunkie

Commore Dam

1

Knockenae Plantation

Tennoch Hill

West Uplaw

South Uplaw

54

D   44   E   45   F

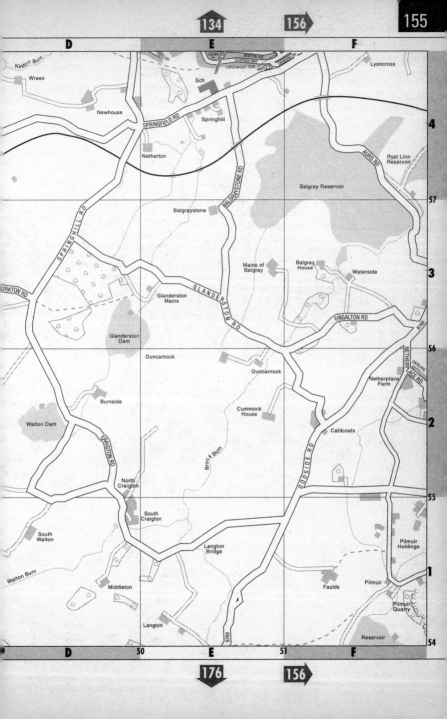

Kirkton Burn
Wraes
Newhouse
Lyoncross
SPRINGFIELD RD
Springhill
Sch
CEDAR PL
NEWTON AVE
GLYFFNIA WAY
LARCHWOOD TERR
MAPLE DR
RED DR
Springhill
Netherton

4

AURS RD
Ryat Linn
Reservoir

BALGRAYSTONE RD

Balgray Reservoir

57

SPRINGHILL RD

Balgraystone

KIRKTON RD

Mains of
Balgray
Balgray
House
Waterside

3

GLANDERSTON RD

Glanderston
Mains

FINGALTON RD

B769

Glanderston
Dam

56

NETHERPLACE RD
CAPELRIG COTTS

Duncarnock

Duncarnock

Netherplace
Farm

Burnside

Walton Dam

CRAIGTON RD

Cummock
House

DODSIDE RD

Caldcoats

2

North
Craigton

South
Craigton

Broc k Burn

55

South
Walton

Pilmuir
Holdings

Langton
Bridge

Walton Burn

Middleton

Faulds

Pilmuir

1

Pilmuir
Quarry

Langton

B769

Reservoir

54

D   50   E   51   F

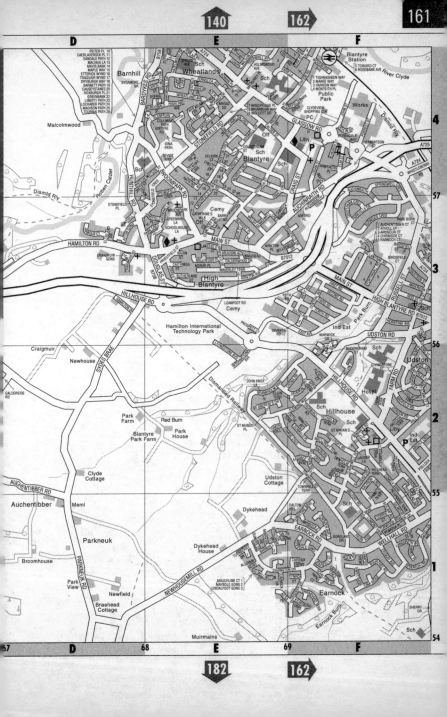

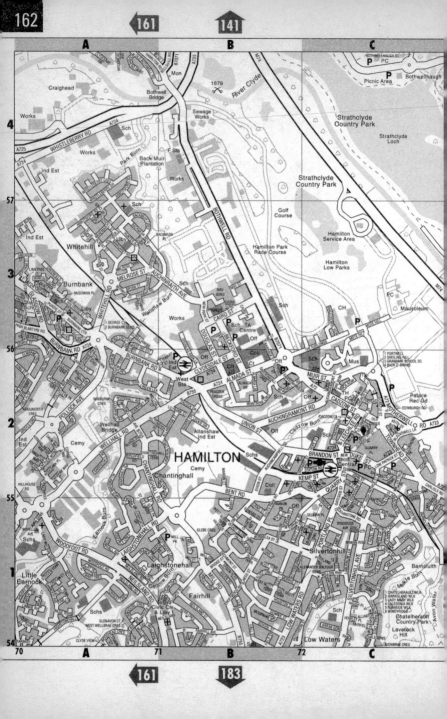

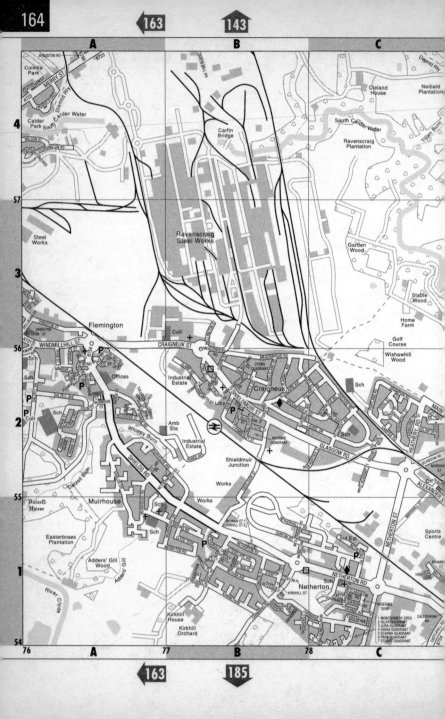

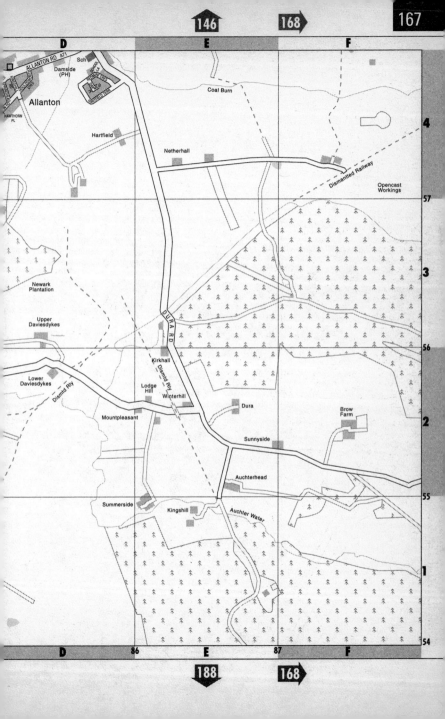

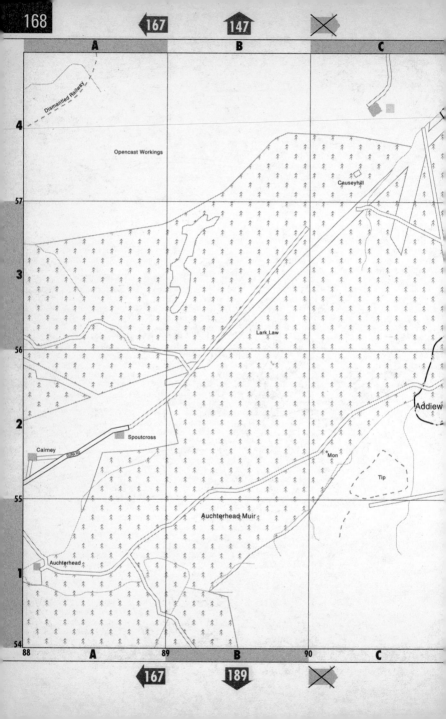

A
B
C

4

Dismantled Railway

Opencast Workings

Causeyhill

57

3

Lark Law

56

Addiew

2

Spoutcross

Cairney

Mon

Tip

55

Auchterhead Muir

1

Auchterhead

54

88
A
89
B
90
C

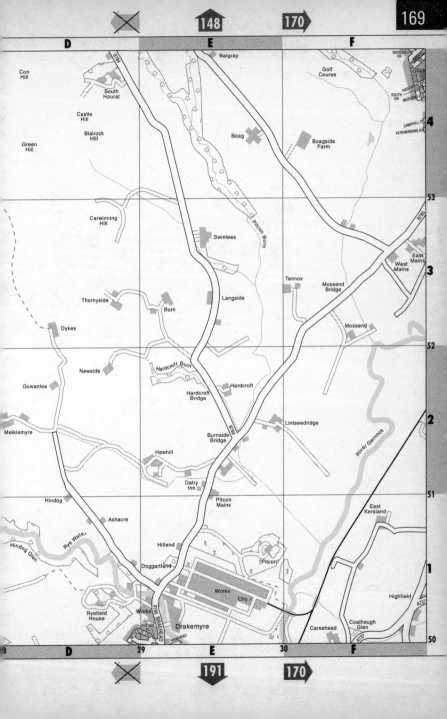

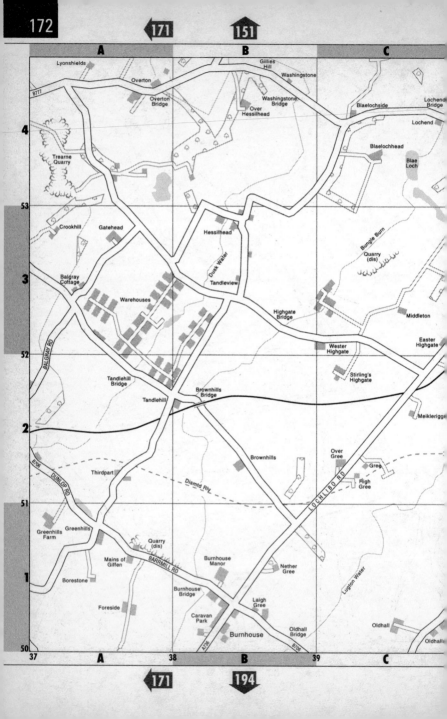

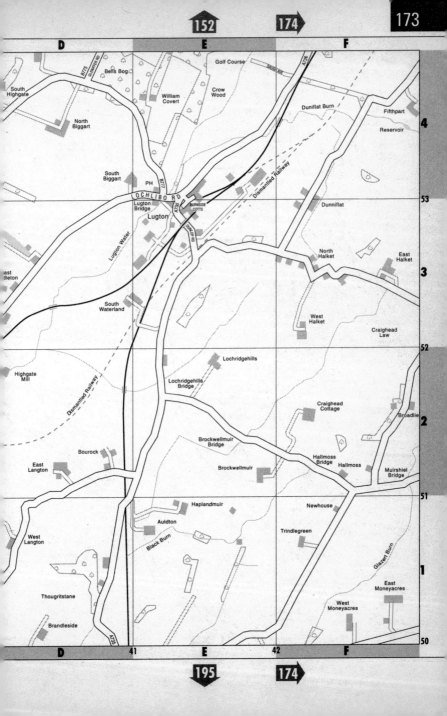

D   E   F

Golf Course

Bells Bog

South Highgate

William Covert

Crow Wood

Dunflat Burn

Fifthpart

North Biggart

Reservoir

4

South Biggart

PH

LOCHLIBO RD

Lugton Bridge

Lugton

BURNSIDE COTTS

Dunniflat

53

Lugton Water

DUNLOP RD

North Halket

East Halket

Dismantled Railway

3

East ...dleton

South Waterland

West Halket

Craighead Law

52

Highgate Mill

Lochridgehills

Dismantled Railway

Lochridgehills Bridge

Craighead Cottage

Broadlie

2

Bourock

Brockwellmuir Bridge

East Langton

Brockwellmuir

Hallmoss Bridge

Hallmoss

Muirshiel Bridge

51

Haplandmuir

Newhouse

West Langton

Auldton

Trindlegreen

Black Burn

Glazert Burn

1

Thougritstane

West Moneyacres

East Moneyacres

Brandleside

50

D   41   E   42   F

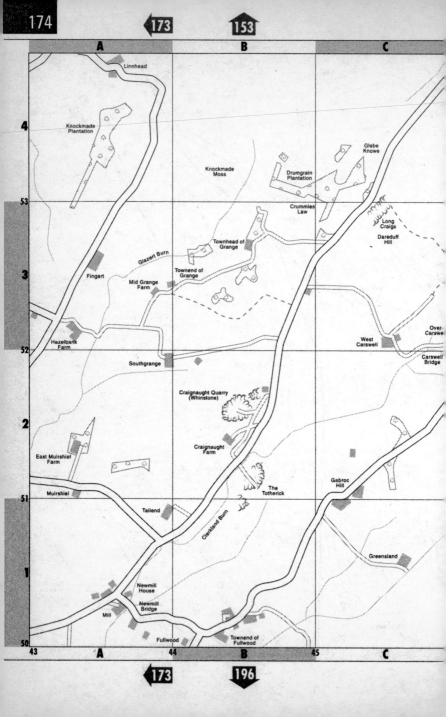

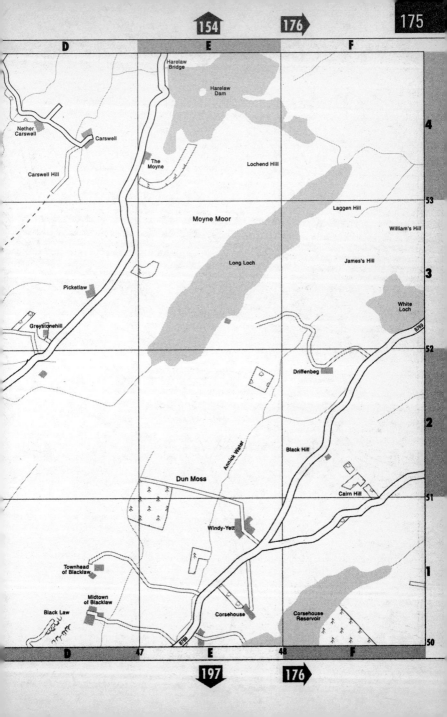

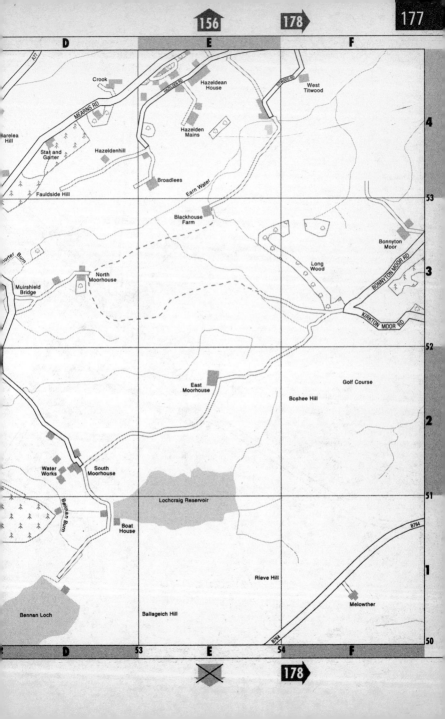

D
E
F

4

53

3

52

2

51

1

50

Crook

Hazeldean House

West Titwood

MEARNS RD

Harelea Hill

Star and Garter

Hazeldenhill

Hazelden Mains

Fauldside Hill

Broadlees

Earn Water

Blackhouse Farm

Bonnyton Moor

Shorter Burn

Long Wood

North Moorhouse

Muirshield Bridge

BONNYTON MOOR RD

KIRKTON MOOR RD

East Moorhouse

Golf Course

Boshee Hill

Water Works

South Moorhouse

Lochcraig Reservoir

Bennan Burn

Boat House

B764

Bennan Loch

Ballageich Hill

Rieve Hill

Melowther

B764

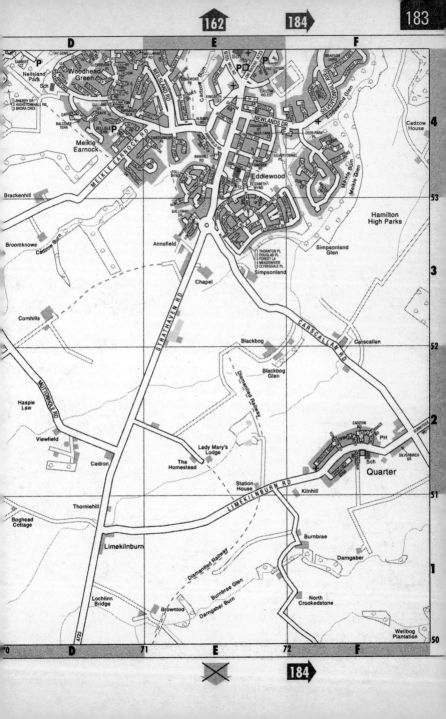

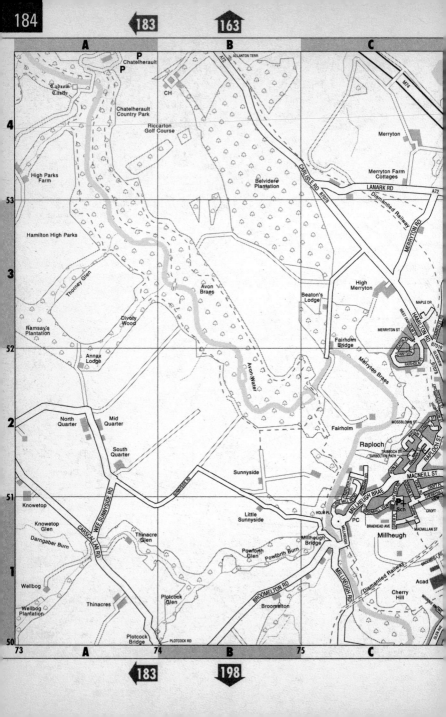

A   B   C

P Chatelherault
P
Cadzow
Castle
CH
ATLANTON TERR

4   Chatelherault
Country Park
Riccarton
Golf Course
Merryton

Belvidere
Plantation
Merryton Farm
Cottages
LANARK RD
High Parks
Farm
Dismantled Railway
53   CARLISLE RD B7078   A72

Hamilton High Parks

MERRYTON RD

3   Thorney Glen   Avon
Braes   Beaton's
Lodge   High
Merryton   MAPLE DR
Divoty
Wood   HAMILTON RD
WEST
Ramsay's
Plantation   MERRYTON ST
52   Annax
Lodge   Fairholm
Bridge   FAIRHOLM
Avon Water   Merryton Braes

MOSSBLOWN ST
2   North
Quarter   Mid
Quarter   Fairholm   Raploch
TARBOLTON PATH   RAPLOCH ST
South
Quarter   MACNEILL ST
Sunnyside

51   Knowetop   Little
Sunnyside   HOLM PL
PC   MILLHEUGH BRAE   P
Sch   CROFT
Knowetop Glen   Thinacre
Glen   BRAEHEAD AVE   MACMILLAN ST
Darngaber Burn   CARSCALLAN RD   WEE SUNNYSIDE RD   Powforth
Glen   Millheugh
Bridge   Millheugh
Powforth Burn

1   Wellbog   Dismantled Railway
MILLHEUGH RD   Cherry
Hill   Acad
Wellbog
Plantation   Thinacres   Plotcock
Glen   BROOMELTON RD   Broomelton
Plotcock
Bridge   PLOTCOCK RD
50
73   A   74   B   75   C

164
186

D   **E**   **F**

Sewage Works

Randalls Orchard

Carbarns Orchard

Carbarnswood

Lower Carbarns

Carbarns Wood

CAMERON CRES

GIGHA QUADRANT

MONTGOMERY CRES

ALLERSHAW TOWER 1
BIRKSHAW TOWER 2
CAPLAW TOWER 3

North Lodge

Castlehill

CASTLEHILL RD

B754

LINGHOPE PL

4

Upper Carbarns

Hall Gill

Cambusnethan House

Highmainshead Wood

53

Junction 7

Tannery's Burn

River Clyde

LANARK RD

Highlees

Prince's Lodge

Whittrick Burn

Nursery

3

SUMMERLEE RD

Skelly Gill

Sewage Works

Tilework Cottage

Nursery

Nursery

52

WILLOWBANK

CHERRYVALE

HAMILTON ST

DUKE ST

Cemy

EAST STATION IND EST

GLENORAN LA
EASTWOOD WAY

Meadowhill

Skellyton Wood

Dismtd Rly

Skellyton

2

P

WELLGATE ST

MONTGOMERY ST

PERCY ST

UNION ST

DRYGATE ST

GORBALS CROSS

PC

Off

Liby

Sta

PLEASANCE

1 GLENBURN WYND
2 PORTLAND WYND
3 SIGHTHILL LOAN
4 PARKNOOK WAY
5 LOMOND WLK
6 HOZIER LOAN
7 CRAIGIE LA
8 GEORGE WAY
9 ALBANY WYND
10 CRAIGMORE WYND
11 BURNS LOAN
12 ABBEY WLK
13 BANK WAY
14 BRAESIDE LA

Larkhall

Golf Course

Milburn Glen

A71

CORNSILLOCH BRAE

A72

MACNEILL ST

CHARING CROSS

BURNSIDE PL

STUART ST

UNION ST

Sch

Burnhead

Milburn Cottage

1 LOMING
2 DOON ST
3 LOVAT PATH
4 ALLOWAY ST
5 BALMORAL PATH
6 MILLBURN LA
7 MOSSGIEL LA
8 WINDSOR PATH
9 CARRICK ST
10 GILLBANK CA
11 CATRINE ST
12 LOCHLEE LOAN

Mill Burn

AYR RD

Cornsilloch

51

BOWMANFLAT

CHERRYHILL VIEW

Leisure Centre

CHARLOTTE PATH

Machan

MACHAN RD

CHURCH ST

JOHN ST

ORCHARD GATE

CLYDE ST

HARELEESHILL RD

HILL ST

SUMMERHILL AVE

BURNHEAD RD

CH

BOLT

Millburn

Shawsburn

13 MAXWELL PATH
14 BRUCE'S LOAN
15 FLEMING WAY
16 ALOA WAY
17 ARRAN PATH
18 DALSERF PATH
19 LOCHNAGAR WAY
20 BLAIR ATHOLL DR
21 TRINITY WAY
22 GLEN FRUIN DR
23 ST ANDREWS PATH
24 LAWRIE WAY
25 KATRIONA PATH
26 CAMERON PATH
27 HAZELDENE LA
28 ROSEMOUNT LA
29 LAUREL LA
30 BRACKEN WAY
31 CAMERONIAN WAY
32 LAMMER WYND

ASHGILLHEAD RD

Nurseries

Stewart Gill

Works

1

MELROSE

WHINNIE KNOWE

ROBERT SMILLIE CRES

Sch

Ind View

GREENELM

REDHOLME

BERTRAM ST

Hareleeshill

KEIR HARDIE RD

BRAESIDE WAY

DUNEATON WYNDE

Shawsrigg

M74

Dismtd Rly

Ashgillhead

50

76   **D**   **77**   **E**   **78**   **F**

199
186

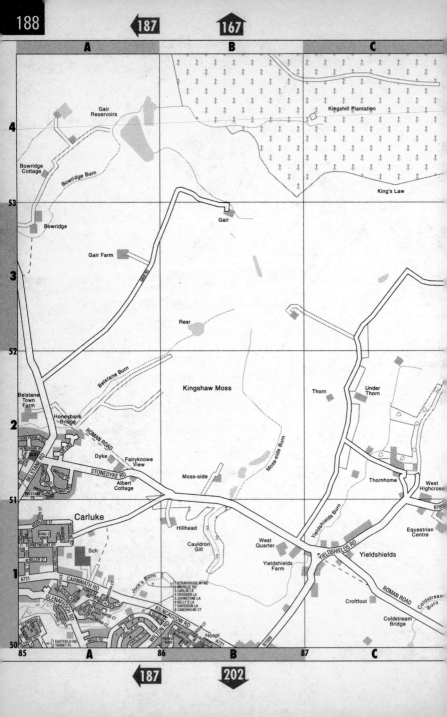

Kingshill Plantation

Gair
Reservoirs

4

Bowridge
Cottage

Bowridge Burn

King's Law

53

Bowridge

Gair

Gair Farm

3

Resr

52

Belstane Burn

Kingshaw Moss

Thorn

Under
Thorn

Beistane
Town
Farm

2

Honeybank
Bridge

ROMAN ROAD

Dyke   Fairyknowe
View

Moss-side Burn

Thornhome

West
Highcross

STONEDYKE RD

Albert
Cottage

Moss-side

51

Carluke

Hillhead

Cauldron
Gill

West
Quarter

Yieldshields Burn

Equestrian
Centre

Sch

B70

CARNWATH RD

Jock's Burn

Yieldshields
Farm

YIELDSHIELDS RD

Yieldshields

1

A721

GLENACLOCH RD

1 STRAGHOUSE WYND
2 MAIRLEE RD
3 CARLIN LA
4 CROSSEN LA
5 JOHNSTONE LA
6 KELLY'S LA
7 DAVIDSON LA
8 CANDIMILNE CT

ROMAN ROAD

Coldstream
Burn

Croftfoot

KILNCADZOW RD

WILTON RD

Hospl

Coldstream
Bridge

1 EASTFIELD RD
2 TARBET PL

A721

B7056

50

85   A   86   B   87   C

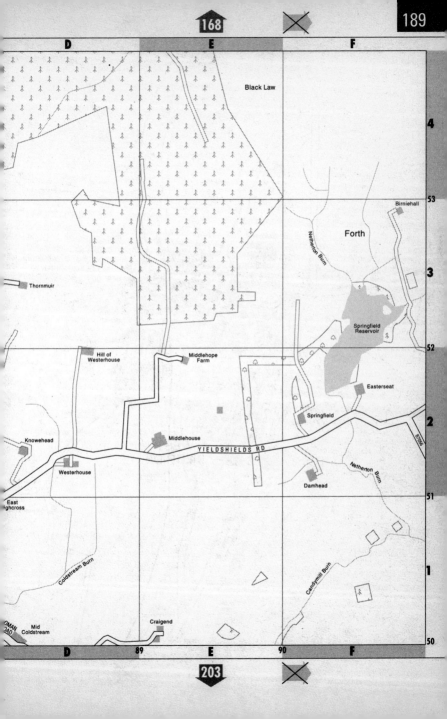

D   E   F

Black Law

4

53

Birniehall

Forth

Netherton Burn

Thornmuir

3

Springfield
Reservoir

52

Hill of
Westerhouse

Middlehope
Farm

Easterseat

Springfield

Middlehouse

2

Knowehead

YIELDSHIELDS RD

B7056

Westerhouse

Netherton Burn

Damhead

East
ighcross

51

Coldstream Burn

Candymill Burn

1

OMAN
OAD

Mid
Coldstream

Craigend

50

D   89   E   90   F

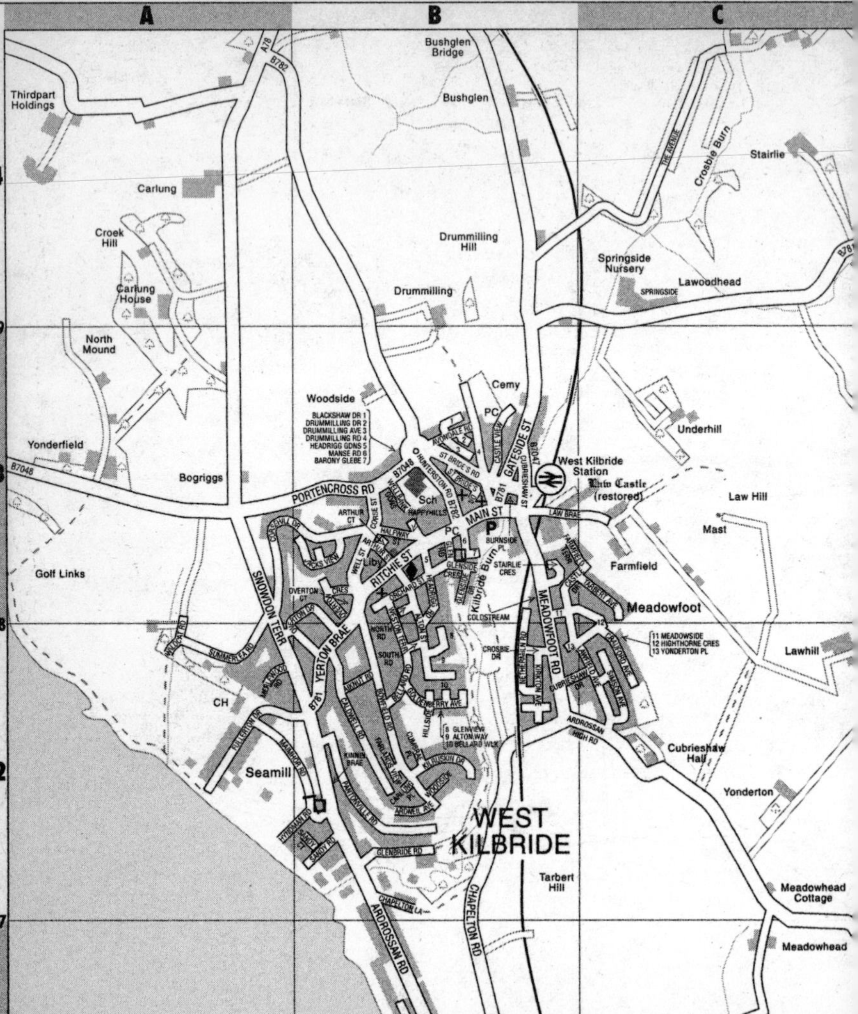

A   B   C

Thirdpart Holdings

Bushglen Bridge

Bushglen

Crosbie Burn

Stairlie

4

Carlung

Croek Hill

Drummilling Hill

Springside Nursery

Lawoodhead

Carlung House

Drummilling

SPRINGSIDE

49

North Mound

Woodside

Cemy

PC

Underhill

BLACKSHAW DR 1
DRUMMILLING DR 2
DRUMMILLING AVE 3
DRUMMILLING RD 4
HEADRIGG GDNS 5
MANSE RD 6
BARONY GLEBE 7

West Kilbride Station

Law Hill

Yonderfield

B7048

Bogriggs

PORTENCROSS RD

Kirk Castle (restored)

Mast

Sch

MAIN ST

Farmfield

3

Golf Links

ARTHUR CT

HAPPYHILLS

RITCHIE ST

BURNSIDE

STAIRLIE CRES

Meadowfoot

OVERTON

GOLDSTREAM

11 MEADOWSIDE
12 HIGHTHORNE CRES
13 YONDERTON PL

Lawhill

48

CH

SOUTH

CROSBIE DR

MEADOWFOOT RD

Cubrieshaw Hall

Seamill

2

8 GLENVIEW
9 ALTONWAY
10 BELLARD WALK

HIGH RD

ARDROSSAN

Yonderton

WEST KILBRIDE

Meadowhead Cottage

GLENBRIDE RD

Tarbert Hill

47

CHAPELTON LA

ARDROSSAN RD

CHAPELTON RD

Meadowhead

1

Chapelton

Kirkland Glen

North Inch

Godrock Burn

Bank Cottages

Kirkland

46

Hotel

19   A   20   B   21   C

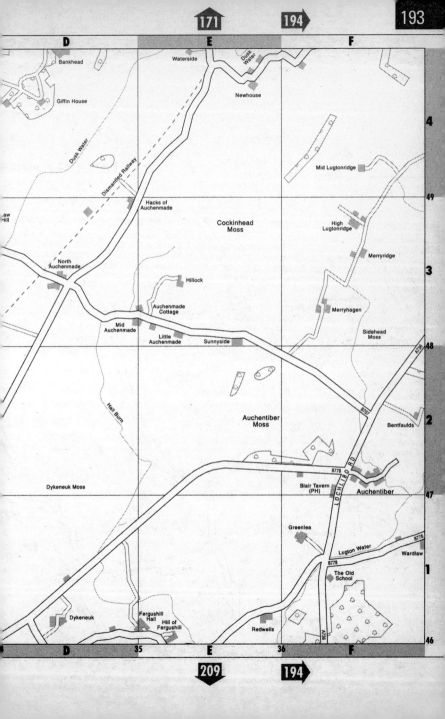

D E F

Bankhead

Waterside

Dusk Water

Giffin House

Newhouse

4

Dusk Water

Mid Lugtonridge

Dismantled Railway

49

-aw -Hill

Hacks of Auchenmade

Cockinhead Moss

High Lugtonridge

North Auchenmade

Merryridge

3

Hillock

Auchenmade Cottage

Merryhagen

Mid Auchenmade

Little Auchenmade

Sunnyside

Sidehead Moss

48

A736

Hall Burn

B702

Auchentiber Moss

Bentfaulds

2

B778

Dykeneuk Moss

LOCHLIBO RD

Blair Tavern (PH)

Auchentiber

47

Greenlea

Lugton Water

B778

Wardlaw

B778

The Old School

1

Dykeneuk

Fergushill Hall

Hill of Fergushill

Redwells

A736

46

D 35 E 36 F

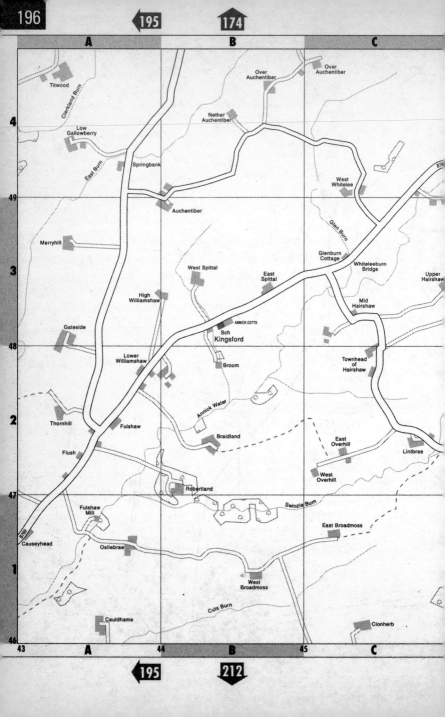

195
174

A **B** **C**

4

Titwood

Clerkland Burn

Over Auchentiber
Over Auchentiber

Low Gallowberry

Nether Auchentiber

East Burn

Springbank

West Whitelee

49

Auchentiber

Merryhill

Glen Burn

Glenburn Cottage

Whiteleeburn Bridge

B76

3

West Spittal

East Spittal

Upper Hairshaw

High Williamshaw

Mid Hairshaw

Gateside

ANNICK COTTS

Sch Kingsford

48

Lower Williamshaw

Broom

Townhead of Hairshaw

Annick Water

2

Thornhill

Fulshaw

Braidland

East Overhill

Lintbrae

Flush

West Overhill

Robertland

47

Swinzie Burn

Fulshaw Mill

East Broadmoss

B708

Causeyhead

Osliebrae

1

West Broadmoss

Cauldhame

Cuts Burn

Cionherb

46

43 **A** 44 **B** 45 **C**

195
212

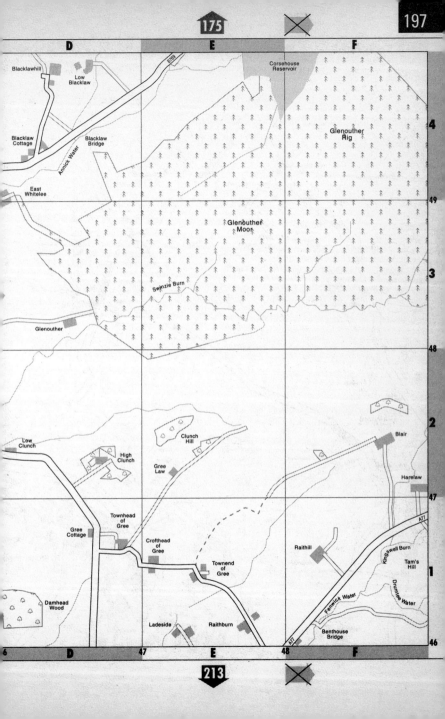

D   E   F

Blacklawhill

Low
Blacklaw

B769

Corsehouse
Reservoir

Glenouther
Rig

4

Blacklaw
Cottage

Blacklaw
Bridge

Arnick Water

East
Whitelee

49

Glenouther
Moor

3

Swinzie Burn

Glenouther

48

Clunch
Hill

2

Low
Clunch

Blair

High
Clunch

Harelaw

Gree
Law

47

Townhead
of Gree

A71

Gree
Cottage

Crofthead
of Gree

Raithill

Kingswell Burn

Tam's
Hill

Townend
of Gree

Drumfea Water

1

Damhead
Wood

Fenwick Water

Ladeside

Raithburn

Benthouse
Bridge

A71

46

6   D   47   E   48   F

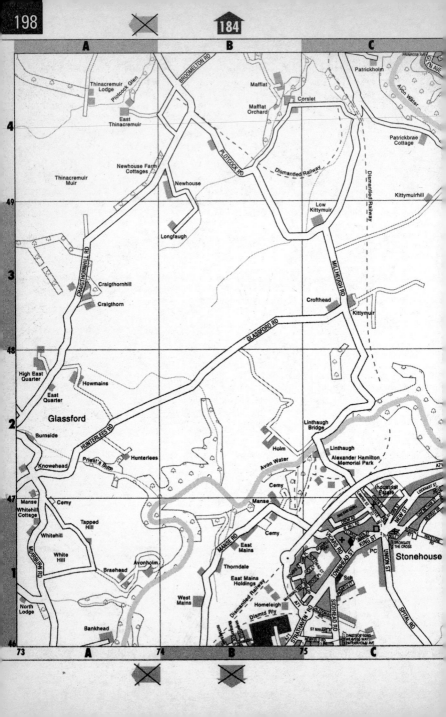

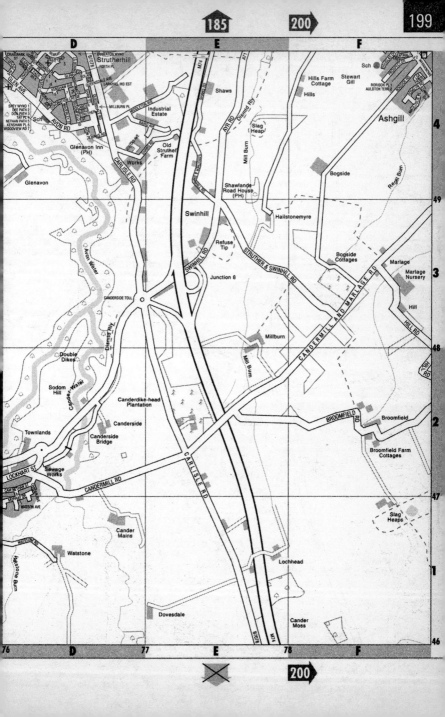

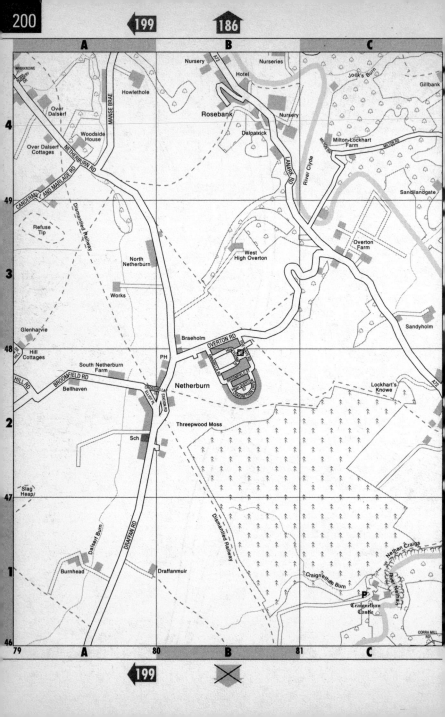

East Coldstream

Callagreen

ROMAN ROAD

Craighead

Candymill Burn

4

wanside

Hill Rigg
Mast

49

KILNCADZOW RD

Mast

Greenbank Farm

Back Burn

westtown

Midtown

Kilncadzow

CARNWATH RD

Hill of Kilncadzow

3

CRAIGENHILL RD

Hole

Muirhead

48

Drums

A721

Collielaw Cottage

2

Collielaw

Birkenhead

Tinto View

47

Fullwood

ROMAN ROAD (course of)

WHITELEES RD

OR RD

Fullwood Burn

Wellhead

1

Cleghorn

Camp Wood

46

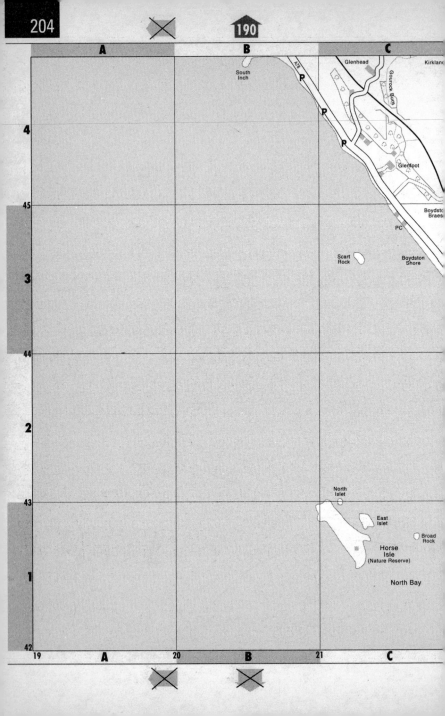

4

45

3

44

2

43

1

42

South
Inch

P

Glenhead

Kirkland

Gourock Burn

P

P

Glenfoot

Boydston
Braes

PC

Scart
Rock

Boydston
Shore

North
Islet

East
Islet

Broad
Rock

Horse
Isle
(Nature Reserve)

North Bay

A78

205

A | B | C

4

Towerlodge

Littlelaught

Meiklelaught

45

West Knockrivoch
Mount

Lochwood

KILN CLAY RD

Bankend

East Knockrivoch
Mount

Knockrivoch

Diddup

3

Stevenston or
Ashgrove Loch

South Knockrivoch
Mount

The Craigs | Loch Craigs

44

Glen
Banks

Golf
Course

Ford

Lochcraigs

Sharphill

Corsankell

Glen Burn

CH

Filter
Station

Hill

2

SHARPHILL
IND EST

Mast

Middlepart

Fellie Hill

Greenhead
Holdings

43

1 ISLAY CRES
2 KEIR VARDIE PL
3 JEAN ARMOUR PL
4 ABBOTSFORD PL
5 TALISMAN WLK
6 MUNRO WLK

Quarrel Burn

MIDDLEPART

MAXWELL PL 1
CLEMENTS PL 2
OAKLAND DR 3
ABCHURLIE DR 4
ASHGROVE AVE 5
ABERELAW AVE 6

Sch

HILLHEAD RD

Sch

LANDSBOROUGH
PL
Hawk

Schs

Mayfield

1

7 MIDDLEPART CRES
8 DUGUID DR
9 PROSPECTHILL RD
10 McNAY CRES
11 McKERRON PL
12 CLARK PL
13 ADAMS AVE
14 LOCHRANZA PL

Priest
Hill

Kerelaw
Mains

KERELAW RD

Stevenston Burn

Cemy

Sch

HAWKHILL DR

1 JOHN BROGAN PL
MARY LOVE PL
GOSPEL PL
CLYDE VIEW AVE
CAPONCRAIG AVE

GLENCAIRN ST

MOUNT PLEASANT

KILWINNING RD

Ardeer Mains

Ca

HIGH RD

HIGH RD

TOWNHEAD ST

DUBBS RD

42

25 | A | 26 | B | 27 | C

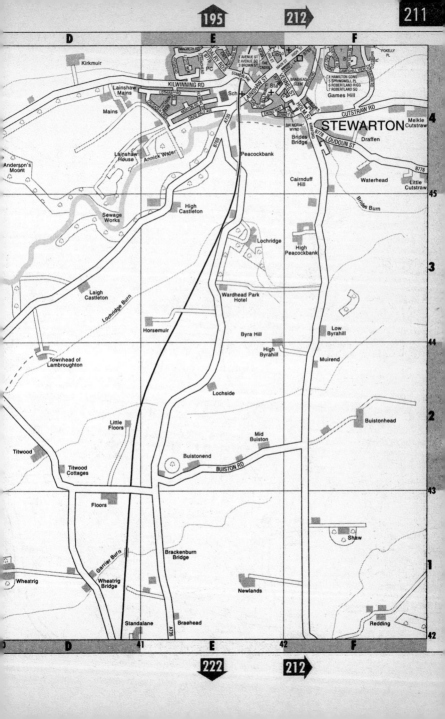

D E F

Kirkmuir

Lainshaw Mains

Mains

Lothianford

KILWINNING RD

MAGRETH RD

DALRY RD

2 AVENUE ST
3 AVENUE SQ
3 BROWN ST.

THE CROSS

PC

Sch

Lainshaw
House

Annick Water

Anderson's
Moont

Sewage
Works

High
Castleton

Laigh
Castleton

Lochridge Burn

Horsemuir

Townhead of
Lambroughton

Little
Floors

Titwood

Titwood
Cottages

Floors

Garrier Burn

Wheatrig

Wheatrig
Bridge

Standalane

Braehead

Brackenburn
Bridge

Buistonend

BUISTON RD

Lochside

Mid
Buiston

Newlands

Byra Hill

High
Byrahill

Wardhead Park
Hotel

Lochridge

Peacockbank

4 HAMILTON GDNS
5 SPRINGWELL PL
6 ROBERTLAND RIGS
7 ROBERTLAND SQ

Games Hill

CUSTRAW RD

STEWARTON

Meikle
Custraw

Draffen

Brides
Bridge

LOUDOUN ST

KINGFORD

Cairnduff
Hill

Brides Burn

Waterhead

Little
Cutstraw

B778

High
Peacockbank

Low
Byrahill

Muirend

Buistonhead

Shaw

Redding

BALMORAL
WYND

B769

A735

STANDALANE

LAINSHAW ST

VENNEL ST

HIGH ST

MAIN ST

4

45

3

44

2

43

1

42

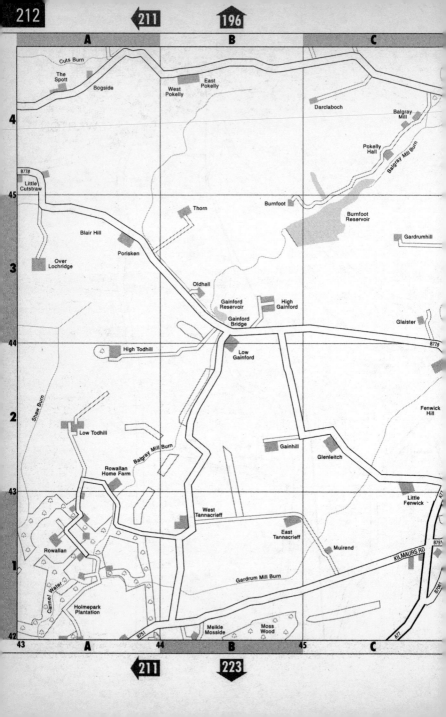

Damhead

Laighmuir

Glassock
Bridge

North
Glassock

South
Glassock

4

45

Pokelly
Hill

Rigghill

Gardrum Mill Burn

Gardrum
Mill

High
Gardrum

Midton

Warnockland

Water
Works

3

Townend

Amlaird

Gardrum

Shelgo Burn

Fenwick Water

Glaister
Bridge

44

BLACKFAULDS
GDNS

Cemy

Skernieland

Waterside

Sch

Waterside
Bridge

Hall
PH

KIRKTON RD

Fenwick

Kirkton
Bridge

Arness

Sch

2

Wyllieland

MAIN RD

POLES RD

Wyllielandhill

Hareshaw

Hareshaw
Mill

Bruntland

43

Laigh
Fenwick

WATERS LA

Midland

Bruntland
Bridge

Craufurdland Water

Hareshawmuir Water

Fenwick
Bridge

Dalsraith
Bridge

Horsehill

Pockinan
Bridge

1

Aikenhead

Dalsraith

Darwhilling

A719

42

202

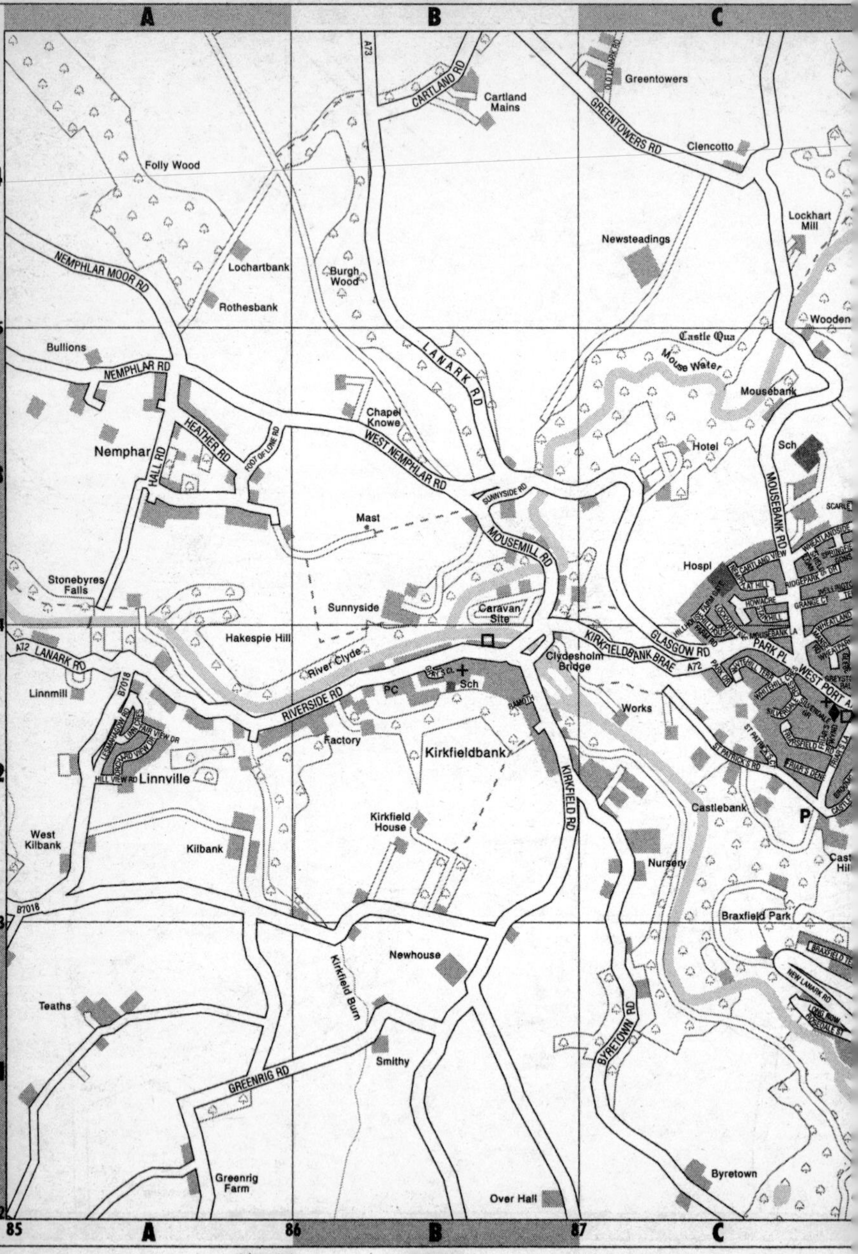

4

Folly Wood

NEMPHLAR MOOR RD

Lochartbank

Rothesbank

Bullions

45

NEMPHLAR RD

HEATHER RD

HALL RD

HOOF OF LOW RD

Nemphar

Chapel Knowe

WEST NEMPHLAR RD

CARTLAND RD

A73

Cartland Mains

LANARK RD

Burgh Wood

SUNNYSIDE RD

Mast

3

MOUSEMILL RD

Stonebyres Falls

Sunnyside

Hakespie Hill

44

A72 LANARK RD

Linnmill

B7018

RIVERSIDE RD

River Clyde

Caravan Site

Clydesholm Bridge

PO

Sch

KIRKFIELDBANK BRAE

GLASGOW RD

A72

Factory

Kirkfieldbank

Works

HILL VIEW RD

HILL VIEW DR

Linnville

2

West Kilbank

Kilbank

Kirkfield House

KIRKFIELD RD

Castlebank

Nursery

Cast Hil

P

43

B7016

Braxfield Park

NEW LANARK RD

Kirkfield Burn

Newhouse

BYRETOWN RD

Teaths

1

GREENRIG RD

Smithy

Greenrig Farm

Over Hall

Byretown

42

Greentowers

GREENTOWERS RD

Ciencotto

Lockhart Mill

Newsteadings

Castle Qua

Mouse Water

Wooden

Mousebank

Hotel

Sch

MOUSEBANK ROW

SCARLE

Hospl

PARK PL

WEST PORT

Hosl

SALTCOATS

South Beach
Promenade
South Bay

Eagle
Rock

SOUTH CRESCENT RD 1
BUTE TERR 2
STANLEY PL 3
GALLOWAY PL 4
LAIGHDYKES RD 5
HARLEY PL 6
BROWN PL 7
TAYLOR PL 8
O'CONNOR CT 9
BARNETT CT 10
WELLPARK LA 11
VICTORIA RD 12
BRAEHEAD PL 13
GLADSTONE RD 14
PARKEND RD 15
NINEYARD ST 16
FINDLAY'S BRAE 17
ERSKINE PL 18
BRADSHAW ST 19
QUAY ST 20
GREEN ST 21

West
Shore

Pav   Harbour

Saltcoats
Sta

PCs

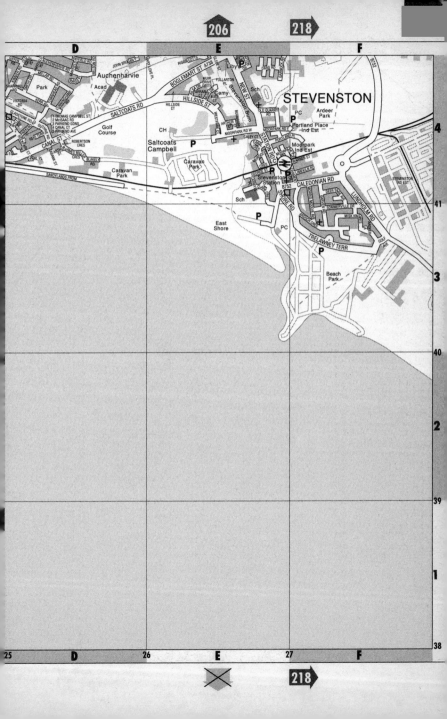

217
207

A
B
C

DUBBS RD

Penny Burn

EYEBROW RD   A78

B79

Nethermains
Bridge

WATERSIDE RD

4

Refuse
Tip

41

3

P

P   PC

Works

Hospl

Stevenston
Site

River Garnock

Golf
Course

CH

40

Bogside

Bogside
Race Course
(disused)

Crooky's
Point

2

River Irvine

39

Bogside
Flats

1

Irvine
Harbour

River Irvine

HARBOUR ST

38   BEACH DR

P

Leisure
Centre

28   A   29   B   30   C

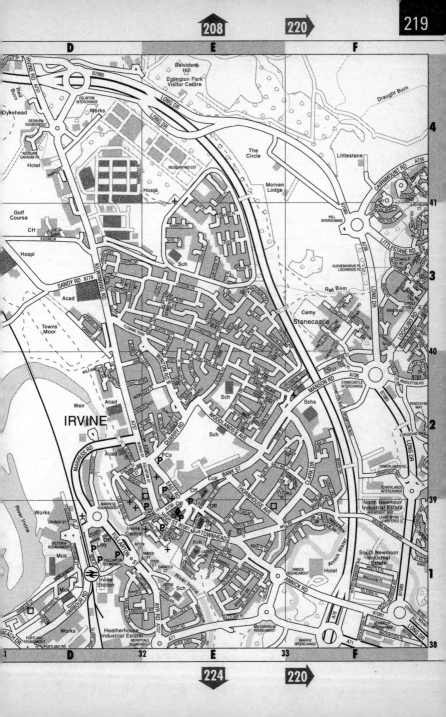

219
209

219
225

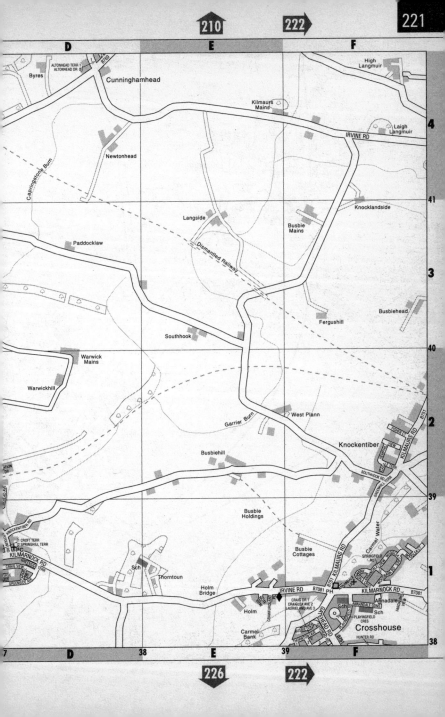

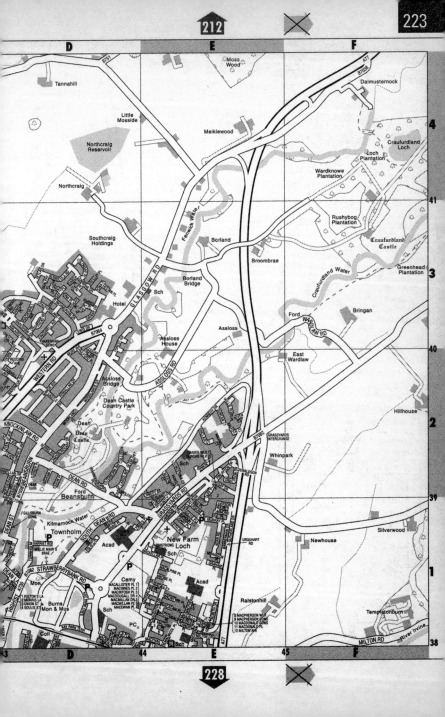

219

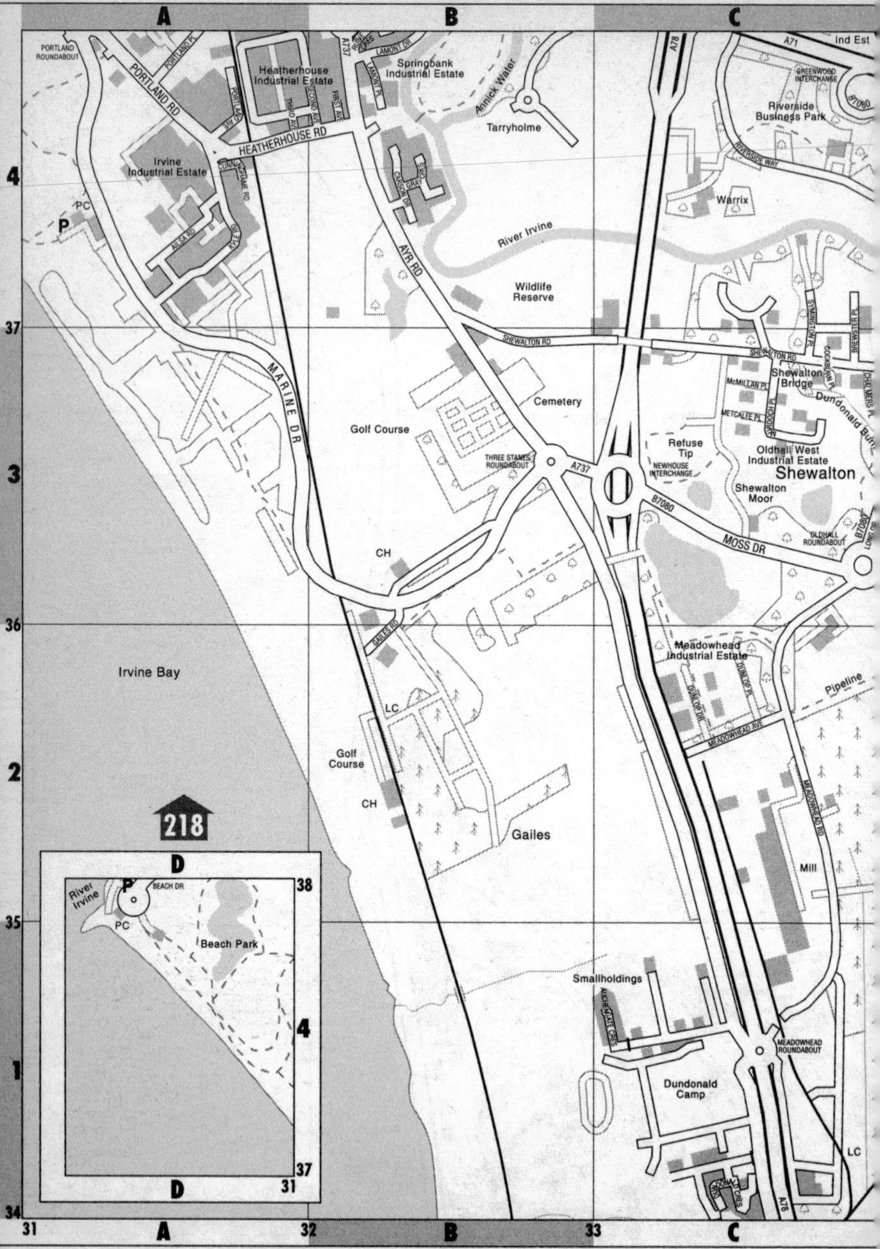
A
B
C
PORTLAND ROUNDABOUT
PORTLAND PL
PORTLAND RD
Heatherhouse Industrial Estate
THIRD AVE
SECOND AVE
FIRST AVE
HEATHERHOUSE RD
A737
LAMONT DR
LAMONT PL
Springbank Industrial Estate
Annick Water
Tarryholme
A78
A71
Ind Est
GREENWOOD INTERCHANGE
B7080
Riverside Business Park
RIVERSIDE WAY
Irvine Industrial Estate
CUNNINGHAME RD
AILSA RD
KYLE RD
CARSON DR
GRAY CRES
PC
P
Warrix
River Irvine
AYR RD
Wildlife Reserve
SHEWALTON RD
SYMINGTON PL
BREWSTER PL
COCKBURN PL
CHALMERS PL
Shewalton Bridge
McMILLAN PL
METCALFE PL
MURDOCH PL
Dundonald Burn
MARINE DR
Cemetery
Golf Course
Refuse Tip
Oldhall West Industrial Estate
Shewalton
THREE STANES ROUNDABOUT
A737
NEWHOUSE INTERCHANGE
Shewalton Moor
B7080
MOSS DR
OLDHALL ROUNDABOUT
LONG RD
CH
GAILES RD
Meadowhead Industrial Estate
DUNLOP DR
DUNLOP PL
Irvine Bay
Pipeline
LC
MEADOWHEAD AVE
Golf Course
CH
MEADOWHEAD RD
Gailes
Mill
218
D
River Irvine
P
BEACH DR
38
PC
Beach Park
4
37
31
Smallholdings
MEADOWHEAD ROUNDABOUT
Dundonald Camp
LC
A78
4
37
3
36
2
35
1
34
31
32
33

229

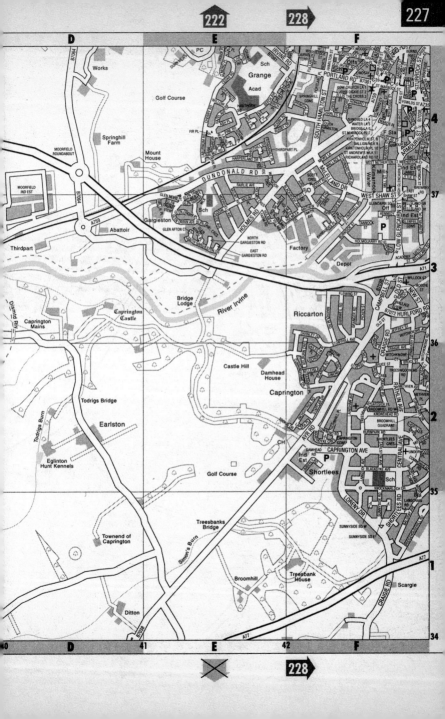

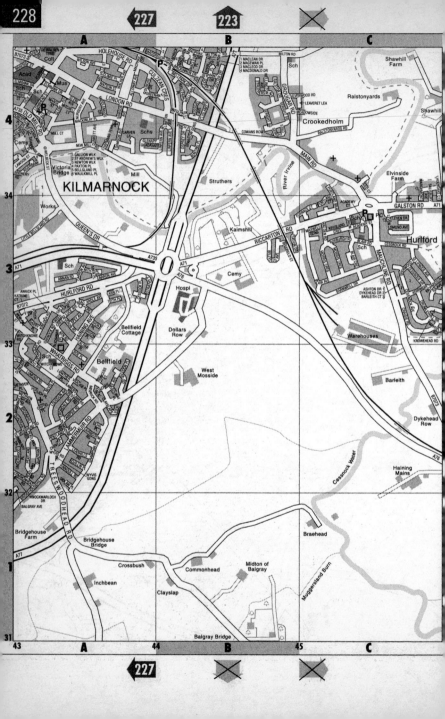

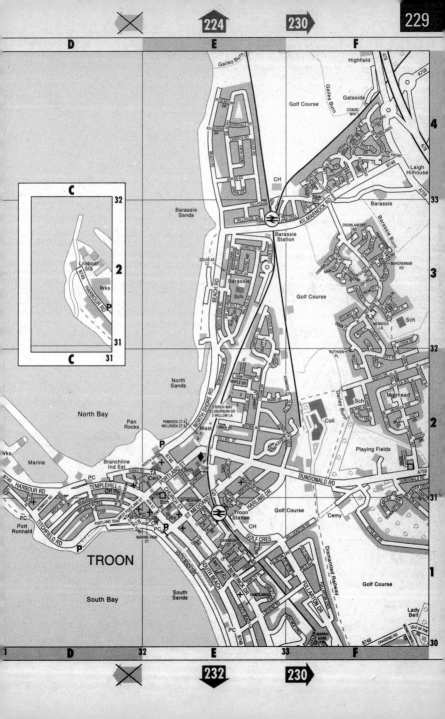

TROON

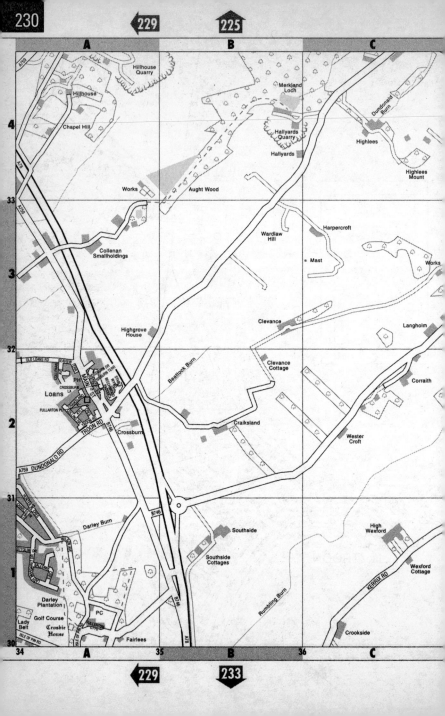

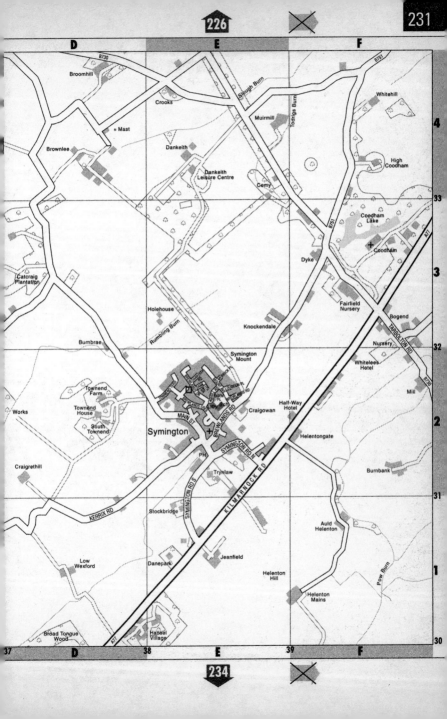

B730

Broomhill

Crooks

Slaugh Burn

Todrigs Burn

Whitehill

Mast

Muirmill

High Coodham

Brownlee

Dankeith

B751

Dankeith Leisure Centre

Cemy

Coodham Lake

A77

Catcraig Plantation

Dyke

Coodham

3

Holehouse

Rumbling Burn

Fairfield Nursery

Bogend

Bumbrae

Knockendale

TARBOLTON RD

Nursery

32

Symington Mount

B730

Symington

Townend Farm

Townend House

South Townend

MAIN ST

BREWLANDS RD

Craigowan

Half-Way Hotel

Whitelees Hotel

Mill

Works

SYMINGTON RD S

SYMINGTON RD

Helentongate

2

Craigrethill

PH

Trynlaw

KILMARNOCK RD

Helentongate

Burnbank

KERRIX RD

Stockbridge

31

Low Wexford

Danepark

Jeanfield

Auld Helenton

Pow Burn

Helenton Hill

1

Broad Tongue Wood

A77

Hansel Village

Helenton Mains

30

229

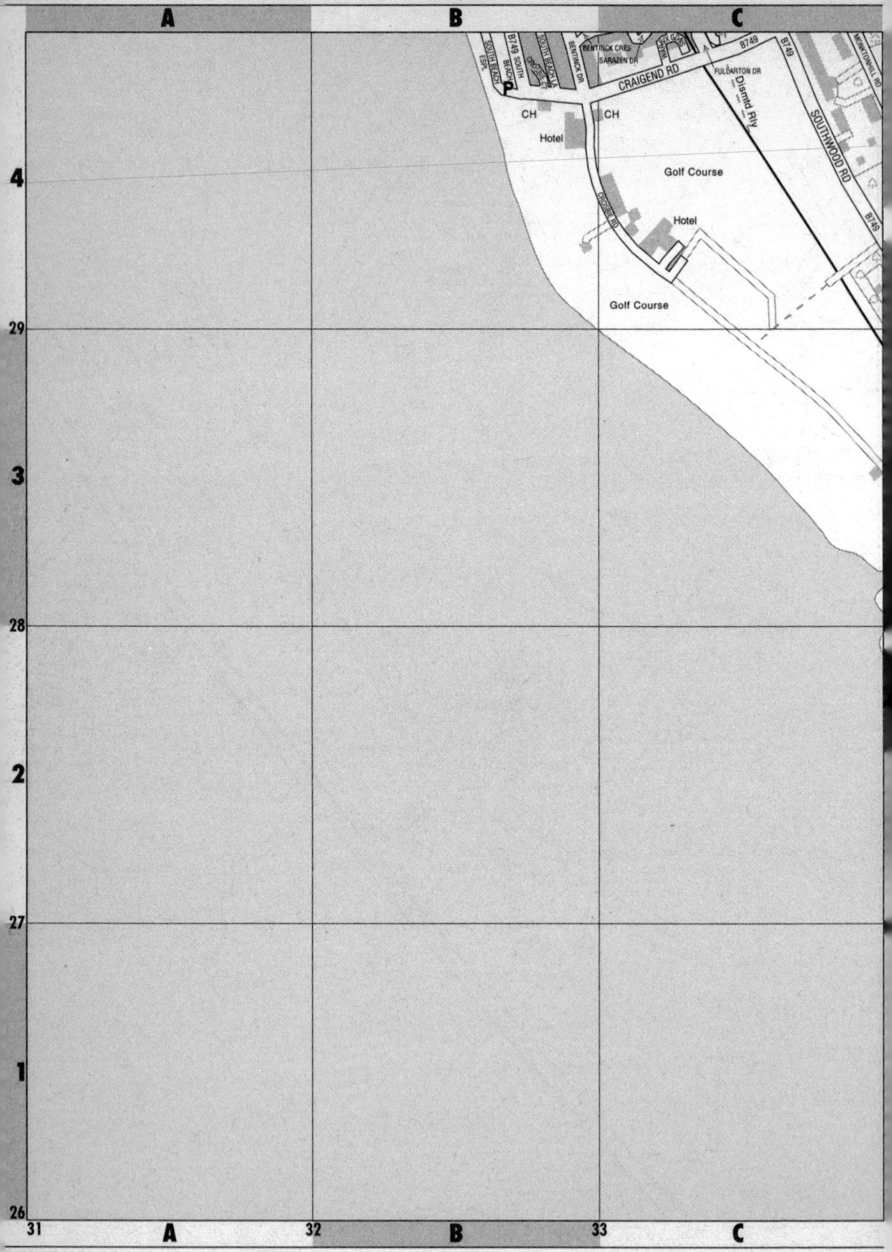
A
B
C
SOUTH BEACH ESPL
B749 SOUTH BEACH
CROSBIE CT
SOUTH BEACH LA
BENTINCK DR
BENTINCK CRES
SARAZEN DR
CRAIGEND RD
FULLARTON DR
Dismtd Rly
B749
B749
SOUTHWOOD RD
MONKTONHILL RD
B749
P
CH
CH
Hotel
Golf Course
CROSBIE RD
Hotel
Golf Course
4
29
3
28
2
27
1
26
31
A
32
B
33
C

235

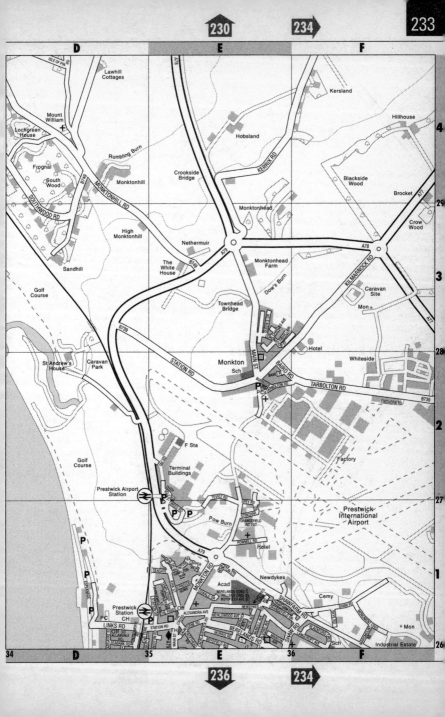

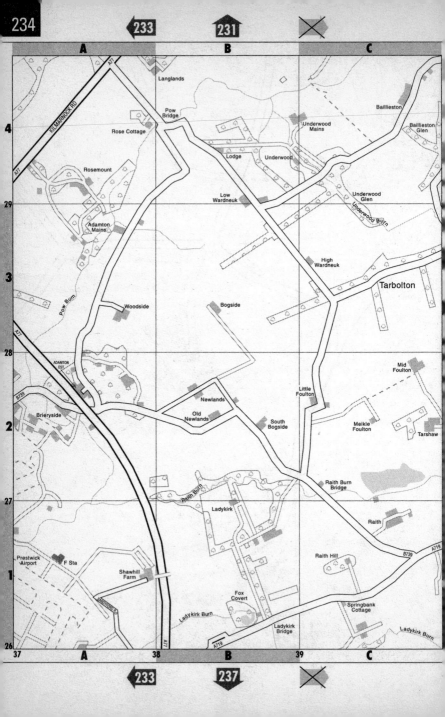

232
236

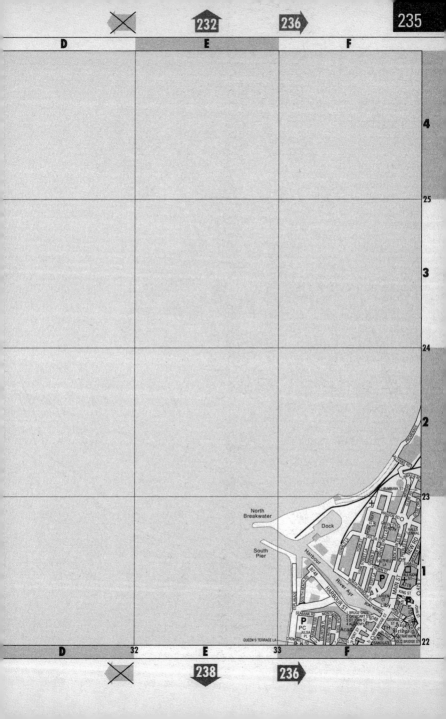

4

25

3

24

2

23

North
Breakwater

Dock

South
Pier

Harbour

River Ayr

1

HARBOUR ST

QUEEN'S TERRACE LA

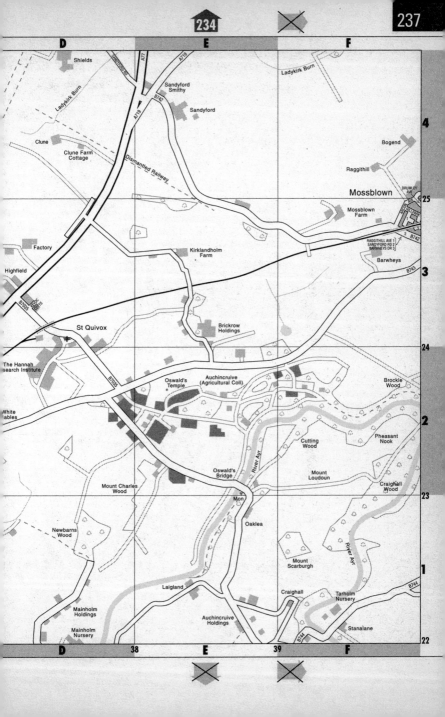

AYR

QUEEN'S TERRACE LA 1
CROMWELL RD 2
AILSA PL 3
BRUCE CRES 4
DOUGLAS LA 5
DOUGLAS ST 6
HOPE ST 7
LORNE ARC 8
BLACKFRIARS WLK 9
KYLE CTR 10
BARNS TERRACE LA 11
DALBLAIR ARC 12

KILLOCH PL 13
BURNS STATUE SQ 14
SMITH ST 15
PARKHOUSE ST 16

Low Green

Seafield

Playing Fields

Golf Course

Slaphouse Burn
Slaphouse

Slaphouse Bridge

Belleisle

Hotel

Belleisle Park

Belleisle Bridge

Cunning Park

Longhill Point

Greenan

Golf Course

Rozelle

Rozelle Park

Nursery

Mill

River Doon

Doonfoot

Doonbank Farm

Longhill

Burton Smithy

High Greenan

Dismantled Railway

Alloway

Heritage Cen

River Doon

Dismtd Rly

Liby

Mus

EXPLANATION OF THE STREET INDEX REFERENCE SYSTEM

Street names are listed alphabetically and show the locality, the page number and a reference to the square in which the name falls on the map page.

Example:	Canal St. Pais..113 E2

Canal St	This is the full street name, which may have been abbreviated on the map.
Pais	This is the abbreviation for the town, village or locality in which the street falls.
113	This is the page number of the map on which the street name appears.
E2	The letter and figure indicate the square on the map in which the centre of the street falls..The square can be found at the junction of the vertical column carrying the appropriate letter and the horizontal row carrying the appropriate figure.

ABBREVIATIONS USED IN THE INDEX
Road Names

Approach	App	Green	Gn
Arcade	Arc	Grove	Gr
Avenue	Ave	Heights	Hts
Boulevard	Bvd	Industrial Estate	Ind Est
Buildings	Bldgs	Junction	Junc
Business Park	Bsns Pk	Lane	La
Business Centre	Bsns Ctr	North	N
Broadway	Bwy	Orchard	Orch
Causeway	Cswy	Parade	Par
Centre	Ctr	Park	Pk
Circle	Circ	Passage	Pas
Circus	Cir	Place	Pl
Close	Cl	Precinct	Prec
Common	Comm	Promenade	Prom
Corner	Cnr	Retail Park	Ret Pk
Cottages	Cotts	Road	Rd
Court	Ct	South	S
Courtyard	Ctyd	Square	Sq
Crescent	Cres	Stairs	Strs
Drive	Dr	Steps	Stps
Drove	Dro	Street,Saint	St
East	E	Terrace	Terr
Embankment	Emb	Trading Estate	Trad Est
Esplanade	Espl	Walk	Wlk
Estate	Est	West	W
Gardens	Gdns	Yard	Yd

Key to abbreviations of Town, Village and Rural locality names used in the index of street names.

Addiewell	Add	168	C2
Airdrie	Aird	123	D4
Airth	Air	14	B2
Alexandria	Alex	27	E3
Allanton	Alla	167	D4
Alloa	All	10	B3
Alva	Alva	5	D3
Arden	Arden	18	B3
Ardrossan	Ard	205	D1
Armadale	Arm	107	F4
Ashgill	Ash	199	F4
Auldhouse	Auld	180	B1
Avonbridge	Avon	87	F4
Ayr	Ayr	238	B4
Banknock	Bank	38	C2
Bannockburn	Bann	7	F1
Barrhead	Barr	134	C1
Bearsden	Bear	75	F3
Beith	Beith	150	A1
Bishopbriggs	Bish	78	B2
Bishopton	Bishop	72	A2
Blackridge	Blac	107	E2
Bonhill	Bonh	28	A2
Bonnybridge	Bon	40	A3
Bridge of Allan	B of A	2	A4
Bridge of Weir	B of W	110	C4
Calderbank	Calder	123	D2
Caldercruix	Cald	105	D3
California	Cali	66	C3
Cambus	Camb	9	D4
Cambusbarron	Cam	6	B3
Cardross	Card	48	A4
Carluke	Car	188	A1
Chapelhall	Chap	123	F1
Chapelton	Chapel	181	E1
Clackmannan	Clack	10	C2
Cleland	Cle	144	A1
Clydebank	Clyde	74	A1
Coatbridge	Coat	122	B3
Cowie	Cowie	12	B4
Coylton	Coy	239	F2
Crossford	Cro	201	D1
Crosshouse	Cross	221	F1
Cumbernauld	Cumb	62	B3
Dalry	Dalry	191	D4
Denny	Den	21	F1
Dumbarton	Dumb	49	F1
Dunblane	Dun	1	B4
Dundonald	Dund	225	F1
Dunipace	Duni	21	E2
Dunlop	Dunlop	195	E4
Duntocher	Dunt	74	A4
Eaglesham	Eagle	178	C3
East Kilbride	E Kil	159	E2
Eastfield	East	127	E2
Erskine	Ersk	73	D1
Fallin	Fall	8	B2
Falkirk	Falk	42	B3
Fauldhouse	Fau	147	F4
Fenwick	Fen	213	D2
Fishcross	Fish	5	F2
Forth	For	189	F3
Gartocharn	Gart	20	C4
Glasgow	Glasg	117	E3
Glassford	Glass	198	A2
Glenboig	Glen	101	F3
Glenmavis	Glenm	102	C2
Gourock	Gour	44	B4
Grangemouth	Gran	24	C2
Greengairs	Gree	83	F1
Greenock	Green	46	A3
Hamilton	Ham	162	B2
Harthill	Hart	127	F3
Hattonrig	Hat	142	A3
Helensburgh	Helen	16	A1
Holytown	Holy	143	D3
Houston	Hous	91	D1
Howwood	How	130	C3
Hurlford	Hurl	228	C3
Inchinnan	Inch	93	E3
Irvine	Irvine	219	D2
Johnstone	John	111	F1
Kilbarchan	Kilbar	111	D2
Kilbirnie	Kilb	149	D1
Kilmacolm	Kil	89	E4
Kilmarnock	Kilmk	228	A4
Kilmaurs	Kilm	222	B4
Kilncadzow	Kilnc	203	D3
Kilsyth	Kils	60	B4
Kilwinning	Kilw	207	F1
Kirkintilloch	Kirk	79	F4
Lanark	Lan	215	E2
Langbank	Lang	70	A4
Larbert	Larb	23	D2
Larkhall	Lark	185	D2
Laurieston	Laur	42	C2
Law	Law	186	C3
Lennoxtown	Lennox	57	E4
Linwood	Lin	112	A3
Lochwinnoch	Loch	129	D2
Menstrie	Men	3	F3
Milngavie	Miln	55	D2
Milton of Campsie	M of C	58	B3
Mossblown	Moss	237	F4
Motherwell	Mother	163	E4
Muirhead	Muir	100	B4
Neilston	Neil	154	C3
New Sauchie	N Sau	5	E1
Newmains	New	166	A3
Newton Mearns	Newt M	156	B2
Old Kilpatrick	O Kill	73	D3
Paisley	Pais	113	E1
Plains	Plains	104	A2
Plean	Plea	12	B2
Port Glasgow	P Glasg	47	F1
Prestwick	Pres	236	A4
Quarter	Quart	183	F2
Renfrew	Ren	94	C1
Rhu	Rhu	15	E3
Rosneath	Ros	15	D2
Salsburgh	Sals	125	E1
Saltcoats	Salt	216	B4
Shewalton	Shew	224	C3
Shieldhill	Shi	66	B3
Shotts	Shot	146	C3
Slamannan	Slam	86	A3
Springside	Spring	220	C1
Stenhousemuir	Sten	23	E2
Stepps	Stepps	99	E3
Stevenston	Steven	217	F4
Stewarton	Stew	211	F4
Stirling	Stir	7	E4
Stonehouse	Stone	198	C1
Strathblane	Strath	31	E2
Symington	Sym	231	E2
Tannochside	Tan	141	D4
Tarbolton	Tar	234	C3
Thorntonhall	Thorn	158	B2
Tillicoultry	Till	5	F4
Torwood	Tor	22	C3
Troon	Troon	229	D1
Tullibody	Tull	4	B2
Twechar	Twe	59	F2
Uddingston	Udd	140	C3
Uplawmoor	Uplaw	153	D2
West Kilbride	W Kil	190	B2
Westfield	West	87	F1
Wishaw	Wish	165	D2

242

Abbey Cl. Pais — Alloway Dr. Clyde

Abbey Cl. Pais 113 F2
Abbey Craig Rd. N Sau 5 D1
Abbey Dr. Glasg 95 F2
Abbey Mill. Stir 7 E4
Abbey Pl. Aird 123 E2
Abbey Rd. John 112 B1
Abbey Rd Pl. Stir 7 E4
Abbey Rd. Stir 2 B1
Abbey Wlk. Lark 185 D2
Abbeycraig Rd. Glasg 100 C1
Abbeydale Way. Glasg 138 B2
Abbeygate. Kilw 207 F2
Abbeygreen. Kilw 207 F2
Abbeygreen St. Glasg 100 C1
Abbeyhill St. Glasg 118 C4
Abbeylands Rd. Dunt 74 B3
Abbot Ct. Pres 236 B3
Abbot Rd. Bann 7 E2
Abbot St. Glasg 116 C1
Abbot St. Green 45 E2
Abbot St. Pais 113 F3
Abbot's Ave. Kilw 207 F1
Abbot's Pl. Kilw 207 F2
Abbot's Wlk. Kilw 207 F2
Abbots Cres. Ayr 238 A1
Abbots Ct. Falk 42 B4
Abbots Moss Dr. Falk 41 F1
Abbots Rd. Falk 42 B4
Abbots Terr. Aird 123 E2
Abbots Way. Ayr 238 B2
Abbotsburn Way. Pais 113 E4
Abbotsford Ave. Glasg 138 A4
Abbotsford Ave. Ham 162 A4
Abbotsford Ave. Lark 185 D1
Abbotsford. Bish 78 B1
Abbotsford Brae. E Kil 159 F2
Abbotsford Cres. Ham 162 A3
Abbotsford Cres. Pais 132 C4
Abbotsford Cres. Shot 146 C3
Abbotsford Cres. Wish 165 E2
Abbotsford Ct. Cumb 82 C4
Abbotsford Dr. Helen 25 C4
Abbotsford Dr. Klrk 79 F4
Abbotsford Gdns. Falk 24 A1
Abbotsford La. Hat 141 F3
Abbotsford Pl. Cumb 82 C4
Abbotsford Pl. Glasg 117 D2
Abbotsford Pl. Glasg 117 D3
Abbotsford Pl. Holy 143 D3
Abbotsford Pl. Salt 206 A1
Abbotsford Pl. Stir 2 B1
Abbotsford Rd. Bear 75 E3
Abbotsford Rd. Chap 123 F1
Abbotsford Rd. Clyde 74 A1
Abbotsford Rd. Cumb 82 C4
Abbotsford Rd. Ham 162 A3
Abbotsford Rd. Wish 165 E2
Abbotsford St. Falk 42 A4
Abbotsford Terr. Lan 215 E2
Abbotshall Ave. Glasg 74 C2
Abbotsinch Rd. Inch 93 F1
Abbott Cres. Clyde 94 B4
Aberconway St. Clyde 94 B4
Abercorn Ave. Glasg 114 C4
Abercorn Cres. Ham 162 C1
Abercorn Dr. Ham 162 C1
Abercorn Ind Est. Pais 113 F3
Abercorn Pl. Glasg 76 C1
Abercorn Rd. Newt M 156 B3
Abercorn St. Dunt 74 C4
Abercorn St. Pais 113 F3
Abercrombie Cres. Coat 120 C3
Abercrombie Dr. Bear 75 D4
Abercrombie Pl. Kils 36 A1
Abercrombie Pl. Men 3 F3
Abercrombie St. Falk 41 F3
Abercromby Cres. E Kil 160 A2
Abercromby Cres. Helen 16 C2
Abercromby Dr. Ayr 238 B2
Abercromby Dr. B of A 2 A4
Abercromby Dr. Glasg 117 F3
Abercromby Pl. E Kil 160 A2
Abercromby Pl. Stir 7 D4
Abercromby Pl. Tull 4 A1
Abercromby Pl W. Helen 16 B2
Abercromby Sq. Glasg 117 F3
Abercromby St E. Helen 16 C1
Abercromby St. Glasg 117 F3
Aberdalgie Rd. Glasg 120 A4
Aberdeen Rd. Chap 123 E2
Aberdour St. Glasg 118 B4
Aberfeldy Ave. Plains 103 F2
Aberfeldy St. Glasg 118 B4
Aberfeldy Terr. Irvine 220 A3
Aberfoyle Rd. Green 46 A1
Aberfoyle St. Glasg 118 B4
Aberlady Rd. Glasg 115 F3
Aberlady St. Cle 144 A1
Aberlour Pl. Irvine 219 F3
Abernethy Dr. Lin 112 A3
Abernethy Pk. E Kil 159 E1
Abernethy St. Glasg 118 B4
Abernethyn Rd. New 166 A3
Aberuthven Dr. Glasg 119 D2
Abiegail Pl. Udd 140 B1
Aboukir St. Glasg 115 F4
Aboyne Ave. Stir 2 B2
Aboyne Dr. Pais 113 F1
Aboyne St. Glasg 115 F3
Acacia Dr. Barr 134 A3
Acacia Dr. Beith 171 D4
Acacia Dr. Pais 113 D1
Acacia Pl. John 132 A4
Academy Brae. Beith 171 D4
Academy Ct. Hurl 228 C3
Academy Ct. Irvine 219 D2
Academy Pk. Aird 123 D4
Academy Pk. Glasg 116 B2
Academy Pl. Bann 7 F1
Academy Rd. Glasg 136 B1
Academy Rd. Irvine 219 D2
Academy Rd. Stir 7 D4
Academy St. Aird 123 D4
Academy St. All 9 F4
Academy St. Ayr 235 F1
Academy St. Coat 122 A4
Academy St. Glasg 119 D2
Academy St. Glasg 119 D3
Academy St. Hurl 228 C3
Academy St. Kilmk 227 F3
Academy St. Lark 185 D2
Academy St. Troon 229 E1
Academy Terr. Hat 142 A3
Acer Cres. Pais 113 D1
Achamore Rd. Glasg 74 C2
Acherhill Gdns. Glasg 95 D4
Achnasheen Rd. Chap 124 A3
Achray Ct. All 10 B3
Achray Dr. Pais 113 D1
Achray Dr. Stir 2 A2
Achray Pl. Coat 101 E1
Achray Pl. Miln 54 B2
Achray Rd. Cumb 82 B3
Acorn Cres. Lar 23 E1
Acorn Ct. Glasg 117 F2
Acorn St. Glasg 117 F2
Acre Dr. Glasg 76 A1
Acre Rd. Glasg 76 A1
Acre Valley Rd. Lennox 57 D1
Acredyke Cres. Glasg 98 B4
Acredyke Pl. Glasg 98 B3
Acredyke Rd. Glasg 98 B4
Acredyke Rd. Glasg 137 F4
Acres The. Lark 185 D1
Adair Ave. Salt 205 F1
Adam Ave. Aird 123 D4
Adam Cres. Sten 23 F1
Adam St. Falk 42 B3
Adam St. Gour 44 C4
Adam St. Green 46 A2
Adam's Gate. Troon 229 F3
Adams Ave. Salt 205 F1
Adams Court La. Glasg 117 D3
Adams Ct. Troon 229 F3
Adams Pl. Kils 60 B4
Adams Wlk. Irvine 219 F1
Adamslie Cres. Klrk 79 D4
Adamslie Dr. Klrk 79 D4
Adamson Pl. Stir 2 A2
Adamson St. Hat 142 B3
Adamswell St. Glasg 97 F2
Adamswell Terr. Muir 81 D1
Adamton Est. Pres 234 A2
Adamton Road N. Pres 236 B4
Adamton Road S. Pres 236 B3
Adamton Terr. Pres 236 B4
Addie St. Mother 163 F4
Addiewell Pl. Coat 122 A2
Addiewell St. Glasg 119 D4
Addison Gr. Glasg 135 F2
Addison Pl. Glasg 135 F2
Addison Rd. Glasg 96 B2
Addison Rd. Glasg 135 F2
Adelaide Rd. E Kil 180 B4
Adelaide St. Gour 44 C4
Adelaide St. Helen 16 C1
Adele St. Mother 163 F2
Adelphi St. Glasg 117 E3
Admiral St. Glasg 116 C3
Admiralty Gdns. Kil 73 D3
Admiralty Gr. O Kill 73 D3
Admiralty Pl. O Kill 73 D3
Affric Ave. Plains 104 A2
Affric Dr. Falk 24 B1
Affric Dr. Pais 114 A1
Affric Loan. Shot 146 C3
Afton Ave. Kilmk 223 D2
Afton Ave. Pres 236 B3
Afton Cres. Bear 76 A2
Afton Ct. Ayr 239 D3
Afton Ct. Irvine 219 D1
Afton Ct. Stir 7 E3
Afton Dr. Bank 39 E4
Afton Dr. Ren 94 C1
Afton Gdns. Troon 229 F2
Afton Gdns. Udd 161 D3
Afton Pl. Ard 205 E2
Afton Rd. Cumb 62 A2
Afton Rd. Steven 217 E4
Afton St. Glasg 136 C4
Afton St. Lark 185 E1
Afton View. Kirk 58 C1
Agamemnon St. Clyde 73 F1
Agnew Ave. Coat 122 B4
Agnew Gr. Tan 141 E3
Agnew La. Glasg 117 D1
Aikenhead House. Glasg 137 E3
Aikenhead Rd. Glasg 137 E4
Aikman Pl. E Kil 160 A2
Aikman Rd. Mother 163 D3
Aiknut Rd. W Kil 190 B2
Ailean Dr. Glasg 119 F2
Ailean Gdns. Glasg 119 F2
Aileymill Gdns. Gour 44 C2
Ailort Pl. E Kil 159 F2
Ailort Ave. Glasg 137 D3
Ailort Loan. Wish 165 F3
Ailsa Ave. Ash 199 F4
Ailsa Ave. Mother 163 D4
Ailsa Cres. Mother 163 D4
Ailsa Ct. Coat 121 F2
Ailsa Ct. Ham 161 E1
Ailsa Dr. Dunt 74 B3
Ailsa Dr. Glasg 136 C4
Ailsa Dr. Glasg 137 F3
Ailsa Dr. Glasg 157 E4
Ailsa Dr. Kirk 58 C1
Ailsa Dr. Pais 133 E4
Ailsa Dr. Steven 217 E4
Ailsa Dr. Udd 141 D2
Ailsa Gdns. Ard 205 E2
Ailsa Pl. Ayr 235 F1
Ailsa Pl. Coat 121 F2
Ailsa Pl. Kilmk 223 D3
Ailsa Rd. Bish 78 A1
Ailsa Rd. Coat 121 F2
Ailsa Rd. Gour 44 B3
Ailsa Rd. Irvine 224 A4
Ailsa Rd. Ren 94 B1
Ailsa Rd. Salt 206 A1
Ailsa Rd. Troon 229 D2
Ailsa St. Pres 236 A4
Ailsa Tower. Glasg 138 C2
Ailsa View. Stew 195 F1
Ainsdale Ct. Kilw 207 D2
Ainslie Rd. Cumb 62 B2
Ainslie Rd. Glasg 115 D4
Airbles Cres. Mother 163 E3
Airbles Dr. Mother 163 E3
Airbles Farm Rd. Mother 163 E3
Airbles Rd. Mother 163 E3
Airbles St. Mother 163 F3
Aird Ave. Kilmk 227 F4
Aird's La. Glasg 117 E3
Airdale Ave. Glasg 136 B1
Airdrie Rd. Cald 105 E1
Airdrie Rd. Car 187 F2
Airdrie Rd. Cumb 81 F2
Airdrie Rd. Cumb 82 A3
Airdrie Rd. Cumb 82 A4
Airdrie Rd. Kils 60 B4
Airdrie Rd. Law 187 F2
Airdrie Rd. Plains 103 F1
Airdriehill Rd. Aird 103 E2
Airdriehill St. Aird 103 E1
Airgold Dr. Glasg 74 C2
Airlie Ave. Bear 75 F4
Airlie Ct. Ayr 238 C3
Airlie Dr. Hat 142 A3
Airlie Gdns. Glasg 138 B2
Airlie La. Glasg 96 A2
Airlie Rd. Glasg 120 A2
Airlie St. Glasg 96 A2
Airlink Ind Est. Pais 113 F4
Airlour Rd. Glasg 136 C3
Airth Ct. Mother 142 B1
Airth Dr. Glasg 115 F2
Airth Dr. Stir 7 E2
Airth La. Glasg 115 F2
Airthrey Ave. B of A 2 A3
Airthrey Ave. Glasg 95 F2
Airthrey Dr. Sten 24 A2
Airthrey La. Glasg 95 F2
Airthrey Rd. B of A 2 B3
Airthrey Rd. Stir 2 B3
Airyligg Dr. Eagle 178 C3
Aitchison Dr. Lar 23 D2
Aitchison St. Aird 122 C4
Aitken Cres. Stir 7 D1
Aitken Dr. Beith 150 B1
Aitken Dr. Slam 86 A3
Aitken Gdns. Falk 41 F3
Aitken La. Alex 27 F4
Aitken Pl. Lan 215 D2
Aitken Rd. Falk 41 E3
Aitken Rd. Ham 183 F4
Aitken St. Aird 103 D1
Aitken St. Dalry 191 E4
Aitken St. Glasg 118 B4
Aitken Terr. Falk 41 E3
Aitkenbar Circ. Dumb 50 A3
Aitkenbar Dr. Dumb 50 A3
Aitkenbrae Dr. Pres 236 B4
Aitkenhead Ave. Coat 121 D2
Aitkenhead Rd. Chap 123 E1
Aitkenhead Rd. Coat 121 D1
Aitkenhead Rd. Tan 121 D1
Akarit Rd. Sten 23 F1
Alasdair Ct. Barr 134 B1
Alba Way. Ham 183 E3
Albans Cres. Mother 163 D4
Albany Ave. Glasg 119 E3
Albany Dr. Glasg 138 A3
Albany Dr. Lan 215 D2
Albany. E Kil 160 B2
Albany Pl. Udd 141 D1
Albany Quadrant. Glasg 119 E3
Albany Rd. Ham 183 E4
Albany St. Coat 121 F4
Albany St. Glasg 118 A2
Albany Terr. Glasg 138 C2
Albany Way. Pais 113 F4
Albany Wynd. Lark 185 D2
Albert Ave. Glasg 117 D1
Albert Ave. Stew 195 F1
Albert Cres. Aird 123 D4
Albert Cross. Glasg 116 C2
Albert Ct. Stew 195 F1
Albert Dr. Bear 76 A2
Albert Dr. Glasg 116 B2
Albert Dr. Glasg 138 A3
Albert Dr. Helen 16 C1
Albert Dr. Lark 185 D1
Albert Pl. Aird 123 D4
Albert Pl. Stew 195 F1
Albert Pl. Stir 7 D4
Albert Quadrant. Holy 143 D3
Albert Rd. Clyde 74 A2
Albert Rd. East 127 F3
Albert Rd. Falk 42 A2
Albert Rd. Glasg 117 D1
Albert Rd. Gour 44 B4
Albert Rd. Kilbar 111 E3
Albert Rd. Klrk 79 E2
Albert Rd. Ren 94 B2
Albert St. Alex 27 F2
Albert St. Coat 122 A4
Albert St. Ham 162 A3
Albert St. Helen 16 C1
Albert St. Mother 163 F4
Albert Terr. Ayr 239 D4
Albert Terr. Ham 162 A3
Albert Wynd. Stew 195 F1
Alberta Ave. Coat 121 F4
Alberta Ave. E Kil 180 B4
Alberta Cres. E Kil 180 B4
Alberta Pk. E Kil 180 B4
Alberta Pl. E Kil 180 B4
Albion Gate. Glasg 117 E4
Albion Gate. Pais 113 E3
Albion St. Coat 122 B3
Albion St. Glasg 117 E4
Albion St. Glasg 119 F2
Albion St. Mother 163 F3
Albion St. Pais 113 F3
Albion Way. E Kil 180 C3
Alcaig Rd. Glasg 115 F1
Alcath Rd. New 166 A3
Alder Ave. Ham 162 C1
Alder Ave. Klrk 79 D3
Alder Bank. Ayr 239 E3
Alder Bank. Tan 121 E1
Alder Cres. E Kil 180 B3
Alder Ct. Barr 134 B1
Alder Ct. E Kil 180 B3
Alder Gn. Irvine 220 A2
Alder La. Holy 143 E3
Alder Pl. E Kil 180 B3
Alder Pl. Glasg 136 B3
Alder Pl. John 112 A1
Alder Pl. Kilmk 227 E4
Alder Rd. Clyde 74 A3
Alder Rd. Cumb 62 B1
Alder Rd. Dumb 49 F2
Alder Rd. Glasg 136 B3
Alder Rd. M of C 58 A2
Alderbank Rd. P Glasg 47 D1
Alderbrae Rd. P Glasg 47 D1
Alderman Pl. Glasg 95 E3
Alderman Rd. Glasg 95 D3
Alderside Ave. Mother 164 B2
Alderside Gdns. Udd 140 C4
Alderside Pl. Udd 141 D2
Alderstocks. E Kil 180 C3
Alderston Ave. Ayr 236 A2
Alderston Pk. Ayr 236 A2
Alderston Pl. Ayr 236 A2
Alderston Pl. Hat 141 F2
Aldersyde Ave. Mother 164 B2
Aldersyde Ave. Troon 229 F2
Aldersyde Pl. Udd 140 B1
Aldersyde Terr. Cle 144 B1
Alderwood Rd. P Glasg 47 D1
Aldrin Rd. Helen 25 D4
Alexander Ave. Eagle 178 C3
Alexander Ave. Falk 42 C3
Alexander Ave. Steven 206 C1
Alexander Ave. Tan 141 E3
Alexander Ave. Twe 59 F2
Alexander
Balfour Gdns. Ham 162 B1
Alexander Dr. B of A 2 A4
Alexander
Fleming Ave. Kilb 148 C1
Alexander Gdns. Ham 163 D1
Alexander Pl. Irvine 219 E2
Alexander Pl. Kirk 80 A4
Alexander Pl. Rhu 15 E3
Alexander Rd. Shot 146 B3
Alexander St. Aird 122 C4
Alexander St. Alex 49 E4
Alexander St. Clyde 74 A1
Alexander St. Coat 122 A4
Alexander St. Dumb 50 A2
Alexander St. Wish 165 D1
Alexander Terr. Neil 154 B3
Alexandra Ave. Klrk 79 E2
Alexandra Ave. Pres 233 E1
Alexandra Ave. Stepps 99 E3
Alexandra Cross. Glasg 118 A4
Alexandra Ct. Glasg 118 A4
Alexandra Dr. All 9 F4
Alexandra Dr. Pais 113 D2
Alexandra Dr. Ren 94 B2
Alexandra Gdns. Klrk 79 E2
Alexandra Par. Glasg 118 A4
Alexandra Park St. Glasg 118 A4
Alexandra Pk. Kirk 79 E2
Alexandra Pl. Stir 2 B1
Alexandra Rd. Klrk 79 E2
Alexandra St. Klrk 79 E4
Alexandra Terr. Ayr 236 A2
Alexandra Terr. Kilw 207 E2
Alexandria Quadrant. Holy 143 D3
Alford Ave. Klrk 79 D4
Alford Pl. Irvine 219 F3
Alford Pl. Lin 111 F3
Alford Quadrant. Wish 165 D3
Alford St. Glasg 97 E2
Alfred La. Glasg 96 C2
Algie St. Glasg 136 C4
Algoma Pl. E Kil 180 A4
Alice Ave. Hat 142 A2
Alice St. Pais 113 F1
Aline Ct. Barr 134 A2
Alison Lea. E Kil 160 B2
Allan Ave. Car 187 F2
Allan Ave. Ren 94 C1
Allan Barr Ct. Falk 42 A1
Allan Cres. Alex 27 E2
Allan Cres. Dumb 50 A3
Allan Cres. Duni 21 E2
Allan Ct. E Kil 179 F4
Allan Dr. E Kil 179 F4
Allan Pk. Stir 7 D4
Allan Pl. Ayr 236 B2
Allan Pl. Dumb 50 A2
Allan Pl. Glasg 118 A1
Allan Sq. Irvine 219 F1
Allan St. Coat 121 E3
Allan St. Glasg 118 A1
Allan St. Mother 163 F4
Allanbank Rd. Lar 23 E1
Allanbank St. Alla 166 C4
Allandale Ave. Holy 143 F3
Allandale Cotts. Bon 39 E1
Allander Ave. Bish 77 D4
Allander Dr. Lennox 78 A4
Allander Gdns. Bish 77 F2
Allander Rd. Miln 55 D1
Allander St. Glasg 97 E2
Allands Ave. Inch 93 E3
Allanfauld Rd. Cumb 61 F1
Allanfauld Rd. Kils 36 B1
Allanshaw Gdns. Ham 162 A2
Allanshaw Gr. Ham 162 A1
Allanshaw St. Ham 162 B2
Allanton Ave. Glasg 114 C2
Allanton Dr. Glasg 115 E3
Allanton Gr. Wish 165 D3
Allanton Lea. Ham 183 E4
Allanton Pl. Ham 162 C1
Allanton Rd. Alla 166 C4
Allanton Rd. Shot 146 B1
Allanton Terr. Ham 184 B4
Allanvale. Dunlop 195 D4
Allanvale Rd. B of A 1 C4
Allanvale Rd. Pres 236 A4
Allanwater Gdns. B of A 2 A4
Allanwood Ct. B of A 2 A4
Allbany Cres. Holy 142 C3
Allendale. E Kil 159 E2
Allender Rd. Bear 75 E1
Allenfield Rd. Ayr 239 E3
Allershaw Pl. Wish 185 F4
Allershaw Rd. Wish 185 F4
Allershaw Tower. Wish 185 F4
Allerton Gdns. Glasg 119 F2
Alleysbank Rd. Glasg 118 A1
Allison Ave. Ersk 72 C1
Allison Dr. Glasg 139 D3
Allison Pl. Glasg 117 D1
Allison Pl. Muir 100 C2
Allison Pl. Newt M 156 B2
Allison St. Ayr 236 A1
Allison St. Glasg 117 D1
Allnach Pl. Glasg 120 C4
Alloa Rd. B of A 3 D2
Alloa Rd. N Sau 5 E2
Alloa Rd. Sten 23 F2
Alloa Rd. Sten 24 A2
Alloa Rd. Tull 4 B2
Alloway Ave. Kilmk 228 A4
Alloway. Ayr 238 C1
Alloway Cres. Bon 39 F3
Alloway Cres. Glasg 137 F3
Alloway Cres. Pais 134 B4
Alloway Ct. Kirk 59 D1
Alloway Dr. Clyde 74 B2

Alloway Dr. Cowie	12 B4	Anderson Dr. Ren	94 B2
Alloway Dr. Glasg	137 F3	Anderson Dr. Salt	206 A1
Alloway Dr. Kirk	59 D1	Anderson Dr. Stev	211 E4
Alloway Dr. Newt M	157 D2	Anderson Gdns. Udd	140 C1
Alloway Dr. Pais	134 A4	Anderson La. Aird	123 D4
Alloway Gdns. Kirk	161 E1	Anderson Pl. Kilmk	223 E1
Alloway Gdns. Kirk	59 D1	Anderson Pl. Stir	7 D2
Alloway Pk. Ayr	238 C4	Anderson Rd. Bishop	72 A2
Alloway Pl. Ard	205 E2	Anderson St. Aird	123 D4
Alloway Pl. Glasg	238 C4	Anderson St. Bon	40 A3
Alloway Place La. Ayr	238 C4	Anderson St. Glasg	96 A1
Alloway Quadrant. Kirk	59 D1	Anderson St. Ham	161 F3
Alloway Rd. E Kil	160 C2	Anderson St. Mother	163 F3
Alloway Rd. Glasg	136 B3	Anderson St P Glasg	47 E1
Alloway St. Ayr	238 C4	Anderson Terr. Ard	205 E1
Alloway St. Lark	185 E1	Anderson Terr. Bank	39 D2
Alloway Terr. Kirk	58 C1	Anderston Quay. Glasg	116 C3
Alloway Wynd. Holy	143 F2	Andrew Ave. Kirk	79 E2
Alma La. Falk	42 A3	Andrew Ave. Ren	94 C2
Alma St. Falk	42 A3	Andrew Cres. Sten	23 E2
Alma St. Glasg	118 A3	Andrew Dr. Clyde	94 B4
Alma Terr. Falk	42 A3	Andrew Pl. Car	187 F2
Almada La. Ham	162 B2	Andrew Sillars Ave. Glasg	139 D2
Almada La. Ham	162 B2	Andrew St. E Kil	159 F1
Almada St. Ham	162 B2	Andrew's La. Glasg	117 E3
Almond Ave. Ren	94 C1	Andrews St. Pais	113 F3
Almond Cres. Pais	112 C1	Anford Pl. Udd	161 F3
Almond Dr. Stir	7 E3	Angela Way. Udd	140 C2
Almond Dr. Bank	38 C1	Angle Gate. Glasg	95 E2
Almond Dr. Bishop	72 A1	Angle St. Stone	198 C1
Almond Dr. E Kil	160 A1	Angus Ave. Aird	123 D3
Almond Dr. Kirk	79 D3	Angus Ave. Bish	78 B1
Almond Pl. Coat	101 E1	Angus Ave. E Kil	160 A1
Almond Pl. Holy	143 D3	Angus Ave. Glasg	115 E2
Almond Rd. Kilmk	227 E4	Angus Ave. Ham	163 D2
Almond Rd. Bear	75 E1	Angus Ave. Mother	163 E4
Almond Rd. Cumb	62 C2	Angus Ave. Pres	236 B3
Almond Rd. Stepps	99 E3	Angus Gdns. Tan	140 C4
Almond St. Glasg	98 B1	Angus Oval. Glasg	115 D2
Almond Terr. East	127 E3	Angus Pl. E Kil	160 A1
Almond Vale. Tan	141 D4	Angus Pl. Glasg	115 D2
Almond Way. Mother	163 F2	Angus Rd. Car	188 A1
Almondbank. Plains	103 F2	Angus Rd. Gour	44 C3
Almswall Rd. Kilw	207 F2	Angus Rd. P Glasg	47 E1
Alness Cres. Glasg	119 D3	Angus St. Alex	27 F2
Alness St. Ham	162 B1	Angus St. Clyde	94 C4
Alness Terr. Ham	162 B1	Angus St. Glasg	97 F2
Alnwick Dr. Eagle	178 B2	Angus Wlk. Tan	141 D4
Alpha Way. Lark	185 E1	Ann Ct. Ham	162 A3
Alpha Ctr. Clyde	94 B4	Ann St. Green	45 F3
Alpine Gr. Tan	140 C4	Ann St. Green	45 F3
Alsatian Ave. Clyde	74 B1	Ann St. Ham	162 A3
Alsh Terr. Ham	162 A1	Ann St. John	112 A2
Alston Ave. Coat	122 A2	Annabella Rd. Ash	200 B2
Alston Gdns. Bear	75 D4	Annan Ave. E Kil	179 F4
Altnacraeg Gdns. Muir	81 D2	Annan Cr. Falk	42 C2
Altoft Pl. Dalry	191 D4	Annan Dr. Bear	75 E2
Alton Rd. Pais	114 B2	Annan Dr. Glasg	138 B4
Alton St. W Kil	190 B3	Annan Dr. Pais	112 C1
Altow Way. W Kil	190 B2	Annan Glade. Mother	164 A2
Altonhead Dr. Spring	210 A1	Annan Gr. Mother	164 A2
Altonhead Terr. Spring	221 E4	Annan Pl. John	131 E4
Altonhill Ave. Kilmk	222 C2	Annan Rd. Kilmk	228 A3
Altry Pl. Ayr	238 A1	Annan St. Mother	164 A2
Altyre St. Glasg	118 C2	Annandale Cres. Cross	221 F1
Aluckitha Ave. Dumb	50 A2	Annandale Gdns. Cross	221 F1
Alva Gdns. Glasg	115 F1	Annandale. Gree	83 F1
Alva Gdns. Bear	75 E4	Annandale St. Glasg	117 F4
Alva Pl. Kirk	79 F2	Annandale View. Cross	221 F1
Alva Terr. Green	45 D4	Annandale Way. Irvine	220 A3
Alvord Ave. Pres	233 E1	Annanhill Ave. Kilmk	222 B1
Alwyn Ave. Hous	111 E4	Annanhill Pl. Kilw	207 D2
Alwyn Ct. E Kil	159 F2	Annbank St. Glasg	117 F3
Alwyn Dr. E Kil	159 F2	Annbank St. Lark	184 C2
Alyssum Cres. Mother	163 E4	Anne Ave. Ren	94 B2
Alyth Cres. Glasg	158 B4	Anne Cres. Kirk	79 E2
Alyth Gdns. Glasg	115 F2	Anne Dr. B of A	2 A3
Alyth Gdns. Glasg	158 A4	Anne St. Alt	23 F2
Ambassador Way. Ren	94 B1	Annerley Ct. Coat	121 F3
Amber Terr. Ham	142 A2	Annerley Pl. Coat	121 F3
Ambleside. E Kil	180 A3	Annes Ct. Glasg	117 F3
Amethyst Ave. Hat	142 A2	Annet Rd. Bank	39 E3
Amisfield St. Glasg	96 C3	Annette St. Glasg	117 D2
Amlaird Rd. Kilmk	223 D3	Annfield Dr. Stir	7 E3
Amochrie Dr. Pais	133 D4	Annfield Gdns. Stir	7 D3
Amulree Pl. Glasg	119 D2	Annfield Gdns. Udd	140 B1
Amulree St. Glasg	119 D2	Annfield Glen Rd. Ayr	239 D2
Ancaster Dr. Glasg	95 F3	Annfield Pl. Glasg	117 F4
Ancaster La. Glasg	95 F3	Annfield Rd. Pres	236 A4
Anchor Ave. Pais	114 A2	Annfield Terr. Pres	236 A4
Anchor Cres. Pais	114 A2	Annick Cotts. Stew	196 B3
Anchor Dr. Pais	114 A2	Annick Cres. Stew	211 F4
Anchor La. Glasg	117 E4	Annick Ct. Irvine	219 E4
Anchor Wynd. Pais	114 A2	Annick Dr. Bear	75 E1
Ancroft St. Glasg	97 D2	Annick Dr. Irvine	220 A1
Andersen Ct. E Kil	180 C3	Annick Pl. Kilmk	228 A3
Andersen. E Kil	180 C3	Annick Pl. Troon	229 F2
Anderson Ave. Kils	36 A1	Annick Rd. Irvine	219 F4
Anderson Cres. Ayr	239 D2	Annick Rd. Irvine	220 A1
Anderson Cres. Call	66 C5	Annick Roundabout. Irvine	219 E1
Anderson Ct. Hat	125 F4	Annick St. Glasg	119 D3
Anderson Cres. Pres	236 C4	Annick St. Glasg	139 E3
Anderson Ct. Hat	142 A1	Annick View. Irvine	219 F1
Anderson Dr. Den	21 F1	Anniesdale Ave. Stepps	99 E3
Anderson Dr. Irvine	219 D2		
Anderson Dr. Newt M	156 B2		

Annieshill View. Plains	104 A1	Arden St. Plains	104 A1
Anniesland Cres. Glasg	95 D3	Arden Terr. Ham	162 B1
Anniesland Ind Est. Glasg	95 E3	Ardencaple Dr. Helen	16 A1
Anniesland Rd. Glasg	95 E3	Ardencaple Quadrant. Helen	16 A1
Annieston. Twe	59 F2	Ardenclutha Ave. Ham	162 A2
Anniversary Ave. E Kil	180 B4	Ardenclutha Dr. P Glasg	47 D1
Annpit Rd. Ayr	236 A2	Ardenconnel Ho. Rhu	15 E3
Annsfield Rd. Ham	183 E4	Ardenconnel Way. Rhu	15 E3
Ansdell Ave. Udd	161 E4	Ardencraig Cres. Glasg	137 E1
Anson Ave. Falk	41 F2	Ardencraig Gdns. Glasg	138 A1
Anson St. Glasg	117 F2	Ardencraig La. Glasg	137 E1
Anson Way. Ren	94 B1	Ardencraig Pl. Glasg	137 F1
Antermony Rd. M of C	58 C3	Ardencraig Quadrant. Glasg	137 F1
Antigua St. Green	46 A2	Ardencraig Rd. Glasg	137 E1
Antigua Way. E Kil	159 D1	Ardencraig St. Glasg	138 A1
Anton Cres. Kils	60 C4	Ardencraig Terr. Glasg	137 F1
Antonine Ave. Mother	163 E4	Ardenlea St. Glasg	118 A2
Antonine Gdns. Dunt	74 A3	Ardenlea. Tan	140 C4
Antonine Rd. Falk	41 E3	Ardery St. Glasg	96 A1
Antonine Gr. Bon	39 F2	Ardessie St. Glasg	76 B1
Antonine Rd. Kirk	59 F1	Ardfern Rd. Chap	124 A3
Antonine Rd. Bear	75 D3	Ardfern St. Glasg	119 D2
Antonine St. Falk	41 E3	Ardfin Cl. Pres	236 B3
Antrim La. Lark	185 D2	Ardfin Rd. Pres	236 B3
Anwoth St. Glasg	119 D2	Ardgare. Rhu	15 E3
Apollo Path. Holy	143 D3	Ardgay Pl. Glasg	119 D2
Appin Ct. Kirk	59 D1	Ardgay St. Glasg	119 D2
Appin Rd. Glasg	118 B4	Ardgay Way. Glasg	138 A2
Appin Terr. Glasg	138 B2	Ardgour Ct. Ham	161 F3
Appin Terr. Ham	161 F2	Ardgour Dr. Lin	112 A3
Appin Terr. Shot	147 D2	Ardgour Par. Holy	143 E1
Appin Way. Glenm	102 C3	Ardgour Pl. Kilmk	222 C2
Appin Way. Udd	141 D2	Ardgour Rd. Kilmk	222 C2
Appleby Cl. E Kil	179 F3	Ardgowan Ave. Pais	113 F2
Appleby St. Glasg	97 D2	Ardgowan Ct. Pais	114 B2
Applecross Gdns. Muir	80 C2	Ardgowan Dr. Tan	140 C4
Applecross Quadrant. Wish	165 D3	Ardgowan Pl. Shot	146 C3
Applecross Rd. Kirk	59 D1	Ardgowan St. Green	45 F3
Applecross St. Glasg	97 D2	Ardgowan St. P Glasg	47 D1
Appledore Cres. Udd	141 D2	Ardgowan St. Pais	113 F2
Apsley La. Glasg	96 A1	Ardgowan Terrace La. Glasg	96 B1
Apsley St. Glasg	96 A1	Ardgryfe Cres. Hous	91 E1
Aqua Ave. Ham	161 F1	Ardholm St. Glasg	119 D3
Aquila Way. Car	187 E1	Ardhu Pl. Glasg	75 D2
Arabum Dr. E Kil	180 C3	Ardlamont Sq. Lin	112 B3
Aranthrue Cres. Ren	94 B2	Ardlaw St. Glasg	115 F3
Aranthrue Dr. Ren	94 B2	Ardle Ave. Kilmk	228 A3
Aray St. Glasg	96 B3	Ardle Rd. Glasg	136 C3
Arbroath Ave. Glasg	115 D2	Ardlui Gdns. Miln	54 B2
Arbroath Cres. Stir	2 A2	Ardlui Rd. Ayr	236 A2
Arbroath Gr. Ham	162 A1	Ardlui St. Glasg	118 C2
Arbuckle Pl. Plains	104 A2	Ardmaleish Cres. Glasg	137 F1
Arbuckle Rd. Caid	104 A2	Ardmaleish Dr. Glasg	137 E1
Arbuckle Rd. Plains	104 A2	Ardmaleish Rd. Glasg	137 E1
Arbuckle St. Kilmk	228 A4	Ardmaleish St. Glasg	137 E1
Arbuthnot St. Falk	41 F3	Ardmaleish Terr. Glasg	137 F1
Arcade. Stir	7 D4	Ardmay Cres. Glasg	137 E4
Arcadia Dr. Glasg	117 F3	Ardmillan. Kilw	207 D1
Arcadia St. Hat	142 A4	Ardmillan St. Glasg	118 C4
Arcan Cres. Glasg	75 D1	Ardmore Ct. Irvine	220 A3
Arch Way. Kils	36 B1	Ardmore Pl. Green	46 B1
Archerfield Ave. Glasg	119 D1	Ardmore Rd. Green	46 B1
Archerfield Cres. Glasg	119 D1	Ardmore Rd. P Glasg	47 E1
Archerfield Dr. Glasg	119 D1	Ardmore Rd. Pais	68 B4
Archerfield Gr. Glasg	119 D1	Ardmory Ave. Glasg	137 E4
Archerhill Ave. Glasg	95 D3	Ardmory La. Glasg	138 A4
Archerhill Cotts. Glasg	95 D4	Ardmory Pl. Glasg	138 A4
Archerhill Cres. Glasg	95 D4	Ardnahoe Ave. Glasg	137 E4
Archerhill Rd. Glasg	95 D4	Ardnahoe Pl. Glasg	137 E4
Archerhill Sq. Glasg	94 C4	Ardneil Ave. W Kil	190 B2
Archerhill Terr. Glasg	95 D4	Ardneil Ct. Ard	205 D2
Archers Ave. Stir	7 E2	Ardneil Rd. Glasg	115 F3
Archibald Dr. Dalry	191 D4	Ardnish St. Glasg	115 F4
Archibald Terr. M of C	58 C3	Ardo Gdns. Glasg	116 A3
Archibald Pl. Hat	142 B2	Ardoch Cres. Dumb	49 E2
Archray Rd. Cumb	82 A3	Ardoch Cres. Steven	217 E3
Arcon Ave. Moss	237 F3	Ardoch Gdns. Glasg	138 C3
Ard La. New	165 F3	Ardoch Gr. Glasg	138 C3
Ard Loan. Holy	143 D3	Ardoch Path. New	165 F3
Ard Rd. Ren	94 A2	Ardoch Rd. Bear	76 A2
Ard St. Glasg	119 D2	Ardoch St. Glasg	97 E2
Ardardan Cotts. Card	25 F1	Ardoch Way. Muir	80 C1
Ardargie Dr. Glasg	139 E4	Ardochrig. E Kil	180 C3
Ardargie Gr. Glasg	139 E4	Ardressie Pl. Glasg	96 B3
Ardargie Pl. Glasg	139 E4	Ardrossan High Rd. W Kil	190 C2
Ardayre Rd. Pres	236 A4	Ardrossan Rd. Salt	216 C4
Ardbeg Ave. Bish	78 B1	Ardrossan Rd. W Kil	190 B1
Ardbeg Ave. Glasg	138 C2	Ardshiel Rd. Glasg	115 F4
Ardbeg Ave. Kilmk	222 D2	Ardsloy La. Glasg	95 D2
Ardbeg Cl. Irvine	219 F3	Ardsloy Pl. Glasg	95 D2
Ardbeg La. Glasg	117 D1	Ardtoe Cres. Stepps	99 F3
Ardbeg Rd. Green	46 B1	Ardtoe Pl. Stepps	99 F3
Ardbeg St. Glasg	117 D1	Arduthie Rd. Glasg	115 F4
Ardchoille Dr. Steven	206 C1	Ardvreck Pl. Sten	24 A2
Ardchoille La. Steven	206 C1	Ardwell Rd. Glasg	115 F2
Ardconnel St. Glasg	135 F2	Argosy Way. Ren	94 B1
Ardeer La. Steven	217 F3	Argus Ave. Chap	123 E1
Arden La. Glasg	135 F1	Argyle Cres. Aird	123 E4
Arden Ct. Ham	162 B1	Argyle Cres. Ham	161 F2
Arden Gr. Kils	36 B1	Argyle Gdns. Lennox	57 F4
Arden Hill. Rhu	15 D2	Argyle Pk. Ayr	236 A1
Arden Pl. Glasg	135 F1	Argyle Pl. Kils	36 B1
Arden Rd. Green	46 B1	Argyle Pl. Salt	216 C4
Arden Rd. Ham	162 B1	Argyle Rd. Bear	75 F4
		Argyle Rd. Gour	44 C3
		Argyle Rd. Salt	216 C4
		Argyle St E. Helen	16 B1

Argyle St. Glasg	116 C4
Argyle St. Glasg	117 D4
Argyll St. Green	45 F3
Argyll St. Pais	113 E2
Argyle St. Stone	198 C1
Argyll Arc. Glasg	117 E4
Argyll Ave. Dumb	50 B2
Argyll Ave. Falk	42 B3
Argyll Ave. Inch	93 F1
Argyll Ave. Ren	94 A2
Argyll Ave. Stir	2 B1
Argyll Est. Alex	27 E4
Argyll Gdns. Lark	185 D2
Argyll Pl. All	10 B4
Argyll Pl. Dumb	50 B2
Argyll Pl. E Kil	160 B2
Argyll Pl. Hat	141 F1
Argyll Rd. Ros	15 D2
Argyll St. Alex	27 E4
Argyll St. All	10 B4
Arisaig Dr. Bear	76 A2
Arisaig Dr. Glasg	119 E2
Arisaig Pl. Glasg	115 F2
Arisdale Cres. Newt M	156 C3
Ark La. Glasg	117 F4
Arkaig Ave. Plains	103 F2
Arkaig St. Wish	165 D1
Arkle Terr. Glasg	138 C2
Arkleston Cres. Pais	114 A4
Arkleston Rd. Pais	114 A3
Arkleston Rd. Pais	114 A4
Arkleston Rd. Ren	114 A4
Arklet Rd. Glasg	115 F4
Arkwright Way. Irvine	219 E2
Arlington St. Glasg	96 C1
Armadale Ct. Glasg	118 A4
Armadale Path. Glasg	118 A4
Armadale Pl. Glasg	118 A4
Armadale Rd. Rhu	15 F2
Armadale St. Glasg	118 A4
Amine Path. Holy	143 E2
Armour Ave. Aird	122 C4
Armour Ave. Irvine	12 B4
Armour Ct. Kirk	59 D1
Armour Ct. Udd	161 D3
Armour Dr. Ayr	239 E3
Armour Dr. Kirk	59 D1
Armour Gdns. Kirk	59 D1
Armour Gr. Mother	164 A2
Armour Pl. Ard	205 E2
Armour Pl. Holy	143 E2
Armour Pl. John	112 A2
Armour Pl. Kirk	59 D1
Armour Pl. Lin	112 B3
Armour Pl. Stew	195 F1
Armour St. Glasg	117 F3
Armour St. John	112 A2
Armour St. Kilmk	227 F4
Armstrong Cres. Tan	141 D4
Armstrong Gr. E Kil	180 B4
Armstrong Rd. Helen	25 D4
Armstrong Rd. Kilmk	223 E1
Arnbrae Rd. Kils	36 A1
Arness Terr. Kilmk	222 C2
Arngask Rd. Glasg	115 F4
Arnhall Pl. Glasg	115 F2
Arnhem St. Glasg	139 E3
Arnholm Pl. Glasg	115 F2
Arnisdale Pl. Glasg	120 A4
Arnisdale Rd. Glasg	120 A4
Arnisdale Way. Glasg	138 A2
Arniston St. Glasg	118 C4
Arniston Way. Pais	114 B4
Arnol Pl. Glasg	119 F4
Arnold Ave. Bish	78 A1
Arnold St. Glasg	97 D3
Arnot St. Falk	42 B2
Arnothill Ct. Falk	41 F3
Arnothill. Falk	42 A3
Arnothill Gdns. Falk	42 A2
Arnothill La. Falk	41 F3
Arnothill Mews. Falk	42 A2
Arnott Dr. Coat	122 A2
Arnott Quadrant. Mother	142 B1
Arnprior Gdns. Glasg	138 D3
Arnprior Pl. Ayr	238 C1
Arnprior Quadrant. Glasg	137 E2
Arnprior Rd. Glasg	137 E2
Arnprior St. Glasg	137 E2
Arnside Ave. Glasg	136 B2
Arnswell. N Sau	5 E1
Arnum Gdns. Car	187 F1
Arnum Pl. Car	187 F1
Arnwood Dr. Glasg	96 A3
Aron Terr. Glasg	138 C3
Aros Dr. Glasg	115 F2
Aros La. Glasg	115 F2
Aros Rd. Rhu	15 D2
Arran Ave. Coat	122 B2
Arran Ave. Dumb	49 F3
Arran Ave. Inch	93 F1
Arran Ave. Kilmk	223 D2
Arran Ave. P Glasg	69 D4

Arran Cres. Beith

Arran Cres. Beith 150 D1
Arran Ct. All 10 A3
Arran Cres. Steven 217 E4
Arran Dr. Aird 102 C1
Arran Dr. Cumb 82 B4
Arran Dr. Glasg 115 F2
Arran Dr. Glasg 136 B1
Arran Dr. Glenm 102 C3
Arran Dr. John 111 E1
Arran Dr. Kirk 58 C1
Arran Dr. Pais 133 F4
Arran. E Kil 160 B1
Arran Gdns. Car 201 F4
Arran Gdns. Ham 162 C1
Arran Gdns. Troon 229 E4
Arran La. Muir 81 D1
Arran La. Salt 205 E1
Arran Path. Lark 185 C1
Arran Pk. Pres 236 A3
Arran Pl. Clyde 74 B1
Arran Pl. Coat 122 B2
Arran Pl. Irvine 219 D3
Arran Pl. Lin 112 A3
Arran Pl. Salt 205 E1
Arran Rd. Gour 44 B3
Arran Rd. Mother 163 E4
Arran Rd. Ren 94 B1
Arran Rd. Troon 229 E4
Arran Terr. Ayr 235 F1
Arran Terr. Falk 41 E2
Arran Terr. Glasg 137 F3
Arran Tower. Glasg 138 C2
Arran View. Kilie 60 B4
Arran View. Stew 195 F1
Arranview Ct. Ayr 236 A2
Arranview St. Chap 123 F1
Arrochar Ct. Glasg 96 C4
Arrochar Dr. Glasg 76 B1
Arrochar Path. Glasg 76 B1
Arrochar St. Glasg 76 B1
Arrol Cres. All 10 B4
Arrol Dr. Ayr 238 C4
Arrol Pk. Ayr 238 C3
Arrol Pl. E Kil 181 D3
Arrol Pl. Glasg 118 A2
Arrol St. Glasg 114 C4
Arrothill Dr. Kilmk 227 E4
Arrotshole Rd. E Kil 159 D2
Arrowsmith Ave. Glasg 96 B4
Artarman Rd. Rhu 15 F2
Arthur Ave. Aird 123 D3
Arthur Ave. Barr 134 A1
Arthur Ct. W Kil 190 B3
Arthur Pl. Newt M 157 F3
Arthur Rd. Pais 133 F4
Arthur St. Alex 27 D2
Arthur St. Ayr 238 C4
Arthur St. Glasg 96 B1
Arthur St. Green 45 F4
Arthur St. Ham 162 B3
Arthur St. Newt M 157 F3
Arthur St. Pais 113 E3
Arthur St. Salt 217 D4
Arthur St. Steven 217 E4
Arthur St. W Kil 190 B3
Arthur's Dr. Sten 23 F1
Arthurlie Ave. Barr 134 B1
Arthurlie Ave. Uplaw 153 D2
Arthurlie Dr. Glasg 136 B1
Arthurlie Dr. Newt M 156 B2
Arthurlie Dr. Uplaw 153 D2
Arthurlie Pl. Salt 216 C4
Arthurlie St. Barr 134 B1
Arthurlie St. Glasg 115 F4
Arthurston Rd. Bonh 28 A4
Arundel Dr. Bish 78 A2
Arundel Dr. Glasg 137 D4
Ascaig Cres. Glasg 115 F1
Ascog Rd. Bear 75 F1
Ascog St. Glasg 117 D1
Ascot Ave. Glasg 95 F3
Ascot. Glasg 96 A3
Ash Ave. E Kil 180 B3
Ash Ct. E Kil 180 B3
Ash Dr. Beith 150 A1
Ash Gr. All 10 B3
Ash Gr. Bish 98 A4
Ash Gr. Kirk 79 D3
Ash Gr. Law 186 C3
Ash Gr. Sten 23 F1
Ash Gr. Tan 141 D4
Ash Pl. Bank 38 C1
Ash Pl. John 112 A1
Ash Pl. Kilmk 227 E4
Ash Rd. Clyde 74 B1
Ash Rd. Cumb 62 C3
Ash Rd. Dumb 49 F2
Ash Rd. Glasg 120 A2
Ash Terr. Stir 6 C3
Ash Wlk. Glasg 138 B2
Ash Wlk. Holy 143 D3
Ashbrae Gdns. Stir 7 D1
Ashburn Gate. Gour 44 B4
Ashburn Gdns. Gour 44 B4
Ashburn Gdns. Miln 54 C1

Ashburn Loan. Lark 185 D2
Ashburn Rd. Miln 54 C1
Ashburn La. Glasg 96 A3
Ashburton Pk. E Kil 180 A4
Ashburton Rd. Glasg 96 A3
Ashby Cres. Bear 75 F1
Ashcroft Ave. Lennox 57 F4
Ashcroft Dr. Glasg 137 F3
Ashcroft. E Kil 160 B3
Ashcroft Wlk. Lennox 57 F4
Ashdale Ave. Salt 205 F1
Ashdale Dr. Glasg 115 F2
Ashdale Rd. Kilmk 222 C2
Ashdene St. Glasg 97 D4
Asher Rd. Chap 123 F1
Ashfield. Bish 78 A2
Ashfield Cotts. Gart 20 A2
Ashfield Rd. Law 187 D3
Ashfield Rd. Miln 55 D1
Ashfield Rd. Newt M 157 F3
Ashfield St. Glasg 97 E2
Ashgill Pl. Glasg 97 E3
Ashgill Rd. Glasg 97 E3
Ashgillhead Rd. Ash 185 F1
Ashgrove. Aird 123 E4
Ashgrove Ave. Gour 44 B4
Ashgrove. Coat 122 A2
Ashgrove. Cald 105 D3
Ashgrove. Coat 122 A2
Ashgrove. Irvine 219 E3
Ashgrove La. P Glasg 47 E1
Ashgrove. Muir 80 C1
Ashgrove Rd. Ard 205 E2
Ashgrove Rd. Hat 142 A4
Ashgrove Rd. Kilw 207 E2
Ashgrove St. Ayr 239 D4
Ashgrove St. Glasg 118 A1
Ashgrove Workshops. Kilw 207 E2
Ashiestiel Ct. Cumb 82 C4
Ashiestiel Pl. Cumb 82 C4
Ashiestiel Rd. Cumb 82 C4
Ashkirk Dr. Ash 199 F4
Ashkirk Dr. Glasg 115 F2
Ashland Ave. Ham 183 E3
Ashlea Dr. Glasg 136 B2
Ashlea Gdns. Plains 103 F2
Ashley Dr. Tan 141 D3
Ashley La. Glasg 96 C1
Ashley Pk. Udd 141 E3
Ashley Rise. Bonh 27 F1
Ashley St. Bon 39 F3
Ashley St. Glasg 96 C1
Ashley Terr. All 10 A4
Ashmore Rd. Glasg 136 C3
Ashton Dr. Helen 25 C4
Ashton Dr. Hurl 128 C4
Ashton Gn. E Kil 159 F1
Ashton La N. Glasg 96 B1
Ashton Pl. Gour 44 B4
Ashton Pl. Glasg 96 B1
Ashton Rd. Gour 44 B4
Ashton Rd. Glasg 118 A1
Ashton St. Mother 142 B1
Ashton Terr. Gour 44 B4
Ashton View. Dumb 49 D2
Ashton Way. Pais 132 C4
Ashtree Ct. O Kili 73 D3
Ashtree Dr. Glasg 136 B2
Ashtree Rd. Glasg 136 B4
Ashvale Cres. Glasg 97 F2
Ashworth Terr. Ham 162 C2
Aspen Dr. Glasg 98 A2
Aspen Pl. John 112 A1
Aspen Rd. Ayr 239 E3
Aspen Way. Ham 162 C1
Asquith Pl. Hat 142 B3
Assloss Rd. Kilmk 223 E2
Aster Dr. Glasg 138 A2
Aster Gdns. Glasg 135 E2
Aster Gdns. Mother 163 F3
Athelstane Dr. Cumb 82 B4
Athelstane Rd. Glasg 95 F4
Athena Way. Tan 141 D4
Athole Gdns. Glasg 96 B2
Athole La. Glasg 96 B2
Athole La. Gour 44 B2
Athole St. Helen 16 C1
Athole Terr. Gour 44 B2
Atholl Ave. Glasg 114 C4
Atholl Ave. Lennox 57 D1
Atholl Cres. Glasg 114 C3
Atholl Ct. Kirk 59 D1
Atholl Dr. Cumb 81 F4
Atholl Dr. Glasg 157 E4
Atholl Gdns. Bear 75 F4
Atholl Gdns. Bish 77 F2
Atholl Gdns. Glasg 135 E4
Atholl Gdns. Kilw 207 F2
Atholl La. Muir 81 D1
Atholl Pl. Coat 122 A2
Atholl Pl. Lin 112 A3
Atholl Pl. Stir 1 C1
Atlas Pl. Glasg 97 F2
Atlas Rd. Glasg 97 F2
Atlas Sq. Glasg 97 F2

Atlas St. Clyde 94 A4
Attercliffe Ave. Wish 164 B1
Attlee Ave. Clyde 74 C1
Attlee Pl. Clyde 74 C1
Attow Rd. Glasg 136 A3
Auburn Dr. Barr 134 B1
Auchans Ave. Dund 225 F1
Auchans Dr. Dund 225 F1
Auchans Pl. Fen 213 D2
Auchans Rd. Lin 92 C1
Auchenbeg Cres. Ayr 239 D2
Auchenbothie Rd. Kil 68 C3
Auchenbothie Rd. P Glasg .. 68 C3
Auchencar Dr. Kilmk 222 C2
Auchencrow St. Glasg 120 B4
Auchencruive. Miln 76 B4
Auchendarroch St. Green .. 46 B2
Auchendavie Rd. Kirk 59 D1
Auchendon Cres. Ayr 238 B2
Auchendore Ave. P Glasg .. 69 D4
Auchenfoil La. P Glasg 68 B4
Auchenfoil Rd. Kil 67 F3
Auchenfoil Rd. P Glasg 68 B4
Auchengate Cres. Shew ... 224 C1
Auchengate. Troon 229 F4
Auchengeich Rd. Muir 80 B2
Auchengilloch. E Kil 180 C3
Auchenglen Dr. Muir 80 C1
Auchenglen Rd. Car 201 F2
Auchengreoch Ave. John . 131 E4
Auchengreoch Rd. John . 131 E3
Auchenharvie Pl. Irvine ... 219 F3
Auchenharvie Pl. Salt 206 A1
Auchenharvie Rd. Salt ... 217 D4
Auchenhove Cres. Kilb ... 149 D2
Auchenhowie Rd. Bish 76 B4
Auchenhowie Rd. Miln 76 B4
Auchenkilns Rd. Cumb 82 B3
Auchenkilns
      Roundabout. Cumb 82 B4
Auchenleck La. P Glasg ... 68 C4
Auchenleck Rd. P Glasg ... 68 C4
Auchenlodment Rd. John . 112 A1
Auchenreoch Ave. Dumb ... 50 A3
Auchenreoch. M of C 59 D3
Auchentibber Rd. Ham ... 161 D2
Auchentorlie Quadrant. Pais 114 A2
Auchentorlie St. Glasg 95 F1
Auchentoshan Ave. Dunt .. 73 F3
Auchentoshan Terr. Glasg .. 97 F1
Auchentrae Cres. Ayr 238 B3
Auchinairn Rd. Bish 98 A4
Auchinairn Rd. Glasg 98 B4
Auchinbaird. N Sau 5 E1
Auchinbee Farm Rd. Cumb . 61 D2
Auchinbee Way. Cumb 61 D2
Auchincampbell Rd. Ham . 162 B2
Auchincarroch Rd. Bonh 28 A4
Auchincarroch Rd. Gart 20 C2
Auchincloch Dr. Bank 38 C1
Auchincruive Ave. Pres ... 236 B3
Auchingill Pl. Glasg 100 B1
Auchingill Rd. Glasg 100 B1
Auchingramont Rd. Ham . 162 B2
Auchinlea Dr. Cle 144 B1
Auchinlea Rd. Glasg 99 F1
Auchinleck Ave. Glasg 98 C3
Auchinleck Cres. Glasg 98 C3
Auchinleck Dr. Glasg 98 C3
Auchinleck Gdns. Glasg 98 C3
Auchinleck Rd. Dunt 74 A4
Auchinleck Rd. Glasg 98 C4
Auchinleck Terr. Dunt 74 A4
Auchinloch Rd. Kirk 79 E2
Auchinloch St. Glasg 97 F2
Auchinraith Ave. Ham 162 B3
Auchinraith Rd. Udd 161 F3
Auchinraith Terr. Udd 161 F3
Auchinvole Cres. Kils 60 A3
Auchmannoch Ave. Glasg 114 C3
Auchmead Rd. Gour 44 C2
Auchmountain Rd. Green ... 46 B2
Auchmountain Rd. Green ... 46 C1
Auchnacraig Rd. Dunt 74 B4
Auchneagh Ave. Green 45 F2
Auchneagh Cres. Green 45 F2
Auchneagh Farm La. Green . 45 D3
Auchneagh Farm Rd. Green . 45 D3
Auchneagh Rd. Green 45 D2
Auchter Ave. New 166 B3
Auchter Rd. Wish 165 F2
Auchterburn Rd. Alla 166 C4
Auckland Pk. E Kil 159 E1
Auckland Pl. Clyde 73 E2
Auckland St. Glasg 97 D2
Auld Clay Rd. Ard 206 C4
Auld Kirk Rd. Glasg 139 E2
Auld Rd The. Cumb 62 A2
Auld St. Clyde 73 F2
Auld's Brae. Aird 123 D4
Auldbar Rd. Glasg 115 F2
Auldbar Terr. Pais 114 A1
Auldburn Rd. Glasg 136 A3
Auldearn Rd. Glasg 99 E4
Auldgirth Rd. Glasg 115 F2
Auldhame St. Coat 121 F4
Auldhouse Ave. Glasg 136 A3

Auldhouse Rd. Auld 180 B1
Auldhouse Rd. Glasg 136 B3
Auldhouse Terr. Glasg 136 B3
Auldlea Rd. Beith 150 A1
Auldton Terr. Ash 185 F1
Aultbea St. Glasg 97 D4
Aultmore Rd. Glasg 119 F4
Aurs Cres. Barr 134 B1
Aurs Dr. Barr 134 B1
Aurs Glen. Barr 134 B1
Aurs Pl. Barr 134 C1
Aurs Rd. Barr 134 C1
Aurs Rd. Newt M 155 F4
Aursbridge Cres. Barr 134 B1
Aursbridge Dr. Barr 134 B1
Austen La. Glasg 95 F3
Austen Rd. Glasg 95 F3
Austine Dr. Ham 183 F4
Avenel Rd. Glasg 75 F1
Avenue End Rd. Glasg 99 D3
Avenue Oak. Miln 75 F4
Avenue Pk. B of A 1 C4
Avenue Sq. Stew 211 E4
Avenue St. Glasg 118 A1
Avenue St. Stew 211 E4
Avenue St. Stew 195 E1
Avenue The. B of A 2 A4
Avenue The. Sten 24 B1
Avenue The. W Kil 190 B3
Avenuehead Rd. Muir 101 D4
Avenuepark St. Glasg 96 C3
Aviemore Gdns. Bear 76 A3
Aviemore Rd. Glasg 115 F2
Avils Hill. Kilb 149 D1
Avils Pl. Kilb 149 D1
Avoch Dr. Glasg 100 A1
Avoch St. Glasg 100 A1
Avon Ave. Bear 76 A2
Avon Ave. Car 187 F1
Avon Ave. Gree 84 B2
Avon Ct. Falk 42 B1
Avon Ct. Irvine 220 A2
Avon Dr. Hat 142 B2
Avon Dr. Lin 112 A3
Avon Pk. Avon 87 F3
Avon Pl. Coat 101 E1
Avon Pl. Kilmk 228 A3
Avon Pl. Lark 199 D4
Avon Rd. Bish 98 A4
Avon Rd. Glasg 136 A1
Avon Rd. Lark 199 D4
Avon St. Ham 162 C2
Avon St. Lark 184 C2
Avon St. Mother 163 F3
Avon Tower. Mother 163 F3
Avon Wynd. New 165 F3
Avonbank Cres. Ham 183 F4
Avonbank Rd. Glasg 137 F4
Avonbank Rd. Lark 184 C2
Avonbrae Cres. Ham 183 F4
Avonbridge Rd. Sals 86 A4
Avondale Ave. E Kil 159 F1
Avondale Dr. Pais 114 A3
Avondale Pl. E Kil 181 D4
Avondale Rd. W Kil 190 B3
Avondale St. Glasg 99 D3
Avonhead Ave. Cumb 82 B4
Avonhead Gdns. Cumb 82 B4
Avonhead Pl. Cumb 82 B4
Avonhead Rd. Cumb 82 B4
Avonhead. E Kil 180 B3
Avonmouth Pl. Gour 44 C3
Avonside Dr. Dunl 201 E3
Avonside Gr. Ham 162 C2
Avonspark St. Glasg 98 A2
Aylmer Rd. Glasg 136 C3
Ayr Ct. Aird 123 D3
Ayr La. Gour 44 C2
Ayr Rd. Ash 185 F1
Ayr Rd. Glasg 157 D4
Ayr Rd. Irvine 224 B4
Ayr Rd. Kilmk 227 F2
Ayr Rd. Newt M 156 B2
Ayr Rd. Pres 236 B4
Ayr Rd. Shew 224 B4
Ayr St. Glasg 97 F2
Ayr St. Troon 229 E1
Ayr Terr. Gour 44 C2
Ayton Pk. N. E Kil 160 A2
Ayton Pk. S. E Kil 160 A2
Aytoun Dr. Ersk 72 C2
Aytoun Rd. Glasg 116 C2

Baads Rd. Cald 106 B1
Baberton Way. Kilw 207 D2
Babylon Ave. Hat 142 A2
Babylon Dr. Hat 142 A2
Babylon Pl. Hat 142 A2
Babylon Rd. Hat 142 A2
Back Cswy. Glasg 118 B3
Back Hawkhill Ave. Ayr .. 236 A1
Back o' Dykes Rd. Kirk 80 A4
Back O Hill. Hous 91 D1
Back O' Hill Rd. Bish 56 C1
Back O' Hill Rd. Stir 2 A1
Back O'Barns. Ham 162 C2
Back Peebles St. Ayr 235 F1

Back Rd. Alva 4 C4
Back Row. Ham 162 C2
Back Sneddon St. Pais ... 113 F3
Back St. Alex 27 E1
Backbrae St. Kils 60 B4
Backburn. Beith 171 D4
Backmuir Cres. Ham 162 A3
Backmuir Pl. Ham 162 B1
Backmuir Rd. Glasg 75 D2
Backmuir Rd. Ham 162 A3
Backwood Ct. Clack 10 C3
Badenheath Pl. Cumb 81 E3
Badenheath Terr. Cumb ... 81 F2
Badenoch Rd. Kirk 59 E1
Bagnell St. Glasg 97 F3
Bahamas Way. E Kil 159 F1
Baidland Ave. Beith 191 F3
Baillie Dr. Bear 76 A4
Baillie Dr. E Kil 160 B2
Baillie Fyfe Way. Wish ... 186 A4
BailliePl. Kilmk 222 B1
Baillie Wynd. Tan 141 D4
Baillie Dr. E Kil 160 B2
Baillie Dr. Udd 141 D2
Baillie Gdns. Wish 165 F2
Baillie Pl. E Kil 160 B2
Baillie Waugh Rd. Stir 7 F2
Baillies La. Aird 123 D4
Bailliesmuir Pl. New 166 A4
Baillieston Ave. Kilb 170 A4
Baillieston Rd. Glasg 119 F2
Baillieston Rd. Udd 120 A1
Bain Cres. Helen 16 C2
Bain St. Glasg 117 F3
Baine Dr. Laur 42 C2
Baine St. Green 45 E3
Baird Ave. Aird 103 D1
Baird Ave. Glasg 114 C4
Baird Ave. Helet 16 A1
Baird Ave. Kilw 207 F2
Baird Ave. Lark 199 E4
Baird Brae. Glasg 97 D2
Baird Cres. Alex 27 E4
Baird Cres. Cumb 82 A4
Baird Ct. Clyde 74 A1
Baird Ct. Kilw 207 D2
Baird Dr. Bear 75 E3
Baird Dr. Ersk 72 C2
Baird Hill. E Kil 180 C4
Baird Pl. Hat 142 A4
Baird Pl. Kilmk 223 D1
Baird Pl. Pres 233 E2
Baird Pl. Wish 165 F2
Baird Rd. Dunl 201 E3
Baird Rd. Ham 223 D1
Baird St. Coat 122 A4
Baird St. Falk 42 A3
Baird St. Glasg 97 E1
Baird Terr. East 127 E3
Baird Terr. Pais 162 B2
Bairds Cres. Ham 162 B2
Bairdsland View. Hat 142 A3
Bairds Ford Ct. Falk 42 A4
Bairns Ford Ct. Falk 42 A4
Bairns Ford Dr. Falk 42 A4
Baker St. Glasg 116 C1
Baker St. Green 46 A2
Baker St. Stir 7 D4
Bakewell Rd. Glasg 120 A3
Balaclava St. Glasg 117 D4
Balado Rd. Glasg 100 B1
Balbeg St. Glasg 115 E3
Balbeggie St. Glasg 119 E2
Balblair Rd. Glasg 115 F1
Balcarres Ave. Glasg 96 B3
Balcastle Gdns. Kils 36 A1
Balcastle Rd. Slam 86 A3
Balcomie Cres. Troon 230 A1
Balcomie Cres. Glasg 99 D1
Balcomie Terr. Ham 183 D4
Baldernock Rd. Miln 55 E1
Baldinnie Rd. Glasg 99 E1
Baldorran Cres. Cumb 61 D2
Baldoran Cres. Glasg 119 F4
Baldric Rd. Glasg 115 E3
Baldovan Cres. Glasg 99 E1
Baldovie Rd. Glasg 95 E3
Baldragon Rd. Glasg 100 B1
Baldric Rd. Glasg 95 E3
Baldwin Ave. Glasg 95 E2
Balerno Dr. Glasg 115 F2
Balfarg Rd. Eagle 178 C3
Balfleurs St. Miln 55 D2
Balfluig St. Glasg 100 A1
Balfour Ave. Beith 171 D4
Balfour Ave. Beith 171 D4
Balfour Cres. Plean 13 E2
Balfour Cres. Pres 236 B3
Balfour Ct. Kilmk 223 E2
Balfour St. All 10 A4
Balfour St. Bann 7 E1
Balfour St. Glasg 96 C3
Balfour St. P Glasg 46 B3
Balfour St. Stir 1 C1
Balfour Terr. E Kil 180 C4

245
Balfour Wynd. Lark — Bearhope St. Green

Balfour Wynd. Lark 185 E1
Balfron Cres. Ham 161 F2
Balfron Rd. Glasg 115 F4
Balfron Rd. Green 46 B1
Balfron Rd. Pais 114 B3
Balgair Dr. Pais 114 A3
Balgair St. Glasg 97 D2
Balgair Terr. Glasg 119 D3
Balglass St. Glasg 97 D3
Balgonie Ave. Pais 113 D1
Balgonie Dr. Pais 113 E1
Balgonie Rd. Glasg 115 F2
Balgonie Woods. Pais 113 E1
Balgownie Cres. Glasg 136 A1
Balgray Ave. Kilb 170 A4
Balgray Ave. Kilmk 227 F1
Balgray Cres. Barr 134 C1
Balgray Rd. Beith 172 A3
Balgray Rd. Kilb 170 A4
Balgray Rd. Newt M 156 A3
Balgray Way. Irvine 220 A3
Balgraybank St. Glasg 98 A2
Balgrayhill Rd. Glasg 97 F3
Balgraystone Rd. Barr 155 E4
Balgraystone Rd. Newt M 155 E4
Balintore St. Glasg 119 D3
Baliol La. Glasg 96 C1
Baliol St. Glasg 96 C1
Baljaffray Rd. Bear 75 D4
Ballachalairy Yett. Strath 30 B2
Ballagan Pl. Miln 54 B1
Ballaig Ave. Bear 75 E3
Ballaig Cres. Stepps 99 E3
Ballantay Quadrant. Glasg 138 A2
Ballantay Rd. Glasg 138 A2
Ballantay Terr. Glasg 138 A2
Ballantine Ave. Glasg 115 D4
Ballantine Dr. Ayr 238 C3
Ballantrae Cres. Newt M 157 D2
Ballantrae Dr. Newt M 157 D2
Ballantrae Rd. Ham 161 F3
Ballater Cres. Wish 165 D3
Ballater Dr. Bear 76 A1
Ballater Dr. Inch 93 E4
Ballater Dr. Pais 114 A1
Ballater Dr. Stir 2 B2
Ballater Pl. Glasg 117 E2
Ballater St. Glasg 117 E2
Ballater Way. Glen 101 E3
Ballayne Dr. Muir 81 D2
Ballengeich Pass. Stir 2 A1
Ballengeich Rd. Stir 1 C1
Ballentrae Wynd. Holy 143 D3
Ballerup Terr. E Kil 180 C3
Ballewan Cres. Strath 31 D2
Ballindalloch Dr. Glasg 118 A4
Ballindalloch La. Glasg 118 A4
Ballinkier Ave. Bank 38 C2
Balloch Gdns. Glasg 115 F2
Balloch Rd. Alex 27 E4
Balloch Rd. Bonh 27 E4
Balloch Rd. Chap 124 A3
Balloch Rd. Cumb 61 E1
Balloch Rd. Green 46 A1
Balloch Rd. Shot 146 C3
Balloch View. Cumb 61 F1
Ballochmill Rd. Glasg 138 B4
Ballochmyle. E Kil 160 B2
Ballochney La. Aird 102 C1
Ballochney Rd. Plains 103 F2
Ballochney St. Aird 102 C1
Ballochnie Dr. Plains 104 A2
Ballogie Rd. Glasg 137 D4
Ballot Rd. Irvine 219 E2
Balmalloch Rd. Kils 36 B1
Balmartin Rd. Glasg 76 B1
Balmedie. Ersk 73 D1
Balmeg Ave. Glasg 157 E4
Balmerino Pl. Bish 98 B4
Balminnoch Pk. Ayr 238 B1
Balmoral Ave. Glenm 102 C3
Balmoral Cres. Coat 121 E2
Balmoral Cres. Inch 93 F3
Balmoral Dr. Bear 76 A1
Balmoral Dr. Falk 41 F2
Balmoral Dr. Glasg 138 C3
Balmoral Dr. Glasg 139 D4
Balmoral Gdns. Tan 120 C1
Balmoral Gdns. Udd 140 B1
Balmoral Path. Lark 185 E1
Balmoral Pl. E Kil 159 E1
Balmoral Pl. Gour 43 F3
Balmoral Pl. Sten 23 F2
Balmoral Pl. Stir 7 D4
Balmoral Rd. John 112 A1
Balmoral Rd. Kilmk 222 C1
Balmoral St. Falk 41 F2
Balmoral St. Glasg 95 D2
Balmoral Wynd. Stew 211 F4
Balmore Ct. Kil 89 E4
Balmore Dr. Ham 183 D4
Balmore Pl. Glasg 97 D3
Balmore Rd. Bish 77 E4
Balmore Rd. Bish 77 F4
Balmore Rd. Glasg 97 D3
Balmore Rd. Green 46 B1
Balmore Sq. Glasg 97 D3
Balmuildy Rd. Bish 77 E3
Balmuildy Rd. Glasg 77 E3
Balmulzier Rd. Slam 86 A4
Balornock Rd. Glasg 98 A3
Balquhatstone Cres. Slam 86 A3
Balquhidderock. Stir 7 E2
Balquidder Ct. Aird 103 D1
Balrossie Dr. Kil 89 D4
Balruddery Pl. Bish 98 B4
Balshagray Ave. Glasg 95 F2
Balshagray Cres. Glasg 95 F1
Balshagray Dr. Glasg 95 F2
Balshagray La. Glasg 95 F2
Balshagray Pl. Glasg 95 F2
Baltic Ct. Glasg 118 A2
Baltic La. Glasg 118 A2
Baltic Pl. Glasg 117 F2
Baltic St. Glasg 118 A2
Balure Cres. Fall 8 B2
Balure St. Glasg 118 B4
Balvaird Cres. Glasg 138 A4
Balvaird Dr. Glasg 138 A4
Balvenie St. Coat 122 A2
Balveny St. Glasg 99 E1
Balvicar Dr. Glasg 116 C1
Balvicar St. Glasg 116 C1
Balvie Ave. Glasg 75 D1
Balvie Ave. Glasg 136 B1
Balvie Cres. Miln 54 C1
Balvie Rd. Miln 54 C1
Banavie Rd. Glasg 96 A2
Banavie Rd. New 165 F3
Banchory Ave. Glasg 136 A3
Banchory Ave. Glenm 102 C3
Banchory Ave. Inch 93 E4
Banchory Cres. Bear 76 A1
Banchory Pl. Tull 4 B2
Banchory Rd. Wish 165 D3
Bandeath Rd. Fall 8 B2
Baneberry Path. E Kil 159 E2
Banff Ave. Aird 123 D2
Banff Pl. E Kil 180 B4
Banff Pl. Gour 44 B3
Banff Quadrant. Wish 165 D3
Banff Rd. Gour 44 B3
Banff St. Glasg 99 D1
Bangorshill St. Glasg 135 F2
Bank Ave. Miln 55 D2
Bank Ct. Irvine 219 F2
Bank Pk. E Kil 180 B4
Bank Pl. Irvine 219 F2
Bank Pl. Kilmk 227 F4
Bank Rd. East 127 F3
Bank Rd. Glasg 139 E4
Bank St. Aird 123 D4
Bank St. Alex 27 F3
Bank St. All 10 A3
Bank St. Barr 134 B1
Bank St. Coat 121 F3
Bank St. Falk 42 A3
Bank St. Glasg 96 C1
Bank St. Glasg 139 D3
Bank St. Green 45 F2
Bank St. Irvine 219 E2
Bank St. Irvine 219 F2
Bank St. Kilb 149 D1
Bank St. Kilmk 227 F4
Bank St. Neil 154 B4
Bank St. Pais 113 F2
Bank St. Pais 113 F3
Bank St. Pres 236 A4
Bank St. Slam 86 A3
Bank St. Stir 7 D4
Bank St. Troon 229 D1
Bank View. Chap 123 E1
Bank Way. Lark 185 D2
Bankbrae Ave. Glasg 135 D3
Bankend. B of W 110 C4
Bankend Pl. Kilmk 223 D3
Bankend Rd. B of W 110 C3
Bankend Rd. Dumb 49 F2
Bankend St. Glasg 99 D1
Bankfaulds Ave. Kilb 149 D1
Bankfield Dr. Ham 183 E4
Bankfoot Dr. Glasg 115 D2
Bankfoot Rd. Glasg 115 D2
Bankfoot Rd. Pais 113 D3
Bankglen Rd. Glasg 75 D2
Bankhall St. Glasg 117 D1
Bankhead Ave. Aird 123 E4
Bankhead Ave. Coat 121 E2
Bankhead Ave. Glasg 95 D3
Bankhead Ave. Hat 142 A2
Bankhead Ave. Spring 221 D1
Bankhead Cres. Bank 39 E3
Bankhead Dr. Glasg 138 A4
Bankhead Pl. Aird 123 E4
Bankhead Pl. Coat 121 E2
Bankhead Pl. Stew 195 F1
Bankhead Rd. E Kil 158 B4
Bankhead Rd. Glasg 137 F4
Bankhead Rd. Kilw 207 F2
Bankhead Rd. Kirk 80 A4
Bankhead Rd. N Sau 5 E2
Bankhead Terr. Lan 215 D1
Bankholm Pl. Thorn 157 F3
Bankier Rd. Bank 38 C2
Bankier Terr. Bank 38 C2
Banknock St. Glasg 118 C3
Banks Rd. Kirk 58 B1
Bankside Ave. John 111 F2
Bankside Ct. Den 21 F1
Bankside. Falk 42 B4
Bankside Gdns. Kilb 149 D2
Banktop Pl. John 111 F2
Bankview Cres. Kirk 79 D4
Bankview Dr. Kirk 79 D4
Bannachra Cres. Alex 27 E3
Bannachra Dr. Helen 16 A1
Bannatyne Ave. Glasg 118 A4
Bannatyne St. Lan 215 D2
Banner Dr. Glasg 75 E1
Banner Rd. Glasg 75 E1
Bannercross Ave. Glasg 120 A3
Bannercross Dr. Glasg 120 A3
Bannercross Gdns. Glasg 120 A3
Bannerman Dr. Hat 142 B3
Bannerman Dr. Kilmk 223 E1
Bannerman Pl. Clyde 74 A1
Bannoch Pl. Kilw 208 A2
Bannoch Rd. Kilw 208 A1
Bannoch Rd. Kilw 208 A2
Bannock Rd. Fall 8 B2
Bannockburn Dr. Lark 185 E1
Bannockburn Pl. Kilmk 223 D2
Bannockburn Rd. Cowie 12 B4
Bannockburn Rd. Stir 7 E2
Bannockburn St. Green 45 E2
Bannockburn
Station Rd. Fall 8 A2
Bantaskin St. Glasg 96 B4
Bantaskine Dr. Falk 41 F2
Bantaskine Gdns. Falk 41 F2
Bantaskine St. Falk 41 F2
Banton Pl. Bon 40 A2
Banton Pl. Glasg 120 A4
Banton Rd. Kils 37 E1
Banyan Cres. Tan 121 E1
Bar Hill Pl. Kils 60 A4
Barassie Cres. Cumb 61 F3
Barassie Ct. Udd 140 C1
Barassie Dr. B of W 110 B3
Barassie. E Kil 159 E2
Barassie Pl. Kilmk 227 F2
Barassie St. Troon 229 E2
Barassiebank La. Troon 229 E3
Barbadoes Pl. Kilmk 227 F3
Barbadoes Rd. Kilmk 227 F3
Barbados Gn. E Kil 159 D1
Barbae Pl. Udd 141 D2
Barbana Rd. E Kil 158 C1
Barbegs Cres. Kils 60 C2
Barberry Ave. Newt M 135 D1
Barberry Dr. Beith 171 D4
Barberry Gdns. Glasg 135 D1
Barbeth Gdns. Cumb 82 A3
Barbeth Pl. Cumb 82 A3
Barbeth Pl. Irvine 220 A3
Barbeth Rd. Cumb 82 A3
Barbeth Way. Cumb 82 A3
Barbour Ave. Stir 7 E2
Barbour's Pk. Stew 211 F4
Barbreck Rd. Glasg 116 C1
Barcaldine Ave. Muir 80 A1
Barcapel Ave. Newt M 156 C4
Barcaple Flats. Newt M 156 C4
Barclaven Rd. Kil 89 F4
Barclay Ave. John 112 A1
Barclay Ct. O Kill 73 D3
Barclay Dr. Helen 16 B2
Barclay Dr. Kilmk 223 E1
Barclay Pl. Stew 195 E1
Barclay Rd. Mother 163 D3
Barclay Sq. Ren 94 A1
Barclay St. Glasg 97 F3
Barclay St. O Kill 73 D3
Barcraigs Dr. Pais 133 F4
Bard Ave. Glasg 95 D4
Bardowie St. Glasg 97 D2
Bardrain Ave. John 112 B1
Bardrain Rd. Pais 133 E4
Bardrainney Ave. P Glasg 68 C4
Bardrill Dr. Bish 77 F1
Bardykes Rd. Udd 161 D4
Barefield St. Lark 185 D2
Barfillan Dr. Glasg 115 F3
Bargaran Rd. Glasg 115 D2
Bargarran Rd. Ersk 72 C2
Bargarron Dr. Pais 114 A4
Barge Ct. Rhu 15 E3
Bargeddie St. Glasg 98 B1
Bargeny. Kilw 207 D1
Bargrennan Rd. Troon 229 F3
Barhill La. Twe 59 F2
Barhill Rd. Ersk 73 D1
Barhill Terr. Twe 60 A2
Barholm Sq. Glasg 99 E1
Barke Rd. Cumb 62 A2
Barkin Ct. Falk 42 A1
Barkly Terr. E Kil 180 B4
Barlae Ave. Eagle 178 C4
Barlanark Ave. Glasg 119 E3
Barlanark Cres. Glasg 119 E4
Barlanark Pl. Glasg 119 D3
Barlanark Pl. Glasg 119 F4
Barlanark Rd. Glasg 119 F4
Barlandfauld St. Kils 60 C4
Barleith Ct. Hurl 228 C3
Barleyhill. Bon 40 A3
Barlia Dr. Glasg 137 F2
Barlia St. Glasg 137 F2
Barlia Terr. Glasg 137 F2
Barloan Cres. Dumb 50 A3
Barloan Pl. Dumb 50 A3
Barloch Ave. Miln 55 D1
Barloch Rd. Miln 55 D1
Barloch St. Glasg 97 E2
Barlogan Ave. Glasg 115 F3
Barlogan Quadrant. Glasg 115 F3
Barmore Ave. Car 202 A4
Barmouth Ave. Gour 44 C3
Barmulloch Rd. Glasg 98 A2
Barn Gn. Kilbar 111 D2
Barn Rd. Stir 7 D4
Barnard Gdns. Bish 78 A2
Barnbeth Rd. Glasg 115 D1
Barncluith Rd. Ham 162 C1
Barnego Rd. Duni 21 E2
Barnes Rd. Glasg 97 D3
Barnes St. Barr 134 A1
Barnett Cres. Salt 216 C4
Barnett Ct. Salt 216 C4
Barnett Path. Udd 161 E4
Barnflat St. Glasg 118 A1
Barnford Cres. Ayr 239 D1
Barnhill Dr. Ham 161 E1
Barnhill Dr. Tull 4 B1
Barnhill Rd. Dumb 50 B2
Barnhill St. Green 46 B2
Barnkirk Ave. Glasg 75 D2
Barns Cres. Ayr 238 C4
Barns Pk. Ayr 238 C4
Barns St. Ayr 238 C4
Barns St. Clyde 94 B4
Barns Street La. Ayr 238 C4
Barns Terr. Ayr 238 C4
Barns Terrace La. Ayr 238 C4
Barnscroft. Kilbar 111 D2
Barnsdale Rd. Stir 7 D2
Barnsford Ave. Inch 93 D2
Barnsford Rd. Inch 93 D2
Barnswood Pl. Udd 141 D2
Barnton La. Falk 42 A2
Barnton St. Glasg 118 C4
Barnton St. Stir 7 D4
Barnweil Rd. Kilmk 227 F3
Barnweil Rd. Pres 236 B3
Barnweill Dr. Hurl 228 C3
Barnwell Rd. Stir 2 B2
Barnwell Terr. Glasg 115 F4
Barochan Cres. Pais 113 D2
Barochan Rd. Glasg 115 D2
Barochan Rd. Hous 91 D3
Barochan Rd. Hous 111 E4
Barochan Rd. Lang 71 D1
Baron Ct. Ham 163 D1
Baron Rd. Pais 114 A3
Baron St. Ren 94 B1
Baronald Dr. Glasg 96 A3
Baronald Gate. Glasg 96 A3
Baronald St. Glasg 118 A1
Barone Dr. Newt M 157 E4
Baronhall Dr. Udd 161 E4
Baronhill. Cumb 62 A3
Barons Gate. Udd 140 C2
Barons Rd. Mother 164 B1
Baronscourt Dr. Lin 112 C2
Baronscourt Gdns. Lin 112 C2
Baronscourt Rd. Lin 112 C2
Barony Ct. Glasg 120 A3
Barony Ct. Irvine 219 F3
Barony Ct. Salt 205 E1
Barony Dr. Glasg 120 A3
Barony Gdns. Glasg 120 A3
Barony Glebe. W Kil 190 B3
Barony Pl. Cumb 60 C1
Barony Rd. Pres 236 B3
Barony Terr. Kilb 170 A4
Barony Wynd. Glasg 120 A3
Barr Ave. Neil 154 C4
Barr Cres. Dunt 74 A3
Barr Gr. Tan 141 D4
Barr Pl. Newt M 156 B3
Barr Pl. Pais 113 E2
Barr St. Ard 205 E1
Barr St. Glasg 97 D2
Barr St. Mother 163 F4
Barr Terr. E Kil 159 F1
Barr's Brae. Kil 69 E1
Barr's Brae. P Glasg 68 B4
Barra Ave. Ren 94 B1
Barra Ave. Wish 165 F3
Barra Cres. Clyde 73 E3
Barra Cres. Irvine 220 B1
Barra Dr. Aird 123 F3
Barra Gdns. Clyde 73 E3
Barra La. Irvine 220 B1
Barra Pl. Irvine 220 B1
Barra Pl. Sten 24 A2
Barra Rd. Clyde 73 E3
Barra St. Glasg 96 B4
Barra Wynd. Irvine 220 B1
Barrachnie Cres. Glasg 119 F3
Barrachnie Ct. Glasg 119 F3
Barrachnie Rd. Glasg 119 F3
Barrack St. Glasg 117 F3
Barrack St. Ham 162 B2
Barraston Rd. Lennox 57 D1
Barrcraig Rd. B of W 110 B4
Barrhead Rd. Glasg 135 E4
Barrhead Rd. Newt M 156 A3
Barrhead Rd. Pais 114 A1
Barrhill Cres. Kilbar 111 E2
Barrhill Ct. Kirk 80 A4
Barrhill Rd. Ersk 93 D4
Barrhill Rd. Gour 44 B4
Barrhill Rd. Kirk 80 A4
Barrie Quadrant. Clyde 74 A2
Barrie Rd. E Kil 160 B3
Barrie Rd. Glasg 115 D4
Barrie Rd. Sten 23 F2
Barrie St. Mother 163 F3
Barrie Terr. Salt 205 E1
Barriedale Ave. Ham 162 A2
Barrington Ave. Beith 150 A1
Barrington Dr. Glasg 96 C1
Barrisdale Rd. Glasg 96 B4
Barrisdale Rd. New 165 F3
Barrisdale Way. Glasg 138 A2
Barrland Dr. Glasg 136 B2
Barrland St. Glasg 117 D2
Barrmill Rd. Beith 171 E4
Barrmill Rd. Beith 172 A1
Barrmill Rd. Glasg 136 A3
Barrochan Interchange. Lin 111 F2
Barrochan Rd. Lin 111 F3
Barrowfield St. Glasg 118 A3
Barrs Brae La. P Glasg 47 E1
Barrs Cres. Card 48 A4
Barrs Ct. Card 26 A1
Barrs La. Car 187 F2
Barrs Terr. Card 48 A4
Barrwood Pl. Tan 141 D4
Barrwood St. Glasg 98 C1
Barry Gdns. Udd 161 E3
Barscube Ave. P Glasg 68 C4
Barscube Terr. Pais 114 A1
Barshaw Dr. Pais 114 A3
Barshaw Pl. Pais 114 B3
Barshaw Rd. Glasg 114 C3
Barskiven Rd. John 112 C2
Barskiven Rd. Pais 112 C2
Barterholm Rd. Pais 113 F1
Bartholomew St. Glasg 118 A2
Bartiebeith Rd. Glasg 119 F4
Bartlands Pl. Eagle 178 C2
Barton Ave. Bonh 28 A4
Bartonhall Rd. Wish 165 E1
Bartonholm Terr. Kilw 207 F1
Barty's Rd. Hat 142 B3
Barwheys Dr. Moss 237 F3
Barwood Hill. Dumb 50 A3
Bassett Ave. Glasg 95 D4
Bassett Cres. Glasg 95 D4
Bastion Wynd. Stir 7 D4
Bath La. Glasg 117 D4
Bath Pl. Ayr 238 C4
Bath Sq. Salt 216 B4
Bath St. Glasg 117 D4
Bath St. Gour 44 C4
Bath St. Kilmk 222 C1
Bath Villas. Salt 216 B4
Bathgate St. Glasg 118 A3
Bathgo Ave. Pais 114 C2
Bathurst Dr. Ayr 239 D1
Bathville Rd. Kilb 149 D1
Bathwick Way. Pais 132 C4
Baton Rd. Shot 146 B3
Batson St. Glasg 117 D1
Battery Park Ave. Green 45 D4
Battery Park Dr. Green 45 D4
Battismains. Lan 215 E2
Battle Pl. Glasg 136 C4
Battlefield Ave. Glasg 137 D4
Battlefield Gdns. Glasg 137 D4
Battlefield Rd. Glasg 137 D4
Bavelaw St. Glasg 99 E1
Bawhirley Rd. Green 46 B2
Baxter Cres. Den 21 E1
Baxter La. Alex 27 F4
Baxter La. Lan 215 D2
Baxter St. Fall 8 B2
Baxter St. Green 46 B2
Baxter's Wynd. Falk 42 A2
Bay St. P Glasg 47 E1
Bay View Rd. Gour 44 C4
Bayfield Ave. Glasg 75 D2
Bayfield Terr. Glasg 75 D2
Bayne St. Stir 2 A1
Beach Dr. Irvine 218 C1
Beach Rd. Troon 229 E3
Beaconsfield Rd. Glasg 96 A3
Beagle Cres. Ayr 238 B2
Bean Row. Falk 42 A2
Beansburn. Kilmk 223 D2
Beanshields Rd. Car 201 F2
Beard Cres. Muir 100 C3
Beardmore Cotts. Inch 93 F3
Beardmore Pl. Clyde 73 F2
Beardmore St. Clyde 73 F2
Beardmore Way. Ersk 73 E1
Bearford Dr. Glasg 115 D3
Bearhope St. Green 45 F3

246

Bearsden Rd. Glasg — Birnam Cres. Bear

Bearsden Rd. Glasg 95 F4
Bearside Rd. Stir 7 D2
Beaton Ave. Bann 7 E1
Beaton Rd. Bonh 27 F4
Beaton Rd. Glasg 116 C1
Beaton St. Lark 184 C3
Beaton Terr. Irvine 219 E3
Beatrice Dr. Holy 142 C3
Beatrice Gdns. Hous 111 E4
Beattock St. Glasg 118 B3
Beattock Wynd. Ham 162 A2
Beatty Ave. Stir 2 A1
Beatty Pl. Helen 17 D1
Beatty St. Clyde 73 F2
Beauclerc St. Alva 5 D4
Beaufield Gdns. Kilm 222 A4
Beaufort Ave. Glasg 136 B3
Beaufort Dr. Kirk 79 D4
Beaufort Dr. Sten 24 A2
Beaufort Gdns. Bish 77 F1
Beauly Cres. Kil 89 E4
Beauly Cres. Kilmk 228 A3
Beauly Ct. Falk 42 B1
Beauly Dr. Pais 112 C1
Beauly Pl. Coat 122 A2
Beauly Pl. E Kil 159 E1
Beauly Pl. Glasg 96 B3
Beauly Pl. Holy 143 D3
Beauly Pl. Muir 80 B1
Beauly Rd. Glasg 120 A2
Beaumont Dr. Sten 24 A1
Beaumont Gate. Glasg 96 B2
Beckford St. Ham 162 B3
Beda Pl. Fall 8 B3
Bedale Rd. Glasg 119 F2
Bedcow View. Kirk 79 F4
Bedford Ave. Clyde 74 B1
Bedford Ct. All 10 A3
Bedford La. Glasg 117 D3
Bedford Pl. All 10 A3
Bedford St. Glasg 117 D3
Bedford St. Green 45 E4
Bedlay Ct. Muir 81 D2
Bedlormie Dr. Blac 107 E1
Beech Ave. B of W 90 B1
Beech Ave. Bear 76 A4
Beech Ave. Beith 150 A1
Beech Ave. Glasg 116 A2
Beech Ave. Glasg 120 A3
Beech Ave. Glasg 138 B2
Beech Ave. Glasg 138 C3
Beech Ave. Holy 143 D2
Beech Ave. Irvine 219 E1
Beech Ave. John 112 B1
Beech Ave. Kilmk 227 E4
Beech Ave. Lark 185 E1
Beech Ave. Newt M 156 C2
Beech Ave. Pais 114 A1
Beech Ave. Plea 12 B2
Beech Cres. Dunl 21 E2
Beech Cres. Holy 143 E4
Beech Cres. Lar 41 E4
Beech Cres. Newt M 156 C2
Beech Ct. Coat 121 F2
Beech Dr. Cald 104 C2
Beech Dr. Clyde 74 A3
Beech Gdns. Glasg 120 A3
Beech Gr. Ayr 239 E4
Beech Gr. E Kil 180 A3
Beech Gr. Law 186 C3
Beech Gr. Muir 101 D3
Beech Gr. Rhu 15 E3
Beech Gr. Wish 165 E4
Beech La. Stir 2 A2
Beech Pl. Bish 98 A4
Beech Pl. Gour 44 B3
Beech Pl. Udd 161 F4
Beech Rd. Bish 98 A4
Beech Rd. Holy 143 E4
Beech Rd. John 111 E1
Beech Rd. Kirk 79 E3
Beech Terr. Lark 185 D1
Beechbank Ave. Aird 102 C1
Beechburn Cres. Loch 129 E2
Beeches Ave. Dunt 73 F3
Beeches Rd. Dunt 73 F3
Beeches Terr. Dunt 74 A3
Beeches The. Hous 91 E1
Beeches The. Kilbar 111 E3
Beeches The. Lan 215 D1
Beeches The. Newt M 156 C3
Beechfield Dr. Car 202 A4
Beechfield Rd. Beith 170 C4
Beechgrove Ave. Tan 141 E4
Beechgrove. Muir 80 C1
Beechgrove Pl. Helen 25 C4
Beechgrove
Quadrant. Holy 143 D3
Beechgrove St. Glasg 118 A1
Beechlands Ave. Glasg 136 C1
Beechlands Dr. Newt M 157 E3
Beechmount Ct. Shot 147 D1
Beechmount Rd. Kirk 79 E2
Beechtree Terr. M of C 58 B3
Beechwood Ave. Glasg 138 B3
Beechwood Ave. Ham 183 D4
Beechwood Ave. Lang 70 B4
Beechwood Ave. Newt M 157 E3
Beechwood Cres. Wish 165 E1
Beechwood Ct. Bear 75 F2
Beechwood Dr. Bonh 28 A1
Beechwood Dr. Coat 122 B3
Beechwood Dr. Glasg 95 F2
Beechwood Dr. Ren 94 B1
Beechwood Gdns. Hat 142 B2
Beechwood Gdns. Muir 80 C1
Beechwood Gr. Barr 134 B1
Beechwood. Kilw 207 E3
Beechwood La. Bear 75 F2
Beechwood. Lark 185 D3
Beechwood. N Sau 5 E1
Beechwood. N Sau 5 F1
Beechwood
Paddock. Troon 230 A2
Beechwood Pl. Glasg 95 F2
Beechwood Pl. Hat 142 B2
Beechwood Rd. Cumb 82 C4
Beechworth Dr. Holy 143 E1
Beecroft Pl. Udd 140 C1
Begg Ave. Falk 41 F2
Beggs Terr. Ard 205 E2
Bell Dr. Clyde 94 C4
Beith Rd. Beith 170 B3
Beith Rd. Beith 191 F4
Beith Rd. Green 45 F1
Beith Rd. How 131 D4
Beith Rd. John 111 F1
Beith St. Glasg 96 A1
Beith St. Glasg 96 B1
Belgowan St. Hat 141 F4
Belgrave La. Glasg 96 C2
Belgrave St. Hat 141 F3
Belhaven Rd. Ham 161 F2
Belhaven Rd. Wish 165 D2
Belhaven St. P Glasg 47 D1
Belhaven Terr. Glasg 96 B2
Belhaven Terr W. Glasg 96 B2
Belhaven Terr. Wish 165 D2
Belhaven Terrace La. Glasg 96 B2
Belhaven
Terrace West La. Glasg 96 B2
Bell Cres. Irvine 219 E3
Bell Gn E. E Kil 180 C4
Bell Gn W. E Kil 180 C4
Bell St. Aird 122 C4
Bell St. Clyde 94 B4
Bell St. Glasg 117 E3
Bell St. Green 46 C1
Bell St. Hat 142 A4
Bell St. Ren 94 B2
Bell St. Wish 165 D2
Bell Trees Rd. How 130 B1
Bell View Ct. Ren 94 B2
Bell's Wynd. Falk 42 A2
Bell's Wynd. Lan 215 E3
Bellahouston Dr. Glasg 115 F2
Bellairs Pl. Udd 140 B1
Bellard Rd. W Kil 190 B2
Bellard Wlk. W Kil 190 B2
Bellas Pl. Plains 104 A1
Bellcraig Ct. Thorn 158 A3
Belleaire Dr. Green 45 E4
Bellefield Rd. Lan 215 D3
Belleisle Ave. Udd 140 C4
Belleisle Cl. Kilw 207 E2
Belleisle Cres. B of W 110 B3
Belleisle Pl. Gour 44 A3
Belleisle Pl. Kilmk 227 F2
Belleisle St. Glasg 117 D1
Bellesleyhill Ave. Ayr 236 A2
Bellesleyhill Rd. Ayr 236 A2
Bellevale Ave. Ayr 239 D3
Bellevale Quadrant. Ayr 238 C3
Bellevue Ave. Kirk 79 D4
Bellevue Cres. Ayr 238 C4
Bellevue Gdns. Kilmk 222 B1
Bellevue La. Ayr 238 C4
Bellevue Rd. All 9 F3
Bellevue Rd. Ayr 238 C4
Bellevue Rd. Kilmk 222 B1
Bellevue Rd. Kirk 79 D4
Bellevue Rd. Pres 236 B4
Bellevue St. Ayr 238 C4
Bellevue St. Falk 42 B2
Bellfield Ave. Hurl 228 B3
Bellfield Cres. Barr 134 A2
Bellfield Ct. Barr 134 A2
Bellfield Ct. Hurl 228 B3
Bellfield Dr. Wish 165 E1
Bellfield La. Pres 236 A4
Bellfield Rd. Bann 7 F1
Bellfield Rd. Kirk 79 D4
Bellfield Rd. Stir 7 D3
Bellfield St. Glasg 118 A3
Bellflower Ct. E Kil 159 E2
Bellflower Gdns. Glasg 135 E2
Bellflower Gr. E Kil 159 E2
Bellgrove St. Glasg 117 F3
Bellisle Terr. Ham 183 D4
Bellrock Ave. Pres 236 A3
Bellrock Cres. Glasg 119 D4
Bellrock Ct. Glasg 119 D4
Bellrock Path. Glasg 119 D4
Bellrock Rd. Ayr 236 A2
Bellrock St. Glasg 119 D4
Bellscroft Ave. Glasg 137 F4
Bellsdyke Rd. Air 24 B3
Bellsdyke Rd. Aird 123 D3
Bellsdyke Rd. Lar 23 E2
Bellsdyke Rd. Sten 23 E2
Bellsfield Dr. Udd 161 F3
Bellshaugh Gdns. Glasg 96 B3
Bellshaugh La. Glasg 96 B3
Bellshaugh Pl. Glasg 96 B3
Bellshaugh Rd. Glasg 96 B2
Bellshill Rd. Hat 141 F2
Bellshill Rd. Mother 142 B1
Bellshill Rd. Tan 141 D3
Bellshill Rd. Tan 141 E1
Bellshill Rd. Udd 141 D3
Bellshill Rd. Udd 141 E1
Bellside Rd. Chap 123 F1
Bellside Rd. Chap 144 A4
Bellside Rd. Cle 144 B1
Bellsland Dr. Kilmk 227 F3
Bellsland Gr. Kilmk 227 F3
Bellsland Pl. Kilmk 228 A4
Bellsmeadow Rd. Falk 42 B2
Bellsmyre Ave. Dumb 50 A3
Belltree Ave. Stew 211 E4
Belltrees Cres. Pais 113 D2
Bellvue Cres. Hat 141 F2
Bellvue Cres. Pres 236 B4
Bellwood St. Glasg 136 C4
Bellziehill Farm. Tan 141 F3
Belman's Cl. Beith 150 A1
Belmont Ave. Ayr 239 D3
Belmont Ave. Shi 66 C4
Belmont Ave. Udd 140 C4
Belmont Cres. Ayr 239 D3
Belmont Cres. Glasg 96 C2
Belmont Cres. Kilm 222 A4
Belmont Ct. Kirk 79 E4
Belmont Dr. Ayr 239 D3
Belmont Dr. Barr 134 B1
Belmont Dr. E Kil 180 A4
Belmont Dr. Glasg 136 A2
Belmont Dr. Glasg 138 A4
Belmont Dr. Shot 147 D1
Belmont La. Glasg 96 C2
Belmont Pl E. Ayr 239 D3
Belmont Pl W. Ayr 239 D3
Belmont Rd. Ayr 239 D3
Belmont Rd. Glasg 97 F3
Belmont Rd. Glasg 138 C2
Belmont Rd. Kil 89 E4
Belmont Rd. Pais 114 A3
Belmont St. Clyde 74 A1
Belmont St. Coat 101 E1
Belmont St. Falk 42 B2
Belmont St. Glasg 96 C2
Belmont St. Kils 36 B1
Belmont St. Wish 186 A3
Belses Dr. Glasg 115 E3
Belstane Pk. Car 187 F2
Belstane Pl. Udd 141 D2
Belstane Rd. Car 188 A2
Belstane Rd. Cumb 82 C3
Belsyde Ave. Glasg 75 D1
Beltane St. Glasg 116 C4
Beltane St. Wish 165 D1
Beltrees Ave. Glasg 115 D1
Beltrees Cres. Glasg 115 D1
Beltrees Rd. Glasg 115 D1
Belvidere Cres. Bish 78 A1
Belvidere Cres. Hat 142 A2
Belvidere Rd. Hat 142 A2
Belvidere Terr. Ayr 236 A1
Belville Ave. Green 46 B2
Belville St. Green 46 A2
Belvoir Pl. Udd 161 E4
Bemersyde Ave. Glasg 136 A3
Bemersyde. Bish 78 B1
Bemersyde Pl. Lark 185 D1
Bemersyde Rd. Pais 132 C4
Ben Alder Dr. Pais 114 B1
Ben Bouie Dr. Helen 16 C1
Ben Buie Way. Pais 114 B1
Ben Hope Ave. Pais 114 B1
Ben Lawers Dr. Cumb 61 D1
Ben Lawers Dr. Pais 114 B1
Ben Ledi Ave. Pais 114 B1
Ben Ledi Cres. Cumb 61 D1
Ben Loyal Ave. Pais 114 B1
Ben Lui Dr. Pais 114 B1
Ben Lui Pl. Cumb 61 D1
Ben More Dr. Cumb 61 D1
Ben More Dr. Pais 114 B1
Ben Nevis Rd. Pais 114 B1
Ben Nevis Way. Cumb 61 D1
Ben Vane Ave. Pais 114 B1
Ben Venue Rd. Cumb 61 D1
Ben Venue Way. Pais 114 B1
Ben Wyvis Dr. Pais 114 B1
Benalder St. Glasg 96 B1
Benarty Gdns. Bish 78 A1
Benbain Pl. Irvine 220 A3
Benbecula. E Kil 160 B1
Benbecula Rd. Kilmk 223 D3
Bencleuch Pl. Irvine 220 A2
Bencloich Ave. Lennox 57 F4
Bencloich Cres. Lennox 33 F1
Bencloich Rd. Lennox 57 F4
Bencloich St. Lennox 33 F1
Benclutha. P Glasg 47 F1
Bencroft Dr. Glasg 137 F3
Bendigo Pl. Lan 215 D2
Benford Ave. Holy 143 E2
Benford Knowe. Holy 143 F2
Bengairn St. Glasg 118 B4
Bengal Pl. Glasg 136 B4
Bengal St. Glasg 136 B4
Benhar Pl. Glasg 118 C4
Benhar Rd. East 126 C1
Benhar Rd. Shot 147 D3
Benholm St. Glasg 118 C2
Benmore La. Gour 44 C2
Benmore. Pres 236 B3
Benmore Tower. Glasg 138 C2
Bennan House. Pres 236 A3
Bennan Sq. Glasg 117 E1
Bennoch Pl. Pres 236 B3
Benrig Ave. Kilm 222 A4
Bensley Ave. Irvine 219 F3
Bensley Rise. Irvine 219 F2
Benson St. Coat 122 A2
Benston Pl. John 111 F1
Benston Rd. John 111 F1
Bent Cres. Tan 141 E3
Bent Rd. Chap 123 E2
Bent Rd. Ham 162 B2
Bentfield Ave. Ayr 238 C3
Bentfield Dr. Pres 236 A3
Bentfoot Rd. Wish 186 B4
Benthall St. Glasg 117 E2
Bentheads. Bann 11 F4
Bentinck Cres. Troon 229 F1
Bentinck Dr. Troon 229 E1
Bentinck St. Glasg 96 C1
Bentinck St. Green 45 E4
Bentinck St. Kilmk 227 F4
Bents Rd. Glasg 120 A3
Benty's La. Car 201 F4
Benvie Gdns. Bish 78 A1
Benview Ave. P Glasg 68 C4
Benview. Bann 7 E1
Benview Rd. Newt M 157 F4
Benview Rd. P Glasg 68 C4
Benview St. Glasg 96 C2
Benview Terr. Fish 5 F2
Benview Terr. Pais 114 A1
Benvue Rd. Lennox 57 F4
Berchem Pl. Salt 216 C4
Bereland Ave. Pres 236 B4
Berelands Cres. Glasg 137 F4
Berelands Gdns. Pres 233 E1
Berelands Pl. Glasg 137 F4
Berelands Rd. Pres 233 E1
Beresford Ave. Glasg 95 F2
Beresford Gr. Irvine 219 F3
Beresford La. Ayr 238 C4
Beresford Terr. Ayr 238 C4
Berkeley St. Glasg 116 C4
Berkeley St. Stir 7 D2
Berkeley
Terrace La. Glasg 116 C4
Berkley Dr. Udd 140 B1
Berl Ave. Hous 111 E4
Bernadette Ave. Holy 143 E1
Bernadette St. Holy 143 E2
Bernard Path. Glasg 118 A2
Bernard St. Glasg 118 A2
Bernard Terr. Glasg 118 A2
Bernard's Wynd. Lan 215 D2
Berneray St. Glasg 97 E4
Berridale Ave. Glasg 137 D3
Berridale Rd. Troon 229 E4
Berriedale Ave. Glasg 120 A2
Berriedale. E Kil 179 F4
Berriedale Quadrant. Wish 165 D3
Berry Dr. Irvine 219 F2
Berryburn Rd. Glasg 98 B2
Berryhill Ave. Irvine 220 A3
Berryhill. Cowie 12 C4
Berryhill Dr. Glasg 136 A1
Berryhill Pl. Shot 147 D1
Berryhill Rd. Cumb 61 F1
Berryhill Rd. Glasg 136 A1
Berryknowe Ave. Muir 100 B4
Berryknowe. Kirk 80 A4
Berryknowes Ave. Glasg 115 E3
Berryknowes La. Glasg 115 E3
Berryknowes Rd. Glasg 115 E3
Berryyards Rd. Green 45 F2
Bertram Dr. Sals 125 E1
Bertram Pl. Shot 146 B3
Bertram St. East 127 E3
Bertram St. Glasg 116 C1
Bertram St. Ham 162 A3
Bertram St. Lark 185 E1
Bertram St. Shot 146 C3
Bervie St. Glasg 115 F3
Berwick Cres. Aird 122 C3
Berwick Cres. Lin 111 F4
Berwick Dr. Glasg 115 D2
Berwick Dr. Glasg 138 B3
Berwick Pl. Coat 122 A2
Berwick Pl. E Kil 160 B2
Berwick Pl. Gour 44 B2
Berwick Rd. Gour 44 B2
Berwick Rd. P Glasg 47 E1
Berwick St. Coat 122 A2
Berwick St. Ham 162 A3
Bessemer Dr. E Kil 181 D3
Beta Ctr. Clyde 94 B4
Betula Dr. Clyde 74 A3
Bevan Ct. Ard 205 D2
Bevan Dr. Alva 5 E4
Bevan Gdns. Kilw 207 F2
Bevan Gr. John 111 F1
Beveridge Terr. Hat 142 B2
Beverley Rd. Glasg 136 B3
Bevin Ave. Clyde 74 B1
Bideford Cres. Glasg 119 E2
Bield The. Wish 165 E1
Biggar Rd. Chap 123 F1
Biggar Rd. Holy 143 F4
Biggar St. Glasg 118 A3
Biggart Rd. Pres 236 B4
Bigholm Rd. Beith 150 B1
Bigton St. Glasg 99 D1
Bilby Terr. Irvine 219 E3
Billings Rd. Mother 163 D3
Bilsland Dr. Glasg 97 D3
Bilsland Pl. Alex 27 E1
Bimson Pl. Irvine 219 D1
Binend Rd. Glasg 135 E4
Binnie La. Gour 44 C4
Binnie Pl. Glasg 117 F3
Binnie Pl. Gran 24 C1
Binnie St. Gour 44 C4
Binniehill Rd. Cumb 61 E1
Binniehill Rd. Slam 85 F2
Binns Rd. Glasg 99 E1
Birch Ave. Newt M 157 F3
Birch Ave. Stir 6 C3
Birch Brae. Ham 162 C1
Birch Cotts. Helen 16 B1
Birch Cres. John 112 A1
Birch Cres. Newt M 157 F3
Birch Ct. Coat 121 F2
Birch Dr. Glasg 139 E3
Birch Dr. Kirk 79 E3
Birch Gr. Lark 185 D3
Birch Gr. Tan 141 D4
Birch Knowe. Bish 98 A4
Birch Pl. Kilmk 227 E4
Birch Pl. Udd 161 E4
Birch Quadrant. Aird 123 E4
Birch Rd. Ayr 239 E2
Birch Rd. Clyde 74 A3
Birch Rd. Cumb 62 C2
Birch Rd. Dumb 49 F2
Birch St. Glasg 117 E2
Birch St. Holy 143 D3
Birch View. Bear 76 A3
Birch Way. Troon 229 E2
Birchfield Dr. Glasg 95 D2
Birchfield Rd. Ham 162 A2
Birchgrove. Hous 91 E1
Birchlea Dr. Glasg 136 B2
Birchview Dr. Thorn 157 F2
Birchwood Ave. Glasg 119 F2
Birchwood Dr. Pais 113 D1
Birchwood. N Sau 5 E1
Birchwood Pl. Glasg 119 F2
Birchwood Rd. Uplaw 153 D2
Birdsfield Ct. Ham 161 F3
Birdsfield Dr. Udd 161 F3
Birdsfield St. Ham 161 F3
Birdston Rd. Glasg 98 B3
Birdston Rd. M of C 58 B2
Birgidale Ave. Glasg 137 E1
Birgidale Rd. Glasg 137 E1
Birgidale Terr. Glasg 137 E1
Birkdale Cl. Kilw 207 E2
Birkdale Ct. Udd 140 C1
Birkdale. E Kil 159 E2
Birken Rd. Kirk 79 F2
Birkenburn Rd. Cumb 62 C3
Birkenshaw Rd. Glen 81 F1
Birkenshaw St. Glasg 118 A4
Birkenshaw Way. Pais 113 F4
Birkfield Loan. Car 188 B1
Birkfield Pl. Car 188 B1
Birkhall Ave. Glasg 115 D2
Birkhall Ave. Inch 93 E4
Birkhall Dr. Bear 75 F1
Birkhill Ave. Bish 78 A1
Birkhill Gdns. Bish 78 A1
Birkhill Rd. Cam 6 C3
Birkhill Rd. Car 201 E1
Birkhill Rd. Ham 183 E4
Birkhill Rd. Stir 6 C3
Birkmyre Ave. P Glasg 47 D1
Birkmyre Rd. Glasg 115 F3
Birks Ct. Law 186 C3
Birks Hill. Irvine 220 A2
Birks Pl. Lan 215 D3
Birks Rd. Lark 199 D4
Birks Rd. Law 186 C2
Birkscairn Pl. Irvine 220 B1
Birkscairn Way. Irvine 220 B1
Birkshaw Brae. Wish 186 A4
Birkshaw Pl. Wish 186 A4
Birkshaw Tower. Wish 185 F4
Birkwood St. Glasg 118 A1
Birmingham Rd. Ren 94 A1
Birnam Ave. Bish 78 A1
Birnam Cres. Bear 76 A3

247
Birnam Ct. Falk
Braehead Rd. Pais

Birnam Ct. Falk 24 B1
Birnam Gdns. Bish 78 A1
Birnam Pl. Ham 161 F2
Birnam Rd. Glasg 118 B2
Birness Dr. Glasg 136 B4
Birnie Ct. Glasg 98 B2
Birnie Rd. Glasg 98 B2
Birniehill Rd. Cle 145 D3
Birniehill Roundabout. E Kil 181 D4
Birniewell Rd. Slam 86 A3
Birnock Ave. Ren 94 C1
Birrell Rd. Miln 54 C2
Birrens Rd. Mother 163 E4
Birsay Rd. Glasg 97 D4
Bishop Gdns. Bish 77 F1
Bishop Gdns. Ham 183 F4
Bishop La. Glasg 117 D4
Bishopdale. E Kil 159 E2
Bishopmill Pl. Glasg 98 B2
Bishopmill Rd. Glasg 98 B2
Bishops Gate. Thorn 158 B2
Bishops Pk. Thorn 158 A2
Bishopsgate Dr. Bish 97 F4
Bishopsgate Gdns. Bish 97 F4
Bishopsgate Pl. Bish 97 F4
Bishopsgate Rd. Bish 97 F4
Bishopbriggs Ind Est. Bish 98 A4
Bisland Ct. Glasg 97 D3
Bissett Cres. Dunt 73 F3
Black O' Hill
Roundabout. Cumb 61 D1
Black St. Aird 103 D1
Black St. Glasg 97 E1
Blackadder Pl. E Kil 179 E4
Blackbog Rd. Glenm 82 C1
Blackbraes Rd. E Kil 160 A2
Blackburn Cres. Dumb 49 E2
Blackburn Cres. Kirk 80 A4
Blackburn Dr. Ayr 238 C3
Blackburn Pl. Ayr 238 C3
Blackburn Rd. Ayr 238 C3
Blackburn Sq. Barr 134 B1
Blackburn St. Glasg 116 C3
Blackbyres Ct. Barr 134 B2
Blackbyres Rd. Pais 134 B3
Blackcraig Ave. Glasg 75 D2
Blackcroft Ave. Chap 123 F3
Blackcroft Gdns. Glasg 119 E2
Blackcroft Rd. Glasg 119 E2
Blackcroft Terr. Sals 125 D1
Blackdyke Rd. Kirk 79 F4
Blackfarm Rd. Newt M 156 C2
Blackfaulds Dr. Fen 213 D2
Blackfaulds Gdns. Fen 213 D2
Blackfaulds Rd. Glasg 137 F4
Blackford Cres. Pres 233 F1
Blackford Rd. Pais 114 A2
Blackfriars St. Glasg 117 E4
Blackfriars Wlk. Ayr 238 C4
Blackhall Ct. Pais 114 A2
Blackhall La. Pais 113 F2
Blackhall St. Pais 114 A2
Blackhall St. Shot 147 D2
Blackhill Dr. Helen 16 B2
Blackhill Pl. Glasg 98 B1
Blackhill Rd. Blac 107 F2
Blackhill Rd. Glasg 76 C1
Blackhill St. Ayr 239 D3
Blackhill View. Law 187 D2
Blackhouse Ave. Newt M 156 C2
Blackhouse Gdns. Newt M 156 C2
Blackhouse Pl. Ayr 239 E4
Blackhouse Rd. Newt M 156 C2
Blackie St. Glasg 96 B1
Blacklands Ave. Kilw 207 F1
Blacklands Cres. Kilw 207 F1
Blacklands Pl. Kirk 79 F2
Blacklands Rd. E Kil 159 E1
Blacklaw Dr. E Kil 181 D4
Blacklaw La. Pais 113 F3
Blackmill Cres. Sten 24 A2
Blackmoor Pl. Holy 143 D2
Blackmoss Dr. Hat 142 A2
Blackmuir Pl. Tull 4 B2
Blackness St. Coat 122 A2
Blackshaw Dr. W Kil 190 B3
Blackstone Ave. Glasg 135 E4
Blackstone Cres. Glasg 115 E1
Blackstone Rd. Lin 113 D4
Blackstoun Ave. Lin 112 A3
Blackstoun Oval. Pais 113 D3
Blackstoun Rd. Pais 113 D3
Blackswell La. Ham 162 C2
Blacksyke Ave. Kilmk 227 F2
Blackthorn Ave. Beith 150 A1
Blackthorn Ave. Kirk 79 D3
Blackthorn Gr. Kirk 79 D3
Blackthorn Rd. Cumb 62 C2
Blackthorn Rd. Tan 141 E4
Blackthorn St. Glasg 97 F3
Blacktongue Farm Rd. Gree 83 F1
Blackwood Ave. Kilmk 227 F3
Blackwood Ave. Lin 112 A3
Blackwood Ave. Newt M 156 C2
Blackwood. E Kil 180 B3
Blackwood Gdns. Mother 142 B1
Blackwood Rd. Cumb 60 C1
Blackwood Rd. Miln 54 C2
Blackwood St. Barr 134 A1
Blackwood St. Glasg 95 F4
Blackwoods Cres. Hat 142 B2
Blackwoods Cres. Muir 80 C1
Bladda La. Pais 113 F2
Blades Ct. Muir 101 D3
Bladnoch Dr. Glasg 75 E1
Blaefaulds Cres. Den 39 E4
Blaeloch Ave. Glasg 137 E1
Blaeloch Dr. Glasg 137 E1
Blaeloch Terr. Glasg 137 D1
Blaeshill Rd. E Kil 179 F4
Blair Atholl Dr. Lark 185 E1
Blair Ave. Hurl 228 C3
Blair Cres. Glasg 120 A2
Blair Cres. Hurl 228 C3
Blair Dr. M of C 58 B3
Blair Gdns. Gour 43 F3
Blair Gdns. Lennox 57 D1
Blair House. Cumb 62 A2
Blair Linn View. Cumb 83 D3
Blair Path. Mother 163 F3
Blair Rd. Beith 191 F4
Blair Rd. Coat 121 F4
Blair Rd. Cro 201 D1
Blair Rd. Glasg 114 C3
Blair Rd. Hurl 228 C3
Blair Rd. Kilw 207 F3
Blair St. Glasg 118 C3
Blair St. Kilmk 222 C1
Blair Terr. Sten 24 A2
Blairafton Wynd. Kilw 207 E3
Blairatholl Ave. Glasg 96 A2
Blairatholl Gdns. Glasg 96 A2
Blairbeth Dr. Glasg 137 D4
Blairbeth Pl. Glasg 138 A3
Blairbeth Rd. Glasg 138 B3
Blairbeth Terr. Glasg 138 B3
Blairdardie Rd. Glasg 75 E1
Blairdenan Ave. Muir 81 D2
Blairdenon Cres. Falk 41 F2
Blairdenon Dr. Cumb 61 E2
Blairdenon Dr. N Sau 5 D1
Blairdenon Rd. Alva 4 C3
Blairdenon Way. Irvine 220 A1
Blairforkie Dr. B of A 1 C4
Blairgowrie Rd. Glasg 115 E2
Blairgrove Ct. Coat 121 F3
Blairhall Ave. Glasg 136 C4
Blairhill Ave. Kirk 80 A3
Blairhill Pl. Coat 121 F4
Blairhill St. Coat 121 F4
Blairholm Dr. Hat 142 A2
Blairlands Dr. Beith 191 F4
Blairlinn Rd. Cumb 82 C3
Blairlogie St. Glasg 99 D1
Blairmore Cres. Green 46 B1
Blairmore Rd. Green 46 B1
Blairmuckhole and
Forrestdyke Rd. Sals 126 C4
Blairpark Ave. Coat 121 F4
Blairquhomrie Cotts. Bonh 20 C1
Blairston Ave. Udd 141 D1
Blairston Gdns. Udd 141 D1
Blairtum Dr. Glasg 138 A3
Blairtummock Rd. Glasg 119 E4
Blairtummock Rd. Glasg 119 F4
Blake Rd. Cumb 62 A1
Blakely Rd. Salt 217 D4
Blane Ave. Strath 31 D2
Blane Cres. Strath 31 D2
Blane Dr. Miln 55 D2
Blane Pl. Strath 31 D2
Blane St. Coat 122 A4
Blanefield Ave. Pres 236 B3
Blaneview. Stepps 99 E2
Blantyre Cres. Dunt 73 F4
Blantyre Ct. Ersk 73 D2
Blantyre Dr. Bishop 72 A2
Blantyre Farm Rd. Udd 140 B3
Blantyre Gdns. Cumb 60 C1
Blantyre Mill Rd. Udd 141 D1
Blantyre Pl. Coat 121 F2
Blantyre Rd. Udd 141 D1
Blantyre St. Coat 121 F2
Blantyre St. Glasg 96 B1
Blaven Ct. Glasg 120 B2
Blaven Head. Irvine 220 A2
Blawarthill St. Glasg 94 C3
Bleachfield. Falk 42 A3
Bleachfield. Miln 55 D2
Bleeze Rd. Dalry 191 D4
Blenheim Ave. E Kil 180 B4
Blenheim Ave. Stepps 99 F3
Blenheim Ct. Kils 36 C1
Blenheim Ct. Pais 113 E3
Blenheim Pl. Sten 23 F3
Blenheim Rd. Car 188 A1
Blindwells. Alva 4 B2
Blinkbonnie Terr. Slam 86 A3
Blinkbonny Rd. Falk 41 F2
Blinny Ct. Shot 147 D2
Blochairn Rd. Glasg 98 A1
Bloomgate. Lan 215 D2
Bluebell Gdns. Glasg 138 A1
Bluebell Gdns. Mother 142 B1
Bluebell Way. Aird 102 C1
Bluebell Way. Car 201 F4
Bluebell Way. Lennox 57 F4
Bluebell Wlk. Holy 143 D2
Blueknowes Rd. Law 186 C3
Bluevale St. Glasg 118 A3
Blyth Rd. Glasg 119 F3
Blythe Pl. Glasg 119 E3
Blythswood Ave. Ren 94 B2
Blythswood Dr. Pais 113 F3
Blythswood Rd. Ren 94 B2
Blythswood Sq. Glasg 117 D4
Blythswood St. Glasg 117 D4
Bo'ness Rd. Chap 123 E1
Bo'ness Rd. Holy 143 E4
Boardwalk The. E Kil 181 D4
Boat Vennel. Ayr 235 F1
Boclair Ave. Bear 75 F2
Boclair Cres. Bear 76 A2
Boclair Cres. Bish 78 A1
Boclair Rd. Bear 76 B3
Boclair Rd. Bish 78 A1
Boclair Rd. Glasg 76 B3
Boclair St. Glasg 95 F4
Bodden Sq. Holy 143 F4
Boden Quadrant. Mother 142 B1
Boden St. Glasg 118 A2
Bodesbeck Ct. Irvine 220 A2
Bodmin Gdns. Muir 80 C2
Bog Rd. Bank 38 C2
Bog Rd. Falk 42 B3
Bog Rd. Falk 42 C2
Bogany Terr. Glasg 137 F1
Bogbain Rd. Glasg 120 A4
Bogend Rd. Bann 11 F4
Bogend Rd. Lar 23 D4
Bogend Rd. Tor 22 C4
Bogfoot Rd. Sals 125 D1
Boggknowe. Tan 140 B4
Boghall Rd. Car 202 A4
Boghall Rd. Glasg 120 A2
Boghall St. Glasg 99 D1
Boghall St. Stone 198 C1
Boghead Ave. Dumb 50 A2
Boghead. Beith 171 D4
Boghead Rd. Dumb 50 A2
Boghead Rd. Glasg 98 A2
Boghead Rd. Kirk 79 D3
Bogiewood Rd. P Glasg 47 D1
Bogle St. Green 46 A2
Boglemart St. Steven 217 E4
Bogleshole Rd. Glasg 138 C4
Boglestone Ave. P Glasg 68 C4
Bogmoor Rd. Glasg 95 E1
Bogmoor Rd. Glasg 115 E4
Bogs View. Hat 141 F2
Bogside Rd. Ash 199 F4
Bogside Rd. Kils 60 B4
Bogside Rd. P Glasg 68 C4
Bogside Rd. Stepps 99 D3
Bogside St. Glasg 118 A2
Bogston La. Green 46 C1
Bogstonhill Rd. Hous 91 D1
Bogton Ave. Glasg 136 C2
Bogton Avenue La. Glasg 136 C2
Bohun Ct. Bann 7 E2
Boleyn Rd. Glasg 116 C1
Bolingbroke. E Kil 160 B2
Bolivar Terr. Glasg 137 E4
Bolton Dr. Glasg 137 D4
Bolton Terr. Lennox 57 F4
Boman Pl. Stew 195 E1
Bon Accord Cres. Shot 146 C3
Bon Accord Rd. Newt M 157 F3
Bon Accord Sq. Clyde 94 A4
Bonar Cres. B of W 110 C4
Bonar La. B of W 110 C4
Bonar Law Ave. Helen 16 A1
Bonawe St. Glasg 96 C2
Boness St. Glasg 118 A2
Bonhill Rd. Dumb 50 A2
Bonhill St. Glasg 97 D2
Bonkle Gdns. New 166 A3
Bonkle Rd. New 166 A3
Bonnar St. Glasg 118 A2
Bonnaughton Rd. Bear 75 D3
Bonnet Ct. Stew 211 F4
Bonnet Rd. Lan 215 D2
Bonnhill View. Alex 27 F2
Bonnington Ave. Lan 215 D2
Bonnybridge Rd. Bank 39 F3
Bonnybridge Rd. Bon 39 F3
Bonnyfield Rd. Bon 39 F3
Bonnyhill Rd. Bon 40 B2
Bonnyhill Rd. Falk 41 D2
Bonnyholm Ave. Glasg 115 D2
Bonnyrigg Dr. Glasg 136 A3
Bonnyside Rd. Bon 40 A3
Bonnyton Dr. Eagle 178 B3
Bonnyton Foot. Irvine 220 A3
Bonnyton Moor Rd. Eagle 178 A4
Bonnyton Pl. Irvine 220 A3
Bonnyton Pl. Kilmk 222 B1
Bonnyton Rd. Cross 222 B1
Bonnyton Rd. Kilmk 222 B1
Bonnyton Row. Irvine 220 A3
Bonnyview Gdns. Bon 40 A3
Bonnywood Ave. Bon 40 A4
Bontine Ave. Dumb 49 E2
Bonyton Ave. Glasg 94 C3
Boon Dr. Glasg 75 D1
Booth Pl. Falk 42 A2
Boquhanran Pl. Clyde 74 A2
Boquhanran Rd. Clyde 73 F1
Boquhanran Rd. Clyde 74 A2
Borden La. Glasg 95 F3
Borden Rd. Glasg 95 F3
Border Ave. Salt 216 C4
Border Pl. Salt 216 C4
Border St. Green 46 B2
Border Way. Kirk 79 F4
Bore Rd. Aird 123 D4
Boreland Dr. Glasg 95 D3
Boreland Dr. Ham 161 F1
Boreland Pl. Glasg 95 D3
Borestone Ave. Kilb 170 A4
Borestone Cres. Stir 7 D2
Borestone Ct. Stir 7 D1
Borestone Pl. Stir 7 D1
Borgie Cres. Glasg 139 D3
Borland Cres. Eagle 178 C3
Borland Rd. Bear 76 A2
Borron St. Glasg 97 E2
Borrowdale. E Kil 179 F3
Borrowlea Rd. Stir 7 E4
Borrowmeadow Rd. Stir 7 F4
Borthwick Dr. E Kil 179 E4
Borthwick St. Glasg 99 D1
Bosfield Cnr. E Kil 159 F2
Bosfield Pl. E Kil 159 F2
Bosfield Rd. E Kil 159 F2
Boston Dr. Helen 16 C2
Boswell Ct. Glasg 136 C4
Boswell Dr. Udd 161 E4
Boswell Pk. Ayr 238 C4
Boswell Pk. E Kil 160 B2
Boswell Sq. Glasg 114 C4
Bosworth Rd. E Kil 160 A3
Botanic Cres. Glasg 96 B2
Botanic Crescent La. Glasg 96 B2
Bothkennar Rd. Air 24 C2
Bothkennar Rd. Sten 24 C2
Bothlin Dr. Stepps 99 E3
Bothlyn Ave. Kirk 79 F4
Bothlyn Cres. Muir 100 C4
Bothlyn Rd. Muir 100 B4
Bothwell La. Glasg 96 C1
Bothwell La. Glasg 117 D4
Bothwell Pl. Coat 121 F4
Bothwell Pl. Pais 132 C4
Bothwell Rd. Car 187 F2
Bothwell Rd. Ham 162 B3
Bothwell Rd. Udd 140 C2
Bothwell St. Glasg 117 D4
Bothwell St. Glasg 138 C3
Bothwell St. Ham 162 B3
Bothwellhaugh
Quadrant. Hat 141 F2
Bothwellhaugh Rd. Hat 142 A1
Bothwellpark Rd. Tan 141 E2
Bothwellshields Rd. Chap 124 B1
Boturich Dr. Bonh 19 F1
Boundary Rd. Pres 236 B2
Bourhill Ct. Wish 164 B1
Bourne Cres. Inch 93 E4
Bourne Ct. Inch 93 E4
Bourne St. Ham 162 C2
Bournemouth Rd. Gour 44 C3
Bourock Sq. Barr 134 C1
Bourtree Pk. Ayr 239 D4
Bourtree Rd. Ham 161 F1
Bouverie St. Clyde 94 C3
Bouverie St. Glasg 137 F4
Bouverie St. P Glasg 47 E1
Bow Rd. Green 45 E2
Bow St. Stir 7 D4
Bowden Dr. Glasg 115 D3
Bowden Pk. E Kil 180 B4
Bower St. Glasg 96 C2
Bowerwalls St. Barr 134 C2
Bowes Cres. Glasg 119 F2
Bowes Rigg. Stew 195 F1
Bowfield Ave. Glasg 114 C3
Bowfield Cres. Glasg 114 C3
Bowfield Dr. Glasg 115 D3
Bowfield Pl. Glasg 114 C3
Bowfield Rd. How 130 C3
Bowfield Rd. W Kil 190 B2
Bowhouse Gdns. All 10 A3
Bowhouse Rd. All 10 A3
Bowhouse Rd. Chap 123 F3
Bowhouse Rise. Irvine 220 A3
Bowhousebog
Or Liquo. Shot 146 A1
Bowhousebog Rd. Shot 146 A1
Bowhousebrae Rd. Chap 123 F3
Bowie St. Dumb 49 F2
Bowling Green La. Glasg 95 E2
Bowling Green Rd. Glasg 95 E2
Bowling Green Rd. Glasg 119 E2
Bowling Green Rd. Glasg 137 D3
Bowling Green Rd. Muir 100 B4
Bowling Green St. Hat 142 A3
Bowling Green View. Glasg 139 F2
Bowling St. Coat 121 F4
Bowman Rd. Ayr 238 C3
Bowman St. Glasg 117 D1
Bowmanflat. Lark 185 D2
Bowmont Hill. Bish 78 A2
Bowmont Pl. E Kil 179 E4
Bowmont Pl. Glasg 139 E3
Bowmont Terr. Glasg 96 B2
Bowmore Ct. Irvine 220 A3
Bowmore Gdns. Glasg 138 C2
Bowmore Gdns. Tan 140 C4
Bowmore Rd. Glasg 115 F3
Bowmore Wlk. Shot 147 D2
Bowmount Gdns. Glasg 96 B2
Bowyer Vennel. Hat 141 F3
Boyd Ct. Kilmk 223 D1
Boyd Dr. Mother 163 D4
Boyd Orr Cres. Kilm 222 A4
Boyd Orr Rd. Salt 206 A1
Boyd St. Falk 42 A3
Boyd St. Glasg 117 E1
Boyd St. Kilmk 223 D1
Boyd St. Pres 236 B4
Boydston Rd. Ard 205 E2
Boydstone Pl. Glasg 136 A3
Boydstone Rd. Glasg 135 F3
Boyle St. Clyde 94 B4
Boylestone Rd. Barr 134 A2
Boyndie St. Glasg 120 A4
Brabloch Cres. Pais 113 F3
Bracadale Dr. Glasg 120 B2
Bracadale Gdns. Glasg 120 B2
Bracadale Gr. Glasg 120 B2
Bracadale Rd. Glasg 120 B2
Bracco Rd. Cald 105 E1
Brachelston St. Green 45 E2
Bracken Pk. Ayr 239 E2
Bracken Rd. P Glasg 69 D4
Bracken St. Glasg 97 D3
Bracken St. Holy 143 D2
Bracken Terr. Udd 141 D2
Bracken Way. Lark 185 E1
Brackenbrae Ave. Bish 77 F1
Brackenbrae Rd. Bish 77 F1
Brackendene. Hous 91 E1
Brackenhill Ave. Kilmk 223 D3
Brackenhill Dr. Ham 183 E4
Brackenhill Rd. Law 187 D3
Brackenhirst Rd. Glenm 102 C4
Brackenhurst St. Dumb 50 B3
Brackenknowe Rd. Gree 83 E2
Brackenlees Rd. Air 24 C3
Brackenlees Rd. Gran 24 C2
Brackenrig Cres. Eagle 157 F1
Brackenrig Rd. Glasg 135 F1
Brackla Ave. Clyde 94 C4
Bradan Ave. Ayr 239 D1
Bradan Ave. Clyde 94 C4
Bradan Rd. Troon 229 D1
Bradbury St. Sten 24 A1
Bradda Ave. Glasg 138 B2
Bradfield Ave. Glasg 96 B3
Bradshaw Cres. Ham 161 F2
Bradshaw St. Salt 216 C4
Brady Cres. Muir 81 D2
Brae The. Bann 7 E1
Brae The. Cam 6 B3
Braedale Ave. Aird 123 E4
Braedale Ave. Mother 163 E3
Braedale Cres. New 166 A3
Braedale Pl. New 166 B3
Braedale Rd. Lan 215 D3
Braeface Rd. Cumb 61 F1
Braefield Dr. Glasg 136 A2
Braefoot Ave. Miln 76 A4
Braefoot Cres. Law 186 C3
Braefoot Cres. Pais 133 F4
Braefoot Ct. Law 186 C3
Braefoot. Irvine 219 F3
Braehead. All 4 B1
Braehead. Alva 5 D4
Braehead Ave. Ayr 236 B1
Braehead Ave. Coat 121 E2
Braehead Ave. Dunt 74 A4
Braehead Ave. Lark 184 C1
Braehead Ave. Loch 129 E2
Braehead Ave. Miln 54 C1
Braehead Ave. Neil 154 B4
Braehead Ave. Tull 4 B1
Braehead. Beith 171 D4
Braehead. Bonh 28 A2
Braehead Cres. Ayr 236 B1
Braehead Cres. Dunt 74 A4
Braehead Ct. Kilmk 223 D1
Braehead. Dalry 191 E4
Braehead Dr. Hat 141 F2
Braehead Glebe. Stew 211 F4
Braehead. Irvine 219 F3
Braehead Loan. Car 202 A4
Braehead. Loch 129 E2
Braehead Pl. Dalry 191 E4
Braehead Pl. Hat 141 F2
Braehead Pl. Rhu 15 F3
Braehead Pl. Salt 216 C4
Braehead Quadrant. Holy 143 E2
Braehead Quadrant. Neil 154 B4
Braehead Rd. Ayr 236 B1
Braehead Rd. Cumb 62 A2
Braehead Rd. Dunt 74 A4
Braehead Rd. Fen 213 D2
Braehead Rd. P Glasg 68 C4
Braehead Rd. Pais 133 E4

Braehead Rd. Stir 7 E2
Braehead Rd. Thorn 158 B2
Braehead Rd. Glasg 117 E2
Braehead St. Kirk 58 B1
Braehead Terr. Kirk 222 B3
Braehead. Udd 161 E3
Braehouse. Rhu 15 E2
Braemar Ave. Clyde 73 F2
Braemar Cres. Bear 75 F1
Braemar Cres. Car 188 A2
Braemar Cres. Falk 42 B3
Braemar Cres. Pais 113 F1
Braemar Ct. Glasg 136 C2
Braemar Dr. Falk 42 B3
Braemar Dr. John 112 A1
Braemar Gdns. Duni 7 E2
Braemar Pl. Sten 24 A2
Braemar Rd. Glasg 138 C2
Braemar Rd. Inch 93 F3
Braemar Sq. Ayr 236 B1
Braemar St. Glasg 136 C4
Braemar St. Ham 162 A3
Braemar View. Clyde 73 F3
Braemore Rd. Stew 195 E1
Braemount Ave. Pais 133 E3
Braes Ave. Clyde 74 B1
Braes O' Yetts. Kirk 80 A4
Braes Rd. Salt 216 C4
Braes The. Tull 4 B2
Brae View. Den 39 E4
Brae View. Shi 66 C4
Braesburn Ct. Cumb 62 C3
Braesburn Pl. Cumb 62 C3
Braesburn Rd. Cumb 62 C3
Braeside Ave. Glasg 138 B4
Braeside Ave. Miln 79 E4
Braeside Ave. Muir 80 C1
Braeside Cres. Barr 134 C1
Braeside Cres. Coat 120 C3
Braeside Gdns. Ham 163 F4
Braeside. Irvine 219 F3
Braeside. Shi 66 B3
Braeside La. Gour 44 B2
Braeside La. Lark 185 D2
Braeside. N Sau 5 E1
Braeside Pl. Glasg 139 D2
Braeside Rd. Ayr 236 B1
Braeside Rd. Gour 44 B2
Braeside Rd. Holy 143 E2
Braeside. Shi 66 B3
Braeside St. Glasg 96 C2
Braeside St. Kilmk 228 A4
Braeside Way. Lark 185 D1
Braeval Ave. Pais 133 D4
Braeview Dr. Pais 133 D4
Braeview Gdns. Pais 133 D4
Braeview. Lar 23 E1
Braeview. Laur 42 C2
Braeview Pl. E Kil 160 A2
Braeview Rd. Pais 133 D4
Braid Sq. Glasg 97 D1
Braid's Rd. Pais 113 F1
Braidbar Cl. Glasg 136 B2
Braidbar Farm Rd. Glasg .. 136 B2
Braidbar Rd. Glasg 136 B2
Braidcraft Pl. Glasg 135 E4
Braidcraft Rd. Glasg 115 E1
Braidcraft Terr. Glasg 115 E1
Braidfauld Gdns. Glasg ... 118 C2
Braidfauld Pl. Glasg 118 C1
Braidfauld St. Glasg 118 C2
Braidfield Gr. Dunt 74 A3
Braidfield Rd. Dunt 74 A3
Braidfute. Lan 215 E3
Braidholm Cres. Glasg 136 B2
Braidholm Rd. Glasg 136 B2
Braidhurst Ind Est. Mother 142 B2
Braidhurst St. Mother 163 F4
Braidley Cres. E Kil 180 C3
Braidpark Dr. Glasg 136 C2
Braidwood Pl. Lin 111 F3
Braidwood Rd. Car 201 E1
Braidwood Rd. John 201 F3
Braidwood Rd. Kilw 207 F2
Braidwood St. Wish 165 E4
Bramblehedge Path. Bonh . 27 F4
Brambling Ct. Wish 165 D1
Bramley Pl. Kirk 79 F2
Brampton. E Kil 179 F3
Branchal Rd. Wish 165 F3
Branchalfield Dr. Wish 165 F3
Branchalmuir Cres. New .. 165 F3
Branchock Ave. Glasg 139 E2
Branchton Rd. Gour 44 A3
Brancumhall Rd. E Kil 160 B2
Brand St. Glasg 96 C3
Brandon Arc. Mother 163 F3
Brandon Dr. Bear 75 F4
Brandon Gdns. Glasg 138 C3
Brandon Par E. Mother ... 163 F3
Brandon Par S. Mother ... 163 F3
Brandon St. Hat 141 F2
Brandon St. Coat 121 F2
Brandon St. Glasg 117 F3
Brandon St. Ham 162 C2
Brandon St. Mother 163 F3
Brandon Way. Coat 121 E2
Brandyhill. Fish 5 F2
Brankholm Brae. Ham 161 E2
Brannock Ave. Holy 143 E2
Brannock Pl. Holy 143 E2
Brannock Rd. Holy 143 E2
Branshill Pl. N Sau 10 A4
Branshill Rd. N Sau 10 A4
Brassey St. Glasg 96 C3
Braxfield Rd. Lan 215 D1
Braxfield Terr. Lan 214 C1
Breadalbane Cres. Mother 142 B1
Breadalbane Gdns. Glasg 138 B2
Breadalbane St. Glasg 116 C4
Breadie Dr. Miln 75 F4
Bream Pl. Hous 111 E4
Breamish Pl. E Kil 179 F3
Brechin Rd. Bish 78 B1
Brechin St. Glasg 116 C4
Breck Ave. Pais 132 B4
Bredi land Rd. Lin 112 A3
Bredi land Rd. Pais 112 A3
Bredin Way. Mother 163 D4
Bredisholm Cres. Tan 121 E1
Bredisholm Dr. Glasg 120 B2
Bredisholm Rd. Coat 120 C2
Bredisholm Rd. Glasg 120 C2
Bredisholm Terr. Glasg ... 120 C2
Brenfield Ave. Glasg 136 C2
Brenfield Dr. Glasg 136 C2
Brenfield Rd. Glasg 137 D2
Brent Cres. Hous 111 E4
Brent Ct. E Kil 159 F2
Brent Rd. E Kil 159 F2
Brentham Ave. Stir 7 D3
Brentham Cres. Stir 7 D3
Brentwood Ave. Glasg 135 D2
Brentwood Dr. Glasg 135 D2
Brentwood Sq. Glasg 135 D2
Brereton St. Glasg 117 E1
Breslin Terr. East 127 E3
Bressay. E Kil 159 F2
Bressay Pl. Kilmk 223 D3
Bressay Rd. Glasg 119 F3
Bressay Wynd. New 165 F3
Breton Ct. Falk 42 B2
Breval Cres. Dunt 74 A4
Brewery Rd. Kilmk 227 F4
Brewster St. John 111 F2
Brewlands Cres. Sym 231 E2
Brewlands Dr. Sym 231 E2
Brewlands Rd. Sym 231 E2
Brewster Ave. Pais 114 A4
Briar Pl. Den 21 E1
Briar Pl. Shew 231 E2
Briar Bank. M of C 58 A3
Briar Dr. Clyde 74 A2
Briar Gr. Ayr 238 C3
Briar Neuk. Bish 98 A4
Briar Pl. Gour 44 B3
Briar Rd. Glasg 136 B3
Briar Rd. Kirk 79 F4
Briarbush Way. Udd 140 A4
Briarcroft Pl. Glasg 100 A4
Briarhill Ct. Pres 236 B4
Briarhill Rd. Pres 236 B4
Briarlea Dr. Glasg 136 B2
Briarlea Pl. All 4 C1
Briarwell La. Milo 55 D1
Briarwell Rd. Milo 75 F4
Briarwood Ct. Glasg 119 F1
Briarwood Rd. Mother 164 C2
Brick La. Pais 113 F3
Bridesburn Pl. Stew 195 F1
Bridge Cres. Den 21 E1
Bridge End. Shot 146 B3
Bridge La. Milo 207 D3
Bridge of Weir Rd. B of W .110 C4
Bridge Of Weir Rd. Hous .. 91 D1
Bridge Of Weir Rd. Kilbar . 89 F3
Bridge Of Weir Rd. Kilbar .111 E3
Bridge Of Weir Rd. Lin ... 112 A3
Bridge Pl. Den 21 E1
Bridge Pl. Milo 55 D2
Bridge Pl. Shot 147 D2
Bridge Rd. P Glasg 68 C4
Bridge St. Alex 27 F2
Bridge St. Bon 40 A3
Bridge St. Cald 84 C1
Bridge St. Clyde 73 F2
Bridge St. Dumb 49 F2
Bridge St. Glasg 117 D3
Bridge St. Glasg 139 D3
Bridge St. Ham 162 B1
Bridge St. Kilb 149 D3
Bridge St. Lin 112 A3
Bridge St. Pais 113 F2
Bridge St. Pres 236 A4
Bridgeacre Gdns. Glasg .. 119 F3
Bridgebar St. Barr 134 C2
Bridgeburn Dr. Muir 80 C1
Bridgeford Ave. Hat 142 B4
Bridgegait. Milo 76 B4
Bridgegate. Glasg 117 E3
Bridgegate. Irvine 219 E1
Bridgehaugh Rd. Stir 2 A1
Bridgehousehill Rd. Kilmk 227 F1
Bridgend Ave. P Glasg 68 C4
Bridgend. Bishop 72 A2
Bridgend Cotts. Kirk 80 A4
Bridgend. Dalry 191 E4
Bridgend La. Kilw 207 F2
Bridgend La. Kilw 207 F2
Bridgend Rd. Green 46 B1
Bridgend Rd. Kilb 149 D1
Bridgend. Stew 211 F4
Bridgend View. Car 187 F1
Bridgend Wlk. Uplaw 153 D2
Bridgepark. Salt 205 E1
Bridgewater
        Shopping Ctr. Ersk 73 E1
Bridgeway Ct. Kirk 79 F4
Bridgeway Pl. Kirk 79 F4
Bridgeway Rd. Kirk 79 F4
Bridgeway Terr. Kirk 79 F4
Bridie Terr. E Kil 160 B2
Brierie Ave. Hous 91 D1
Brierie Gdns. Hous 111 D4
Brierie Hills. Hous 91 D1
Brierie La. Hous 111 D4
Brierie-Hill Ct. Hous 111 D4
Brierie-Hill Gr. Hous 111 D4
Brierie-Hill Rd. Hous 111 D4
Briery Ct. Kilb 170 A4
Brierybank Ave. Lan 215 D2
Brig O'Lee Terr. Neil 154 B3
Brig-O-Doon Gr. Cowie 12 C4
Brigbrae Ave. Hat 142 B2
Brigham Pl. Glasg 96 C4
Brighton Pl. Glasg 116 B3
Brighton St. Glasg 116 B3
Brightside Ave. P Glasg ... 69 D4
Brightside Ave. Udd 140 C3
Brigside Gdns. Ham 163 D1
Bringan Rd. Kilmk 222 C3
Brisbane Ct. Glasg 136 B2
Brisbane Rd. Bishop 72 A2
Brisbane St. Clyde 73 E2
Brisbane St. Glasg 137 D4
Brisbane St. Green 45 E3
Brisbane Terr. E Kil 180 B4
Britannia Pl. Ayr 236 A1
Britannia Way. Ren 94 B1
Briton St. Glasg 116 A4
Broad La. Udd 161 E4
Broad Sq. Udd 161 E4
Broad St. All 10 A3
Broad St. Den 21 F1
Broad St. Glasg 118 A3
Broad St. Stir 7 D4
Broad Way The. Mother .. 164 C2
Broadcroft. Kirk 79 F4
Broadcroft Rd. Kirk 58 B1
Broadfield Ave. P Glasg ... 69 D4
Broadford St. Glasg 97 E1
Broadford Terr. Gour 44 C2
Broadleys Ave. Bish 77 F1
Broadlie Ct. Neil 154 B4
Broadlie Dr. Glasg 95 D3
Broadlie Rd. Neil 154 B4
Broadloan. Ren 94 A1
Broadmoss Ave. Newt M . 157 E2
Broadstone Ave. P Glasg . 47 D1
Broadway. Ard 205 E2
Broadwood Dr. Glasg 137 D3
Broadwood Pk. Ayr 239 D1
Broadwood
        Roundabout. Cumb 81 F4
Brock Oval. Glasg 135 E3
Brock Pl. Glasg 135 F3
Brock Pl. Stir 7 D1
Brock Rd. Glasg 135 E3
Brock Terr. Glasg 135 E3
Brockburn Rd. Glasg 115 D1
Brockburn Terr. Glasg 135 E4
Brockburn Terr. Glasg 135 E4
Brocklinn Pk. E Kil 179 F4
Brockly View. Kilb 149 D2
Brockville St. Glasg 118 C3
Brock Ave. Bon 40 A4
Brodick Ave. Mother 163 D4
Brodick Ct. Kilw 207 E2
Brodick Dr. E Kil 159 E2
Brodick Dr. Gour 43 F3
Brodick Pl. Falk 41 E2
Brodick Pl. Kilmk 222 B1
Brodick Rd. Kilmk 222 B1
Brodie Ave. Troon 229 E2
Brodie Park Ave. Pais 113 F1
Brodie Park Cres. Pais ... 113 F1
Brodie Park Gdns. Pais .. 113 F1
Brodie Pl. E Kil 159 D2
Brodie Pl. Kilmk 222 B1
Brodie Pl. Stone 198 C1
Brodie Rd. Glasg 99 F4
Brodie St. Falk 42 A2
Brogan Cres. Mother 163 D4
Broich The. Alva 4 C4
Bron Way. Cumb 62 A1
Bronte Pl. Sten 24 A2
Brook St. Alva 5 D3
Brook St. Clyde 73 F2
Brook St. Glasg 117 F3
Brook St. Men 3 F3
Brookbank Terr. Car 188 A1
Brooke Ave. Bonh 28 A4
Brookfield Pl. Alva 5 D3
Brookfield Rd. P Glasg 68 C4
Brooklands. Alex 27 E3
Brooklands Ave. Udd 140 C4
Brooklands. E Kil 159 D1
Brooklea Dr. Glasg 136 B3
Brooklime Dr. E Kil 159 E2
Brooklyn Pl. Wish 186 A4
Brookside Dr. Glasg 118 A3
Broom Ave. Inch 93 D4
Broom Cliff. Newt M 156 C2
Broom Cres. Barr 134 A3
Broom Cres. E Kil 180 B3
Broom Ct. Stir 7 E2
Broom Dr. Lark 185 D3
Broom Gdns. Kirk 79 D3
Broom Path. Glasg 119 F2
Broom Pk. E. Men 4 A3
Broom Pk W. Men 4 A3
Broom Pk. B of W 110 C4
Broom Pl. Coat 121 F2
Broom Pl. Holy 143 E2
Broom Pl. Kilmk 228 A3
Broom Pl. Cumb 62 B3
Broom Rd E. Newt M 157 D2
Broom Rd. Glasg 136 B3
Broom Rd. Newt M 157 D3
Broom Rd. Ros 15 D2
Broom Rd. Stir 7 E2
Broom Terr. John 112 A1
Broom Wynd. Shot 146 C3
Broomage Ave. Lar 23 D2
Broomage Cres. Lar 23 D2
Broomage Dr. Lar 23 D2
Broomage Pk. Lar 23 E1
Broomberry Dr. Gour 44 C4
Broomburn Dr. Newt M .. 157 D3
Broomcroft Rd. Newt M .. 157 D3
Broomdyke Way. Pais 113 E4
Broomelton Rd. Quart ... 184 B1
Broomfield Ave. Glasg ... 138 B4
Broomfield Ave. Newt M 156 C1
Broomfield Gdns. Ayr 238 C3
Broomfield La. Glasg 97 F3
Broomfield Pl. Glasg 97 F3
Broomfield Rd. Ash 199 F2
Broomfield Rd. Ayr 238 C3
Broomfield Rd. Glasg 97 F3
Broomfield Rd. Lark 199 D4
Broomfield Rd. Newt M .. 157 D3
Broomfield St. Aird 123 D4
Broomfield St. Aird 200 B2
Broomfield St. Kilw 207 E2
Broomfield Terr. Tan 120 C1
Broomgate. Lan 215 D2
Broomhill Ave. Glasg 95 F1
Broomhill Ave. Glasg 139 D4
Broomhill Ave. Newt M .. 156 C1
Broomhill Cres. Bon 28 A1
Broomhill Cres. Hat 141 F2
Broomhill Dr. Dumb 50 A3
Broomhill Dr. Glasg 95 F2
Broomhill Dr. Dumb 50 A3
Broomhill Dr. Glasg 95 F2
Broomhill Farm Mews. Kirk 58 C1
Broomhill Gdns. Glasg 95 F1
Broomhill Gdns. Newt M 156 C2
Broomhill La. Glasg 95 F1
Broomhill Path. Glasg 95 F1
Broomhill Pl. Duni 21 E2
Broomhill Pl. Glasg 95 F1
Broomhill Pl. Stir 5 C3
Broomhill Quadrant. Kilmk 228 A2
Broomhill Rd. Bon 40 A4
Broomhill Rd E. Kilmk 228 A2
Broomhill Rd. Lark 185 D1
Broomhill Rd W. Kilmk ... 227 F2
Broomhill St. East 127 E3
Broomhill St. Green 45 F2
Broomhill Terr. Glasg 95 F1
Broomhill View. Lark 184 C1
Broomill Way. Green 46 A3
Broomieknowe Dr. Glasg 138 A3
Broomieknowe Rd. Glasg 138 A3
Broomieknowe. Tull 4 B2
Broomielaw. Glasg 117 D3
Broomknoll St. Aird 123 D4
Broomknowe. Cumb 81 E2
Broomknowe Rd. Pais 133 D4
Broomknowes Ave. Kirk .. 79 F2
Broomknowes Rd. Glasg .. 98 A2
Broomlands Ave. Inch 93 E4
Broomlands
        Busway. Irvine 220 A1
Broomlands Cres. Inch 93 F4
Broomlands Ct. Irvine 220 A1
Broomlands Dr. Irvine 219 E1
Broomlands Gdns. Inch ... 93 E4
Broomlands Pl. Irvine 219 F1
Broomlands Rd. Cumb 83 D4
Broomlands Rd. Irvine ... 220 A1
Broomlands St. Pais 113 E2
Broomlands Way. Inch 93 F4
Broomlea Cres. Inch 93 E4
Broomlee Rd. Cumb 82 C3
Broomley Cres. Alex 27 E4
Broomley Dr. Glasg 136 B1
Broomley La. Glasg 136 B1
Broomloan Ct. Glasg 116 A3
Broomloan Pl. Glasg 116 A3
Broomloan Rd. Glasg 116 A3
Broompark Ave. Pres 236 B4
Broompark Ave. Udd 161 E3
Broompark Cir. Glasg 117 F4
Broompark Cres. Aird 103 D2
Broompark Cres. Pres ... 236 B4
Broompark Dr. Glasg 117 F4
Broompark Dr. Inch 93 E4
Broompark Dr. Newt M .. 157 D2
Broompark Gdns. Den 21 F1
Broompark La. Glasg 117 F4
Broompark Rd. Mother .. 164 B2
Broompark Rd. Udd 161 E4
Broompark St. Glasg 117 F4
Broomridge Rd. Stir 7 E2
Broomside Cres. Mother 163 F2
Broomside St. Mother 163 F2
Broomside Rd. Bon 40 A2
Broomstone Ave. Newt M 156 C2
Broomton Rd. Glasg 98 B4
Broomward Dr. John 112 A2
Brora Dr. Bear 76 A2
Brora Dr. Glasg 136 B1
Brora Dr. Ren 94 C2
Brora Gdns. Bish 78 A1
Brora Rd. Bish 78 A1
Brora St. Glasg 98 B1
Brosdale Ct. Falk 42 A1
Brougham St. Green 45 F4
Broughton Dr. Glasg 96 C4
Broughton E Kil 180 C3
Broughton Gdns. Glasg ... 76 C1
Broughton Pl. Coat 122 A2
Broughton Pl. Ham 162 A2
Broughton Rd. Glasg 76 C1
Brouster Gate. E Kil 159 F1
Brouster Hill. E Kil 159 F1
Brouster Pl. E Kil 159 F1
Brown Ave. All 4 C1
Brown Ave. Dumb 50 B2
Brown Ave. Ren 94 C4
Brown Ave. Stir 2 A1
Brown Ave. Troon 229 E2
Brown Pl. Glasg 139 D3
Brown Pl. Salt 205 F1
Brown Rd. Cumb 61 F1
Brown St. Bonh 28 A4
Brown St. Car 187 F2
Brown St. Coat 122 A2
Brown St. Falk 41 E3
Brown St. Glasg 117 D4
Brown St. Greer 46 B2
Brown St. Lark 185 D2
Brown St. Mother 163 F4
Brown St. New 166 A2
Brown St. P Glasg 47 D1
Brown St. Pais 113 F3
Brown St. Ren 94 A1
Brown St. Shot 147 D2
Brown St. Stew 211 E4
Brown St. Wish 173 F2
Brown Wlk. Irvine 219 F3
Brownhill Dr. Kilb 149 D3
Brownhill Rd. Glasg 136 A2
Brownhill View. New 166 B3
Brownieside Pl. Plains ... 104 B1
Brownlee Rd. Law 186 C2
Brownlie St. Glasg 137 D4
Brownmuir Ave. Eagle ... 178 C2
Brownsburn Rd. Aird 123 D1
Brownsdale Rd. Glasg 137 F4
Brownsfield Cres. Inch 93 D3
Brownsfield Rd. Inch 93 D3
Brownshill Ave. Coat 121 F2
Brownside Ave. Barr 134 A3
Brownside Ave. Car 188 A3
Brownside Ave. Glasg ... 134 A3
Brownside Cres. Barr 134 A3
Brownside Dr. Barr 134 A3
Brownside Dr. Glasg 134 A3
Brownside Gr. Barr 134 A3
Brownside Mews. Glasg 134 A3
Brownside Rd. Camb 138 C2
Brownside Rd. Glasg 138 C2
Brownside Ave. Pais 133 F3
Bruar Way. New 165 F3
Bruart Ave. Sten 23 F2
Bruce Ave. Dund 225 F1
Bruce Ave. John 131 F4
Bruce Ave. Mother 163 E4
Bruce Ave. Pais 114 A4
Bruce Ave. Pres 236 A3

249
Bruce Cres. Ayr
Cairnwood Dr. Aird

Bruce Cres. Ayr 238 C4
Bruce Cres. Kilmk 227 F2
Bruce Cres. Plea 12 B2
Bruce Cres. Sten 24 A2
Bruce Ct. Aird 123 F4
Bruce Dr. Fall 8 B3
Bruce Dr. Sten 23 F2
Bruce La. Pres 236 A3
Bruce Loan. Wish 186 B3
Bruce Pl. E Kil 180 C4
Bruce Rd. Bishop 72 A2
Bruce Rd. Glasg 116 C2
Bruce Rd. Holy 143 D1
Bruce Rd. Pais 114 A4
Bruce Rd. Ren 94 A1
Bruce St. All 10 B4
Bruce St. Bann 7 F1
Bruce St. Clyde 74 A1
Bruce St. Coat 122 A4
Bruce St. Dumb 50 A1
Bruce St. Falk 42 B3
Bruce St. Green 45 F3
Bruce St. Hat 142 A3
Bruce St. Kilmk 227 F2
Bruce St. P Glasg 47 E1
Bruce St. Plains 104 A1
Bruce St. Plea 12 B2
Bruce St. Stir 2 A1
Bruce Terr. Cam 6 B3
Bruce Terr. E Kil 180 C4
Bruce Terr. Irvine 219 E3
Bruce Terr. Udd 140 C1
Bruce's Loan. Lark 185 E1
Brucefield Pl. Glasg 120 B4
Brucehill Rd. Dumb 49 E2
Brunel Way. E Kil 180 C4
Brunstane Rd. Glasg 100 A1
Brunswick La. Glasg 117 E4
Brunswick St. Glasg 117 E4
Brunton St. Glasg 137 D3
Brunton Terr. Glasg 137 D2
Bruntsfield Ave. Glasg 135 D2
Bruntsfield Ave. Kilw 207 D2
Bruntsfield Gdns. Glasg 135 D2
Bryan St. Ham 162 A3
Bryce Ave. Sten 24 A1
Bryce Gdns. Lark 185 D2
Bryce Knox Ct. Irvine 220 A3
Bryce Pl. E Kil 180 B3
Brydson Pl. Lin 112 A3
Brymner St. Green 46 A3
Bryon Ct. Udd 141 D1
Bryony The. Tull 4 A1
Bryson Ct. Ham 183 E4
Bryson St. Dunt 74 C4
Bryson St. Falk 42 A3
Buccleuch Ave. Glasg 114 C4
Buccleuch Ave. Newt M 157 E4
Buccleuch Dr. Bear 75 F4
Buccleuch La. Glasg 97 D1
Buccleuch St. Glasg 97 D1
Buccleugh St. Green 45 F3
Buchan Gn. E Kil 160 A2
Buchan Rd. Holy 143 D1
Buchan Rd. Troon 229 F2
Buchan St. Ham 183 E4
Buchan St. Wish 165 D3
Buchan Terr. Glasg 138 C2
Buchanan Ave. Bishop 72 A2
Buchanan Ave. Bonh 28 A4
Buchanan Bsns Pk. Stepps 99 F3
Buchanan Cres. Bish 98 B4
Buchanan Cres. Ham 162 A1
Buchanan Ct. Falk 42 A4
Buchanan Ct. Stepps 99 F3
Buchanan Dr. Bear 76 A2
Buchanan Dr. Bish 98 B4
Buchanan Dr. Glasg 138 B3
Buchanan Dr. Glasg 138 C3
Buchanan Dr. Kirk 79 E2
Buchanan Dr. Law 187 D3
Buchanan Dr. Newt M 156 C4
Buchanan Dr. Stir 2 A2
Buchanan Gdns. Glasg 119 F1
Buchanan Pl. Kilmk 228 A3
Buchanan Pl. Lennox 57 D1
Buchanan Rd. Helen 17 D1
Buchanan St. Aird 123 D4
Buchanan St. Coat 121 F3
Buchanan St. Dumb 50 A1
Buchanan St. Glasg 117 D4
Buchanan St. Glasg 117 E4
Buchanan St. Glasg 120 A2
Buchanan St. Green 45 D2
Buchanan St. John 111 F1
Buchanan St. Miln 55 D1
Buchandyke Rd. E Kil 160 A2
Buchlyvie Gdns. Bish 97 F4
Buchlyvie Rd. Glasg 114 C3
Buchlyvie St. Glasg 120 A4
Buckie. Ersk 73 D2
Buckie Wlk. Hat 142 A3
Buckingham Ct. Ham 161 F2
Buckingham Dr. Glasg 138 B4
Buckingham Dr. Glasg 139 D4
Buckingham St. Glasg 96 B2
Buckingham Terr. Glasg 96 B2
Bucklaw Gdns. Glasg 115 E2
Bucklaw Pl. Glasg 115 E2
Bucklaw Terr. Glasg 115 E2
Buckley St. Glasg 97 E3
Bucksburn Rd. Glasg 98 B2
Buckthorne Pl. Glasg 135 D2
Buddon St. Glasg 118 B2
Budhill Ave. Glasg 119 D3
Budshaw Ave. Chap 123 E1
Buiston Rd. Spring 211 E2
Bull Rd. Newt M 157 F3
Bull's Cl. Lan 215 D2
Bulldale Rd. Glasg 94 C3
Bulldale St. Glasg 94 C3
Bullionslaw Dr. Glasg 138 B3
Bulloch Ave. Glasg 136 B1
Bulloch Cres. Den 21 E1
Bullwood Ave. Glasg 134 C4
Bullwood Ct. Glasg 115 D1
Bullwood Dr. Glasg 114 C1
Bullwood Gdns. Glasg 114 C1
Bullwood Pl. Glasg 114 C1
Bunbury Terr. E Kil 180 B4
Bunessan St. Glasg 115 F3
Bunhouse Rd. Glasg 96 B1
Buntine Cres. Stir 7 D2
Bunting Pl. Kilmk 228 B4
Burbank. Miln 55 D1
Burbank Terr. P Glasg 68 B4
Burgh Hall La. Glasg 96 A1
Burgh Hall St. Glasg 96 A1
Burgh La. Glasg 96 B2
Burgh Mews. All 10 A3
Burgh Rd. Pres 236 A4
Burgh Wlk. Gour 44 C4
Burghead Dr. Glasg 115 F4
Burghead Pl. Glasg 115 F4
Burgher St. Glasg 118 B3
Burghmuir Rd. Stir 7 D3
Burleigh Rd. Udd 141 D2
Burleigh St. Coat 122 A2
Burleigh St. Glasg 116 A4
Burleigh Way. All 10 B3
Burley Pl. E Kil 158 C1
Burlington Ave. Glasg 96 A3
Burmola St. Glasg 97 D2
Burn Cres. Chap 123 E1
Burn Cres. Holy 143 D2
Burn Dr. Stir 7 E2
Burn La. Holy 143 D2
Burn Rd. Car 187 F2
Burn Rd. Salt 216 B4
Burn St. Alex 27 F2
Burn Street La. Bonh 27 F2
Burn Terr. Glasg 138 C4
Burn View. Cumb 62 B2
Burn's Cres. Aird 123 D3
Burn's Pl. Steven 206 C1
Burnacre Gdns. Udd 140 C4
Burnbank Braes. Car 187 F1
Burnbank Ctr. Ham 162 A3
Burnbank Dr. Barr 134 B1
Burnbank Gdns. Ham 162 A3
Burnbank Pl. Ayr 239 D2
Burnbank Pl. Glasg 97 D1
Burnbank Pl. Sten 195 F1
Burnbank Quadrant. Aird 122 C4
Burnbank Rd. Ayr 239 D2
Burnbank Rd. Falk 42 A4
Burnbank Rd. Ham 162 A2
Burnbank St. Aird 122 C4
Burnbank St. Coat 122 A4
Burnbank St. Steven 217 E4
Burnbank Terr. Glasg 97 D1
Burnbank Terr. Kils 36 B1
Burnblea Gdns. Ham 162 C1
Burnblea St. Ham 162 B1
Burnbrae Ave. Bear 76 A4
Burnbrae Ave. Lin 112 B3
Burnbrae Ave. Muir 81 D1
Burnbrae Dr. Glasg 138 B3
Burnbrae Dr. Irvine 220 B3
Burnbrae Dr. John 112 B2
Burnbrae. Dunt 74 A3
Burnbrae Gdns. Alva 5 D3
Burnbrae Gdns. Falk 42 A3
Burnbrae. N Sau 10 B4
Burnbrae Pl. E Kil 159 E1
Burnbrae Rd. Falk 42 A3
Burnbrae Rd. Hart 127 F3
Burnbrae Rd. John 112 B2
Burnbrae Rd. Kirk 80 A4
Burnbrae Rd. Muir 80 A2
Burnbrae Rd. Shot 146 C2
Burnbrae Rd. Stepps 79 F1
Burnbrae Rd. Udd 161 E4
Burnbrae St. Dunt 74 B4
Burnbrae St. Glasg 98 A2
Burnbrae St. Lark 184 C2
Burnbrae. Twe 59 F2
Burncleuch Ave. Glasg 139 D2
Burncrooks Ave. E Kil 159 E1
Burncrooks Ct. Dunt 73 F3
Burndale La. Kil 89 E4
Burndyke Ct. Glasg 116 B4
Burndyke Sq. Glasg 116 B4
Burnee. Fish 5 F2
Burness Ave. Ayr 238 C1
Burnet Rose Ct. E Kil 159 E2
Burnet Rose Gdns. E Kil 159 E2
Burnet Rose Pl. E Kil 159 E2
Burnett Rd. Glasg 119 F4
Burnett Terr. Ayr 236 A1
Burnfield Ave. Glasg 136 A2
Burnfield Cotts. Glasg 136 A2
Burnfield Dr. Glasg 136 A2
Burnfield Gdns. Glasg 136 B2
Burnfield Pl. Falk 42 B4
Burnfield Rd. Glasg 136 A2
Burnfoot Ave. Troon 229 E3
Burnfoot. Card 48 A4
Burnfoot Cres. Glasg 138 B3
Burnfoot Cres. Pais 133 E4
Burnfoot Dr. Glasg 115 D3
Burnfoot La. Ard 205 D2
Burnfoot La. Falk 42 A2
Burnfoot Pl. Kilmk 222 C2
Burnfoot Rd. Aird 122 C4
Burnfoot Rd. Loch 129 D1
Burnfoot Way. Troon 229 E3
Burngreen. Kils 60 B4
Burngreen Terr. Cumb 62 A3
Burnhall Pl. Wish 165 E1
Burnhall Rd. Wish 165 E1
Burnhall St. Wish 165 E1
Burnham Rd. Glasg 95 D2
Burnhaven. Ersk 73 D1
Burnhead La. Falk 42 B2
Burnhead La. P Glasg 68 B4
Burnhead Rd. Aird 103 E1
Burnhead Rd. Cumb 61 E1
Burnhead Rd. Glasg 136 C3
Burnhead Rd. Lar 23 E2
Burnhead Rd. Lark 185 E1
Burnhead Rd. P Glasg 68 B4
Burnhead St. Green 46 A1
Burnhead St. Tan 141 E4
Burnhill Quadrant. Glasg 137 F4
Burnhill St. Glasg 137 F4
Burnhouse Ave. Dalry 191 D4
Burnhouse Cotts. Dunlop 195 D4
Burnhouse Cres. Ham 162 A1
Burnhouse Rd. Auld 180 A1
Burnhouse Rd. Ham 162 A1
Burnhouse St. Glasg 96 B3
Burniebrae. Aird 122 C4
Burniebrae Rd. Chap 123 F2
Burnlea Cres. Hous 91 D2
Burnlea Pl. Steven 206 C1
Burnlip Rd. Glen 102 A2
Burnmouth Ct. Glasg 119 F3
Burnmouth Rd. Glasg 119 F3
Burnock Pl. E Kil 179 F4
Burnpark Ave. Tan 140 B4
Burnpark Rd. Kilmk 227 F2
Burns Ave. Bishop 72 A2
Burns Ave. Kilmk 223 D2
Burns Ave. Salt 205 F2
Burns Cres. Hart 127 F3
Burns Cres. Irvine 220 A3
Burns Cres. Laur 42 C2
Burns Ct. Kirk 59 D1
Burns Dr. John 131 F4
Burns Dr. Kirk 59 D1
Burns Gdns. Udd 140 B1
Burns Gr. Glasg 136 A1
Burns La. Chap 123 E2
Burns Loan. Lark 185 D2
Burns Pk. E Kil 160 A2
Burns Pl. Kilw 207 F2
Burns Pl. Shot 146 A3
Burns Prec. Kilmk 227 F4
Burns Rd. Chap 123 F2
Burns Rd. Cumb 62 A1
Burns Rd. Gour 44 B2
Burns Rd. Kirk 59 D1
Burns Rd. Troon 229 F2
Burns Sq. Ard 205 E2
Burns Sq. Gour 44 B2
Burns St. Alex 27 E1
Burns St. Alex 27 F4
Burns St. Clyde 73 F2
Burns St. Ham 162 B1
Burns St. Irvine 219 D2
Burns St. Stir 2 A1
Burns Statue Sq. Ayr 238 C4
Burns Terr. Ard 205 E2
Burns Terr. Cowie 12 B4
Burns Walk. Hat 142 A4
Burns Way. Holy 143 E2
Burnside Ave. Barr 134 A2
Burnside Ave. Calder 123 D1
Burnside Ave. Hat 142 B2
Burnside Ave. Kilbar 111 E3
Burnside Ave. Kirk 79 D4
Burnside Ave. P Glasg 68 C4
Burnside. Bear 75 E4
Burnside Cotts. Beith 173 E3
Burnside Cres. Bonh 27 F4
Burnside Cres. Dunt 74 A4
Burnside Cres. Ham 161 F3
Burnside Cres. Plea 12 B2
Burnside Cres. Shot 146 B3
Burnside Ct. Bear 75 E4
Burnside Ct. Glasg 138 B3
Burnside Ct. Mother 164 A2
Burnside Gate. Glasg 138 B3
Burnside Gdns. Kilbar 111 D1
Burnside Gdns. Newt M 157 E4
Burnside Gdns. Pres 233 E1
Burnside Gr. John 111 F1
Burnside Ind Est. Kils 60 B4
Burnside La. Ham 162 C1
Burnside Pl. Dumb 50 A1
Burnside Pl. Irvine 219 D2
Burnside Pl. Lark 185 D2
Burnside Pl. Pais 113 D4
Burnside Pl. Sten 24 A2
Burnside Pl. Troon 229 E2
Burnside Pl. W Kil 190 B3
Burnside Quadrant. Holy 143 D3
Burnside Rd. Aird 102 B1
Burnside Rd. Glasg 138 B2
Burnside Rd. Gour 44 C3
Burnside Rd. Holy 143 E2
Burnside Rd. John 112 B1
Burnside Rd. Men 3 F3
Burnside Rd. Newt M 157 D3
Burnside Rd. Pres 233 E2
Burnside St. Dumb 50 A1
Burnside St. Kilb 170 A3
Burnside St. Kilmk 227 F3
Burnside St. Mother 164 A2
Burnside St. N Sau 5 E1
Burnside St. Stir 7 E3
Burnside Terr. Falk 41 F3
Burnside View. Coat 121 F3
Burnside Wlk. Coat 121 F3
Burnstone Ave. Cumb 61 D1
Burntbroom Dr. Glasg 119 F2
Burntbroom Gdns. Glasg 119 F2
Burntbroom Rd. Glasg 119 F1
Burntbroom St. Glasg 119 E4
Burntshields Rd. Kilbar 110 B1
Burnwood Dr. Chap 124 A3
Burra Gdns. Bish 78 B1
Burrell Ct. Glasg 116 B1
Burrell's La. Glasg 117 F4
Burrelton Rd. Glasg 136 C3
Burstenman's Brae. Beith 207 F4
Burton La. Car 187 F1
Burton La. Glasg 117 D1
Busbie View. Cross 221 F1
Busbiehead. Irvine 220 A3
Busbiehill Pl. Kilmk 222 B1
Busby Pl. Kilw 207 F2
Busby Rd. E Kil 158 B4
Busby Rd. Hat 141 F2
Busby Rd. Newt M 157 F3
Busby Rd. Newt M 157 F4
Bush Cres. Wish 165 E1
Bushelhead Rd. Car 201 F3
Bushes Ave. Pais 113 E1
Busheyhill St. Glasg 139 D3
Bute Ave. Mother 163 E4
Bute Ave. P Glasg 69 D4
Bute Ave. Ren 94 B1
Bute Cres. Bear 75 F1
Bute Cres. Pais 133 E4
Bute Cres. Shot 146 B3
Bute Ct. Green 45 D3
Bute Ct. Irvine 220 B1
Bute Ct. Steven 217 E4
Bute Dr. John 111 E1
Bute. E Kil 160 B1
Bute Gdns. Glasg 96 B1
Bute Gdns. Glasg 136 C2
Bute La. Glasg 96 B1
Bute Pl. Ard 205 E1
Bute Rd. Inch 93 E1
Bute Rd. Kirk 80 A4
Bute St. Coat 122 A2
Bute St. Falk 42 A3
Bute St. Gour 44 B3
Bute St. Ham 162 A3
Bute Terr. Glasg 138 A3
Bute Terr. Salt 205 F1
Bute Terr. Tan 141 D4
Bute Tower. Glasg 138 C2
Butt Ave. Helen 16 C2
Butterbiggins Rd. Glasg 117 D2
Butterburnpark St. Ham 162 B1
Butterfield Pl. Glasg 117 D2
Buttermere. E Kil 179 F3
By Pass Rd. Beith 150 B1
By-Pass Rd. Bank 39 F3
Byars Rd. Kirk 79 D4
Byrebush Rd. Glasg 115 E1
Byrehill Ave. Kilw 207 D1
Byrehill Ave. Kilw 207 F1
Byrehill Pl. Kilw 207 D1
Byrehill Rd. Kilw 207 E1
Byrehill Rd. Kilw 218 C4
Byres Ave. Pais 114 A3
Byres Cres. Pais 114 A3
Byres Loch. Kilw 207 E2
Byres Rd. Glasg 96 B1
Byres Rd. Holy 143 F2
Byres Rd. John 112 B1
Byres Rd. Kilw 207 E2
Byresknowe La. Holy 143 D1
Byrestone Ave. Newt M 157 E2
Byretown Rd. Lan 214 C1
Byron Rd. Shot 146 A3
Byron St. Clyde 74 A2
Byron St. Glasg 95 F1
Byshot St. Glasg 97 E2

Cable Depot Rd. Clyde 73 F1
Cables Dr. Bonh 27 F3
Cabrach Loan. New 165 F3
Cadder Ct. Bish 78 A3
Cadder Pl. Glasg 96 C4
Cadder Rd. Bish 78 A3
Cadder Rd. Glasg 96 C4
Cadder Way. Bish 78 A3
Caddlehill St. Green 45 E3
Cadell Dr. Sten 24 A3
Cadell Gdns. E Kil 160 B3
Cadger's Sheuch. Kils 61 D4
Cadgers Loan. Plea 12 A1
Cadoc St. Glasg 139 D3
Cadogan St. Glasg 117 D4
Cadzow Ave. Glasg 157 D4
Cadzow Cres. Coat 121 F2
Cadzow Dr. Glasg 139 D3
Cadzow Dr. Hat 142 B2
Cadzow Gn. E Kil 159 E1
Cadzow Ind Est. Ham 183 E4
Cadzow La. Ham 162 C2
Cadzow Rd. Quart 183 F2
Cadzow St. Ham 162 C2
Cadzow St. Lark 185 D2
Cadzow St. Mother 163 E3
Caerlaverock Ave. Pres 236 B4
Caerlaverock Pl. Udd 161 E3
Caerlaverock Rd. Pres 236 B4
Caird Ave. Green 45 E4
Caird Dr. Glasg 96 A1
Caird Gdns. Ham 162 B3
Caird Pk. Ham 162 B3
Caird St. Ham 162 B3
Caird Terr. Bear 75 E4
Cairn Ave. Ren 94 C1
Cairn Cl. Stew 195 E1
Cairn Cres. Ayr 238 B1
Cairn Ct. E Kil 159 F2
Cairn Dr. Lin 112 A3
Cairn Pl. E Kil 159 F2
Cairn St. Glasg 97 F3
Cairn View. Aird 122 C3
Cairn View. Kirk 80 A4
Cairnbairn Ct. Car 187 F2
Cairnban St. Glasg 115 E3
Cairnbrook Ind Est. Glasg 120 B4
Cairnbrook Rd. Glasg 120 B4
Cairncurran Ct. Green 45 F2
Cairndhu Ave. Helen 16 A1
Cairndhu Gdns. Helen 16 A1
Cairndow Ave. Glasg 136 C2
Cairndow Avenue La. Glasg 136 C2
Cairndow Ct. Glasg 136 C2
Cairnduff Pl. Stew 195 F1
Cairndyke Cres. Aird 123 D3
Cairney Pl. New 166 B3
Cairneymount Rd. Car 188 A1
Cairnfore Ave. Troon 229 F3
Cairngorm Cres. Barr 134 B1
Cairngorm Cres. Bear 75 D3
Cairngorm Cres. Pais 133 F4
Cairngorm Cres. Wish 164 C2
Cairngorm Ct. Irvine 220 A3
Cairngorm Gdns. Cumb 61 D1
Cairngorm Rd. Glasg 136 B3
Cairngorm Rd. Kilmk 228 A2
Cairnhill Ave. Aird 123 D3
Cairnhill Cir. Glasg 114 C2
Cairnhill Cres. Coat 122 B2
Cairnhill Ct. Car 188 A1
Cairnhill Dr. Glasg 114 C2
Cairnhill Pl. Glasg 114 C2
Cairnhill Rd. Aird 123 D3
Cairnhill Rd. Bear 75 F1
Cairnhope Ave. Aird 122 C3
Cairnlea Dr. Glasg 116 A3
Cairnlea Gdns. Hat 142 A2
Cairnlea Rd. Miln 54 C1
Cairnmount Rd. Irvine 219 F4
Cairnmuir Rd. E Kil 159 E3
Cairnoch Hill. Cumb 61 E1
Cairnoch Way. Bann 7 F1
Cairnoch Wlk. Den 21 E1
Cairnryan. E Kil 159 E2
Cairns Ave. Glasg 139 D3
Cairns Dr. Miln 55 D1
Cairns Rd. Bishop 72 A2
Cairns Rd. Glasg 139 D2
Cairns St. Mother 163 F3
Cairns Terr. Kilmk 222 C1
Cairns The. Men 4 A3
Cairnsgarroch Way. Irvine 220 A1
Cairnsmore Dr. Ayr 238 B1
Cairnsmore Dr. Bear 75 D4
Cairnsmore Rd. Glasg 74 C1
Cairnsmore Way. Irvine 220 A1
Cairnswell Ave. Glasg 139 E2
Cairnswell Pl. Glasg 139 E2
Cairntoul Ct. Cumb 61 D1
Cairntoul Dr. Glasg 95 D3
Cairntoul Pl. Glasg 95 D3
Cairnview Rd. M of C 58 B3
Cairnwood Dr. Aird 122 C3

Caithness Rd. E Kil 160 B2
Caithness Rd. Gour 44 B2
Caithness Row. Lan 215 D1
Caithness St. Glasg 96 C2
Caithness St. Udd 161 E3
Cala Sona Ct. Wish 185 F4
Calcots Path. Glasg 100 B1
Calcots Pl. Glasg 100 B1
Caldarvan St. Glasg 97 D2
Calder Ave. Barr 134 B1
Calder Ave. Cald 104 C2
Calder Ave. Coat 122 A2
Calder Ave. New 166 B4
Calder Ave. Troon 229 F3
Calder Ct. Coat 122 A2
Calder Ct. Stir 7 E3
Calder Dr. Glasg 139 D3
Calder Dr. Hat 142 B2
Calder Dr. Loch 129 E2
Calder Dr. Shot 147 D2
Calder Gate. Bish 77 F2
Calder Pl. Falk 42 B1
Calder Pl. Glasg 120 A2
Calder Pl. Kilm 228 A3
Calder Rd. Alla 166 C4
Calder Rd. Hat 142 B2
Calder Rd. Pais 113 D3
Calder Rd. Udd 140 B3
Calder St. Calder 122 C2
Calder St. Coat 122 B3
Calder St. Glasg 117 D1
Calder St. Loch 129 E2
Calder St. Udd 161 E4
Calder Tower. Mother 163 F3
Calder View. New 166 B4
Calder View. Mother 163 F4
Calderbank Rd. Calder 123 D2
Calderbank Rd. Mother 163 F4
Calderbank View. Glasg 120 B2
Calderbanks Aves. Lan 140 C4
Caldercruix Rd. Cald 105 E4
Caldercuilt Rd. Glasg 76 B3
Calderglen Ave. Udd 140 B2
Calderglen Rd. E Kil 160 B1
Caldergrove. Mother 163 F3
Calderhaugh La. Loch 129 D1
Calderhead Rd. Shot 146 B4
Calderpark Ave. Glasg 120 A1
Calderpark Ave. Loch 129 E2
Calderpark Cres. Glasg 120 A1
Calderpark St. Loch 129 E2
Calderrigg Pl. Aird 123 F4
Calderside Rd. Ham 160 C2
Caldervale St. Chap 123 E2
Calderview Ave. Coat 122 C2
Calderwood Ave. Glasg 120 A2
Calderwood Dr. Glasg 120 A2
Calderwood Dr. Udd 161 E3
Calderwood Gdns. E Kil 160 C2
Calderwood Gdns. Glasg 120 A2
Calderwood Pl. Kilw 207 F3
Calderwood Rd. E Kil 160 C2
Calderwood Rd. Glasg 136 B3
Calderwood Rd. Glasg 138 B4
Calderwood Sq. E Kil 160 A2
Caldon Rd. Irvine 219 E2
Caldwell Ave. Glasg 95 D3
Caldwell Ave. Lin 112 A3
Caldwell Gr. Hat 142 A4
Caldwell Pl. Rhu 15 F3
Caldwell Quadrant. Mother 163 D4
Caldwell Rd. Car 188 C2
Caldwell Rd. W Kil 190 B2
Caledon La. Glasg 96 B1
Caledon St. Glasg 96 B2
Caledonia Ave. Glasg 117 E2
Caledonia Ave. Glasg 138 A4
Caledonia Cres. Ard 205 E1
Caledonia Cres. Gour 44 C4
Caledonia Cres. Gour 45 D4
Caledonia Ct. Pais 113 E3
Caledonia Dr. Glasg 120 A2
Caledonia Dr. Holy 143 E2
Caledonia Rd. Ard 205 E1
Caledonia Rd. Ayr 239 E3
Caledonia Rd. Beith 150 A1
Caledonia Rd. Salt 216 C4
Caledonia Rd. Shot 146 C3
Caledonia St. Clyde 73 D2
Caledonia St. Glasg 117 E2
Caledonia St. Pais 113 E3
Caledonia Terr. Dumb 49 E2
Caledonia Way E. Inch 93 F1
Caledonia Way. W Inch 93 E1
Caledonia Wlk. Ham 162 C1
Caledonian Ave. Hat 141 F2
Caledonian Ave. Stone 198 C1
Caledonian Cres. Glasg 96 C1
Caledonian Ct. E Kil 180 C4
Caledonian Gdns. All 9 F3
Caledonian Pl. Kilb 170 A4
Caledonian Rd. All 9 F3
Caledonian Rd. Kilb 170 B4
Caledonian Rd. Lark 185 D2

Caledonian Rd. Steven 217 F4
Caledonian Rd. Wish 165 D1
Caley Brae. Udd 140 C3
Caley Ct. Steven 217 E4
Calhill Rd. Glasg 115 D1
Calfmuir Rd. Kirk 80 A3
Calgary Pk. E Kil 180 A3
Calgary Pl. E Kil 180 B4
Calgary St. Glasg 97 E1
California Terr. Cali 66 C3
Callaghan Wynd. Udd 140 B1
Callander Dr. Lar 41 E4
Callander St. Glasg 97 D2
Callander Way. Falk 42 A1
Callendar Pl. Ayr 236 B2
Callendar Rd. Falk 42 B2
Callender Riggs. Falk 42 B2
Callender Bsns Pk. Falk 42 C2
Callender Rd. Chap 123 E1
Callender Rd. Pres 236 B3
Callieburn Rd. Bish 98 A4
Callon St. Aird 123 D4
Cally Ave. Glasg 75 D2
Calside Ave. Pais 113 F2
Calside. Pais 113 F2
Calton Cres. Stir 7 D2
Calton Entry. Glasg 117 F3
Calvay Cres. Glasg 119 E4
Calvay Rd. Glasg 119 F4
Calvinston Rd. Pres 236 B3
Cam'nethan St. Stone 198 C1
Cambourne Rd. Muir 80 C2
Cambridge Ave. Clyde 74 A2
Cambridge Ave. Gour 45 D4
Cambridge Rd. Gour 45 D4
Cambridge Rd. Ren 94 B1
Cambridge St. Glasg 117 D4
Camburn St. Glasg 118 C3
Cambus Pl. Glasg 99 E1
Cambusdoon Dr. Ayr 238 C1
Cambusdoon Pl. Kilw 207 E2
Cambusdoon Rd. Glasg 99 E1
Cambuskeith Rd. Steven 206 C2
Cambuskenneth
Gdns. Glasg 119 E3
Cambuskenneth Pl. Glasg 99 E1
Cambuslang Ind Est. Glasg 139 D4
Cambuslang Rd. Glasg 138 B4
Cambuslang Rd. Glasg 138 C4
Cambuslea Rd. Ayr 236 A2
Cambusmoon Terr. Gart 20 C4
Cambusnethan St Wish 165 F2
Camden St. Glasg 117 E2
Camelon Cres. Udd 161 E4
Camelon Rd. Falk 41 F3
Cameron Ave. Bishop 72 A2
Cameron Cres. E Kil 158 C4
Cameron Cres. Ham 162 B2
Cameron Ct. Aird 123 F4
Cameron Ct. Glasg 138 A4
Cameron Dr. Alex 27 F4
Cameron Dr. Bear 76 A2
Cameron Dr. Kilm 223 E1
Cameron Dr. Newt M 156 C4
Cameron Dr. Tan 141 D4
Cameron Path. Lark 185 E1
Cameron Pl. Stem 24 A1
Cameron Sq. Dunt 74 B3
Cameron St. Clyde 94 B4
Cameron St. Coat 122 A4
Cameron St. Glasg 114 C4
Cameron St. Mother 163 E3
Cameron Terr. Slam 86 A2
Cameronian Ct. Lan 215 E3
Cameronian Dr. Car 188 A1
Cameronian Pl. Hat 141 F2
Cameronian St. Stir 7 D4
Cameronian Way. Lark 185 E1
Camis Eskan House. Card 25 E4
Camlachie St. Glasg 118 C3
Camp Rd. Glasg 117 F1
Camp Rd. Glasg 120 A3
Camp Rd. Mother 163 F2
Camp St. Mother 163 F3
Campbell Ave. Bishop 72 A2
Campbell Ave. Dumb 50 B2
Campbell Ave. Miln 55 D1
Campbell Ave. Salt 216 C4
Campbell Ave. Steven 206 B1
Campbell Cres. Alex 27 E4
Campbell Cres. Laur 42 C2
Campbell Cres. Newt M 156 C3
Campbell Cres. Udd 141 D2
Campbell Ct. Ayr 239 E4
Campbell Ct. Green 45 F4
Campbell Ct. Stir 6 C2
Campbell Dr. Bear 134 B1
Campbell Dr. Dumb 50 B2
Campbell Dr. Helen 25 D4
Campbell Dr. Troon 229 E3
Campbell La. Ham 162 C2
Campbell Pl. E Kil 180 C4
Campbell Pl. Irvine 225 D4

Campbell Pl. Lennox 57 D1
Campbell St. Bonh 27 F2
Campbell St. Glasg 96 C4
Campbell St. Green 45 F3
Campbell St. Ham 162 C2
Campbell St. Hat 142 A3
Campbell St. Helen 16 B2
Campbell St. John 111 F1
Campbell St. Klmk 227 F2
Campbell St. Ren 94 B3
Campbell St. Wish 165 E1
Campbell Terr. Dumb 50 B2
Campbeltown Dr. Kilmk 222 C2
Camperdown Ct. Helen 17 D3
Camphill Ave. Glasg 136 C4
Camphill Ave. Klrk 79 E4
Camphill Ct. Kilb 170 A4
Camphill Cres. Kilm 79 E2
Camphill Gdns. Bishop 72 B2
Camphill. Pais 113 E2
Campie Terr. Gran 24 C1
Campion Pl. Ayr 239 D2
Campie Rd. Mother 163 F4
Camps Cres. Ren 94 C1
Campsie Ave. Barr 134 B1
Campsie Cres. Kilm 79 E3
Campsie Cres. Aird 122 C4
Campsie Cres. Kilm 79 E3
Campsie Dene Rd. Strath 31 D2
Campsie Dr. Bear 75 F4
Campsie Dr. Inch 93 F1
Campsie Dr. Miln 55 D1
Campsie Dr. Pais 133 E4
Campsie Dr. Ren 114 A4
Campsie Gdns. Newt M 157 E4
Campsie Pl. Muir 100 B4
Campsie Rd. Kilmk 228 A3
Campsie Rd. E Kil 159 F1
Campsie Rd. M of C 58 A1
Campsie Rd. P Glasg 69 D3
Campsie Rd. Wish 164 C2
Campsie St. Glasg 98 A3
Campsie View. Cumb 63 F2
Campsie View. Dr. Strath 31 D2
Campsie View. Ham 161 F1
Campsie View. Kirk 79 D4
Campsie View. Muir 100 B4
Campsie View. Stepps 99 E3
Campsie View. Tan 141 D4
Campsie Wlk. Irvine 220 A2
Campsie Way. Irvine 220 A2
Campus Pl. Glasg 99 D1
Camsail Ave. Helen 16 A2
Camsail Rd. Ros 15 E2
Cambusmore Pl. Glasg 99 E1
Camsdale Ave. Sals 125 D1
Camstradden Dr E. Bear 75 E2
Camstradden Dr W. Bear 75 E2
Canal Ave. John 112 A1
Canal Cres. Steven 217 E4
Canal Ct. Salt 217 D4
Canal La. Kils 60 B4
Canal Pl. Salt 217 D4
Canal Rd. John 112 A1
Canal St. Falk 41 E3
Canal St. Falk 42 A4
Canal St. Glasg 97 E1
Canal St. John 112 B2
Canal St. Kirk 58 B1
Canal St. Pais 113 E2
Canal St. Ren 94 B2
Canal St. Salt 217 D4
Canal Terr. Pais 113 F2
Canavan Ct. Stir 7 E2
Canberra Ave. Clyde 73 D2
Canberra Ct. Glasg 136 C2
Canberra Dr. E Kil 180 B4
Cander Ave. Stone 199 D2
Cander Rigg. Bish 78 A2
Cander St. Lark 199 D3
Candermill &
Marlage Rd. Ash 199 F3
Candermill Rd. Ash 199 D2
Candermill Rd. Stone 199 D2
Canderside Toll. Ash 199 E3
Candimilne. All 10 A3
Candleriggs. Glasg 117 F3
Candren Rd. Lin 112 C3
Candren Rd. Pais 113 D2
Candren Rd. Pais 113 D3
Caneluk Ave. Car 188 A1
Canmore Pl. Glasg 118 C2
Canmore Cres. Sten 45 D2
Canmore Pl. Sten 23 F2
Canmore Pl. Glasg 118 B2
Canmore Pl. Stew 195 F1
Canmore St. Glasg 118 C2
Cannerton Cres. M of C 58 A3
Cannich Dr. Pais 114 A1
Cannich Pl. New 165 F3
Canniesburn Rd. Bear 75 D2

Canniesburn Toll. Bear 75 F2
Cannons Way. Falk 24 A1
Canon Ct. Holy 143 E1
Canonbie St. Glasg 100 B1
Canongate. E Kil 160 B2
Canonsburgh. E Kil 160 B4
Canthill Gdns. Shot 146 A2
Cantieslaw Dr. E Kil 160 A2
Canton Way. Glasg 116 B4
Canyon Rd. Wish 164 B1
Capel Ave. Newt M 156 C3
Capel Gr. E Kil 160 A2
Capel Pl. Irvine 220 A1
Capelrig Ciotts. Newt M 155 F2
Capelrig Dr. E Kil 160 A2
Capelrig Dr. Newt M 156 C3
Capelrig Rd. Newt M 156 C3
Capelrig St. Glasg 135 F2
Caplaw Pl. Wish 185 F4
Caplaw Rd. Pais 133 E3
Caplaw Rd. Uplaw 132 B1
Caplaw Tower. Wish 185 F4
Caplethill Rd. Barr 134 A3
Caplethill Rd. Pais 134 A3
Caponcraig Ave. Steven 206 B1
Cappielow Ind Est. Green 46 B2
Capringstone Foot. Irvine 220 A2
Caprington Ave. Kilmk 227 F2
Caprington Pl. Kilmk 227 F2
Caprington St. Glasg 99 D1
Captain St. Green 45 F2
Cara Dr. Glasg 116 B3
Caravelle Way. Ren 94 B1
Carbarns Rd. Wish 164 B1
Carbarns E. Wish 164 B1
Carbarns W. Wish 164 B1
Carbarns. Wish 164 C1
Carberry Rd. Glasg 116 B1
Carberth Pl. Miln 54 C1
Carberth St. Glasg 97 D2
Carbisdale St. Glasg 97 F3
Carbost St. Glasg 76 B1
Carbrook Pl. Plea 12 B2
Carbrook St. Glasg 98 A1
Carbrook St. Pais 113 E2
Carcluie Cres. Ayr 239 D1
Cardarrach St. Glasg 98 A2
Cardean Rd. Holy 142 C3
Cardell Ave. Pais 113 D2
Cardell Cres. Chap 123 E1
Cardell Dr. Pais 113 D2
Cardell Rd. Pais 113 D2
Cardon Pl. Irvine 220 A1
Cardonald Dr. Glasg 115 D2
Cardonald Gdns. Glasg 115 D2
Cardonald Place Rd. Glasg 115 D2
Cardow Cres. Irvine 220 A3
Cardow Rd. Glasg 98 B2
Cardowan Dr. Stepps 99 F3
Cardowan Dr. Glasg 119 D4
Cardowan Rd. Glasg 99 F3
Cardowan Rd. Glasg 119 D3
Cardross Ave. P Glasg 68 C4
Cardross Cres. Green 46 B1
Cardross Ct. Glasg 117 F4
Cardross Pl. Green 46 B1
Cardross Rd. Alex 27 D1
Cardross Rd. Card 25 E4
Cardross Rd. Card 26 C4
Cardross Rd. Dumb 49 E2
Cardross Rd. Dumb 26 C4
Cardross St. Glasg 117 F4
Cardrowan Rd. Plea 12 B1
Cardwell Rd. Gour 44 C4
Cardwell St. Glasg 117 D2
Cardyke St. Glasg 98 A2
Careloch Rd. P Glasg 68 C4
Careston Pl. Bish 78 B1
Carey Gdns. Cle 144 B1
Carey Rd. Salt 205 F2
Carfin Dr. Car 201 E1
Carfin Mill Rd. Holy 143 E1
Carfin Rd. Holy 143 E2
Carfin Rd. Mother 143 E2
Carfin St. Coat 122 A2
Carfin St. Glasg 117 D1
Carfin St. Holy 143 D2
Carfrae St. Glasg 116 B4
Cargil Ave. Kilmk 222 B3
Cargill Dr. Pres 236 B3
Cargill Sq. Bish 98 B4
Cargill Sq. Glasg 118 C2
Carham Cres. Glasg 115 E3
Carham Dr. Glasg 115 E3
Carharn Dr. Glasg 236 B3
Caribou Gn. E Kil 180 A4
Carillon Rd. Glasg 116 B3
Carisbrooke Cres. Bish 78 A3
Carlaverock Rd. Glasg 136 C4
Carleith Quadrant. Glasg 115 E4
Carleith Terr. Dunt 73 F3
Carleston St. Glasg 97 F2
Carleton Dr. Glasg 96 A2
Carleton Gate. Glasg 96 A2
Carleton Gdns. Glasg 96 A2
Carlibar Ave. Glasg 94 C3
Carlibar Dr. Barr 134 B2

Carlibar Gdns. Barr 134 B2
Carlibar Rd. Barr 134 B2
Carlibar Ave. B of A 2 A3
Carlile Pl. Pais 113 E3
Carlin La. Carl 188 A1
Carlisle La. Aird 123 E4
Carlisle Rd. Aird 123 E3
Carlisle Rd. Ash 199 E2
Carlisle Rd. Chap 123 E3
Carlisle Rd. Chap 143 E4
Carlisle Rd. Cle 144 B1
Carlisle Rd. Ham 163 D1
Carlisle Rd. Lark 184 C1
Carlisle Rd. Lark 199 E2
Carlisle St. Glasg 97 E2
Carlowrie Ave. Udd 140 B3
Carlton Ct. Glasg 117 D3
Carlton Pl. Glasg 117 D3
Carlung Pl. W Kil 190 B2
Carlyle Ave. Glasg 114 C4
Carlyle Dr. E Kil 160 A1
Carlyle Terr. E Kil 160 A1
Carlyle Terr. Glasg 118 A1
Carmaben Rd. Glasg 119 F4
Carman Rd. Alex 27 E1
Carman Rd. Card 48 B4
Carmel Ave. Kilmk 222 B1
Carmel Dr. Spring 221 D1
Carmel Pl. Kilm 222 A4
Carmel Pl. Kilb 170 B4
Carmel Terr. Kilmk 222 B1
Carmen View. Dumb 50 A3
Carment Dr. Glasg 136 B4
Carment Dr. Steven 217 F4
Carmichael Path. Glen 101 E3
Carmichael Pl. Glasg 136 C4
Carmichael St. Glasg 116 B3
Carmichael St. Green 45 E3
Carmichael St. Law 186 C3
Carmichael Way. Law 186 C3
Carmichael Ave. Dumb 26 B4
Carmunnock
By-Pass. E Kil 158 C1
Carmunnock Rd. E Kil 159 D2
Carmunnock Rd. E Kil 159 E2
Carmunnock Rd. Glasg 137 E3
Carmunnock Thorn 158 A3
Carmyle Ave. Glasg 139 D4
Carmyle Pl. Steven 217 E4
Carna Dr. Glasg 137 E3
Carnarvon St. Glasg 96 C1
Carnaughton Pl. Alva 4 C3
Carnbooth Ct. Glasg 158 B3
Carnbroe Rd. Coat 122 B2
Carnbroe Rd. Hat 122 B1
Carneddans Rd. Miln 54 B2
Carnegie Dr. Falk 42 B1
Carnegie Hill. E Kil 180 B4
Carnegie Pl. E Kil 180 B4
Carnegie Rd. Glasg 115 D3
Carnell Cres. Pres 236 B4
Carnell Terr. Pres 236 B4
Carnock Cres. Barr 134 A1
Carnock Gdns. Miln 54 C1
Carnock St. Glasg 135 E4
Carnock St. Cowie 12 B4
Carnock St. Green 46 A2
Carnoustie Ave. Gour 44 C4
Carnoustie Cres. Bish 78 B1
Carnoustie Cres. E Kil 180 A3
Carnoustie Ct. Kilw 207 D2
Carnoustie Ct. Udd 140 C1
Carnoustie Pl. Hat 142 A4
Carnoustie Pl. Glasg 116 C3
Carnoustie St. Glasg 116 C3
Carntyne Path. Glasg 118 B4
Carntyne Pl. Glasg 118 B4
Carntyne Rd. Glasg 118 C3
Carntynehall Rd. Glasg 118 C3
Carnwadric Rd. Glasg 135 F2
Carnwath Ave. Glasg 137 E4
Carnwath Rd. Car 188 A1
Carnwath Rd. Kilnc 203 E3
Caroline Cres. Alva 5 D3
Caroline St. Glasg 119 D3
Carolside Ave. Newt M 157 F4
Carolside Dr. Glasg 75 F3
Carolside Gdns. Newt M 157 F4
Caradale Ave. Cumb 81 F4
Carradale Cres. Cumb 81 F4
Carradale Dr. Pres 236 B3
Carradale Gdns. Bish 78 B1
Carradale Gdns. Car 202 A4
Carradale Pl. Lin 112 A3
Carradale St. Coat 121 F4
Carranbuie Rd. Car 187 F2
Carrbridge Dr. Glasg 96 B2
Carresbrook Ave. Kirk 80 A2
Carriagehill Ave. Pais 113 F1
Carriagehill Dr. Pais 113 F1
Carrick Ave. Ayr 239 D3
Carrick Ave. Salt 206 C3
Carrick Ct. Kirk 80 A4
Carrick Cres. Glasg 158 B3
Carrick Cres. Wish 165 D3

251
Carrick Ct. Kirk
Cherry Pl. Holy

Carrick Ct. Kirk 59 D1
Carrick Ct. Stir 7 E3
Carrick Dr. Coat 121 E4
Carrick Dr. Glasg 119 F2
Carrick Dr. Glasg 138 A3
Carrick Dr. Irvine 219 D3
Carrick Gdns. Ayr 238 C3
Carrick Gdns. Car 202 A4
Carrick Gdns. Ham 161 F1
Carrick Gdns. Hat 142 A4
Carrick Gdns. Udd 161 E3
Carrick Gr. Glasg 119 F2
Carrick La. Gour 44 C2
Carrick Pk. Ayr 238 C3
Carrick Pl. Ard 205 E2
Carrick Pl. Coat 121 E4
Carrick Pl. Falk 41 E2
Carrick Pl. Glen 101 F3
Carrick Pl. Hat 142 A4
Carrick Pl. Lark 185 D2
Carrick Pl. Pres 236 A4
Carrick Pl. Sten 24 A2
Carrick Rd. Ayr 238 C3
Carrick Rd. Bish 78 B1
Carrick Rd. Bishop 72 B1
Carrick Rd. Cumb 62 A2
Carrick Rd. E Kil 159 F2
Carrick Rd. Glasg 137 F3
Carrick Rd. Troon 229 E4
Carrick Road La. Ayr 238 C3
Carrick St. Ayr 238 C4
Carrick St. Glasg 117 D4
Carrick St. Lark 185 E1
Carrick Terr. Dumb 49 D2
Carrick Terr. Gour 44 C2
Carrick Vale. Cle 144 B1
Carrick View. Glen 101 F3
Carrick Way. Udd 141 D2
Carrickarden Rd. Bear 75 F2
Carrickstone Rd. Cumb 61 F3
Carrickstone View. Cumb 61 F3
Carrington St. Glasg 96 C1
Carrochan Cres. Bonh 27 F4
Carrochan Rd. Bonh 27 F4
Carroglen Gdns. Glasg 119 E3
Carroglen Gr. Glasg 119 E3
Carron Ave. Kilmk 228 A3
Carron Cres. Bear 75 E2
Carron Cres. Bish 78 A1
Carron Cres. Glasg 97 E3
Carron Cres. Kirk 79 F2
Carron Ct. Glasg 139 E3
Carron Ct. Ham 162 A1
Carron Dr. Bishop 72 B1
Carron Ind Est. Sten 24 A1
Carron Pl. Coat 101 E1
Carron Pl. E Kil 180 C3
Carron Pl. Glasg 97 F3
Carron Pl. Irvine 219 E3
Carron Pl. Stir 7 D1
Carron Rd. Falk 42 A4
Carron St. Glasg 97 F3
Carron St. Wish 165 D1
Carron Way. Holy 143 E2
Carron Way. Pais 114 A4
Carronbank Ave. Sten 24 A1
Carronbank Cres. Den 21 F2
Carronbank Ct. Sten 24 A1
Carrongrove Ave. Sten 24 A1
Carrongrove Rd. Sten 24 A1
Carronhall Ave. Sten 24 B2
Carronlea Dr. Sten 24 A1
Carronshore Rd. Sten 24 A1
Carronside Pl. Duni 21 F2
Carronside St. Falk 42 A4
Carronvale Ave. Lar 23 E1
Carronvale Rd. Lar 23 E1
Carronview. Lar 23 E1
Carrour Gdns. Bish 77 F1
Carruth Dr. Kil 89 E4
Carruth Rd. B of W 110 B4
Carsaig Dr. Glasg 115 F3
Carsaig Loan. Glen 101 E3
Carscallan Rd. Ham 183 F3
Carscallan Rd. Quart 184 A1
Carse Terr. All 9 F4
Carse View. Air 14 C2
Carsebridge Rd. N Sau 10 B4
Carsegreen Ave. Pais 133 D4
Carseloch Rd. Ayr 238 C1
Carsemeadow. Kil 89 F1
Carseview. Bann 7 F1
Carseview Dr. Bear 76 A3
Carseview. Tull 4 A1
Carsewood Ave. How 130 C3
Carson Dr. Irvine 224 B4
Carson Rd. Bonh 27 F4
Carstairs St. Glasg 118 A1
Carswell Ct. Dalry 191 D4
Carswell Gdns. Glasg 116 C1
Carswell Rd. Newt M 156 A3
Cart La. Pais 113 F3
Cart St. Clyde 94 A4
Cartcraigs Rd. Glasg 136 A3
Carters Pl. Irvine 219 E1
Cartha Cres. Pais 114 A2
Cartha St. Glasg 136 C4
Cartland Ave. Car 201 F4
Cartland Rd. Lan 214 B4
Cartland View. Lan 214 C3
Cartsbridge Rd. Newt M 157 F3
Cartsburn St. Green 46 A2
Cartside Ave. Inch 93 D2
Cartside Ave. John 111 E1
Cartside Dr. Thorn 158 A3
Cartside Pl. Newt M 157 F3
Cartside Quadrant. Glasg 137 D4
Cartside Rd. Newt M 157 F3
Cartside St. Glasg 136 C4
Cartvale La. Pais 113 F3
Cartvale Rd. Glasg 137 D4
Cartview Ct. Newt M 157 F3
Carvale Ave. Sals 125 D1
Carvel Dr. Green 45 E2
Carwinshoch View. Ayr 238 B3
Carwood Ct. Green 46 B2
Carwood St. Green 46 B2
Caskie Dr. Udd 140 C1
Cassels Gr. Mother 142 B1
Cassels St. Car 187 F1
Cassels St. Mother 163 F4
Cassillis St. Ayr 238 C4
Cassley Ave. Ren 94 C1
Castburn Rd. Cumb 62 C3
Castings Ave. Falk 42 A4
Castings Ct. Falk 42 A4
Castings Ct. Falk 42 C3
Castings Dr. Falk 42 A3
Castings Rd. Falk 42 C3
Castle Ave. Bonh 19 F1
Castle Ave. Helen 16 A1
Castle Ave. Holy 143 D3
Castle Ave. John 112 A1
Castle Ave. Sten 24 B2
Castle Ave. Steven 206 C1
Castle Ave. Udd 140 C2
Castle
Chimmins Ave. Glasg 139 E2
Castle Chimmins Rd. Glasg 139 E2
Castle Cres. Bishop 72 A1
Castle Cres. Den 21 E1
Castle Cres. Falk 42 B4
Castle Cres. Tor 22 C4
Castle Ct. Falk 42 B4
Castle Ct. Kirk 79 E4
Castle Ct. Men 3 F3
Castle Ct. Stir 7 D4
Castle Dr. Dund 225 F1
Castle Dr. Falk 42 B4
Castle Dr. Holy 143 D3
Castle Dr. Kilb 149 D1
Castle Dr. Kilmk 223 D2
Castle Dr. Sten 23 F1
Castle Dr. W Kil 190 B3
Castle Gait. Pais 113 F2
Castle Gate. Newt M 157 D2
Castle Gate. Udd 140 C2
Castle Gdns. Gour 44 C4
Castle Gdns. Muir 80 C1
Castle Gr. Kilb 149 D1
Castle Gr. Kils 36 B1
Castle Mains Rd. Miln 54 B1
Castle Pl. Falk 42 B4
Castle Pl. Udd 140 C3
Castle Quadrant. Aird 123 E4
Castle Rd. Aird 123 E4
Castle Rd. Ard 205 E2
Castle Rd. B of W 90 B1
Castle Rd. Dumb 50 A1
Castle Rd. Falk 42 B4
Castle Rd. Green 46 B1
Castle Rd. John 112 B2
Castle Rd. Men 3 F3
Castle Rd. Newt M 156 B2
Castle Rd. P Glasg 47 E1
Castle Rd. Stir 2 B2
Castle Sq. Clyde 73 F2
Castle St. All 10 A3
Castle St. Chap 123 E1
Castle St. Clyde 73 F2
Castle St. Dumb 49 F2
Castle St. Glasg 96 B1
Castle St. Glasg 97 F1
Castle St. Glasg 120 A2
Castle St. Glasg 138 A4
Castle St. Ham 162 C2
Castle St. Irvine 219 D2
Castle St. Pais 113 E2
Castle Terr. B of W 110 C4
Castle Terr. Cross 221 F2
Castle Terr. Den 21 E1
Castle View. Fall 8 B2
Castle View. New 166 A3
Castle View. W Kil 190 B3
Castle Way. Coat 120 C3
Castle Way. Cumb 62 B2
Castle Wlk. Ayr 238 B2
Castle Wynd. Quart 183 F2
Castle Wynd. Stir 7 D4
Castle Wynd. Udd 141 D1
Castlebank Cres. Glasg 96 A1
Castlebank Ct. Glasg 95 F3
Castlebank Gdns. Glasg 95 F3
Castlebank St. Glasg 96 A1
Castlebank Villas. Glasg 95 F3
Castlebay Dr. Glasg 77 E1
Castlebay Pl. Glasg 97 E4
Castlebay St. Glasg 97 E4
Castlebrae. Dumb 49 E3
Castlecary Rd. Cumb 62 B4
Castlecroft Gdns. Udd 140 C3
Castlefern Rd. Glasg 138 A2
Castlefield Gdns. E Kil 180 A3
Castlegait. Stir 7 D4
Castlegate. Lan 215 D2
Castleglen Rd. E Kil 159 D2
Castlegreen Cres. Dumb 50 A1
Castlegreen La. Dumb 50 A1
Castlegreen St. Dumb 50 A1
Castlehill Ave. P Glasg 69 D4
Castlehill Ave. Slam 86 A3
Castlehill Cres. Ayr 239 D3
Castlehill Cres. Bank 38 C1
Castlehill Cres. Ham 162 C2
Castlehill Cres. Ham 163 E1
Castlehill Cres. Kil 89 E4
Castlehill Cres. Law 187 D2
Castlehill Cres. Ren 94 B2
Castlehill Dr. Newt M 156 C2
Castlehill Gdns. Ham 162 C1
Castlehill Quadrant. Dumb 49 E3
Castlehill Rd. Ayr 239 D3
Castlehill Rd. Bear 75 E3
Castlehill Rd. Car 187 F3
Castlehill Rd. Dumb 49 E3
Castlehill Rd. Kil 89 E4
Castlehill Rd. Stew 195 F1
Castlehill Rd. Wish 186 A4
Castlehill View. Kils 36 B1
Castlelaurie St. Falk 42 B4
Castlelaw Gdns. Glasg 119 D3
Castlelaw St. Glasg 119 D3
Castlemilk Arc. Glasg 137 E2
Castlemilk Cres. Glasg 137 F3
Castlemilk Dr. Glasg 137 F1
Castlemilk Dr. Glasg 137 F2
Castlemilk Rd. Glasg 137 F3
Castlemount Ave. Newt M 156 C2
Castleton Ave. Bish 97 F4
Castleton Ave. Newt M 157 D2
Castleton Cres. Newt M 156 C2
Castleton Ct. Glasg 137 F1
Castleton Ct. Newt M 156 C2
Castleton Dr. Newt M 156 C2
Castleton Gr. Newt M 156 C2
Castleview Ave. Pais 133 D4
Castleview. B of A 2 A2
Castleview. Cumb 62 C4
Castleview Dr. B of A 2 A4
Castleview Dr. Pais 133 D4
Castleview. Dund 225 F2
Castleview. Lennox 32 C2
Castleview Pl. Pais 133 D4
Castleview Terr. Bank 39 D2
Catacol Ave. Salt 205 F1
Cathay St. Glasg 97 E4
Cathburn Rd. New 166 B3
Cathcart Cres. Pais 114 A2
Cathcart Pl. Glasg 137 F4
Cathcart Rd. Glasg 117 D1
Cathcart Rd. Glasg 137 F4
Cathcart Sq. Green 45 F3
Cathcart St. Ayr 235 F1
Cathcart St. Green 46 A3
Cathedral Sq. Glasg 117 F4
Cathedral St. Glasg 117 E4
Catherine Pl. Kilm 222 B3
Catherine St. Bann 7 E1
Catherine St. Kirk 79 E4
Catherine St. Mother 163 F2
Catherine Way. Holy 142 C2
Catherine's Wlk. Udd 161 E3
Cathkin Ave. Glasg 138 B4
Cathkin Ave. Glasg 138 C3
Cathkin By-Pass. Glasg 138 B2
Cathkin Ct. Glasg 137 F1
Cathkin Dr. Newt M 157 E4
Cathkin Gdns. Tan 120 C1
Cathkin Pl. Glasg 138 C3
Cathkin Pl. Kilw 207 D2
Cathkin Rd. Glasg 136 C4
Cathkin Rd. Glasg 138 B1
Cathkin Rd. Tan 120 C1
Cathkin View. Glasg 139 D4
Cathkinview Pl. Glasg 137 D4
Cathkinview Rd. Glasg 137 D4
Catrine Cres. Mother 164 A2
Catrine. E Kil 159 E1
Catrine St. Lark 185 E1
Catriona Way. Holy 143 D2
Catter Gdns. Miln 54 C2
Cauldhame Cres. Cam 6 B3
Cauldstream Pl. Miln 54 C1
Causeway The. B of A 2 B3
Causewayhead Rd. Stir 2 B2
Causewayside Cres. Glasg 119 D2
Causewayside St. Glasg 119 D1
Causeyfoot Dr. Kilb 149 D1
Causeyside St. Pais 113 F2
Causeystanes. Udd 161 E4
Cavendish Ct. Troon 229 E1
Cavendish Dr. Newt M 156 C3
Cavendish La. Troon 229 E1
Cavendish Pl. Glasg 117 D2
Cavendish Pl. Troon 229 E1
Cavendish St. Glasg 117 D2
Cavin Dr. Glasg 137 F2
Cavin Rd. Glasg 137 F2
Cawder Gdns. B of A 1 C4
Cawder Rd. B of A 1 C4
Cawdor Cres. Bishop 72 A1
Cawdor Cres. Green 45 D2
Cawdor Pl. Green 45 D2
Cawdor Way. E Kil 159 E2
Cayton Gdns. Glasg 119 F2
Cecil St. Coat 122 A3
Cecil St. Glasg 96 B2
Cecil St. Newt M 157 F4
Cecil St. Stir 7 D3
Cedar Ave. Beith 171 D4
Cedar Ave. Clyde 73 E2
Cedar Ave. John 132 A4
Cedar Ave. Stir 6 C3
Cedar Ave. Tan 141 D4
Cedar Cres. Green 46 C1
Cedar Cres. Ham 162 C1
Cedar Ct. E Kil 180 B3
Cedar Ct. Glasg 97 D1
Cedar Ct. Kilbar 111 D2
Cedar Dr. E Kil 180 B3
Cedar Dr. Kirk 79 E3
Cedar Dr. M of C 58 B3
Cedar Dr. Tan 141 E4
Cedar Gdns. Glasg 138 B2
Cedar Gdns. Holy 143 E2
Cedar Gdns. Law 186 C3
Cedar Gr. Card 48 A4
Cedar Gr. Lar 23 E1
Cedar La. Aird 123 E4
Cedar La. Holy 143 D2
Cedar Pl. Barr 155 E4
Cedar Pl. E Kil 180 B3
Cedar Pl. Gour 44 B3
Cedar Pl. Udd 140 B1
Cedar Rd. Ayr 239 E3
Cedar Rd. Bank 38 C1
Cedar Rd. Bish 98 A4
Cedar Rd. Cumb 62 B2
Cedar Rd. Irvine 219 E2
Cedar Rd. Kilmk 227 E4
Cedar St. Glasg 97 D1
Cedar Wlk. Bish 98 A4
Cedars The. Tull 4 A1
Cedarwood Ave. Newt M 156 C3
Cedarwood Rd. Newt M 156 C2
Cedric Pl. Glasg 95 E4
Cedric Rd. Glasg 95 E4
Celandine Bank. Ayr 239 E2
Celtic St. Glasg 96 B4
Cemetery Rd. Glasg 115 F2
Cemetery Rd. Shot 147 D2
Cemetery Rd. Udd 161 E3
Centenary Ave. Aird 122 B4
Centenary Ct. Clyde 74 A1
Centenary Gdns. Coat 122 A3
Centenary Gdns. Ham 162 C1
Centenary Pl. Ard 205 E2
Centenary Quadrant. Holy 143 D3
Central Ave. Ard 205 E2
Central Ave. Clyde 74 A1
Central Ave. Glasg 95 F1
Central Ave. Glasg 119 F2
Central Ave. Glasg 138 C3
Central Ave. Ham 161 F3
Central Ave. Holy 142 C3
Central Ave. Holy 143 D1
Central Ave. Kilb 170 A4
Central Ave. Kilmk 227 F2
Central Ave. Tan 141 E3
Central Ave. Troon 229 F2
Central Cres. Ash 199 F4
Central Dr. Sten 23 F2
Central Path. Glasg 119 F2
Central Quadrant. Ard 205 E2
Central Rd. Pais 113 F3
Central Way. Cumb 61 F1
Central Way. Pais 113 F3
Centre
Roundabout The. E Kil 159 F1
Centre St. Chap 123 E1
Centre St. Glasg 117 D3
Centre St. Glen 101 E3
Centre The. Barr 134 A1
Ceres Gdns. Bish 78 B1
Cessnock Ave. Hurl 228 C3
Cessnock Dr. Hurl 228 C3
Cessnock Pl. Ayr 239 E3
Cessnock Pl. Glasg 139 E3
Cessnock Rd. Hurl 228 C3
Cessnock Rd. Stepps 99 D2
Cessnock Rd. Troon 229 E2
Cessnock St. Glasg 116 B3
Cessock Pl. Kilmk 228 A3
Chacefield St. Bon 40 A3
Chacefield Wood. Bank 39 F4
Chalmers Ave. Ayr 239 D3
Chalmers Cres. E Kil 180 C4
Chalmers Ct. Glasg 117 F3
Chalmers Dr. E Kil 180 C4
Chalmers Gate. Glasg 117 F3
Chalmers Pl. Glasg 117 F3
Chalmers Pl. Shew 224 C3
Chalmers Rd. Ayr 239 D3
Chalmers St. Clyde 74 A1
Chalmers St. Glasg 117 F3
Chalmers St. Gour 44 C4
Chalmerston Rd. Cam 1 A2
Chalton Rd. B of A 2 A4
Chamberlain La. Glasg 95 F3
Chamberlain Rd. Glasg 95 F3
Chambers Dr. Sten 24 A1
Chancellor St. Glasg 96 B1
Chantinghall Rd. Ham 162 A2
Chantinghall Terr. Ham 162 A2
Chapel Cres. Sten 24 A2
Chapel Ct. Glasg 137 F4
Chapel Dr. Sten 23 F2
Chapel La. Falk 42 A3
Chapel La. Irvine 219 E1
Chapel Rd. Dunt 74 A3
Chapel Rd. Hous 91 D2
Chapel Rd. New 166 B1
Chapel St. Aird 123 D4
Chapel St. Car 187 F1
Chapel St. Cle 144 A1
Chapel St. Glasg 96 C3
Chapel St. Glasg 137 F4
Chapel St. Gour 44 C4
Chapel St. Green 46 A2
Chapel St. Lennox 57 E4
Chapelacre Gr. Helen 16 C1
Chapelcross Ave. Aird 103 D1
Chapelgill Pl. Irvine 220 A2
Chapelhill Mount. Ard 205 E3
Chapelhill Rd. Pais 114 A1
Chapelknowe Rd. Holy 143 F1
Chapelpark Rd. Ayr 238 C2
Chapelside Ave. Aird 123 D4
Chapelside Rd. E Kil 160 A3
Chapelton Ave. Bear 75 F2
Chapelton Ave. Dumb 50 A3
Chapelton Gdns. Bear 75 F2
Chapelton Gdns. Dumb 50 A3
Chapelton La. W Kil 190 B2
Chapelton Rd. Cumb 82 B3
Chapelton Rd. W Kil 190 B1
Chapelton St. Glasg 97 D3
Chapelton St. P Glasg 47 D1
Chapeltoun Terr. Spring 210 C2
Chapelwell St. Salt 216 C4
Chapland Rd. Lan 215 D3
Chaplet Ave. Glasg 95 E4
Chapman Ave. Glen 101 E3
Chapman St. Glasg 117 D1
Chapmans Terr. Kilmk 228 A4
Chappell St. Barr 134 A2
Charing Cross La. Glasg 116 C4
Charing Cross. Lark 185 D2
Charles Ave. B of A 2 A3
Charles Ave. Pres 233 E3
Charles Ave. Ren 94 B2
Charles Cres. Car 188 A1
Charles Cres. Kirk 79 E2
Charles Dr. Lar 41 E4
Charles Dr. Troon 229 F1
Charles Path. Chap 123 E1
Charles Pl. Green 45 F3
Charles Pl. Kilmk 227 F4
Charles Quadrant. Holy 143 D3
Charles Rodger Pl. B of A 2 A3
Charles St. All 9 F4
Charles St. Glasg 97 F1
Charles St. Kilmk 227 F4
Charles St. Kils 36 B1
Charles St. Mother 164 B2
Charles St. Shot 147 D2
Charles St. Stir 7 D3
Charleson Row. Kils 60 C2
Charlotte Ave. Lennox 78 A4
Charlotte Path. Lark 185 D1
Charlotte Pl. Pais 113 F1
Charlotte St. Ayr 238 C4
Charlotte St. Dumb 49 E2
Charlotte St. Glasg 117 E3
Charlotte St. Helen 16 C1
Charlotte St. Shot 147 D2
Charlotte Street La. Ayr 238 C4
Charter St. Stir 7 D2
Chartershall Rd. Bann 7 D1
Chartershall Rd. Bann 11 D3
Chartwell Rd. Bishop 72 A2
Chassels St. Coat 122 A4
Chateau Gr. Ham 163 D1
Chatelherault Ave. Glasg 138 C3
Chatelherault Cres. Ham 162 C1
Chatelherault Wlk. Ham 162 C1
Chatham. E Kil 180 B4
Chattan Ave. Stir 2 A2
Chatton St. Glasg 76 B1
Cheapside St. Eagle 178 C3
Cheapside St. Glasg 116 C4
Chelmsford Dr. Glasg 96 A3
Cherry Bank. Kirk 79 D3
Cherry Cres. Clyde 74 A2
Cherry Gdns. Irvine 219 F3
Cherry Hill Rd. Ayr 239 D1
Cherry La. Bank 38 C1
Cherry La. Troon 229 E2
Cherry Pl. Bish 98 A4
Cherry Pl. Holy 143 D3

Cherry Pl. John

Cherry Pl. John 112 A1
Cherry Pl. M of C 58 A2
Cherry Pl. Tan 141 E4
Cherry Rd. Kilmk 227 E3
Cherrybank Rd. Glasg 136 C3
Cherrybank Wlk. Aird 122 B4
Cherryhill View. Lark 184 C2
Cherrytree Cres. Lark 185 D3
Cherrywood Dr. Beith 150 B1
Cherrywood Rd. John 112 B1
Chester Rd. Gour 44 C3
Chester St. Glasg 119 D3
Chesterfield Ave. Glasg 96 A3
Chesters Cres. Mother 163 E4
Chesters Pl. Glasg 138 A4
Chesters Rd. Bear 75 E2
Chestnut Ave. Beith 171 D4
Chestnut Ave. Bishop 71 F3
Chestnut Ave. Cumb 62 C3
Chestnut Cres. Duni 21 E2
Chestnut Cres. E Kil 180 B3
Chestnut Cres. Ham 162 C1
Chestnut Cres. Tan 141 E4
Chestnut Ct. Cumb 62 C3
Chestnut Ct. M of C 58 A3
Chestnut Dr. Clyde 74 A3
Chestnut Dr. Kirk 79 D3
Chestnut Gr. Bar 187 F1
Chestnut Gr. Glen 101 E3
Chestnut Gr. Lark 185 D3
Chestnut Gr. Mother 163 E2
Chestnut Gr. Sten 23 F2
Chestnut Gr. Udd 161 E4
Chestnut La. Miln 54 C1
Chestnut Pl. Cumb 62 C3
Chestnut Pl. John 132 A4
Chestnut Rd. Ayr 239 E3
Chestnut Rd. Glasg 97 E3
Cheviot Ave. Barr 134 B1
Cheviot Cres. Wish 164 C2
Cheviot Ct. Aird 103 D1
Cheviot Ct. Irvine 220 A2
Cheviot Dr. Newt M 156 B2
Cheviot Gdns. Bear 75 E4
Cheviot Head. Irvine 219 F2
Cheviot Pl. Kilmk 228 A2
Cheviot Rd. Glasg 136 B3
Cheviot Rd. Ham 162 C1
Cheviot Rd. Lark 185 E1
Cheviot Rd. Pais 113 F1
Cheviot St. Udd 161 E4
Cheviot Way. Irvine 220 A2
Chillin Pl. Lark 185 E1
Chirnside Ct. Ham 161 F3
Chirnside Pl. Glasg 115 D3
Chirnside Rd. Glasg 115 D3
Chisholm Ave. Bishop 72 B2
Chisholm Ave. Stir 2 A2
Chisholm Dr. Newt M 156 C3
Chisholm St. Coat 122 A4
Chisolm St. Glasg 117 E3
Chriss Ave. Ham 183 E4
Christchurch Pl. E Kil 180 A4
Christian St. Glasg 136 B4
Christie Gdns. Salt 216 C4
Christie La. Pais 113 F3
Christie St. Hat 142 B3
Christie St. Pais 113 F3
Christopher St. Glasg 98 A1
Chromars Pl. Green 45 F2
Chryston Rd. Kirk 80 B3
Chryston Rd. Muir 100 B4
Chryston Rd. Twe 80 B3
Chuckie La. Kilbar 111 E3
Church Ave. Card 48 A4
Church Ave. Glasg 138 B3
Church Ave. New 166 A2
Church Ave. Stepps 99 E3
Church Cres. Aird 103 F1
Church Cres. Ham 183 E3
Church Ct. Ayr 236 A1
Church Ct. Dumb 49 F2
Church Dr. Kirk 79 E3
Church Gr. N Sau 5 E1
Church Hill. Pais 113 F3
Church La. Car 187 F1
Church La. Coat 122 A4
Church La. Duni 21 E2
Church La. Kilmk 227 F3
Church La. Kils 60 B4
Church Pl. Cald 104 C2
Church Pl. Falk 42 A3
Church Pl. Kill 73 D3
Church Pl. Rhu 15 E2
Church Pl. Salt 205 E1
Church Rd. B of W 110 C4
Church Rd. Cald 66 C3
Church Rd. Glasg 136 B1
Church Rd. Kil 89 F1
Church Rd. Muir 100 B4
Church Rd. New 166 B3
Church Rd. Newt M 157 F3
Church Rd. Rhu 15 E3
Church St. Alex 27 F2
Church St. All 10 A3
Church St. Bon 40 B2
Church St. Clyde 74 A2
Church St. Coat 122 A4
Church St. Dumb 49 F2
Church St. East 127 E3
Church St. Glasg 96 B1
Church St. Glasg 120 B2
Church St. Gour 44 C4
Church St. Ham 162 C2
Church St. Holy 143 F2
Church St. Irvine 219 D1
Church St. John 111 F2
Church St. Kilbar 111 D2
Church St. Kilmk 222 C1
Church St. Kils 60 B4
Church St. Kilw 207 F2
Church St. Lark 185 D1
Church St. Loch 129 E1
Church St. P Glasg 47 E1
Church St. Sten 23 F2
Church St. Sten 24 B1
Church St. Troon 229 E1
Church St. Udd 140 C3
Church St. Udd 161 F4
Church View Ct. Lennox 33 E1
Church View Gdns. Hat 142 A3
Church View. Glasg 139 D4
Church Wlk. Den 21 F1
Churchill Ave. E Kil 159 F1
Churchill Ave. John 131 E4
Churchill Ave. Kilw 208 A2
Churchill Cres. Ayr 239 E4
Churchill Cres. Udd 141 D2
Churchill Dr. Ard 205 E2
Churchill Dr. B of A 2 A3
Churchill Dr. Bishop 72 A2
Churchill Dr. Glasg 96 A2
Churchill Pl. Kilbar 111 D2
Churchill Rd. Kil 89 E4
Churchill Sq. Helen 17 D1
Churchill St. All 9 F4
Churchill Way. Glasg 77 F1
Circus Dr. Glasg 117 F4
Circus Pl. Glasg 117 F4
Circus Place La. Glasg 117 F4
Citadel Pl. Ayr 235 F1
Citadel Pl. Mother 163 E2
Citadel Way. Troon 229 F4
Citizen La. Glasg 117 E4
Citrus Cres. Tan 141 E4
Cityford Cres. Glasg 137 F3
Cityford Dr. Glasg 137 F3
Civic St. Glasg 97 D1
Civic Way. Kirk 79 E4
Clachan Dr. Glasg 115 F4
Clachan Rd. Ros 15 D2
Clachan The. Wish 165 D2
Clackmannan Rd. All 10 B3
Claddens Pl. Kirk 79 F2
Claddens Quadrant. Glasg . 97 E3
Claddens St. Glasg 97 D3
Claddoch Cotts. Card 25 E3
Cladence Gr. E Kil 180 C1
Clair Rd. Bish 78 B1
Claire St. New 166 A3
Clairinch Gdns. Ren 94 B1
Clairmont Gdns. Glasg 96 C1
Clamp Rd. Mother 164 B2
Clamps Ct. E Kil 181 D4
Clamps Terr. E Kil 181 D4
Clamps Wood. E Kil 181 D4
Clanrye Dr. Coat 122 A2
Clapperhow Rd. Holy 143 D1
Clare St. Glasg 98 A1
Claremont. All 9 F4
Claremont Ave. Kirk 79 D4
Claremont Cres. Kilw 207 E2
Claremont Dr. B of A 2 B4
Claremont Dr. Miln 55 D1
Claremont Gdns. Miln 55 D1
Claremont Pass. Glasg 96 C1
Claremont Pl. Glasg 96 C1
Claremont St. Bon 39 F3
Claremont St. Glasg 116 C4
Claremont Terr. Glasg 96 C1
Claremont
    Terrace La. Glasg 96 C1
Claremount Ave. Glasg ... 136 B1
Clarence Dr. Glasg 96 A2
Clarence Dr. Pais 114 A2
Clarence Gdns. Glasg 96 A2
Clarence La. Glasg 96 A2
Clarence St. Clyde 74 B2
Clarence St. Green 45 F3
Clarence St. Pais 114 A3
Clarendon Pl. Ayr 239 E3
Clarendon Pl. Glasg 97 D1
Clarendon Pl. Stir 7 D4
Clarendon Rd. Stir 7 D4
Clarendon Rd. Wish 164 C2
Clarendon St. Glasg 97 D1
Clarinda Ave. Falk 41 D3
Clarinda Cres. Kirk 59 D1
Clarinda Pl. Holy 143 E2
Clarion Cres. Glasg 95 D4
Clark Dr. Irvine 219 F2
Clark Cres. Steven 217 E4
Clark Dr. Irvine 219 F2
Clark Pl. Lennox 78 B4
Clark Pl. Newt M 156 A2
Clark St. Aird 123 D4
Clark St. Clyde 73 F2
Clark St. John 111 F2
Clark St. Kilmk 227 F4
Clark St. New 165 F3
Clark St. Pais 113 E3
Clark St. Ren 94 A2
Clark St. Stir 7 D4
Clark Way. Hat 141 F4
Clarke Ave. Ayr 238 C3
Clarkston Ave. Glasg 136 C2
Clarkston Dr. Aird 123 E4
Clarkston Rd. Glasg 136 C2
Clarkwell Rd. Ham 161 F2
Clarkwell Terr. Ham 161 F2
Clathic Ave. Bear 76 A2
Claud Rd. Pais 114 A3
Claude Ave. Glasg 139 F2
Claude St. Lark 185 D2
Clavens Rd. Glasg 114 C3
Claverhouse Pl. Pais 114 A2
Claverhouse Rd. Glasg 114 C4
Clavering St E. Pais 113 E3
Clavering St W. Pais 113 E2
Clay Cres. Hat 142 B4
Clay Cres. Kilmk 222 C1
Clay Rd. Hat 142 B4
Clayhouse Rd. Stepps 99 F2
Claymore Dr. Bann 7 E2
Claymore Dr. House 111 E4
Claypotts Pl. Glasg 99 D1
Claypotts Rd. Glasg 99 D1
Clayslaps Rd. Glasg 96 B1
Clayslaps View. Klimk 228 A2
Claythorn Ave. Glasg 117 F3
Claythorn Cir. Glasg 117 F3
Claythorn Ct. Glasg 117 F3
Claythorn Pk. Glasg 117 F3
Claythorn Pk. Glasg 117 F3
Claythorn St. Glasg 117 F3
Claythorn Terr. Glasg 117 F3
Clayton Ave. Irvine 219 E2
Clayton Path. Hat 142 A4
Clayton Terr. Glasg 117 F4
Clearfield Ave. Ham 162 A2
Cleaves The. Tull 4 A1
Cleddans Cres. Dunt 74 B3
Cleddans Rd. Dunt 74 B3
Cleddans Rd. Kirk 58 C1
Cleddans View. Clyde 74 B2
Cleddens Ct. Bish 78 A1
Cleeves Ave. Beith 191 F3
Cleeves Quadrant. Glasg . 135 D3
Cleeves Rd. Glasg 135 D3
Cleghorn Ave. Lan 215 D3
Cleghorn Rd. Lan 215 D3
Cleghorn St. Glasg 97 D2
Cleish Ave. Bear 75 E4
Cleland La. Glasg 117 E3
Cleland Pl. E Kil 160 A2
Cleland Rd. Car 188 A1
Cleland Rd. Holy 143 E1
Cleland Rd. Holy 144 A1
Cleland Rd. Wish 165 D2
Cleland St. Glasg 117 E3
Clelland Ave. Bish 98 A4
Clem Attlee Gdns. Lark ... 185 D1
Clements St. Steven 206 C1
Clerkland Rd. Stew 195 E1
Clerwood St. Glasg 118 B3
Cleuch Ave. Tull 4 A1
Cleuch Dr. Alva 5 D4
Cleuch Gdns. Newt M 157 E4
Cleughearn Rd. Auld 180 B1
Clevans Rd. B of W 110 B4
Clevedon Cres. Glasg 96 A3
Clevedon
    Crescent La. Glasg 96 A3
Clevedon Dr. Glasg 96 B2
Clevedon Dr. Glasg 138 B3
Cleveden Drive La. Glasg .. 96 B2
Clevedon Gdns. Glasg 96 B3
Cleveland La. Glasg 96 A3
Cleveland La. Glasg 116 C4
Cleveland St. Glasg 116 C4
Cliff Rd. Glasg 96 C1
Clifford Gdns. Glasg 116 A3
Clifford La. Glasg 116 B3
Clifford Pl. Glasg 116 B3
Clifford St. Glasg 116 B3
Clifton Pl. Coat 122 B3
Clifton Pl. Glasg 116 C4
Clifton Rd. Glasg 96 B3
Clifton St. Glasg 96 C1
Clifton Terr. Glasg 138 C2
Clifton Terr. John 112 A1
Climie Pl. Kilmk 228 A4
Clincart Rd. Glasg 137 D4
Clincarthill Rd. Glasg 138 A4
Clippens Rd. Lin 111 F4
Clippens Rd. Lin 112 A3
Clive St. Shot 146 C3
Cloak Rd. Kil 69 E2
Cloan Ave. Glasg 75 D1
Cloan Cres. Bish 78 A2
Clober Farm La. Miln 54 C2
Clober Rd. Miln 55 D1
Cloberfield Gdns. Miln 54 C2
Cloberfield. Miln 54 C2
Cloberhill Rd. Glasg 75 E1
Cloch Brae. Gour 44 A3
Cloch Rd. Gour 43 F3
Cloch St. Glasg 119 D4
Clochbar Ave. Miln 54 C2
Clochbar Gdns. Miln 54 C1
Clochoderick Ave. Kilbar .. 111 D1
Clochranhill Rd. Ayr 236 C1
Clockerhill Pl. Holy 143 F2
Cloister Ave. Aird 123 E2
Clonbeith St. Glasg 99 F1
Cloncaird. Kilw 207 E1
Closeburn St. Glasg 97 E3
Cloth St. Barr 134 B1
Clouden Rd. Cumb 62 A1
Cloudhowe Terr. Udd 140 B1
Clouston La. Glasg 96 C2
Clouston St. Glasg 96 C2
Clova Pl. Udd 140 C3
Clova St. Glasg 135 F2
Clove Mill Wynd. Lark 184 C1
Clover Leaf Path. Alex 27 F2
Cloverbank St. Glasg 98 A1
Clovergate. Bish 77 F1
Cloverhill. Ayr 239 E3
Cloverhill Pl. Muir 100 B4
Cloverhill Terr. E Kil 159 F1
Cloverhill View. E Kil 159 E1
Cloves The. Men 4 A3
Clunie Ave. Shot 146 C3
Clune Brae. P Glasg 47 F1
Clune Pk. E Kil 180 A4
Clune Rd. Glasg 99 F1
Clunie Rd. Glasg 115 F2
Cluny Ave. Bear 76 A1
Cluny Ave. Dunt 74 B4
Cluny Dr. Bear 76 A1
Cluny Dr. Pais 114 A3
Cluny Gdns. Glasg 95 F2
Cluny Gdns. Glasg 120 A2
Cluny Villas. Glasg 95 F2
Clunie Pk. E Kil 180 A4
Clutha St. Glasg 116 B3
Clyde Ave. Barr 134 B1
Clyde Ave. Ham 163 E1
Clyde Ave. Lennox 78 A4
Clyde Ave. Udd 140 C1
Clyde Cres. Lan 215 D3
Clyde Cres. Lar 23 D2
Clyde Pl. Glasg 117 D3
Clyde Pl. Ard 205 E2
Clyde Pl. Glasg 117 D3
Clyde Pl. Glasg 139 E2
Clyde Pl. John 131 E4
Clyde Pl. Kilmk 228 A3
Clyde Pl. Troon 229 F3
Clyde Rd. Gour 44 C3
Clyde Rd. Pais 114 A4
Clyde Shopping Ctr. Clyde . 74 A1
Clyde Sq. Green 45 F3
Clyde St. Car 187 F1
Clyde St. Coat 122 B4
Clyde St E. Helen 16 C1
Clyde St W. Helen 16 C1
Clyde St. Falk 41 F3
Clyde St. Glasg 117 E3
Clyde St. Ren 94 B3
Clyde Terr. Ard 205 E2
Clyde Tower. Mother 163 F3
Clyde Valley Ave. Mother . 163 F2
Clyde View. Ham 162 A1
Clyde View. Pais 114 A1
Clyde Way. Pais 114 A4
Clyde Wynds. Green 45 E2
Clydebrae Dr. Udd 140 C1
Clydebrae St. Glasg 116 A1
Clydeford Dr. Glasg 118 C2
Clydeford Dr. Udd 140 C4
Clydeford Rd. Glasg 139 D4
Clydeholm Rd. Glasg 95 E1
Clydeholm Terr. Clyde 94 B3
Clydesdale Ave. Ham 183 E3
Clydesdale Ave. Ren 94 A1
Clydesdale Ave. Wish 164 B1
Clydesdale Pl. Ham 183 E3
Clydesdale Rd. Ham 183 E3
Clydesdale St. Holy 142 C2
Clydesdale St. Lark 185 D2
Clydeshore Rd. Dumb 49 F2
Clydeside
    Expressway. Glasg 116 C4
Clydeside Ind Est. Glasg .. 95 F1
Clydeside Rd. Glasg 117 F1
Clydesmill Dr. Glasg 139 D2
Clydesmill Gr. Glasg 139 D4
Clydesmill Pl. Glasg 139 D4
Clydesmill Rd. Glasg 139 D4
Clydeview. Dumb 49 F1
Clydeview Rd. Green 46 A1
Clydeview Rd. P Glasg 68 C4
Clydeview
    Shopping Ctr. Udd ... 161 F4
Clydeview Terr. Glasg 139 E4
Clydeview. Udd 141 E1
Clynder Rd. Green 46 B1
Clynder St. Glasg 116 A3
Clyth Dr. Glasg 136 B1
Co-Operative Terr. John ... 112 A2
Coach Cl. Kils 61 D4
Coach Pl. Kils 60 C4
Coach Rd. Kils 60 C4
Coal Wynd. Bann 7 E1
Coalburn Rd. Tan 141 D3
Coalburn St. Gree 83 F1
Coalgate. All 10 A3
Coalhall Ave. Holy 143 D1
Coalhill Pl. Ard 205 D2
Coalhill St. Glasg 118 A3
Coalpots Way. Pais 5 F2
Coatbank St. Coat 122 A3
Coatbank Way. Coat 122 A3
Coatbridge Rd. Aird 102 A2
Coatbridge Rd. Coat 101 D2
Coatbridge Rd. Coat 120 C3
Coatbridge Rd. Glasg 120 C3
Coatbridge Rd. Glen 101 F3
Coatbridge Rd. Glenm 102 B2
Coathill St. Coat 122 A2
Coats Cres. Glasg 120 A3
Coats Dr. Pais 113 D2
Coats St. Coat 122 A3
Coats Pl. Dund 225 F1
Cobbett Rd. Mother 163 D3
Cobblebrae Cres. Falk 24 A1
Cobblerigg Way. Udd 160 C3
Cobbleton Rd. Holy 142 C1
Cobden Rd. Glasg 97 F1
Cobden St. Alva 5 D3
Cobden St. Alva 5 D2
Cobham St. Green 46 C1
Cobington Pl. Glasg 99 D1
Cobinshaw St. Glasg 119 D3
Coblecrook Gdns. Alva 4 C3
Coblecrook La. Alva 4 C3
Coblecrook Pl. Alva 4 C3
Coburg St. Glasg 117 D3
Cochno Rd. Dunt 74 A4
Cochno St. Clyde 94 B3
Cochran St. Pais 113 F2
Cochrane Ave. Dund 225 F1
Cochrane Ave. Falk 42 A2
Cochrane Cres. Alva 4 C4
Cochrane Ct. Miln 76 B4
Cochrane Dr. Dund 225 F1
Cochrane Pl. Helen 17 D1
Cochrane Pl. Kilw 207 F2
Cochrane Pres. Ava 236 A4
Cochranes The. Ava 5 D4
Cochrie Pl. Tull 4 A2
Cockburn Pl. Coat 121 F2
Cockburn Pl. Shew 224 C3
Cockburn St. Falk 42 A2
Cochrane St. Barr 134 A1
Cochrane St. Falk 141 F3
Cochrane St. Irvine 219 D1
Cochrane St. Kilb 149 D2
Cochranemill Rd. John 111 E1
Cochranes The. Ava 5 D4
Cochrie Pl. Coat 121 F2
Coers Loan. Shot 147 D2
Colbert St. Glasg 117 F2
Colbreggan Ct. Dunt 74 B3
Colchester Dr. Glasg 96 A3
Coldgreen Ave. Kilb 149 D1
Coldingham Ave. Clyde 94 C3
Coldstream Cres. Wish ... 165 E3
Coldstream Dr. Glasg 138 B3
Coldstream Dr. Pais 113 D2
Coldstream Pl. Glasg 97 F2
Coldstream Rd. Clyde 74 A1
Coldstream St. Udd 161 E4
Colebrooke Pl. Glasg 96 C2
Colebrooke St. Glasg 96 C2
Colebrooke St. Glasg 139 D3

253

Colebrooke Terr. Glasg | Craigie La. Lark

Colebrooke Terr. Glasg 96 C2
Coleburn Ct. Irvine 219 F3
Coleridge Ave. Udd 141 D2
Coleridge. E Kil 180 A4
Colfin St. Glasg 100 B1
Colgrain St. Glasg 97 D3
Colgrave Cres. Glasg 118 C2
Colinbar Circ. Barr 134 A1
Colinslee Ave. Pais 113 F1
Colinslee Cres. Pais 113 F1
Colinslee Dr. Pais 113 F1
Colinslie Rd. Glasg 135 E4
Colinton Pl. Glasg 119 D4
Colintraive Ave. Glasg 98 C2
Colintraive Cres. Glasg 98 C2
Coll Ave. P Glasg 69 D4
Coll Ave. Ren 94 B1
Coll. E Kil 181 E4
Coll Gdns. Irvine 225 D4
Coll Pl. Glasg 98 A1
Coll St. Glasg 98 A1
Coll St. New 165 F3
Colla Gdns. Bish 78 B1
Collace Ave. B of W 110 B4
College Cres. Falk 42 B4
College La. Glasg 117 E4
College Pk. Troon 229 F4
College St. Dumb 49 F2
College St. Glasg 117 E4
College Way. Dumb 49 F2
College Wynd. Kilmk 227 F4
Collenan Ave. Troon 230 A2
Collessie Dr. Glasg 99 E1
Collier St. John 111 F2
Colliertree Rd. Aird 123 E4
Collina St. Glasg 96 B3
Collingwood Ct. Falk 41 F3
Collingwood Pl. Helen 17 D1
Collingwood Terr. Gour 44 C3
Collins Dr. Troon 230 A2
Collins Rd. Helen 25 D4
Collins St. Dunt 74 B3
Collins St. Glasg 117 F4
Collyland Rd. N Sau 5 E2
Collylinn Rd. Bear 75 F2
Colmonell Ave. Glasg 94 C4
Colonsay Ave. P Glasg 69 D4
Colonsay Ave. Ren 94 B1
Colonsay Dr. Newt M 156 A3
Colonsay. E Kil 181 E4
Colonsay House. Pres 236 A3
Colonsay Pl. Kilmk 223 D3
Colonsay Rd. Glasg 115 F3
Colonsay Rd. Pais 133 E4
Colonsay Terr. Falk 42 A1
Colquhoun Ave. Glasg 115 D4
Colquhoun Ct. Glasg 116 B2
Colquhoun Dr. Alex 27 F4
Colquhoun Dr. Bear 75 F3
Colquhoun. Dumb 50 A2
Colquhoun Rd. Dumb 50 C1
Colquhoun Rd. Kilmk 223 E1
Colquhoun Sq. Helen 16 B1
Colquhoun St. Dumb 50 A2
Colquhoun St. Helen 16 B1
Colquhoun St. Stir 7 E3
Colsnaur. Men 4 A3
Colson Pl. Hat 142 B2
Colston Ave. Bish 97 F4
Colston Dr. Bish 97 F4
Colston Gdns. Aird 123 E4
Colston Gdns. Bish 97 F4
Colston Path. Bish 97 F4
Colston Pl. Aird 123 E4
Colston Pl. Bish 97 F4
Colston Rd. Aird 123 E4
Colston Rd. Glasg 97 F4
Colston Terr. Aird 123 E4
Colt Ave. Coat 101 F1
Colt Pl. Coat 122 A4
Colt Terr. Coat 122 A4
Coltmuir Cres. Bish 97 F4
Coltmuir Dr. Bish 97 F4
Coltmuir Gdns. Bish 97 F4
Coltmuir St. Glasg 97 D3
Coltness Ave. Alla 166 C4
Coltness Dr. Hat 142 A2
Coltness La. Glasg 119 E4
Coltness Rd. Wish 165 E3
Coltness St. Glasg 119 E4
Coltpark Ave. Bish 97 F4
Coltpark La. Bish 97 F4
Coltsfoot Dr. Glasg 135 D2
Coltswood Ct. Coat 122 A4
Coltswood Rd. Coat 122 A4
Columba Cres. Mother 142 B1
Columba Path. Udd 161 E4
Columba St. Glasg 116 A4
Columba St. Green 45 E2
Columba St. Helen 16 B1
Columbia Pl. E Kil 180 A4
Columbia Way. E Kil 180 A4
Columbine Way. Car 201 F4
Colvend St. Glasg 117 F2
Colville Dr. Glasg 138 B3
Colvilles Pl. E Kil 181 D3
Colvilles Rd. E Kil 181 D3
Colwood Ave. Glasg 135 D2
Colwood Gdns. Glasg 135 D2
Colwood Pl. Glasg 135 D2
Colwood Sq. Glasg 135 D2
Colwyn Ct. Aird 103 D1
Colzium View. Kils 60 C4
Combe Quadrant. Hat 141 F2
Comedie Rd. Stepps 99 F2
Comely Bank. Ham 161 F2
Comely Park Terr. Falk 42 A2
Comely Pl. Falk 42 A2
Comelybank La. Dumb 49 E2
Comelybank Rd. Dumb 49 F2
Comelypark Pl. Glasg 118 A3
Comelypark St. Glasg 118 A3
Commerce St. Glasg 117 D3
Commercial Ct. Glasg 117 E3
Commercial Rd. Barr 134 B2
Commercial Rd. Glasg 117 E3
Common Gn. Ham 162 C2
Commonhead Ave. Aird 102 C1
Commonhead La. Aird 102 C1
Commonhead Rd. Coat 120 C4
Commonhead Rd. Glasg 120 C4
Commonhead Rd. Kilmk 228 A2
Commonhead St. Aird 102 C1
Commonside St. Aird 102 C1
Commore Ave. Barr 134 B1
Commore Dr. Glasg 95 D4
Commore Pl. Neil 154 B3
Community Ave. Hat 142 A1
Community Pl. Hat 142 A2
Community Rd. Hat 142 A1
Comrie Cres. Ham 161 F2
Comrie Rd. Stepps 99 E3
Comrie St. Glasg 119 D2
Cona St. Glasg 135 F2
Conan Ct. Glasg 139 E3
Condorrat
Interchange. Cumb 82 B4
Condorrat Rd. Cumb 82 A2
Condorrat Rd. Glen 82 A2
Condorrat Rd. Glenm 102 B3
Condorrat Ring Rd. Cumb 82 B4
Coneyhill Rd. B of A 2 A4
Coneypark Cres. Bank 38 B2
Coneypark Pl. Bank 38 B2
Coneypark. Stir 6 C3
Congress Rd. Glasg 116 B4
Conifer Pl. Klrk 79 D3
Coningsby Pl. All 10 A3
Conisborough Path. Glasg 99 F1
Conisborough Rd. Glasg 100 A1
Coniston Dr. Hat 142 A2
Coniston. E Kil 179 F3
Conistone Cres. Glasg 119 F2
Connal St. Glasg 118 A2
Connell Cres. Miln 55 E1
Connell Ct. Kilb 149 D1
Conner Ave. Falk 42 A4
Conniston St. Glasg 118 C4
Connor Rd. Barr 134 A2
Connor St. Aird 103 F1
Conon Ave. Bear 75 E2
Consett La. Glasg 119 E4
Consett St. Glasg 119 E4
Constable Rd. Stir 7 D3
Constarry Rd. Kils 60 C2
Container Way. Green 45 F3
Content Ave. Ayr 239 D4
Content St. Ayr 236 A1
Contin Pl. Glasg 96 B3
Convair Way. Ren 94 B1
Conval Way. Pais 113 E4
Conway Ct. Falk 41 F2
Coo La. Eagle 178 C3
Coodham Pl. Kilw 207 E2
Cook Rd. Bonh 28 A4
Cook St. Glasg 117 D3
Coolgardie Gn. E Kil 180 B4
Coolgardie Pl. E Kil 180 B4
Cooper's Well St. Glasg 96 B1
Cooperage La. Falk 42 A3
Copenhagen Ave. E Kil 180 C3
Copland Pl. Alva 4 C4
Copland Pl. Glasg 116 A3
Copland Quadrant. Glasg 116 A3
Copland Rd. Glasg 116 A3
Coplaw St. Glasg 117 D2
Copperfield La. Tan 141 D4
Coral Terr. Hat 142 A2
Coralmount Gdns. Klrk 79 F4
Coranbae Pl. Ayr 238 A1
Corbett Ct. Glasg 118 C2
Corbett St. Glasg 119 D2
Corbie Pl. Miln 54 B1
Corbiewood Dr. Bann 11 F4
Corbiston Way. Cumb 62 A1
Cordiner St. Glasg 137 D4
Corentin Ct. Falk 42 B2
Corkerhill Gdns. Glasg 115 F2
Corkerhill Pl. Glasg 115 F1
Corkerhill Rd. Glasg 115 E2
Corlaich Ave. Glasg 137 F4
Corlaich Dr. Glasg 137 F4
Corlic St. Green 46 A1
Corlic Way. Kil 89 E4
Cormack Ave. Lennox 57 E1
Cormorant Ave. Hous 111 E4
Corn Exchange Rd. Stir 7 D4
Corn St. Glasg 97 D1
Cornaig Rd. Glasg 135 D4
Cornalee Gdns. Glasg 135 D4
Cornalee Pl. Glasg 135 D4
Cornalee Rd. Glasg 135 D4
Cornelia St. Mother 142 A1
Cornelian Terr. Hat 142 A2
Cornhaddock St. Green 45 F2
Cornhill. Ayr 239 D2
Cornhill Cres. Stir 7 D2
Cornhill Dr. Coat 121 F4
Cornhill St. Glasg 98 A3
Cornock Cres. Clyde 74 A2
Cornock St. Clyde 74 A2
Cornsilloch Brae. Ash 186 A2
Cornton Cres. B of A 2 A3
Cornton Rd. B of A 2 A2
Cornton Rd. Stir 2 A2
Cornwall Ave. Glasg 138 B3
Cornwall Ct. E Kil 159 F1
Cornwall St. E Kil 159 F1
Cornwall St. Glasg 116 B3
Cornwall St S. Glasg 116 B3
Cornwall Way. E Kil 159 F1
Coronation Ave. Lark 199 D4
Coronation Cres. Lark 199 D4
Coronation Pl. Gran 24 C2
Coronation Pl. Lark 199 D4
Coronation Pl. Muir 100 C4
Coronation Rd E. Holy 142 C2
Coronation Rd. Holy 142 C2
Coronation St. Pres 233 E3
Coronation St. Wish 165 E2
Coronation Way. Bear 76 A1
Corpach Pl. Glasg 100 B1
Corporation St. Falk 42 B2
Corra Linn. Ham 162 A2
Corran Ave. Newt M 156 B3
Corran St. Glasg 118 C4
Correen Gdns. Bear 75 D4
Corrie Ave. Sten 23 F2
Corrie Brae. Kils 36 B1
Corrie Cres. Kilmk 222 C2
Corrie Cres. Salt 205 F1
Corrie Ct. Ham 161 F1
Corrie Dr. Mother 163 D4
Corrie Dr. Pais 114 C2
Corrie Gr. Glasg 136 C2
Corrie House. Pres 236 A3
Corrie Pl. Falk 41 E2
Corrie Pl. Helen 16 C2
Corrie Pl. Klrk 79 F2
Corrie Pl. Troon 229 F4
Corrie Rd. Kils 36 B1
Corrie View. Cumb 81 F4
Corrie Way. Lark 185 D1
Corrour Rd. Glasg 136 C4
Corrour Rd. Newt M 156 B3
Corruna Ct. Car 188 A1
Corse Ave. Spring 221 D1
Corse Dr. Barr 134 A2
Corse Pl. Cross 226 C4
Corse Rd. Glasg 114 C3
Corse St. W Kil 190 B3
Corsebar Ave. Pais 113 E1
Corsebar Cres. Pais 113 E1
Corsebar Dr. Pais 113 E1
Corsebar La. Pais 113 D1
Corsebar Rd. Pais 113 D1
Corsebar Way. Pais 113 E2
Corsefield Rd. Loch 128 C1
Corseford Ave. John 131 E4
Corsehill Dr. W Kil 190 A3
Corsehill. Kilw 208 A2
Corsehill Mount Rd. Irvine 225 D4
Corsehill Mount
Roundabout. Irvine 225 E4
Corsehill Pk. Ayr 238 C3
Corsehill Pk. Irvine 225 E4
Corsehill Pl. Ayr 238 C3
Corsehill Pl. Glasg 120 B4
Corsehill Pl. Stew 195 F1
Corsehill Rd. Ayr 238 C3
Corsehill St. Glasg 120 B4
Corsehill Terr. Spring 220 C1
Corsehillbank St. Stew 195 E1
Corselet Rd. Barr 135 D1
Corselet Rd. Glasg 135 D2
Corserine Bank. Irvine 219 F2
Corserine Rd. Ayr 238 A1
Corsewall Ave. Glasg 119 F2
Corsewall St. Coat 121 F4
Corsford Dr. Glasg 135 E3
Corsliehill Rd. Hous 90 C4
Corsock Ave. Ham 161 F1
Corsock St. Glasg 118 B4
Corston St. Glasg 118 B4
Cortachy Ave. Sten 24 A2
Cortachy Pl. Bish 78 B1
Coruisk Dr. Newt M 157 E4
Corunna St. Glasg 116 C4
Coshneuk Rd. Stepps 99 D2
Cosy Neuk. Lark 185 E1
Cottage Cres. Falk 41 F3
Cottar St. Glasg 96 C4
Cotter Dr. Kilmk 228 B4
Cotton Ave. Lin 112 A3
Cotton St. Glasg 118 A1
Cotton St. Pais 113 F2
Coulport Pl. Helen 16 A1
Coulter Ave. Coat 121 F4
Coulter Ave. Wish 165 E4
Coulthard Dr. Pres 236 B3
Countess St. Salt 216 C4
County Ave. Glasg 138 C4
County Dr. Lan 215 E2
County Pl. Pais 113 F3
County Sq. Pais 113 F3
Couper St. Glasg 97 E1
Coursington Cres. Mother 164 A4
Coursington Gdns. Mother 163 F4
Coursington Pl. Mother 163 F4
Coursington Rd. Mother 163 F4
Coursington Rd. Mother 164 A4
Court Rd. P Glasg 47 E1
Courthill. Alva 5 D4
Courthill Ave. Glasg 137 D3
Courthill. Bear 75 E3
Courthill Cres. Kils 60 C4
Courthill Pl. Dalry 191 E4
Courthill St. Dalry 191 E4
Courtrai Ave. Helen 16 A1
Coustonholm Rd. Glasg 136 B4
Couther Quadrant. Aird 103 D1
Covanburn Ave. Ham 162 C1
Cove Cres. Shot 146 C3
Cove Pl. Helen 16 A1
Cove Rd. Gour 44 C4
Coveland Dr. Glasg 138 A2
Covenant Cres. Lark 185 D1
Covenant Pl. Wish 164 B1
Covenanter Rd. East 127 E2
Covenanters Way. Wish 186 B3
Coventry Dr. Glasg 118 A4
Cow Wynd. Falk 42 A2
Cowal Cres. Gour 44 A3
Cowal Cres. Kirk 59 D1
Cowal Dr. Lin 112 A3
Cowal St. Glasg 96 B4
Cowal View. Gour 44 A3
Cowan Cres. Ayr 236 B2
Cowan Cres. Barr 134 B2
Cowan La. Glasg 96 C1
Cowan Rd. Cumb 61 E1
Cowan St. Bon 40 A3
Cowan St. Glasg 96 C1
Cowan Wilson Ave. Udd 161 E4
Cowan Wynd. Tan 141 D4
Cowan Wynd. Wish 186 B4
Cowane St. Stir 7 D4
Cowans Row. Hurl 228 B4
Cowcaddens Rd. Glasg 97 D1
Cowcaddens St. Glasg 117 E4
Cowden Dr. Bish 78 A2
Cowden St. Glasg 115 E4
Cowdenhill Cir. Glasg 95 E4
Cowdenhill Pl. Glasg 95 E4
Cowdenhill Rd. Glasg 95 E4
Cowdray Cres. Ren 94 B2
Cowgate. Klrk 79 E4
Cowglen Rd. Glasg 135 E4
Cowie Rd. Bann 12 A4
Cowiehall Rd. Cowie 12 B4
Cowlairs Ind Est. Glasg 97 E3
Cowlairs Rd. Glasg 97 F2
Coxdale Ave. Klrk 79 D4
Coxhill St. Glasg 97 E2
Coxithill Rd. Stir 7 D2
Coxton Pl. Glasg 99 E1
Coyle Pk. Troon 229 F3
Coylebank. Pres 236 B3
Coylton Cres. Ham 161 F1
Coylton Rd. Glasg 136 C3
Crabb Quadrant. Mother 142 B1
Cragdale. E Kil 159 E2
Craggan Dr. Glasg 95 D3
Crags Ave. Pais 113 F1
Crags Cres. Pais 113 F1
Crags Rd. Pais 113 F1
Cragwell Pk. E Kil 158 C4
Craig Ave. Alex 27 E4
Craig Ave. Dalry 191 D4
Craig Cotts. Cross 226 B4
Craig Cres. Kirk 80 A4
Craig Cres. Stir 2 B2
Craig Ct. B of A 2 A3
Craig Dr. Cross 226 C4
Craig Gdns. Newt M 156 B3
Craig Hill. E Kil 180 B4
Craig Pl. Newt M 156 A3
Craig Rd. Glasg 137 D3
Craig Rd. Lin 111 F4
Craig Rd. Neil 154 B3
Craig Rd. Troon 229 D2
Craig St. Aird 122 C4
Craig St. Blac 107 F2
Craig St. Coat 121 F2
Craig St. Udd 161 F4
Craig View. Spring 221 D1
Craigallian Ave. Glasg 139 E2
Craigallian Ave. Miln 55 D2
Craiganour La. Glasg 136 B3
Craigard Pl. Glasg 138 B2
Craigash Quadrant. Miln 54 C2
Craigash Rd. Miln 54 C2
Craigbank Cres. Eagle 178 C3
Craigbank Dr. Glasg 135 D3
Craigbank Gr. Eagle 178 C3
Craigbank. N Sau 5 E1
Craigbank Rd. Lark 199 D4
Craigbank St. Lark 185 D1
Craigbanzo St. Dunt 74 B4
Craigbarnet Ave. Lennox 78 A4
Craigbarnet Cres. Stepps 99 D2
Craigbarnet Rd. Miln 54 B1
Craigbet Ave. Kil 89 F1
Craigbet Cres. Kil 89 F1
Craigbet Pl. Kil 89 F1
Craigbo Ave. Glasg 76 B1
Craigbo Ct. Glasg 96 B4
Craigbo Dr. Glasg 76 B1
Craigbo Pl. Glasg 96 B4
Craigbo Rd. Glasg 76 B1
Craigbo St. Glasg 76 B1
Craigbog Ave. John 131 E4
Craigburn Ave. Hous 111 E4
Craigburn Cres. Hous 111 E4
Craigburn Ct. Ash 185 F1
Craigburn Ct. Falk 41 F1
Craigburn Pl. Hous 111 F4
Craigburn St. Ham 183 E4
Craigdene Dr. Steven 206 C1
Craigdhu Ave. Miln 54 C1
Craigdhu Rd. Bear 75 F4
Craigdhu Rd. Miln 54 C1
Craigdonald Pl. John 111 F2
Craigellan Rd. Glasg 136 B3
Craigelvan Ave. Cumb 81 F3
Craigelvan Ct. Cumb 81 F3
Craigelvan Dr. Cumb 81 F3
Craigelvan Gdns. Cumb 81 F3
Craigelvan Gr. Cumb 81 F3
Craigelvan Pl. Cumb 81 F3
Craigelvan View. Cumb 81 F3
Craigenbay Cres. Klrk 79 F3
Craigenbay Rd. Klrk 79 F3
Craigenbay St. Glasg 98 A2
Craigencart Ct. Dunt 73 F3
Craigend Cres. Miln 54 C1
Craigend Dr. Coat 121 E2
Craigend Dr W. Miln 54 C1
Craigend Pl. Glasg 95 F3
Craigend Rd. Auld 179 F1
Craigend Rd. Stir 7 D2
Craigend Rd. Troon 232 C4
Craigend St. Glasg 95 F3
Craigendmuir Rd. Stepps 99 F2
Craigendmuir St. Glasg 98 B1
Craigendon Oval. Pais 133 E3
Craigendon Rd. Pais 133 E3
Craigendoran Ave. Helen 25 C4
Craigends Ave. Kil 89 F2
Craigends Dr. Kilbar 111 D2
Craigends Pl. Kil 89 F2
Craigends Rd. Hous 111 F4
Craigends Rd. Kilb 170 A3
Craigenfeoch Ave. John 111 E1
Craigenhill Rd. Kilnc 203 D3
Craigenlay Ave. Strath 31 E2
Craigens Rd. Chap 124 B2
Craigfaulds Ave. Pais 113 D1
Craigfell Ct. Ham 161 F1
Craigfern Dr. Strath 31 E2
Craigfin Ct. Pres 236 B3
Craigflower Ave. Glasg 135 D2
Craigflower Gdns. Glasg 135 D2
Craigflower Rd. Glasg 135 D2
Craigford Dr. Bann 7 E1
Craigforth Cres. Stir 1 C1
Craighalbert Rd. Cumb 61 E2
Craighalbert
Roundabout. Cumb 61 E2
Craighalbert Way. Cumb 61 E2
Craighall Pl. Ayr 239 D1
Craighall Quadrant. Neil 154 B3
Craighall Rd. Glasg 97 D1
Craighall St. Stir 1 C1
Craighaw St. Dunt 74 B4
Craighead Ave. Glasg 98 B2
Craighead Ave. M of C 58 B3
Craighead Rd. Bishop 72 A1
Craighead Rd. M of C 58 B3
Craighead St. Aird 123 F4
Craighead Way. Barr 134 A1
Craighill Dr. Newt M 157 E3
Craighill Gr. Newt M 157 E3
Craighill View. Blac 107 F2
Craighirst Dr. Dunt 74 A4
Craighirst Rd. Miln 54 B1
Craighlaw Ave. Newt M 157 E1
Craighlaw Dr. Newt M 157 E1
Craigholm Rd. Ayr 239 E4
Craigholme. Hous 91 E1
Craighorn Dr. Falk 41 F1
Craighorn. Men 4 A3
Craighorn Rd. Alva 4 C3
Craighouse St. Glasg 99 D1
Craighton Gdns. Lennox 57 F4
Craigie Ave. Ayr 239 D4
Craigie Ave. Kilmk 227 F2
Craigie Ct. Lar 23 D1
Craigie Dr. Newt M 156 C2
Craigie La. Lark 185 D2

Craigie Lea. Ayr

Craigie Lea. Ayr 239 D4
Craigie Pk. Kirk 79 F3
Craigie Pl. Cross 226 C4
Craigie Pl. Kilmk 227 F2
Craigie Rd. Ayr 238 A1
Craigie Rd. Hurl 228 C3
Craigie Rd. Kilmk 227 F1
Craigie Rd. Kilmk 227 F2
Craigie St. Glasg 117 D1
Craigie St. Pres 236 A4
Craigie Way. Ayr 239 E4
Craigiebar Dr. Pais 133 E4
Craigieburn Gdns. Glasg 96 A4
Craigieburn Rd. Cumb 61 F1
Craigiehall Ave. Inch 93 D4
Craigiehall Cres. Inch 93 D4
Craigiehall Pl. Glasg 116 B3
Craigiehall St. Glasg 116 C3
Craigiehall Way. Inch 93 D4
Craigieknowes St. Green 46 B2
Craigielea Cres. Miln 54 C3
Craigielea Dr. Pais 113 E3
Craigielea Pk. Ren 94 B2
Craigielea Rd. Bear 73 F4
Craigielea Rd. Ren 94 B2
Craigielea St. Glasg 118 A4
Craigielinn Ave. Pais 133 E4
Craigievar Ave. Sten 24 A2
Craigievar St. Glasg 99 F1
Craigilinn Terr. Bac 107 E2
Craiglea Ave. Cross 226 C4
Craiglea Pl. Aird 123 E4
Craiglea Terr. Plains 103 F2
Craiglee. E Kil 180 C3
Craiglea Wk. Falk 41 F1
Craigleith. Fish 5 F2
Craigleith St. Glasg 118 C3
Craiglockhart St. Glasg 99 E1
Craiglomond Gdns. Alex 27 E4
Craiglynn Gdns. Bonh 27 F4
Craigmaddie Gdns. Lennox .. 78 A4
Craigmaddie Rd. Bish 58 A1
Craigmaddie
Terrace La. Glasg 96 C1
Craigmark Pl. Irvine 219 F3
Craigmarloch Ave. Lennox .. 78 A4
Craigmillar Ave. Miln 55 D2
Craigmillar Pl. Sten 23 E2
Craigmillar Rd. Glasg 137 D4
Craigmochan Ave. Aird 102 C1
Craigmont Dr. Glasg 96 C3
Craigmont St. Glasg 96 C3
Craigmore Rd. Bear 75 D4
Craigmore St. Glasg 118 B3
Craigmore Wynd. Lark 185 D2
Craigmount Ave. Pais 133 E3
Craigmount St. Kirk 79 E4
Craigmuir Cres. Glasg 114 C3
Craigmuir Gdns. Udd 161 D3
Craigmuir Pl. Glasg 114 C3
Craigmuir Rd. Glasg 114 C3
Craigmuir Rd. Glasg 161 D3
Craigmuschat Rd. Gour 44 C4
Craignaw Pl. Irvine 220 A1
Craigneil Dr. Pres 236 B4
Craigneil St. Glasg 99 F1
Craigneith Cres. Ash 200 B2
Craigneithan Rd. Car 187 F2
Craigneithan Rd. Newt M 157 D2
Craigneuk Ave. Aird 123 E3
Craigneuk St. Mother 164 B3
Craignethan Rd. Glasg 138 A2
Craigomus Cres. Men 3 F3
Craigpark Ave. Pres 236 A4
Craigpark Dr. Glasg 118 A4
Craigpark. Glasg 118 A4
Craigpark St. Dunt 74 A3
Craigpark Way. Tan 141 D4
Craigs Ave. Dunt 74 B3
Craigs Pl. Salt 217 D4
Craigs The. Green 45 E4
Craigsdow Rd. Troon 229 F3
Craigsheen Ave. E Kil 158 B4
Craigsliel Pl. Ayr 238 B2
Craigside Ct. Cumb 81 F4
Craigside Rd. Cumb 81 F4
Craigskeen Pl. Pres 236 B3
Craigson Pl. Aird 123 F3
Craigspark. Aird 205 E2
Craigstewart Cres. Ayr 238 B1
Craigston Ave. Ayr 239 E3
Craigston Dr. John 111 F1
Craigston Rd. John 111 F1
Craigstone View. Kils 60 C4
Craigthornhill Rd. Glasg 198 A3
Craigton Ave. Barr 134 C1
Craigton Ave. Miln 54 C1
Craigton Cotts. Miln 54 B1
Craigton Cres. Alva 4 C3
Craigton Cres. Newt M 156 A3
Craigton Dr. Barr 134 C1
Craigton Dr. Glasg 115 E5
Craigton Pl. Glasg 115 F3
Craigton Pl. Udd 140 B1
Craigton Rd. Glasg 115 F4
Craigton Rd. Kilb 170 C3

Craigton Rd. Miln 54 C2
Craigton Rd. Newt M 155 D2
Craigton St. Dunt 74 B4
Craigvicar Gdns. Glasg 119 E2
Craigview Ave. John 111 F1
Craigview. N Sau 5 E1
Craigview Rd. Mother 163 F4
Craigview Terr. John 111 E1
Craigwell. All 10 A3
Craigwell Pl. Ayr 238 C4
Craigwell Rd. Ayr 238 C4
Craigwell Ave. Glasg 138 B3
Craiksland Pl. Troon 230 A2
Crail St. Glasg 118 B3
Cramalt Ct. Irvine 220 A2
Crammond Ave. Coat 121 E2
Cramond Ave. Ren 94 C1
Cramond Ct. Falk 42 A1
Cramond Pl. Irvine 219 F1
Cramond St. Glasg 117 F1
Cramond Terr. Glasg 119 D3
Cramond Way. Irvine 219 F1
Cranberry Moss Rd. Kilw ... 207 E1
Cranberry Moss Rd. Kilw ... 207 E2
Cranberry Pl. Kilw 207 D1
Cranbrooke Dr. Glasg 96 B4
Crandleyhill Rd. Pres 236 A3
Cranesbill Ct. Ayr 239 D2
Cranmog Dr. Dumb 50 C1
Cranmog Way. Kilw 207 E2
Cranston St. Glasg 116 C4
Cranworth La. Glasg 96 B2
Cranworth St. Glasg 96 B2
Crarae Ave. Bear 75 F1
Crathes Ave. Sten 24 A2
Crathes Ct. Glasg 136 C2
Crathie Ct. Car 187 F2
Crathie Dr. Duni 21 E2
Crathie Dr. Glasg 96 A1
Crathie Dr. Glenm 102 C2
Crathie Dr. Salt 205 E1
Crathie Quadrant. Wish 165 D3
Crathie Rd. Kilmk 222 C1
Crauford Ave. W Kil 190 C2
Craufurd Cres. Beith 150 A2
Craufurdland Rd. Kilmk 223 D3
Craven Gr. Irvine 219 F3
Craw Pl. Loch 129 E1
Craw Rd. Pais 113 E2
Crawberry Rd. Green 46 A1
Crawford Ave. Kilm 79 F2
Crawford Ave. Pres 236 B3
Crawford Cres. Udd 140 B1
Crawford Cres. Udd 140 C4
Crawford Dr. E Kil 160 A2
Crawford Dr. Glasg 75 D1
Crawford Dr. Helen 16 C2
Crawford Gdns. Mother 163 E3
Crawford Hill. E Kil 160 A1
Crawford Rd. Hous 91 E1
Crawford Rd. Miln 54 C2
Crawford Rd. Air 14 B2
Crawford St. Glasg 96 A1
Crawford St. Ham 162 A3
Crawford St. Mother 163 E3
Crawford St. P Glasg 47 E1
Crawford Ave. Glasg 138 A3
Crawford Dr. Pais 113 D3
Crawford Gdns. Glasg 138 B2
Crawford St. Green 45 F3
Crawfordland Pl. Cross 221 E1
Crawfurds View. Loch 129 E2
Crawhin Gdns. Green 45 E2
Crawriggs Ave. Kirk 79 E3
Creamery Rd. Wish 165 E5
Crebar Dr. Barr 134 B1
Crebar St. Glasg 135 F2
Credon Dr. Aird 123 D2
Credon Dr. Cross 226 C4
Credon Gdns. Glasg 138 B2
Cree Ave. Bish 78 A2
Cree Gdns. Glasg 118 C3
Cree Pl. E Kil 159 D1
Creebank Pl. Troon 229 F3
Creelshaugh Rd. Fen 213 D2
Creighton Gr. E Kil 159 F1
Creighton Ct. Kilmk 223 D3
Creinch Dr. Bonh 19 F1
Creran Ct. Ham 162 A1
Creran Ct. Pres 236 B3
Creran Dr. Bank 39 E3
Creran Dr. Ren 94 A2
Creran Path. New 165 F3
Crescent Dr. Glasg 95 D3
Crescent St. Green 46 A2
Crescent The. Clyde 73 D4
Crescent The. Bear 54 B1
Crescent The. Stew 195 F1
Crescent The. Thorn 158 A3
Cresswell La. Glasg 96 B2
Cresswell St. Glasg 96 B2
Crest Ave. Glasg 95 D4
Crestlea Ave. Pais 133 F4
Creveul Ct. Alex 27 F3
Crichton Ave. Dalry 191 D4

Crichton Ct. Glasg 137 F1
Crichton St. Coat 122 A4
Crichton St. Glasg 97 F2
Crickefield La. Hous 91 E2
Criffel Pl. Holy 143 E2
Criffel Pl. Kilmk 228 A2
Criffell Gdns. Glasg 119 E2
Criffell Rd. Glasg 119 E2
Crimea St. Glasg 117 D4
Crimond Pl. Kils 36 A1
Crimond Pl. Shi 66 C4
Crinan Cres. Coat 101 E5
Crinan Gdns. Bish 78 B1
Crinan Pl. Coat 205 E3
Crinan Pl. Coat 101 E1
Crinan Pl. Hat 142 A2
Crinan Rd. Bish 78 B1
Crinan St. Glasg 118 A4
Crindledyke Cres. New 166 A3
Cringate Gdns. Bear 75 F1
Cripps Ave. Clyde 74 B1
Crisswell Cl. Gour 44 B1
Crissvell Cres. Gour 44 B1
Crocus Bank. Ayr 239 D2
Crocus Gr. Irvine 219 E2
Croe Pl. Kilmk 228 A2
Croft. Lark 184 C1
Croft Pl. Lark 184 C2
Croft Rd. Bish 77 F4
Croft Rd. E Kil 180 C4
Croft Rd. Glasg 139 D3
Croft Rd. Lark 184 C2
Croft St. Bonh 27 F2
Croft St. Kilmk 222 C1
Croft Terr. Spring 220 C1
Croft Wynd. Udd 141 D3
Croft's Rd. Tull 4 A2
Croftbank Ave. Udd 141 D1
Croftbank Cres. Udd 140 C3
Croftbank Cres. Udd 141 D1
Croftbank St. Glasg 97 F2
Croftburn Dr. Glasg 137 E2
Croftcot Ave. Hat 141 F2
Croftcroighn Rd. Glasg 99 D1
Croftend Ave. Glasg 137 F3
Croftend La. Glasg 137 F3
Croftfoot Cres. Glasg 138 A2
Croftfoot Dr. Glasg 137 F2
Croftfoot Pl. Duni 21 E2
Croftfoot Quadrant. Glasg .. 137 F2
Croftfoot Rd. Glasg 137 E2
Croftfoot St. Glasg 138 A2
Croftfoot Terr. Glasg 137 F2
Crofthead Ave. Kilmk 223 D3
Crofthead Cotts. Neil 154 B4
Crofthead Cres. Hat 141 F2
Crofthead Ct. Irvine 220 A1
Crofthead Dr. Lennox 33 E1
Crofthead. Irvine 220 A2
Crofthead Pl. Hat 141 F2
Crofthead Pl. Newt M 156 C2
Crofthead Rd. Ayr 239 E3
Crofthead Rd. Prem 233 E1
Crofthead St. Udd 140 C3
Crofthill Ave. Udd 140 C3
Crofthill Rd. Glasg 137 F3
Crofthouse Dr. Glasg 137 F2
Croftmont Ave. Glasg 137 F2
Croftmoraig Ave. Muir 81 D2
Crofton Ave. Glasg 137 E2
Croftpark Ave. Glasg 137 E3
Croftpark Cres. Ham 161 F3
Croftpark Rd. Dunt 74 A4
Croftpark St. Hat 142 A3
Croftshaw Rd. Alva 5 D4
Croftside Ave. Glasg 137 F2
Croftspar Ave. Glasg 119 E3
Croftspar Dr. Glasg 119 E3
Croftspar Pl. Glasg 119 E3
Croftwood Ave. Glasg 137 E2
Croftwood. Bish 78 A2
Croftwood Rd. Ham 162 B3
Crogal Cres. Chap 123 E1
Cromalt Cres. Bear 75 E4
Cromarty Ave. Bish 78 B1
Cromarty Ave. Glasg 136 C3
Cromarty Cres. Bear 75 F4
Cromarty Gdns. Glasg 137 D1
Cromarty Pl. E Kil 160 B2
Cromarty Pl. Muir 80 C2
Cromarty Rd. Aird 122 C3
Crombie Gdns. Glasg 120 A2
Cromdale Rd. Kilmk 228 A2
Cromdale Rd. P Glasg 69 D3
Cromdale St. Glasg 115 F3
Cromer Gdns. Glasg 96 C3
Cromer St. Glasg 96 C3
Cromer Way. Pais 113 E4
Crompton Ave. Glasg 137 D3
Crompton Way. Irvine 219 F2
Cromwell Rd. Ayr 235 F1
Cromwell Rd. Falk 42 B2
Cromwell Rd W. Falk 42 B2

Cromwell St. Glasg 97 D3
Crona Dr. Ham 161 F2
Cronberry Quadrant. Glasg 114 C2
Cronberry Terr. Glasg 114 C2
Cronin Pl. Hat 142 A4
Cronulla Pl. Kils 60 C4
Crookedshields Rd. E Kil ... 160 A4
Crookfur Cottage
Homes. Newt M 156 B3
Crookfur Rd. Newt M 156 B3
Crookston Ct. Glasg 115 D2
Crookston Ct. Glasg 114 C2
Crookston Dr. Glasg 114 C2
Crookston Gdns. Glasg 114 C2
Crookston Gr. Glasg 115 D2
Crookston Path. Glasg 114 C2
Crookston Pl. Glasg 114 C2
Crookston Quadrant. Glasg 115 D2
Crookston Rd. Glasg 135 D4
Crookston Terr. Glasg 115 D2
Crookstonhill Path. Glasg ... 114 C2
Crophill. N Sau 5 E1
Crosbie Ct. Troon 232 B4
Crosbie Dr. Pais 132 C4
Crosbie Dr. W Kil 190 B2
Crosbie La. Glasg 96 B4
Crosbie Pl. Troon 232 C4
Crosbie St. Glasg 96 B4
Crosbie Terr. Pres 236 B4
Crosbie Wood. Pais 113 D1
Cross Arthurlie St. Barr 134 A2
Cross. Beith 171 D4
Cross Brae. Shi 66 B3
Cross Gates. Hat 142 A2
Cross Key's La. Lan 215 D2
Cross Rd. Pais 113 D2
Cross Shore St. Green 46 A3
Cross St. Falk 24 A1
Cross St. Glasg 119 E1
Cross St. Pais 113 E2
Cross The. Dalry 191 E4
Cross The. Glasg 117 E3
Cross The. Kilmk 227 F4
Cross The. Pres 233 E1
Cross The. Stew 211 E4
Cross The. Stone 198 C1
Crossart St. Sals 125 D1
Crossbank Ave. Glasg 117 F1
Crossbank Dr. Glasg 117 E1
Crossbank Rd. Glasg 117 E1
Crossbank Terr. Glasg 117 E1
Crossburn Ave. Miln 54 C1
Crossburn. Ayr 238 A1
Crossburn La. Troon 230 A2
Crossburn La. Troon 230 A2
Crossclyde View. Car 201 E1
Crossdene Rd. Cross 226 C4
Crossdykes. Kirk 80 A4
Crossen La. Car 188 A1
Crossflat Cres. Pais 114 A3
Crossford Dr. Glasg 76 C1
Crossgate. Kirk 58 B1
Crossgates Ave. Cle 144 A2
Crossgates. Bishop 72 A2
Crossgates St. Lark 184 C2
Crosshill Ave. Glasg 117 D1
Crosshill Ave. Kirk 79 E3
Crosshill Dr. Cle 144 A2
Crosshill Dr. Glasg 138 A3
Crosshill Pl. P Glasg 68 C3
Crosshill Rd. Bish 78 C3
Crosshill Rd. Bish 78 B1
Crosshill Rd. P Glasg 68 C3
Crosshill Rd. P Glasg 68 C3
Crosshill St. Aird 122 C3
Crosshill St. Coat 121 D2
Crosshill St. Lennox 33 E1
Crosshill St. Mother 163 F3
Crosshouse Rd. E Kil 180 A3
Crosshouse Rd. Kilm 222 A3
Crosshouse Rd. Lennox 33 D2
Crossing La. Ash 200 A2
Crosslaw Ave. Lan 215 D2
Crosslaw Ave. Lan 215 D2
Crosslee Cres. Hous 91 E1
Crosslee Pk. Hous 111 E4
Crosslee Rd. B of W 111 D4
Crosslee St. Glasg 115 E3
Crosslees Dr. Glasg 135 F2
Crosslees Pk. Glasg 135 F2
Crosslees Rd. Glasg 135 F1
Crosslet Ave. Dumb 50 B2
Crosslet Rd. Dumb 50 B2
Crosslet Rd. Dumb 50 A2
Crossloan Rd. Glasg 115 F4
Crossloan Terr. Glasg 115 F3
Crossmill Ave. Barr 134 B2
Crossmyloof Gdns. Glasg . 116 B1
Crosspoint Dr. Glasg 76 C1
Crossroads. Beith 170 B2
Crossroads. Beith 170 B2
Crosstobs Rd. Glasg 115 D1
Crossveggate. Miln 55 D1
Crossview Ave. Glasg 119 E3
Crossview Pl. Glasg 119 E3
Crossways. Hous 91 E1
Crosveggate. Miln 55 D1
Crovie Rd. Glasg 135 D4

Crow Ave. Holy 143 D3
Crow Av. Glasg 95 F3
Crow Rd. Glasg 96 A1
Crow Rd. Lennox 33 D3
Crow Rd. Stone 198 C1
Crow Wood Rd. Muir 100 A4
Crow Wood Terr. Muir 100 A4
Crow-Wood Cres. Calder .. 123 D1
Crow-Wood Rd. Calder ... 123 D1
Crowfall View. Tan 121 E1
Crowflats Rd. Udd 140 C3
Crowhill Cres. Aird 102 C1
Crowhill Rd. Bish 97 F4
Crowhill St. Glasg 97 F3
Crowlin Cres. Glasg 119 D4
Crown Ave. Clyde 74 A2
Crown Cir. Glasg 96 B2
Crown Gdns. Al 9 F4
Crown Gdns. Glasg 96 B2
Crown Rd N. Glasg 96 B2
Crown Rd S. Glasg 96 B2
Crown St. Ayr 235 F1
Crown St. Calder 123 D2
Crown St. Coat 122 B4
Crown St. Glasg 117 E2
Crown St. Glasg 117 D3
Crown St. Glasg 119 F2
Crown St. Green 45 F3
Crown Terr. Glasg 96 B2
Crownest Loan. Lar 23 F1
Crownpoint Rd. Glasg 117 F3
Crowwood Dr. Aird 123 E4
Croy Ave. Newt M 157 D3
Croy. E Kil 159 E2
Croy Pl. Glasg 98 B3
Croy Rd. Coat 121 F2
Croy Rd. Glasg 98 B3
Cruachan Ave. Ren 94 B1
Cruachan Ave. Stir 2 A2
Cruachan Dr. Barr 134 B3
Cruachan Dr. Shi 66 A4
Cruachan Pl. Kilmk 228 A2
Cruachan Rd. Bear 75 D4
Cruachan Rd. Glasg 138 B2
Cruachan St. Glasg 135 F3
Cruachan Way. Barr 134 B3
Cruden St. Glasg 115 F3
Cruickshank Dr. Shi 66 A4
Cruickshank's Ct. Den 21 F1
Crum Ave. Glasg 136 A2
Crum Cres. Stir 7 E2
Crummock Gdns. Beith 150 B1
Crummock St. Beith 150 B1
Crusader Cres. Stew 211 E4
Cubie St. Glasg 117 F3
Cubrieshaw Dr. W Kil 190 B2
Cubrieshaw St. W Kil 190 B3
Cuckoo Way. Holy 143 D3
Cuilen La. Car 188 A1
Cuilhill Rd. Coat 121 D4
Cuillin Ct. Falk 42 B1
Cuillin Pl. Irvine 220 A2
Cuillin Pl. Kilmk 228 A2
Cuillin Way. Barr 134 B3
Cuillins The. Muir 81 D2
Cuillins The. Udd 123 D1
Cuilmuir Terr. Kils 60 C2
Cuilmuir View. Kils 60 C2
Cuilt Rd. Strath 30 B2
Cuilts Rd. Strath 30 A2
Culbin Dr. Glasg 94 D4
Culbin Dr. Glasg 95 D4
Culcreuch Ave. Bank 39 D3
Culcreuch Ct. Bank 39 D3
Culcreuch. Ersk 73 D2
Cullen La. E Kil 180 C4
Cullen Pl. Tan 141 D4
Cullen Rd. E Kil 180 B4
Cullen Rd. Mother 163 B3
Cullen St. Alex 27 F4
Cullen St. Glasg 119 D2
Cullins Rd. Glasg 139 D2
Cullion Way. Holy 144 A3
Culloch Rd. Bear 75 E4
Culloch Rd. Slam 123 D1
Cullochrig Rd. Glenm 82 C1
Culloden Pl. Kilmk 223 D3
Culmuir Pl. Sten 24 A3
Culross Hill. E Kil 159 E1
Culross Pl. Coat 122 C4
Culross Pl. E Kil 159 E1
Culross St. Glasg 118 B3
Culross Way. Muir 81 D2
Cult Rd. Kirk 79 F2
Cultenhove Cres. Stir 7 D1
Cultenhove Pl. Stir 7 D2
Cultenhove Rd. Stir 7 D2
Culterfell Path. Cle 144 A1
Cults St. Glasg 115 F3
Culvain Ave. Bear 75 D4
Culzean Ave. Coat 121 F2
Culzean Ave. Pres 236 B4
Culzean Cres. Glasg 120 A2

255
Culzean Cres. Kilmk Dewar Wlk. Car

Culzean Cres. Kilmk 228 B4
Culzean Cres. Newt M 157 D2
Culzean Dr. E Kil 159 E2
Culzean Dr. Glasg 119 E2
Culzean Dr. Gour 43 F3
Culzean. Glenm 102 C3
Culzean Pl. E Kil 159 E2
Culzean Pl. Kilw 207 E1
Culzean Pl. Sten 23 F2
Culzean Rd. Ayr 238 B2
Cumberland Arc. Glasg 117 E2
Cumberland Ave. Helen 16 A2
Cumberland Pl. Coat 121 E2
Cumberland Pl. Glasg 117 E2
Cumberland Rd. Gour 44 C2
Cumberland Rd. Rhu 15 E3
Cumberland St. Glasg 117 D3
Cumberland St. Glasg 117 E2
Cumberland Terr. Rhu 15 E3
Cumberland Wlk. Gour 44 C2
Cumbernauld Rd. Bank 39 D2
Cumbernauld Rd. Cumb 81 E2
Cumbernauld Rd. Glasg 118 B4
Cumbernauld Rd. Muir 81 D2
Cumbernauld Rd. Muir 100 B4
Cumbernauld Rd. Stepps 99 E3
Cumbrae Ave. P Glasg 69 D4
Cumbrae Cres. Aird 122 C3
Cumbrae Cres N. Dumb 49 E3
Cumbrae Cres S. Dumb 49 E3
Cumbrae Ct. Clyde 74 A1
Cumbrae Ct. Green 45 D3
Cumbrae Ct. Irvine 225 E4
Cumbrae Dr. Falk 41 E2
Cumbrae Dr. Kilmk 223 D3
Cumbrae Dr. Mother 163 E4
Cumbrae. E Kil 160 B1
Cumbrae House. Pres 236 A3
Cumbrae Pl. Aird 122 C2
Cumbrae Pl. Gour 44 B3
Cumbrae Pl. W Kil 190 B2
Cumbrae Rd. Pais 133 F4
Cumbrae Rd. Ren 94 B1
Cumbrae Rd. Salt 205 F1
Cumbrae St. Glasg 119 D4
Cumlodden Dr. Glasg 96 B4
Cumming Dr. Glasg 137 D4
Cumnock Dr. Barr 134 B1
Cumnock Dr. Ham 161 E1
Cumnock Rd. Glasg 98 C3
Cumroch Rd. Lennox 33 E1
Cunard St. Clyde 94 A4
Cuninghame Dr. Salt 206 A1
Cuninghame Rd. Ard 205 E2
Cuninghame Rd. Kilbar 111 D2
Cuninghame Rd. Salt 217 D4
Cunning Park Dr. Ayr 238 B2
Cunningair Dr. Mother 163 F2
Cunningham Cres. Ayr 239 E3
Cunningham Dr. Dunt 73 F3
Cunningham Dr. East 127 E3
Cunningham Dr. Glasg 136 C2
Cunningham Gdns. Falk 42 C3
Cunningham Pl. Ayr 239 E3
Cunningham Rd. Glasg 114 C4
Cunningham Rd. Sten 24 A2
Cunningham Rd. Stir 7 E4
Cunningham St. Mother 163 E3
Cunningham Watt Rd. Stew 195 E1
Cunninghame Dr. Kilmk 227 F2
Cunninghame Rd. E Kil 159 F1
Cunninghame Rd. Glasg 138 B4
Cunninghame Rd. Irvine 224 A4
Cunninghame Rd. Pres 236 B4
Cupar Dr. Green 44 C2
Cuparhead Ave. Coat 121 F2
Cuppleton Brae. How 130 A1
Curfew Rd. Glasg 75 E1
Curle St. Glasg 95 E1
Curlew Cres. Green 45 D2
Curlew La. Green 45 D2
Curlew Pl. John 131 E4
Curling Cres. Glasg 137 E4
Curlinghaugh Cres. Wish 165 E2
Curlingmire. E Kil 180 C4
Curran Ave. Wish 164 C1
Currie Ct. Ard 205 E1
Currie St. Glasg 96 C3
Currieside Ave. Shot 146 C2
Currieside Pl. Shot 146 B2
Curtecan Pl. Ayr 238 C3
Curtis Ave. Glasg 137 E4
Curzon St. Glasg 96 C3
Cushenquarter Dr. Plea 12 B2
Customhouse Pl. Green 46 A3
Custonhall Pl. Den 21 E1
Cuthbert Pl. Kilmk 223 D1
Cuthbert St. Tan 141 D4
Cuthbertson St. Glasg 117 D1
Cuthelton Dr. Glasg 118 C2
Cuthelton St. Glasg 118 B2
Cuthelton Terr. Glasg 118 B2
Cutsburn Pl. Stew 211 F4
Cutsburn Rd. Stew 211 F4
Cutstraw Rd. Stew 211 F4
Cuttyfield Pl. Sten 24 B2
Cypress Ave. Beith 150 B1
Cypress Ave. Tan 141 D4
Cypress Ave. Udd 140 B1
Cypress Cres. E Kil 180 B3
Cypress Ct. E Kil 180 B3
Cypress Ct. Ham 162 C1
Cypress Ct. Kirk 79 D3
Cypress Gdns. Irvine 219 F3
Cypress Pl. E Kil 180 B3
Cypress St. Glasg 97 E3
Cyprus Ave. John 112 A1
Cyril St. Pais 114 A2

Daer Ave. Ren 94 C1
Daer Way. Ham 162 A2
Daer Wlk. Lark 199 D4
Daffodil Way. Mother 163 F4
Dairsie Gdns. Bish 98 B4
Dairsie St. Glasg 136 C2
Daisy Cotts. Ayr 236 A2
Daisy St. Glasg 117 D1
Daisybank. Beith 170 B3
Dakota Way. Ren 94 B1
Dalbeth Pl. Glasg 118 C1
Dalbeth Rd. Glasg 118 C1
Dalblair Arc. Ayr 238 C4
Dalblair Rd. Ayr 238 C4
Dalcharn Pl. Glasg 120 A4
Dalcross St. Glasg 96 B1
Dalcruin Gdns. Muir 81 D2
Dalderse Ave. Falk 42 A3
Daldowie Ave. Glasg 119 E2
Daldowie Rd. Glasg 120 A1
Daldowie St. Coat 121 F2
Dale Ave. E Kil 180 B3
Dale Cres. Irvine 219 E2
Dale Ct. Wish 164 B1
Dale Dr. Holy 143 D2
Dale St. Glasg 117 F2
Dale St. Glasg 118 A2
Dale Way. Glasg 138 A2
Daleview Ave. Glasg 96 A3
Daleview Dr. Newt M 157 E3
Daleview Gr. Newt M 157 E3
Dalfoil Ct. Glasg 114 C2
Dalgain Ct. Irvine 220 A3
Dalgarroch Ave. Clyde 94 C4
Dalgleish Ave. Dunt 73 F3
Dalgleish Ct. Stir 7 D4
Dalgraig Cres. Udd 140 B1
Dalhousie Gdns. Bish 78 A1
Dalhousie La. Glasg 97 D1
Dalhousie Rd. Kilbar 111 D1
Dalhousie St. Glasg 97 D1
Dalilea Dr. Glasg 100 B1
Dalilea Path. Glasg 100 B1
Dalilea Pl. Glasg 100 B1
Dalintober St. Glasg 117 D3
Daljarrock. Kilw 207 D1
Dalkeith Ave. Bish 78 A2
Dalkeith Ave. Glasg 116 A2
Dalkeith Rd. Bish 78 A2
Dallas Ct. Troon 229 E1
Dallas La. Troon 229 E1
Dallas Pl. Troon 229 E1
Dallas Rd. Troon 229 E1
Dalmacoulter Rd. Aird 103 D2
Dalmahoy Cres. B of W 110 B3
Dalmahoy St. Glasg 118 C4
Dalmahoy Way. Kilw 207 D2
Dalmailing Ave. Irvine 220 A1
Dalmailington Ave. Irvine 220 A1
Dalmally St. Glasg 96 C2
Dalmally St. Green 46 C1
Dalmarnock Ct. Glasg 118 A2
Dalmarnock Rd. Glasg 118 A1
Dalmary Dr. Pais 114 A3
Dalmellington Ct. Ham 161 E1
Dalmellington Rd. Ayr 239 E2
Dalmeny Ave. Glasg 136 B2
Dalmeny Dr. Barr 134 A1
Dalmeny Rd. Ham 162 B1
Dalmeny St. Glasg 117 F1
Dalmilling Cres. Ayr 236 B1
Dalmilling Dr. Ayr 236 C1
Dalmilling Rd. Ayr 236 C1
Dalmoak Rd. Green 46 B1
Dalmonach Rd. Bonh 27 F2
Dalmore Cres. Helen 16 A2
Dalmore Dr. Alva 4 C3
Dalmore Pl. Irvine 219 F3
Dalmore Way. Irvine 219 F3
Dalmorglen Pk. Stir 6 C3
Dalnair Pl. Miln 54 B1
Dalnair St. Glasg 96 B1
Dalness St. Glasg 119 D2
Dalnottar Ave. O Kill 73 D3
Dalnottar Dr. O Kill 73 D3
Dalnottar Gdns. O Kill 73 D3
Dalnottar Hill Rd. O Kill 73 D3
Dalnottar Terr. O Kill 73 D3
Dalreoch Ave. Glasg 120 B3
Dalreoch Ct. Dumb 49 E2
Dalreoch Path. Glasg 120 B3
Dalriada Cres. Mother 142 B1
Dalriada Dr. Lennox 78 B4
Dalriada Rd. Gour 44 B2
Dalriada St. Glasg 118 B2
Dalry Gdns. Ham 161 E1
Dalry La. Ard 205 E2
Dalry Rd. Ard 205 E2
Dalry Rd. Beith 171 D4
Dalry Rd. Kilb 170 A4
Dalry Rd. Kilw 207 E2
Dalry Rd. Salt 206 A1
Dalry Rd. Stew 195 E1
Dalry Rd. Tan 141 D4
Dalry St. Glasg 119 D2
Dalrymple Ct. Irvine 219 F2
Dalrymple Dr. E Kil 159 F1
Dalrymple Dr. Irvine 219 F2
Dalrymple Dr. Newt M 157 D2
Dalrymple Pl. Irvine 219 E2
Dalrymple St. Green 45 F3
Dalrymple St. Green 46 A3
Dalserf Cres. Glasg 136 A1
Dalserf Path. Lark 185 E1
Dalserf St. Glasg 118 A3
Dalsetter Ave. Glasg 75 D1
Dalsetter Pl. Glasg 75 D1
Dalshannon Pl. Cumb 82 A4
Dalshannon Rd. Cumb 82 A4
Dalshannon View. Cumb 82 A4
Dalshannon Way. Cumb 82 A4
Dalsholm Rd. Glasg 96 A4
Dalskeith Ave. Pais 113 D3
Dalskeith Cres. Pais 113 D3
Dalskeith Rd. Pais 113 D3
Dalswinton St. Glasg 120 B4
Dalton Ave. Clyde 74 C1
Dalton Hill. Ham 161 F1
Dalton St. Glasg 118 C3
Dalvait Gdns. Bonh 27 F4
Dalvait Rd. Bonh 27 F4
Dalveen Ct. Barr 134 B1
Dalveen Dr. Tan 140 C4
Dalveen Quadrant. Aird 122 B3
Dalveen St. Glasg 118 C3
Dalveen Way. Glasg 138 B2
Dalwhinnie Ave. Udd 140 B1
Dalwood Rd. Pres 236 A4
Daly Gdns. Udd 140 C1
Dalzell Ave. Mother 164 A2
Dalzell Dr. Mother 164 A2
Dalziel Dr. Glasg 116 B2
Dalziel Rd. Glasg 114 C4
Dalziel St. Ham 162 A3
Dalziel St. Mother 163 F4
Damhead Rd. Kilmk 227 F2
Dampark. Dunlop 195 E4
Damshot Cres. Glasg 115 E1
Damshot Rd. Glasg 135 E4
Damside. Ayr 235 F1
Danby Rd. Glasg 119 F2
Danes Cres. Glasg 95 D3
Danes Dr. Glasg 95 E2
Danes La N. Glasg 95 E2
Danes La S. Glasg 95 E2
Daniel McLaughlin Pl. Kirk 58 C1
Dankeith Dr. Sym 231 E2
Dankeith Rd. Sym 231 E2
Darg Rd. Steven 217 E4
Dargarvel Ave. Glasg 116 A2
Dargavel Ave. Bishop 72 A2
Dargavel Rd. Bishop 72 B4
Dargavel Rd. Ersk 72 C1
Dark Brig Rd. Cro 201 D1
Darkwood Cres. Pais 113 D3
Darkwood Dr. Pais 113 D3
Darleith Rd. Card 26 A1
Darleith St. Glasg 118 C3
Darley Cres. Troon 229 E1
Darley Pl. Ham 183 D4
Darley Pl. Troon 229 E1
Darlington View. Stew 195 F1
Darluith Rd. Lin 111 F3
Darmeid Pl. Alla 167 D4
Darnaway Ave. Glasg 99 E1
Darnaway St. Glasg 99 E1
Darndaff Rd. Green 46 A1
Darngaber Gdns. Quart 183 F2
Darngaber Rd. Quart 183 F2
Darngavil Rd. Plains 103 F3
Darnick St. Glasg 98 A1
Darnley Cres. Bish 77 F2
Darnley Dr. Kilmk 227 F3
Darnley Gdns. Glasg 116 C1
Darnley Path. Glasg 135 F3
Darnley Pl. Glasg 116 C1
Darnley Rd. Barr 134 C2
Darnley Rd. Glasg 116 C1
Darnley St. Glasg 116 C2
Darnley St. Stir 7 D4
Darnshaw Cl. Irvine 220 B3
Darrach Dr. Duni 21 D1
Darroch Ave. Gour 44 C4
Darroch Dr. Ersk 72 C2
Darroch Dr. Gour 44 C4
Darroch Way. Cumb 62 A2
Dartford St. Glasg 97 D2
Dartmouth Ave. Gour 44 C3
Darvel Cres. Pais 114 C2
Darvel Dr. Newt M 157 D3
Darvel St. Glasg 134 C3
Darwin Pl. Clyde 73 E2
Darwin Rd. E Kil 180 B4
Dava St. Glasg 116 A4
Davaar Dr. Coat 121 E4
Davaar Dr. Kilmk 223 D3
Davaar Dr. Mother 142 B1
Davaar Dr. Pais 133 F4
Davaar. E Kil 160 B1
Davaar Pl. Newt M 156 B3
Davaar Rd. Gour 44 B2
Davaar Rd. Ren 94 B1
Davaar Rd. Salt 205 F1
Davaar St. Glasg 118 A2
Davan Loan. New 165 F3
Davarr Pl. Falk 41 E2
Daventry Dr. Glasg 96 A3
Davey St. Green 45 E3
David Dale Ave. Stew 211 E4
David Gage St. Kilw 207 F3
David Orr St. Kilmk 222 C1
David Pl. Glasg 119 F2
David Pl. Pais 114 A4
David St. Coat 122 B4
David St. Glasg 118 A3
David St. Sals 125 D1
David Way. Pais 114 A4
David's Cres. Kilw 207 E1
David's Loan. Falk 24 B1
Davidson Ave. Beith 170 B3
Davidson Cres. Twe 59 F2
Davidson Dr. Gour 44 C4
Davidson Gdns. Glasg 95 F2
Davidson La. Car 188 A1
Davidson Pl. Ayr 236 A1
Davidson Pl. Glasg 119 E3
Davidson Quadrant. Dunt 73 F4
Davidson Rd. Bonh 27 F4
Davidson St. Aird 122 C4
Davidson St. Bann 7 E1
Davidson St. Clyde 94 C4
Davidson St. Coat 122 A2
Davidson St. Glasg 118 A2
Davidston Pl. Kirk 79 F2
Davieland Rd. Glasg 136 A1
Davies Quadrant. Mother 142 B1
Davington Dr. Ham 161 E1
Daviot St. Glasg 115 E3
Dawsholm Ind Est. Glasg 96 A4
Dawson Ave. All 9 F4
Dawson Ave. E Kil 159 D1
Dawson Pl. Glasg 97 D2
Dawson Rd. Glasg 97 D2
Dawson St. Falk 42 A4
De Morville Pl. Beith 171 D4
De Walden Terr. Kilmk 223 D1
Deacons Rd. Kils 60 C4
Dealston Rd. Barr 134 A2
Dean Cres. Ham 162 B1
Dean Cres. Muir 80 B1
Dean Cres. Stir 2 B1
Dean Ct. Kilmk 222 C1
Dean La. Kilmk 223 D1
Dean Park Ave. Udd 141 D1
Dean Park Dr. Glasg 139 E2
Dean Park Rd. Ren 94 C1
Dean Pl. Cross 226 C4
Dean Rd. Kilb 149 D1
Dean Rd. Kilmk 223 D2
Dean St. Clyde 74 B1
Dean St. Hat 142 A3
Dean St. Kilmk 223 D1
Dean St. Stew 195 F1
Dean Terr. Kilmk 223 D2
Deanbrae St. Udd 140 C3
Deanfield Quadrant. Glasg 114 C3
Deanhill La. Kilmk 223 D2
Deanpark Gdns. Ren 94 C2
Deans Ave. Glasg 139 E2
Deanside Rd. Glasg 115 D4
Deanston Dr. Glasg 136 C4
Deanwood Ave. Glasg 136 C2
Deanwood Rd. Glasg 136 C2
Deas Rd. Shot 146 B3
Dechmont Ave. Glasg 139 E2
Dechmont Ave. Mother 163 E4
Dechmont Cotts. Glasg 139 F2
Dechmont. E Kil 180 B3
Dechmont Gdns. Udd 140 B1
Dechmont Pl. Glasg 139 E2
Dechmont Rd. Tan 120 C1
Dechmont St. Glasg 118 B2
Dechmont St. Ham 162 B1
Dechmont View. Hat 141 F2
Dechmont View. Tan 141 D4
Dee Ave. Kilmk 228 A2
Dee Ave. Pais 112 C1
Dee Ave. Ren 94 C2
Dee Dr. Pais 112 C1
Dee Path. Holy 143 D3
Dee Path. Lark 199 D4
Dee Pl. E Kil 179 F3
Dee Pl. John 131 E4
Dee St. Coat 101 E1
Dee St. Glasg 118 B4
Dee St. Green 45 D3
Dee St. Shot 146 B3
Dee Terr. Ham 183 D4
Deedes St. Aird 122 B3
Deep Dale. E Kil 159 E2
Deepdene Rd. Bear 75 E1
Deepdene Rd. Muir 80 C1
Deer Park Ave. Steven 217 F4
Deer Park Ct. Ham 183 E4
Deer Park Pl. Ham 183 F4
Deerdykes Ct N. Cumb 81 F3
Deerdykes Ct S. Cumb 81 F3
Deerdykes Pl. Cumb 81 F3
Deerdykes Rd. Cumb 81 F3
Deerdykes View. Cumb 81 E3
Deerpark. N Sau 5 F1
Deeside Dr. Car 188 A2
Delfie Dr. Green 45 D2
Delhi Ave. Clyde 73 E2
Dell The. Hat 142 B2
Dellburn St. Mother 164 A3
Dellingburn St. Green 46 A2
Delny Pl. Glasg 119 F4
Delph Rd. Tull 4 B1
Delphwood Cres. Tull 4 B1
Delves Pk. Lan 215 D2
Delves Rd. Lan 215 D2
Delvin Rd. Glasg 137 D3
Dempsey Rd. Hat 141 F2
Dempster St. Green 45 F2
Den La. Shot 146 B3
Denbak Ave. Ham 162 A1
Denbeck St. Glasg 118 C3
Denbrae St. Glasg 118 C3
Denewood Ave. Pais 133 E4
Denham St. Glasg 97 D2
Denholm Cres. E Kil 180 C4
Denholm Dr. Glasg 136 B1
Denholm Dr. Wish 165 E3
Denholm Gdns. Green 45 E3
Denholm Gdns. Quart 183 F2
Denholm Gn. E Kil 180 C4
Denholm St. Green 45 E3
Denholm Terr. Green 45 E3
Denholm Terr. Ham 161 F2
Denholm Way. Beith 171 D4
Denmark St. Glasg 97 E2
Denmark St. Glasg 97 E3
Denmilne Gdns. Glasg 120 B4
Denmilne Path. Glasg 120 B4
Denmilne Rd. Glasg 120 B4
Denmilne St. Glasg 120 B4
Denniston Pl. Lan 215 E3
Dennistoun Cres. Helen 25 D4
Dennistoun Rd. Lang 70 B4
Dennistoun St. Hat 142 A3
Denny Rd. Bank 39 F3
Denny Rd. Lar 23 D1
Denny Way. Alex 27 E1
Dennyholm Wynd. Kilb 149 D1
Denovan Rd. Duni 21 F2
Denovan Rd. Tor 21 F2
Dentdale. E Kil 159 E2
Deramore Ave. Newt M 157 D4
Derby St. Glasg 116 C4
Derby Terrace La. Glasg 116 C4
Deroran Pl. Stir 6 C3
Derrywood Rd. M of C 58 B3
Dervaig Gdns. Gree 84 B2
Derwent Ave. Falk 41 F2
Derwent Dr. Coat 101 E1
Derwent St. Glasg 97 D2
Derwentwater. E Kil 179 F3
Despard Ave. Glasg 119 F2
Despard Gdns. Glasg 119 F2
Deveron Ave. Glasg 136 B1
Deveron Cres. Ham 161 F2
Deveron Rd. Bear 75 E1
Deveron Rd. E Kil 160 A1
Deveron Rd. Holy 143 D3
Deveron Rd. Kilmk 228 A3
Deveron Rd. Troon 229 F3
Deveron St. Coat 101 E1
Deveron St. Glasg 98 B1
Devilla Ct. Pres 236 B3
Devlin Gr. Udd 161 F4
Devol Ave. P Glasg 47 D1
Devol Cres. Glasg 135 D4
Devol Rd. Kil 68 B3
Devol Rd. P Glasg 68 B3
Devon Ct. Tull 4 A1
Devon Dr. Bishop 72 B2
Devon Dr. Men 4 C2
Devon Gdns. Bish 77 F2
Devon Gdns. Car 187 F1
Devon Pl. Camb 4 A1
Devon Pl. Glasg 117 D2
Devon Rd. All 10 B3
Devon Rd. Gour 44 B2
Devon St. Glasg 117 D2
Devon Village. Fish 5 F2
Devon Way. Mother 163 D3
Devonbank. Fish 5 F2
Devondale Ave. Udd 140 B1
Devonhill Ave. Ham 183 E4
Devonport Pk. E Kil 180 A4
Devonshire
Gardens La. Glasg 96 A2
Devonshire Terr. Glasg 96 A2
Devonshire
Terrace La. Glasg 96 A2
Devonview Pl. Aird 122 C3
Devonview St. Aird 122 C3
Devonway. Clack 10 C3
Dewar Cl. Tan 121 D1
Dewar Wlk. Car 201 D1

Dewshill Cotts. Sals

Dewshill Cotts. Sals 126 A2
Dhuhill Dr E. Helen 16 C2
Diamond St. Ham 142 A2
Diana Ave. Clap 95 D4
Diana Quadrant. Holy 143 D3
Diana Vernon Ct. Helen 25 C4
Dick Cres. Irvine 219 E3
Dick Ct. Stone 198 C1
Dick Quad. Card 48 A4
Dick Rd. Kilmrk 228 A4
Dick St. Glasg 96 C2
Dick Terr. Irvine 219 E3
Dickburn Cres. Bon 39 F3
Dickens Ave. Clyde 74 A2
Dickies Wells. Alva 5 E4
Dicks Pk. E Kil 180 B4
Dickson Dr. Irvine 219 E3
Dickson Sq. Cle 144 A1
Dickson St. Lark 185 D1
Diddup Dr. Salt 206 A1
Differ Ave. Twe 59 F1
Dillchip Terr. Bonh 27 F2
Dillichip Cl. Bonh 27 F1
Dillichip Gdns. Bonh 27 F2
Dillichip Loan. Bonh 27 F2
Dilwara Ave. Glasg 95 F1
Dimity St. John 111 F2
Dimsdale Cres. Wish 165 E1
Dimsdale Rd. Wish 165 E1
Dinard Dr. Glasg 136 B2
Dinart St. Glasg 98 B1
Dinduff St. Glasg 100 B1
Dingwall Dr. Gour 44 C2
Dinmont Ave. Pais 112 C1
Dinmont Cres. Mother 142 B1
Dinmont Pl. Glasg 116 C1
Dinmont Rd. Glasg 116 B1
Dinmont Way. Pais 112 C1
Dinmurchie Rd. Troon 229 F3
Dinnet Way. New 165 F3
Dinwiddie St. Glasg 98 B1
Dinyra Pl. Glen 101 E3
Dippin Pl. Salt 205 F1
Dipple Ct. Kilb 149 D1
Dipple Pl. Glasg 75 D1
Dipple Pl. Kilb 149 D1
Dipple View. Kilb 149 D2
Dirleton Dr. Glasg 136 C4
Dirleton Dr. Pais 113 D1
Dirleton Gate. Bear 75 E1
Dirleton Gdns. All 9 F4
Dirleton La. All 9 F3
Dirrans Terr. Kilw 207 F1
Ditton Dr. Kilmk 227 F4
Divernia Way. Barr 155 E4
Divernwell. N Sau 5 E1
Divert Rd. Gour 44 B3
Divert Wlk. Gour 44 B3
Dixon Ave. Dumb 49 E2
Dixon Ave. Glasg 117 D1
Dixon Dr. Dumb 49 E1
Dixon Pl. E Kil 159 D2
Dixon Rd. Glasg 117 E1
Dixon Rd. Helen 16 C2
Dixon St. Coat 122 A2
Dixon St. Glasg 117 D3
Dixon St. Ham 162 B2
Dixon St. Pais 113 F2
Dobbie Ave. Lar 23 E1
Dobbie's Loan. Glasg 97 F1
Dobbies Ct. Law 187 D3
Dochart Ave. Ren 94 C1
Dochart Dr. Coat 101 E1
Dochart Pl. Falk 42 B1
Dochart St. Glasg 98 C1
Dock Breast. Green 46 A3
Dock Rd. Aird 205 D1
Dock St. Clyde 94 B4
Dock St. Sten 24 B1
Dockhead Pl. Salt 216 C4
Dockhead St. Salt 216 C4
Dodhill Pl. Glasg 95 D3
Dodside Gdns. Glasg 119 E2
Dodside Pl. Glasg 119 E2
Dodside Rd. Newt M 155 F2
Dodside St. Glasg 119 E2
Dolan St. Glasg 120 A3
Dollar Ave. Falk 42 A4
Dollar Gdns. Falk 42 A4
Dollar Pk. Mother 164 A2
Dollar Pl. Glasg 96 B4
Dolphin Rd. Glasg 116 B1
Dominica Gn. E Kil 180 D1
Don Ave. Ren 94 C1
Don Ct. Ham 183 D4
Don Dr. Pais 112 C1
Don Path. Lark 199 D4
Don Pl. John 131 E4
Don St. Glasg 98 B1
Don St. Green 45 E3
Donald Cres. Troon 229 E3
Donald Terr. Ham 162 B1
Donald Way. Tan 141 A3
Donald's Ct. Green 46 A3
Donaldfield Rd. B of W 110 C4
Donaldson Ave. Kils 60 C4
Donaldson Ave. Salt 216 C4
Donaldson Ave. Steven 206 C1

Donaldson Cres. Klrk 79 E4
Donaldson Dr. Irvine 219 E3
Donaldson Dr. Ren 94 B2
Donaldson Pl. Aird 123 D4
Donaldson Pl. Cam 6 B3
Donaldson Pl. Klrk 79 E4
Donaldson Rd. Kilmk 223 E2
Donaldson Rd. Lark 185 E1
Donaldson St. Ham 162 A3
Donaldson St. Klrk 79 E4
Donaldswood Rd. Pais 133 E4
Doncaster St. Glasg 97 D2
Dongola Rd. Ayr 239 D4
Donnelly Way. Mother 164 B2
Donnies Brae. Neil 154 C4
Doo'cot Brae. All 10 A4
Doon Ave. Pres 236 A3
Doon Cres. Bear 75 E2
Doon Ct. Irvine 219 E1
Doon Pl. Kilmk 228 A2
Doon Pl. Kirk 58 C1
Doon Pl. Salt 206 A2
Doon Rd. Wish 231 E2
Doon Pl. Troon 229 F3
Doon Rd. Kirk 59 D1
Doon Side. Cumb 62 A1
Doon St. Clyde 74 B2
Doon St. Lark 185 E1
Doon St. Mother 164 A2
Doon Way. Kirk 59 D1
Doonfoot Rd. Ayr 238 C2
Doonfoot Rd. Glasg 136 B3
Doonholm Pl. Ayr 238 C1
Doonholm Rd. Ayr 238 C1
Dora St. Glasg 117 F3
Dorain Rd. Holy 143 E2
Dorchester Ave. Glasg 96 A3
Dorchester Ct. Glasg 96 A3
Dorchester Pl. Glasg 96 A3
Dorian Dr. Newt M 157 E4
Dorlin Rd. Stepps 99 F3
Dornal Ave. Glasg 115 E2
Dornal Ave. Clyde 94 C4
Dornie Dr. Troon 229 F3
Dornford Ave. Glasg 119 E1
Dornford Rd. Glasg 119 E1
Dornie Cl. Stew 195 E1
Dornie Dr. Glasg 139 D4
Dornie Path. New 166 B3
Dornie Wynd. Shot 147 D2
Dornoch Ave. Glasg 136 B4
Dornoch Pk. Ayr 238 C3
Dornoch Pl. Bish 78 B1
Dornoch Pl. E Kil 169 E1
Dornoch Pl. Muir 80 B1
Dornoch Rd. Bear 75 E1
Dornoch Rd. Holy 143 D3
Dornoch St. Glasg 117 F3
Dornoch Way. Aird 122 C2
Dornoch Way. Cumb 62 A3
Dornoch Way. Kirk 41 F1
Dorset Rd. Gour 44 C2
Dorset Sq. Glasg 116 C4
Dorset St. Glasg 116 C4
Dosk Ave. Glasg 94 C4
Dosk Pl. Glasg 94 C4
Double Edges Rd. Neil 154 B3
Dougalston Ave. Miln 55 D1
Dougalston Cres. Miln 55 D1
Dougalston Gdns N. Miln 55 D1
Dougalston Gdns S. Miln 55 D1
Dougalston Rd. Glasg 76 C1
Douglas Ave. Beith 191 E3
Douglas Ave. Glasg 119 D1
Douglas Ave. Glasg 96 B1
Douglas Ave. Glasg 138 B3
Douglas Ave. John 112 A1
Douglas Ave. Klrk 79 E3
Douglas Ave. Lang 70 B4
Douglas Cres. Aird 123 D3
Douglas Cres. Ersk 72 C2
Douglas Cres. Ham 183 E3
Douglas Cres. Tan 141 D4
Douglas Ct. Wish 181 D4
Douglas Dr. Troon 229 E3
Douglas Dr. Ash 199 F4
Douglas Dr E. Helen 16 C2
Douglas Dr. E Kil 179 F4
Douglas Dr. Glasg 119 E1
Douglas Dr. Glasg 138 C3
Douglas Dr. Ham 162 A3
Douglas Dr. Helen 16 B2
Douglas Dr. Newt M 156 C3
Douglas Dr. Steven 206 D1
Douglas Dr. Udd 141 D1
Douglas Gdns. Bear 75 F2
Douglas Gdns. Glasg 136 B1
Douglas Gdns. Klrk 79 E3
Douglas Gdns. Udd 140 C3
Douglas La. Glasg 42 C1
Douglas Muir Dr. Miln 54 B1
Douglas Muir Rd. Dunt 74 B4
Douglas Muir Rd. Miln 54 B1

Douglas Park Cres. Bear 76 A3
Douglas Park La. Ham 162 B2
Douglas Pl. Bear 75 F3
Douglas Pl. Coat 121 F3
Douglas Pl. Ham 183 E3
Douglas Pl. Klrk 79 E3
Douglas Pl. Sten 23 F2
Douglas Pl. Dumb 50 A2
Douglas Rd. Ren 114 A4
Douglas St. Aird 123 D3
Douglas St. Ayr 238 C4
Douglas St. Bann 7 F1
Douglas St. Blac 71 E1
Douglas St. Glasg 117 D4
Douglas St. Ham 162 B2
Douglas St. Kilmk 227 F4
Douglas St. Lark 185 D2
Douglas St. Miln 55 D1
Douglas St. Mother 163 E3
Douglas St. Pais 113 E3
Douglas St. Stir 2 A1
Douglas St. Tan 141 D4
Douglas St. Udd 161 E3
Douglas Terr. Glasg 116 B4
Douglas Terr. Inch 93 F1
Douglas Terr. Stir 6 C3
Douglas View. Coat 121 F2
Douglasdale. E Kil 159 F1
Douglehill Pl. P Glasg 68 B4
Douglehill Rd. P Glasg 68 A4
Douglehill Terr. P Glasg 68 B4
Dougray Pl. Barr 134 B1
Dougrie Dr. Glasg 137 F2
Dougrie Gdns. Glasg 137 F2
Dougrie Pl. Glasg 137 F2
Dougrie Rd. Glasg 137 E2
Dougrie St. Glasg 137 F2
Dougrie Terr. Glasg 137 E2
Doune Cres. Bish 78 A2
Doune Cres. Newt M 157 E4
Doune Cres. Sten 24 A2
Doune Gardens La. Glasg ... 96 C2
Doune Gdns. Glasg 96 C2
Doune Gdns. Gour 44 A3
Doune Quadrant. Glasg 96 C2
Doune Terr. Coat 101 E1
Doura Dr. Irvine 219 F3
Doura Pl. Irvine 219 E3
Dove Pl. E Kil 179 F3
Dove Wynd. Bell 141 F4
Dovecot. Glasg 136 B4
Dovecot La. Kilw 207 F2
Dovecot La. Lan 215 D2
Dovecot Pl. Tull 4 A2
Dovecot Rd. Tull 4 A2
Dovecote View. Kirk 79 F4
Dovecothall St. Barr 134 B2
Dovecotwood. Kils 36 B1
Dovehill. All 10 A4
Doveholm Ave. Dumb 50 A3
Doveholm. Dumb 50 A3
Dover St. Coat 101 E1
Dover St. Glasg 116 C4
Dowan Pl. Stir 6 C3
Dowan Rd. Bish 55 F1
Dowanfield Rd. Cumb 61 F2
Dowanhill St. Glasg 96 B1
Dowanside La. Glasg 96 B2
Dowanside Rd. Glasg 96 B2
Downcraig Dr. Glasg 137 E1
Downcraig Gr. Glasg 137 E1
Downcraig Terr. Glasg 137 E1
Downfield Dr. Ham 183 D4
Downfield Gdns. Udd 140 C1
Downfield St. Glasg 118 C2
Downhill St. Glasg 96 B1
Downie St. Ham 162 B1
Downiebrae Rd. Glasg 118 A1
Downs Cres. All 9 F3
Downs St. Glasg 97 F3
Downcraig St. Glasg 115 D1
Draffan Rd. Ash 200 A1
Draffan Rd. Cro 200 A1
Draffen St. Mother 163 F4
Draffen St. Mother 163 F4
Drake St. Glasg 117 F3
Drakemire Ave. Glasg 137 E2
Drakemire Dr. Glasg 137 E2
Dreghorn Rd. Shew 225 E3
Dreghorn St. Glasg 118 B4
Dresling Rd. Green 45 F2
Drimnin Rd. Stepps 80 A3
Drip Rd. Stir C1
Drive David Gray. Kirk 59 D1
Drive Rd. Glasg 115 F4
Drochil St. Glasg 100 A1
Drochmore St. Kirk 79 D4
Drossie Rd. Falk 42 A2
Drove Hill. Cumb 61 F3
Drove Loan. Bon 39 F3
Drove Loan Cres. Bank 39 F4
Drove Loan. Bon 39 F3
Druid Dr. Kilw 207 F2
Drum Mains Pk. Cumb 81 E4
Drumadoon Dr. Helen 16 C1
Drumalbing Terr. Lennox 57 F4
Drumbathie Rd. Aird 123 E4

Drumbeg Dr. Glasg 135 D3
Drumbeg Pl. Glasg 135 D3
Drumbeg Terr. Miln 54 B1
Drumbottie Rd. Glasg 98 A3
Drumbreck Pl. Klrk 79 F2
Drumbrock Rd. Miln 54 B1
Drumby Cres. Newt M 157 E4
Drumby Dr. Newt M 157 E4
Drumcarn Dr. Miln 54 C1
Drumcavel Rd. Muir 100 C4
Drumchapel Gdns. Glasg 75 D1
Drumchapel Pl. Glasg 75 D1
Drumchapel Rd. Glasg 75 D1
Drumchapel
Shopping Ctr. Glasg 74 C2
Drumclair Ave. Slam 86 A3
Drumclair Pl. Aird 123 E4
Drumclog Ave. Miln 55 D2
Drumclog Gdns. Glasg 98 A4
Drumclog Pl. Kilmk 223 D2
Drumcross Rd. Bishop 72 B2
Drumcross Rd. Glasg 115 E1
Drumduff. E Kil 180 B3
Drumellan Rd. Ayr 239 D1
Drumelzier Ct. Irvine 220 A2
Drumfin Ave. Caid 104 C2
Drumfork Ct. Helen 25 C4
Drumfork Rd. Helen 25 D4
Drumfrochar Pl. Green 45 F2
Drumfrochar Rd. Green 45 E2
Drumgarve Ct. Helen 16 B1
Drumgelloch St. Aird 123 E4
Drumgray Gdns. Gree 83 E1
Drumgray La. Gree 83 E1
Drumhead Pl. Glasg 116 C1
Drumhead Rd. Glasg 116 C1
Drumhill. Kirk 59 D1
Drumilaw Cres. Glasg 138 A3
Drumilaw Rd. Glasg 138 A3
Drumilaw Way. Glasg 138 A3
Drumillan Hill. Gour 44 B1
Drumkinnon Rd. Alex 27 E4
Drumlaken Path. Glasg 76 B1
Drumlaken Pl. Glasg 76 B1
Drumlaken St. Glasg 76 A1
Drumlanford Rd. Troon 229 F3
Drumlanrig Pl. Glasg 100 B1
Drumlanrig Pl. Sten 23 F2
Drumlanrig
Quadrant. Glasg 120 B4
Drumley Ave. Moss 237 F3
Drumleyhill Dr. Hurl 228 C3
Drumlin Dr. Miln 76 A4
Drumloch Gdns. E Kil 180 C3
Drumlochy Rd. Glasg 99 D3
Drummilling Ave. W Kil 190 B3
Drummilling Dr. W Kil 190 B3
Drummilling Rd. W Kil 190 B3
Drummond Ave. Glasg 137 F4
Drummond Cres. Ayr 236 C1
Drummond Dr. Pais 114 B2
Drummond Dr. Wish 165 E2
Drummond Hill. E Kil 160 A2
Drummond House. Cumb 62 A2
Drummond La. Stir 7 D3
Drummond Pl. Blac 107 E2
Drummond Pl. Bon 40 A4
Drummond Pl. E Kil 160 A2
Drummond Pl. Kilmk 223 E1
Drummond Pl. Stir 7 D3
Drummond Place La. Stir 7 D3
Drummond Rd. Glasg 55 D4
Drummore Rd. Glasg 137 F4
Drummur Foot. Irvine 220 A3
Drumnessie Ct. Cumb 81 F4
Drumnessie Rd. Cumb 81 F4
Drumnessie View. Cumb 81 F4
Drumore Ave. Chap 123 E1
Drumover Dr. Glasg 118 C2
Drumoyne Ave. Glasg 115 F3
Drumoyne Cir. Glasg 115 F3
Drumoyne Dr. Glasg 115 F4
Drumoyne Pl. Glasg 115 F3
Drumoyne Quadrant. Glasg 115 F3
Drumoyne Rd. Glasg 115 F3
Drumoyne Sq. Glasg 115 F4
Drumpark St. Coat 121 E2
Drumpark St. Glasg 95 E2
Drumpark St. Stir 7 D2
Drumpellier Ave. Coat 121 E2
Drumpellier Ave. Cumb 82 B4
Drumpellier Ave. Glasg 120 A2
Drumpellier Cres. Coat 121 E3
Drumpellier Gdns. Cumb 82 B4
Drumpellier Pl. Cumb 82 B4
Drumpellier Pl. Coat 121 E4
Drumpellier Pl. Cumb 82 B4
Drumpellier Pl. Glasg 120 A2
Drumpellier St. Glasg 98 B1
Drumreoch Dr. Glasg 137 F4
Drumreoch Pl. Glasg 137 F4
Drumsgend Rd. Slam 86 B3
Drumry Rd. Clyde 74 B1
Drumry Rd E. Glasg 74 C1
Druma Ave. Pais 113 E3
Drums Cres. Pais 113 E3

Drums Rd. Glasg 115 D2
Druns Terr. Green 45 D4
Drumsack Ave. Muir 100 B4
Drumsargard Rd. Glasg 138 B3
Drumshangie St. Aird 103 D1
Drumshangie Terr. Gour 44 C4
Drumshaw Dr. Glasg 139 E4
Drumslea. Green 45 D4
Drumtrocher St. Kils 60 B4
Drumvale Dr. Muir 80 C1
Drunslea. Green 45 D4
Drury St. Glasg 117 D4
Dryad St. Glasg 135 F3
Drybridge Rd. Dund 225 F1
Dryburgh Ave. Den 21 E1
Dryburgh Ave. Glasg 138 A3
Dryburgh Rd. Bear 75 E1
Dryburgh Gdns. Glasg 96 C2
Dryburgh Hill. E Kil 159 E1
Dryburgh La. E Kil 159 E1
Dryburgh Pl. Coat 121 F4
Dryburgh Rd. Wish 165 D2
Dryburgh Way. Udd 161 E4
Dryburgh Wlk. Muir 81 D2
Dryburn Ave. Glasg 115 E4
Dryden St. Ham 162 A3
Drygate. Glasg 117 F4
Drygate St. Lark 185 D2
Drygrange Rd. Glasg 99 E1
Drymen Pl. Kirk 79 E2
Drymen Rd. Bear 75 F2
Drymen Rd. Bonh 19 F1
Drymen St. Glasg 115 F3
Drynoch Pl. Glasg 97 D4
Drysdale St. All 10 A3
Drysdale St. Glasg 94 C3
Duart Ave. Pres 236 B4
Duart Cres. Pres 236 B4
Duart Dr. E Kil 159 E2
Duart Dr. Newt M 157 D3
Duart Dr. John 112 B1
Duart St. Glasg 96 B4
Dubbs Rd. Kilw 207 D1
Dubbs Rd. P Glasg 68 C4
Dubbs Rd. Steven 206 C1
Dubs Rd. Barr 134 C2
Dublon St. Glasg 98 C4
Duchal Dr. Kilm 163 D1
Duchal Rd. P Glasg 68 A4
Duchall Pl. Glasg 95 D2
Duchess Ct. Ham 163 D1
Duchess Pl. Glasg 138 B4
Duchess Palace. Glasg 138 B4
Duchess Pk. Helen 16 A2
Duchess Rd. Glasg 118 B1
Duchray Dr. Glasg 114 C2
Duchray La. Glasg 98 B1
Duchray St. Glasg 98 B1
Ducraig St. Glasg 119 D3
Duddingston Ave. Kilw 207 D2
Dudhope St. Glasg 99 E1
Dudley Dr. Coat 101 E1
Dudley Dr. Glasg 96 A2
Dudley Rd. Kilw 207 D1
Duff Cres. Stir 1 C1
Duff Pl. Kilmk 223 E2
Duff St. Salt 206 A1
Duff St. Green 46 A3
Duffus Pl. Glasg 139 E4
Duffus St. Glasg 100 A1
Duffus Terr. Glasg 139 E4
Duguid Dr. Salt 206 A1
Duich Gdns. Glasg 76 C1
Duisdale Rd. Glasg 139 E4
Duke St. Alva 5 D4
Duke St. Bann 7 E1
Duke St. Den 21 E1
Duke St. Glasg 118 A3
Duke St. Ham 162 C2
Duke St. Lark 185 D2
Duke St. Mother 163 F4
Duke St. New 166 B3
Duke St. Pais 113 F1
Duke St. Stir 2 A1
Duke Terr. Ayr 236 A1
Duke's Pl. Glasg 138 B3
Dukes Gate. Udd 140 C3
Dukes Pl. Ham 183 E3
Dukes Rd. Glasg 138 B3
Dukes Rd. Troon 229 D2

Dulfatur
Roundabout. Cumb 61 F3
Dulnain St. Glasg 139 E4
Dulsie Rd. Glasg 98 B3
Dumbarton Rd. Bonh 20 A1
Dumbarton Rd. Clyde 73 D4
Dumbarton Rd. Clyde 92 C4
Dumbarton Rd. Dumb 73 D4
Dumbarton Rd. Dunt 74 A3
Dumbarton Rd. Glasg 95 E2
Dumbarton Rd. O Kil 72 B4
Dumbarton Rd. Stir 6 C4
Dumbarton Rd. Stir 7 D4

257
Dumbreck Ave. Glasg Eastwood Ave. Glasg

Dumbreck Ave. Glasg 116 A2
Dumbreck Ct. Glasg 116 A2
Dumbreck Pl. Glasg 116 A2
Dumbreck Rd. Glasg 116 A2
Dumbreck Sq. Glasg 116 A2
Dumbreck Terr. Kils 59 F4
Dumbrock Cres. Strath 31 E2
Dumbrock Dr. Strath 31 D2
Dumbrock Rd. Strath 31 E2
Dumbuck Cres. Dumb 50 B1
Dumbuck Rd. Dumb 50 A3
Dumbuck Rd. Dumb 50 B2
Dumbuie Ave. Dumb 50 A2
Dumfries Cres. Aird 122 C3
Dumfriespark. Ayr 239 D1
Dumgoyne Ave. Miln 54 C1
Dumgoyne Ct. Aird 103 D1
Dumgoyne Dr. Bear 75 E4
Dumgoyne Gdns. Miln 54 C1
Dumgoyne Pl. Newt M 157 E4
Dumgoyne Rd. Kilmk 228 A2
Dumyat Ave. Tull 4 A1
Dumyat Dr. Falk 41 F2
Dumyat Rd. Alva 4 C3
Dumyat Rd. Men 3 F3
Dumyat Rd. Stir 2 B2
Dumyat St. All 4 C1
Dunagoil Rd. Glasg 137 E1
Dunagoil St. Glasg 137 F1
Dunagoil Terr. Glasg 137 F1
Dunalastair Dr. Stepps 99 E3
Dunalistair Dr. Stepps 99 D3
Dunan Pl. Glasg 119 F4
Dunard Ct. Car 187 F2
Dunard Rd. Glasg 138 A4
Dunard St. Glasg 96 C2
Dunard Way. Pais 113 E4
Dunaskin St. Glasg 96 B1
Dunbar Ave. Coat 121 E2
Dunbar Ave. Glasg 138 B4
Dunbar Ave. John 131 F4
Dunbar Ave. Sten 23 F2
Dunbar Dr. Mother 164 A2
Dunbar Gate. Duni 21 F2
Dunbar Hill. E Kil 159 E1
Dunbar Pl. E Kil 159 E1
Dunbar Rd. Pais 113 D1
Dunbar St. Ham 162 A3
Dunbeath Ave. Newt M 156 C3
Dunbeith Pl. Glasg 96 B3
Dunbeth Ave. Coat 122 A4
Dunbeth Ct. Coat 122 A4
Dunbeth Rd. Coat 122 A4
Dunblane Dr. E Kil 159 F1
Dunblane Pl. Coat 121 F2
Dunblane Pl. E Kil 159 F1
Dunblane St. Glasg 97 D1
Dunbrach Rd. Cumb 61 E1
Dunbreck Ave. Cald 105 D3
Dunbritton Rd. Dumb 50 B2
Duncairn Ave. Bon 39 F3
Duncan Ave. Glasg 95 E2
Duncan Ave. Sten 24 A2
Duncan Ct. Kilmk 223 E2
Duncan Dr. Irvine 219 E1
Duncan Graham St. Lark 185 D2
Duncan La. Glasg 95 E2
Duncan La N. Glasg 95 E2
Duncan La S. Glasg 95 E2
Duncan McIntosh Rd. Cumb 62 B4
Duncan Rd. Helen 16 C2
Duncan Rd. P Glasg 47 D1
Duncan St. Bon 39 F3
Duncan St. Clyde 74 A2
Duncan St. Green 45 F3
Duncan's Cl. Lan 215 D2
Duncansby Rd. Glasg 119 E3
Duncanson Ave. All 10 A4
Duncarnock Ave. Neil 154 C4
Duncarnock Cres. Neil 154 C4
Duncarron Pl. Den 21 F1
Dunchattan Gr. Troon 229 F1
Dunchattan Pl. Glasg 117 F4
Dunchattan St. Glasg 117 F4
Dunchattan Way. Troon 229 F1
Dunchurch Rd. Pais 114 B3
Dunclutha Dr. Udd 141 D1
Dunclutha St. Glasg 118 A1
Duncolm Pl. Miln 54 B1
Duncombe Ave. Dunt 74 A4
Duncombe St. Glasg 96 B4
Duncombe View. Clyde 74 B2
Duncraig Cres. John 131 E4
Duncrub Dr. Bish 77 F1
Duncruin St. Glasg 96 B4
Duncruin Terr. Glasg 96 B4
Duncryne Ave. Glasg 119 F2
Duncryne Gdns. Glasg 119 F2
Duncryne Pl. Bish 97 F4
Duncryne Rd. Gart 20 C4
Duncryne Rd. Glasg 119 E2
Dundaff Ct. Den 21 E1
Dundaff Hill. Cumb 61 E1
Dundarroch St. Lar 23 D1
Dundas Ave. Lennox 78 A4
Dundas Cotts. Bon 39 D1
Dundas La. Glasg 117 E4
Dundas Pl. E Kil 159 F1
Dundas Rd. Stir 2 A2
Dundas St. Glasg 117 E4
Dundas Wlk. Kilmk 223 E2
Dundashill. Glasg 97 D1
Dundasvale Ct. Glasg 97 D1
Dundee Dr. Glasg 115 D2
Dundee Pl. Falk 42 A4
Dundonald Ave. John 111 E1
Dundonald Cres. Newt M 157 D2
Dundonald Cres. Shew 224 C1
Dundonald Dr. Ham 183 E4
Dundonald Pl. Neil 154 B4
Dundonald Rd. Glasg 96 B2
Dundonald Rd. Irvine 220 B1
Dundonald Rd. Kilmk 227 E4
Dundonald Rd. Pais 114 A4
Dundonald Rd. Troon 229 F2
Dundonald St. Udd 161 E4
Dundrennan Rd. Glasg 136 C4
Dundyvan La. Wish 165 D1
Dundyvan Rd. Coat 121 F3
Dundyvan St. Wish 165 D1
Dundyvan Way. Coat 121 F3
Dunean St. Glasg 96 C1
Dunearn Pl. Pais 114 A2
Duneaton Wynde. Lark 185 D1
Dunedin Ct. E Kil 180 A4
Dunedin Dr. E Kil 180 A4
Dunedin Rd. Lark 185 D1
Dunellan Dr. Dunt 74 A4
Dunellan Rd. Miln 54 B1
Dunellan St. Glasg 115 F3
Dungavel Gdns. Ham 183 F4
Dungavel Rd. Kilmk 228 A2
Dungeonhill Rd. Glasg 120 B4
Dunglass Ave. E Kil 159 F2
Dunglass Ave. Glasg 95 E2
Dunglass La. Glasg 95 E2
Dunglass La N. Glasg 95 E2
Dunglass La S. Glasg 95 E2
Dunglass Pl. Miln 54 C2
Dunglass Rd. Bishop 72 B1
Dunglass Sq. E Kil 159 F2
Dunglass View. Strath 31 E2
Dungoil Ave. Cumb 61 D2
Dungoil Rd. Kirk 79 F4
Dungourney Dr. Green 45 E4
Dungoyne St. Glasg 96 B4
Dunholme Pk. Clyde 73 E2
Dunira St. Glasg 118 C2
Dunivaig St. Glasg 119 F4
Dunkeld Ave. Glasg 138 A4
Dunkeld Dr. Bear 76 A2
Dunkeld Gdns. Bish 78 A1
Dunkeld La. Muir 81 D1
Dunkeld Pl. Coat 121 F2
Dunkeld Pl. Falk 24 B1
Dunkeld Pl. Ham 161 F2
Dunkeld St. Glasg 118 B2
Dunkenny Rd. Glasg 74 C2
Dunkirk St. Cald 105 D3
Dunlin Cres. Hous 91 E1
Dunlin Ct. Tan 141 F4
Dunlin. E Kil 159 F2
Dunlop Cres. Ayr 236 C1
Dunlop Cres. Irvine 220 A1
Dunlop Cres. Ren 94 B2
Dunlop Cres. Udd 141 D1
Dunlop Ct. Ham 183 F4
Dunlop Dr. Shew 224 C2
Dunlop Gr. Tan 121 D1
Dunlop Pl. Miln 54 C2
Dunlop Pl. Shew 224 C2
Dunlop Rd. Beith 172 A2
Dunlop Rd. Dunlop 173 E3
Dunlop Rd. Stew 195 E1
Dunlop St. Fen 213 D2
Dunlop St. Glasg 117 E3
Dunlop St. Glasg 139 F3
Dunlop St. Green 45 E2
Dunlop St. Kilmk 222 C1
Dunlop St. Lin 112 B3
Dunlop St. Ren 94 B2
Dunlop St. Stew 195 F1
Dunlop Terr. Ayr 236 B1
Dunmar Cres. All 4 C1
Dunmar Dr. All 4 C1
Dunmore Dr. Miln 76 B4
Dunmore St. Clyde 94 B4
Dunn Mews. Kilmk 227 E4
Dunn St. Clyde 73 F2
Dunn St. Dunt 73 F3
Dunn St. Glasg 118 A2
Dunn St. Green 45 F2
Dunn St. Pais 114 A2
Dunn Terr. East 127 F3
Dunnachie Dr. Coat 121 D2
Dunnet Ave. Glenm 102 C3
Dunnett Ave. Kilmk 228 A4
Dunnichen Gdns. Bish 78 B1
Dunnikier Wlk. Cumb 60 C1
Dunning Pl. Falk 24 B1
Dunning St. Glasg 118 B2
Dunnotar Wlk. New 165 F3
Dunnottar Cres. E Kil 159 E2
Dunnottar Dr. Sten 23 F2
Dunnottar St. Bish 78 B1
Dunnottar St. Glasg 99 D1
Dunns Wood Rd. Cumb 62 B3
Dunolly Dr. Newt M 156 C3
Dunolly St. Glasg 98 A1
Dunoon Ave. Kilmk 222 C2
Dunottar Ave. Coat 122 A1
Dunphail Dr. Glasg 100 B1
Dunphail Rd. Glasg 120 B4
Dunragit St. Glasg 118 B4
Dunrobin Ave. John 112 B1
Dunrobin Ave. Sten 23 F3
Dunrobin Cres. E Kil 159 E2
Dunrobin Ct. E Kil 159 E2
Dunrobin Dr. E Kil 159 E2
Dunrobin Dr. Gour 43 F3
Dunrobin Pl. Coat 121 F4
Dunrobin Rd. Aird 123 F4
Dunrobin St. Glasg 118 A3
Dunrod Hill. E Kil 159 F2
Dunrod St. Glasg 119 D2
Duns Cres. Wish 165 E4
Duns Path. Coat 122 B2
Dunscore Brae. Ham 161 F1
Dunside Dr. Glasg 135 D3
Dunsiston Rd. Chap 124 A2
Dunskaith St. Glasg 120 B4
Dunsmore Rd. Bishop 72 A2
Dunsmuir St. Glasg 116 A4
Dunster Gdns. Bish 78 A2
Dunster Rd. Stir 2 B2
Dunswin Ave. Clyde 73 F2
Dunsyre Pl. Glasg 76 C1
Dunsyre St. Glasg 118 C4
Duntarvie Cres. Glasg 120 B4
Duntarvie Pl. Glasg 120 A4
Duntarvie Quadrant. Glasg 120 B4
Duntarvie Rd. Glasg 120 A4
Dunterlie Ave. Glasg 95 D3
Dunterlie Ct. Barr 134 B2
Duntiblae Rd. Kirk 80 A4
Duntiglennan Rd. Dunt 74 A3
Duntilland Ave. Sals 125 D1
Duntilland Rd. Chap 124 C4
Duntilland Rd. Sals 125 E3
Duntocher Rd. Bear 75 D3
Duntocher Rd. Clyde 74 A2
Duntocher Rd. Miln 74 C4
Duntonknoll. Irvine 219 E2
Duntreath Ave. Glasg 74 C1
Duntreath Terr. Kils 60 B4
Duntroon Pl. Hat 142 A2
Duntroon St. Glasg 118 A4
Dunure Courts. Kilw 207 E2
Dunure Cres. Bon 40 A3
Dunure Dr. Glasg 137 F3
Dunure Dr. Ham 161 E1
Dunure Dr. Kilmk 228 A4
Dunure Dr. Newt M 157 D3
Dunure Pl. Coat 121 F2
Dunure Pl. Newt M 157 D2
Dunure Rd. Ayr 238 B1
Dunure St. Bon 40 A3
Dunure St. Coat 121 F2
Dunure St. Glasg 96 B4
Dunvegan Ave. Coat 101 E1
Dunvegan Ave. Gour 43 F3
Dunvegan Ave. John 112 B1
Dunvegan Ave. Sten 23 F2
Dunvegan Ct. All 10 A3
Dunvegan Dr. Bish 78 A2
Dunvegan Dr. Falk 24 B1
Dunvegan Dr. Newt M 157 D3
Dunvegan Dr. Stir 2 A2
Dunvegan. Glenm 102 C2
Dunvegan Pl. Bon 39 F3
Dunvegan Pl. E Kil 159 E2
Dunvegan Pl. Irvine 219 E3
Dunvegan Pl. Tan 140 B4
Dunvegan Quadrant. Ren 94 A2
Dunwan Ave. Glasg 94 C4
Dunwan Pl. Glasg 94 C4
Dura Rd. Alla 167 E3
Durban Ave. Clyde 73 E2
Durham Rd. Gour 44 C3
Durham St. Glasg 116 B3
Durisdeer Dr. Ham 161 F1
Durness Ave. Bear 76 A2
Duror St. Glasg 119 D3
Durris Gdns. Glasg 119 E2
Durrockstock Cres. Pais 132 C4
Durrockstock Rd. Pais 133 D4
Durrockstock Rd. Pais 132 C4
Durrockstock Way. Pais 132 C4
Durward Ave. Glasg 116 B1
Durward Cres. Pais 112 C1
Durward Ct. Glasg 116 B1
Durward. E Kil 160 C2
Durward Way. Pais 112 C1
Duthie Rd. Gour 45 D4
Duthil St. Glasg 115 E3
Dyce La. Glasg 96 A1
Dyers' Wynd. Pais 113 F3
Dyfrig St. Shot 146 C3
Dyfrig St. Udd 161 E4
Dyke Rd. Glasg 95 D4
Dyke St. Coat 121 D2
Dyke St. Glasg 120 B3
Dykebar Ave. Glasg 95 D3
Dykebar Cres. Pais 114 A1
Dykehead Cres. Aird 102 C1
Dykehead Dr. Hurl 228 C3
Dykehead La. Glasg 119 E4
Dykehead Rd. Aird 103 D2
Dykehead Rd. Coat 121 D3
Dykehead Rd. Cumb 61 E3
Dykehead Rd. Kils 59 F4
Dykehead Sq. Ham 161 F2
Dykehead St. Glasg 119 E4
Dykemuir Pl. Glasg 98 A2
Dykemuir Quadrant. Glasg 98 A2
Dykemuir St. Glasg 98 A2
Dykeneuk Rd. P Glasg 68 B4
Dykes Pl. Salt 205 F1
Dykes The. Kilb 170 A4
Dykesfield Pl. Salt 205 F1
Dykesmains Rd. Salt 205 F1
Dysart Way. Chap 124 A3

Eagle Cres. Bear 75 D3
Eagle St. Glasg 97 E1
Eaglesham Ct. Glasg 116 C3
Eaglesham Path. Glen 101 E3
Eaglesham Pl. Glasg 116 C3
Eaglesham Rd. E Kil 158 C1
Eaglesham Rd. Eagle 179 E4
Eaglesham Rd. Newt M 156 B2
Eaglesham Rd. Newt M 157 F3
Eaglesham Rd. Thorn 179 E4
Earl Ave. Cald 105 D3
Earl Haig Rd. Glasg 114 C4
Earl La. Glasg 95 E2
Earl Of Mar Ct. All 10 A3
Earl Pl. B of W 110 B3
Earl Pl. Glasg 95 E2
Earl St. Glasg 95 D2
Earl View. Holy 143 D2
Earl's Gate. Udd 140 C2
Earl's Hill. Cumb 61 D2
Earlbank Ave. Glasg 95 E2
Earlbank La N. Glasg 95 E2
Earlbank La S. Glasg 95 E2
Earls Ct. All 10 A3
Earls Way. Ayr 238 B1
Earlsburn Ave. Stir 7 D2
Earlsburn Rd. Kirk 79 F2
Earlscourt. Muir 80 C1
Earlshill Dr. Bann 7 F1
Earlspark Ave. Glasg 136 C3
Earlston Ave. Kilmk 227 F2
Earlston Cres. Coat 122 B2
Earlston St. Wish 165 E3
Earn Ave. Bear 76 A2
Earn Ave. Ren 94 C1
Earn Ave. Tan 141 F3
Earn Cres. Wish 165 D1
Earn Ct. All 10 B3
Earn Gdns. Lark 199 D4
Earn Loan. Holy 143 D3
Earn Pl. Bank 39 E3
Earn Pl. Kilmk 228 A3
Earn Rd. Newt M 156 B4
Earn Rd. Troon 229 F2
Earn St. Glasg 98 C1
Earn Terr. Shot 146 C3
Earncraig Gn. Irvine 220 A2
Earnhill Rd. Gour 44 B3
Earnock Ave. Mother 163 E3
Earnock Rd. Ham 161 F1
Earnock St. Glasg 98 B2
Earnock St. Ham 162 A2
Earnside St. Glasg 119 D3
Easdale Dr. Glasg 119 D2
Easdale. E Kil 181 D4
Easdale Path. Glen 101 E3
Easdale Pl. Newt M 156 A3
Easdale Rise. Ham 161 F2
East Academy St. Wish 165 D1
East Ave. Car 187 E1
East Ave. Ham 161 F3
East Ave. Holy 143 D1
East Ave. Plains 104 A2
East Ave. Ren 94 B2
East Ave. Tan 141 E3
East Barmoss Ave. P Glasg 68 C4
East Bams St. Clyde 94 B4
East Bath La. Glasg 117 E4
East Blackhall St. Green 46 A2
East Boreland Pl. Den 21 F1
East Bowhouse Head. Irvine 220 A3
East Bowhouse Way. Irvine 220 A3
East Breast. Green 46 A3
East Bridge St. Falk 42 B2
East Broomlands. Irvine 220 A1
East Buchanan St. Pais 113 F3
East Burnside St. Kils 60 B4
East Campbell St. Glasg 117 F3
East Castle St. All 10 A3
East Crawford St. Green 46 B2
East Dean St. Hat 142 A3
East Dr. Lar 23 E1
East Faulds Rd. Lan 215 F3
East Gargieston Ave. Kilmk 227 E3
East Gartferry Rd. Muir 80 C1
East Gate. Glen 101 E4
East Gate. Wish 165 E2
East George St. Coat 122 A4
East Glebe Terr. Ham 162 B1
East Gr. Troon 229 F2
East Greenlees Ave. Glasg 139 E2
East Greenlees Cres. Glasg 139 E2
East Greenlees Dr. Glasg 139 E2
East Greenlees Rd. Glasg 139 D2
East Hallhill Rd. Glasg 120 B3
East Hamilton St. Green 46 B2
East Hamilton St. Wish 165 D1
East High St. Aird 123 D4
East High St. Kirk 58 B1
East India Breast. Green 46 A3
East Kilbride Rd. E Kil 158 C2
East Kilbride Rd. Glasg 138 C2
East Kilbride Rd. Thorn 158 B2
East Kirkland. Dalry 191 E4
East La. Pais 114 A2
East Lennox Dr. Helen 16 C2
East Link Rd. B of A 2 B3
East Machan St. Lark 185 D1
East Main St. East 127 F3
East Main St. Hart 127 F3
East Mains. Men 4 A3
East Mains Rd. E Kil 159 F2
East Milton Gr. E Kil 159 D1
East Montrose St. Helen 16 C1
East Murrayfield. Bann 7 F1
East Netherton St. Kilmk 227 F4
East Park Cres. Kilm 222 A4
East Park Dr. Kilm 222 A4
East Park Rd. Ayr 236 A2
East Rd. Holy 143 D2
East Rd. Irvine 219 E1
East Rd. Kilbar 111 D2
East Rd. P Glasg 68 C4
East Rd. Pres 236 B3
East Rossdhu Dr. Helen 16 C2
East Scott Terr. Ham 162 B1
East Shaw St. Green 45 F3
East Shaw St. Kilmk 227 F3
East Springfield Terr. Bish 98 A4
East St. Green 46 C1
East Station Ind Est. Lark 185 D2
East Stewart Pl. Coat 122 B4
East Stewart St. Coat 122 B3
East Stewart St. Green 46 A2
East Stirling St. Alva 5 D4
East Thomson St. Clyde 74 A2
East Thornlie St. Wish 165 D1
East Union St. Troon 229 E2
East Vennel. All 10 A3
East Wellbrae Cres. Ham 162 A1
East Wellington St. Glasg 118 B3
East William St. Green 46 B2
East Woodside Ave. P Glasg 69 D4
Eastburn Dr. Falk 42 B2
Eastburn Rd. Glasg 98 A3
Eastcote Ave. Glasg 95 F2
Eastcroft. Glasg 138 A4
Eastcroft St. Lar 23 D1
Eastcroft Terr. Glasg 98 A2
Eastend Ave. Holy 143 D1
Eastend. Loch 129 E2
Easter Cornton Rd. Stir 2 A2
Easter Craigs. Glasg 118 A4
Easter Cres. Wish 165 F2
Easter Garngaber Rd. Kirk 79 F3
Easter Livilands. Stir 7 E2
Easter Mews. Udd 140 C3
Easter Queenslie Rd. Glasg 119 F4
Easter Rd. Shot 146 B3
Easter Rd. Thorn 158 A3
Easter Wood Cres. Tan 121 E1
Eastergreens Ave. Kirk 79 E4
Easterhill Pl. Glasg 118 C2
Easterhill Rd. Helen 16 C2
Easterhill St. Glasg 119 D1
Easterhouse Pl. Glasg 120 B4
Easterhouse Quadrant. Glasg 120 B4
Easterhouse Rd. Glasg 120 B4
Eastermains. Kirk 59 D1
Eastern Cres. Kilb 170 A4
Easterton Ave. Thorn 158 A3
Easterton Cres. Cowie 12 C4
Easterton Dr. Cowie 12 C4
Easterton Gr. Cowie 12 C4
Eastfield Ave. Glasg 138 C3
Eastfield Cres. Dumb 50 A1
Eastfield Pl. Dumb 50 A1
Eastfield Rd. Cald 105 D3
Eastfield Rd. Car 202 A4
Eastfield Rd. Cumb 61 E2
Eastfield Rd. Glasg 97 F2
Eastfield Terr. Hat 142 B2
Eastgate. Muir 101 D3
Eastlea Pl. Aird 123 D3
Eastmuir St. Glasg 119 D3
Eastmuir St. Wish 165 F2
Easton Ct. Stir 2 A1
Easton Dr. Shi 66 B4
Easton Pl. Coat 122 A3
Eastside. Kirk 58 B1
Eastvale Pl. Glasg 116 B4
Eastwood Ave. Glasg 136 B1

Eastwood Ave. Glasg 136 B4
Eastwood Ave. Irvine 219 E2
Eastwood Cres. Glasg 135 F2
Eastwood Dr. New 166 A3
Eastwood La. Helen 25 C4
Eastwood Rd. Muir 80 C1
Eastwood Toll. Glasg 136 A1
Eastwood View. Glasg 139 F3
Eastwood Way. Lark 185 D2
Eastwoodmains Rd. Glasg 136 B1
Eastwoodmains
    Rd. Newt M 157 E4
Easwald Bank. Kilbar 111 E1
Ebenezer Pl. Call 66 C3
Ebroch Dr. Kils 60 C4
Ebroch Pk. Kils 60 C4
Eccles St. Glasg 97 F3
Eck Path. Holy 143 D3
Eckford St. Glasg 119 D2
Eday St. Glasg 97 E3
Edderton Pl. Glasg 120 A4
Eddington Dr. Newt M 156 B2
Eddleston Pl. Glasg 139 F3
Edelweiss Rd. Glasg 119 F4
Eden Ct. Kilw 207 D2
Eden Dr. E Kil 179 F3
Eden Gdns. E Kil 179 F3
Eden Gr. E Kil 179 F4
Eden La. Glasg 98 B1
Eden Pk. Udd 140 C1
Eden Pl. Glasg 139 E3
Eden Pl. Kilrk 228 A3
Eden Pl. Ren 94 C1
Eden St. Glasg 98 B1
Edenhall Rd. Ayr 238 A2
Edenkill Pl. Strath 31 E2
Edenside. Cumb 62 A4
Edenwood St. Glasg 118 C3
Edgam Dr. Glasg 115 E3
Edgefauld Ave. Glasg 97 F2
Edgefauld Dr. Glasg 97 F2
Edgefauld Pl. Glasg 97 F3
Edgefauld Rd. Glasg 98 A2
Edgehill La. Glasg 96 A2
Edgehill Rd. Bear 75 F3
Edgehill Rd. Glasg 96 A2
Edgemont Pk. Ham 183 E4
Edgemont St. Glasg 136 C4
Edinbeg Ave. Glasg 137 F4
Edinbeg Pl. Glasg 137 F4
Edinburgh Dr. Gour 43 F3
Edinburgh Rd. East 127 E3
Edinburgh Rd. Glasg 119 E4
Edinburgh Rd. Ham 162 C2
Edinburgh Rd. Holy 143 E4
Edington Gdns. Muir 80 C2
Edington St. Glasg 97 D1
Edison Pl. Kilw 207 F1
Edison St. Glasg 114 C4
Edmiston Ave. Pres 236 A4
Edmiston Dr. Glasg 136 B4
Edmiston Dr. Lin 112 A4
Edmonstone Dr. Kils 60 B4
Edmonton Terr. E Kil 180 B4
Edmund Kean. E Kil 160 B3
Edrom Ct. Glasg 118 C3
Edrom Path. Glasg 118 C3
Edrom St. Glasg 118 C3
Edward Ave. Ren 94 C2
Edward Ave. Sten 23 F2
Edward Ave. Stir 2 B1
Edward Dr. Helen 16 B2
Edward Pl. Gour 24 C2
Edward Rd. Stir 2 A1
Edward St. Clyde 94 B4
Edward St. Coat 120 C3
Edward St. Ham 162 B1
Edward St. Kils 36 B1
Edward St. Mother 163 F2
Edwin St. Glasg 116 B3
Edzell Ct. Glasg 95 E1
Edzell Dr. John 112 B1
Edzell Dr. Newt M 156 C2
Edzell Gdns. Bish 98 B4
Edzell Pl. Glasg 95 E2
Edzell Row. Kilw 207 D2
Edzell St. Coat 121 E2
Edzell St. Glasg 95 E1
Egidia Ave. Glasg 136 B1
Egilsay Cres. Glasg 97 E4
Egilsay Pl. Glasg 97 E4
Egilsay St. Glasg 97 E4
Egilsay Terr. Glasg 97 E4
Eglinton Cres. Troon 229 F3
Eglinton Ct. Glasg 117 D3
Eglinton Ct. Salt 216 C4
Eglinton Dr. Eagle 178 C2
Eglinton Dr. Glasg 136 B1
Eglinton Dr. Troon 229 F3
Eglinton Interchange. Kilw 219 D1
Eglinton Pl. Ayr 235 F1
Eglinton Pl. Kilw 207 F2
Eglinton Pl. Salt 216 C4
Eglinton Rd. Ard 205 E2
Eglinton Sq. Ard 205 E2
Eglinton St. Beith 171 D4
Eglinton St. Coat 122 A4

Eglinton St. Glasg 117 D2
Eglinton St. Irvine 219 E2
Eglinton St. Salt 216 C4
Eglinton Terr. Ayr 235 F1
Egmont Pk. E Kil 180 A4
Eider Ave. E Kil 180 A3
Eider Gr. E Kil 180 A3
Eider Pl. Auld 180 A2
Eighth St. Tan 120 C1
Eildon Dr. Barr 134 B1
Eildon Rd. Kirk 79 F4
Eileen Gdns. Bish 78 A1
Eilt Wlk. New 165 F3
Elba Ct. Ayr 236 A1
Elba Gdns. Ayr 236 A1
Elba St. Ayr 236 A1
Elcho St. Glasg 117 F3
Elder Ave. Beith 171 D4
Elder Dr. Tan 141 D4
Elder St. Glasg 115 F4
Elderbank. Bear 75 F2
Elderbank Gdns. Glasg 115 F4
Elderpark Gr. Glasg 115 F4
Elderpark St. Glasg 115 F4
Elderslea Rd. Car 202 A4
Elderslie Cres. Kilmk 227 F2
Elderslie St. Glasg 116 C4
Eldin Pl. B of W 110 C3
Eldon Pl. John 112 A1
Eldon Ct. Glasg 96 A1
Eldon Gdns. Bish 77 F1
Eldon Pl. Green 45 E4
Eldon St. Glasg 96 C1
Eldon St. Gour 45 E4
Elgin Ave. E Kil 160 B4
Elgin Ave. Stew 195 E1
Elgin Dr. Stir 7 E2
Elgin Gdns. Glasg 157 F4
Elgin Pl. Aird 122 C3
Elgin Pl. Coat 122 A2
Elgin Pl. E Kil 159 F2
Elgin Pl. Falk 42 A2
Elgin Pl. Kils 36 B1
Elgin Terr. Ham 161 F2
Elgin Way. Hat 142 A3
Elgin Way. Stew 99 B1
Elie St. Glasg 96 B1
Eliot Cres. Ham 162 B1
Eliot Terr. Ham 162 B1
Elizabeth Ave. Lar 23 E1
Elizabeth Ave. M of C 58 A3
Elizabeth Cres. Falk 41 D3
Elizabeth Cres. Glasg 136 A2
Elizabeth Quadrant. Holy .. 142 B3
Elizabeth St. Glasg 116 B3
Elizabeth St. Stir 7 D3
Elizabeth Wynd. Ham 183 E4
Ellangowan Way. Ren 94 B1
Ella Gdns. Hat 142 B2
Elleangowan Rd. Glasg 136 B4
Ellangowan Rd. Miln 55 D1
Ellergreen Rd. Bear 75 F3
Ellerslie St. John 112 A2
Ellesmere St. Glasg 97 D2
Elliot Ave. Glasg 136 B2
Elliot Ave. Pais 132 C4
Elliot Cres. E Kil 160 A1
Elliot Dr. Glasg 136 B2
Elliot Pl. Ash 200 A2
Elliot Pl. Glasg 116 C4
Elliot St. Glasg 116 C4
Elliot Terr. Falk 42 A4
Ellis St. Coat 122 A3
Ellis St. Kilmk 227 F4
Ellis Way. Mother 163 F3
Ellisland Ave. Clyde 74 B2
Ellisland Cres. Glasg 137 F3
Ellisland Dr. Kirk 228 B4
Ellisland Dr. Udd 161 D3
Ellisland. E Kil 160 C4
Ellisland Pl. Ayr 239 D3
Ellisland Pl. Salt 206 A2
Ellisland Rd. Cumb 62 A1
Ellisland Rd. Glasg 136 F3
Ellisland Sq. Ayr 239 D3
Ellisland Wynd. Holy 143 E2
Ellismuir Farm Rd. Glasg . 120 B2
Ellismuir Pl. Glasg 120 B3
Ellismuir St. Coat 121 F2
Elliston Ave. Glasg 135 E3
Elliston Cres. Glasg 135 E3
Elliston Dr. Glasg 135 E3
Elliston Pl. Glasg 135 E3
Elm Dr. Lin 112 A3
Ellrig. E Kil 180 B3
Elm Ave. Kirk 79 E3
Elm Ave. Ren 94 B2
Elm Bank. Bish 78 A1
Elm Bank. Kirk 58 B1
Elm Cres. Tan 141 E4
Elm Dr. Cumb 62 C2

Elm Dr. Glasg 139 E3
Elm Dr. John 112 A1
Elm Dr. Shi 66 B3
Elm Gdns. Bear 75 F3
Elm Gdns. Troon 230 A1
Elm Gr. All 10 B3
Elm Gr. Lang 70 B4
Elm Gr. Lar 23 E1
Elm La E. Glasg 95 E2
Elm La W. Glasg 95 E2
Elm Park. Ard 205 E2
Elm Pl. E Kil 180 B3
Elm Quadrant. Aird 123 E4
Elm Rd. B of W 110 C4
Elm Rd. Clyde 74 A3
Elm Rd. Dumb 49 F2
Elm Rd. Glasg 138 A2
Elm Rd. Holy 143 D3
Elm Rd. Pais 114 A1
Elm St. Coat 122 B3
Elm St. Glasg 95 E2
Elm St. Lennox 57 F4
Elm St. Mother 163 E3
Elm St. Newt M 157 F3
Elm St. Udd 161 C1
Elm St. Udd 161 F4
Elm Terr. Gour 44 C3
Elm View. Ct. Hat 142 B2
Elm Wlk. Bear 75 F3
Elmbank Ave. Kilmk 228 A4
Elmbank Ave. Tan 141 D4
Elmbank Cres. Bank 39 E3
Elmbank Cres. Glasg 117 D4
Elmbank Cres. Ham 162 A2
Elmbank Dr. Bonh 27 F3
Elmbank Dr. Kilmk 228 A4
Elmbank Dr. Lark 185 E1
Elmbank. Men 4 A3
Elmbank Rd. Lang 70 B4
Elmbank Rd. Stir 2 A2
Elmbank St. Ayr 236 A2
Elmbank St. Car 202 A4
Elmbank St. Glasg 117 D4
Elmbank St. Hat 142 A2
Elmbank Street La. Glasg . 117 D4
Elmbank Terr. Irvine 219 D2
Elmfoot St. Glasg 117 E1
Elmhurst. Mother 163 E2
Elmira Rd. Muir 100 B4
Elmore Ave. Glasg 137 D3
Elms Pl. Beith 150 A4
Elms Pl. Steven 206 C1
Elms The. Glasg 137 D2
Elmslie Ct. Glasg 120 B2
Elmvale Row. Glasg 97 F3
Elmvale St. Glasg 98 A3
Elmway. Lark 185 D3
Elmwood Ave. Glasg 95 F2
Elmwood Ave. Newt M 156 C3
Elmwood Ct. Udd 141 D1
Elmwood Gdns. Kirk 79 D3
Elmwood La. Glasg 95 F2
Elmwood Rd. Shot 147 D1
Elphin St. Glasg 76 B1
Elphinstone Cres. Air 14 C2
Elphinstone Cres. E Kil 180 C3
Elphinstone Mews. Kil 89 E4
Elphinstone Pl. Glasg 116 B4
Elphinstone Rd. Newt M .. 157 D4
Elrig Rd. Glasg 137 D3
Elsinore Path. E Kil 180 C3
Elspeth Gdns. Bish 78 B1
Elswick Dr. Cald 105 D2
Eltham St. Glasg 97 D2
Elvan Pl. E Kil 179 F4
Elvan St. Glasg 118 C3
Elvan St. Mother 163 E3
Elwan Tower. Mother 163 F3
Embo Dr. Glasg 95 D3
Emerald Terr. Hat 142 A2
Emerson Rd. Bish 78 A1
Emerson Rd W. Bish 78 A1
Emily Dr. Mother 163 F2
Emma Jay Rd. Hat 142 A3
Empress Dr. Helen 16 A2
Empress Rd. Rhu 15 E3
Endfield Ave. Glasg 96 A3
Endrick Bank. Bish 78 A1
Endrick Dr. Bank 39 F3
Endrick Dr. Bear 75 F2
Endrick Dr. Bonh 19 F1
Endrick Dr. Pais 114 A3
Endrick Gdns. Miln 54 C1
Endrick St. Glasg 97 F3
Endrick Rd. Stir 141 D4
Endrick Rd. Green 46 A1
Endrick St. Glasg 97 E2
Engelen Dr. All 10 A3
Englestone Ave. Pres 236 A3
English St. Mother 164 B2
Ennerdale. E Kil 179 F3
Ennisfree Rd. Udd 161 E4
Ensay St. Glasg 98 B3
Enterkin St. Glasg 118 C2
Enterkine. Kilw 207 D1
Eribol Wlk. Holy 143 E2
Eriboll Pl. Glasg 97 D4

Eriboll St. Glasg 97 D4
Ericht Pl. Shot 146 C3
Ericht Rd. Glasg 136 B3
Eriska Ave. Glasg 95 D3
Eriskay Ave. Ham 161 F1
Eriskay Ave. Newt M 156 A3
Eriskay Ave. P Glasg 69 D2
Eriskay Cres. Newt M 156 A3
Eriskay Ct. Falk 42 B1
Eriskay Ct. Irvine 225 E4
Eriskay Pl. Kilmk 223 D3
Erradale St. Glasg 97 D4
Errogie St. Glasg 120 A4
Erskin View. O Kill 73 D3
Erskine Ave. Glasg 116 A2
Erskine Cres. Aird 122 C3
Erskine Ct. Aird 123 F4
Erskine Ferry Rd. O Kill ... 73 D3
Erskine Pl. Clack 10 C3
Erskine Pl. Kilmk 223 E4
Erskine Rd. Salt 216 C4
Erskine Rd. Newt M 157 D3
Erskine Sq. Glasg 114 C4
Erskine St. Alva 5 E4
Erskine St. Alva 10 A4
Erskine Way. Shot 146 C2
Erskinefauld Rd. Lin 112 A3
Ervie St. Glasg 120 B4
Escart Rd. Car 187 F2
Esdaile Ct. Holy 143 D2
Esk Ave. Ren 94 C1
Esk Dale. E Kil 159 E2
Esk Rd. Troon 229 F3
Esk St. Glasg 114 C4
Esk Way. Pais 112 C1
Eskbank St. Glasg 119 D3
Eskdale Dr. Glasg 138 B4
Eskdale. Newt M 157 D3
Eskdale Rd. Bear 75 F2
Eskdale St. Glasg 117 D1
Esmond St. Glasg 96 B1
Espedair St. Pais 113 F2
Esperanto Rd. Pres 236 C4
Espleside Cres. Coat 121 E4
Esplanade. Ayr 238 C4
Esplanade. Green 45 E4
Esplanade. Pres 233 D1
Esselmont Ave. Glasg 95 E3
Essenside Ave. Glasg 75 E1
Essex Dr. Glasg 95 F2
Essex La. Glasg 95 F2
Essex Rd. Gour 44 C2
Esslemont Ave. Glasg 95 E2
Esson Pl. Kilmk 223 D2
Estate Ave. Falk 42 A4
Estate Quadrant. Glasg 139 E4
Estate Rd. Glasg 119 E1
Etive Ave. Bear 76 A2
Etive Ave. Ham 162 A1
Etive Cres. Bish 78 A1
Etive Cres. Cumb 82 A3
Etive Cres. Cumb 82 A3
Etive Ct. Cumb 82 A3
Etive Ct. Dunt 74 B3
Etive Dr. Aird 123 E3
Etive Dr. Bishop 72 B1
Etive Dr. Glasg 82 A3
Etive Dr. Glasg 136 B1
Etive Pl. Cumb 82 A3
Etive Pl. Irvine 219 E3
Etive Pl. Stir 2 A2
Etive St. Glasg 119 D3
Etive St. Wish 165 D1
Etive Way. Shot 147 D2
Etna Rd. Falk 42 B4
Etna St. Mother 164 B2
Ettrick Ave. Hat 142 A4
Etterick Wynd. Udd 161 E4
Ettrick Cres. Glasg 138 B4
Ettrick Cres. Kilmk 222 C2
Ettrick Ct. Falk 42 A1
Ettrick Ct. Glasg 139 F2
Ettrick Dr. Bear 75 E4
Ettrick Dr. Bishop 72 B1
Ettrick Hill. E Kil 160 A2
Ettrick Oval. Pais 132 C4
Ettrick Pl. Ayr 236 A2
Ettrick Pl. Glasg 136 B4
Ettrick Pl. Kilmk 222 C2
Ettrick Sq. Cumb 61 F1
Ettrick St. Wish 165 D1
Ettrick Terr. John 131 E4
Euchan Pl. Troon 229 F3
Evan Cres. Glasg 136 B1
Evan Dr. Glasg 136 B1
Evanlea. Lar 23 E2
Evanton Dr. Glasg 135 F2
Evanton Pl. Glasg 135 F2
Evelyn Terr. Kilw 207 F1
Everard Ct. Bish 97 F4
Everard Dr. Bish 97 F4
Everard Pl. Bish 97 F4
Everard Quadrant. Bish 97 F4
Everglades The. Muir 100 A4
Eversley St. Glasg 119 D2

Everton Rd. Glasg 115 E1
Ewart Cres. Ham 162 A1
Ewart Terr. Ham 162 A1
Ewenfield Ave. Ayr 239 D2
Ewenfield Gdns. Ayr 239 D2
Ewenfield Pk. Ayr 238 C2
Ewenfield Rd. Ayr 239 D2
Ewing Ave. Falk 42 A4
Ewing Cres. Ham 183 E4
Ewing Ct. Stir 7 E2
Ewing Dr. Falk 42 A4
Ewing Pl. Glasg 118 B3
Ewing Pl. Loch 129 E2
Ewing St. Glasg 138 A4
Ewing St. Kilbar 111 D2
Ewing Way. Stew 211 E4
Ewing Wlk. Miln 55 E1
Excelsior St. Mother 164 B2
Exeter Dr. Glasg 96 A1
Exeter La. Glasg 96 A1
Exeter St. Coat 122 A3
Exhibition Way. Glasg 116 C4
Exmouth Pl. Gour 44 C3
Eynort St. Glasg 97 D4

Factory Rd. Mother 163 F3
Fagan Ct. Udd 140 C1
Failley Rd. Dunt 74 B4
Failford Pl. Kilmk 223 D2
Failford Pl. Lin 223 D2
Fair Oaks. E Kil 158 C4
Fair View Dr. Lan 214 A2
Fair Way. Card 48 A4
Fairbairn Cres. Glasg 136 A1
Fairbairn Path. Glasg 118 C2
Fairbairn St. Glasg 118 C2
Fairfax Ave. Glasg 137 E3
Fairfield Ave. Bon 40 A3
Fairfield Ct. Newt M 157 F3
Fairfield Dr. Newt M 157 E3
Fairfield Gdns. Glasg 115 F4
Fairfield. N Sau 5 E1
Fairfield Pk. Ayr 238 C4
Fairfield Pl. E Kil 159 E1
Fairfield Pl. Glasg 115 F4
Fairfield Pl. Ham 183 E4
Fairfield Pl. Udd 141 D1
Fairfield Rd. Ayr 238 C4
Fairfield St. Glasg 115 F4
Fairford Dr. Cumb 82 A2
Fairgreen Pl. Barn 11 F4
Fairhaven Rd. Glasg 96 C4
Fairhaven Sq. Kilw 207 D2
Fairhaven. Troon 229 F4
Fairhill Ave. Glasg 135 E4
Fairhill Ave. Ham 162 B1
Fairhill Pl. Ham 183 E4
Fairhill Rd. Stir 7 D1
Fairholm Ave. Ham 163 E1
Fairholm St. Glasg 119 D3
Fairholm St. Lark 184 C2
Fairley St. Glasg 116 A3
Fairlie Ave. Kilmk 227 E4
Fairlie Dr. Falk 41 E3
Fairlie Park Dr. Glasg 96 A1
Fairlie St. Falk 41 E3
Fairlie View. Cross 226 C3
Fairmount Dr. N Sau 5 E1
Fairview Ct. Miln 56 B2
Fairview Cr. Wish 65 D2
Fairway. Bear 75 E3
Fairways. Irvine 219 D4
Fairways. Lark 185 E2
Fairways Pl. Bon 40 A4
Fairweather Pl. Newt M ... 156 B3
Fairyburn Rd. All 9 F4
Fairyhill Pl. Kilmk 227 E3
Fairyhill Rd. Kilmk 227 E3
Fairyknowe Gdns. Udd 141 D1
Faith Ave. Kil 89 F1
Falcon Cres. Green 45 D3
Falcon Cres. Pais 113 D3
Falcon Dr. Lar 23 D2
Falcon La. Green 45 D3
Falcon Rd. John 131 E3
Falcon Terr. Glasg 96 B4
Falcon Terrace La. Glasg .. 96 B4
Falconbridge Rd. E Kil 160 B2
Falconer Ct. Stir 7 D2
Falconer St. P Glasg 67 F3
Falconer Terr. Ham 162 B1
Faldfield St. Glasg 117 D2
Falkirk Rd. Bon 40 B3
Falkirk Rd. Lar 42 C3
Falkirk St. Ayr 238 A2
Falkirk Rd. Ren 94 B1
Falkirk Rd. Lar 23 F2
Falkirk Rd. Stir 2 A1
Falkland Ave. Newt M 157 E4
Falkland Cres. Bish 98 B4
Falkland Dr. E Kil 159 E1
Falkland La. Glasg 95 F2
Falkland Park Rd. Ayr 236 A2

Falkland Pk. E Kil 159 E1
Falkland Pl. Ayr 236 A2
Falkland Pl. Coat 122 A2
Falkland Pl. E Kil 159 E1
Falkland Pl. Sten 23 F2
Falkland Rd. Ayr 236 A2
Falkland St. Glasg 96 A2
Falloch Pl. New 165 F3
Falloch Rd. Bear 75 E1
Falloch St. Glasg 137 D4
Falloch Rd. Miln 54 C2
Fallside Ave. Tan 141 E3
Fallside Rd. Tan 141 D1
Fallside Rd. Udd 141 D2
Falmouth Dr. Gour 44 C3
Falside Ave. Pais 113 F1
Falside Rd. Pais 119 D1
Falside Rd. Pais 113 F1
Falstaff. E Kil 160 B3
Fancy Farm Pl. Green 44 C2
Fancy Farm Rd. Green 45 D2
Fara St. Glasg 96 C4
Faraday Ave. Wish 165 D3
Faransay Pl. Kilmk 223 D3
Fardalehill View. Cross 221 F1
Farden Pl. Pres 236 B3
Farie St. Glasg 138 A4
Farlands View. W Kil 190 B2
Farm Cres. Holy 143 F2
Farm Ct. Udd 141 D2
Farm La. Hat 117 E2
Farm Pk. Klrk 79 E2
Farm Rd. Clyde 73 E2
Farm Rd. Cowie 12 B4
Farm Rd. Dunt 74 B4
Farm Rd. Fail 4 B3
Farm Rd. Glasg 116 A3
Farm Rd. Ham 161 F2
Farm Rd. Kilmk 222 C2
Farm Rd. Udd 140 B1
Farm St. Falk 24 A1
Farm St. Mother 163 E4
Farm Terr. Ham 161 F2
Farme Cross. Glasg 118 A1
Farmeloan Rd. Glasg 138 A4
Farmfield Terr. W Kil 190 B3
Farmgate Sq. Hat 141 F2
Farmington Ave. Glasg 119 E3
Farmington Gate. Glasg 119 E3
Farmington Gdns. Glasg 119 E3
Farmington Gr. Glasg 119 E3
Farndale. E Kil 159 E2
Farm Dr. Glasg 137 E2
Farnell St. Glasg 97 D1
Farquhar Rd. P Glasg 47 E2
Farquhar Sq. Blac 107 E2
Farrell Pl. Ayr 236 B2
Farrier Ct. John 111 F2
Faskally Ave. Bish 77 F2
Faskally Wlk. New 165 F3
Faskin Cres. Glasg 134 C4
Faskin Pl. Glasg 134 C4
Faskin Rd. Glasg 134 C4
Faskine Ave. Aird 122 C1
Faskine Ave. Calder 123 D1
Faskine Cres. Aird 122 C1
Fasque Pl. Glasg 74 C2
Fastnet St. Glasg 119 D4
Fauldhouse St. Glasg 117 E2
Faulds. Glasg 120 B3
Faulds. Glasg 120 B3
Faulds Park Rd. Gour 43 F3
Faulds St. Coat 121 F2
Fauldshead Rd. Ren 94 B2
Fauldspark Cres. Glasg 120 B3
Fauldswood Cres. Pais 113 D1
Fauldswood Dr. Pais 113 D1
Fearmore Rd. Glasg 96 B4
Fearnoch. Pres 236 B3
Fells The. Lennox 57 F4
Fellsview Ave. Kirk 54 C4
Fencedyke Way. Irvine 220 A2
Fendoch St. Glasg 119 D2
Fenella St. Glasg 119 D3
Fennsbank Ave. Glasg 138 B2
Fenton St. All 10 A4
Fenwick Dr. Barr 134 B1
Fenwick Dr. Ham 183 F4
Fenwick Pl. Glasg 136 A1
Fenwick Rd. Glasg 136 B2
Fenwick Rd. Giff 136 B2
Fenwickland Ave. Ayr 239 D2
Fenwickland Pl. Ayr 239 D2
Ferclay St. Dunt 74 B4
Fereneze Ave. Barr 134 A2
Fereneze Ave. Newt M 157 E4
Fereneze Ave. Ren 114 A4
Fereneze Cres. Glasg 95 D4
Fereneze Cres. Ham 161 F2
Fereneze Dr. Pais 133 E4
Fereneze Rd. Neil 154 B4
Fergus Ave. Pais 113 D3
Fergus Dr. Green 46 C2
Fergus Dr. Green 45 D2
Fergus Dr. Pais 113 D3
Fergus Gdns. Ham 162 C1
Fergus La. Glasg 96 C2

Fergus Pl. Green 45 D2
Fergus Rd. Green 45 D2
Fergushill Rd. Kilw 208 A2
Fergusilie. Pais 113 D2
Ferguslie Park Ave. Pais 113 D3
Ferguslie Park Cres. Pais ... 113 D2
Ferguslie Wlk. Pais 113 D2
Ferguson Ave. Miln 55 D1
Ferguson Ave. Ren 94 B2
Ferguson Ave. Ren 94 B2
Ferguson Dr. Den 24 A3
Ferguson Dr. Mother 163 F2
Ferguson St. Ayr 236 B2
Ferguson St. John 111 F2
Ferguson St. Ren 94 B2
Ferguson St. Stir 1 C1
Ferguson Pl. E Kil 160 B3
Ferguson Rd. Cumb 61 F1
Ferguson Terr. M of C 58 B3
Ferguston Rd. Bear 75 F2
Fern Ave. Bish 98 A4
Fern Ave. Inch 93 D4
Fern Ave. Kirk 80 A4
Fern Brae. Ayr 239 E2
Fern Dr. Barr 134 A2
Fern La. Glasg 95 F3
Fern Lea Gr. Sten 24 B2
Fern Pl. Kilmk 227 E4
Fern St. Mother 164 A2
Fernan St. Glasg 118 C3
Fernbank Ave. Glasg 139 E2
Fernbank. Pres 236 A3
Fernbank St. Glasg 97 F3
Fernbrae Ave. Glasg 138 B2
Fernbrae Way. Glasg 138 A2
Ferncroft Dr. Glasg 137 E3
Ferndale Ct. Glasg 96 B4
Ferndale Dr. Glasg 96 B4
Ferndale. Gdns. Glasg 96 B4
Ferndale. Lark 185 D1
Ferndale Pl. Glasg 96 B4
Ferness Oval. Glasg 98 B4
Ferness Pl. Glasg 98 B4
Ferness Rd. Glasg 98 B4
Ferngrove Ave. Glasg 96 A3
Fernhill Grange. Udd 141 D1
Fernhill Rd. Glasg 138 A2
Ferniegair Ave. Helen 16 A1
Fernieshaw Rd. Cle 144 C1
Fernlea. Bear 75 F2
Fernleigh Pl. Muir 80 C1
Fernleigh Rd. Glasg 136 B3
Fernside Wlk. Ham 162 C1
Fernslea Ave. Udd 161 E4
Ferry Loan. Alex 27 F3
Ferry Orch. Stir 2 B1
Ferry Rd. Air 9 F2
Ferry Rd. Bishop 72 A2
Ferry Rd. Card 48 A3
Ferry Rd. Glasg 95 F2
Ferry Rd. Ren 94 B3
Ferry Rd. Ros 15 D2
Ferry Rd. Stir 2 B1
Ferry Rd. Udd 140 C3
Ferry Rd. Udd 141 D1
Ferryden Ct. Glasg 95 F1
Ferryden St. Glasg 95 F1
Fersit St. Glasg 136 B3
Fetlar Dr. Glasg 137 E3
Fetlar Rd. Bridge 223 D3
Fetlar Rd. B of W 110 B4
Fettercairn Ave. Glasg 74 C2
Fettercairn Gdns. Bish 78 B1
Fettes St. Glasg 118 C4
Fiddison Pl. Pres 236 C3
Fiddoch Ct. New 165 F4
Fidra St. Glasg 118 C4
Field Gr. Thorn 157 F3
Field Rd. Dunt 74 B4
Field Rd. Lark 185 D1
Field Rd. Thorn 157 F3
Field St. Ham 162 B1
Fielden Pl. Glasg 118 A3
Fielden St. Glasg 118 A3
Fieldhead Dr. Glasg 136 A3
Fieldhead Sq. Glasg 136 A3
Fields La. Hous 91 D2
Fife Ave. Aird 123 D3
Fife Ave. Glasg 115 D2
Fife Cres. Udd 141 D1
Fife Dr. Gour 44 A3
Fife Rd. Gour 44 B3
Fife Way. Bish 98 B4
Fife Way. Aird 123 E4
Fifth Ave. Glasg 95 F3
Fifth Ave. Ren 94 B3
Fifth Ave. Stepps 99 D3
Fifth Rd. Blan 161 F3
Finart Dr. Pais 114 A1
Finaven Gdns. Bear 75 D4
Finch Pl. John 131 E4
Finch Pl. Kilmk 228 B4
Finch Rd. Green 45 D3
Findhorn Ave. Pais 112 C1

Findhorn Ave. Ren 94 C2
Findhorn Ct. E Kil 179 E4
Findhorn. Ersk 73 D1
Findhorn Pl. E Kil 179 E4
Findhorn Pl. Falk 42 B1
Findhorn Pl. Troon 229 F3
Findhorn Rd. Pres 233 F2
Findhorn St. Glasg 118 B4
Findlay St. Kils 60 B4
Findlay St. Mother 163 F3
Findlay's Brae. Salt 216 C4
Findochty. Ersk 73 D1
Findochty St. Glasg 99 F1
Fingal La. Glasg 96 B4
Fingal St. Glasg 96 B4
Fingalton Rd. Newt M 155 F3
Fingask St. Glasg 119 E2
Finglas Ave. Pais 114 A1
Finglen Gdns. Miln 54 C1
Finglen Pl. Glasg 135 D3
Fingleton Ave. Barr 134 B1
Finhaven St. Glasg 118 C2
Finistere Ave. Falk 42 A2
Finlarig Ct. Sten 23 F2
Finlarig St. Glasg 120 B4
Finlas Ave. Ayr 239 D2
Finlas St. Glasg 97 E2
Finlay Dr. Glasg 118 A4
Finlay Dr. Lin 111 F3
Finlay Rise. Miln 76 B4
Finlayson Dr. Aird 123 F4
Finlayson Dr. Kilmk 223 E2
Finlayson Quadrant. Aird ... 123 F4
Finlaystone Cres. Kilb 69 E1
Finlaystone Rd. Kilb 69 F2
Finlaystone Rd. P Glasg 69 D4
Finlaystone St. Coat 121 F4
Finnart Cres. Gour 44 B3
Finnart Rd. Green 45 E3
Finnart Sq. Glasg 117 F2
Finnart St. Glasg 117 F2
Finnart St. Green 45 E3
Finneston La. Green 46 A3
Finneston St. Green 46 A3
Finneston Way. Green 46 A3
Finnick Glen. Ayr 239 D2
Finnie Terr. Gour 44 B3
Finnie Terr. Spring 220 C1
Finnie Wynd. Mother 164 A2
Finnieston Quay. Glasg 96 C1
Finnieston St. Glasg 116 C4
Finsbay St. Glasg 115 F3
Fintrie Terr. Ham 161 F2
Fintry Ave. Pais 133 F4
Fintry Cres. Barr 134 B1
Fintry Cres. Bish 78 B1
Fintry Dr. Glasg 137 E4
Fintry Gdns. Bear 75 D4
Fintry Pl. Irvine 220 A1
Fintry Rd. Green 46 A1
Fintry Terr. Irvine 219 D3
Fintry Wlk. Irvine 220 A1
Fir Bank Ave. Lark 185 D1
Fir Bank. Ayr 239 E3
Fir Ct. Coat 121 F2
Fir Ct. E Kil 180 A4
Fir Gr. Tan 141 E4
Fir La. Lar 23 E1
Fir Pk. St. Mother 163 F2
Fir Pl. Cle 144 A1
Fir Pl. Glasg 138 C2
Fir Pl. John 112 A1
Fir Pl. Kilmk 227 E4
Fir St. Green 46 C1
Fir Terr. Gour 44 B3
Fir View. Calder 123 D1
Firbank Ave. Lennox 78 A4
Firbank Terr. Barr 134 C1
Firdon Cres. Glasg 75 D1
Firhill Ave. Aird 122 C3
Firhill Dr. Pres 233 E3
Firhill Rd. Glasg 97 D2
Firhill St. Glasg 97 D2
Firlee. E Kil 179 F4
Firpark Rd. Bish 98 A4
Firpark St. Glasg 117 F4
Firpark Terr. Cam 6 B3
Firpark Terr. Ham 117 F4
Firs Cres. Bann 7 E1
Firs Entry. Bann 7 E1
Firs Rd. Tull 4 B1
Firs St. Tull 42 B3
Firs The. Bann 7 E1
Firs The. Bann 7 E1
Firs The. Glasg 137 D2
First Ave. Bear 76 A2
First Ave. Bonh 27 F3
First Ave. Dumb 50 B3
First Ave. Glasg 136 C1
First Ave. Irvine 224 B4
First Ave. Ren 94 B1
First Ave. Stepps 79 E1
First Ave. Stepps 99 D2
First Gdns. Glasg 116 A2
First Rd. Ham 161 F3
First St. Tan 140 C4

First Terr. Clyde 74 A2
Firth Cres. Gour 44 B3
Firth Gdns. Troon 229 E4
Firth Rd. Troon 229 E4
Firth View Terr. Ard 205 E2
Firthview Terr. Dumb 49 E2
Firtree Pl. New 166 A3
Firtree Rd. New 166 A3
Firwood Dr. Glasg 137 E3
Firwood Rd. Newt M 156 C2
Fischer Gdns. Lin 112 C3
Fisher Ave. Kils 60 B4
Fisher Ave. Lin 112 C2
Fisher Cres. Dunt 74 A3
Fisher Ct. Cross 221 F2
Fisher Ct. Glasg 117 F4
Fisher Dr. Lin 112 C2
Fisher Pl. Helen 17 D1
Fisher St. Lark 185 D1
Fisher Way. Lin 112 C2
Fishers Rd. Ren 94 B3
Fisherwood Rd. Alex 27 F4
Fishescoates Ave. Glasg 138 B3
Fishescoates Gdns. Glasg .. 138 B3
Fitzalan Dr. Pais 114 A3
Fitzalan Rd. Ren 94 A1
Fitzroy La. Glasg 116 C4
Fitzroy Pl. Glasg 116 C4
Five Roads. Kilw 208 A2
Five Ways Rd. Ash 200 B2
Fladda. E Kil 159 D1
Flanders St. Dunt 74 B4
Flatterton La. Gour 44 B1
Flatterton Rd. Gour 44 B1
Flax Mill Rd. East 127 F3
Flax Rd. Udd 141 D3
Flaxfield Gr. Mother 142 B1
Flaxmill Ave. Mother 164 B2
Fleck Ave. Salt 206 A1
Fleet Ave. Ren 94 C1
Fleet St. Glasg 119 D2
Fleming Ave. Clyde 94 B4
Fleming Ave. Muir 100 B4
Fleming Cres. Salt 206 A2
Fleming Ct. Car 187 F1
Fleming Ct. Clyde 74 A1
Fleming Ct. Ham 161 F2
Fleming Ct. Mother 164 A2
Fleming Dr. Sten 24 A2
Fleming Gdns. Falk 41 F3
Fleming Pl. Blac 107 F2
Fleming Pl. E Kil 180 C4
Fleming Rd. Bishop 72 A2
Fleming Rd. Cumb 61 F1
Fleming Rd. Hous 91 D1
Fleming St. Glasg 118 A3
Fleming St. Kilmk 227 F3
Fleming St. Pais 113 F4
Fleming Terr. Irvine 219 D3
Fleming Terr. Ham 161 F2
Fleming Way. Lark 185 E1
Flemington Ind Est. Glasg .. 139 F2
Flemington St. Glasg 97 E2
Flenders Ave. Newt M 157 E3
Flenders Rd. Newt M 157 E3
Fletcher Ave. Gour 44 C4
Fleurs Ave. Glasg 116 A2
Fleurs Rd. Glasg 116 A2
Flinders Pl. E Kil 180 A4
Flint Mill La. Green 46 A1
Floyd St. Coat 121 F3
Floors Rd. Newt M 157 E1
Floors St. John 111 F2
Floorsburn Cres. John 111 F1
Flora Gdns. Bish 78 B1
Florence Dr. Glasg 136 B2
Florence Gdns. Glasg 138 B2
Florence Gdns. Glasg 138 B2
Florence St. Glasg 117 E2
Florence St. Glasg 117 E3
Florence St. Green 46 C2
Florida Ave. Glasg 137 D4
Florida Cres. Glasg 137 D4
Florida Dr. Glasg 137 D4
Florida Gdns. Glasg 120 A3
Florida Sq. Glasg 137 D4
Florida St. Glasg 137 D4
Flowerdale Pl. Glasg 135 D2
Flowerhill St. Aird 123 D4
Flures Ave. Inch 93 F4
Flures Cres. Inch 93 F4
Flures Dr. Inch 93 F4
Flures Pl. Inch 93 F4
Fochabers Dr. Glasg 115 E3
Fogo Pl. Glasg 96 B3
Foinavon Rd. Quart 183 F2
Foot Of Lone Rd. Lan 214 A3
Footfield Rd. Hat 141 F2
Forbes Ave. Lar 23 E1
Forbes Ct. Falk 42 C3
Forbes Dr. Glasg 117 F3
Forbes Dr. Mother 143 E4
Forbes Pl. Pres 236 B2
Forbes Pl. Kilmk 223 D1
Forbes Pl. Pais 113 F2
Forbes St. Falk 42 B2

Forbes St. All 9 F3
Forbes St. Glasg 117 F3
Forbes Wlk. Kilmk 223 D1
Ford Ave. Irvine 225 E4
Ford Rd. Bonh 40 A3
Ford Rd. Glasg 96 B2
Ford Rd. Newt M 156 B2
Forde Cres. Steven 206 C1
Fordneuk St. Glasg 118 A3
Fordoun St. Glasg 120 B4
Fordyce Ct. Newt M 156 B2
Fordyce St. Glasg 96 B1
Fore Row. Ham 162 C2
Fore St. Glasg 95 E2
Fore St. P Glasg 47 E1
Forebraes. All 10 A4
Foregate Sq. Kilmk 222 C1
Foregate The. Kilmk 222 C1
Forehill Rd. Ayr 239 E3
Forehouse Rd. Kilbar 110 B2
Foremount
    Terrace La. Glasg 96 B2
Forest Ave. Ham 183 E3
Forest Dr. Bear 75 D4
Forest Dr. Udd 141 D2
Forest Gdns. Kirk 79 D2
Forest Gr. Kilmk 223 D3
Forest Kirk. Car 202 A4
Forest La. Ham 183 E3
Forest Pk. Cro 201 D1
Forest Pk. Kirk 79 D2
Forest Pl. Pais 113 F1
Forest Rd. Cumb 62 C2
Forest Rd. Cumb 62 C3
Forest Rd. Lark 185 D2
Forest View. Cumb 62 B2
Forest Way. Ayr 239 E3
Forester Gr. All 4 C1
Forestfield Gdns. Cald 105 D2
Foresthall Dr. Glasg 98 A2
Foresthall Gdns. Glasg 98 A2
Forfar Ave. Glasg 115 D2
Forfar Cres. Bish 98 B4
Forfar Rd. Gour 44 C2
Forgan Gdns. Bish 98 B4
Forge Dr. Coat 121 F4
Forge Pl. Glasg 98 A1
Forge Rd. Aird 123 F3
Forge St. Glasg 98 A1
Forge St. Kilmk 222 C2
Forge Vennal. Kilw 207 E2
Forgewood Rd. Mother 142 B1
Forglen Cres. B of A 2 A3
Forglen Rd. B of A 2 A3
Forglen St. Glasg 100 A1
Formby Dr. Glasg 76 B1
Forres Ave. Glasg 136 B2
Forres Cres. Hat 142 A3
Forres Gate. Glasg 136 B1
Forres Quadrant. Wish 165 D3
Forres St. Glasg 76 C1
Forres St. Udd 161 E3
Forrest Cres. Ham 162 A1
Forrest Dr. Hat 142 B2
Forrest Pl. East 127 F3
Forrest Rd. Cald 106 A1
Forrest Rd. Lan 215 D3
Forrest Rd. Sais 126 A3
Forrest St. Air 2 A1
Forrest St. Aird 123 E4
Forrest St. Glasg 118 A3
Forrest St. Shot 146 B3
Forrester Ct. Bish 97 F4
Forrester Pl. Air 14 B2
Forrestfield Cres. Newt M .. 156 C3
Forrestfield Gdns. Newt M . 156 C3
Forrestfield Rd. Cald 106 A3
Forrestfield St. Glasg 98 A1
Forrestlea Rd. Car 202 A4
Forsyth Gr. Green 45 D3
Forsyth St. Aird 123 E4
Forsyth St. Green 45 E3
Fort Matilda Pl. Green 45 D4
Fort Matilda Terr. Green 45 D4
Fort St. Ayr 235 F1
Fort St. Mother 163 D4
Fort St. Mother 163 E4
Fortacre Pl. Irvine 220 A3
Forteviot Ave. Glasg 120 B3
Forteviot Pl. Glasg 120 B3
Forth Ave. Lar 23 D2
Forth Ave. Pais 112 C1
Forth Cres. All 10 B3
Forth Ct. E Kil 179 F4
Forth Ct. Stir 7 E4
Forth Ct. E Kil 179 F4
Forth Ct. Stir 2 A1
Forth Gr. E Kil 179 F4
Forth Pl. John 131 E4
Forth Pl. Lark 199 D4
Forth Rd. Bear 75 E1
Forth Rd. Ham 161 F3
Forth Rd. Lennox 78 A4
Forth St. Camb 9 D4
Forth St. Clyde 94 B4

Forth St. Fall 8 B2
Forth St. Glasg 116 C2
Forth St. Green 45 D3
Forth St. Stir 7 D4
Forth Terr. Men 183 D4
Forth View. Stir 2 A1
Forthvale. Men 4 A3
Forthview. Renn 7 F1
Forthview Ct. Falk 41 F1
Forties Rd. Hous 111 E4
Fortieth Ave. E Kil 180 C3
Fortingale Ave. Glasg 96 B3
Fortingale Pl. Glasg 96 B3
Fortingall Rd. Ham 161 F3
Fortissat Ave. Shot 146 B3
Fortisset Rd. Sals 126 A1
Fortrose St. Glasg 96 A1
Fossil Gr. Kirk 59 D1
Foswell Pl. Glasg 74 C3
Fotheringay La. Glasg .. 116 C1
Fotheringay Rd. Glasg . 116 C1
Fothringham Rd. Ayr ... 239 D4
Foulburn Rd. Cle 145 E1
Foulis La. Glasg 95 F3
Foulis St. Glasg 95 F3
Foulsykes Rd. Wish 165 F2
Foundry La. Barr 134 B1
Foundry Loan. Lar 23 D1
Foundry Rd. Bon 40 A3
Foundry Rd. Cle 144 B1
Foundry Rd. Shot 146 C2
Foundry St. Falk 42 A4
Fountain Cres. Inch 93 E3
Fountain Dr. Inch 93 E2
Fountain Rd. B of A 2 A4
Fountain
  Bsns Ctr The. Coat ... 122 A3
Fountainwell Ave. Glasg .. 97 E2
Fountainwell Dr. Glasg .. 97 E1
Fountainwell Pl. Glasg .. 97 E2
Fountainwell Rd. Glasg .. 97 E1
Fountainwell Sq. Glasg .. 97 F1
Fountainwell Terr. Glasg .. 97 F1
Four Acres Dr. Kilm 222 A4
Fourlanatowns. Hous 91 D1
Fourth Ave. Dumb 50 C2
Fourth Ave. Ren 94 B1
Fourth Ave. Stepps 79 E1
Fourth Ave. Stepps 99 D3
Fourth Gdns. Glasg 116 A2
Fourth St. Tan 120 C1
Fowlds St. Kilm 227 F4
Fowler Pl. E Kil 181 D3
Fowlis Dr. Newt M 156 B3
Fox Gr. Mother 163 D4
Fox St. Glasg 117 D3
Fox St. Green 45 E4
Foxbar Cres. Pais 132 C4
Foxbar Dr. Glasg 95 D3
Foxbar Dr. Pais 132 C4
Foxbar Rd. Pais 132 C4
Foxes Gr. Kirk 79 F3
Foxglove Pl. Ayr 239 E2
Foxglove Pl. Glasg 135 D2
Foxhills Pl. Glasg 76 C1
Foxley St. Glasg 119 E3
Foyers Terr. Glasg 98 A2
Franchi Dr. Sten 23 F3
Francis St. Glasg 117 D2
Frankfield Rd. Stepps 99 F3
Frankfield St. Glasg 98 C1
Frankfort St. Glasg 116 C1
Franklin Pl. E Kil 159 D1
Franklin St. Salt 205 F1
Franklin St. Glasg 117 F2
Fraser Ave. Bishop 77 E4
Fraser Ave. Dumb 50 B2
Fraser Ave. Glasg 138 B4
Fraser Ave. John 112 A1
Fraser Ave. Newt M 156 C2
Fraser Ave. Troon 229 E3
Fraser Cres. Ham 162 A2
Fraser Ct. Aird 123 F4
Fraser Gdns. Kirk 79 D4
Fraser Pl. Stir 2 C2
Fraser St. Cle 144 A1
Fraser St. Glasg 138 C3
Fraser Wik. Kilm 223 E2
Frazer Ave. Helen 16 A2
Frazer St. Glasg 118 A3
Frederick St. Coat 121 F4
Freeland Cl. Glasg 135 D3
Freeland Ct. Glasg 135 D3
Freeland Dr. B of W 90 B1
Freeland Dr. Inch 93 E3
Freeland La. E Kil 180 C4
Freeland Pl. Kirk 79 E4
Freeland Rd. Inch 93 D4
Freelands Cres. Clyde .. 73 E3
Freelands Ct. Clyde 73 E2
Freelands Rd. Clyde 73 E3
Freesia Ct. Mother 163 F3
French St. Clyde 73 F2
French St. Glasg 117 F2
French St. Ren 94 A1

French St. Wish 165 D2
Freuchie St. Glasg 120 A4
Frew Terr. Irvine 219 E3
Friar Ave. Bish 78 A2
Friar's Dene. Lan 214 C2
Friar's La. Lan 214 C2
Friar's Wynd. Lan 214 C2
Friars Croft. Irvine 219 D2
Friars Croft. Kirk 79 F4
Friars Lawn. Klw 207 E2
Friars Pl. Glasg 95 E4
Friars St. Stir 7 D4
Friars Way. Aird 123 E2
Friarscourt Ave. Glasg .. 95 E4
Friarscourt Rd. Muir 80 A1
Friarsfield Rd. Lan 214 C2
Friarton Rd. Glasg 136 C3
Friendship Gdns. Sten .. 24 B2
Friendship Way. Ren 94 B1
Frobisher Ave. Falk 41 F2
Frobisher Pl. Helen 17 D1
Frood St. Mother 142 B1
Fruin Ave. Newt M 156 C3
Fruin Rd. Glasg 74 C1
Fruin Rise. Ham 161 F1
Fruin St. Glasg 97 E2
Fudstone Dr. Kilb 170 A4
Fulbar Ave. Ren 94 B2
Fulbar Cres. Pais 112 C1
Fulbar Ct. Ren 94 B2
Fulbar Gdns. Pais 112 C1
Fulbar La. Ren 94 B2
Fulbar Rd. Glasg 115 E4
Fulbar Rd. Lin 112 C2
Fulbar St. Ren 94 B2
Fullarton Ave. Dund 225 F1
Fullarton Ave. Glasg ... 119 D1
Fullarton Cres. Troon .. 229 F1
Fullarton Dr. Troon 229 F1
Fullarton La. Glasg 119 D1
Fullarton Pl. Coat 121 F2
Fullarton Pl. Steven 217 E4
Fullarton Pl. Troon 230 A2
Fullarton Rd. Glasg 119 D1
Fullarton Rd. Troon 229 F1
Fullarton Rdabout. Irvine 219 D1
Fullarton St. Ayr 238 C4
Fullarton St. Coat 121 F2
Fullarton St. Irvine 219 D1
Fullarton St. Kilmk 227 F4
Fullers Gate. Dunt 74 B4
Fullerton Cryd. Troon .. 230 A1
Fullerton Dr. W Kil 190 A2
Fullerton La. Green 46 C2
Fullerton Sq. Ard 205 E1
Fullerton St. Pais 113 E3
Fulmar Ct. Bish 77 F1
Fulmar Pl. E Kil 159 E2
Fulmar Pl. John 131 E3
Fulshaw Ave. Ayr 236 C1
Fulton Cres. Kilbar 111 D2
Fulton Dr. Hous 111 D1
Fulton Gdns. Hous 111 D1
Fulton Rd. Miln 55 D1
Fulton St. Glasg 95 F4
Fulton's La. Kilmk 222 C1
Fulwood Ave. Glasg 94 C4
Fulwood Ave. Lin 94 C4
Fulwood Ind Est. Ham . 162 A3
Fulwood Pl. Glasg 94 C4
Furlongs The. Ham 162 C3
Furnace Ct. Hurl 228 C3
Furnace Rd. Quart 183 F2
Fyfe Park Terr. P Glasg 47 F1
Fyfe Shore Rd. P Glasg 47 F1
Fyffe Park Rd. P Glasg . 47 F1
Fyne Ave. Tan 141 F3
Fyne Ct. Ham 162 A1
Fyne La. Shot 146 C3
Fyne Way. Holy 143 D3
Fyneart St. Wish 165 F2
Fynloch Pl. Dunt 73 F4
Fyvie Ave. Glasg 136 A3

Golf Ct. Glasg 136 C1
Gaberston Ave. All 10 B4
Gadie St. Green 46 A1
Gadie Ave. Ren 94 C1
Gadiel St. Glasg 88 B4
Gadloch Ave. Stepps 79 E1
Gadloch Gdns. Kirk 79 E2
Gadloch St. Glasg 98 A3
Gadloch View. Stepps ... 79 E1
Gadsburn Ct. Glasg 98 B3
Gadshill St. Glasg 97 F1
Gael St. Green 45 E2
Gagarin Terr. Kilw 207 F2
Gailes Pk. Udd 140 C1
Gailes Pl. Kilmk 227 F2
Gailes Rd. Shew 224 E2
Gailes Rd. Troon 229 E4
Gailes St. Glasg 118 A2
Gain and
  Shankburn Rd. Glen .. 82 B1
Gain and
  Shankburn Rd. Glenm 82 B1

Gain Rd. Glen 82 A1
Gainburn Cres. Cumb 81 F3
Gainburn Ct. Cumb 81 F3
Gainburn Gdns. Cumb .. 81 F3
Gainburn Pl. Cumb 81 F3
Gainburn View. Cumb ... 81 F3
Gainford Pl. Kilmk 222 C2
Gainside Rd. Glen 101 E3
Gair Cres. Car 188 A2
Gair Cres. Wish 165 D1
Gair Rd. Car 188 A3
Gair Wynd. Shot 147 D2
Gairbraid Ave. Glasg 96 B3
Gairbraid Ct. Glasg 96 B3
Gairbraid Pl. Glasg 96 B3
Gairbraid Terr. Coat ... 121 D3
Gairdoch Dr. Sten 24 B2
Gairdoch St. Falk 42 A4
Gairloch Gdns. Kirk 59 D1
Gaitskell Ave. Alex 27 E4
Gala Ave. Ren 94 C1
Gala Cres. Wish 165 D3
Gala St. Glasg 98 C1
Galbraith Cres. Law 187 D3
Galbraith Dr. Glasg 115 F4
Galbraith Dr. Miln 75 F4
Galdenoch St. Glasg 99 D1
Gallacher Ave. Pais 113 D1
Gallacher Cres. Bonh ... 19 F1
Gallacher Ct. Pais 113 E3
Gallahill Ave. P Glasg ... 69 D4
Gallamuir Dr. Plea 12 B2
Gallamuir Rd. Plea 12 B3
Gallan Ave. Glasg 76 C1
Gallion Wlk. Kilmk 227 F4
Galloway Ave. Ayr 236 B1
Galloway Ave. Ham 183 E4
Galloway Dr. Glasg 138 A2
Galloway Dr. Ham 183 E3
Galloway Pl. Salt 216 C4
Galloway Rd. Aird 122 C2
Galloway Rd. E Kil 160 B2
Galloway St. Falk 42 A3
Galloway St. Glasg 97 F3
Gallowflat St. Glasg ... 114 B2
Gallowgate. Glasg 117 F3
Gallowhill Ave. Kirk 79 E3
Gallowhill Dr. Kirk 79 E4
Gallowhill Lark 185 D1
Gallowhill Rd. E Kil 158 C4
Gallowhill Rd. Kirk 79 E3
Gallowhill Rd. Pais 215 D2
Gallowhill Rd. Pais 114 A3
Galrigside Rd. Kilmk ... 227 E4
Galston Ave. Newt M ... 157 D3
Galston Ct. Ham 183 F4
Galston Rd. Hurl 228 C3
Galston St. Glasg 119 E1
Galt Ave. Irvine 219 E2
Galt Pl. E Kil 180 B4
Galt St. Green 46 B2
Gameshill View. Stew .. 211 F4
Gamrie Dr. Glasg 135 D4
Gamrie Gdns. Glasg ... 135 D4
Gamrie Rd. Glasg 135 D4
Gannochy Dr. Bish 78 B1
Gantock Cres. Glasg .. 119 E2
Ganton Ct. Kilw 207 D2
Garden St. Ayr 235 F1
Garden Pl. Troon 229 D2
Garden Square La. Kilw 207 F2
Garden Square Wlk. Aird 122 B4
Garden St. Ayr 235 F1
Garden St. Falk 42 B3
Garden St. Kilm 222 C1
Garden Terr. Falk 42 B3
Garden Veteran's Cotts. Ersk 72 C3
Gardenhall Ct. E Kil ... 179 F4
Gardenhall. E Kil 179 F4
Gardenside Ave. Glasg 139 D4
Gardenside Ave. Udd . 140 C3
Gardenside Cres. Glasg 139 D4
Gardenside. Hat 142 A2
Gardenside Pl. Glasg . 139 D4
Gardenside Rd. Ham .. 162 B1
Gardenside St. Udd 140 C3
Gardner St. Pres 236 B4
Gardner Gr. Tan 141 D4
Gardner St. Glasg 96 B2
Gardrum Gdns. Bth 66 B4
Gardrum Pl. Kilmk 222 C2
Gardyne St. Glasg 100 A1
Gare Rd. Ros 15 D2
Garelet Pl. Irvine 220 A1
Gareloch Ave. Pais 113 D1
Gareloch Cres. Aird ... 102 A3
Gareloch La. P Glasg ... 68 B4
Gareloch Rd. Green 46 A2
Gareloch Rd. Helen 16 F2
Gareloch Rd. P Glasg ... 68 C4
Gareloch Rd. Rhu 15 E3
Garfield Ave. Hat 142 B3
Garfield Dr. Hat 142 B2
Garfield St. Glasg 118 A3
Garforth Rd. Glasg 119 F2
Gargrave Ave. Glasg .. 119 F2
Garion Dr. Glasg 95 D3
Garrieston Rd. Glasg .. 119 F3

Garmouth Ct. Glasg 116 A4
Garmouth Gdns. Glasg 116 A4
Garmouth St. Glasg 115 F4
Garnet St. Glasg 97 D1
Garnethill St. Glasg 97 D1
Garngaber Ave. Kirk 79 E3
Garngaber Ct. Kirk 79 F3
Garngrew Rd. Bank 38 C2
Garnhall Farm Rd. Cumb 62 C4
Garnie Ave. Ersk 93 E4
Garnie La. Inch 93 E4
Garnie Oval. Ersk 73 E1
Garnie Pl. Ersk 73 E1
Garnieland Rd. Ersk 73 E1
Garnieland Rd. Inch 93 F4
Garnkirk La. Stepps 99 F3
Garnock St. Ardr 99 F3
Garnock St. Dalry 191 E4
Garnock St. Glasg 97 F1
Garnock St. Kilb 149 D1
Garnock View. Kilw 207 F2
Garpel Way. Loch 129 D1
Garrallan. Kilw 207 E1
Garrawy Rd. Helen 16 C1
Garrell Gr. Kils 36 B1
Garrell Pl. Kils 36 B1
Garrell Pl. Kils 60 B4
Garrell Rd. Kils 60 B4
Garrell Way. Cumb 61 F1
Garrell Way. Kils 60 B4
Garrier Pl. Kilmk 222 B1
Garrier Rd. Spring 220 C1
Garrioch Cres. Glasg 96 B3
Garrioch Gate. Glasg ... 96 B3
Garrioch Quadrant. Glasg 96 B3
Garrioch Rd. Glasg 96 C2
Garriochmill Rd. Glasg . 96 C2
Garrion Bsns Pk. Wish 186 A4
Garrion Pl. Ash 185 F1
Garrion St. Wish 186 B3
Garrowhill Dr. Glasg .. 119 F3
Garry Ave. Bear 76 A1
Garry Dr. Pais 113 D1
Garry Pl. Falk 42 B1
Garry Pl. Kilmk 228 A3
Garry Pl. Troon 229 F3
Garry St. Glasg 137 D4
Garry Way. Shot 146 C3
Garryhorn. Pres 236 B3
Garscadden Rd. Glasg .. 75 D1
Garscadden Rd S. Glasg 94 C4
Garscadden St. Glasg ... 95 D4
Garscadden View. Clyde 74 B2
Garscube Cross. Glasg . 97 D1
Garscube Rd. Glasg 97 D1
Garshake Ave. Dumb 50 B3
Garshake Rd. Dumb 50 B3
Garshake Terr. Dumb ... 50 B3
Gartartan Rd. Glasg ... 114 C3
Gartcarron Hill. Cumb .. 61 E2
Gartcloss Rd. Coat 101 E1
Gartcloss Gdns. Bann .. 11 F4
Gartconnell Dr. Bear 75 F3
Gartconnell Gdns. Bear . 75 F3
Gartconnell Rd. Bear 75 F3
Gartconner Ave. Kirk 80 A4
Gartcosh Rd. Coat 101 D1
Gartcosh Rd. Coat 120 C3
Gartcosh Wlk. Hat 141 F3
Gartcows Ave. Falk 42 A2
Gartcows Cres. Falk 42 A2
Gartcows Dr. Falk 42 A2
Gartcows Gdns. Falk 41 F2
Gartcows Pl. Falk 42 A2
Gartcows Rd. Falk 42 A2
Gartcraig Rd. Glasg ... 118 C4
Gartferry Ave. Bear 123 D3
Gartferry Rd. Muir 80 C1
Gartferry Rd. Muir 80 C1
Gartferry St. Glasg 98 A2
Gartfield St. Aird 123 D3
Gartgill Rd. Coat 101 F2
Gartgill La. Falk 42 A2
Garth St. Glasg 117 E4
Garthamlock Rd. Glasg . 99 F1
Garthill Gdns. Falk 42 A2
Garthland Dr. Ard 205 E2
Garthland Dr. Glasg ... 118 A4
Garthland La. Pais 113 F3
Gartlea Ave. Aird 123 D4
Gartlea Rd. Aird 123 D4
Gartleahill. Aird 123 D3
Gartliston Rd. Glenb ... 101 F2
Gartliston Terr. Coat ... 101 F1
Gartloch Rd. Glasg 99 D1
Gartloch Rd. Glasg 100 B2
Gartly St. Glasg 136 C2
Gartmore Gdns. Tan ... 140 C4
Gartmore La. Muir 81 D1
Gartmore Rd. Pais 114 B2
Gartmore Terr. Glasg . 138 C2

Gartmorn Rd. N Sau 5 E1
Gartness Dr. Chap 123 F3
Gartness Rd. Chap 124 A2
Gartocher Rd. Glasg ... 119 E3
Gartocher Terr. Glasg . 119 E3
Gartons Rd. Glasg 98 B2
Gartsherrie Ave. Glasg 101 F3
Gartsherrie Rd. Coat .. 121 F4
Gartshore Cres. Twe ... 59 F1
Gartshore Gdns. Cumb . 60 C3
Garturk St. Coat 122 A2
Garturk St. Glasg 117 D1
Garvald Ct. Glasg 118 A2
Garvald La. Den 21 E1
Garvald St. Glasg 118 A2
Garvald St. Green 46 B2
Garvally Cres. All 10 A4
Garve Ave. Glasg 137 D3
Garvel Cres. Glasg 119 F3
Garvel Pr. Miln 54 C1
Garvel Rd. Glasg 119 F3
Garvel Rd. Miln 54 C1
Garven Ct. Kilmk 228 A4
Garvin Rd. Steven 217 F3
Garvin Ave. Gour 44 C3
Garvock Dr. Glasg 136 A3
Garvock Dr. Green 45 E2
Garwhitter Dr. Miln 55 D1
Gas St. John 112 A2
Gascoyne. E Kil 180 B4
Gask Pl. Glasg 74 C2
Gaskin Path. Stepps 99 F3
Gasworks Rd. Car 187 E2
Gatehead Rd. Cross ... 221 F1
Gatehouse St. Glasg .. 119 D2
Gates Rd. Loch 129 E2
Gateshead Pl. Kilbar .. 111 D2
Gateside Ave. Bon 40 B3
Gateside Ave. Glasg .. 139 E3
Gateside Ave. Green 45 D2
Gateside Ave. Kils 60 A4
Gateside Cres. Aird 123 D4
Gateside Cres. Barr ... 134 A1
Gateside Gdns. Green .. 45 D2
Gateside Gr. Green 45 C2
Gateside La. Hag 219 F3
Gateside Pk. Kils 60 A4
Gateside Pl. Kilmk 227 F2
Gateside Rd. Barr 134 A1
Gateside Rd. Mother .. 164 C2
Gateside St. Ham 162 C2
Gateside St. Glasg 118 A3
Gateside St. W Kil 190 B3
Gateway The. E Kil 160 A2
Gaudry Ave. Glasg 115 E2
Gauldry St. Pais 113 F3
Gavell Rd. Kils 60 A4
Gavin Hamilton Ct. Ayr 239 E3
Gavin St. Mother 163 F3
Gavin's Mill Rd. Miln 55 D1
Gavinburn Gdns. O Kil . 73 D4
Gavinburn Pl. O Kil 73 D4
Gavinburn St. O Kil 73 D4
Gavins Rd. All 4 C1
Gavins Rd. Dunt 74 A3
Gavinton St. Glasg 136 C3
Gayne Dr. Glen 82 B1
Gean Ct. Cumb 62 C2
Gean Rd. All 9 F4
Gearholm Rd. Ayr 238 B2
Geary St. Glasg 76 B1
Geddes Hill. E Kil 160 A2
Geddes Rd. Glasg 98 B3
Geelong Gdns. Lennox .. 33 E1
Geils Ave. Dumb 50 C2
Geils Quadrant. Dumb .. 50 C2
Geilsland Rd. Beith 171 E4
Geilston Pk. Card 48 A1
Geirston Rd. Kilb 148 C1
Gelston St. Glasg 119 D2
Gemini Gr. Holy 143 D3
Gemmel Pl. Newt M ... 156 B3
Gemmell Cres. Ayr 236 B1
Gemmell Way. Stone .. 198 C1
General Roy Way. Car . 202 B4
Generals Gate. Udd 140 C3
Gentle Row. Dunt 73 F3
George Aitken Ct. Ard . 205 E2
George Ave. Clyde 74 B2
George Cres. Clyde 74 B2
George Ct. Ham 162 A3
George Ct. Pais 113 F2
George Gray St. Glasg 138 A2
George La. Pais 113 F2
George Mann Terr. Glasg 138 A2
George Pl. Pais 113 F2
George Reith Ave. Glasg 95 F3
George Sq. Ayr 236 A1
George Sq. Glasg 117 E4
George St. Aird 122 C4
George St. Alva 5 D3
George St. Ayr 235 F1
George St. Barr 134 A2
George St. Bonh 27 F2

George St. Chap ... 123 E2
George St. Falk ... 42 A3
George St. Glasg ... 117 E4
George St. Glasg ... 120 A2
George St. Ham ... 162 A3
George St. Helen ... 16 C1
George St. Holy ... 143 D2
George St. How ... 130 C3
George St. John ... 111 F2
George St. Lar ... 23 E2
George St. Laur ... 42 C2
George St. Mother ... 163 F2
George St. Pais ... 113 E2
George St. Steven ... 217 E4
George Street La. Bonh ... 27 F2
George Terr. Irvine ... 219 E2
George Way. Lark ... 185 D2
George's Ave. Ayr ... 236 A2
Gerald Terr. Sten ... 23 F2
Gerard Pl. Hat ... 142 A4
Gertrude Pl. Barr ... 134 A1
Ghillies La. Mother ... 142 B1
Gibb St. Chap ... 123 E1
Gibb St. Cle ... 144 A1
Gibbdun Pl. Bank ... 39 F4
Gibbon Cres. E Kil ... 160 B2
Gibbshill Pl. East ... 127 E3
Gibshill Rd. Green ... 46 C1
Gibson Ave. Dumb ... 50 A2
Gibson Cres. John ... 111 F1
Gibson La. Kil ... 69 E1
Gibson Quadrant. Mother ... 142 B1
Gibson St. Ren ... 94 A4
Gibson St. Dumb ... 50 A2
Gibson St. Glasg ... 96 C1
Gibson St. Glasg ... 117 F3
Gibson St. Helen ... 222 B1
Gibson St. Sals ... 125 D1
Gibsongray St. Falk ... 42 A4
Giffen Rd. Salt ... 217 D4
Giffnock Park Ave. Glasg ... 136 B2
Gifford Dr. Glasg ... 115 D3
Gigha Cres. Irvine ... 220 A1
Gigha Gdns. Car ... 202 A4
Gigha La. Irvine ... 220 A1
Gigha Pl. Irvine ... 220 A1
Gigha Quadrant. Wish ... 164 C1
Gigha Terr. Irvine ... 220 A1
Gigha Wynd. Irvine ... 220 A1
Gilbert St. Glasg ... 116 B4
Gilbertfield Path. Glasg ... 99 D1
Gilbertfield Path. Glasg ... 99 D1
Gilbertfield Pl. Glasg ... 99 D1
Gilbertfield Rd. Glasg ... 139 F2
Gilbertfield St. Glasg ... 99 D1
Gilburn Pl. Shot ... 146 C2
Gilchrist Dr. Falk ... 41 F2
Gilchrist St. Coat ... 122 A4
Gilderdale. E Kil ... 159 E1
Gilfillan Ave. Salt ... 206 A1
Gilfillan Pl. Wish ... 186 B4
Gilfillan Way. Pais ... 132 C4
Gilhill St. Glasg ... 96 B4
Gill Pk. Den ... 21 F1
Gill Rd. Wish ... 186 B3
Gill Rd. Wish ... 186 B3
Gillbank Ave. Car ... 187 E1
Gilbank La. Lark ... 185 E1
Gillburn Rd. Kil ... 69 E1
Gillburn St. Wish ... 186 B3
Gillburn Pl. Helen ... 16 B2
Gillespie Pl. Bann ... 7 D1
Gillies Cres. E Kil ... 160 B3
Gillies Ct. Aird ... 123 F4
Gillies St. Stir ... 7 E2
Gillies Hill. Cam ... 6 A3
Gillies La. Glasg ... 120 B2
Gillies St. Troon ... 229 E2
Gilmartin Rd. Lin ... 111 F3
Gilmerton St. Glasg ... 119 D2
Gilmour Ave. Dunt ... 74 A4
Gilmour Ave. Thorn ... 158 A1
Gilmour Cres. Eagle ... 178 C3
Gilmour Cres. Glasg ... 137 F4
Gilmour Dr. Ham ... 161 F1
Gilmour Pl. Coat ... 121 F4
Gilmour Pl. Glasg ... 117 E2
Gilmour Pl. Hat ... 141 F3
Gilmour St. Alex ... 27 E3
Gilmour St. Clyde ... 74 B3
Gilmour St. Eagle ... 178 C3
Gilmour St. Green ... 46 B1
Gilmour St. Kilmk ... 228 A4
Gilmour St. Pais ... 113 F3
Gilmour St. Stew ... 195 F1
Gilmourton Cres. Newt M ... 156 B2
Gilroy Cl. Lan ... 215 E3
Gilsay Ct. Falk ... 42 B1
Gimmerscroft Cres. Aird ... 123 F3
Girdle Gate. Irvine ... 219 F3
Girdle Toll. Irvine ... 220 A3
Girdons Dr. Glasg ... 119 E2
Girvan St. Glasg ... 118 B4
Glade The. Lark ... 185 D1
Gladney Ave. Clyde ... 94 C4
Gladsmuir Rd. Glasg ... 115 D3

Gladstone Ave. Barr ... 134 A1
Gladstone Ave. John ... 131 E4
Gladstone Ct. Ham ... 162 A3
Gladstone Pl. Stir ... 7 D3
Gladstone Rd. Salt ... 217 D4
Gladstone Rd. Sten ... 23 E2
Gladstone St. Glasg ... 97 D1
Gladstone St. Ham ... 142 A3
Glaive Ave. Bann ... 7 E2
Glaive Rd. Glasg ... 75 E1
Glamis Ave. Car ... 187 F1
Glamis Ave. E Kil ... 159 F2
Glamis Ave. John ... 112 A1
Glamis Ave. Newt M ... 156 C3
Glamis Dr. Green ... 45 D3
Glamis Gdns. Bish ... 78 A2
Glamis Pl. Green ... 45 D3
Glamis Rd. Glasg ... 118 B2
Glanderston Ave. Barr ... 134 C1
Glanderston Ave. Newt M ... 156 A3
Glanderston Dr. Glasg ... 95 D4
Glanderston Gate. Newt M ... 156 A3
Glanderston Rd. Newt M ... 155 E3
Glasgow and
 Edinburgh Rd. Calder ... 123 D1
Glasgow and
 Edinburgh Rd. Chap ... 144 A4
Glasgow and
 Edinburgh Rd. Coat ... 121 E2
Glasgow and
 Edinburgh Rd. Glasg ... 120 B3
Glasgow and
 Edinburgh Rd. Sals ... 125 D1
Glasgow La. Ard ... 205 E1
Glasgow Rd. Barr ... 39 E2
Glasgow Rd. Bann ... 11 E4
Glasgow Rd. Bart ... 134 B2
Glasgow Rd. Clyde ... 94 B4
Glasgow Rd. Coat ... 121 E3
Glasgow Rd. Cumb ... 62 A2
Glasgow Rd. Den ... 21 F1
Glasgow Rd. Dumb ... 50 B1
Glasgow Rd. Dumb ... 74 B3
Glasgow Rd. E Kil ... 160 A4
Glasgow Rd. Eagle ... 178 C4
Glasgow Rd. Falk ... 41 E3
Glasgow Rd. Glasg ... 114 B2
Glasgow Rd. Glasg ... 117 F1
Glasgow Rd. Glasg ... 120 A2
Glasgow Rd. Glasg ... 138 C1
Glasgow Rd. Glasg ... 139 F4
Glasgow Rd. Kilmk ... 223 E3
Glasgow Rd. Kils ... 60 B4
Glasgow Rd. Kirk ... 58 B1
Glasgow Rd. Klrk ... 79 D4
Glasgow Rd. Milln ... 55 D1
Glasgow Rd. Mother ... 164 C2
Glasgow Rd. Newt M ... 157 E1
Glasgow Rd. P Glasg ... 47 F1
Glasgow Rd. Ren ... 94 C1
Glasgow Rd. Stir ... 7 D1
Glasgow Rd. Strath ... 31 D2
Glasgow Rd. Tan ... 140 A4
Glasgow Rd. Udd ... 140 C4
Glasgow Rd. Udd ... 161 F4
Glasgow Rd. Wish ... 164 C2
Glasgow St. Ard ... 205 E1
Glasgow St. Glasg ... 96 C1
Glasgow St. Helen ... 16 B1
Glasgow St. Kilb ... 170 A4
Glasgow Vennel. Irvine ... 219 E1
Glassel Rd. Glasg ... 100 B1
Glasserton Pl. Glasg ... 136 C3
Glasserton Rd. Glasg ... 136 C3
Glassford Rd. Stone ... 198 B3
Glassford St. Ham ... 117 E4
Glassford St. Milln ... 55 D1
Glassford St. Mother ... 164 A2
Glasshouse Loan. All ... 10 A3
Glassock Rd. Kilmk ... 222 C3
Gaudhall Ave. Muir ... 100 C4
Glazert Pl. M of C ... 58 A2
Glebe Ave. Coat ... 121 E2
Glebe Ave. E Kil ... 158 B4
Glebe Ave. Irvine ... 225 E4
Glebe Ave. Kilmk ... 222 B4
Glebe Ave. Stir ... 7 D4
Glebe Ave. Udd ... 141 D1
Glebe Cres. Aird ... 123 E4
Glebe Cres. Alva ... 5 D4
Glebe Cres. Ayr ... 235 F1
Glebe Cres. E Kil ... 158 B4
Glebe Cres. Ham ... 162 B1
Glebe Cres. Stir ... 7 D4
Glebe Ct. Beith ... 171 C3
Glebe Ct. Glasg ... 117 F4
Glebe Ct. Lar ... 89 E4
Glebe Gdns. Bonh ... 27 F2
Glebe Gdns. Hous ... 91 D1
Glebe Hollow. Udd ... 141 D1
Glebe La. Newt M ... 156 B2
Glebe Pk. Dumb ... 50 A3
Glebe Pl. Glasg ... 137 F4
Glebe Pl. Glasg ... 139 D3
Glebe Pl. Salt ... 216 C4

Glebe Rd. Ayr ... 235 F1
Glebe Rd. Beith ... 171 D4
Glebe Rd. Kil ... 89 E4
Glebe Rd. Kilmk ... 228 A4
Glebe Rd. Newt M ... 156 B2
Glebe St. Den ... 21 F1
Glebe St. E Kil ... 159 F1
Glebe St. Falk ... 42 A3
Glebe St. Glasg ... 97 E1
Glebe St. Glasg ... 117 F4
Glebe St. Ham ... 162 B1
Glebe St. Hat ... 141 F3
Glebe St. Kilw ... 207 F2
Glebe St. Ren ... 94 B2
Glebe St. Salt ... 216 C4
Glebe St. Steven ... 206 B1
Glebe Terr. All ... 10 A3
Glebe Terr. Fen ... 213 D2
Glebe The. Alva ... 5 D4
Glebe The. Irvine ... 225 E4
Glebe The. Lan ... 214 C2
Glebe The. Udd ... 141 D1
Glebe Wynd. Udd ... 141 D1
Glebefield Rd. Rhu ... 15 F3
Glebelands Way. Beith ... 171 D4
Gleddoch Rd. Glasg ... 114 C3
Gledstane Rd. Bishop ... 72 A1
Glen Affric Ave. Glasg ... 135 E2
Glen Affric Dr. Chap ... 123 E1
Glen Affric Dr. Glasg ... 135 E2
Glen Affric. E Kil ... 160 A1
Glen Affric Pl. Kilmk ... 227 E3
Glen Affric Way. Chap ... 123 E1
Glen Alton Ct. Kilmk ... 227 E3
Glen Alby Pl. Glasg ... 135 E2
Glen Almond. E Kil ... 160 B1
Glen Arroch. E Kil ... 160 A1
Glen Ave. Bonh ... 28 A4
Glen Ave. Glasg ... 119 D3
Glen Ave. Gour ... 44 C3
Glen Ave. Mur ... 80 C1
Glen Ave. Neil ... 154 C4
Glen Ave. P Glasg ... 47 D1
Glen Avon Dr. Chap ... 123 E1
Glen Bervie. E Kil ... 160 A1
Glen Brae. B of W ... 110 B4
Glen Brae. Falk ... 42 C1
Glen Cally. E Kil ... 160 A1
Glen Cannich. E Kil ... 160 A1
Glen Carron. E Kil ... 160 A1
Glen Clova. E Kil ... 160 A1
Glen Clunie Ave. Glasg ... 135 E2
Glen Clunie Dr. Glasg ... 135 E2
Glen Clunie Pl. Glasg ... 160 B1
Glen Clunie Pl. Glasg ... 135 E2
Glen Cona Dr. Glasg ... 135 E2
Glen Creran Cres. Neil ... 154 B3
Glen Cres. Clyde ... 74 A4
Glen Cres. Falk ... 42 A1
Glen Ct. Coat ... 121 E3
Glen Ct. Mother ... 164 A2
Glen Derry. E Kil ... 160 B2
Glen Dessary. E Kil ... 181 D4
Glen Devon. E Kil ... 160 B1
Glen Doll. E Kil ... 160 A1
Glen Doll Rd. Neil ... 154 A3
Glen Douglas Dr. Cumb ... 61 E2
Glen Douglas Pl. Green ... 45 E2
Glen Douglas Rd. Green ... 45 E2
Glen Douglas Way. Green ... 45 E2
Glen Dr. Helen ... 16 A2
Glen Dr. Holy ... 143 D3
Glen Dye. E Kil ... 160 A1
Glen Eagles. E Kil ... 160 A1
Glen Esk Dr. Glasg ... 135 E2
Glen Esk. E Kil ... 160 B1
Glen Etive Pl. Glasg ... 138 C1
Glen Falloch Cres. Neil ... 154 B3
Glen Falloch. E Kil ... 160 A1
Glen Farg. E Kil ... 160 A1
Glen Farrar. E Kil ... 160 A1
Glen Farrar Wlk. Kilmk ... 227 E3
Glen Feshie. E Kil ... 181 D4
Glen Finlet Rd. Neil ... 154 B3
Glen Fruin Dr. Lark ... 185 E1
Glen Fruin Pl. Chap ... 123 E1
Glen Fruin Rd. Green ... 45 E2
Glen Fyne Rd. Cumb ... 61 E2
Glen Gairn Cres. Neil ... 154 B3
Glen Gairn. E Kil ... 160 B1
Glen Garrell Pl. Kils ... 36 B1
Glen Garry. E Kil ... 181 D4
Glen Gdns. Falk ... 42 A2
Glen Gdns. John ... 112 B2
Glen Gr. E Kil ... 180 B4
Glen Gr. Kils ... 36 B1
Glen Isla Ave. Neil ... 154 B3
Glen Isla. E Kil ... 160 B1
Glen Kinglas Ave. Green ... 45 E1
Glen Kinglas Rd. Green ... 45 E1
Glen La. Pais ... 113 F3
Glen La. Uplaw ... 153 D2
Glen Lednock Dr. Cumb ... 61 D2
Glen Lee. E Kil ... 160 B1
Glen Lethnot. E Kil ... 160 B1
Glen Livet Pl. Glasg ... 135 E2
Glen Lochay Gdns. Cumb ... 61 D2
Glen Loy Pl. Glasg ... 135 E2

Glen Luce Dr. Glasg ... 119 E2
Glen Luss Rd. Green ... 45 E1
Glen Luss Way. Green ... 45 E1
Glen Lyon Ct. Cumb ... 61 D2
Glen Lyon. E Kil ... 160 B1
Glen Lyon Rd. Neil ... 154 B3
Glen Mallie. E Kil ... 160 B1
Glen Mark. E Kil ... 160 B1
Glen Mark Rd. Neil ... 154 B3
Glen Markie Dr. Glasg ... 135 E2
Glen More. E Kil ... 160 A1
Glen Moriston. E Kil ... 160 A1
Glen Moriston Rd. Glasg ... 135 E2
Glen Moy. E Kil ... 160 B1
Glen Muir Rd. Neil ... 154 B3
Glen Nevis. E Kil ... 181 D4
Glen Nevis Pl. Glasg ... 138 B1
Glen Nevis Pl. Kilmk ... 227 E3
Glen Ochil Rd. Chap ... 123 E1
Glen Ogilvie. E Kil ... 160 B1
Glen Ogle St. Glasg ... 119 E2
Glen Orchy Dr. Glasg ... 135 E2
Glen Orchy Pl. Chap ... 123 E1
Glen Orchy Pl. Glasg ... 135 E2
Glen Orchy Pl. Kilmk ... 227 E3
Glen Orrin Ave. Kilmk ... 227 E3
Glen Orrin Way. Kilmk ... 227 E3
Glen Pl. Newt M ... 157 E4
Glen Prosen. E Kil ... 160 B1
Glen Quoich. E Kil ... 160 B2
Glen Rannoch Dr. Chap ... 123 E1
Glen Rd. Aird ... 123 E3
Glen Rd. Bishop ... 72 A2
Glen Rd. Cald ... 104 C2
Glen Rd. E Kil ... 158 C3
Glen Rd. Glasg ... 119 D4
Glen Rd. Holy ... 143 E4
Glen Rd. Lennox ... 33 D1
Glen Rd. O Kil ... 73 D3
Glen Rd. Plea ... 12 B1
Glen Rd. Shot ... 146 C2
Glen Rd. Tor ... 22 B4
Glen Rd. Wish ... 190 B3
Glen Rd. Wish ... 165 D4
Glen Rinnes Dr. Neil ... 154 B3
Glen Roy Dr. Neil ... 154 B3
Glen Sax Dr. Ren ... 94 C1
Glen Shee Ave. Neil ... 154 B3
Glen Shee Cres. Chap ... 123 E1
Glen Shee. E Kil ... 160 B1
Glen Shiel Cres. Kilmk ... 227 E3
Glen Shirva Rd. Twe ... 59 F2
Glen St. Barr ... 134 B2
Glen St. Glasg ... 116 C4
Glen St. Green ... 45 E4
Glen St. Holy ... 143 E2
Glen St. Mother ... 142 C1
Glen St. Pais ... 113 F3
Glen Tanner. E Kil ... 160 B1
Glen Tarbert Dr. Neil ... 154 B3
Glen Tennet. E Kil ... 160 B1
Glen Terr. Den ... 21 E1
Glen Trool Wlk. Kilmk ... 227 E4
Glen Truim View. Kilmk ... 227 E3
Glen Turret. E Kil ... 160 B1
Glen Urquhart. E Kil ... 160 A1
Glen View. Bank ... 39 E3
Glen View. Cumb ... 62 B2
Glen View. Ham ... 183 E4
Glenacre Cres. Tan ... 140 C4
Glenacre Dr. Aird ... 123 E3
Glenacre Dr. Glasg ... 137 E2
Glenacre Quadrant. Glasg ... 137 E2
Glenacre Rd. Cumb ... 82 C4
Glenacre St. Glasg ... 137 E2
Glenacre Terr. Glasg ... 137 E2
Glenafeoch Rd. Car ... 188 A1
Glenafton View. Ham ... 183 D4
Glenalla Cres. Ayr ... 238 B1
Glenallan Way. Pais ... 132 C4
Glenalmond Rd. Glasg ... 119 D2
Glenalmond St. Glasg ... 119 D2
Glenan Gdns. Helen ... 16 B1
Glenapp Ave. Pais ... 114 A1
Glenapp Pl. Glasg ... 100 B4
Glenapp Pl. Kilw ... 207 E1
Glenapp Pl. Kilw ... 207 E1
Glenapp Pl. Muir ... 80 C2
Glenapp Quadrant. Kilmk ... 228 A4
Glenapp Rd. Pais ... 114 A1
Glenapp St. Glasg ... 117 D2
Glenarklet Dr. Pais ... 114 A1
Glenarn Rd. Rhu ... 15 F2
Glenartney. Hous ... 91 D1
Glenartney Rd. Muir ... 80 B1
Glenashdale Way. Pais ... 114 A1
Glenavon Ct. Ham ... 162 A1
Glenavon Rd. Glasg ... 96 B4
Glenbank Ave. Klrk ... 79 E2
Glenbank Ct. Glasg ... 135 F1
Glenbank Dr. Glasg ... 135 D1
Glenbank. Falk ... 42 A1
Glenbank Rd. Klrk ... 79 E2
Glenbank St. Glasg ... 97 F1
Glenbarr St. Glasg ... 118 A3
Glenbervie Cres. Cumb ... 61 F3
Glenbervie Cres. Lar ... 23 D2
Glenbervie Dr. Kilw ... 207 D2
Glenbervie Dr. Lar ... 23 D2
Glenbervie Pl. Glasg ... 76 C1

Glenbervie Pl. Gour ... 44 A3
Glenbo Dr. Bank ... 39 F4
Glenbog Farm Rd. Glen ... 101 F3
Glenbog New Rd. Glen ... 101 F3
Glenbog Rd. Glen ... 101 E3
Glenbog Rd. Glen ... 101 D4
Glenbrae Ct. Falk ... 42 A2
Glenbrae La. Green ... 46 A1
Glenbrae Rd. Green ... 46 A1
Glenbrae Rd. P Glasg ... 68 B4
Glenbride Rd. W Kil ... 190 B2
Glenbrittle Dr. Pais ... 114 A1
Glenbrittle Way. Pais ... 114 A1
Glenbuck Ave. Glasg ... 98 C3
Glenbuck Dr. Glasg ... 98 C3
Glenburn Ave. Glasg ... 120 B3
Glenburn Ave. Glasg ... 138 C3
Glenburn Ave. Holy ... 143 E3
Glenburn Ave. Muir ... 80 C1
Glenburn Cres. M of C ... 58 B3
Glenburn Cres. Pais ... 133 E4
Glenburn Cres. Tan ... 141 E4
Glenburn Dr. Kil ... 69 E1
Glenburn Gdns. Bish ... 77 F1
Glenburn Gdns. Glen ... 101 D3
Glenburn La. Glasg ... 96 C4
Glenburn Rd. Bear ... 75 F3
Glenburn Rd. E Kil ... 159 D2
Glenburn Rd. Falk ... 42 B1
Glenburn Rd. Glasg ... 136 A1
Glenburn Rd. Ham ... 162 A2
Glenburn Rd. Kil ... 69 E1
Glenburn Rd. Pais ... 133 E4
Glenburn Rd. Pres ... 236 E4
Glenburn St. Glasg ... 96 C4
Glenburn St. P Glasg ... 47 D1
Glenburn Terr. Car ... 201 F1
Glenburn Terr. Holy ... 143 E1
Glenburn Way. E Kil ... 158 C2
Glenburn Wlk. Glasg ... 120 B3
Glenburn Wynd. Lark ... 185 D2
Glencairn Dr. Falk ... 42 A1
Glencairn Ave. Mother ... 164 B2
Glencairn Dr. Glasg ... 116 C1
Glencairn Dr. Glasg ... 137 F4
Glencairn Dr. Muir ... 80 C1
Glencairn Gdns. Glasg ... 116 C1
Glencairn Gdns. Glasg ... 139 E3
Glencairn La. Glasg ... 116 C1
Glencairn Rd. Ayr ... 239 D3
Glencairn Rd. Cumb ... 62 B1
Glencairn Rd. Dumb ... 49 E2
Glencairn Rd. Gour ... 44 C2
Glencairn Rd. Holy ... 143 E1
Glencairn Rd. Lang ... 70 F4
Glencairn Rd. Pais ... 114 A4
Glencairn St. Kilmk ... 227 F3
Glencairn St. Falk ... 31 D3
Glencairn St. Helen ... 16 C1
Glencairn St. Kilmk ... 227 F3
Glencairn St. Mother ... 163 F3
Glencairn St. Salt ... 216 C4
Glencairn St. Steven ... 206 C1
Glencairn St. Stir ... 7 D2
Glencairn Terr. Kilmk ... 222 A4
Glencalder Cres. Hat ... 142 B2
Glencally Ave. Pais ... 114 A1
Glencart St. John ... 111 E1
Glencleland Rd. Mother ... 164 B2
Glenclora Dr. Pais ... 114 A1
Glencloy St. Glasg ... 96 B4
Glencoats Cres. Pais ... 113 D2
Glencoe Dr. Holy ... 143 D3
Glencoe Pl. Ham ... 183 D4
Glencoe Rd. Car ... 202 A4
Glencoe Rd. Glasg ... 138 B2
Glencoe St. Stir ... 2 A1
Glencoe St. Glasg ... 95 F4
Glenconner Pl. Ayr ... 239 D3
Glenconner Rd. Ayr ... 239 D3
Glenconner Way. Kirk ... 59 D1
Glenconer Rd. Ayr ... 199 D4
Glencorse Rd. Pais ... 113 E1
Glencorse St. Glasg ... 118 C4
Glencraig St. Aird ... 122 C4
Glencroft Rd. Glasg ... 137 E3
Glencroft Terr. Pen ... 213 D2
Glencryan Rd. Cumb ... 62 A2
Glendale Ave. Aird ... 123 E3
Glendale Cres. Ayr ... 239 E2
Glendale Cres. Bish ... 98 B4
Glendale Dr. Bish ... 98 B4
Glendale Pl. Bish ... 98 B4
Glendale Pl. Glasg ... 118 A3
Glendale St. Glasg ... 118 A3
Glendaruel Ave. Bear ... 76 A3
Glendaruel Rd. Glasg ... 139 F1
Glendee Gdns. Ren ... 94 B1
Glendee Rd. Ren ... 94 B1
Glendenning Rd. B of W ... 110 B3
Glendevon Pl. Clyde ... 73 F2
Glendevon Pl. Ham ... 183 D4

262

Glendevon Sq. Glasg Greenhead Rd. Dumb

Glendevon Sq. Glasg 99 D1
Glendinning Pl. Eagle 178 B2
Glendinning Rd. Glasg 75 F1
Glendorch Ave. Wish 165 E4
Glendore St. Glasg 95 F1
Glendoune Rd. Newt M 157 F3
Glendower Way. Pais 132 C4
Glenduffhill Rd. Glasg 119 F3
Gleneagles Ave. Cumb 62 A3
Gleneagles Ave. Kilw 207 E2
Gleneagles Dr. Bish 78 A2
Gleneagles Dr. Gour 44 A3
Gleneagles Gdns. Bish 78 A2
Gleneagles La N. Glasg 95 E2
Gleneagles La S. Glasg 95 E2
Gleneagles Pk. Udd 140 C1
Glenelg Cres. Kirk 59 D1
Glenelg Path. Glen 101 E3
Glenelg Quadrant. Glasg 100 B1
Glenelm Pl. Hat 142 A3
Glenfarg Cres. Bear 76 A2
Glenfarg Rd. Glasg 138 A2
Glenfarg Rd. Ham 183 D4
Glenfarg St. Glasg 97 D1
Glenfarm Rd. Holy 143 F2
Glenfield Ave. Pais 133 F4
Glenfield Cres. Pais 133 F3
Glenfield Gdns. Kilmk 227 F3
Glenfield Pl. Kilmk 227 F3
Glenfield Rd. E Kil 181 D3
Glenfield Rd. Pais 133 E3
Glenfinlas St. Helen 16 C1
Glenfinnan Dr. Glasg 76 B2
Glenfinnan Dr. Glasg 96 B3
Glenfinnan Pl. Glasg 96 B3
Glenfinnan Rd. Glasg 96 B3
Glenfruin Cres. Pais 114 A1
Glenfruin Rd. Udd 161 E4
Glenfuir Rd. Falk 41 F3
Glenfuir St. Falk 41 E3
Glengarnock
Workshops. Kilb 170 B4
Glengarriff Rd. Hat 142 A4
Glengarry Dr. Glasg 115 E3
Glengavel Cres. Glasg 98 C3
Glengavel Gdns. Wish 165 E4
Glengowan Rd. B of W 110 B4
Glengowan Rd. Cald 105 D2
Glengyre St. Glasg 100 B1
Glenhead Cres. Dunt 74 A4
Glenhead Cres. Glasg 97 E3
Glenhead Rd. Clyde 74 A3
Glenhead Rd. Kirk 79 E2
Glenhead St. Glasg 97 E3
Glenholme Ave. Pais 113 D1
Glenhove Rd. Cumb 62 A1
Glenhuntly Rd. P Glasg 47 E1
Glenhuntly Terr. P Glasg 47 E1
Gleniffer Ave. Glasg 95 D3
Gleniffer Cres. John 112 B1
Gleniffer Ct. Aird 103 D1
Gleniffer Dr. Barr 134 A3
Gleniffer Rd. John 132 B2
Gleniffer Rd. Pais 133 D4
Gleniffer Rd. Ren 114 A4
Gleniffer Rd. Uplaw 152 B2
Gleniffer View. Clyde 74 B2
Gleniffer View. Neil 154 B4
Gleninver Rd. Green 45 D2
Glenisla Ave. Muir 81 D2
Glenisla St. Glasg 118 B2
Glenkirk Dr. Glasg 75 D1
Glenlee St. Ham 161 F3
Glenleith Pl. Irvine 220 B1
Glenlivet Pl. Kilmk 223 D2
Glenlivet Rd. Neil 154 B3
Glenlora Dr. Glasg 135 D4
Glenlora Terr. Glasg 135 D4
Glenluce Gdns. Muir 81 D2
Glenluce Terr. E Kil 159 E1
Glenluggie Rd. Kirk 80 A4
Glenlui Ave. Glasg 138 A3
Glenlyon Ct. Ham 183 D4
Glenlyon Gr. Irvine 219 F3
Glenlyon Pl. Glasg 138 B2
Glenmalloch Pl. John 112 B2
Glenmanor Ave. Muir 80 C1
Glenmare Ave. Kirk 80 A4
Glenmavis Cres. Car 188 A1
Glenmavis Rd. Aird 102 C1
Glenmavis St. Glasg 97 D1
Glenmore Ave. Glasg 137 F4
Glenmore Ave. Hat 142 A2
Glenmore Dr. Bon 39 F3
Glenmore Rd. Holy 143 E2
Glenmoss Ave. Ersk 72 C1
Glenmosston Rd. Kil 89 F4
Glenmount Pl. Ayr 238 A1
Glenmuir Ct. Ayr 236 B1
Glenmuir Dr. Glasg 135 D3
Glenmuir Pl. Ayr 236 B1
Glenmuir Rd. Ayr 236 B1
Glenochil Pk. Men 4 C2
Glenochil Rd. Falk 42 A2
Glenochil Terr. Men 4 C2
Glenoran La. Lark 185 D2
Glenoran Rd. Helen 16 A2
Glenorchard Rd. Bish 56 B1
Glenorrin Way. Neil 154 B3
Glenpark. Aird 123 F3
Glenpark Ave. Glasg 136 A1
Glenpark Ave. Pres 236 B3
Glenpark Dr. P Glasg 47 D1
Glenpark Gdns. Glasg 138 C4
Glenpark Pl. Ayr 239 D2
Glenpark Rd. Glasg 118 A3
Glenpark Rd. Loch 129 E2
Glenpark St. Glasg 118 A3
Glenpark St. Wish 165 D2
Glenpark Terr. Glasg 138 C4
Glenpath. Dumb 50 B2
Glenpatrick Rd. John 112 B1
Glenraith Path. Glasg 99 D2
Glenraith Rd. Glasg 99 D1
Glenraith Sq. Glasg 99 D2
Glenraith Wlk. Glasg 99 E2
Glenriddel Rd. Ayr 239 D3
Glenriddet Ave. Kilb 170 A4
Glenshee St. Glasg 118 B2
Glenshee Terr. Ham 183 D4
Glenshiel Ave. Pais 114 A1
Glenshira Ave. Pais 114 A1
Glenside Ave. Glasg 115 D1
Glenside Cres. W Kil 190 B3
Glenside Dr. Glasg 138 C3
Glenside Gr. W Kil 190 B3
Glenside Rd. Dumb 50 B3
Glenside Rd. P Glasg 68 B4
Glenspean St. Glasg 136 B3
Glentanar Pl. Glasg 97 D4
Glentanar Rd. Glasg 97 D4
Glentarbert Rd. Glasg 138 B2
Glentore Quadrant. Aird 103 D1
Glenturret St. Glasg 119 D2
Glentyan Ave. Kilbar 111 D2
Glentyan Dr. Glasg 135 D3
Glentyan Terr. Glasg 135 D4
Glentye Gdns. Falk 41 F1
Glenview. Aird 123 E3
Glenview Ave. Bank 38 C2
Glenview Ave. Cald 105 D2
Glenview Cres. Muir 81 D2
Glenview Dr. Falk 41 F1
Glenview. Duni 21 D2
Glenview. Kirk 79 E4
Glenview. Lark 184 C2
Glenview. Men 4 A3
Glenview Pl. Udd 140 B1
Glenview St. Glenm 102 C2
Glenview Terr. Green 45 E2
Glenview. W Kil 190 B2
Glenville Ave. Glasg 136 A2
Glenville Gate. Thorn 158 A3
Glenville Terr. Thorn 158 A3
Glenward Ave. Lennox 57 F4
Glenwell St. Glenm 102 C2
Glenwinnel Rd. Alva 4 C4
Glenwood Ave. Aird 123 E2
Glenwood Bsns Ctr. Glasg 137 F2
Glenwood Ct. Kirk 79 D3
Glenwood Dr. Glasg 135 F1
Glenwood Gdns. Kirk 79 D3
Glenwood Pl. Kirk 79 D3
Glenwood Rd. Kirk 79 D3
Glenyards Rd. Bon 40 A1
Glidden Ct. Wish 186 B4
Glorat Ave. Lennox 57 F4
Gloucester Ave. Glasg 138 B3
Gloucester Ave. Newt M 157 E4
Gloucester St. Glasg 117 D3
Glowrorum Dr. Bank 39 F4
Glynwed Ct. Falk 42 B4
Goatfell View. Troon 229 F4
Gockston Rd. Pais 113 E4
Goddard Pl. New 166 A3
Godfrey Ave. Den 21 E1
Godfrey Cres. Lar 23 E1
Gogar Loan. B of A 3 E3
Gogar Pl. Glasg 118 C4
Gogar Pl. Stir 7 E1
Gogar St. Glasg 118 C4
Goil Ave. Tan 141 E3
Goil Way. Holy 143 D3
Goldberry Ave. Glasg 95 D3
Goldcraig Ct. Irvine 220 A3
Goldenacre Pl. Plains 103 F2
Goldenberry Ave. W Kil 190 B2
Goldie Pl. Steven 206 B1
Goldie Rd. Udd 141 D2
Golf Ave. Hat 142 A2
Golf Ave. Steven 217 F3
Golf Course Rd. B of W 110 B4
Golf Course Rd. Bish 77 F4
Golf Cres. Troon 229 E1
Golf Dr. Glasg 74 C1
Golf Dr. P Glasg 68 B4
Golf Dr. Pais 114 B2
Golf Gdns. Lark 185 E1
Golf Pl. Green 45 E4
Golf Pl. Hat 142 A2
Golf Pl. Helen 17 D1
Golf Pl. Irvine 219 D3
Golf Pl. Troon 229 E1
Golf Rd. Bishop 72 A2
Golf Rd. Glasg 138 A2
Golf Rd. Gour 44 B3
Golf Rd. Newt M 157 E4
Golf View. Clyde 73 F2
Golffields Rd. Irvine 219 E1
Golfhill Dr. Bonh 27 F3
Golfhill Dr. Glasg 118 A4
Golfhill Dr. Helen 16 C1
Golfhill Quadrant. Aird 103 D1
Golfhill Rd. Mother 164 C2
Golfview. Bear 75 E3
Golfview Dr. Coat 121 E4
Golfview Pl. Coat 121 E3
Golsbie Ave. Aird 122 C2
Golspie St. Glasg 116 A4
Goodview Gdns. Lark 185 E1
Goosecroft Rd. Stir 7 D4
Goosedubbs. Glasg 117 E3
Gooseholm Cres. Dumb 50 A3
Gooseholm Rd. Dumb 50 A3
Gopher Ave. Tan 141 D4
Gorbals Cross. Glasg 117 E3
Gorbals Cross. Lark 185 D2
Gorbals St. Glasg 117 E3
Gordon Ave. Bishop 72 A2
Gordon Ave. Glasg 114 C4
Gordon Ave. Glasg 119 F3
Gordon Ave. Glasg 136 C1
Gordon Cres. B of A 2 A4
Gordon Cres. Newt M 156 C3
Gordon Cres. Stir 1 C1
Gordon Ct. Aird 123 F4
Gordon Dr. All 10 B4
Gordon Dr. E Kil 160 A2
Gordon Dr. Glasg 136 C2
Gordon La. Glasg 117 D4
Gordon Pl. Falk 41 F3
Gordon Pl. Hat 141 F1
Gordon Rd. Glasg 136 C1
Gordon Rd. Ham 161 F2
Gordon Rd. Kilmk 222 C2
Gordon St. Ayr 236 A2
Gordon St. Glasg 117 D4
Gordon St. Green 45 F2
Gordon St. Pais 113 F2
Gordon Terr. Ayr 239 D4
Gordon Terr. Ham 161 F2
Gordon Terr. Udd 140 B1
Gorebridge St. Glasg 118 C4
Goremire Rd. Car 202 A4
Gorget Ave. Glasg 75 E1
Gorget Pl. Glasg 75 E1
Gorget Quadrant. Glasg 75 D1
Gorrie St. Den 21 E1
Gorse Cres. B of W 110 C4
Gorse Pk. Ayr 239 E2
Gorse Pl. Tan 141 D4
Gorsehall St. Cle 144 A1
Gorsewood. Bish 77 F1
Gorstan Pl. Glasg 96 B3
Gorstan St. Glasg 96 B4
Goschen Terr. Ayr 236 A1
Gosford La. Glasg 95 D2
Gottries Rd. Irvine 219 D1
Goudie St. Pais 113 E4
Gough St. Glasg 118 B4
Goukscroft Pk. Ayr 238 B2
Gould St. Ayr 236 B1
Gourlay Dr. Wish 186 B3
Gourlay. E Kil 160 B3
Gourlay St. Glasg 97 E2
Gourlay St. Glasg 97 F2
Gourock St. Glasg 117 D2
Govan Dr. Alex 27 E3
Govan Rd. Glasg 115 F4
Govan Rd. Glasg 116 B3
Govanhill St. Glasg 117 D1
Govanhill St. Glasg 117 E1
Gowan Ave. Falk 42 A3
Gowan Brae. Cald 105 D3
Gowan La. Falk 42 A3
Gowanbank Gdns. John 111 F1
Gowanbank Rd. Ayr 239 D1
Gowanbrae. Kirk 79 E3
Gowanhill Gdns. Stir 1 C1
Gowanlea Ave. Glasg 75 D1
Gowanlea Dr. Glasg 136 B2
Gowanlea Dr. Slam 86 A3
Gowanlea Terr. Tan 141 D4
Gowanside Pl. Car 187 E1
Gower Pl. Ayr 239 D2
Gower St. Glasg 116 B2
Gower Terr. Glasg 116 B3
Gowkhall Ave. Holy 143 F2
Gowkhouse Rd. Kil 89 F4
Goyle Ave. Glasg 75 E2
Grace Ave. Coat 120 C3
Grace St. Glasg 116 C4
Gracie Cres. Fall 8 B2
Gradion Pl. Falk 42 A2
Graeme Pl. Falk 41 F1
Graffham Ave. Glasg 136 C2
Grafton Pl. Glasg 117 E4
Graham Ave. Clyde 74 A2
Graham Ave. E Kil 159 F1
Graham Ave. Glasg 139 E3
Graham Ave. Ham 183 E4
Graham Ave. Lar 23 D2
Graham Ave. Stir 2 B2
Graham Cres. Card 48 A4
Graham Dr. Miln 54 C1
Graham Pl. Ash 185 F1
Graham Pl. Helen 17 D1
Graham Pl. Kilmk 223 E1
Graham Pl. Kils 36 B1
Graham Rd. Car 201 D1
Graham Rd. Dumb 49 E2
Graham Sq. Glasg 117 F3
Graham St. Aird 123 D4
Graham St. B of A 2 A4
Graham St. Barr 134 A2
Graham St. Green 45 E3
Graham St. Ham 162 C2
Graham St. Holy 143 D3
Graham St. John 111 F1
Graham St. Wish 165 D1
Graham Terr. Air 14 B2
Graham Terr. Bish 98 A4
Graham Terr. Stew 195 E1
Graham View. Alex 27 F1
Grahamfield Pl. Beith 171 D4
Grahams Ave. Loch 129 E2
Grahams Rd. Falk 42 A3
Grahamsdyke Cres. Bon 40 A2
Grahamsdyke Rd. Bon 40 A2
Grahamsdyke Rd. Kirk 58 C1
Grahamsdyke St. Laur 42 C2
Grahamshill Ave. Aird 123 E4
Grahamshill St. Aird 123 E4
Grahamston Ave. Kilb 170 A4
Grahamston Cres. Pais 134 B4
Grahamston Ct. Pais 134 B4
Grahamston Pk. Barr 134 A3
Grahamston Pl. Pais 134 B4
Grahamston Rd. Barr 134 B3
Grahamston Rd. Pais 134 B3
Graigleith View. Tull 4 B2
Graignestock Pl. Glasg 117 F3
Graignestock St. Glasg 117 F3
Graigside Pl. Cumb 81 F4
Grainger Rd. Bish 78 B1
Grammar School Sq. Ham 162 C2
Grampian Ave. Pais 133 E4
Grampian Cres. Glasg 119 D2
Grampian Ct. Irvine 220 A2
Grampian Pl. Glasg 119 D2
Grampian Rd. Kilmk 228 A2
Grampian Rd. P Glasg 69 D3
Grampian Rd. Stir 6 C3
Grampian Rd. Wish 164 C2
Grampian St. Glasg 119 D2
Grampian Way. Barr 134 B1
Grampian Way. Bear 75 D4
Grampian Way. Bear 75 E4
Grampian Way. Cumb 61 D1
Gran St. Clyde 94 C4
Granary Rd. Falk 42 A4
Granary Sq. Falk 42 A4
Granby La. Glasg 96 B2
Grandtuly Dr. Glasg 96 B3
Grange Ave. Ayr 239 D1
Grange Ave. Falk 42 B3
Grange Ave. Miln 55 D1
Grange Ave. Wish 164 C1
Grange Ct. Lan 214 C3
Grange Dr. Falk 42 B3
Grange Gdns. B of A 2 B4
Grange Gdns. Udd 141 D1
Grange Pl. Alex 27 F3
Grange Pl. Kilmk 227 F4
Grange Rd. All 9 F3
Grange Rd. B of A 2 B3
Grange Rd. Bear 75 F3
Grange Rd. Glasg 137 D4
Grange Rd. Steven 206 B1
Grange St. Kilmk 227 F4
Grange St. Mother 164 A2
Grange Terr. Kilmk 227 E4
Grangemouth Rd. Falk 42 C3
Grangemuir Rd. Pres 236 A4
Grangeneuk Gdns. Cumb 61 E1
Granger Rd. Bonh 27 F4
Granger Rd. Kilmk 227 F3
Grangeview. Lar 23 F1
Grant Cres. Alex 27 E1
Grant Ct. Aird 123 F4
Grant Ct. Ham 183 E4
Grant Pl. Coat 122 B2
Grant Pl. Kilmk 223 E1
Grant Pl. Stir 2 A2
Grant St. All 9 F3
Grant St. Glasg 96 C1
Grant St. Green 46 B2
Grant St. Helen 16 B1
Grantholm Ave. Holy 143 D3
Grantlea Gr. Glasg 119 E2
Grantlea Terr. Glasg 119 E2
Grantley Gdns. Glasg 136 B4
Grantley St. Glasg 136 B4
Grantoften Path. E Kil 180 C3
Granton St. Glasg 117 F1
Grantown Gdns. Glenm 102 C3
Granville St. Clyde 74 A2
Granville St. Glasg 116 C4
Granville St. Helen 16 C1
Grasmere. E Kil 179 F3
Grassyards
Interchange. Kilmk 223 E2
Grassyards Rd. Kilmk 223 E1
Grathellen Ct. Mother 164 A4
Gray Cres. Irvine 224 B4
Gray Dr. Bear 75 F2
Gray St. Alex 27 F3
Gray St. Cle 144 A1
Gray St. Glasg 96 C1
Gray St. Green 46 A2
Gray St. Kirk 80 A4
Gray St. Lark 185 D2
Gray St. Pres 236 B4
Gray St. Shot 147 D2
Gray's Cl. Lan 214 B2
Gray's Rd. Tan 141 D3
Grayshill Rd. Cumb 81 F3
Graystale Rd. Stir 7 D2
Graystonelee Rd. Shot 146 B3
Graystones. Kilw 207 F3
Great Dovehill. Glasg 117 E3
Great George La. Glasg 96 B2
Great George St. Glasg 96 B2
Great George St. Glasg 96 C1
Great Hamilton St. Pais 113 F1
Great Kelvin La. Glasg 96 C1
Great Western Rd. Clyde 74 B2
Great Western Rd. Glasg 96 B2
Great Western Rd. Kil 73 E3
Great Western Terr. Glasg 96 B2
Great Western
Terrace La. Glasg 96 B2
Green Ave. Irvine 219 E2
Green Bank. Dalry 191 E4
Green Bank Rd. Cumb 61 E1
Green Dale. Wish 165 E3
Green Farm Rd. Lin 112 A3
Green Gdns. Cle 144 B1
Green Loan. Holy 143 D2
Green Pl. Calder 123 D1
Green Pl. Udd 141 D1
Green Rd. Glasg 138 A4
Green Rd. Pais 113 D2
Green St. Ayr 235 F1
Green St. Clyde 74 A2
Green St. Glasg 117 F3
Green St. Salt 216 C4
Green St. Stone 198 C1
Green St. Udd 141 D1
Green Street La. Ayr 235 F1
Green
Street La Bsns Pk. Ayr 235 F1
Green The. Alva 5 D4
Green The. Glasg 117 F2
Greenacre Ct. Bann 7 F1
Greenacre Pl. Bann 7 F1
Greenacres. Ard 205 F2
Greenacres. Mother 163 E3
Greenacres View. Mother 163 E3
Greenan Ave. Glasg 137 F4
Greenan Gr. Ayr 238 A2
Greenan Pk. Ayr 238 A2
Greenan Pl. Ayr 238 B2
Greenan Rd. Ayr 238 B2
Greenan Rd. Kilmk 228 A4
Greenan Terr. Pres 236 B4
Greenan Way. Ayr 238 A2
Greenbank Ave. Newt M 157 D4
Greenbank Dr. Pais 133 E4
Greenbank Pl. Falk 41 E2
Greenbank Rd. Falk 41 E2
Greenbank Rd. Irvine 219 E1
Greenbank Rd. Wish 165 E2
Greenbank St. Glasg 138 A4
Greenbank Terr. Car 187 F1
Greenbank. Udd 161 E4
Greencraig Ave. Shi 66 B3
Greendyke St. Glasg 117 E3
Greenend Ave. John 111 E1
Greenend Pl. Glasg 119 E4
Greenend View. Hat 141 F3
Greenfarm Rd. Newt M 156 A3
Greenfaulds Cres. Cumb 83 D4
Greenfaulds Rd. Cumb 82 C4
Greenfaulds Rd. Cumb 83 D4
Greenfield Ave. Ayr 238 B1
Greenfield Ave. Glasg 119 D4
Greenfield Cres. Wish 165 E2
Greenfield Dr. Irvine 219 E1
Greenfield Dr. Wish 165 E2
Greenfield Pl. Glasg 119 D3
Greenfield Quadrant. Holy 143 F2
Greenfield Rd. Car 187 F2
Greenfield Rd. Glasg 119 E3
Greenfield Rd. Ham 162 A3
Greenfield Rd. Newt M 157 F3
Greenfield St. All 10 A4
Greenfield St. Bon 40 A3
Greenfield St. Glasg 115 F4
Greenfield St. Wish 165 E2
Greenfoot. Kilw 207 F2
Greengairs Ave. Glasg 115 E4
Greengairs Rd. Gree 83 F1
Greenhall Pl. Udd 161 E3
Greenhead. Alva 5 D3
Greenhead Ave. Dumb 50 A2
Greenhead Ave. Steven 206 C1
Greenhead Gdns. Dumb 50 A2
Greenhead Rd. Bear 75 F2
Greenhead Rd. Dumb 50 B2

Greenhead Rd. Inch 93 E3
Greenhead Rd. Lennox 57 F4
Greenhead Rd. Wish 165 E1
Greenhead St. Glasg 117 F2
Greenhead St. Glasg 117 F3
Greenhill
  and Wilson's Rd. Chap . 144 C4
Greenhill
  and Wilson's Rd. Cle ... 144 C3
Greenhill Ave. Glasg 136 B1
Greenhill Ave. Muir 100 C4
Greenhill. Bish 98 B4
Greenhill Cres. John 112 B1
Greenhill Cres. Lin 112 B3
Greenhill Ct. Glasg 138 A4
Greenhill Ct. Irvine 220 A3
Greenhill Dr. Lin 112 B3
Greenhill Rd. Blac 107 F2
Greenhill Rd. Bon 40 A2
Greenhill Rd. Glasg 138 A4
Greenhill Rd. Pais 113 E3
Greenhill St. Glasg 138 A4
Greenhill Terr. Cross 221 F2
Greenhills Cres. E Kil 180 A3
Greenhills Rd. E Kil 180 B3
Greenholm Ave. Newt M . 157 F4
Greenholm Ave. Udd 140 C4
Greenholm St. Kilrnk 227 F3
Greenholme Ct. Glasg 137 D3
Greenholme St. Glasg 137 D3
Greenhorn's Well Ave. Falk . 41 F2
Greenhorn's Well Cres. Falk . 41 F2
Greenhorn's Well Dr. Falk . 41 F2
Greenknowe Dr. Law 186 C3
Greenknowe Rd. Glasg ... 136 A3
Greenknowe St. Wish 186 A3
Greenlaw Ave. Pais 114 A3
Greenlaw Ave. Wish 165 E3
Greenlaw Cres. Pais 114 A3
Greenlaw Dr. Pais 114 A3
Greenlaw Ind Est. Pais ... 113 F3
Greenlaw Rd. Glasg 95 E4
Greenlaw Rd. Newt M 156 B3
Greenlea Rd. Muir 100 A4
Greenlea St. Glasg 95 F3
Greenlees Ct. Dalry 191 D4
Greenlees Gdns. Glasg 138 C2
Greenlees Rd. Glasg 139 D2
Greenlees Rd. Glasg 139 D2
Greenloan Ave. Glasg 115 E4
Greenloan View. Lark 185 D1
Greenmoss Pl. Hat 142 B3
Greenmount Dr. Shi 66 A3
Greenmount. Glasg 97 D4
Greenock Ave. Glasg 137 D3
Greenock Rd. Bishop 71 E3
Greenock Rd. Green 46 C1
Greenock Rd. Hous 83 E3
Greenock Rd. Inch 93 E3
Greenock Rd. K 69 E4
Greenock Rd. Lang 70 B4
Greenock Rd. P Glasg 47 E1
Greenock Rd. Pais 113 E4
Greenrig Rd. Lan 214 A1
Greenrig St. Glasg 98 B2
Greenrigg Cotts. Hart 127 F3
Greenrigg Rd. Cumb 62 A1
Greenrigg St. Udd 140 C3
Greens Ave. Kirk 79 E4
Greens Cres. Kirk 79 E4
Greens Rd. Cumb 82 C3
Greenshields Rd. Glasg ... 120 A3
Greenside Ave. Kilb 190 A4
Greenside Ave. Pres 236 B4
Greenside Ave. Spring 221 D1
Greenside Cl. Lan 215 D2
Greenside Cres. Glasg 96 C2
Greenside. irvine 220 A2
Greenside La. Lan 215 D2
Greenside Pl. Bear 75 D4
Greenside Rd. Dunt 74 A4
Greenside Rd. E Kil 158 C4
Greenside Rd. Holy 143 E4
Greenside Rd. Wish 165 E1
Greenside St. Al 10 A3
Greenside St. Glasg 98 C2
Greenside St. Holy 143 F2
Greenside Terr. Spring 221 D1
Greenside Way. Irvine 220 A2
Greentowers Rd. Lan 215 F2
Greentree Dr. Glasg 119 F2
Greentree Pk. Ayr 239 E2
Greenview St. Glasg 136 B4
Greenville La. Udd 161 E3
Greenways Ave. Pais 113 D1
Greenways Ct. Pais 113 D1
Greenwood Ave. Glasg 139 F3
Greenwood Ave. Muir 80 C1
Greenwood Ave. Stir 7 D2
Greenwood Cres. Coat 122 B3
Greenwood Ct. Newt M ... 157 F4
Greenwood Dr. Bear 76 A2
Greenwood
  Interchange. Shew 224 C4
Greenwood Quadrant. Clyde 74 B2
Greenwood Rd. Irvine 220 B1

Greenwood Rd. Newt M 157 E4
Greenwood St. Shot 146 C3
Greenyards
  Interchange. Cumb 62 B1
Greer Quadrant. Clyde ... 74 A2
Grenada Pl. E Kil 159 D1
Grenadier Gdns. Mother . 163 E2
Grendon Ct. Stir 7 D3
Grendon Gdns. Stir 7 D3
Grenville Dr. Glasg 138 C2
Grenville Rd. Gour 44 C3
Greta Meek La. M of C ... 58 B3
Grey Pl. Green 45 F3
Greyfriars Rd. Udd 140 B4
Greyfriars St. Glasg 118 C4
Greygoran. N Sau 5 E1
Greystone Ave. Glasg 138 B3
Greystone Bauks. Lan 214 C2
Greywood St. Glasg 95 F4
Grier Pl. Lark 184 C1
Griers Wlk. Shew 224 C4
Grierson Cres. Cam 6 B3
Grierson La. Glasg 118 B4
Grierson St. Glasg 118 B4
Grieve Croft. Udd 140 C1
Grieve Rd. Cumb 62 A2
Grieve Rd. Green 45 D3
Griffiths St. Falk 42 A2
Griffiths Way. Law 186 C2
Griqua Terr. Udd 141 D1
Grodwell Dr. Alva 4 C4
Grogarry Rd. Glasg 75 D2
Grosvenor Cres. Glasg 96 B2
Grosvenor
  Crescent La. Glasg 96 B2
Grosvenor La. Glasg 96 B2
Grosvenor La. Green 46 B2
Grosvenor Rd. Green 46 B2
Grosvenor Terr. Glasg 96 B2
Grougar Dr. Kilmk 223 D2
Grougar Rd. Hurl 228 B4
Grove Cres. Lark 185 D1
Grove Park Gdns. Glasg .. 97 D1
Grove Pk. Kirk 79 E2
Grove St. Den 21 E1
Grove The. B of W 110 C3
Grove The. Bishop 72 A2
Grove The. Glasg 157 D4
Grove The. Kilbar 111 D2
Grove The. Neil 154 B3
Grove Way. Hat 141 F2
Grove Wood. Tan 121 E1
Grove Wynd. Holy 143 E2
Grovebum Ave. Glasg 136 A2
Grovepark Ct. Glasg 97 D1
Grovepark St. Glasg 97 D2
Grudie St. Glasg 120 A4
Gryfe Rd. B of W 110 C3
Gryfe Rd. P Glasg 68 C4
Gryfe St. Green 46 A1
Gryfebank Ave. Hous 91 F1
Grylewood Cres. Hous 91 D1
Gryffe Ave. B of W 90 B1
Gryffe Ave. Ren 94 A3
Gryffe Cres. Pais 112 C1
Gryffe Gr. B of W 110 B4
Gryffe Pk. B of W 90 B1
Gryffe Rd. Kil 89 E4
Gryffe St. Glasg 137 D4
Guildford St. Glasg 99 E1
Guiltreehill. Ayr 239 D1
Gullane Cres. Cumb 61 F3
Gullane Ct. Ham 183 D4
Gullane Pl. Kilw 207 D2
Gullane St. Glasg 96 A1
Guilland Ave. Dund 225 F1
Guilliland Pl. Irvine 219 E1
Gullin Dr. Pres 236 C2
Gunn Quadrant. Hat 141 F2
Guthrie Dr. Tan 121 D1
Guthrie Pl. E Kil 159 F1
Guthrie Pl. Lennox 57 E1
Guthrie Rd. Salt 217 D4
Guthrie St. Glasg 96 B3
Guthrie St. Ham 162 A2
Guy Mannering Rd. Helen . 25 C4

Habbieauld Rd. Kilrn 222 A4
Haberlea Ave. Glasg 135 E2
Haberlea Gdns. Glasg 135 E1
Haddington Gdns. Irvine . 220 A3
Haddow Gr. Tan 141 D4
Haddow St. Ham 162 A2
Hadrian Terr. Mother 163 E4
Hagart Rd. Hous 91 D1
Hagg Cres. John 111 F2
Hagg Pl. John 111 F2
Hagg Rd. John 111 F1
Hagg St. Glasg 116 B1
Haggs La. Glasg 116 B1
Haggs Rd. Glasg 116 B1
Haggswood Ave. Glasg 116 B1
Haghill Rd. Glasg 118 B4
Hagtholm Pl. Lan 215 F4
Haghill Rd. Coat 122 A2
Haghorn Ave. Kilb 170 A4
Haig Ave. Stir 2 A1

Haig Dr. Glasg 119 F2
Haig St. Glasg 98 A2
Haig St. Green 45 F3
Hailes Ave. Glasg 119 E3
Haining Ave. Kilmk 223 E2
Haining Rd. Ren 94 B2
Haining Rd. Ren 94 B1
Hairmyres Pk. E Kil 179 F4
Hairmyres
  Roundabout. E Kil 158 C1
Hairmyres St. Glasg 117 E1
Hairst St. Ren 94 B2
Halbeath Ave. Glasg 74 C2
Halbert St. Glasg 116 C1
Halberts Cres. Stir 7 D1
Haldane Ave. B of A 2 A3
Haldane Ct. Bonh 27 F4
Haldane La. Glasg 95 E2
Haldane Pl. E Kil 180 C4
Haldane St. Glasg 95 E2
Haldane Terr. Bonh 19 F1
Halfmerk N. E Kil 160 A1
Halfmerk S. E Kil 160 A1
Halfway St. W Kil 190 B3
Halgreen Ave. Glasg 74 C2
Halifax Way. Ren 94 B1
Halkett Cres. Alex 27 F4
Hall Bar Gdns. Car 201 F2
Hall La. Troon 230 A2
Hall Pl. Lan 215 D2
Hall Rd. Lan 214 A3
Hall Rd. Rhu 15 E3
Hall St. Alex 49 E4
Hall St. Bonh 27 F2
Hall St. Clyde 74 A1
Hall St. Glasg 162 B1
Hall St. Holy 143 D2
Hallbrae St. Glasg 98 C1
Hallcraig St. Aird 123 D4
Halley Dr. Clyde 94 C4
Halley Pl. Clyde 94 C4
Halley Sq. Clyde 94 C4
Halley St. Clyde 94 C4
Hallforest St. Glasg 99 D1
Hallhill Cres. Glasg 119 F4
Hallhill Rd. Glasg 119 D3
Hallhill Rd. Glasg 119 E4
Hallhill Rd. Glasg 119 F3
Hallhill Rd. Glasg 120 A3
Hallhill Rd. John 131 E4
Halliburton Cres. Glasg .. 119 F4
Halliburton Terr. Glasg ... 120 A4
Halidale Cres. Ren 94 C1
Hallinan Gdns. Wish 164 C1
Hallpark. N Sau 10 B4
Hallrule Dr. Glasg 115 E3
Halls Vennal. Ayr 235 F1
Hallside Ave. Glasg 139 F3
Hallside Cres. Glasg 139 F3
Hallside Dr. Glasg 139 F3
Hallside Gdns. Wish 165 F2
Hallside Pl. Glasg 117 E2
Hallside Rd. Glasg 139 F2
Hallside St. How 130 C3
Hallydown Dr. Glasg 95 E3
Halpin Ct. Tan 141 E3
Halton Gdns. Glasg 119 F3
Hamersley Pl. E Kil 180 A4
Hamilcomb Rd. Hat 142 A2
Hamill Dr. Kils 60 C4
Hamilton Ave. Glasg 116 B2
Hamilton Ave. Sten 23 F2
Hamilton Cres. Ayr 239 D4
Hamilton Cres. Bear 75 F4
Hamilton Cres. Bishop 71 F2
Hamilton Cres. Camb 139 E3
Hamilton Cres. Ren 94 B3
Hamilton Cres. Steven ... 206 C1
Hamilton Ct. Kilm 222 A4
Hamilton Ct. Pais 113 F1
Hamilton Dr. Aird 103 D1
Hamilton Dr. Ersk 72 C2
Hamilton Dr. Glasg 42 A2
Hamilton Dr. Glasg 96 C2
Hamilton Dr. Glasg 136 B1
Hamilton Dr. Glasg 139 D3
Hamilton Dr. Mother 163 D3
Hamilton Dr. Mother 142 B2
Hamilton Dr. Udd 141 D1
Hamilton Gate. Green 45 E3
Hamilton Gdns. Stew 195 F1
Hamilton Park Ave. Glasg 96 C2
Hamilton Pl. E Kil 180 C4
Hamilton Pl. Ham 183 E3
Hamilton Pl. Holy 143 E2
Hamilton Rd. E Kil 161 D3
Hamilton Rd. Glasg 138 B4
Hamilton Rd. Glasg 139 E3
Hamilton Rd. Hat 141 F2
Hamilton Rd. Lark 184 C3
Hamilton Rd. Mother 163 E3

Hamilton Rd. Sten 23 E3
Hamilton Rd. Udd 141 D1
Hamilton Rd. Udd 161 D3
Hamilton St. Car 187 F1
Hamilton St. Clyde 94 B4
Hamilton St. Dumb 50 A2
Hamilton St. Falk 41 E3
Hamilton St. Glasg 117 E1
Hamilton St. Kilw 207 F2
Hamilton St. Lark 185 D2
Hamilton St. Pais 113 F3
Hamilton St. Salt 216 C4
Hamilton Terr. Clyde 94 B4
Hamilton View. Tan 141 D4
Hamilton Way. Green 45 F3
Hamilton Way. Pres 233 E1
Hamiltonhill Rd. Glasg ... 97 D2
Hamlet. E Kil 160 A3
Hampden Dr. Glasg 137 D3
Hampden Terr. Glasg 137 D4
Hampden Terr. Glasg 137 D4
Hampden Way. Ren 94 B1
Hangingshaw Pl. Glasg ... 137 E4
Hanover Cl. Glasg 137 D4
Hanover Ct. Glasg 117 E4
Hanover Ct. Pais 114 A3
Hanover Gdns. Bish 78 A1
Hanover Gdns. Pais 113 E4
Hanover St. Glasg 117 E4
Hanover St. Helen 25 C4
Hanson St. Glasg 117 F4
Hapland Ave. Glasg 115 E1
Hapland Rd. Glasg 115 E1
Happyhills. W Kil 190 B3
Haran Rd. Bonh 19 F1
Harbour Ind Est. Ard 205 E1
Harbour La. Pais 113 F3
Harbour Pl. Ard 205 D1
Harbour Pl. Ard 216 A1
Harbour Pl. Irvine 219 D2
Harbour Pl. Pais 113 F3
Harbour Rd. Troon 229 D2
Harbour Rd. Ard 205 D1
Harbour St. Ayr 235 F1
Harbour St. Irvine 219 D2
Harbour St. Salt 216 C4
Harburn Pl. Glasg 74 C2
Harburn Rd. Glasg 94 C3
Harcourt Dr. Glasg 118 A4
Hardacres. Lan 215 D3
Hardgate Dr. Glasg 115 E4
Hardgate Gdns. Glasg 115 E4
Hardgate Pl. Glasg 115 E4
Hardgate Rd. Glasg 115 E4
Hardie Ave. Glasg 138 B4
Hardie Ct. Stir 7 D2
Hardie St. Alex 27 E4
Hardie St. Ham 162 A1
Hardie St. Mother 163 F4
Hardie St. Udd 161 E3
Hardmuir Gdns. Kirk 58 C1
Hardridge Ave. Glasg 115 F1
Hardridge Pl. Glasg 115 F1
Hardridge Rd. Glasg 115 F1
Hardy Hill. Helen 17 D1
Harebell Pl. Ayr 239 D2
Harefield Dr. Glasg 95 D3
Harelaw Ave. Barr 134 B1
Harelaw Ave. Glasg 136 C2
Harelaw Ave. Neil 154 B3
Harelaw Cres. Pais 133 E4
Hareleeshill Rd. Lark 185 E1
Hareshaw Dr. Kilmk 223 D3
Hareshaw Gdns. Kilmk ... 223 D3
Harestanes Gdns. Kirk 59 D1
Harestanes Rd. Car 202 B1
Harestone Ave. Lark 165 E1
Harestone Rd. Wish 165 E1
Harhill St. Glasg 116 A4
Harkins Ave. Udd 161 E3
Harkness Ave. M of C 58 A3
Harland Cotts. Glasg 95 E2
Harland St. Glasg 95 E2
Harlaw Gdns. Bish 78 B1
Harley Ct. Falk 42 A4
Harley Pl. Salt 205 F4
Harley St. Glasg 116 C3
Harling Dr. Troon 229 E1
Harmetray St. Glasg 97 E3
Harmony Ct. Glasg 116 A4
Harmony Pl. Glasg 116 A4
Harmony Row. Glasg 116 A4
Harmony Sq. Glasg 116 A4
Harmsworth St. Glasg 95 F1
Harper Cres. Wish 165 F2
Harpercroft. Kilmk 227 E4
Harport St. Glasg 135 F2
Harriet Pl. Glasg 136 B4
Harriet Rd. Kilmk 223 D1
Harriet St. Glasg 136 B4
Harrington Rd. E Kil 159 E1
Harris Cr. Newt M 156 A3
Harris Cres. O Kill 73 D3
Harris Ct. All 10 A3
Harris Ct. Irvine 225 E4

Harris Dr. O Kill 73 D3
Harris Gdns. O Kill 73 E3
Harris Pl. Kilmk 223 D3
Harris Quadrant. Wish ... 165 F3
Harris Rd. Glasg 76 C1
Harris Rd. O Kill 73 E3
Harris Rd. P Glasg 69 D4
Harris Terr. Irvine 225 E4
Harrison Dr. Glasg 116 A3
Harrow Pl. Falk 41 F1
Harrow Ct. Glasg 74 C2
Harrow Pl. Glasg 74 C2
Hart St. Glasg 118 C3
Hart St. Lin 112 B3
Hart Wynd. Bann 7 F1
Hartfield Cres. Neil 154 C4
Hartfield Ct. Dumb 50 A2
Hartfield Gdns. Dumb 50 A2
Hartfield Rd. Ayr 238 C3
Hartfield Terr. Alla 167 D2
Hartfield Terr. Pais 114 A1
Harthall. Ayr 236 C1
Harthill Rd. Blac 107 E1
Hartlaw Cres. Glasg 115 D3
Hartree Ave. Clyde 94 B4
Hartstone Pl. Glasg 135 D4
Hartstone Rd. Glasg 135 D4
Hartstone Terr. Glasg 135 D4
Hartwood Gdns. Shot 146 A1
Hartwood Rd. Shot 145 F1
Harvest Dr. Mother 163 E2
Harvey Gdns. Ard 205 E2
Harvey Sq. Loch 129 E1
Harvey St. Ard 205 E2
Harvey St. Glasg 97 E1
Harvey Terr. Loch 129 E1
Harvey Way. Hat 142 B4
Harvey Wynd. Stir 2 A1
Harvie Ave. Newt M 156 B3
Harvie St. Glasg 116 B3
Harwood Gdns. Muir 81 D2
Harwood St. Glasg 118 C4
Hastie St. Glasg 96 B1
Hastings. E Kil 180 A4
Hatfield Ct. Kil 89 E4
Hatfield Dr. Glasg 95 C3
Hathaway Dr. Glasg 136 A1
Hathaway La. Glasg 96 C3
Hathaway St. Glasg 96 C3
Hathersage Ave. Glasg ... 120 A3
Hathersage Dr. Glasg 120 A3
Hathersage Gdns. Glasg . 120 A3
Hatton Gdns. Glasg 115 D2
Hatton Pl. Holy 143 E1
Hatton Terr. Holy 143 E1
Hattonhill. Holy 143 E1
Hattonrigg Rd. Hat 142 A4
Haugh Gdns. Falk 24 A1
Haugh Pl. Ham 162 C1
Haugh Rd. Glasg 118 B4
Haugh Rd. Stir 2 A1
Haugh St. Falk 24 A1
Haughburn Pl. Glasg 135 D4
Haughburn Rd. Glasg 135 D4
Haughburn Terr. Glasg ... 135 E4
Haughton Ave. Kils 60 C4
Haughview Rd. Mother ... 163 D3
Haugland Rd. Ard 205 D3
Havelock La. Glasg 96 B1
Havelock Pk. E Kil 159 D1
Havelock Pl. Helen 16 C1
Havelock St. Helen 96 B1
Havelock St. Helen 16 C1
Haven Pk. E Kil 179 F3
Havoc Rd. Dumb 49 E2
Hawbank Rd. E Kil 159 D2
Hawbank
  Roundabout. E Kil 159 D1
Hawick Ave. Pais 113 D1
Hawick Cres. Lark 185 D1
Hawick Dr. Coat 122 B2
Hawick St. Clyde 94 B4
Hawick St. Wish 165 E3
Hawkhead Ave. Pais 114 B1
Hawkhead Rd. Pais 114 A2
Hawkhill Ave. Ayr 236 A1
Hawkhill Avenue La. Ayr . 236 A1
Hawkhill Dr. All 10 B3
Hawksland Wlk. Ham 162 C1
Hawkwood Ayr 239 D1
Hawkwood Rd. Aird 101 E4
Hawley Rd. Falk 42 B2
Hawthorn Ave. Bear 76 A4
Hawthorn Ave. Bish 98 A4
Hawthorn Ave. Dumb 49 D3
Hawthorn Ave. Ersk 93 F4
Hawthorn Ave. John 112 A1
Hawthorn Ave. Kirk 79 E3
Hawthorn Ave. New 166 B3
Hawthorn Cres. Beith 171 D4
Hawthorn Cres. Ersk 93 F4
Hawthorn Cres. Inch 93 F4
Hawthorn Cres. Stir 1 C1
Hawthorn Ct. Kilw 207 F1

264

Hawthorn Ct. Newt M

Hilltop Rd. Gour

Hawthorn Ct. Newt M 157 F3
Hawthorn Dr. Aird 123 E3
Hawthorn Dr. Ayr 239 E2
Hawthorn Dr. Bank 38 C1
Hawthorn Dr. Barr 155 E4
Hawthorn Dr. Coat 122 B3
Hawthorn Dr. Duni 21 E2
Hawthorn Dr. East 127 F3
Hawthorn Dr. Falk 41 F2
Hawthorn Dr. Fall 8 B2
Hawthorn Dr. Holy 143 D2
Hawthorn Dr. Shot 147 E2
Hawthorn Dr. Steven 206 C2
Hawthorn Dr. Wish 165 E2
Hawthorn Gdns. Hat 142 B2
Hawthorn Gdns. Lark 185 E1
Hawthorn Gdns. Newt M 157 F3
Hawthorn Gdns. Pres 236 B4
Hawthorn Gr. Law 186 C3
Hawthorn Hill. Ham 162 C1
Hawthorn Pl. Alla 167 D4
Hawthorn Pl. Troon 229 E2
Hawthorn Pl. Udd 161 F4
Hawthorn Quadrant. Glasg .. 97 E3
Hawthorn Rd. Cumb 62 C2
Hawthorn Rd. Inch 93 F4
Hawthorn Rd. Newt M 157 F3
Hawthorn Sq. Kilmk 227 E4
Hawthorn St. Clyde 74 A2
Hawthorn St. Glasg 97 E3
Hawthorn St. Lennox 57 E1
Hawthorn Terr. E Kil 180 A3
Hawthorn Terr. Tan 141 D4
Hawthorn Way. Inch 93 F4
Hawthorn Way. M of C 58 B3
Hawthorn Wlk. Glasg 138 B3
Hawthornden Gdns. Glasg .. 76 C1
Hawthorne Pl. Gour 44 A3
Hawthorne Pl. Lar 23 E1
Hawthornhill Rd. Dumb 49 E3
Hay Ave. Bishop 72 B2
Hay Dr. John 112 A2
Hay Hill. Ayr 236 C1
Hay St. Green 45 F2
Hayburn Cres. Glasg 96 A2
Hayburn Gate. Glasg 96 A1
Hayburn La. Glasg 96 A2
Hayburn St. Glasg 96 A1
Hayfield. Falk 42 B4
Hayfield Rd. Falk 42 B4
Hayfield St. Glasg 117 E2
Hayfield Terr. Bank 39 F4
Hayhill Rd. Thorn 179 E4
Hayle Gdns. Muir 80 C2
Haylnn St. Glasg 95 F1
Haymarket St. Glasg 118 C4
Hayocks Rd. Steven 206 C1
Haypark Rd. Bank 39 E3
Haystack Pl. Klrk 79 F2
Hayston Cres. Glasg 97 D3
Hayston Rd. Klrk 79 D4
Hayston St. Glasg 97 D3
Haywood St. Glasg 97 E3
Hazel Ave. Ard 205 E2
Hazel Ave. Bear 76 A4
Hazel Ave. Dumb 49 D3
Hazel Ave. Glasg 136 C2
Hazel Ave. John 112 A1
Hazel Ave. Kilmk 227 E4
Hazel Ave. Klrk 79 E3
Hazel Bank. M of C 58 A2
Hazel Cres. Duni 21 E2
Hazel Dene. Bish 98 A4
Hazel Gdns. Mother 163 F2
Hazel Gr. Falk 42 B4
Hazel Gr. Kilw 208 A2
Hazel Gr. Klrk 79 E3
Hazel Gr. Law 186 C3
Hazel Path. Cle 144 A1
Hazel Pk. Ham 162 C1
Hazel Rd. Bank 38 C1
Hazel Rd. Cumb 62 B2
Hazel Terr. Gour 44 B3
Hazel Terr. Tan 141 D4
Hazelbank Gdns. Stir 2 A1
Hazelbank. Holy 143 D3
Hazelbank. Plains 103 F2
Hazelbank Wlk. Aird 122 B4
Hazeldean Cres. Wish 165 E3
Hazelden Rd. Newt M 177 E4
Hazeldene La. Lark 185 E1
Hazelhead. E Kil 160 A1
Hazellea Dr. Glasg 136 C2
Hazelmere Rd. Kil 89 D4
Hazelton. Mother 163 E3
Hazelwood Ave. B of W 110 C4
Hazelwood Ave. Newt M 156 C2
Hazelwood Ave. Pais 132 C4
Hazelwood Dr. Udd 161 E4
Hazelwood Gdns. Glasg 138 B2
Hazelwood La. B of W 110 B4
Hazelwood Rd. Ayr 238 C3
Hazelwood Rd. B of W 110 B3
Hazelwood Rd. Glasg 116 B2
Hazlitt St. Glasg 97 D3
Head St. Beith 171 E4
Headhouse Ct. E Kil 180 B4
Headhouse Gn. E Kil 180 C4
Headlesscross Rd. Shot 147 F1
Headrigg Gdns. W Kil 190 B3
Headrigg Rd. W Kil 190 B3
Headsmuir Ave. Car 187 E1
Heath Ave. Bish 98 A4
Heath Ave. Klrk 79 E2
Heath Rd. Lark 185 D2
Heathcliffe Ave. Udd 140 B1
Heathcot Ave. Glasg 74 C1
Heathcot Pl. Glasg 74 C1
Heather Ave. Alex 27 F3
Heather Ave. Barr 134 A3
Heather Ave. Bear 75 F4
Heather Ave. Dunt 74 A4
Heather Ave. Holy 143 D3
Heather Ave. Shi 66 B3
Heather Dr. Klrk 79 D2
Heather Gdns. Klrk 79 D2
Heather Pk. Ayr 239 E2
Heather Pl. John 112 A1
Heather Pl. Kilmk 227 E4
Heather Pl. Klrk 79 D2
Heather Rd. Lan 214 A3
Heather Row. Car 187 F2
Heather St. Cald 105 D3
Heather Way. Holy 143 D2
Heatherbank Wlk. Aird 122 B4
Heatherbrae. Bish 77 F1
Heatherdale Gdns. Bank 39 F4
Heatherhouse Rd. Irvine 224 A4
Heatherstane Bank. Irvine . 220 B1
Heatherstane Way. Irvine .. 220 B1
Heathery Knowe. E Kil 180 C4
Heathery Rd. Wish 164 C2
Heatheryknowe Rd. Coat ... 120 C4
Heatheryknowe Rd. Glasg . 120 C4
Heathfield Ave. Muir 81 D1
Heathfield Dr. Miln 55 D2
Heathfield Rd. Ayr 236 B2
Heathfield St. Glasg 119 E4
Heathfield. Wish 186 A4
Heathpark. Pres 236 B3
Heathside Rd. Glasg 136 B2
Heathwood Dr. Glasg 136 A2
Hecla Ave. Glasg 74 C2
Hecla Pl. Glasg 74 C2
Hecla Sq. Glasg 74 C2
Hector Rd. Glasg 136 B4
Hedges The. Falk 41 F3
Heggies Ave. P Glasg 69 D4
Heights Rd. Blac 107 E2
Helen St. Glasg 116 A3
Helen Way. Bonh 27 F1
Helen's Terr. Kilw 207 F1
Helena Pl. Newt M 157 F4
Helensburgh Dr. Glasg 95 F3
Helenslea. Glasg 139 F2
Helenslea Pl. Hat 141 F2
Helenslee Cres. Dumb 49 E2
Helenslee Ct. Dumb 49 E2
Helenslee Rd. Dumb 49 E2
Helenslee Rd. Lang 70 B4
Helenvale Ct. Glasg 118 B3
Helenvale St. Glasg 118 B2
Helmsdale Ave. Udd 140 B2
Helmsdale Ct. Glasg 139 E3
Hemlock St. Glasg 95 F4
Hemmingen Ct. Car 187 F2
Hemphill View. Cross 221 F2
Henderland Rd. Bear 75 F1
Henderson Ave. All 10 A4
Henderson Ave. Glasg 139 F3
Henderson Pl. Alva 5 D4
Henderson Rd. Troon 229 E1
Henderson St. Aird 123 D4
Henderson St. B of A 2 A4
Henderson St. Clyde 94 C4
Henderson St. Coat 121 F3
Henderson St. Glasg 96 C2
Henderson St. Pais 113 E3
Henderson Terr. Gour 44 C3
Hendry St. Falk 42 A4
Hennings The. N Sau 5 E1
Henrietta St. Glasg 95 E2
Henry Bell Gn. E Kil 180 C4
Henry Bell St. Helen 16 C1
Henry St. Alva 5 D3
Henry St. Barr 134 A2
Hepburn Hill. Ham 183 E4
Hepburn Rd. Glasg 115 D4
Herald Ave. Glasg 75 E1
Herald Gr. Mother 163 E2
Herald St. Ard 216 A4
Herald Way. Ren 94 B1
Herbert St. Glasg 96 C2
Herbertshire St. Den 21 F1
Herbertson Cres. Irvine 219 E2
Herbertson St. Glasg 117 D3
Herbertson St. Udd 161 F4
Hercules Way. Ren 94 B1
Herdshill Ave. Shi 66 B3
Heriot Ave. Pais 132 C4
Heriot Cres. Bish 78 A2
Heriot Rd. Klrk 79 E2
Heritage Ct. Newt M 156 C3
Heritage Dr. Sten 24 A2
Heritage View. Coat 121 F4
Heritage Way. Coat 121 F4
Herma St. Glasg 96 C4
Hermes Way. Holy 142 C3
Hermiston Ave. Glasg 119 E3
Hermiston Pl. Glasg 119 E3
Hermiston Pl. Holy 143 D3
Hermiston Rd. Glasg 119 D3
Hermitage Ave. Glasg 95 E3
Hermitage Cres. Coat 122 A2
Hermitage Rd. B of A 2 C3
Herndon Ct. Newt M 157 D3
Heron Ct. Dunt 74 A3
Heron Pl. John 131 E4
Heron Rd. Green 45 D2
Heron Way. Ren 94 B1
Heronswood. Kilw 207 F3
Herries Rd. Glasg 116 B1
Herriet St. Glasg 116 C2
Herriot Ave. Kilb 149 D2
Herriot St. Coat 121 F4
Herschell St. Glasg 95 F3
Hertford Ave. Glasg 96 A3
Hervey St. All 10 A4
Hestan Pl. Kilmk 223 D3
Heugh St. Falk 42 A2
Hewett Cres. Hous 91 E1
Hexham Gdns. Glasg 116 B1
Heyford Pl. Cam 6 B3
Heys St. Barr 134 B1
Hibernia St. Green 45 E2
Hickman St. Glasg 117 E1
Hickory Cres. Tan 141 E4
Hickory St. Glasg 97 F3
High Avon St. Lark 184 C2
High Banton Rd. Kils 37 E2
High Barholm. Kilbar 111 D2
High Barrwood Rd. Kils 60 C4
High Beeches. E Kil 158 C4
High Blantyre Rd. Ham 161 F3
High Burnside Ave. Coat 121 F3
High Calside. Pais 113 F2
High Carnegie Rd. P Glasg . 68 C4
High Coats. Coat 122 A4
High Common Rd. E Kil 181 D4
High Craigends. Kils 60 C4
High Flender Rd. Newt M .. 157 E3
High Glencairn St. Kilmk 227 F4
High Graighall Rd. Glasg 97 D1
High Kirk View. John 111 F1
High Mains Ave. Dumb 50 B2
High Meadow. Car 188 B1
High Mill Rd. Car 188 A1
High Overton St. Ash 200 B2
High Parks Cres. Ham 183 E3
High Parksail. Ersk 93 E4
High Patrick St. Ham 162 C2
High Pleasance. Lark 185 D2
High Rd. Ayr 236 C2
High Rd. Mother 163 F4
High Rd. Pais 113 E2
High Rd. Salt 206 A1
High Rd. Steven 206 B1
High Row. Bish 78 A3
High St. Air 14 B2
High St. Aird 122 C4
High St. All 10 A3
High St. Ayr 238 C4
High St. Bon 40 A3
High St. Car 187 F1
High St. Clack 10 C2
High St. Dumb 49 F2
High St. Falk 42 A2
High St. Glasg 117 E4
High St. Glasg 138 A4
High St. Green 45 F3
High St. Holy 143 F2
High St. Irvine 219 E1
High St. John 111 F2
High St. Kil 69 E1
High St. Kilb 149 D2
High St. Kilmk 223 D1
High St. Lan 215 D2
High St. Loch 129 E1
High St. Neil 154 C4
High St. Pais 113 F2
High St. Ren 94 C2
High St. Shot 146 C2
High St. Slam 86 A4
High St. Stew 195 F1
High Station Rd. Falk 42 A2
High View Gr. Shi 66 B3
High Whitehills Rd. E Kil 180 C3
Highburgh Ave. Lan 215 D2
Highburgh Ct. Lan 215 D2
Highburgh Dr. Glasg 138 B3
Highburgh Rd. Glasg 96 B1
Highcraig Ave. John 111 E1
Highcroft Ave. Glasg 137 E3
Highcross Ave. Coat 121 E2
Highet Gdns. Irvine 219 D2
Highet St. Kilmk 222 C1
Highfield Ave. Kilmk 223 D2
Highfield Ave. Kirk 58 C1
Highfield Ave. Pais 133 E4
Highfield Ave. Pres 236 B4
Highfield Cres. Mother 164 A4
Highfield Cres. Pais 133 E4
Highfield Ct. Kirk 58 C1
Highfield Dr. Glasg 96 A3
Highfield Dr. Glasg 138 B2
Highfield Dr. Newt M 157 E4
Highfield Dr. Steven 206 C1
Highfield Gr. Kirk 58 C1
Highfield Pl. E Kil 159 F2
Highfield Pl. Glasg 96 A3
Highfield Pl. Irvine 219 F3
Highfield Rd. Ayr 239 D2
Highfield Rd. Kirk 58 C1
Highfield Rd. Lark 185 D2
Highfield St. Kilw 207 F2
Highholm Ave. P Glasg 47 D1
Highholm St. P Glasg 47 D1
Highland Ave. Udd 161 E4
Highland Dr. Lar 23 E2
Highland Dykes Cres. Bon 40 A3
Highland Dykes Dr. Bon 40 A3
Highland La. Glasg 116 B4
Highland Pk. Kils 36 B1
Highland Pl. Kils 36 B1
Highland Rd. Miln 55 D1
Highlandman's Rd. Rhu 15 F3
Highstonehall Rd. Ham 162 A1
Highthorne Cres. W Kil 190 C3
Hilary Cres. Ayr 239 D3
Hilary Dr. Glasg 119 F3
Hilda Cres. Glasg 98 C2
Hill Ave. Newt M 156 B2
Hill Cres. Newt M 157 F3
Hill Dr. Eagle 178 C2
Hill House Rd. Bank 39 F4
Hill Interchange. Irvine 219 F3
Hill La. Ard 205 E1
Hill Pl. All 10 A4
Hill Pl. Ard 205 E1
Hill Pl. Hat 141 F2
Hill Pl. Holy 143 E1
Hill Pl. Shot 146 C3
Hill Rd. Ash 199 F3
Hill Rd. Cumb 61 F1
Hill Rd. East 127 E3
Hill Rd. How 130 C3
Hill Rd. Kils 36 B1
Hill Rd. Stone 198 C1
Hill St. Alex 27 E3
Hill St. All 10 A4
Hill St. Ard 205 E1
Hill St. Cald 104 C3
Hill St. Chap 123 E1
Hill St. Dumb 49 E2
Hill St. Glasg 97 D1
Hill St. Green 46 A2
Hill St. Ham 161 F2
Hill St. Irvine 219 E1
Hill St. Kilmk 222 C1
Hill St. Lark 185 D1
Hill St. Salt 216 C4
Hill St. Stir 7 D2
Hill St. Wish 165 D2
Hill Street Ind Est. Ard 205 E1
Hill Terr. Holy 143 E1
Hill View. Dumb 50 C1
Hill View. E Kil 180 C4
Hill View Rd. Lan 214 A2
Hillary Ave. Glasg 138 B3
Hillary Rd. Lar 23 F1
Hillbank Rd. Kilmk 222 C2
Hillbank St. Bonh 27 F2
Hillcrest Ave. Coat 122 B3
Hillcrest Ave. Cumb 82 C4
Hillcrest Ave. Dunt 74 A4
Hillcrest Ave. Glasg 136 C2
Hillcrest Ave. Glasg 139 D4
Hillcrest Ave. Mother 164 C2
Hillcrest Ave. Pais 133 E3
Hillcrest Ct. Cumb 61 F1
Hillcrest Dr. All 10 B3
Hillcrest Dr. Newt M 157 D3
Hillcrest Dr. Steven 206 C1
Hillcrest. E Kil 158 B4
Hillcrest. Muir 100 B4
Hillcrest Pl. Bank 39 E4
Hillcrest Pl. Kilw 207 F2
Hillcrest Rd. Bear 75 F2
Hillcrest Rd. Falk 41 F1
Hillcrest Rd. Glasg 139 E4
Hillcrest Rd. Kils 59 F4
Hillcrest Rd. Tan 141 D4
Hillcrest St. Miln 55 D1
Hillcrest Terr. Udd 141 D2
Hillcrest View. Lark 185 D2
Hillcroft Terr. Bish 97 F4
Hillend Cres. Dunt 73 F4
Hillend Cres. Newt M 157 E3
Hillend Dr. Green 46 B2
Hillend Pl. Green 46 B2
Hillend Rd. Glasg 97 D4
Hillend Rd. Glasg 138 A3
Hillend Rd. Newt M 157 E3
Hillfoot. Alex 27 E1
Hillfoot Ave. Bear 75 F3
Hillfoot Ave. Dumb 50 B2
Hillfoot Ave. Glasg 138 A4
Hillfoot Ave. Wish 165 E4
Hillfoot Cres. Ayr 239 D3
Hillfoot Cres. Wish 165 E4
Hillfoot Dr. Bear 75 F3
Hillfoot Dr. Coat 121 E3
Hillfoot Dr. How 130 C3
Hillfoot Dr. Wish 165 E4
Hillfoot Gdns. Tan 140 C4
Hillfoot Gdns. Wish 165 E4
Hillfoot. Hous 111 F4
Hillfoot Rd. Aird 123 D3
Hillfoot Rd. Ayr 239 E3
Hillfoot St. Glasg 118 A4
Hillfoot Terr. Car 188 A1
Hillfoots Rd. B of A 2 C2
Hillhead Ave. Bank 38 C2
Hillhead Ave. Car 188 A1
Hillhead Ave. Glasg 138 A2
Hillhead Ave. Holy 143 D1
Hillhead Ave. Muir 80 C1
Hillhead Cres. Ham 161 F2
Hillhead Cres. Holy 143 D1
Hillhead Dr. Aird 123 D3
Hillhead Dr. Falk 41 F1
Hillhead Dr. Holy 143 D1
Hillhead Pl. Glasg 138 A2
Hillhead Rd. Glasg 98 B4
Hillhead Rd. Kirk 58 C1
Hillhead Rd. Steven 206 C2
Hillhead Sq. Kilmk 222 C2
Hillhead St. Glasg 96 B1
Hillhead St. Miln 55 D1
Hillhead Terr. Ham 161 F2
Hillhouse Cres. Ham 161 F2
Hillhouse Farm Gate. Lan .. 214 C3
Hillhouse Farm Rd. Lan 214 C2
Hillhouse Gate. Car 202 B4
Hillhouse Gdns. Troon 229 E3
Hillhouse Pl. Stew 195 E1
Hillhouse Rd. Ham 161 F2
Hillhouse Rd. Troon 229 E3
Hillhouse St. Glasg 98 A3
Hillhouse Terr. Ham 161 F2
Hillhouseridge Rd. Shot 146 B3
Hillington Gdns. Glasg 115 E2
Hillington Park Cir. Glasg ... 115 E3
Hillington Quadrant. Glasg . 115 D3
Hillington Rd. Glasg 115 D4
Hillington Rd. Ren 94 C1
Hillington Rd S. Glasg 115 D3
Hillington Terr. Glasg 115 D3
Hillkirk Pl. Glasg 97 F2
Hillkirk St. Glasg 97 F2
Hillmoss. Kilm 222 A4
Hillneuk Ave. Bear 76 A3
Hillneuk Dr. Bear 76 A3
Hillocks Pl. Troon 229 F4
Hillpark Ave. Pais 113 E1
Hillpark Cres. Bann 7 E1
Hillpark Dr. Bann 7 E1
Hillpark Dr. Glasg 136 B3
Hillpark Dr. Kilmk 222 C1
Hillpark. Moss 237 F3
Hillpark Rise. Kilw 207 D2
Hillrigg Ave. Aird 123 E4
Hillrigg. Gree 83 E1
Hillsborough Rd. Glasg 119 F3
Hillshaw Foot. Irvine 220 B1
Hillshaw Gn. Irvine 220 B1
Hillside Ave. Alex 27 E2
Hillside Ave. Bear 75 F3
Hillside Ave. Kil 69 E1
Hillside Ave. Newt M 157 E4
Hillside Cotts. Beith 191 F4
Hillside Cotts. Glen 101 F3
Hillside Cres. Coat 121 F2
Hillside Cres. Ham 162 B1
Hillside Cres. Holy 143 E2
Hillside Cres. Neil 154 B4
Hillside Cres. Pres 236 B4
Hillside Ct. Glasg 135 F2
Hillside Ct. Steven 217 E4
Hillside Dr. Barr 134 A2
Hillside Dr. Bear 76 A3
Hillside Dr. Bish 78 A1
Hillside Dr. Blac 107 E2
Hillside Dr. P Glasg 47 D1
Hillside Gr. Barr 134 A1
Hillside Gr. Bish 98 B4
Hillside. Hous 111 F4
Hillside. Kils 60 C2
Hillside. N Sau 5 E1
Hillside Pk. Dunt 74 A3
Hillside Pl. Blac 107 E2
Hillside Pl. Holy 143 E2
Hillside Quadrant. Glasg 136 A3
Hillside Rd. Barr 134 A2
Hillside Rd. Card 26 A1
Hillside Rd. Glasg 136 A3
Hillside Rd. Gour 44 B4
Hillside Rd. Green 46 A1
Hillside Rd. Neil 154 B4
Hillside Rd. Pais 114 A1
Hillside St. Steven 217 E4
Hillside Terr. All 10 A4
Hillside Terr. Ham 162 B1
Hillside Terr. M of C 58 A3
Hillside. W Kil 190 B2
Hillswick Cres. Glasg 97 D4
Hilltop Ave. Hat 142 A4
Hilltop Cres. Gour 44 C3
Hilltop Pl. Ayr 239 E3
Hilltop Rd. Gour 44 C3

Hilltop Rd. Muir 80 C1
Hillview Ave. Kils 60 C4
Hillview Ave. Lennox 57 F4
Hillview Cotts. Twe 59 F2
Hillview Cres. Hat 142 A4
Hillview Cres. Lark 185 D1
Hillview Cres. Tan 140 C4
Hillview Dr. B of A 2 A3
Hillview Dr. Helen 16 B2
Hillview Dr. Newt M 157 F4
Hillview Dr. Udd 140 B1
Hillview Gdns. Bish 98 B4
Hillview. Gree 83 F1
Hillview. Kils 37 E2
Hillview Pl. Fall 8 B2
Hillview Pl. Newt M 156 B2
Hillview Pl. Newt M 157 F4
Hillview Rd. B of W 110 C4
Hillview Rd. Bon 40 B2
Hillview Rd. John 112 B1
Hillview Rd. Lar 23 E2
Hillview St. Glasg 118 C3
Hillview Terr. All 10 B3
Hilton. Cowie 12 C4
Hilton Cres. All 10 B4
Hilton. Ct. Bish 78 A2
Hilton Gdns. Glasg 95 F4
Hilton Pk. Bish 77 F2
Hilton Rd. All 10 B4
Hilton Rd. Bish 78 A2
Hilton Rd. Miln 54 C1
Hilton Terr. Bish 191 D4
Hilton Terr. Fall 8 B2
Hilton Terr. Glasg 95 F4
Hilton Terr. Glasg 138 C2
Hiltonbank St. Ham 162 A2
Hindog Pl. Daly 191 D4
Hindsland Rd. Lark 185 D1
Hinshaw St. Glasg 97 D2
Hinshelwood Dr. Glasg 116 A3
Hinshelwood Pl. Glasg 116 A3
Hirsel Pl. Udd 141 D4
Hirst Gdns. Shot 146 B3
Hirst Rd. East 126 B2
Hirst Rd. Sals 126 B2
Hirstrigg Cotts. Sals 126 A2
Hobart Cres. Clyde 73 E3
Hobart Quadrant. Wish ... 165 F2
Hobart Rd. E Kil 180 B4
Hobart St. Glasg 97 D2
Hobden St. Glasg 98 A2
Hoddam Ave. Glasg 138 A2
Hoddam Terr. Glasg 138 A2
Hodge St. Falk 42 A2
Hoey Dr. Wish 186 B4
Hogan Ct. Dunt 73 F3
Hogarth Ave. Glasg 118 B4
Hogarth Ave. Salt 205 F1
Hogarth Cres. Glasg 118 B4
Hogarth Dr. Glasg 118 B4
Hogarth Gdns. Glasg 118 B4
Hogg Ave. John 111 F1
Hogg Rd. Chap 123 D4
Hogganfield St. Glasg 98 B1
Holburne Pl. Men 4 A4
Hole Farm Rd. Green 45 E2
Holehouse La. Glasg 136 B3
Holeburn Rd. Glasg 136 B3
Holehills Dr. Aird 103 D1
Holehills Pl. Aird 103 D1
Holehouse Brae. Neil 154 B4
Holehouse Dr. Glasg 95 D3
Holehouse Dr. Kilb 149 D2
Holehouse Rd. Eagle 178 C3
Holehouse Rd. Kilmk 228 A4
Holehouse Rd. Thorn 179 D4
Holehouse Terr. Neil 154 B4
Holland St. Glasg 117 D4
Hollandbush Ave. Bank 38 C2
Hollandbush Cres. Bank ... 38 C2
Hollandhurst Rd. Coat 101 F1
Hollinwell Rd. Glasg 76 B1
Hollow Pk. Ayr 239 D3
Hollowglen Rd. Glasg 119 D3
Hollows Ave. Pais 132 C4
Hollows Cres. Pais 132 C4
Holly Ave. M of C 58 A3
Holly Ave. Sten 23 F2
Holly Bank. Ayr 239 E3
Holly Dr. Dumb 49 D2
Holly Dr. Glasg 98 A2
Holly Gr. Bank 38 C1
Holly Gr. Holy 142 C3
Holly Pl. John 132 A4
Holly Pl. Kilmk 222 B1
Holly St. Aird 123 E3
Holly St. Clyde 74 B2
Hollybank Pl. Glasg 139 D2
Hollybank St. Glasg 98 A4
Hollybrook St. Glasg 117 D1
Hollybush Ave. Pais 133 D4
Hollybush Rd. Glasg 114 C3
Hollymount. Bear 75 F1
Holm Ave. Pais 113 F1
Holm Ave. Udd 140 C4
Holm Cres. Fen 213 D2
Holm Crest. Cro 201 D1

Holm Gdns. Hat 142 B2
Holm La. E Kil 159 F1
Holm Pl. Lark 184 C1
Holm Pl. Lin 112 A4
Holm Place. Lark 184 C1
Holm Rd. Cro 201 D1
Holm St. Car 187 F1
Holm St. Glasg 117 D4
Holm St. Holy 143 D2
Holm St. Stew 211 F4
Holmbank Ave. Glasg 136 B4
Holmbrae Ave. Tan 140 C4
Holmbrae Rd. Tan 140 C4
Holmbyre Rd. Glasg 137 E1
Holmbyre Terr. Glasg 137 E1
Holmes Ave. Ren 94 B1
Holmes Cres. Kilmk 227 E3
Holmes Farm Rd. Kilmk .. 227 E3
Holmes Quadrant. Hat 142 A2
Holmes Rd. Kilmk 227 E3
Holmes Village. Kilmk 227 E3
Holmfauld Rd. Glasg 95 F1
Holmfauldhead Dr. Glasg . 115 F4
Holmfauldhead Pl. Glasg . 115 F4
Holmfield. Kirk 79 F4
Holmhead Cres. Glasg 137 D3
Holmhead Kilb 170 A4
Holmhead Pl. Glasg 137 D3
Holmhead Rd. Glasg 137 D3
Holmhill Ave. Glasg 139 D2
Holmhills Dr. Glasg 138 C2
Holmhills Gdns. Glasg 138 C2
Holmhills Gr. Glasg 138 C2
Holmhills Pl. Glasg 138 C2
Holmhills Rd. Glasg 138 C2
Holmhills Terr. Glasg 138 C2
Holmlands Pl. Kilmk 227 E3
Holmlea Dr. Kilmk 227 F3
Holmlea Pl. Kilmk 227 F3
Holmlea Rd. Glasg 137 D4
Holmpark. Bishop 72 A2
Holmquarry Rd. Kilmk 227 F3
Holms Ave. Irvine 220 B1
Holms Cres. Ersk 72 C1
Holms Pl. Muir 100 C4
Holms Rd. Kilb 170 A3
Holmscroft Ave. Green 45 F2
Holmscroft St. Green 45 F2
Holmscroft Way. Green ... 45 F2
Holmston Cres. Ayr 239 E4
Holmston Dr. Ayr 239 E3
Holmston Rd. Ayr 239 E4
Holmswood Ave. Udd 161 E2
Holmwood Ave. Udd 140 C4
Holmwood Gdns. Udd 140 C3
Holmwood Gr. Glasg 137 D2
Holton Cres. N Sau 5 E1
Holton Sq. N Sau 5 E1
Holyknowe Cres. Lennox ... 57 F4
Holyknowe Rd. Lennox 57 F4
Holyoake Ct. Hurl 228 C4
Holyrood Cres. Glasg 96 C1
Holyrood Pl. Sten 23 F2
Holyrood Quadrant. Glasg . 96 C1
Holyrood St. Ham 162 A3
Holytown Rd. Holy 142 C3
Holywell St. Glasg 118 A3
Home Farm Cotts. Den 19 F3
Home Farm Rd. Ayr 239 D1
Honeywell Cres. Chap 123 F1
Hood Cl. Helen 16 A1
Hood St. Clyde 74 B1
Hood St. Green 45 F3
Hookney Terr. Den 19 F1
Hope Ave. Kil 89 F1
Hope Cres. Lark 185 D2
Hope St. Ayr 238 C4
Hope St. Car 188 A1
Hope St. Falk 42 A3
Hope St. Glasg 117 D4
Hope St. Green 46 A2
Hope St. Ham 162 C2
Hope St. Helen 25 C4
Hope St. Lan 215 D2
Hope St. Mother 163 F3
Hope St. New 166 A2
Hope St. Stir 1 C1
Hopefield Ave. Glasg 96 B3
Hopehill Rd. Glasg 97 D2
Hopeman Ave. Glasg 135 F2
Hopeman Dr. Glasg 135 F2
Hopeman Path. Glasg 135 F2
Hopeman Rd. Glasg 135 F2
Hopeman St. Glasg 135 F2
Hopepark Terr. Bon 39 F3
Hopetoun Bank. Irvine 220 B1
Hopetoun Dr. B of A 2 A4

Hopetoun Pl. Glasg 76 C1
Hopkin's Brae. Kirk 58 B1
Horatius St. Mother 142 A1
Hornal Rd. Udd 141 D2
Hornbeam Dr. Clyde 74 A2
Hornbeam Rd. Cumb 62 C3
Hornbeam Rd. Tan 141 D4
Hornbeam Cres. Glasg 99 E1
Horndean Ct. Bish 78 A2
Hornal St. Udd 97 F3
Hornock Rd. Coat 101 F1
Hornshill Dr. Cle 144 A1
Hornshill Farm Rd. Stepps . 99 F1
Hornshill St. Glasg 98 A2
Horsburgh Ave. Kils 36 B1
Horsburgh St. Glasg 99 E1
Horse Shoe Rd. Bear 75 F2
Horsewood Rd. B of W 110 B4
Horslet St. Coat 121 E2
Horslethill Rd. Glasg 96 B2
Horsley Brae. Wish 186 A2
Horton Pl. Helen 17 D2
Hospital Rd. Wish 186 A4
Hospital St. Coat 122 A2
Hospital St. Glasg 117 D2
Hospitland Dr. Lan 215 E2
Hotspur St. Glasg 96 C2
Houldsworth Cres. Alla ... 167 D4
Houldsworth La. Glasg 116 C4
Houldsworth St. Glasg 116 C4
House O' Muir Rd. Sals 126 A2
Househillmuir Cres. Glasg 135 E4
Househillmuir La. Glasg ... 135 E4
Househillmuir Pl. Glasg ... 135 E4
Househillmuir Rd. Glasg .. 135 D4
Househillwood Cres. Glasg 135 D4
Househillwood Rd. Glasg . 135 D3
Housel Ave. Glasg 95 D2
Houston Cres. Dalry 191 D4
Houston Pl. Glasg 116 C3
Houston Pl. John 112 B1
Houston Rd. B of W 90 B1
Houston Rd. Hous 91 D3
Houston Rd. Hous 111 E4
Houston Rd. Inch 92 B2
Houston Rd. Kil 89 F4
Houston Sq. John 111 F1
Houston St. Green 45 F3
Houston St. Ham 162 B1
Houston St. Ren 94 B2
Houston St. Wish 165 E1
Houston Terr. E Kil 159 E1
Hozierled
Quadrant. Hous 91 D1
Houstonfield Rd. Hous 91 D1
Houstoun Ct. John 111 F2
Houstoun Sq. John 111 F2
Howacre. Lan 214 C3
Howard Ave. E Kil 160 A3
Howard Ct. E Kil 160 A3
Howard Ct. Kilmk 227 F4
Howard Park Dr. Kilmk ... 227 F4
Howard St. Falk 41 F2
Howard St. Glasg 117 D3
Howard St. Kilmk 227 F4
Howard St. Lark 185 E1
Howard St. Pais 114 A2
Howat Cres. Irvine 219 F2
Howat St. Glasg 116 A4
Howatshaws Rd. Dumb 50 B3
Howburn Cres. East 127 E3
Howburn Rd. East 127 E3
Howden Ave. Holy 143 E4
Howden Ave. Kilw 207 D2
Howden Dr. Lin 112 A3
Howden Pl. Holy 143 D3
Howe Rd. Kils 60 B4
Howes St. Coat 122 A2
Howeton. Fish 5 E2
Howford Rd. Glasg 115 D2
Howgate Ave. Glasg 114 C2
Howgate. Kilw 207 E2
Howgate Rd. Ham 183 E4
Howie Bldgs. Newt M 157 F1
Howie Cres. Ros 15 D2
Howie's Pl. Falk 41 D2
Howieshill Ave. Glasg 139 D3
Howieshill Rd. Glasg 139 D3
Howlands Rd. Stir 7 D2
Howlet Pl. Ham 162 C1
Howletnest Rd. Aird 123 E3
Howson Vew. Mother 163 E4
Howth Dr. Glasg 95 F4
Howth Terr. Glasg 95 F4
Hoylake Ct. Coat 140 C1
Hoylake Pk. Udd 140 C1
Hoylake Pl. Glasg 76 C1
Hoylake Sq. Glasg 207 E2
Hozier Cres. Tan 140 C4
Hozier Loan. Lark 185 D2
Hozier Pl. Udd 141 E2
Hozier St. Car 187 F1
Hozier St. Coat 122 A4
Hudson Terr. E Kil 180 B4
Hudson Way. E Kil 180 B4
Hugbeth Ct. Alex 27 E4
Hugh Murray Cr. Glasg .. 139 E3
Hugh Watt Pl. Wish 222 A4
Hughenden Dr. Glasg 96 A2

Hughenden Gdns. Glasg 96 A2
Hughenden La. Glasg 96 A2
Hughenden Rd. Glasg 96 A2
Hugo St. Glasg 96 C3
Hulks Rd. Gree 83 E2
Humbie Ct. Newt M 156 C1
Humbie Gate. Newt M ... 156 C1
Humbie Lawns. Newt M .. 156 C1
Humbie Rd. Eagle 178 B4
Humbie Rd. Newt M 156 C1
Hume Cres. B of A 2 A3
Hume Ct. B of A 2 A3
Hume Dr. Udd 140 C2
Hume Dr. Udd 141 D2
Hume Pl. E Kil 180 B4
Hume Rd. Cumb 62 A2
Hunter Ave. Salt 205 E1
Hunter Cres. Troon 230 A1
Hunter Dr. Irvine 219 D3
Hunter Gdns. Den 21 E1
Hunter Pl. Kilbar 111 D1
Hunter Pl. Kilw 208 A2
Hunter Pl. Milnen 54 C1
Hunter Pl. Shot 147 D2
Hunter Pl. Sten 24 A2
Hunter Rd. Cross 221 F1
Hunter Rd. Glasg 118 B3
Hunter Rd. Ham 162 A3
Hunter Rd. Milnen 54 C1
Hunter St. Aird 103 D1
Hunter St. E Kil 159 F1
Hunter St. Glasg 117 F3
Hunter St. Glasg 117 F4
Hunter St. Hat 142 A3
Hunter St. Pais 113 F3
Hunter St. Pres 236 B4
Hunter St. Shot 146 B3
Hunter's Ave. Ayr 236 A2
Hunter's Ave. Dumb 50 B2
Hunterfield Ct. Lan 215 D2
Hunterhill Ave. Pais 113 F2
Hunterhill Rd. Pais 113 F2
Hunterhill Rd. Glasg 144 B2
Hunters Hill Ct. Glasg 97 F3
Hunters Pl. Green 45 F3
Huntersfield Rd. John 111 E1
Huntershill St. Bish 97 F4
Huntershill St. Glasg 97 F4
Hunterston Rd. W Kil 190 B3
Hunthill La. Udd 161 D3
Hunthill Pl. Thorn 158 A3
Hunting Lodge Gdns. Ham 163 D1
Huntingdon Rd. Glasg 97 F1
Huntingdon Sq. Glasg 97 F1
Huntingtower Rd. Glasg .. 119 F2
Huntley Cres. Stir 1 C1
Huntley Gdns. Glasg 96 B2
Huntly Ave. E Kil 180 B3
Huntly Ave. Glasg 136 B1
Huntly Ave. Hat 142 A3
Huntly Ct. Bish 98 A4
Huntly Ct. Kilmk 227 E3
Huntly Dr. Bear 75 F4
Huntly Dr. Coat 121 E2
Huntly Dr. Glasg 139 D2
Huntly Dr. Gour 44 C2
Huntly Gdns. Glasg 96 B2
Huntly Path. Muir 81 D3
Huntly Pl. Kilmk 223 E1
Huntly Pl. P Glasg 47 D1
Huntly Quadrant. Wish ... 165 D3
Huntly Rd. Glasg 96 B2
Huntly Rd. Glasg 139 D2
Huntly Terr. P Glasg 47 D1
Huntly Terr. Pais 114 A1
Huntly Terr. Shot 147 D2
Hurlawcrook Rd. Chapel .. 180 C1
Hurlethurry Rd. E Kil 181 D2
Hurlet Cotts. Glasg 134 C3
Hurlet Rd. Pais 134 C3
Hurlford Ave. Glasg 94 C4
Hurlford Rd. Kilmk 228 A3
Hurly Hawkin. Bish 98 B4
Hurworth St. Falk 41 F2
Hutcheson Rd. Glasg 136 C3
Hutcheson St. Glasg 117 E4
Hutchison Pl. Glasg 139 F2
Hutchison St. Wish 186 B4
Hutchison Town Ct. Glasg 117 E2
Hutchison Dr. Bear 76 A1
Hutchison Pl. Coat 142 A3
Hutchison St. Ham 162 B1
Hutton Ave. Hous 111 E4
Hutton Dr. Glasg 115 F4
Hutton Pk. All 10 B4
Huxley St. Glasg 96 C3
Hyacinth Way. Car 201 F4
Hydepark St. Glasg 116 C3
Hyndal Ave. Glasg 115 E1
Hyndford Pl. Lan 215 E1
Hyndford Rd. Lan 215 D1
Hyndland Ave. Glasg 96 A1
Hyndland Rd. Glasg 96 A2
Hyndland St. Glasg 96 B1
Hyndlee Dr. Glasg 115 E2
Hyndman Rd. W Kil 190 B2

Hyndshaw Rd. Car 188 A2
Hyndshaw View. Law 187 D2
Hyslop Pl. Clyde 74 A2
Hyslop Rd. Steven 206 C1
Hyslop St. Aird 122 C4

Iain Dr. Bear 75 E3
Iain Rd. Bear 75 E3
Ian Smith Ct. Clyde 94 B4
Ibrox St. Glasg 116 B3
Ibrox Terr. Glasg 116 A3
Ibroxholm Ave. Glasg 116 A3
Ibroxholm Oval. Glasg 116 A3
Ibroxholm Pl. Glasg 116 A3
Ida Quadrant. Hat 141 F3
Iddesleigh Ave. Miln 55 D1
Ilay Ave. Glasg 96 A4
Ilay Ct. Glasg 96 A4
Ilay Rd. Glasg 96 A4
Imperial Dr. Aird 122 C4
Inch Garve. E Kil 160 B1
Inch Keith. E Kil 160 B1
Inch Marnock. E Kil 160 B1
Inch Murrin. E Kil 160 B1
Inchbrae Rd. Glasg 115 E2
Inchcolm Pl. E Kil 159 E1
Inchconnachan Ave. Bonh . 19 F1
Inches Rd. Ard 216 A4
Inches Rd. Salt 205 E1
Inchfad Dr. Glasg 94 C3
Inchfad Pl. Bonh 19 F1
Inchgotrick Rd. Kilmk 227 F2
Inchgower Gr. Rhu 15 E3
Inchgreen St. Green 46 C1
Inchholm La. Glasg 95 F1
Inchholm St. Glasg 95 F1
Inchinnan Rd. Hat 141 F4
Inchinnan Rd. Pais 113 F4
Inchinnan Rd. Ren 94 A2
Inchkeith Pl. Falk 42 A1
Inchkeith Pl. Glasg 119 D4
Inchlee St. Glasg 95 F2
Inchlonaig Dr. Bonh 19 F1
Inchmurrin Ave. Kirk 80 A4
Inchmurrin Cres. Bonh 19 F1
Inchmurrin Dr. Glasg 138 B1
Inchmurrin Dr. Kilmk 223 D3
Inchmurrin Gdns. Glasg .. 138 B1
Inchmurrin Pl. Glasg 138 B1
Inchna. Men 4 A3
Inchneuk Rd. Glen 100 C4
Inchoch St. Glasg 99 F1
Inchrory Pl. Glasg 74 C2
Inchwood Ct. Cumb 82 A4
Inchwood Pl. Cumb 81 F4
Inchwood Rd. Cumb 81 F4
India Dr. Inch 93 E3
India St. Alex 27 F3
India St. Glasg 117 D4
Ingerbreck Ave. Glasg 138 B2
Ingleby Dr. Glasg 118 A4
Ingleby Pl. Neil 154 C4
Inglefield Ct. Aird 123 D4
Inglefield St. Glasg 117 D1
Ingleneuk Ave. Stepps 99 D3
Ingleside. Klrk 79 E3
Ingleston Ave. Duni 21 E3
Ingleston St. Green 46 A2
Inglestone Ave. Glasg 136 A1
Inglewood. All 10 A4
Inglewood Cres. E Kil 180 A4
Inglewood Rd. All 9 F4
Inglis Pl. E Kil 180 C4
Inglis St. Glasg 118 A3
Inglis St. Wish 164 B1
Ingliston Dr. Bishop 71 F2
Ingram Pl. Kilmk 223 D2
Ingram St. Glasg 117 E4
Innishail Rd. Glasg 119 D3
Inkerman Pl. Kilmk 222 C1
Inkerman Rd. Glasg 114 C3
Innellan Dr. Kilmk 222 C2
Inner City Trad Est. Glasg . 97 E1
Innerdale Dr. Wish 165 E3
Innermanse
Quadrant. Holy 143 F3
Innerpeffray Dr. Sten 24 A2
Innerwick Dr. Glasg 115 D3
Innerwood Rd. Kilw 207 F2
Inner Ct. Falk 24 B1
International Ave. Ham ... 161 E2
Inver Ct. Falk 24 B1
Inver Rd. Glasg 119 F4
Inverallan Ct. B of A 1 C4
Inverallan Dr. B of A 1 C4
Inverallan Rd. B of A 1 C4
Inveraray Dr. Bish 78 A2
Inveraray Dr. Sten 23 F3
Inveravon Dr. Mother 163 E3
Inverbervie. Ersk 72 C2
Invercanny Dr. Glasg 75 D2
Invercanny Pl. Glasg 75 D2
Invercargill. E Kil 180 A4
Invercloy Pl. Kilmk 222 C2

266
Inverclyde Gdns. Glasg Kelvinview Ave. Bank

Inverclyde Gdns. Glasg 138 C2
Invercree Wlk. Glen 101 E3
Inveresk Pl. Coat 122 A4
Inveresk Quadrant. Glasg 119 D3
Inveresk St. Glasg 119 D3
Inverewe Ave. Glasg 135 E1
Inverewe Dr. Glasg 135 E1
Inverewe Gdns. Glasg 135 E1
Inverewe Pl. Glasg 135 E2
Invergarry Ave. Glasg 135 E1
Invergarry Ct. Glasg 135 F1
Invergarry Dr. Glasg 135 F1
Invergarry Gdns. Glasg 135 E1
Invergarry Gr. Glasg 135 E1
Invergarry Pl. Glasg 135 F1
Invergarry Quad. Glasg 135 F1
Invergarry View. Glasg 135 F1
Inverglas Ave. Ren 94 C1
Invergordon Ave. Glasg 136 C4
Invergyle Dr. Glasg 115 E3
Inverkar Dr. Pais 113 D1
Inverkar Rd. Ayr 239 D3
Inverkip Dr. Shot 146 C3
Inverkip Rd. Gour 44 B1
Inverkip Rd. Green 45 E2
Inverkip St. Green 45 F3
Inverlair Ave. Glasg 136 C3
Inverleith St. Glasg 118 C4
Inverleven Pl. Irvine 219 F4
Inverlochy St. Glasg 99 E1
Inverness St. Glasg 115 E3
Inveroran Dr. Bear 76 A2
Invershiel Rd. Glasg 76 C1
Invershin Dr. Glasg 96 B3
Inverurie St. Glasg 97 E2
Invervale Ave. Aird 123 F3
Inzievar Terr. Glasg 119 D1
Iona. Aird 123 E3
Iona Ave. E Kil 160 A2
Iona Cres. Clyde 73 E3
Iona Cres. Gour 44 B3
Iona Ct. Irvine 225 E4
Iona Dr. Pais 133 E4
Iona Gdns. Clyde 73 E3
Iona La. Muir 81 D1
Iona Path. Udd 161 E4
Iona Pl. Clyde 73 E3
Iona Pl. Coat 101 E1
Iona Pl. Falk 42 A1
Iona Pl. Irvine 225 E4
Iona Pl. Kilmk 223 D3
Iona Quadrant. Wish 165 F3
Iona Rd. Glasg 138 C2
Iona Rd. New 165 F3
Iona Rd. P Glasg 69 D4
Iona Rd. Ren 94 B1
Iona Ridge. Ham 161 F1
Iona St. Glasg 116 A4
Iona St. Green 45 E2
Iona St. Mother 142 B1
Iona Way. Kirk 80 A4
Iona Way. Stepps 99 F2
Iona Wlk. Gour 44 B3
Iona Wynd. Bonh 27 F1
Iris Ave. Glasg 138 A2
Iris Ct. Ayr 239 E2
Irongray St. Glasg 118 B4
Irvine Cres. Coat 122 B4
Irvine Gdns. M of C 58 A3
Irvine Mains Cres. Irvine 219 E2
Irvine Pl. Kils 36 A1
Irvine Pl. Stir 7 D4
Irvine Rd. Cross 221 F1
Irvine Rd. Kilm 222 A4
Irvine Rd. Kilmk 222 B1
Irvine Rd. Kilw 207 F1
Irvine Rd. Kilw 219 D4
Irvine St. Glasg 118 A2
Irvine St. Glenm 102 C2
Irvine Terr. Ham 183 E4
Irving Ave. Dunt 74 A3
Irving Ct. Dunt 74 A3
Irving Ct. Falk 41 F3
Irving Quadrant. Dunt 74 A3
Irwin St. Green 46 C1
Isabella Gdns. Ham 163 E1
Isla Ave. New 165 F3
Island Rd. Cumb 82 B4
Island View. Ard 205 D2
Islands Cres. Falk 42 A1
Islay. Aird 123 F3
Islay Ave. Glasg 138 C2
Islay Ave. P Glasg 69 D4
Islay Cres. Clyde 73 E3
Islay Cres. Pais 133 E4
Islay Cres. Salt 205 F1
Islay Ct. Ham 161 F1
Islay Ct. Irvine 225 E4
Islay Dr. Clyde 73 E3
Islay Dr. Newt M 156 A3
Islay Gdns. Car 202 A4
Islay Gdns. Lark 185 D2
Islay Pl. Kilmk 223 D3
Islay Quadrant. Wish 164 C1
Islay Rd. Kirk 80 A4
Isle Of Pin Rd. Troon 230 A1
Ivanhoe Cres. Wish 165 E2
Ivanhoe Ct. Car 187 E1
Ivanhoe Dr. Kirk 79 F4
Ivanhoe Dr. Salt 206 A1
Ivanhoe. E Kil 160 B2
Ivanhoe Pl. Holy 143 D3
Ivanhoe Pl. Stir 2 A1
Ivanhoe Rd. Cumb 82 C4
Ivanhoe Rd. Glasg 95 E4
Ivanhoe Rd. Pais 112 C1
Ivanhoe Way. Pais 112 C1
Ivy Cres. Gour 44 C3
Ivy Pl. Ayr 239 E3
Ivy Pl. Holy 143 D2
Ivy Pl. Udd 161 E4
Ivy Rd. Tan 141 E4
Ivy Terr. Holy 143 D3
Ivybank Ave. Glasg 139 E2
Ivybank Cres. P Glasg 47 D1
Ivybank Rd. P Glasg 47 D1
Izatt St. All 10 A4
Jack St. Ham 183 E4
Jack St. Mother 164 A2
Jack's Rd. Salt 205 F1
Jack's Rd. Udd 141 D3
Jacks View. W Kil 190 B3
Jackson Ct. Coat 122 A3
Jackson Pl. Car 187 F2
Jackson St. Coat 122 A4
Jackton Rd. Auld 179 E3
Jackton Rd. Thorn 179 E3
Jacob Pl. Falk 42 A2
Jacob's Ladder Way. Wish 186 B3
Jacobs Dr. Gour 44 B3
Jagger Gdns. Glasg 119 F2
Jail Wynd. Stir 7 D4
Jamaica Dr. E Kil 159 D1
Jamaica La. Green 45 F3
Jamaica St. Glasg 117 D3
Jamaica St. Green 45 F3
James Brown Ave. Ayr 236 C2
James Campbell Rd. Ayr 239 E4
James Cres. Irvine 219 E2
James Croft Dr. Falk 41 F1
James Dempsey Ct. Coat 121 F3
James
Dempsey Gdns. Coat 121 F3
James Dunlop Gdns. Bish 98 A4
James Gray St. Glasg 136 C4
James Hamilton Dr. Hat 142 A3
James Healy Dr. Ham 183 E4
James Hemphill Ct. Lennox 57 F4
James Leeson Ct. M of C 58 B3
James Little St. Kilmk 227 F4
James Miller Cres. Salt 217 D4
James Morrison St. Glasg 117 E3
James Nisbet St. Glasg 97 F1
James St. Alex 27 F3
James St. Alva 5 D3
James St. Ayr 236 A1
James St. Bank 39 D2
James St. Bann 7 E1
James St. Car 187 F1
James St. Dalry 191 D4
James St. Falk 42 A3
James St. Glasg 117 F2
James St. Helen 16 B1
James St. Lar 23 E1
James St. Laur 42 C2
James St. Mother 163 E4
James St. Pres 236 A3
James St. Stir 2 A1
James St. Tan 141 F4
James Sym Cres. Kilmk 227 F3
James View. Holy 142 C2
James Watt La. Glasg 117 D3
James Watt Pl. E Kil 159 D2
James Watt Rd. Miln 54 C2
James Watt St. Glasg 117 D4
James Wilson Pl. Cro 201 D1
Jamieson Ct. Dunt 74 A4
Jamieson Ct. Glasg 117 D1
Jamieson Dr. E Kil 160 A1
Jamieson Gdns. Shot 146 C3
Jamieson Pl. Stew 195 E1
Jamieson St. Glasg 117 D1
Jamieson St. Glasg 117 E1
Jamieson Way. Beith 171 D4
Jane Ct. Lark 185 D1
Jane's Brae. Cumb 82 C4
Jane's
Brae Interchange. Cumb 82 C4
Janebank Ave. Glasg 139 E2
Janefield Ave. John 111 F1
Janefield Pl. Beith 150 A1
Janefield Pl. Lennox 33 E1
Janefield Pl. Udd 161 E3
Janefield St. Glasg 118 B3
Janesmith St. Mother 164 B2
Janetta St. Clyde 74 A2
Jardine St. Glasg 96 C2
Jardine Terr. Green 45 F4
Jardine Terr. Muir 100 C3
Jarvie Ave. Plains 104 A1
Jarvie Cres. Kils 60 B4
Jarvie Pl. Falk 42 A4
Jarvie Way. Pais 132 C4
Jasmine Pl. Cumb 82 A3
Jasmine Rd. Kilmk 227 E4
Jasmine Way. Car 201 F4
Java St. Mother 142 B1
Jean Armour Dr. Clyde 74 B2
Jean Armour La. Gour 44 C2
Jean Armour Pl. Salt 206 A1
Jean Armour Terr. Gour 44 C2
Jean St. P Glasg 47 D1
Jeanette Ave. Ham 183 E4
Jeanie Deans Dr. Helen 25 D4
Jedburgh Ave. Glasg 138 A4
Jedburgh Dr. Pais 113 D1
Jedburgh Gdns. Glasg 96 C2
Jedburgh Pl. Coat 121 F2
Jedburgh Pl. E Kil 159 F1
Jedburgh St. Udd 161 E4
Jedburgh St. Wish 165 E3
Jedworth Ave. Glasg 75 E2
Jedworth Ct. Bear 75 F3
Jedworth Rd. Glasg 75 D2
Jeffrey Pl. Kils 36 B1
Jeffrey St. Kilmk 227 F3
Jellicoe Pl. Helen 17 D1
Jellicoe St. Clyde 73 F2
Jellyholm Rd. N Sau 10 C4
Jennie Lee Dr. Wish 186 A4
Jennys Well Ct. Pais 114 A1
Jennys Well Rd. Pais 114 A1
Jermond Dr. Irvine 219 E3
Jervis Pl. Helen 17 D1
Jervis Terr. E Kil 180 A4
Jerviston Ct. Holy 143 D1
Jerviston Rd. Glasg 99 E1
Jerviston Rd. Holy 143 D1
Jerviston St. Holy 143 D2
Jerviston St. Mother 163 F4
Jerviswood Dr. Lan 215 F4
Jerviswood. Holy 143 D1
Jerviswood Rd. Lan 215 D2
Jessie St. Glasg 117 E1
Jessiman Sq. Ren 94 A1
Jimmy
Sneddon Way. Mother 142 B1
Joanna Terr. Udd 161 E4
Jocelyn Sq. Glasg 117 E3
Jocksthorn Terr. Kilm 222 B3
John Bassy Dr. Bank 38 B2
John Brannan Way. Tan 141 E3
John Brogan Pl. Salt 217 D4
John Brown Pl. Muir 100 B4
John Burnside Dr. Dunt 74 B4
John Davidson Dr. Duni 21 E2
John Dickie St. Kilmk 222 C1
John Ewing Gdns. Lark 185 D2
John Finnie St. Kilmk 227 F4
John Gregor Pl. Loch 129 E1
John Hendry Rd. Udd 141 D2
John Jarvis Sq. Kils 36 B1
John Knox La. Ham 161 E2
John Knox St. Clyde 94 B4
John Knox St. Glasg 117 F4
John Lang St. John 112 A2
John
McEwan Way. Lennox 78 A4
John Murray Ct. Mother 163 F2
John Murray Dr. B of A 2 A4
John Rushforth Pl. Stir 1 C2
John St. Alex 49 E4
John St. Ayr 239 D4
John St. Bank 39 D2
John St. Barr 134 A2
John St. Car 187 F1
John St. Falk 42 A4
John St. Glasg 117 E4
John St. Gour 44 C4
John St. Green 46 A2
John St. Ham 162 C2
John St. Hat 142 A3
John St. Helen 16 B1
John St. Kirk 58 B1
John St. Lark 185 D1
John St. Mother 164 B2
John St. Stir 7 D4
John St. Udd 161 F4
John Street La. Helen 16 B1
John Wilson Dr. Kils 36 A1
John Wilson St. Green 46 B1
John Wood St. P Glasg 47 E1
Johnshaven. Ersk 73 D1
Johnshaven St. Glasg 136 B4
Johnshill. Loch 129 E2
Johnson Ct. Helen 16 C1
Johnson Dr. Glasg 139 D3
Johnston Ave. Clyde 94 B4
Johnston Ave. Kils 60 B4
Johnston Ave. Sten 23 F2
Johnston Ave. Stir 2 A2
Johnston Dr. Troon 229 E3
Johnston Pl. Den 21 E1
Johnston Rd. Muir 101 D3
Johnston St. Aird 123 D4
Johnston St. Bann 7 E1
Johnston St. Green 45 E4
Johnston St. Pais 113 F2
Johnston Terr. Green 45 E4
Johnstone Ave. Glasg 115 D4
Johnstone Dr. Glasg 138 A4
Johnstone Dr. Loch 129 E1
Johnstone La. Car 188 A1
Johnstone Rd. Ham 162 C1
Johnstone St. Alva 5 D3
Johnstone St. Hat 142 B3
Johnstone St. Men 3 F3
Johnstone Terr. Twe 59 F2
Jones Ave. Lar 41 E4
Jonquil Way. Car 201 F4
Joppa St. Glasg 118 C4
Jordan St. Glasg 95 E1
Jordanhill Cres. Glasg 95 E3
Jordanhill Dr. Glasg 95 E3
Jordanhill La. Glasg 95 F3
Jordanvale Ave. Glasg 95 E1
Jowitt Ave. Clyde 74 B1
Jubilee Bank. Kirk 79 E2
Jubilee Dr. Stew 195 F1
Jubilee Gdns. Bear 75 F2
Jubilee Pl. Stew 195 F1
Jubilee Rd. Duni 21 F2
Jubilee Terr. John 111 E1
Julian Ave. Glasg 96 B2
Julian La. Glasg 96 B2
Juniper Ave. E Kil 180 B3
Juniper Ct. Kirk 79 D3
Juniper Dr. M of C 58 A2
Juniper Gn. Ayr 239 E3
Juniper Gr. Ham 162 C1
Juniper Pl. Glasg 119 F2
Juniper Pl. John 132 A4
Juniper Pl. Tan 141 E4
Juniper Rd. Tan 141 E4
Juniper Terr. Glasg 119 F2
Juniper Wynd. Holy 143 D3
Juno La. Gour 44 B2
Juno St. Mother 142 B1
Juno Terr. Gour 44 B2
Jupiter La. Gour 44 B2
Jupiter Pl. Rhu 15 E3
Jupiter St. Mother 142 B1
Jupiter Terr. Gour 44 B2
Jura Ave. Ren 94 B1
Jura Ct. Irvine 225 E4
Jura Dr. Clyde 73 E3
Jura Dr. Kirk 80 A4
Jura Dr. Newt M 156 A3
Jura Dr. Udd 140 B2
Jura. E Kil 181 D4
Jura Gdns. Car 202 A4
Jura Gdns. Clyde 73 E3
Jura Gdns. Ham 162 A1
Jura Gdns. Lark 185 E2
Jura Pl. Clyde 73 E3
Jura Pl. Troon 229 F4
Jura Quadrant. Wish 164 C1
Jura Rd. Clyde 73 E3
Jura Rd. Pais 133 E4
Jura St. Glasg 115 F3
Jura St. Green 45 E2
Jura Wynd. Glen 101 E3
Jutland Ct. Helen 16 A2
Kaim Dr. Glasg 135 E3
Kames Ct. Irvine 220 A3
Kames Rd. Shot 146 C3
Kane Pl. Stone 198 C1
Kane St. Alex 27 E1
Karadale Gdns. Lark 185 D2
Karol Path. Glasg 97 D1
Karriemuir Rd. Bish 78 B1
Katewell Ave. Glasg 74 C2
Katherine St. Aird 123 F4
Kathleen Pk. Helen 16 A2
Katrine Ave. Bish 78 A1
Katrine Ave. Tan 141 E3
Katrine Cres. Aird 102 C1
Katrine Ct. All 10 B3
Katrine Ct. Kilmk 228 A3
Katrine Dr. Newt M 157 D2
Katrine Dr. Pais 113 D1
Katrine Pl. Bank 39 E3
Katrine Pl. Coat 101 E1
Katrine Pl. Glasg 139 D3
Katrine Pl. Irvine 219 E3
Katrine Rd. Green 46 A2
Katrine Rd. Shot 146 C3
Katrine Way. Udd 141 D2
Katrine Wynd. Holy 143 D3
Katriona Path. Lark 185 E1
Kay Gdns. Mother 163 D3
Kay Park Cres. Kilmk 223 D1
Kay Park Terr. Kilmk 223 D1
Kay St. Glasg 97 F2
Kaystone Rd. Glasg 75 D1
Keal Ave. Glasg 95 D4
Keal Cres. Glasg 95 D4
Keal Dr. Glasg 95 D4
Keal Pl. Glasg 95 D4
Kearn Ave. Glasg 75 D1
Kearn Pl. Glasg 75 D1
Keats Pk. Udd 141 D2
Keil Cres. Dumb 49 E2
Keilarsbrae. N Sau 5 E1
Keir Ave. Stir 2 A1
Keir Cres. Wish 165 D2
Keir Dr. Bish 77 F1
Keir Gdns. B of A 2 A4
Keir Hardie Ave. Holy 143 D3
Keir Hardie Ave. Laur 42 C2
Keir Hardie Cres. Kilw 208 A2
Keir Hardie Ct. Bish 78 A1
Keir Hardie Dr. Ard 205 D2
Keir Hardie Dr. Hat 141 F2
Keir Hardie Dr. Kilb 149 D1
Keir Hardie Dr. Kils 60 B4
Keir Hardie Pl. Hat 141 F2
Keir Hardie Pl. Salt 206 A1
Keir Hardie Rd. Alva 5 E4
Keir Hardie Rd. Lark 185 E1
Keir Hardie Rd. Steven 206 C1
Keir Hardie St. Green 46 C1
Keir St. B of A 2 A4
Keir St. Glasg 116 C2
Keir's Wlk. Glasg 139 D3
Keith Ave. Glasg 136 B2
Keith Ave. Stir 7 E2
Keith Ct. Glasg 96 B1
Keith Pl. Kilmk 223 E1
Keith Quadrant. Wish 165 D3
Keith St. Glasg 96 B1
Keith St. Hat 142 A3
Kelbourne Cres. Hat 141 F3
Kelbourne St. Glasg 96 C2
Kelburn Cres. Kilmk 227 F2
Kelburn St. Barr 134 A1
Kelburn Terr. P Glasg 48 A1
Kelburne Dr. Pais 114 A3
Kelburne Gdns. Glasg 120 A2
Kelburne Gdns. Pais 114 A3
Kelburne. Kilw 207 E1
Kelburne Oval. Pais 114 A3
Kelhead Ave. Glasg 114 C2
Kelhead Ave. Glasg 114 C3
Kelhead Dr. Glasg 114 C3
Kelhead Path. Glasg 114 C3
Kelhead Pl. Glasg 114 C3
Kellas St. Glasg 116 A4
Kellie Gr. E Kil 159 E2
Kellie Pl. All 10 A4
Kelliebank. All 9 F3
Kellock Ave. Coat 121 E2
Kellock Cres. Coat 121 E2
Kells Pl. Glasg 74 C2
Kelly Dr. Den 21 F2
Kelly St. Green 45 E3
Kelly's La. Car 188 A1
Kelso Ave. B of W 110 B4
Kelso Ave. Glasg 138 A4
Kelso Ave. Pais 113 D1
Kelso Cres. Wish 165 D3
Kelso Dr. Car 188 B1
Kelso Dr. E Kil 160 A2
Kelso Gdns. Muir 80 C2
Kelso Pl. Clyde 94 C3
Kelso Quadrant. Coat 121 F4
Kelso St. Glasg 94 C4
Kelton St. Glasg 119 D2
Kelvin Ave. Glasg 114 C4
Kelvin Ave. Kilw 207 F1
Kelvin Cres. Bear 75 F1
Kelvin Ct. Glasg 96 A3
Kelvin Dr. Aird 103 D1
Kelvin Dr. Barr 134 B1
Kelvin Dr. Bish 78 A1
Kelvin Dr. E Kil 180 C4
Kelvin Dr. Glasg 96 B2
Kelvin Dr. Kirk 79 D4
Kelvin Dr. Muir 80 C1
Kelvin Dr. Shot 147 D2
Kelvin Gdns. Ham 161 F2
Kelvin Gdns. Kils 60 B4
Kelvin Pl. E Kil 181 D4
Kelvin Rd. Cumb 83 D4
Kelvin Rd. E Kil 181 D4
Kelvin Rd. Hat 142 A4
Kelvin Rd. Miln 54 C2
Kelvin Rd N. Cumb 83 D4
Kelvin Rd. Tan 140 C4
Kelvin St. Coat 122 B3
Kelvin Terr. Twe 59 F2
Kelvin View. Lennox 78 B4
Kelvin View. Twe 59 F2
Kelvin Way. Glasg 96 C1
Kelvin Way. Kils 36 B1
Kelvin Way. Kirk 79 D4
Kelvin Way. Udd 141 D2
Kelvinbridge
Roundabout. Lennox 78 A4
Kelvindale Gdns. Glasg 96 B3
Kelvindale. Lennox 57 E1
Kelvindale Pl. Glasg 96 B3
Kelvindale Rd. Glasg 96 B3
Kelvingrove St. Glasg 116 C4
Kelvinhaugh Pl. Glasg 116 B4
Kelvinhaugh St. Glasg 116 B4
Kelvinhead Rd. Kils 37 F1
Kelvinside Ave. Glasg 96 C2
Kelvinside Cres. Kils 37 F2
Kelvinside Dr. Glasg 96 C2
Kelvinside
Gardens La. Glasg 96 C2
Kelvinside Gdns E. Glasg 96 C2
Kelvinside Gdns. Glasg 96 C2
Kelvinside Terr S. Glasg 96 C2
Kelvinside Terr W. Glasg 96 C2
Kelvinvale. Kirk 58 B1
Kelvinview Ave. Bank 38 C1

267
Kemp Ave. Ren Kinloch Dr. Mother

emp Ave. Ren 94 A1
emp Ct. Ham 162 C2
emp St. Glasg 97 F2
emp St. Ham 162 C2
emper Ave. Falk 42 B2
empock Pl. Gour 44 C4
empock St. Glasg 118 B2
empock St. Gour 44 C4
empsthorn Cres. Glasg 115 D1
empsthorn Rd. Glasg 115 D1
en Rd. Kilmk 228 A3
enbank Cres. B of W 110 B4
enbank Rd. B of W 110 B4
endal Ave. Glasg 96 A3
endal Ave. Glasg 136 B2
endal Dr. Glasg 96 A3
endal Rd. E Kil 179 F3
endoon Ave. Glasg 74 C2
enilburn Ave. Aird 103 D1
enilburn Cres. Aird 103 D1
enilworth Ave. Glasg 136 B4
enilworth Ave. Helen 25 D4
enilworth Ave. Pais 132 C4
enilworth Ave. Wish 165 D2
enilworth Cres. Bear 75 E3
enilworth Cres. Green 45 E2
enilworth Cres. Ham 161 F2
enilworth Cres. Hat 142 A3
enilworth Ct. Car 187 F1
enilworth Ct. Holy 143 D3
enilworth Dr. Aird 123 E4
enilworth Dr. Laur 42 C2
enilworth Dr. Salt 206 A1
enilworth. E Kil 160 C2
enilworth Rd. B of A 2 A4
enilworth Rd. Kirk 79 F4
enilworth Rd. Lan 215 D2
enilworth Way. Pais 112 C1
enmar Gdns. Tan 140 C4
enmar Rd. Ham 162 A3
enmar Terr. Ham 162 A3
enmore Ave. Pres 236 B3
enmore Gdns. Bear 76 A3
enmore Pl. Troon 229 F2
enmore Rd. Cumb 62 A1
enmore Rd. Kil 89 E4
enmore St. Glasg 119 D3
enmore Way. Car 187 F2
enmuir Ave. Glasg 119 F2
enmuir Rd. Glasg 119 F1
enmuir Rd. Glasg 139 E4
enmuir St. Coat 121 E2
enmuir St. Falk 41 D3
enmuiraid Pl. Hat 141 F2
enmuirhill Rd. Glasg 119 E1
enmure Ave. Bish 77 F1
enmure Cres. Bish 77 F1
enmure Dr. Bish 77 F1
enmure Gdns. Bish 77 F1
enmure La. Bish 77 F1
enmure Pl. Sten 23 F2
enmure Rd. Newt M 157 D3
enmure St. Glasg 116 C2
enmure Way. Glasg 138 A2
ennard St. Falk 42 B3
ennedar Dr. Glasg 115 F4
ennedy Ct. Glasg 136 B2
ennedy Ct. Kilmk 223 E2
ennedy Dr. Aird 122 C4
ennedy Dr. Helen 16 B2
ennedy Dr. Kilmk 223 E2
ennedy Gdns. Wish 186 A4
ennedy Rd. Salt 205 F1
ennedy Rd. Troon 229 D1
ennedy St. Kilmk 227 F3
ennedy St. Wish 165 E2
ennedy's La. Green 46 A2
ennelburn Rd. Chap 123 E1
enneth Rd. Mother 163 E3
ennihill. Aird 103 D1
ennihill Quadrant. Aird 103 D1
enningknowes Rd. Stir 6 C3
ennishead Ave. Glasg 135 F3
ennishead Path. Glasg 135 F3
ennishead Pl. Glasg 135 F3
ennishead Rd. Glasg 135 E3
ennishead Rd. Glasg 135 F2
ennisholm Ave. Glasg 135 F3
ennisholm Path. Glasg 135 F3
ennisholm Pl. Glasg 135 F3
ennoway Dr. Glasg 95 F1
ennyhill Sq. Glasg 118 A4
enshaw Ave. Lark 199 D4
enshaw Pl. Lark 199 D4
ensington Dr. Glasg 136 B1
ensington Gate. Glasg 96 B2
ensington Gate La. Glasg 96 B2
ensington Rd. Glasg 96 B2
ent Ct. Helen 17 D2
ent Dr. Glasg 138 B3
ent Dr. Helen 17 D2
ent Pl. E Kil 179 F3
ent Rd. All 9 F4
ent Rd. Glasg 116 C4
ent Rd. Stir 7 D3
ent St. Glasg 117 F3
entallen Rd. Glasg 119 F3
entigern Terr. Bish 98 A4
Kentmere Cl. E Kil 180 A3
Kentmere Dr. E Kil 180 A3
Kentmere Pl. E Kil 180 A3
Keppel Dr. Glasg 137 F3
Keppoch St. Glasg 97 E2
Keppochhill Rd. Glasg 97 E2
Ker Rd. Miln 54 C2
Ker St. Green 45 F3
Kerelaw Ave. Steven 206 C1
Kerelaw Rd. Steven 206 B1
Kerfield Pl. Glasg 74 C2
Kerr Ave. Salt 217 D4
Kerr Cres. Bank 39 D2
Kerr Cres. Ham 162 B1
Kerr Dr. Irvine 219 E1
Kerr Dr. Mother 163 E3
Kerr Gdns. Tan 141 D4
Kerr Pl. Den 21 E1
Kerr Pl. Glasg 117 F3
Kerr Pl. Irvine 219 E1
Kerr Rd. Kilmk 223 E1
Kerr St. Barr 134 A1
Kerr St. Glasg 117 F3
Kerr St. Kirk 79 E4
Kerr St. Pais 113 E3
Kerr St. Udd 161 F4
Kerrera Pl. Glasg 119 E3
Kerrera Rd. Glasg 119 E3
Kerrix Rd. Sym 231 D1
Kerrmuir Ave. Hurl 228 C3
Kerrs La. Salt 216 C4
Kerry Pl. Glasg 74 C2
Kerrycroy Ave. Glasg 137 E4
Kerrycroy Pl. Glasg 137 E4
Kerrycroy St. Glasg 137 E4
Kerrydale St. Glasg 118 A2
Kerrylamont Ave. Glasg 137 F4
Kerse Ave. Beith 191 F4
Kerse Gdns. Falk 42 C3
Kerse Gn Rd. Clack 10 C3
Kerse La. Falk 42 B3
Kerse Pl. Falk 42 B3
Kerse Rd. Fal 7 F3
Kerse Rd. Stir 7 E3
Kersebonny Rd. Cam 6 B4
Kersepark. Ayr 239 D1
Kershaw St. Wish 186 B4
Kersie Rd. Fall 9 D2
Kersie Terr. Air 9 F2
Kersland Cres. Hurl 228 C3
Kersland Dr. Miln 55 D1
Kersland Foot. Irvine 219 F3
Kersland La. Glasg 96 B2
Kersland La. Miln 55 D1
Kersland Rd. Beith 170 B3
Kersland St. Glasg 96 B2
Kerswinning Ave. Kilb 170 A4
Kessington Dr. Bear 76 A2
Kessington Rd. Bear 76 A2
Kessock Dr. Glasg 97 D2
Kestrel Cres. Green 45 D3
Kestrel Ct. Dunt 74 A3
Kestrel Pl. Green 45 D3
Kestrel Pl. John 131 E4
Kestrel Rd. Glasg 95 E3
Keswick Rd. E Kil 179 F3
Kethers La. Mother 163 E4
Kethers St. Mother 163 E3
Keverkae. All 9 F3
Kevoc Cotts. Moss 237 D3
Kew Gdns. Tan 141 D4
Kew La. Glasg 96 B2
Kew Terr. Glasg 96 B2
Keynes Sq. Hat 142 B2
Keystone Ave. Miln 76 A4
Keystone Quadrant. Miln 76 A4
Keystone Rd. Miln 76 A4
Kibbleston Rd. Kilbar 130 C4
Kidsneuk Gdns. Irvine 219 D3
Kidsneuk. Irvine 219 D3
Kidston Dr. Helen 16 A1
Kidston St. Glasg 117 E2
Kier Hardie Ct. Beith 171 D4
Kierhill Rd. Cumb 61 E1
Kilallan Ave. B of W 90 B1
Kilallan Rd. Hous 90 B3
Kilbarchan Rd. B of W 110 C3
Kilbarchan Rd. John 111 E1
Kilbarchan St. Glasg 117 D3
Kilbean Dr. Falk 41 F1
Kilbeck Gdns. Bear 75 E4
Kilbeg Terr. Glasg 135 E2
Kilberry St. Glasg 98 A1
Kilbirnie Pl. Glasg 117 D2
Kilbirnie St. Glasg 117 D2
Kilbirnie Terr. Den 21 E2
Kilblain St. Green 45 F3
Kilbowie Rd. Clyde 74 A2
Kilbowie Rd. Cumb 62 A1
Kilbowie Rd. Dunt 74 A3
Kilbrandon Cres. Ayr 238 A1
Kilbrandon Way. Ayr 238 A1
Kilbrannan Ave. Salt 205 F1
Kilbrannan Dr. Green 45 D2
Kilbreck La. Holy 143 E2
Kilbrennan Dr. Falk 41 D2
Kilbrennan Dr. Mother 163 D4
Kilbrennan Rd. Lin 112 A3
Kilbride Dr. Helen 16 C2
Kilbride Rd. Stew 195 E1
Kilbride St. Glasg 117 E1
Kilbride View. Tan 141 D4
Kilburn Gr. Udd 140 B1
Kilburn Pl. Glasg 95 D3
Kilchattan Dr. Glasg 137 E4
Kilchoan Rd. Glasg 99 E1
Kilcloy Ave. Glasg 75 D2
Kilcreggan View. Green 46 B1
Kilda Dr. Glasg 95 F2
Kildale Rd. Loch 129 D1
Kildale Way. Glasg 137 F4
Kildare Dr. Lan 215 D2
Kildare Pl. Lan 215 D2
Kildare Rd. Lan 215 D2
Kildary Ave. Glasg 137 D3
Kildary Rd. Glasg 137 D3
Kildermorie Rd. Glasg 120 A4
Kildonan Ct. New 165 F4
Kildonan Dr. Glasg 96 A1
Kildonan Dr. Helen 16 C1
Kildonan House. Pres 236 A3
Kildonan Pl. Mother 163 E4
Kildonan Pl. Salt 205 F1
Kildonan St. Coat 122 A4
Kildrostan St. Glasg 116 C1
Kildrum Rd. Cumb 62 B2
Kildrum South
Interchange. Cumb 62 A1
Kildrummy Ave. Sten 23 F2
Kildrummy Pl. E Kil 159 E2
Kilearn Rd. Pais 114 A4
Kilearn Sq. Pais 114 A4
Kilearn Way. Pais 114 A4
Kilfinan Rd. Shot 146 B3
Kilfinan St. Glasg 97 D4
Kilgarth St. Coat 121 E2
Kilgraston Rd. B of W 110 B3
Kilkerran Dr. Glasg 98 C3
Kilkerran Dr. Troon 229 E4
Kilkerran. Kilw 207 D2
Killearn Dr. Glasg 114 C2
Killearn Rd. Green 46 A1
Killearn St. Glasg 97 E2
Killermont Ave. Bear 76 A1
Killermont Ct. Bear 76 A2
Killermont Meadows. Udd 140 C1
Killermont Pl. Kilw 207 D2
Killermont Rd. Bear 76 A1
Killermont St. Glasg 117 E4
Killermont View. Glasg 76 A1
Killiegrew Rd. Glasg 116 B1
Killin Dr. Lin 111 F3
Killin Pl. Troon 229 F2
Killin St. Glasg 119 D2
Killoch Ave. Pais 113 D3
Killoch Dr. Barr 134 B1
Killoch Dr. Glasg 95 D3
Killoch Pl. Irvine 219 F2
Killoch Rd. Pais 113 D3
Killoch Way. Irvine 219 F2
Kilmacolm Pl. Green 46 B1
Kilmacolm Rd. B of W 90 A2
Kilmacolm Rd. Green 46 A1
Kilmacolm Rd. Hous 91 D2
Kilmacolm Rd. Kil 69 D3
Kilmacolm Rd. P Glasg 69 D3
Kilmahew Ave. Card 26 A1
Kilmahew Ct. Card 26 A1
Kilmahew Dr. Card 26 A1
Kilmahew Gr. Card 26 A1
Kilmahew St. Ard 205 E1
Kilmailing Rd. Glasg 137 D3
Kilmair Pl. Glasg 96 B3
Kilmaluag Terr. Glasg 135 E2
Kilmannan Gdns. Miln 54 C2
Kilmany Ct. Salt 205 E1
Kilmany Dr. Glasg 118 C3
Kilmany Gdns. Glasg 118 C3
Kilmardinny Ave. Bear 75 F3
Kilmardinny Cres. Bear 76 A3
Kilmardinny Dr. Bear 75 F3
Kilmardinny Gate. Bear 75 F3
Kilmardinny Gr. Bear 75 F3
Kilmarnock Rd. Cross 222 A1
Kilmarnock Rd. Dund 225 F1
Kilmarnock Rd. Glasg 136 B4
Kilmarnock Rd. Kilm 222 B3
Kilmarnock Rd. Pres 233 F3
Kilmarnock Rd. Spring 221 D1
Kilmarnock Rd. Sym 231 E2
Kilmarnock Rd. Troon 229 F3
Kilmartin La. Car 187 F2
Kilmartin Pl. Glasg 135 F2
Kilmaurs Dr. Glasg 136 C2
Kilmaurs Rd. Cross 221 F1
Kilmaurs Rd. Fen 212 C1
Kilmaurs Rd. Kilmk 222 C2
Kilmaurs Rd. Stew 212 C1
Kilmaurs St. Glasg 115 F3
Kilmeny Cres. Wish 165 E3
Kilmeny Terr. Salt 205 E1
Kilmichael Ave. New 166 A3
Kilmorie Dr. Glasg 137 F4
Kilmory Ave. Tan 141 D4
Kilmory Ct. Falk 41 E2
Kilmory Dr. Newt M 156 C3
Kilmory Gdns. Car 188 A2
Kilmory Pl. Kilmk 222 C2
Kilmory Pl. Troon 229 F3
Kilmory Rd. Car 202 A4
Kilmory Rd. Salt 205 F1
Kilmory Wlk. Stew 195 E1
Kilmuir Cres. Glasg 135 E2
Kilmuir Dr. Glasg 135 F2
Kilmuir Rd. Glasg 135 F2
Kilmuir Rd. Tan 120 C1
Kilmun Rd. Green 46 A2
Kilmun St. Glasg 96 B4
Kiln Ct. Irvine 219 E1
Kilnbank Cres. Ayr 239 E4
Kilnburn Rd. Mother 163 E4
Kilncadzow Rd. Car 188 B1
Kilncadzow Rd. Kilnc 202 C4
Kilncraigs Ct. All 10 B3
Kilncraigs Rd. All 10 B3
Kilnford Cres. Dund 225 E1
Kilnford Dr. Dund 225 F1
Kilnknowie Cotts. How 131 D3
Kilns Pl. Falk 41 F3
Kilns Rd. Falk 42 A3
Kilnside Rd. Pais 114 A2
Kilnwell Quadrant. Mother 163 E4
Kiloran St. Glasg 135 F2
Kilpatrick Ave. Pais 113 D1
Kilpatrick Cres. Pais 133 E4
Kilpatrick Ct. Irvine 220 A2
Kilpatrick Ct. O Kill 73 D3
Kilpatrick Dr. Bear 75 E4
Kilpatrick Dr. Ren 114 A4
Kilpatrick Gdns. Newt M 157 E4
Kilpatrick Pl. Irvine 220 A1
Kilpatrick View. Dumb 50 A2
Kilpatrick Way. Tan 141 D4
Kilrig Ave. Kilw 207 F2
Kilruskin Dr. W Kil 190 B2
Kilsyth Cres. Irvine 220 A2
Kilsyth Rd. Bank 38 B2
Kilsyth Rd. Kils 59 F4
Kilsyth Rd. Kirk 58 C1
Kilsyth Wlk. Irvine 220 A2
Kiltarie Cres. Aird 123 F3
Kiltarie Cres. Chap 124 A3
Kiltearn Rd. Glasg 119 F4
Kiltongue Cotts. Aird 122 B4
Kilvaxter Dr. Glasg 135 F2
Kilwinning Cres. Ham 161 F1
Kilwinning Rd. Dalry 191 D4
Kilwinning Rd. Irvine 219 D3
Kilwinning Rd. Steven 206 C1
Kilwinning Rd. Stew 211 E4
Kilwynet Way. Pais 114 A4
Kimberley Gdns. E Kil 180 B4
Kimberley St. Clyde 73 F3
Kimberley St. Mother 164 B2
Kinalty Rd. Glasg 137 D3
Kinarvie Cres. Glasg 134 C4
Kinarvie Pl. Glasg 134 C4
Kinarvie Rd. Glasg 134 C4
Kinarvie Terr. Glasg 134 C4
Kinbuck St. Glasg 97 E2
Kincaid Dr. Lennox 33 E1
Kincaid Field. M of C 58 B3
Kincaid Gdns. Glasg 139 D3
Kincaid St. Green 45 D4
Kincaid Way. M of C 58 B3
Kincaidston Dr. Ayr 239 E2
Kincardine Dr. Bish 98 B4
Kincardine Pl. Bish 98 B4
Kincardine Pl. E Kil 160 B2
Kincardine Rd. Sten 24 B2
Kincardine Sq. Glasg 99 E1
Kincath Ave. Glasg 138 B2
Kinclaven Ave. Glasg 75 D2
Kincraig St. Glasg 115 E3
Kinellan Rd. Bear 75 F1
Kinellar Dr. Glasg 95 D3
Kinfauns Dr. Glasg 75 D2
Kinfauns Dr. Newt M 156 C3
King Edward La. Glasg 95 F3
King Edward Rd. Glasg 95 F3
King Edward St. Alex 27 F3
King O' Muirs Ave. Men 4 C2
King Pl. Coat 121 D3
King St. Alex 27 E1
King St. Ayr 236 A1
King St. Clyde 94 B4
King St. Coat 121 F3
King St E. Helen 16 C1
King St E. Helen 25 C4
King St. Falk 42 B3
King St. Fall 8 B2
King St. Glasg 117 E3
King St. Glasg 138 A4
King St. Gour 44 C4
King St. Green 45 F3
King St. Ham 162 A2
King St. Kilmk 227 F4
King St. Kils 60 B4
King St. Kilw 207 F2
King St. Lark 185 D2
King St. New 166 A3
King St. P Glasg 47 E1
King St. Pais 113 E3
King St. Shot 146 C2
King St. Sten 23 E1
King St. Sten 23 F2
King St. Stir 7 D4
King St. Stone 198 C1
King St. Wish 165 D1
King Street La. Glasg 138 A4
King Street La. Kils 60 B4
King's Cres. Car 188 A1
King's Cres. Glasg 139 D3
King's Cres. Helen 16 C1
King's Ct. Beith 150 A1
King's Dr. Cumb 61 F3
King's Dr. Glasg 117 F2
King's Dr. Newt M 157 D2
King's Gdns. Newt M 157 D2
King's Inch Rd. Ren 94 C2
King's Park Ave. Glasg 137 E3
King's Park Rd. Glasg 137 D4
King's Park Rd. Stir 7 D4
King's Pk Rd. Stir 6 C3
King's Pl. Glasg 97 D3
King's Rd. Beith 150 A1
King's Rd. John 112 A1
King's View. Cumb 61 F3
King's Way. Dumb 49 E3
Kingarth La. Glasg 117 D1
Kingarth St. Glasg 117 D1
Kingarth St. Ham 183 E4
Kingcase Ave. Pres 236 A3
Kinghorn Dr. Glasg 137 E4
Kinghorn La. Glasg 137 E4
Kinglas Rd. Bear 75 E1
Kings Cres. John 112 B2
Kings Ct. All 10 A4
Kings Ct. Ayr 236 A1
Kings Ct. Falk 42 A2
Kings Dr. Holy 142 C2
Kings Myre. Lan 215 E2
Kings Pk. Lennox 57 E1
Kingsacre Rd. Glasg 137 E4
Kingsbarns Dr. Glasg 137 D4
Kingsborough Gate. Glasg 96 A2
Kingsborough Gdns. Glasg 96 A2
Kingsborough La E. Glasg 96 A2
Kingsborough La. Glasg 96 A2
Kingsbrae Ave. Glasg 137 E4
Kingsbridge Cres. Glasg 137 E3
Kingsbridge Dr. Glasg 137 F3
Kingsburgh Dr. Pais 114 A3
Kingsburn Dr. Glasg 138 A3
Kingsburn Gr. Glasg 138 A3
Kingscliffe Ave. Glasg 137 E3
Kingscourt Ave. Glasg 137 E3
Kingscroft Rd. Pres 236 A4
Kingsdale Ave. Glasg 137 E4
Kingsdyke Ave. Glasg 137 E4
Kingseat Pl. Falk 41 F2
Kingsford Ave. Glasg 136 C2
Kingsford Ct. Newt M 156 B3
Kingsgate Ret Pk. E Kil 160 A3
Kingsheath Ave. Glasg 137 F3
Kingshill Ave. Cumb 60 C1
Kingshill Dr. Glasg 137 E3
Kingshill Rd. Alla 167 D4
Kingshill View. Law 187 D2
Kingshouse Ave. Glasg 137 E3
Kingshurst Ave. Glasg 137 E3
Kingsknowe Dr. Glasg 137 F3
Kingsland Cres. Glasg 115 D3
Kingsland Dr. Glasg 115 E3
Kingsland La. Glasg 115 E3
Kingslea Rd. Hous 91 D1
Kingsley Ave. Glasg 117 D1
Kingsley Ave. Sten 23 F2
Kingsley Ct. Tan 141 D4
Kingslynn Dr. Glasg 137 E3
Kingsmuir Dr. Glasg 137 F3
Kingstables La. Stir 7 D4
Kingston Ave. Aird 123 E4
Kingston Ave. Neil 154 B3
Kingston Ave. Tan 141 D4
Kingston Flats. Kils 36 B1
Kingston Gr. Bishop 72 A2
Kingston Pl. Clyde 73 E2
Kingston Rd. Bishop 72 A2
Kingston Rd. Bishop 72 B2
Kingston Rd. Kils 36 B1
Kingston Rd. Neil 154 B3
Kingston St. Glasg 117 D3
Kingsway Ct. Glasg 95 D3
Kingsway. Dalry 191 D4
Kingsway. E Kil 160 A2
Kingsway. Glasg 95 D3
Kingsway. Gour 44 B3
Kingsway. Kils 36 B1
Kingsway. Kirk 59 D1
Kingswell Ave. Kilmk 223 D3
Kingswell Pk. All 10 B4
Kingswood Dr. Glasg 137 E4
Kingswood Rd. Bishop 71 F2
Kingussie Ave. Stew 195 E1
Kingussie Dr. Glasg 137 E3
Kiniver Dr. Glasg 75 D1
Kinkell Gdns. Kirk 59 D1
Kinloch Ave. Glasg 139 D2
Kinloch Ave. Lin 112 A3
Kinloch Ave. Stew 195 E1
Kinloch Dr. Mother 142 B1

Kinloch La. Gour

Kinloch La. Gour 44 C2
Kinloch Rd. Kilmk 228 A3
Kinloch Rd. Newt M 156 B3
Kinloch Pl. Ren 94 A1
Kinloch St. Glasg 118 B2
Kinloch Terr. Gour 44 C2
Kinloss Pl. E Kil 159 F1
Kinmount Ave. Glasg 137 D4
Kinnaird Ave. Newt M 157 D3
Kinnaird Ave. Sten 24 A2
Kinnaird Cres. Bear 76 A2
Kinnaird Dr. Lin 112 A3
Kinnaird Dr. Sten 23 F2
Kinnaird Pl. Bish 98 A4
Kinnaird Rd. Glasg 118 A2
Kinnell Pl. Ham 161 F1
Kinnell Ave. Glasg 115 E2
Kinnell Cres. Glasg 115 E2
Kinnell Pl. Glasg 115 E2
Kinnell Rd. Salt 217 D4
Kinnin Brae. W Kil 190 B2
Kinning St. Glasg 117 D3
Kinnis Vennel. Kilw 207 E2
Kinnoul Gdns. Bear 75 E4
Kinnoull Pl. Udd 161 E4
Kinnoull Rd. Kilmk 228 A2
Kinpurnie Rd. Pais 114 B3
Kinross Ave. Glasg 115 D2
Kinross Ave. P Glasg 47 E1
Kinross Pk. E Kil 160 B2
Kinsail Dr. Glasg 114 C3
Kinstone Ave. Glasg 95 D3
Kintail Gdns. Kirk 59 D1
Kintessack Pl. Bish 78 B1
Kintillo Dr. Glasg 95 D3
Kintore Pk. Ham 183 D4
Kintore Rd. Glasg 136 C3
Kintore Tower. Glasg 138 C2
Kintra St. Glasg 116 A4
Kintyre Ave. Lin 112 A2
Kintyre Cres. Newt M 156 B3
Kintyre Cres. Plains 104 B2
Kintyre Gdns. Kirk 59 D1
Kintyre Pl. Falk 41 E2
Kintyre Rd. Udd 161 E4
Kintyre St. Glasg 98 A1
Kintyre Terr. Gour 44 A2
Kintyre Wynd. Car 187 F2
Kippen Dr. Thorn 158 A3
Kippen St. Aird 122 C4
Kippen St. Glasg 97 E3
Kipperoch Rd. Bear 49 D4
Kipperoch Rd. Card 49 D4
Kipperoch Rd. Dumb 49 D4
Kippford St. Glasg 119 E2
Kipps Ave. Aird 122 C4
Kirk Ave. Sten 23 F1
Kirk Cres. Kil 73 D4
Kirk Glebe. Neil 154 C4
Kirk Glebe. Stew 211 E4
Kirk La. Bear 75 F3
Kirk La. Glasg 136 B4
Kirk Path. Alla 167 D4
Kirk Pl. Bear 75 F3
Kirk Pl. Cumb 82 A4
Kirk Pl. Udd 140 C3
Kirk Port. Ayr 238 C4
Kirk Rd. Ash 186 A1
Kirk Rd. Bear 75 F3
Kirk Rd. Beith 171 D4
Kirk Rd. Car 187 F1
Kirk Rd. E Kil 158 B4
Kirk Rd. Holy 143 E4
Kirk Rd. Hous 91 E1
Kirk Rd. Shot 146 C2
Kirk Rd. Wish 165 E2
Kirk St. Car 187 F1
Kirk St. Coat 121 F3
Kirk St. Miln 54 C1
Kirk St. Mother 163 F4
Kirk St. Pres 233 E1
Kirk St. Stone 198 C1
Kirk Vennel. Irvine 219 E1
Kirk Wynd. Falk 42 A2
Kirk Wynd. Stir 7 D2
Kirkaig Ave. Ren 94 C1
Kirkbean Ave. Glasg 138 A2
Kirkbrae. Clack 10 C2
Kirkbride Terr. Plea 12 B2
Kirkbriggs Gdns. Glasg 138 A3
Kirkbriggs Way. Glasg 138 A3
Kirkburn Ave. Glasg 139 D2
Kirkburn Dr. Strath 31 E2
Kirkburn Rd. Strath 31 E2
Kirkburn. Slam 68 A4
Kirkcaldy Rd. Glasg 116 B1
Kirkconnel Ave. Cumb 60 C1
Kirkconnel Ave. Glasg 94 C1
Kirkconnel Dr. Glasg 137 F3
Kirkcudbright Pl. E Kil 160 B2
Kirkdale Dr. Glasg 115 F3
Kirkdene Ave. Newt M 157 D3
Kirkdene Bank. Newt M 157 D3
Kirkdene Cres. Newt M 157 D3
Kirkdene Gr. Newt M 157 D2
Kirkdene Pl. Newt M 157 D3
Kirkfield Bank Way. Ham 162 A2
Kirkfield Rd. Lan 214 B2

Kirkfield Rd. Udd 141 D2
Kirkfield Terr. Wish 165 E2
Kirkfieldbank Brae. Lan 214 C2
Kirkford Rd. Muir 80 C1
Kirkford. Stew 211 F4
Kirkgate. All 10 A3
Kirkgate. Irvine 219 E1
Kirkgate. Salt 216 C4
Kirkhall Gdns. Ard 205 E1
Kirkhall Pl. Den 21 F1
Kirkhall Rd. Holy 143 E2
Kirkhill Ave. Glasg 139 D2
Kirkhill Cres. Neil 154 C4
Kirkhill Cres. Pres 236 A3
Kirkhill Dr. Glasg 96 B3
Kirkhill Gate. Newt M 157 D2
Kirkhill Gdns. Glasg 139 D2
Kirkhill Gr. Glasg 139 D2
Kirkhill. Kilw 207 E1
Kirkhill Pl. Glasg 96 B3
Kirkhill Pl. Wish 164 B1
Kirkhill Rd. Muir 100 C3
Kirkhill Rd. Newt M 157 D3
Kirkhill Rd. Tan 140 C4
Kirkhill Rd. Wish 164 B1
Kirkhill St. Wish 164 B1
Kirkhill Terr. Glasg 139 D2
Kirkholm Ave. Ayr 236 A2
Kirkhope Dr. Glasg 75 D1
Kirkhouse Ave. Strath 31 E2
Kirkhouse Cres. Strath 31 E2
Kirkhouse Rd. Strath 31 E2
Kirkinner Rd. Glasg 119 E2
Kirkintilloch Rd. Bish 78 B3
Kirkintilloch Rd. Bish 78 B3
Kirkintilloch Rd. Kirk 80 B4
Kirkintilloch Rd. Lennox 58 A1
Kirkland Ave. Kilmk 222 C2
Kirkland Ave. Strath 31 E2
Kirkland Cres. Dalry 191 D4
Kirkland Dr. Dunk 21 D1
Kirkland Gdns. Kilm 222 B3
Kirkland Gr. John 111 F2
Kirkland La. Bonh 27 F2
Kirkland Rd. Dunlop 195 D4
Kirkland Rd. Kilb 170 A4
Kirkland St. Glasg 96 C2
Kirkland St. Mother 163 E3
Kirkland Terr. Spring 220 C1
Kirklandholm. Pres 236 B3
Kirklandneuk Rd. Ren 94 A2
Kirklands Ave. Kils 60 B4
Kirklands Cres. Udd 141 D2
Kirklands Rd. Lan 215 D2
Kirkle Dr. Newt M 157 D3
Kirklea Ave. Pais 113 D3
Kirklee Cir. Glasg 96 B2
Kirklee Gardens La. Glasg 96 B2
Kirklee Pl. Glasg 96 B2
Kirklee Quadrant. Glasg 96 B2
Kirklee Quadrant La. Glasg 96 B2
Kirklee Rd. Glasg 96 B2
Kirklee Rd. Holy 142 C2
Kirklee Terr. Glasg 96 B2
Kirklee Terrace La. Glasg 96 B2
Kirklee Terrace Rd. Glasg 96 B2
Kirkliston St. Glasg 118 C3
Kirkmichael Ave. Glasg 96 A2
Kirkmichael Gdns. Glasg 96 A2
Kirkmichael Rd. Helen 16 C1
Kirkmuir Dr. Glasg 138 A1
Kirkmuir Dr. Stew 195 E1
Kirkness St. Aird 123 D4
Kirknethan. Wish 164 B1
Kirknewton St. Glasg 119 D3
Kirkoswald Dr. Clyde 74 B2
Kirkoswald. E Kil 160 B2
Kirkoswald Rd. Glasg 136 B3
Kirkoswald Rd. Holy 143 E3
Kirkpatrick Cres. Alex 27 E4
Kirkpatrick St. Glasg 118 A3
Kirkriggs Ave. Glasg 138 A3
Kirkshaws Ave. Coat 121 F2
Kirkshaws Pl. Coat 121 F2
Kirkshaws Rd. Coat 121 F2
Kirkslap. Den 21 F1
Kirkstall Gdns. Bish 78 A2
Kirkstone Cl. E Kil 179 F3
Kirkstone. Newt M 157 D3
Kirkstyle Ave. Car 187 F1
Kirkstyle Cres. Aird 102 C1
Kirkstyle Cres. Neil 154 B4
Kirkstyle. Irvine 220 A3
Kirkstyle La. Neil 154 C4
Kirkstyle Pl. Glenm 102 B2
Kirksyde Ave. Kirk 79 F4
Kirkton Ave. Barr 134 A1
Kirkton Ave. Car 187 F1
Kirkton Ave. Glasg 95 D3
Kirkton Ave. Udd 161 E3
Kirkton Ave. W Kil 190 B2
Kirkton Cres. Card 26 A1
Kirkton Cres. Coat 122 B2
Kirkton Cres. Glasg 95 D3
Kirkton Cres. M of C 58 B3
Kirkton Ct. Car 187 F1
Kirkton Ct. Eagle 178 C2

Kirkton Dr. Eagle 178 C3
Kirkton. Ersk 73 D2
Kirkton Gate. E Kil 159 F1
Kirkton Moor Rd. Eagle 178 A2
Kirkton. O Kil 73 D4
Kirkton Pk. E Kil 159 F1
Kirkton Pl. Coat 122 B2
Kirkton Pl. E Kil 159 F1
Kirkton Pl. Fen 213 D2
Kirkton Pl. Sten 24 B2
Kirkton Pl. Udd 161 E3
Kirkton Rd. Card 26 A1
Kirkton Rd. Dumb 49 E2
Kirkton Rd. Fen 213 D2
Kirkton Rd. Glasg 139 D3
Kirkton Rd. Kilm 222 B3
Kirkton Rd. Kilm 222 C3
Kirkton Rd. Neil 154 C3
Kirkton St. Car 187 F1
Kirkton Terr. Lennox 32 C2
Kirktonfield Rd. Neil 154 C4
Kirktonholm Pl. Kilmk 227 F4
Kirktonholm St. Kilmk 227 F4
Kirktonholme Cres. E Kil 159 E1
Kirktonholme Rd. E Kil 159 E1
Kirktonside. Barr 134 A1
Kirkvale Cres. Newt M 157 D3
Kirkvale Ct. Newt M 157 D3
Kirkvale Dr. Newt M 157 D3
Kirkview Ave. Sals 125 F1
Kirkview Cres. Newt M 156 C2
Kirkview Ct. Cumb 82 A3
Kirkview. Cumb 82 A3
Kirkview Gdns. Tan 140 C4
Kirkville Pl. Glasg 75 D1
Kirkwall Ave. Blan 140 B3
Kirkwall. Cumb 62 A3
Kirkwall Rd. Gour 44 C2
Kirkway. Air 14 B2
Kirkwood Ave. Glasg 137 D3
Kirkwood Ave. Clyde 74 C1
Kirkwood Quadrant. Clyde 74 B1
Kirkwood Rd. Tan 140 C4
Kirkwood St. Coat 121 F3
Kirkwood St. Glasg 116 C3
Kirkwood St. Glasg 138 A4
Kirn Dr. Gour 44 B3
Kirn Rd. Kilmk 222 C1
Kirriemuir Ave. Glasg 115 E2
Kirriemuir. E Kil 160 B3
Kirriemuir Gdns. Bish 78 B1
Kirriemuir Pl. Glasg 115 E2
Kirriemuir Rd. Bish 78 B1
Kirstie Pl. Bonh 27 F1
Kirtle Dr. Ren 94 C1
Kirtle Pl. E Kil 179 F4
Kishorn Pl. Glasg 99 E1
Kitchener St. Wish 165 D2
Kitoch Pl. E Kil 159 F1
Kittoch St. E Kil 159 F1
Kittochside Rd. E Kil 158 C3
Kittyshaw Rd. Dalry 191 D4
Knapdale St. Glasg 97 D4
Knights Way. Den 21 E1
Knightsbridge St. Glasg 95 E4
Knightscliffe Ave. Glasg 95 E4
Knightswood Rd. Glasg 95 E4
Knightswood Terr. Udd 140 C1
Knivysbridge Pl. Hat 141 F2
Knock Way. Pais 114 A4
Knockbuckle Ave. Kil 69 D1
Knockbuckle Rd. Kil 69 D1
Knockburnie Rd. Udd 141 D2
Knockentiber Rd. Spring 221 D1
Knockhall St. Glasg 99 E1
Knockhill Dr. Glasg 137 D4
Knockhill Rd. Ren 94 C1
Knockinlaw Mount. Kilmk 222 C2
Knockinlaw Rd. Kilmk 222 C2
Knockmarloch Dr. Kilmk 227 F2
Knocknair St. P Glasg 68 C4
Knockriovch Pl. Ard 205 F2
Knockriovch Wynt. Ard 205 F2
Knockside Ave. Pais 133 E4
Knoll Croft Rd. Shot 147 D2
Knoll Pk. Ayr 238 C2
Knollpark Dr. Newt M 157 E3
Knowe Cres. Holy 143 E2
Knowe Rd. Green 46 A2
Knowe Rd. Muir 100 B4
Knowe Rd. Pais 114 A4
Knowe St. Miln 54 C1
Knowe The. N Sau 5 E2
Knowe The. Troon 229 F4
Knowefaulds Rd. Tull 4 A2
Knowehead Dr. Udd 140 C3
Knowehead Gdns. Udd 140 C3
Knowehead Rd. Hurl 228 C3
Knowehead Rd. Kilmk 227 F2
Knowehead Rd. Lennox 32 C2
Knowehead Rd. Wish 165 E1
Knowehill Pl. Ayr 238 B1
Knoweholm. Ayr 238 B1
Knownoble St. Cle 144 A1
Knowes Ave. Newt M 156 C3
Knowes Rd. Newt M 156 C3
Knowetap St. Glasg 96 C4
Knowetop Ave. Mother 163 F2

Knowetop Cres. Dumb 49 E3
Knowhead Gdns. Glasg 116 C2
Knowhead Terr. Glasg 116 C2
Knox Ave. B of W 110 B4
Knox Pl. Newt M 156 A2
Knox Pl. Salt 206 A1
Knox St. Aird 123 D4
Knox St. Pais 113 E2
Knoxland Sq. Dumb 50 A1
Knoxland St. Dumb 50 A1
Knoxville Rd. Kilb 149 D1
Kronborg Way. E Kil 180 C3
Kyle Ave. Cowie 12 C4
Kyle Ave. Spring 220 C1
Kyle Cres. Troon 220 A2
Kyle Ct. Glasg 139 D3
Kyle Dr. Troon 229 E3
Kyle Gr. Holy 143 D2
Kyleakin Dr. Udd 140 A1
Kyleakin Rd. Glasg 135 E2
Kyleakin Terr. Glasg 135 E2
Kyle Quadrant. Holy 143 E2
Kyle Quadrant. Wish 164 C1
Kyle Rd. Cumb 62 A2
Kyle Rd. Irvine 224 A4
Kyle Sq. Glasg 137 F3
Kyle St. Ayr 238 C4
Kyle St. Glasg 97 E1
Kyle St. Mother 163 D4
Kyle St. Pres 236 B4
Kyle Terr. Dumb 49 D3
Kylemore Cres. Mother 142 B1
Kylemore La. Gour 44 C2
Kylemore Terr. Gour 44 C2
Kylepark Ave. Udd 140 B3
Kylepark Cres. Udd 140 B3
Kylepark Dr. Udd 140 B4
Kylerhea Rd. Glasg 135 E2
Kyleshill. Salt 216 C4
Kyleswell St. Kilw 207 F2

La Belle Allee. Glasg 96 C1
La Belle Pl. Glasg 96 C1
Laburnum Ave. Beith 171 D4
Laburnum Ave. E Kil 180 B3
Laburnum Cres. Wish 165 D3
Laburnum Ct. E Kil 180 B3
Laburnum Dr. M of C 58 A3
Laburnum Gdns. Kirk 79 D3
Laburnum Gr. Coat 122 B3
Laburnum Gr. Stir 6 C3
Laburnum Lea. Ham 162 C1
Laburnum Pl. John 132 A4
Laburnum Rd. Ayr 239 E3
Laburnum Rd. Bank 39 D3
Laburnum Rd. Cumb 62 B1
Laburnum Rd. Glasg 116 B2
Laburnum Rd. Kilmk 227 E4
Laburnum Rd. Tan 141 E4
Laburnum St. Green 45 F3
Lachlan Cres. Ersk 72 C1
Lacy St. Pais 114 A2
Lade Dr. Lar 41 E4
Lade Rd. Bon 40 A3
Lade Terr. Glasg 115 D2
Lade The. Bonh 27 F3
Ladeside Cl. Newt M 156 B3
Ladeside Cres. Lar 23 F1
Ladeside Ct. Kilb 170 A4
Ladeside Dr. John 111 E1
Ladeside Dr. Kils 36 C1
Ladeside. Kilm 222 B4
Ladeside Rd. Kilm 222 B4
Ladhope Pl. Clyde 94 C4
Lady Ann Cres. Aird 123 E3
Lady Anne St. Glasg 94 C3
Lady Isle Cres. Udd 140 C3
Lady Jane Gate. Udd 140 C2
Lady La. Pais 113 E2
Lady Margaret Dr. Troon 230 A1
Lady Mary Wlk. Ham 162 C2
Lady Watson Gdns. Ham 162 A1
Lady Wilson St. Aird 123 D4
Lady's Gate. Bonh 27 F1
Ladyacre. Kilw 207 F2
Ladyacre Rd. Lan 215 D2
Ladyacres. Inch 93 E3
Ladybank Ct. E Kil 159 F1
Ladybank. Cumb 61 F3
Ladybank Dr. Glasg 115 F2
Ladybank Gdns. E Kil 159 F1
Ladybank Pl. E Kil 159 F1
Ladyburn Ct. Irvine 219 F3
Ladyburn St. Green 46 B2
Ladyburn St. Pais 114 A2
Ladyford Ave. Kilw 207 D2
Ladyha Ct. Irvine 220 A2
Ladyhill Dr. Glasg 120 A2
Ladykirk Cres. Glasg 115 D3
Ladykirk Cres. Pais 113 F2
Ladykirk Dr. Glasg 115 D3
Ladykirk Rd. Pres 236 B3
Ladyland Dr. Kilb 149 D2
Ladyloan Ave. Glasg 74 C2

Ladymuir Circ. Ersk 72
Ladymuir Cres. Glasg 115
Ladysgate Ct. Sten 24
Ladysmill. Falk 42
Ladysmith Ave. Kilbar 111
Ladysmith Rd. Kilb 149
Ladysmith. Mother 164
Ladysneuk Rd. Stir 2
Ladyton. Bonh 27
Ladywell Ct. Lar 23
Ladywell Dr. Tull 4
Ladywell Rd. Mother 163
Ladywell St. Glasg 117
Ladywood. Miln 55
Lagan Rd. Car 188
Laggan Ave. Shot 147
Laggan House. Pres 236
Laggan Quadrant. Aird 102
Laggan Rd. Aird 123
Laggan Rd. Bish 78
Laggan Rd. Glasg 136
Laggan Rd. Newt M 156
Laggan Terr. Ren 94
Laggan Way. New 165
Laggary Pk. Rhu 15
Laggary Rd. Rhu 15
Laidlaw Ave. Holy 142
Laidlaw Gdns. Tan 120
Laidlaw St. Glasg 117
Laidon Rd. Aird 123
Laidon Rd. Aird 102
Laidon Wlk. New 165
Laigh Ct. Beith 150
Laigh Mount. Ayr 238
Laigh Rd. Newt M 157
Laighcartside St. John 112
Laighdykes Rd. Salt 205
Laighland. Pres 236
Laighmuir St. Udd 141
Laighpark Ave. Bishop 72
Laighstonehall Rd. Ham 162
Laightoun Ct. Cumb 82
Laightoun Dr. Cumb 82
Laightoun Gdns. Cumb 82
Lainshaw Ave. Kilmk 227
Lainshaw Dr. Glasg 137
Lainshaw St. Stew 211
Laird La. Glasg 122
Laird St. Coat 122
Laird St. Green 45
Laird Weir. Ard 205
Laird's Hill Ct. Kils 60
Laird's Hill Pl. Kils 60
Lairds Gate. Udd 140
Lairds Hill. Cumb 61
Lairg Dr. Udd 54
Lairhills Rd. E Kil 180
Lake Ave. Lan 215
Lakefield Ct. Udd 161
Lamb St. Glasg 97
Lamb St. Ham 162
Lambert Terr. All 10
Lamberton Ave. Stir 7
Lamberton Dr. Glasg 115
Lamberton Gdns. Irvine 220
Lamberton Rd. Stew 195
Lambhill Quadrant. Glasg 116
Lambhill St. Glasg 116
Lamble Cres. Newt M 156
Lamerton Rd. Cumb 62
Lamford Dr. Ayr 238
Lamington Rd. Glasg 115
Lamlash Cres. Glasg 119
Lamlash Pl. Glasg 119
Lamlash Pl. Helen 16
Lamlash Pl. Mother 163
Lamlash Sq. Glasg 119
Lammer Wynd. Lark 185
Lammerknowes Rd. Kils 37
Lammermoor Ave. Glasg 115
Lammermoor Cres. Kirk 79
Lammermoor Dr. Cumb 82
Lammermoor Rd. Kirk 79
Lammermoor Terr. Wish 165
Lammermuir Ct. Irvine 220
Lammermuir Ct. Pais 133
Lammermuir Dr. Pais 133
Lammermuir Gdns. Bear 75
Lammermuir Pl. Holy 143
Lammermuir Rd. Kilmk 222
Lamond View. Lar 23
Lamont Ave. Bish 78
Lamont Cres. Alex 27
Lamont Cres. Fall 8
Lamont Dr. Irvine 224
Lamont Pl. Irvine 224
Lamont Rd. Glasg 98
Lanark Ave. Aird 123
Lanark Rd. Ash 200
Lanark Rd. Car 187
Lanark Rd. Kilnc 207
Lanark Rd. Lark 185

269

anark St. Glasg Lexwell Ave. John

nark St. Glasg 117 E3
ncaster Ave. Beith 171 D4
ncaster Ave. Calder 123 E1
ncaster Cres. Glasg 96 B2
ncaster
Crescent La. Glasg 96 B2
ncaster Rd. Bish 78 A2
ncaster Terr. Glasg 96 B2
ncaster
Terrace La. Glasg 96 B2
ncaster Way. Ren 94 B1
ncefield Quay. Glasg 116 C4
ncefield St. Glasg 116 C4
ndemer Dr. Glasg 138 A3
ndressy Pl. Glasg 117 F2
ndressy St. Glasg 117 F2
ndsborough Dr. Kilmk 223 D2
ndsborough Pl. Steven 206 C1
ndsdowne Gdns. Ham 162 C2
ndsdowne Rd. Lark 185 E1
ne Gdns. Glasg 96 A2
ne The. Cumb 61 E3
nfine Rd. Pais 114 B2
nfine Terr. Irvine 219 F3
nfine Way. Irvine 220 A3
ng Ave. Bishop 72 B2
ng Ave. Ren 94 B1
ng Rd. Troon 229 F4
ng St. Pais 114 A2
nga St. Glasg 96 C4
ngbank Dr. Kil 69 F1
ngbank Rise. Kil 69 F1
ngbank St. Glasg 117 D3
ngbar Cres. Glasg 119 F4
ngbyres Rd. Cle 144 B1
ngcraig Rd. Kilmk 227 F1
ngcraigs Ct. Pais 133 E4
ngcraigs Dr. Pais 133 E3
ngcraigs Terr. Pais 133 E3
ngcroft Ave. Pres 233 F1
ngcroft Dr. Glasg 139 E2
ngcroft Pl. Glasg 115 E4
ngcroft Rd. Glasg 115 E4
ngcroft Terr. Glasg 115 E4
ngdale Ave. Glasg 98 C2
ngdale. E Kil 159 E2
ngdale. Newt M 157 D3
ngdale Rd. Muir 80 C1
ngdale St. Glasg 98 C2
ngdales Ave. Cumb 61 E1
ngfaulds Cres. Dunt 74 B3
ngford Dr. Glasg 135 D2
ngford Pl. Glasg 135 D2
nghill Dr. Cumb 61 E2
nghill Pl. Den 21 E1
ngholm Cres. Wish 165 D3
ngholm Ct. Muir 81 D1
ngholm Dr. Lin 112 B3
ngholm. E Kil 179 F3
nglands Ave. E Kil 180 C2
nglands Ave. Glasg 115 E4
nglands Brae. Kilmk 222 C1
nglands Ct. E Kil 180 C2
nglands Dr. E Kil 180 C2
nglands Dr. Glasg 115 E4
nglands Pl. E Kil 180 C2
nglands Rd. Auld 180 C2
nglands Rd. Glasg 115 F4
nglands St. Kilmk 222 C1
nglands Terr. Dumb 50 A3
nglands-seafar
Interchange. Cumb 82 C4
nglea Ave. Glasg 138 B2
nglea Gr. Glasg 138 C2
nglea Rd. Glasg 138 C2
nglees Ave. Newt M 157 D3
nglees St. Falk 24 B1
ngley Ave. Glasg 95 D4
ngloan Cres. Coat 121 F3
ngloan Pl. Coat 121 F3
ngloan St. Coat 121 F3
ngmuir Ave. Irvine 220 B3
ngmuir Ave. Kirk 58 C1
ngmuir Ct. Irvine 220 B3
ngmuir Rd. Coat 121 D3
ngmuir Rd. Kirk 59 D1
ngmuir Way. Coat 121 D3
ngmuirhead Rd. Stepps 79 E1
ngness Rd. Glasg 119 D4
ngoreth Ave. Ham 161 F1
ngrig Rd. Glasg 98 A2
ngrig Rd. Newt M 156 B2
ngshaw Cres. Car 187 F1
ngshot St. Glasg 116 B3
ngside Ave. Glasg 136 C4
ngside Ave. Kilmk 227 F2
ngside Ave. Tan 141 E3
ngside Ct. Udd 141 D1
ngside Dr. Blac 107 D2
ngside Dr. Glasg 136 C3
ngside Dr. Kilbar 111 D1
ngside Gdns. Glasg 137 D4
ngside La. Glasg 117 D1
ngside Pk. Kilbar 111 D1
ngside Pl. Glasg 136 C4
ngside Pl. Kilb 149 D1
ngside Rd. Glasg 137 D4
ngside Rd. Udd 141 D1
Langside St. Dunt 74 C3
Langside Terr. P Glasg 68 B4
Langstile Pl. Glasg 114 C3
Langstile Rd. Glasg 114 C3
Langton Cres. Barr 134 B1
Langton Cres. Glasg 115 E1
Langton Gate. Newt M 156 B3
Langton Gdns. Glasg 119 F2
Langton Pl. Newt M 156 B3
Langton Rd. Glasg 115 E1
Langtree Ave. Glasg 136 A1
Lanrig Pl. Muir 100 B4
Lanrig Rd. Muir 100 B4
Lansbury Gdns. Pais 113 E4
Lansbury St. Alex 27 F4
Lansbury Terr. Lark 185 E1
Lansdowne Cres. Glasg 96 C1
Lansdowne Cres. Shot 147 D2
Lansdowne
Crescent La. Glasg 96 C1
Lansdowne Dr. Cumb 61 F2
Lansdowne Dr. Cumb 61 F3
Lansdowne Rd. Ayr 236 A2
Lanton Dr. Glasg 115 D3
Lanton Rd. Glasg 136 C3
Lappin St. Clyde 94 B4
Laputa Pl. Kilmk 227 F2
Larbert Rd. Bon 40 A3
Larbert St. Glasg 97 D1
Larch Ave. Bish 98 A4
Larch Ave. Klrk 79 E3
Larch Cres. Klrk 79 E3
Larch Ct. Cumb 62 C2
Larch Ct. E Kil 180 A3
Larch Ct. Udd 161 E4
Larch Dr. Bank 38 C1
Larch Dr. E Kil 180 A3
Larch Gr. Cumb 62 C2
Larch Gr. Ham 162 C1
Larch Gr. Holy 143 D3
Larch Gr. M of C 58 A3
Larch Gr. Sten 23 F2
Larch House. Pres 236 A3
Larch Pl. E Kil 180 A3
Larch Pl. John 132 A4
Larch Pl. Kilmk 227 E4
Larch Pl. Tan 141 E4
Larch Rd. Cumb 62 C2
Larch Rd. Glasg 116 A2
Larch Terr. Beith 171 E4
Larches The. All 10 A4
Larches The. Muir 81 D2
Larchfield Ave. Glasg 95 D2
Larchfield Ave. Newt M 156 C3
Larchfield Cres. Wish 165 E3
Larchfield Ct. Newt M 156 B2
Larchfield Dr. Glasg 138 B2
Larchfield Gdns. Wish 165 E3
Larchfield Gr. Wish 165 E4
Larchfield La. Shot 147 D1
Larchfield Pl. Glasg 95 D2
Larchfield Pl. Wish 165 E3
Larchfield Rd. Bear 75 F1
Larchgrove Ave. Glasg 119 E3
Larchgrove Pl. Glasg 119 E4
Larchgrove Rd. Glasg 119 E4
Larchwood Rd. Ayr 239 E2
Larchwood Terr. Barr 155 E4
Larghill La. Ayr 239 D3
Largie Rd. Glasg 136 C3
Largo Pl. Glasg 115 F4
Largs Ave. Kilmk 223 D2
Largs Rd. Kilb 148 B1
Larkfield Dr. Udd 161 E3
Larkfield Gr. Gour 44 C2
Larkfield Ind Est. Gour 44 B3
Larkfield Rd. Gour 44 C2
Larkfield Rd. Gour 44 C3
Larkfield Rd. Klrk 79 F3
Larkfield St. Glasg 117 D2
Larkhill Ind Est. Lark 199 D4
Larkin Gdns. Pais 113 E4
Larkin Way. Hat 141 F4
Larksfield Dr. Car 202 A4
Larkspur Dr. E Kil 159 E2
Larkspur Way. Car 201 F4
Lashley Gr. Wish 186 B4
Lasswade St. Clyde 94 C3
Latherton Dr. Glasg 96 B3
Latimer Gdns. Glasg 115 D2
Latta Ct. Pres 236 B3
Latta St. Dumb 50 A2
Lauchlin Pl. Kirk 80 A4
Lauchope Rd. Holy 143 E4
Lauchope St. Chap 123 F1
Laudedale La. Glasg 96 A2
Lauder Cres. Wish 165 D3
Lauder Ct. Kilmk 223 E2
Lauder Dr. Glasg 138 B3
Lauder Dr. Lin 112 A3
Lauder Gdns. Coat 122 B2
Lauder Gdns. Udd 140 B1
Lauder Gn. E Kil 160 A2
Lauder La. Ham 161 F2
Lauder St. Glasg 117 D2
Lauderdale Dr. Newt M 156 B2
Lauderdale Gdns. Glasg 96 A2
Laudervale Gdns. Alex 27 E4
Laughland Dr. Holy 143 E2
Laughlanglen Rd. Ayr 239 D2
Laundry La. Stepps 99 E3
Lauranne Pl. Hat 141 F3
Laurel Ave. Clyde 73 E2
Laurel Ave. Klrk 79 E3
Laurel Bank. Ayr 239 E2
Laurel Bank. Ham 183 E4
Laurel Ct. E Kil 180 B3
Laurel Ct. Falk 41 E3
Laurel Dr. E Kil 180 B3
Laurel Dr. Lark 185 E1
Laurel Dr. Mother 164 C2
Laurel Gdns. Chap 123 F1
Laurel Gdns. Tan 140 C4
Laurel Gr. Bon 39 F2
Laurel Gr. Gree 83 F1
Laurel La. Lark 185 E1
Laurel Pl. Bon 39 F2
Laurel Pl. E Kil 180 B3
Laurel Pl. Glasg 96 A1
Laurel Pl. Kilmk 227 E4
Laurel Sq. Bank 38 C1
Laurel St. Glasg 96 A1
Laurel Way. Barr 134 A2
Laurel Wlk. Glasg 138 B2
Laurelbank Ave. Bon 40 A2
Laurelbank. Coat 122 A4
Laurelbank Rd. Glasg 139 E4
Laurelbank Rd. Muir 100 A4
Laurelhill Gdns. Stir 6 C3
Laurelhill Pl. Stir 7 D3
Laurels The. Newt M 156 B3
Laurels The. Tull 4 A1
Lauren View. Aird 122 C4
Laurence Dr. Bear 75 E3
Laurencecroft Rd. Stir 2 A1
Laurenstone Terr. E Kil 160 A2
Laurie Ct. Tan 141 D4
Laurieland Ave. Cross 221 F1
Laurieston Ct. Dund 225 F1
Laurieston Way. Glasg 138 A2
Lauriston Ct. Salt 205 E1
Lavelle Dr. Coat 122 B4
Lavender Dr. E Kil 180 B3
Lavender La. Car 201 F4
Laverock Ave. Green 45 E2
Laverock Ave. Ham 163 D1
Laverock Rd. Aird 103 D2
Laverock Terr. Muir 80 C1
Laverockhall. Lan 215 D3
Laverockhall St. Glasg 97 F2
Law Brae. W Kil 190 B3
Law Dr. Holy 143 E2
Law Pl. E Kil 159 F3
Law Roundabout. E Kil 159 F2
Law St. Glasg 118 A3
Law View. Wish 186 B3
Lawer Pl. Irvine 220 A2
Lawers Cres. Kilmk 228 A2
Lawers Dr. Bear 75 E4
Lawers La. Holy 143 E2
Lawers Rd. Glasg 136 A3
Lawers Rd. Kilmk 228 A2
Lawers Rd. Ren 94 B1
Lawfield Ave. Newt M 157 D3
Lawfield Ave. W Kil 190 C2
Lawhill Ave. Glasg 137 E2
Lawhill Rd. Law 187 D2
Lawhill Rd. Sym 231 E2
Lawhope Mill Rd. Chap 123 F2
Lawmarnock Cres. B of W 110 B4
Lawmarnock Rd. B of W 110 B4
Lawmoor Ave. Glasg 117 E2
Lawmoor Pl. Glasg 117 E1
Lawmoor Rd. Glasg 117 E2
Lawmoor St. Glasg 117 E2
Lawmuir Cres. Dunt 74 C4
Lawmuir Pl. Hat 142 A1
Lawmuir Rd. Hat 142 A2
Lawmuir Rd. Law 186 C3
Lawn Pk. Miln 55 E1
Lawn St. Pais 113 F3
Lawrence Ave. Glasg 136 B1
Lawrence Ave. Helen 25 D4
Lawrence Dr. Bonh 19 F1
Lawrence St. Glasg 96 B1
Lawrie St. Glasg 96 A1
Lawrie St. New 165 F3
Lawrie St. Stone 198 C1
Lawrie Way. Lark 185 E1
Lawson Ave. Mother 163 F2
Lawson Dr. Ard 205 E2
Lawson St. Ayr 236 A1
Lawson St. Kilmk 228 A4
Lawswell. Fish 5 F2
Lawthorn
Roundabout. Irvine 220 A3
Laxdale Dr. Bank 39 E4
Laxford Ave. Glasg 137 D2
Laxford Pl. Coat 122 B2
Laxford Rd. Ersk 72 C1
Laxford Way. Holy 143 E2
Laxton Dr. Klrk 79 F2
Le Froy Gdns. E Kil 180 B4
Le Froy La. E Kil 180 B4
Lea Ave. Neil 154 B4
Leabank Ave. Pais 133 F4
Leadburn Rd. Glasg 98 B2
Leadburn St. Glasg 118 C4
Leader St. Glasg 98 B1
Leadhills Rd. Kilmk 228 A2
Leaend Rd. Aird 102 C1
Leander Cres. Holy 142 C3
Leander Cres. Ren 94 C1
Learigg Rd. Plains 104 A2
Learmont Pl. Miln 54 C1
Learmonth St. Falk 42 A2
Leathem Pl. Wish 164 B1
Leathen Pl. Ersk 72 C1
Leaveret Lea. Hurl 228 B4
Leckethill Ave. Cumb 81 F4
Leckethill Ct. Cumb 81 F4
Leckethill Pl. Cumb 81 F4
Leckethill View. Cumb 81 F4
Leckie Dr. Ham 162 B2
Leckie St. Glasg 136 B4
Ledaig St. Glasg 118 B4
Ledard Rd. Glasg 137 D4
Ledcameroch Cres. Bear 75 F2
Ledcameroch Pk. Bear 75 E2
Ledcameroch Rd. Bear 75 F2
Ledgate. Kirk 58 B1
Ledgowan Pl. Glasg 96 B4
Ledi Ave. Tull 4 A1
Ledi Dr. Bear 75 D4
Ledi Path. Holy 143 E2
Ledi Rd. Glasg 136 B3
Ledi View. Stir 2 A2
Ledmore Dr. Glasg 74 C2
Ledmore Pl. Falk 42 C1
Lednock Rd. Glasg 115 D3
Lednock Rd. Stepps 99 E3
Ledrish Ave. Bonh 19 F1
Lee Ave. Glasg 98 C1
Lee Cres. Bish 98 A4
Lee Pl. Hat 142 B2
Leebank Dr. Glasg 136 C1
Leeburn Ave. Hous 91 E1
Leechford. Lan 215 D3
Leechlee Rd. Ham 162 C2
Leefield Dr. Glasg 136 C1
Leehill Rd. Bish 97 F4
Leesburn Pl. E Kil 159 F2
Leeside Rd. Bish 97 F4
Leesland. Tan 141 D4
Leeward Circ. E Kil 159 D1
Leeward Pk. Ayr 239 D1
Leewood Dr. Glasg 137 D1
Lefroy St. Coat 121 F4
Legbrannock Ave. Holy 143 E3
Legbrannock Cres. Holy 143 E2
Legbrannock Rd. Holy 143 F3
Leicester Ave. Glasg 96 A3
Leighton St. Glasg 96 C3
Leighton St. Wish 165 D1
Leitch St. Green 46 C2
Leitchland Rd. John 132 B4
Leitchland Rd. Pais 132 B4
Leith Pl. Bank 39 E4
Leith St. Glasg 118 B4
Leithland Ave. Glasg 115 D1
Leithland Rd. Glasg 115 D1
Leman Dr. Hous 111 E4
Leman Gr. Hous 111 E4
Lembert Dr. Newt M 157 E4
Lemmon St. Green 45 E2
Lendal Pl. E Kil 179 F3
Lendale La. Bish 78 A2
Lendalfoot Gdns. Ham 161 E1
Lendel Pl. Glasg 116 B3
Lendrick Ave. Falk 41 F1
Lenihall Dr. Glasg 137 F1
Lenihall Terr. Glasg 137 F1
Lennox Ave. Bishop 72 A2
Lennox Ave. Coat 121 F4
Lennox Ave. Glasg 95 E2
Lennox Ave. Miln 55 D1
Lennox Ave. Stir 7 D2
Lennox Cres. Bish 97 F4
Lennox Cres. Kilmk 222 B1
Lennox Dr. Bear 75 F3
Lennox Dr. Dunt 74 B4
Lennox Dr. Pres 236 B3
Lennox Gdns. Glasg 95 E2
Lennox La E. Glasg 95 E2
Lennox La W. Glasg 95 E2
Lennox Pl. Clyde 73 F2
Lennox Rd. Cumb 61 F1
Lennox Rd. Dumb 50 A2
Lennox Rd. Dumb 50 C1
Lennox Rd. Lennox 33 E1
Lennox St. Alex 27 F3
Lennox St. Alex 49 E4
Lennox St. Dumb 50 A2
Lennox St. Glasg 96 B4
Lennox St. Wish 165 F2
Lennox Terr. Pais 114 A4
Lentran St. Glasg 120 B4
Lenwood Gdns. Bonh 27 F2
Leny St. Glasg 96 C2
Lenzie Pl. Glasg 97 F3
Lenzie Rd. Klrk 79 E4
Lenzie Rd. Stepps 99 E3
Lenzie St. Glasg 97 F3
Lenzie Terr. Glasg 97 F3
Lenziemill Rd. Cumb 83 D4
Leperstone Ave. Kil 69 E1
Leperstone Ave. P Glasg 68 C4
Leperstone Rd. Kil 69 E1
Lesley Pl. Steven 206 C1
Lesley Quadrant. Hat 142 A1
Leslie Ave. Bishop 72 A2
Leslie Ave. Newt M 156 C4
Leslie Cres. Ayr 239 D3
Leslie Pl. Kilmk 223 D1
Leslie Rd. Glasg 116 C2
Leslie Rd. Kilmk 223 D1
Leslie St. Glasg 116 C2
Leslie St. Mother 163 F4
Leslie Terr. Pres 236 B4
Lesmahagow Rd. Lan 214 A2
Lesmuir Dr. Glasg 95 D3
Lesmuir Pl. Glasg 94 C3
Lestrange Terr. Alva 5 D4
Letham Cotts. Air 24 B4
Letham Ct. Glasg 136 C3
Letham Dr. Bish 98 B4
Letham Dr. Glasg 136 C3
Letham Grange. Cumb 62 A3
Letham Oval. Bish 98 B4
Letham Terrs. Air 14 B1
Lethamhill Cres. Glasg 98 C1
Lethamhill Pl. Glasg 98 C1
Lethamhill Rd. Glasg 98 C1
Lethbridge Pl. E Kil 180 B4
Letherby Dr. Glasg 137 D4
Letheron Dr. Wish 165 D3
Lethington Ave. Glasg 136 C4
Lethington Pl. Glasg 136 C4
Lethington Rd. Newt M 157 D4
Letterfearn Rd. Glasg 76 C1
Letterickhills Cres. Glasg 139 F2
Lettoch St. Glasg 116 A3
Levanne Gdns. Gour 43 F3
Levanne Pl. Gour 43 F3
Leven Ave. Bish 78 A1
Leven Ave. Kilmk 223 D2
Leven Ct. All 10 B3
Leven Ct. Barr 134 A3
Leven Ct. Dumb 49 F2
Leven Ct. Hurl 228 C3
Leven Dr. Bear 75 F2
Leven Dr. Ham 183 D4
Leven Dr. Hurl 228 C3
Leven Path. Holy 143 D3
Leven Pl. Ersk 72 C1
Leven Pl. Green 46 B1
Leven Pl. Irvine 219 E3
Leven Pl. Kilmk 223 D2
Leven Pl. Shot 146 C3
Leven Quadrant. Aird 102 C1
Leven Rd. Coat 101 E1
Leven Rd. Green 46 B1
Leven Rd. Lang 70 B4
Leven Rd. Troon 229 F3
Leven Sq. Ren 94 A2
Leven St. Alex 27 F2
Leven St. Alex 49 E4
Leven St. Dumb 50 A2
Leven St. Falk 42 A4
Leven St. Glasg 116 C2
Leven St. Mother 163 F2
Leven Terr. Holy 143 E1
Leven Way. E Kil 179 F3
Leven Way. Pais 112 C1
Levenbank Gdns. Bonh 27 F4
Levencroft Mews. Bonh 27 F2
Levenford Terr. Dumb 49 F2
Levengrove Ct. Dumb 49 F2
Levengrove Terr. Dumb 49 F2
Levenhowe Pl. Bonh 27 F4
Levenhowe Rd. Bonh 27 F4
Lever Rd. Helen 16 C2
Levern Cres. Barr 134 A1
Levern Gdns. Barr 134 A2
Levern Rd. Barr 134 C3
Levernside Ave. Barr 134 A1
Levernside Ave. Glasg 135 E4
Levernside Cres. Glasg 135 E4
Levernside Rd. Glasg 135 E4
Lewis Ave. Ren 94 B1
Lewis Ave. Wish 165 F3
Lewis Cres. Irvine 219 F1
Lewis Cres. Kilbar 111 E1
Lewis Cres. O Kill 73 E3
Lewis Ct. All 10 A3
Lewis Ct. Falk 42 A1
Lewis Dr. Kilmk 223 D3
Lewis Dr. O Kill 73 D3
Lewis Gdns. Bear 75 D3
Lewis Gdns. O Kill 73 E3
Lewis Gr. O Kill 73 E3
Lewis Pl. Newt M 156 A3
Lewis Pl. O Kill 73 E3
Lewis Rd. Green 45 E2
Lewis Rd. P Glasg 69 D4
Lewis Rise. Irvine 220 A1
Lewis Terr. Irvine 220 A1
Lewis Wynd. Irvine 220 A1
Lewiston Dr. Glasg 76 B1
Lewiston Pl. Glasg 76 B1
Lewiston Rd. Glasg 76 B1
Lexwell Ave. John 112 B2

Lexwell Rd. Pais

Lexwell Rd. Pais 112 C1
Leyden Ct. Glasg 96 C3
Leyden Gdns. Glasg 96 C3
Leyden St. Glasg 96 C3
Leys Pk. Ham 162 A2
Leys The. Bean 78 A1
Libberton Way. Ham 162 A2
Liberator Dr. Pres 236 C2
Liberton St. Glasg 118 C4
Liberty Ave. Coat 121 D3
Liberty Path. Udd 161 E4
Liberty Rd. Cald 105 D3
Liberty Rd. Hat 142 A2
Libo Ave. Glasg 115 E1
Libo Ave. Uplaw 153 D2
Libo Pl. Ersk 72 C1
Library La. Glasg 135 F2
Lichtenfels Gdns. Pres 236 C4
Lickprivick Rd. E Kil 180 A3
Liddel Rd. Cumb 61 F1
Liddell Gr. E Kil 180 B4
Liddell St. Glasg 119 E1
Liddells Ct. Bish 98 A1
Liddesdale Pl. Bish 97 F4
Liddesdale Rd. Glasg 97 E4
Liddesdale Sq. Bish 97 F4
Liddesdale Pass. Glasg 97 F4
Liddesdale Pass. Glasg 97 F4
Liddoch Way. Glasg 137 F4
Liff Gdns. Bish 98 B4
Liff Pl. Glasg 100 B1
Lilnock Ave. Hurl 228 C3
Lightburn Pl. Glasg 119 D4
Lightburn Rd. Glasg 118 B3
Lightburn Rd. Glasg 139 F2
Lilac Ave. Clyde 73 E3
Lilac Ave. Cumb 62 C3
Lilac Cres. Tan 141 E4
Lilac Ct. Cumb 62 C3
Lilac Gdns. Bish 98 A4
Lilac Hill. Cumb 62 C3
Lilac Hill. Ham 162 C1
Lilac Pl. Kilm 227 F4
Lilac Way. Holy 143 D3
Lillyburn Pl. Glasg 74 C3
Lily St. Glasg 118 A2
Lilybank Ave. Aird 103 D1
Lilybank Ave. Glasg 169 D2
Lilybank Ave. Muir 100 B4
Lilybank Ct. N Sau 5 E1
Lilybank Gardens La. Glasg . 96 B1
Lilybank Gdns. Glasg 96 B1
Lilybank La. Glasg 96 B1
Lilybank Rd. P Glasg 47 D1
Lilybank Rd. Pres 236 A1
Lilybank St. Ham 162 B2
Lilybank Terr. Glasg 96 B1
Lilybank Terrace La. Glasg .. 96 B1
Lime Cres. Aird 123 D4
Lime Cres. Cumb 62 C2
Lime Gr. Klrk 79 E3
Lime Gr. Lar 23 E1
Lime Gr. Mother 163 F2
Lime Gr. Udd 140 B1
Lime La. Glasg 95 E2
Lime Loan. Holy 143 D2
Lime Pl. Kilmk 227 E4
Lime Rd. Dumb 49 F2
Lime Rd. Falk 41 D2
Lime St. Glasg 95 E2
Lime St. Green 45 F2
Limecraigs Ave. Pais 133 E4
Limecraigs Cres. Pais 133 E4
Limecraigs Rd. Pais 133 E4
Limegrove St. Hat 142 A4
Limekiln Rd. Ayr 236 A2
Limekiln Rd. Steven 217 F4
Limekilnburn Rd. Quart 183 E2
Limekilns Rd. Cumb 82 C3
Limekilns St. Dunt 74 B4
Limelands Quadrant. Cald . 104 C2
Limes The. Glasg 137 D2
Limeside Ave. Glasg 138 B4
Limeside Gdns. Glasg 138 B4
Limetree Ave. Tan 141 E4
Limetree Cres. Newt M 156 B2
Limetree Ct. Ham 162 A3
Limetree Dr. Clyde 74 A2
Limetree Quadrant. Tan 141 E4
Limetree Wlk. M of C 123 E4
Limeview Ave. Pais 133 D4
Limeview Cres. Pais 133 D4
Limeview Rd. Pais 133 D4
Limeview Way. Pais 133 D4
Limonds Ct. Ayr 236 A1
Limonds Wynd. Ayr 236 A1
Limpetlaw. Lan 215 D3
Linacre Dr. Glasg 119 E3
Linacre Gdns. Glasg 119 E3
Linburn Pl. Glasg 115 D3
Linburn Rd. Ersk 113 D4
Linburn Rd. Glasg 114 C3
Linclive Interchange. Lin .. 112 B3
Linclive Terr. Lin 112 B3
Lincoln Ave. Glasg 95 E3
Lincoln Ave. Tan 120 C1
Lincoln Rd. Gour 44 B2

Lincuan Ave. Glasg 157 E4
Lindams. Udd 140 C3
Linden Ave. Duni 21 E2
Linden Ave. Stir 7 E3
Linden Ave. Wish 165 E3
Linden Dr. Bank 38 C1
Linden Dr. Dunt 74 A3
Linden Lea. Ham 162 A2
Linden Lea. M of C 58 A3
Linden Pl. Glasg 95 F4
Linden St. Glasg 95 F4
Linden Way. Glasg 95 F4
Lindores Ave. Glasg 138 B4
Lindores Dr. E Kil 159 E1
Lindores Pl. E Kil 159 E1
Lindores St. Glasg 137 D4
Lindrick Dr. Glasg 76 C1
Lindsay Ave. Kilb 149 D2
Lindsay Dr. Glasg 96 A3
Lindsay Dr. Kilmk 223 E2
Lindsay Dr. Stir 2 A2
Lindsay Gr. E Kil 159 F1
Lindsay Loan. Lan 215 E3
Lindsay Pl. E Kil 160 A1
Lindsay Pl. Glasg 96 A3
Lindsay Pl. John 112 A2
Lindsay Pl. Klrk 79 E2
Lindsay Quadrant. Bonh 28 A1
Lindsay Rd. E Kil 159 F1
Lindsay St. Salt 205 F1
Lindsay St. Ayr 236 B1
Lindsay St. Kilmk 227 F4
Lindsay Terr. Lennox 57 F1
Lindsaybeg Rd. Muir 80 A1
Lindum Cres. Mother 163 D4
Lindum St. Mother 163 D4
Lineside Wlk. Rhu 15 F3
Linfern Ave E. Kilmk 228 B4
Linfern Ave. Kilmk 228 B4
Linfern Ave W. Kilmk 228 B4
Linfern Pl. Ayr 239 D2
Linfern Rd. Glasg 96 B2
Linfield Loan. Udd 141 D3
Linghope Pl. Wish 185 F4
Lingley Ave. Aird 123 D3
Linhope Pl. E Kil 179 F4
Links Cres. Troon 229 F3
Links Rd. Glasg 119 E2
Links Rd. Glasg 137 E2
Links Rd. Pres 233 D1
Links Rd. Salt 205 F1
Links The. Cumb 62 A3
Links View. Lark 185 E1
Linkside Rd. Holy 143 D1
Linkwood Ave. Glasg 74 C2
Linkwood Cres. Glasg 75 D2
Linkwood Ct. Irvine 220 A3
Linkwood Dr. Glasg 75 D2
Linkwood Pl. Glasg 74 C2
Linkwood Pl. Irvine 220 A3
Linlithgow Gdns. Glasg 119 E3
Linlithgow Pl. Sten 23 F2
Linn Cres. Lan 214 A2
Linn Cres. Pais 133 E4
Linn Dr. Glasg 136 C2
Linn Glen. Lennox 57 F4
Linn Park Gdns. John 112 A1
Linn Park Ind Est. Glasg ... 137 D1
Linn Rd. Ard 205 E2
Linn Valley View. Glasg 136 C2
Linnet Ave. John 131 E4
Linnet Rd. Green 45 D2
Linnet Rd. Hat 142 A2
Linnhe Ave. Bish 78 A1
Linnhe Ave. Glasg 137 D2
Linnhe Ave. Ham 162 A1
Linnhe Cres. Wish 165 D1
Linnhe Dr. Barr 134 A3
Linnhe Pl. Ersk 72 C1
Linnhe Pl. Udd 140 B1
Linnhead Dr. Glasg 135 E3
Linnhead Pl. Glasg 95 D2
Linnpark Ave. Glasg 136 C1
Linnpark Ct. Glasg 136 C1
Linnwell Cres. Pais 133 E4
Linrigg Rd. Chap 144 B4
Linside Ave. Pais 114 A2
Lint Brae. Stew 195 F1
Lint Riggs. Falk 42 A3
Linthaugh Rd. Glasg 115 E2
Linthaugh Terr. Glasg 115 E1
Linthill. Lan 215 D3
Linthouse Bldgs. Glasg 115 F4
Linthouse Rd. Glasg 95 F1
Lintie Rd. Holy 143 E2
Lintlaw Dr. Glasg 115 D3
Lintlaw. Udd 140 B1
Lintmill Terr. Neil 154 B3
Linton St. Glasg 118 C4
Lintwhite Cres. B of W 110 C4
Linwood Ave. E Kil 159 D1
Linwood Ave. Newt M 157 E2
Linwood Ct. Glasg 137 D3
Linwood Rd. Pais 112 B2
Linwood Terr. Ham 162 A2
Lion Bank. Kirk 58 B1

Lionthorn Rd. Falk 41 F1
Lipney. Men 4 A3
Lisburn Rd. Ayr 236 A2
Lismore Ave. Mother 163 D4
Lismore Ave. P Glasg 69 D4
Lismore Ave. Ren 94 B1
Lismore Ct. Falk 42 A1
Lismore Dr. Irvine 225 D4
Lismore Dr. Lin 111 F3
Lismore Dr. Pais 133 E4
Lismore. E Kil 181 E4
Lismore Gdns. Kilbar 111 E1
Lismore Hill. Ham 161 E2
Lismore House. Pres 236 A3
Lismore Pl. Muir 81 D2
Lismore Pl. Newt M 156 A3
Lismore Rd. Glasg 96 A3
Lismore Way. Irvine 225 E4
Lister Ct. B of A 2 A3
Lister Gdns. Thorn 158 A3
Lister Pl. Glasg 115 D4
Lister Rd. Glasg 115 D4
Lister St. Cross 222 A1
Lister St. Glasg 97 E1
Litheholm Pl. Clyde 73 F2
Littlemill Ave. Cumb 60 C1
Littlesdale Ave. Pais 132 B4
Littlestane Rd. Irvine 220 A3
Littlestane Rise. Irvine 220 A3
Littlestane
Roundabout. Irvine 220 A3
Littleston Gdns. Ersk 72 C1
Littleton Dr. Glasg 76 B1
Littleton St. Glasg 76 B1
Liviands Ct. Stir 7 D3
Liviands Gate. Stir 7 D3
Liviands La. Stir 7 D3
Livingston Dr. Plains 104 A2
Livingston La. Udd 141 D2
Livingstone Ave. Glasg 115 D4
Livingstone Bvd. Ham 161 E2
Livingstone Cres. E Kil 180 B4
Livingstone Cres. Falk 42 C3
Livingstone Cres. Udd 140 C4
Livingstone Ct. Kilmk 223 E2
Livingstone Dr. E Kil 180 C4
Livingstone Dr. Laur 42 C1
Livingstone Gdns. Lark 185 D2
Livingstone Pk. Kils 36 B1
Livingstone Pl. Aird 123 D4
Livingstone Quadrant. East 127 E2
Livingstone St. Clyde 74 B1
Livingstone St. Ham 161 F2
Livingstone Terr. Irvine ... 219 E3
Livingstone Pk. Kils 36 A1
Lloyd Ave. Glasg 119 D1
Lloyd Dr. Holy 143 D1
Lloyd St. Glasg 118 A1
Lloyd St. Holy 143 A4
Lloyd St. Sten 23 F2
Lloyd Wlk. Stew 211 E4
Lloyds St. Coat 122 A2
Llynallan Rd. East 127 D3
Loach Ave. Irvine 219 E1
Loadingbank Ct. Kilb 170 A4
Loadingbank. Kilb 170 A4
Loan End Cres. Lark 185 F1
Loan Pl. East 127 E3
Loan The. Miln 54 B2
Loanbank Quadrant. Glasg 115 F4
Loancroft Ave. Glasg 120 B2
Loancroft Gate. Udd 140 C3
Loancroft Gdns. Udd 140 C3
Loancroft Pl. Glasg 120 A2
Loanend Cotts. Glasg 139 F1
Loanfoot Ave. Glasg 95 D4
Loanfoot Ave. Kilmk 222 B3
Loanfoot Ave. Neil 154 B3
Loanfoot Gdns. Plea 111 E1
Loanfoot Rd. Udd 161 E3
Loanhead Ave. Bank 39 E3
Loanhead Ave. Holy 143 E2
Loanhead Ave. Lin 112 A3
Loanhead Ave. Ren 94 B2
Loanhead Cres. Holy 143 E2
Loanhead La. Lin 112 A3
Loanhead Rd. Holy 143 E2
Loanhead Rd. Lin 112 A3
Loanhead St. Coat 121 F2
Loanhead St. Glasg 118 C4
Loanhead St. Kilmk 228 A4
Loaning. Lark 185 E1
Loaning The. Ayr 239 D1

Loaning The. Mother 163 E4
Loaning The. Newt M 157 D4
Loaninghead Dr. Dumb 50 A3
Lobnitz Ave. Ren 94 B2
Loccard Rd. Steven 206 B1
Loch Achray Gdns. Glasg .. 119 E2
Loch Achray St. Glasg 119 E2
Loch Assynt. E Kil 181 D4
Loch Awe. Car 201 F2
Loch Awe. E Kil 181 D4
Loch Dr. Helen 16 A1
Loch Earn. Newt M 157 D4
Loch Goil. E Kil 160 A1
Loch Laidon St. Glasg 119 E2
Loch Laxford. E Kil 181 D4
Loch Lea. Kirk 58 C1
Loch Long. E Kil 181 D4
Loch Loyal. E Kil 181 D4
Loch Maree. E Kil 181 D4
Loch Meadie. E Kil 181 D4
Loch Naver. E Kil 181 D4
Loch Park Ave. Car 201 F4
Loch Park. Lark 185 D1
Loch Pl. B of W 110 B4
Loch Rd. B of W 110 B4
Loch Rd. Klrk 79 F4
Loch Rd. Miln 55 D2
Loch Rd. Stepps 99 E2
Loch Shin. E Kil 181 D4
Loch St. Calder 123 D2
Loch Striven. E Kil 160 A1
Loch Torridon. E Kil 181 D4
Loch View. Cald 105 D3
Loch View. Calder 123 D1
Loch Voil St. Glasg 119 E2
Lochaber Cres. Shot 147 D2
Lochaber Dr. Glasg 138 B2
Lochaber Dr. Sten 23 F2
Lochaber Path. Udd 161 E4
Lochaber Pl. E Kil 159 F2
Lochaber Rd. Bear 76 A1
Lochaber Wlk. M of C 58 B4
Lochaline Ave. Pais 113 D1
Lochaline Dr. Glasg 137 D2
Lochaline St. Glasg 58 B4
Lochalsh Cres. M of C 58 B4
Lochalsh Dr. Pais 113 D1
Lochalsh Pl. Udd 140 A1
Lochana The. Ros 15 D2
Lochar Cres. Glasg 115 E1
Lochar Pl. E Kil 179 F4
Lochard Dr. Pais 113 D1
Lochay St. Glasg 119 E2
Lochbrae. N Sau 5 E1
Lochbridge Rd. Glasg 120 A4
Lochbroom Ct. Newt M 156 C3
Lochbroom Dr. Newt M 156 C3
Lochbroom Dr. Pais 113 D1
Lochbuie La. Glenm 102 C2
Lochburn Cres. Glasg 96 C4
Lochburn Pass. Glasg 96 C4
Lochburn Rd. Glasg 96 C4
Lochcraig Ct. Irvine 219 E1
Lochcraigs Rd. Stepps 99 E3
Lochend Ave. Muir 80 B4
Lochend Cres. Bear 75 E2
Lochend Dr. Bear 75 F2
Lochend Rd. Bear 75 F2
Lochend Rd. Coat 101 D1
Lochend Rd. Glasg 100 B1
Lochend Rd. Kilb 170 B4
Lochend Rd. Troon 229 E1
Lochend St. Mother 163 F3
Locher Ave. Hous 91 F1
Locher Cres. Hous 111 F4
Locher Gdns. Hous 111 F4
Locher Rd. Kilbar 110 C2
Locher Way. Hous 111 F4
Locherburn Ave. Hous 111 F4
Locherburn Gr. Hous 111 E4
Locherburn Pl. Hous 111 F4
Locherhill Rd. Glasg 77 D1
Lochfield Cres. Pais 113 F1
Lochfield Dr. Pais 114 A1
Lochfield Gdns. Glasg 100 A3
Lochfield Rd. Pais 113 F1
Lochgilp St. Glasg 96 B4
Lochgoin Ave. Glasg 74 C2
Lochgreen Ave. Troon 229 F4
Lochgreen Pl. Coat 101 E1
Lochgreen Pl. Ham 183 D4
Lochgreen Pl. Kilmk 222 C3
Lochgreen Rd. Falk 41 F1
Lochgreen St. Glasg 98 B2
Lochhead Ave. Den 21 F1
Lochhead Ave. Lin 112 A3
Lochiel Dr. M of C 58 B4
Lochiel La. Glasg 138 B2
Lochiel Rd. Glasg 135 F2
Lochinvar Pl. Bon 40 B2
Lochinvar Rd. Cumb 82 C4
Lochinver Cres. Pais 113 D1
Lochinver Dr. Glasg 137 D3
Lochinver Gr. Glasg 139 D3

Lochknowe St. Car 201 F4
Lochlands Dr. Beith 171 E3
Lochlands Ind Est. Falk ...... 41 C
Lochlea Ave. Clyde .... 74 B
Lochlea Ave. Troon .... 229 F
Lochlea Dr. Ayr .... 239 D
Lochlea. E Kil .... 160 B
Lochlea Rd. Cumb .... 62 B
Lochlea Rd. Glasg .... 138 B
Lochlea Rd. Glasg .... 137 F
Lochlea Rd. Newt M .... 157 F
Lochlea Rd. Salt .... 206 A
Lochlea Way. Holy .... 143 F
Lochleven La. Glasg .... 137 D
Lochleven Rd. Glasg .... 137 D
Lochlibo Ave. Glasg .... 94 C
Lochlibo Ct. Irvine .... 220 A
Lochlibo Cres. Barr .... 134 A
Lochlibo Rd. Barr .... 134 A
Lochlibo Rd. Beith .... 172 C
Lochlibo Rd. Irvine .... 219 E
Lochlibo Rd. Neil .... 154 C
Lochlibo Rd. Stew .... 209 E
Lochlibo Rd. Uplaw .... 152 C
Lochlibo Terr. Barr .... 134 A
Lochmaben Dr. Sten .... 23 F
Lochmaben Rd. Glasg ...... 114 C
Lochmaddy Ave. Glasg ..... 137 D
Lochnagar Dr. Bear .... 75 D
Lochnagar Rd. Kilmk .... 228 A
Lochnagar Way. Lark .... 185 F
Lochpark. Ayr .... 238 E
Lochpark Pl. Den .... 21 F
Lochranza Dr. Helen .... 16 C
Lochranza Pl. Salt .... 206 A
Lochridge Pl. Den .... 21 F
Lochshore
East Ind Est. Kilb .... 170 B
Lochside. Bear .... 75 F
Lochside. Ct. Ayr .... 236 A
Lochside. Muir .... 100 C
Lochside. Ayr .... 236 A
Lochside Rd. Slam .... 86 E
Lochside St. Glasg .... 116 C
Lochslave. Gour .... 45 D
Lochview Cres. Glasg .... 98 C
Lochview Dr. Glasg .... 98 C
Lochview Gdns. Glasg .... 98 C
Lochview Pl. Glasg .... 98 C
Lochview Rd. Bear .... 75 F
Lochview Rd. Coat .... 121 F
Lochview Rd. P Glasg .... 47 C
Lochview Terr. Muir .... 100 C
Lochwinnoch Rd. Kil .... 89 E
Lochwood Gdns. Glasg ..... 120 B
Lochwood Loan. Muir .... 81 D
Lochwood Pl. Irvine .... 219 E
Lochwood St. Glasg .... 98 E
Lochy Ave. Ren .... 94 C
Lochy Gdns. Bish .... 78 A
Lock Pk. Ersk .... 72 C
Lock St. Wish .... 165 E
Lock Sixteen. Falk .... 41 E
Lockerbie Ave. Glasg .... 136 E
Locket Yett View. Hat ...... 141 F
Lockhart Ave. Glasg .... 138 C
Lockhart Ave. Lan .... 214 E
Lockhart Dr. Glasg .... 139 E
Lockhart Pl. Wish .... 165 F
Lockhart Pl. Udd .... 187 E
Lockhart St. Car .... 187 E
Lockhart St. Glasg .... 139 E
Lockhart St. Ham .... 183 E
Lockhart St. Stone .... 199 E
Lockhart Terr. E Kil .... 181 E
Locks St. Coat .... 122 E
Locksley Ave. Cumb .... 82 E
Locksley Ave. Glasg .... 95 E
Locksley Cres. Cumb .... 82 E
Locksley Ct. Cumb .... 82 E
Locksley Pl. Cumb .... 82 E
Locksley Rd. Cumb .... 82 E
Locksley Rd. Pais .... 112 E
Lodge Cres. Kil .... 89 E
Lodge Dr. Sten .... 23 E
Lodge Gdns. Kil .... 89 E
Loftus Sq. Udd .... 141 E
Logan Ave. Newt M .... 156 E
Logan Ct. Troon .... 229 E
Logan Dr. Cumb .... 61 E
Logan Dr. Pais .... 113 E
Logan Gdns. Cle .... 144 E
Logan St. Glasg .... 117 E
Logan St. Udd .... 141 E
Logan Tower. Glasg .... 139 E
Loganlea Ave. New .... 165 E
Loganlea Dr. Holy .... 143 E
Logans Rd. Mozther .... 163 E
Loganswell Dr. Glasg .... 135 E
Loganswell Gdns. Glasg ... 135 E
Loganswell Pl. Glasg .... 135 E
Loganswell Rd. Glasg ...... 135 E

271

Logie Dr. Lar Main St. Barr

Logie Dr. Lar 23 D2
Logie La. B of A 2 B4
Logie Pk. E Kil 160 A2
Logie Rd. Stir 2 B2
Logie Sq. E Kil 160 A2
Lomax St. Glasg 118 B4
Lomond Ave. Hurl 228 C3
Lomond Ave. P Glasg 68 C4
Lomond Ave. Ren 94 A1
Lomond Cres. Alex 27 E4
Lomond Cres. B of W 110 B4
Lomond Cres. Beith 150 B1
Lomond Cres. Cumb 82 B4
Lomond Cres. Pais 133 E4
Lomond Cres. Sten 23 F2
Lomond Cres. Stir 2 A2
Lomond Ct. All 10 B3
Lomond Ct. Barr 134 B1
Lomond Ct. Cumb 82 B4
Lomond Ct. Dumb 49 F2
Lomond Ct. Helen 16 C1
Lomond Dr. Aird 102 C1
Lomond Dr. Alex 27 E4
Lomond Dr. Bann 7 F1
Lomond Dr. Barr 134 A2
Lomond Dr. Bish 78 A2
Lomond Dr. Cumb 82 A4
Lomond Dr. Dumb 50 A3
Lomond Dr. Falk 24 B1
Lomond Dr. Newt M 156 B4
Lomond Dr. Udd 141 D2
Lomond Dr. Wish 165 D1
Lomond. E Kil 180 C3
Lomond Gdns. John 112 B1
Lomond Gr. Cumb 82 B4
Lomond Ind Est. Alex 27 F3
Lomond Pl. Coat 101 F1
Lomond Pl. Cumb 82 A4
Lomond Pl. Ersk 72 C1
Lomond Pl. Irvine 219 E3
Lomond Pl. Stepps 99 F2
Lomond Rd. Alex 27 E4
Lomond Rd. Bear 75 F1
Lomond Rd. Bonh 27 F4
Lomond Rd. Coat 101 E1
Lomond Rd. Green 46 A2
Lomond Rd. Kilmk 228 A2
Lomond Rd. Kirk 79 E3
Lomond Rd. Shot 146 C3
Lomond Rd. Tan 120 C1
Lomond St. All 4 C1
Lomond St. Glasg 97 D3
Lomond St. Helen 16 C1
Lomond View. Cumb 82 B4
Lomond View. Ham 161 F1
Lomond Way. Bank 39 E3
Lomond Way. Holy 143 D3
Lomond Way. Irvine 220 A2
Lomond Wlk. Holy 143 E2
Lomond Wlk. Lark 185 D2
Lomondside Ave. Newt M 157 E4
Lomondview Ind Est. John 111 F2
London Rd. Glasg 118 C1
London Rd. Glasg 119 E1
London Rd. Hurl 228 A4
London Rd. Kilmk 228 A4
London St. Lark 185 D2
London St. Ren 94 B3
Lonend. Pais 113 F2
Loney Cres. Den 39 F4
Long Crags View. Dumb 50 B3
Long Dr. E Kil 181 D4
Long Dr. Irvine 219 F2
Long Dr. Kilw 219 E4
Long Dr. Shew 225 D4
Long Row. Glasg 120 B3
Long Row. Lan 214 C1
Long Row. Men 4 A4
Longay Pl. Glasg 97 E4
Longay St. Glasg 97 E4
Longbank Dr. Ayr 239 D2
Longbank Rd. Ayr 239 D2
Longbar Ave. Beith 170 B3
Longcraigs Ave. Ard 205 E3
Longcroft Dr. Ren 94 B2
Longdales Ave. Falk 42 A4
Longdales Ct. Falk 42 A4
Longdales Pl. Falk 42 A4
Longdales Rd. Falk 42 A4
Longden St. Clyde 94 B4
Longdyke Pl. Sten 24 B2
Longfield Ave. Salt 205 F1
Longfield Pl. Salt 205 F1
Longford Ave. Kilw 207 F1
Longford St. Glasg 118 B4
Longhill Ave. Ayr 238 B1
Longlands Pk. Ayr 238 C2
Longlee. Glasg 120 A2
Longmeadow. John 111 E1
Longpark Ave. Kilmk 222 C1
Longriggend Rd. Cald 85 E1
Longrow Gdns. Irvine 219 F4
Longstone Pl. Glasg 119 D4
Longstone Rd. Glasg 119 D4
Longwill Terr. Cumb 62 A2
Lonmay Rd. Glasg 119 E4
Lonsdale Ave. Glasg 136 B2
Loom Wlk. Kilbar 111 D2
Lora Dr. Glasg 115 F2
Loreny Dr. Kilmk 227 F1
Loretto Pl. Glasg 118 C4
Loretto St. Glasg 118 C4
Lorien Ct. Pres 236 B2
Lorimar Pl. Sten 24 A1
Lorimer Cres. E Kil 180 B4
Lorn Ave. Muir 100 B4
Lorn Dr. Bonh 19 F1
Lorn Pl. Kirk 59 E1
Lorne Arc. Ayr 238 C4
Lorne Cres. Bish 78 B1
Lorne Dr. Lin 112 A3
Lorne Dr. Mother 142 B1
Lorne Gdns. Laur 42 C2
Lorne Gdns. Sals 125 D1
Lorne Pl. Coat 122 B3
Lorne Rd. Glasg 114 C4
Lorne Rd. Lar 23 E1
Lorne St. Glasg 116 B3
Lorne St. Ham 162 B2
Lorne St. Helen 16 B1
Lorne Terr. Glasg 138 C2
Lornshill Cres. All 9 F4
Lorraine Gardens La. Glasg 96 B2
Lorraine Gdns. Glasg 96 B2
Lorraine Rd. Glasg 96 B2
Lorraine Way. Bonh 27 F1
Loskin Dr. Glasg 97 D4
Losshill. Men 4 A3
Lossie Cres. Ren 94 C1
Lossie St. Glasg 98 B1
Lothian Cres. Pais 113 E1
Lothian Cres. Stir 2 B2
Lothian Dr. Newt M 157 E4
Lothian Gdns. Glasg 96 C2
Lothian Rd. Ayr 239 D4
Lothian Rd. Gour 44 B2
Lothian Rd. Stew 211 E4
Lothian St. Glasg 114 C4
Lothian Way. E Kil 160 B2
Louburn. Blac 107 E2
Louden St. Aird 123 D4
Loudens Wlk. Duni 21 E3
Loudon. E Kil 180 C3
Loudon Gdns. John 112 A2
Loudon Rd. Stepps 99 D2
Loudon St. Wish 165 D3
Loudon Terr. Bear 75 E4
Loudonhill Ave. Ham 183 F4
Loudoun Ave. Kilmk 228 A4
Loudoun Cres. Kilw 207 D2
Loudoun Pl. Cross 226 C4
Loudoun Pl. Sym 231 E2
Loudoun St. Stew 211 F4
Loudoun Terr. Pres 236 B4
Louise Gdns. Holy 142 C3
Louisville Ave. Wish 165 E3
Lounsdale Cres. Pais 113 D1
Lounsdale Dr. Pais 113 D1
Lounsdale House. Pais 113 D1
Lounsdale Pl. Glasg 95 D2
Lounsdale Rd. Pais 113 D1
Lourdes Ave. Glasg 115 E2
Lourdes Ct. Glasg 115 E2
Lovat Ave. Miln 75 F4
Lovat Dr. Kirk 79 D4
Lovat Path. Lark 185 E1
Lovat Pl. Glasg 138 B2
Love Ave. Kil 89 F1
Love St. Kilw 208 A2
Love St. Pais 113 F3
Lovers Loan. Alva 5 D4
Lovers Wlk. Stir 2 A1
Low Barholm. Kilbar 111 D1
Low Broadlie Rd. Neil 154 B4
Low Church La. Kilmk 227 F4
Low Craigends. Kils 60 C4
Low Cres. Clyde 94 C4
Low Flender Rd. Newt M 157 E3
Low Glencairn St. Kilmk 227 F3
Low Green Rd. Irvine 219 D1
Low Parksail. Ersk 93 E4
Low Patrick St. Ham 162 C2
Low Pleasance. Lark 185 D2
Low Rd. Ayr 236 C2
Low Rd. Pais 113 E2
Low Waters Rd. Ham 162 B1
Lower Auchingramont
Rd. Ham 162 C2
Lower Bourtree Dr. Glasg 138 B2
Lower Bouverie St. P Glasg 47 E1
Lower Bridge St. Stir 2 A1
Lower Castlehill. Stir 2 A1
Lower Mill Rd. Newt M 157 F3
Lower Millgate. Udd 140 C3
Lower
Stoneymollan Rd. Alex 27 E4
Lower
Sutherland Cres. Helen 16 A2
Lowndes St. Barr 134 B1
Lowther Ave. Bear 75 E4
Lowther Bank. Irvine 220 B1
Lowther Pl. Kilmk 228 A2
Lowther Terr. Glasg 96 B2
Loyal Ave. Ersk 72 C1
Loyal Gdns. Bear 75 D4
Loyal Pl. Ersk 72 C1
Loyne Dr. Ren 94 C1
Luath St. Glasg 116 A4
Lubas Ave. Glasg 137 E4
Lubas Pl. Glasg 137 E4
Lubnaig Dr. Ersk 72 C1
Lubnaig Gdns. Bear 75 E4
Lubnaig Pl. Aird 102 C1
Lubnaig Rd. Glasg 136 C3
Lubnaig Wlk. Holy 143 D3
Luce Ave. Kilmk 228 A3
Luckenhill Dr. Gree 84 B2
Luckiesfauld. Neil 154 B3
Luckingsford Ave. Inch 93 E4
Luckingsford Dr. Inch 93 E4
Luckingsford Rd. Inch 93 E4
Lucy Brae. Tan 140 C4
Ludgate. All 10 A3
Ludovic Sq. John 111 F2
Luffness Gdns. Glasg 119 D1
Lugar Ave. Irvine 220 A3
Lugar Cres. Pres 236 A3
Lugar Dr. Glasg 115 F2
Lugar Pl. Glasg 137 F3
Lugar Pl. Troon 229 F3
Lugar St. Coat 122 A4
Luggie Rd. Car 187 F2
Luggie View. Cumb 82 A4
Luggiebank Pl. Coat 121 D2
Luggiebank Rd. Kirk 58 B1
Luggiebank Rd. Kirk 79 E4
Lugton Ct. Irvine 219 E1
Lugton Rd. Dunlop 195 D4
Luing. Aird 123 F3
Luing Rd. Glasg 115 F3
Lumloch St. Glasg 98 A2
Lumsden La. Glasg 96 B1
Lumsden Pl. Steven 206 C1
Lumsden St. Glasg 96 B1
Lunan Dr. Bish 98 B4
Lunan Pl. Glasg 115 F4
Luncarty Pl. Glasg 119 D2
Luncarty St. Glasg 119 D2
Lunderston Dr. Glasg 135 D4
Lundholm Rd. Steven 217 F4
Lundie Gdns. Bish 98 B4
Lundie St. Glasg 118 C2
Lurg St. P Glasg 68 B4
Luss Ave. Green 46 A1
Luss Brae. Ham 161 F1
Luss Pl. Green 46 A1
Luss Rd. Alex 27 E4
Luss Rd. Glasg 115 F4
Luss Rd. Helen 17 D3
Lusset Glen. O Kill 73 D3
Lusset Rd. O Kill 73 D3
Lusshill Terr. Glasg 120 A1
Lybster Cres. Glasg 138 B2
Lychgate Rd. Tull 4 A1
Lye Brae. Cumb 62 A1
Lyell Ct. E Kil 159 F2
Lyell Gr. E Kil 159 F2
Lyle Cres. Bishop 72 A2
Lyle Gr. Green 45 D4
Lyle Pl. Green 45 D4
Lyle Pl. Pais 113 F1
Lyle Rd. Aird 123 F4
Lyle Rd. Green 45 D4
Lyle Rd. Kil 89 E4
Lyle Sq. Miln 54 C1
Lyle St. Green 45 F2
Lyle St. Green 46 A2
Lylefoot Cres. Green 45 D4
Lylefoot Pl. Green 45 D4
Lylesland Ct. Pais 113 F1
Lylestone Terr. Kilw 208 B4
Lyman Dr. Wish 165 E4
Lymburn Pl. Ayr 239 D4
Lymburn St. Glasg 116 B4
Lymekilns Rd. E Kil 159 E2
Lyndale Pl. Glasg 96 B4
Lyndale Rd. Glasg 96 B4
Lyndhurst
Gardens La. Glasg 96 C2
Lyndhurst Gdns. Glasg 96 C2
Lyne Croft. Bish 78 A2
Lyne St. Wish 165 D3
Lynedoch Cres. Glasg 96 C1
Lynedoch
Crescent La. Glasg 96 C1
Lynedoch Ind Est. Green 46 A2
Lynedoch Pl. Glasg 96 C1
Lynedoch St. Glasg 96 C1
Lynedoch St. Green 45 F2
Lynedoch Terr. Glasg 96 C1
Lynmouth Pl. Gour 44 C3
Lynn Ave. Dalry 191 E4
Lynn Ct. Lark 185 D1
Lynn Dr. Eagle 178 C3
Lynn Dr. Kilb 149 D2
Lynn Dr. Miln 55 E1
Lynn Wlk. Bonh 27 F4
Lynn Wlk. Udd 141 D3
Lynnburn Ave. Hat 142 A3
Lynne Dr. Glasg 76 C1
Lynnhurst. Tan 140 C4
Lynnwood Rd. New 166 B3
Lynton Ave. Glasg 136 A1
Lyon Cres. B of A 2 A3
Lyon Rd. Ersk 72 C1
Lyon Rd. John 112 A2
Lyon Rd. Pais 112 C1
Lyoncross Ave. Barr 134 B2
Lyoncross Cres. Barr 134 B2
Lyoncross Rd. Glasg 115 D1
Lyons Quadrant. Mother 164 B2
Lysa Vale Pl. Hat 141 F3
Lysander Way. Ren 94 B1
Lytham Dr. Glasg 76 C1
Lytham Meadows. Udd 140 C1
Lythgow Way. Lan 215 E3
Lyttelton. E Kil 180 A4

Mabel St. Mother 163 F3
Maberry Cl. Stew 195 E1
Maberry Pl. Troon 229 F3
Macadam Gdns. Hat 142 A3
Macadam Pl. Ayr 236 A1
Macadam Pl. E Kil 180 C4
Macadam Pl. Irvine 219 F1
Macadam Pl. Kilmk 223 E1
Macadam Place. Falk 41 E3
Macadam Sq. Ayr 236 A1
Macalian Pl. Irvine 219 F4
Macallister Pl. Kilmk 223 E1
Macalpine Pl. Kilmk 223 E1
Macandrew Pl. Kilmk 223 E1
Macara Dr. Irvine 219 F2
Macarthur Ave. Glenm 102 B2
Macarthur Cres. E Kil 159 E2
Macarthur Ct. E Kil 159 E2
Macarthur Dr. E Kil 159 E2
Macarthur Gdns. E Kil 159 E2
Macaulay Pl. Helen 16 A1
Macauley Pl. Kilmk 223 E1
Macbeth Dr. Kilmk 223 E1
Macbeth. E Kil 160 A3
Macbeth Gdns. Kilmk 223 E1
Macbeth Pl. Glasg 118 B2
Macbeth Rd. Green 45 D3
Macbeth Rd. Stew 211 E4
Macbeth St. Glasg 118 B2
Maccabe Gdns. Lennox 57 F4
Maccallum Pl. Kilmk 223 E1
Maccrimmon Pk. E Kil 159 D2
Macdairmid Dr. Ham 183 D4
Macdonald Ave. E Kil 159 D2
Macdonald Cres. Twe 60 A2
Macdonald Ct. Beith 171 D4
Macdonald Dr. Kilmk 223 E1
Macdonald Dr. Stir 7 D2
Macdonald Gdns. Kilmk 223 E1
Macdonald Gr. Hat 141 F1
Macdonald Pl. Kilmk 223 E1
Macdonald St. Glasg 138 A4
Macdonald St. Mother 163 F3
MacDonald Wlk. Bonh 27 F4
Macdougal Quadrant. Hat 141 F1
Macdougall Dr. Kilmk 223 E1
Macdougall St. Glasg 136 B4
Macdougall St. Green 46 B2
Macdowall St. John 111 F2
Macdowall St. Pais 113 E3
Macduff. Ersk 73 D1
Macduff Pl. Glasg 118 B2
Macduff St. Glasg 118 B2
Mace Ct. Bann 7 E2
Mace Rd. Glasg 75 E1
Macewan Pl. Kilmk 228 B4
Macfarlane Cres. Falk 42 A3
Macfarlane Dr. Kilmk 223 E1
Macfarlane Rd. Bear 76 A2
Macfie Pl. E Kil 159 D2
Macgregor Dr. Kilmk 228 B4
Machan Ave. Lark 185 D2
Machan Rd. Lark 185 D1
Machanhill. Lark 185 D1
Machanhill View. Lark 185 D1
Machrie Ct. Falk 41 E2
Machrie Dr. Glasg 137 F2
Machrie Dr. Helen 16 C2
Machrie Dr. Newt M 156 C3
Machrie Pl. Kilw 207 E2
Machrie Rd. Glasg 137 F2
Machrie Rd. Kilmk 222 C2
Machrie Rd. Mother 163 D4
Machrie St. Glasg 137 F2
Macinnes Pl. Kilmk 223 E1
Macintosh Pl. E Kil 180 B4
Macintosh Pl. Kilmk 223 E1
Macintyre Pl. Kilmk 223 E1
Macintyre Rd. Pres 233 E1
Macintyre St. Glasg 116 C4
Macivor Cres. E Kil 159 D2
Macivor Pl. Kilmk 223 E1
Mack St. Aird 123 D4
Mackean St. Pais 113 E3
Mackeith St. Glasg 117 F2
Mackellar Pl. Kilmk 223 E1
Mackendrick Pl. Kilmk 228 B4
Mackenzie Dr. Kilbar 111 D1
Mackenzie Dr. Kilmk 223 D1
Mackenzie Gdns. E Kil 159 D2
Mackenzie St. Green 46 B2
Mackenzie Terr. Hat 142 A4
Mackie Ave. Green 46 C1
Mackie Ave. P Glasg 47 D1
Mackie Ave. Stew 195 E1
Mackie Pl. Kilmk 223 E1
Mackie St. Ayr 236 B1
Mackie's Mill Rd. John 132 B4
Mackinlay Pl. Kilmk 228 A4
Mackinlay St. Glasg 117 D2
Mackinnon Dr. Kilmk 228 B4
Mackinnon Terr. Irvine 219 F2
Mackintosh Pl. Irvine 219 F1
Maclachlan Ave. Den 21 E1
Maclachlan Pl. Helen 16 C2
Maclachlan Rd. Helen 16 C2
Maclaren Pl. Kilmk 228 B4
Maclaren Terr. Sten 24 A1
Maclay Ave. Kilbar 111 D1
Maclean Cres. Alva 5 E4
Maclean Ct. E Kil 159 D2
Maclean Ct. Stir 7 E2
Maclean Dr. Kilmk 223 D1
Maclean Gr. E Kil 159 D2
Maclean Pl. E Kil 159 D2
Maclean Sq. Glasg 116 C3
Maclean St. Clyde 94 C4
Maclean St. Glasg 116 B3
Maclean Terr. Blac 107 E2
Maclehose Rd. Cumb 62 B2
Maclellan Rd. Neil 154 C3
Maclellan St. Glasg 116 B3
Macleod Cres. Helen 16 A2
Macleod Dr. Helen 16 B2
Macleod Dr. Kilmk 228 B4
Macleod Pl. E Kil 160 A2
Macleod Pl. Kilmk 228 B4
Macleod St. Glasg 117 F4
Macmillan Dr. Gour 44 B3
Macmillan Dr. Kilmk 223 E1
Macmillan Gdns. Tan 121 D1
Macmillan Pl. Kilmk 223 E1
Macmillan St. Lark 184 C1
Macnab Pl. Kilmk 223 D1
Macnaughton Dr. Kilmk 223 E1
Macneil Pl. Kilmk 223 D1
Macneill Dr. E Kil 159 D2
Macneill Gdns. E Kil 159 D2
Macneill St. Lark 184 C2
Macneish Way. E Kil 159 E2
Macnicol Ct. E Kil 159 D2
Macnicol Pk. E Kil 159 D2
Macnicol Pl. E Kil 159 D2
Macnicol Pl. Kilmk 223 E1
Macphail Dr. Kilmk 223 E1
Macpherson Gdns. Kilmk 223 E1
Macpherson Pk. E Kil 159 E2
Macpherson Pl. Kilmk 223 E1
Macpherson Wlk. Kilmk 223 E1
Macphie Rd. Dumb 50 B2
Macrae Dr. Pres 233 E1
Macrae Gdns. E Kil 159 E2
Macrimmon Pl. E Kil 180 C4
Macrobert Ave. Irvine 220 A1
Mactaggart Rd. Cumb 82 C4
Madeira La. Green 45 E4
Madeira St. Green 45 E4
Madill Pl. Sten 23 F2
Madison Ave. Glasg 137 D3
Madison Path. Udd 161 E4
Madras Pl. Neil 154 C4
Madras St. Glasg 117 F2
Mafeking St. Glasg 116 A3
Mafeking St. Mother 164 B2
Mafeking Terr. Neil 154 B4
Magdalen Way. Pais 132 C4
Maggie Wood's Loan. Falk 41 F3
Magna St. Mother 163 D4
Magnolia Gdns. Holy 143 E2
Magnolia Pl. Tan 141 E4
Magnolia St. Wish 165 D3
Magnus Cres. Glasg 137 D2
Magnus Rd. Hous 111 E4
Mahon Ct. Muir 80 C1
Maid Morville Ave. Irvine 225 E4
Maidens Ave. Newt M 157 D3
Maidens. E Kil 159 E2
Maidland Rd. Glasg 135 E4
Mailerbeg Gdns. Muir 80 C2
Mailie Wlk. Holy 143 E2
Mailing Ave. Bish 78 B1
Mailings Rd. Kils 37 F2
Mainhor Rd. W Kil 190 B2
Main Rd. Ayr 236 C1
Main Rd. Card 48 A4
Main Rd. Cross 226 C3
Main Rd. Cumb 82 A4
Main Rd. Fen 213 D2
Main Rd. Fen 213 F2
Main Rd. Hurl 228 C4
Main Rd. John 112 B2
Main Rd. Kilb 149 D1
Main Rd. Lang 70 B4
Main Rd. Pais 113 E2
Main Rd. Ros 15 D2
Main Rd. Spring 220 C1
Main St. Air 14 B2
Main St. Alex 27 F2
Main St. Ayr 235 F1
Main St. B of W 110 B4
Main St. Bann 7 E1
Main St. Barr 134 B2

272

Main St. Beith Maxwell St. P Glasg

Main St. Beith 150 A1
Main St. Blac 107 E2
Main St. Bon 40 A3
Main St. Bonh 19 F1
Main St. Bonh 27 F3
Main St. Cald 85 D1
Main St. Cald 105 D2
Main St. Calder 123 E1
Main St. Cali 66 C3
Main St. Cam 6 B3
Main St. Camb 9 D4
Main St. Chap 123 F2
Main St. Cle 144 B1
Main St. Coat 122 B3
Main St. Cowie 12 B4
Main St. Cumb 62 A3
Main St. Dalry 191 E4
Main St. Dund 225 F1
Main St. Dunlop 195 D4
Main St. E Kil 159 F1
Main St E. Men 4 A3
Main St. Falk 41 F3
Main St. Falk 42 A4
Main St. Fall 8 C2
Main St. Glasg 117 F2
Main St. Glasg 120 B2
Main St. Glasg 135 F2
Main St. Glasg 138 A4
Main St. Glasg 139 D3
Main St. Glen 101 F3
Main St. Green 46 B2
Main St. Ham 161 F3
Main St. Hat 142 A3
Main St. Holy 143 D3
Main St. Hous 91 D1
Main St. How 130 C3
Main St. Irvine 220 B1
Main St. Kilb 170 A3
Main St. Kilm 222 B4
Main St. Kils 37 E2
Main St. Kils 60 B4
Main St. Kilw 207 F2
Main St. Lar 23 E1
Main St. Lennox 57 E4
Main St. Lennox 78 A4
Main St. Loch 129 E1
Main St. Miln 76 A4
Main St. Muir 80 B1
Main St. N Sau 5 E1
Main St. Neil 154 B4
Main St. New 166 A2
Main St. Newt M 157 F3
Main St. Plains 104 A1
Main St. Plea 12 B2
Main St. Pres 233 E2
Main St. Pres 236 B4
Main St. Sals 125 D1
Main St. Shew 225 E3
Main St. Shi 66 B3
Main St. Shot 147 D2
Main St. Slam 86 A4
Main St. Sten 23 F1
Main St. Sten 24 B2
Main St. Steven 206 B1
Main St. Stew 211 E4
Main St. Stir 7 D2
Main St. Sym 231 E2
Main St. Troon 230 A2
Main St. Tull 4 A1
Main St. Twe 59 F2
Main St. Udd 140 C3
Main St. Udd 141 D1
Main St. Udd 161 E3
Main St. W Kil 190 B3
Main St W. Men 3 F3
Main St. Wish 165 D2
Main St. Wish 186 B3
Mainhead Terr. Cumb 62 A3
Mainhill Ave. Glasg 120 B3
Mainhill Dr. Glasg 120 B3
Mainhill Pl. Glasg 120 B3
Mainhill Rd. Coat 120 C3
Mainholm Cres. Ayr 236 B1
Mainholm Rd. Ayr 236 B1
Mainholm Rd. Moss 239 F4
Mains Ave. Beith 150 A1
Mains Ave. Glasg 136 A1
Mains Ave. Helen 16 A2
Mains Ct. Lan 215 E3
Mains Dr. Ersk 73 E1
Mains Hill. Ersk 73 D1
Mains Pl. Hat 142 A2
Mains Rd. Beith 150 A1
Mains Rd. E Kil 159 F3
Mains Rd. East 127 F3
Mains River. Ersk 73 E1
Mains Wood. Ersk 73 E1
Mainscroft. Ersk 73 E1
Mainshill Ave. Ersk 73 D1
Mainshill Gdns. Ersk 73 D1
Mair Ave. Beith 191 F4
Mair St. Glasg 116 C3
Maitland Ave. Bann 7 E1
Maitland Bank. Lark 185 E2
Maitland Cres. Stir 7 D2
Maitland Ct. Helen 16 B1
Maitland Dr. Lennox 57 D1
Maitland Pl. Ren 94 A1
Maitland St. Glasg 97 D1
Maitland St. Helen 16 B1
Majors Loan. Falk 42 A2
Majors Pl. Falk 42 A2
Malcolm Ct. Stew 195 F1
Malcolm Dr. Sten 23 F2
Malcolm Pl. Helen 17 D1
Malcolm St. Mother 163 E3
Malin Pl. Glasg 118 C4
Mallaig Pl. Glasg 115 E4
Mallaig Rd. Glasg 115 F4
Mallaig Rd. P Glasg 68 C4
Mallaig Terr. Gour 44 C2
Mallard Cres. E Kil 180 A3
Mallard Cres. Green 45 D3
Mallard La. Green 45 D3
Mallard La. Udd 141 D2
Mallard Pl. E Kil 180 A3
Mallard Rd. Dunt 74 A3
Mallard Terr. E Kil 180 A3
Malleable Gdns. Mother 142 B1
Malletsheugh Rd. Newt M 156 A2
Malloch Cres. John 112 A1
Malloch Pl. E Kil 160 A1
Malloch St. Glasg 96 C3
Malov Ct. E Kil 180 C3
Malplaquet Ct. Car 188 A1
Maltbarns St. Glasg 97 D2
Malvaig La. Udd 161 E3
Malvern Ct. Glasg 118 A3
Malvern Way. Pais 113 E4
Mambeg Dr. Glasg 115 F4
Mamore Pl. Glasg 136 B3
Mamore St. Glasg 136 B3
Mamre Dr. Cali 66 C3
Manchester Dr. Glasg 96 A3
Mandela Ave. Falk 42 B4
Mandora Ct. Car 188 A1
Manitoba Cres. E Kil 159 D1
Mannering Ct. Glasg 136 B4
Mannering. E Kil 160 B2
Mannering Rd. Glasg 136 B4
Mannering Rd. Pais 132 C4
Mannering Way. Pais 112 C1
Mannfield Ave. Bon 39 F2
Mannofield. Bear 75 E2
Manor Ave. Kilmk 223 D2
Manor Cres. Gour 44 C4
Manor Cres. Tull 4 A1
Manor Dr. Aird 122 C4
Manor Gate. Newt M 156 C2
Manor Loan. B of A 3 D2
Manor Pk. Ham 162 B1
Manor Powis Cotts. B of A 3 D2
Manor Rd. Glasg 74 C1
Manor Rd. Glasg 95 F2
Manor Rd. Muir 100 C3
Manor Rd. Pais 112 C1
Manor St. Falk 42 A2
Manor View. Calder 123 D1
Manor View. Lark 185 E1
Manor Way. Glasg 138 B2
Manresa Pl. Glasg 97 D1
Manse Ave. Bear 75 F3
Manse Ave. Coat 121 E2
Manse Ave. Udd 141 D1
Manse Brae. Ash 200 A4
Manse Brae. Glasg 137 D3
Manse Brae. Rhu 15 E3
Manse Cres. Hous 91 D1
Manse Cres. Stir 7 D2
Manse Ct. Barr 134 B2
Manse Ct. Kils 60 B4
Manse Ct. Kilw 207 F2
Manse Ct. Law 187 D2
Manse Dr. Bonh 27 F4
Manse Garden's. Bonh 27 F4
Manse Pl. Aird 123 D4
Manse Pl. Bann 7 F1
Manse Pl. Falk 42 A2
Manse Pl. Slam 86 A4
Manse Rd. Bear 75 F3
Manse Rd. Coat 120 C3
Manse Rd. E Kil 158 B4
Manse Rd. Glasg 119 E2
Manse Rd. Glasg 120 C3
Manse Rd. Kils 60 C4
Manse Rd. Lan 214 C2
Manse Rd. Mother 163 F2
Manse Rd. Neil 154 C4
Manse Rd. New 166 A2
Manse Rd. O Kill 72 B4
Manse Rd. Sals 125 E1
Manse Rd. Shot 147 D2
Manse Rd. Stone 198 B1
Manse Rd. W Kil 190 B3
Manse St. Coat 121 F3
Manse St. Kil 89 F4
Manse St. Kilmk 228 A4
Manse St. Ren 94 B2
Manse St. Salt 216 C4
Manse View. Holy 143 F3
Mansefield Ave. Glasg 139 D2
Mansefield Cres. O Kil 73 D3
Mansefield Dr. Udd 140 C3
Mansefield Rd. Newt M 157 E3
Mansefield Terr. Dunlop 195 D4
Mansel St. Glasg 98 A3
Manseview. Lark 185 D1
Manseview Terr. Eagle 178 C3
Mansewood Ct. Glasg 120 B2
Mansewood Dr. Dumb 50 A3
Mansewood Rd. Glasg 136 A3
Mansfield Ave. N Sau 5 E1
Mansfield Cres. Newt M 157 E3
Mansfield Rd. Glasg 114 C4
Mansfield Rd. Ham 183 F3
Mansfield Rd. Hat 141 F2
Mansfield Rd. Loch 129 E2
Mansfield Rd. Newt M 157 F3
Mansfield Rd. Pres 236 A3
Mansfield St. Glasg 96 B1
Mansfield Way. Irvine 220 A3
Mansion Ave. P Glasg 69 D4
Mansion Ct. Glasg 139 D3
Mansion St. Glasg 97 E3
Mansion St. Glasg 139 D3
Mansionhouse Ave. Glasg 139 E4
Mansionhouse Dr. Glasg 119 E3
Mansionhouse Gdns. Glasg 136 C4
Mansionhouse Gr. Glasg 119 F2
Mansionhouse Rd. Falk 41 E3
Mansionhouse Rd. Glasg 119 F2
Mansionhouse Rd. Glasg 136 C4
Mansionhouse Rd. Pais 114 A3
Manson Ave. Pres 233 E1
Manson Pl. E Kil 181 D3
Manson Rd. Irvine 219 F2
Manuel Ave. Beith 171 D4
Manuel Ct. Irvine 225 E4
Manuel Ct. Kilb 170 A4
Manuel Terr. Irvine 225 E4
Maple Ave. Dumb 49 D3
Maple Ave. M of C 58 A3
Maple Ave. Newt M 156 B2
Maple Ave. Sten 23 F2
Maple Bank. Ham 162 C1
Maple Ct. All 10 A3
Maple Ct. Coat 121 F2
Maple Ct. Cumb 62 C3
Maple Dr. Ayr 239 E3
Maple Dr. Barr 155 E4
Maple Dr. Beith 150 A1
Maple Dr. Clyde 74 A3
Maple Dr. John 132 A4
Maple Dr. Kirk 79 D3
Maple Dr. Lark 185 D3
Maple Gr. E Kil 180 A3
Maple Gr. Troon 229 E2
Maple Pl. Bank 38 C1
Maple Pl. Duni 21 E2
Maple Pl. E Kil 180 A3
Maple Pl. Kilmk 227 E4
Maple Pl. Tan 141 E4
Maple Quadrant. Aird 123 E3
Maple Rd. Cumb 62 C3
Maple Rd. Glasg 116 A2
Maple Rd. Green 45 D2
Maple Rd. Holy 143 D3
Maple Terr. E Kil 180 A3
Maple Terr. Irvine 219 E2
Maple Way. Udd 161 E4
Mar Ave. Bishop 72 A2
Mar Dr. Bear 75 F4
Mar Gdns. Glasg 138 B2
Mar Pl. All 10 A4
Mar Pl. N Sau 5 E1
Mar Pl. Stir 7 D4
Mar St. All 10 A3
Marble Ave. Irvine 220 B1
March St. Glasg 116 C1
Marchbank Gdns. Pais 114 B2
Marchburn Ave. Pres 236 C4
Marchdyke Cres. Kilmk 227 F2
Marches The. Lan 215 D3
Marchfield Ave. Pais 113 F4
Marchfield. Bish 77 F2
Marchfield Quadrant. Ayr 236 A3
Marchfield Rd. Ayr 236 A3
Marchglen. Fish 5 F3
Marchglen Pl. Glasg 115 E4
Marchmont Ct. Hurl 228 C4
Marchmont Gdns. Bish 77 F1
Marchmont Rd. Ayr 238 C3
Marchmont Road La. Ayr 238 C4
Marchmont Terr. Glasg 96 B2
Marchside Ct. N Sau 5 E1
Mardale. E Kil 159 E2
Maree Ct. All 10 B3
Maree Dr. Cumb 82 A4
Maree Dr. Glasg 115 F2
Maree Gdns. Bish 78 A1
Maree Pl. Irvine 219 E4
Maree Rd. Pais 113 D1
Maree Way. Udd 161 E4
Maree Wlk. New 165 F3
Marfield St. Glasg 118 C3
Margaret Ave. Bank 39 D2
Margaret Ave. Sals 125 D1
Margaret Ct. Den 21 F1
Margaret Dr. Alex 27 E3
Margaret Dr. Bon 40 A3
Margaret Pl. Hat 141 F3
Margaret Rd. Bann 7 E1
Margaret Rd. Ham 162 A3
Margaret St. Coat 122 A2
Margaret St. Gour 44 C4
Margaret St. Green 45 E4
Margaret Terr. Sten 23 F2
Margaret's Pl. Lark 185 D2
Margaretta Bldgs. Glasg 137 D3
Margaretvale Dr. Lark 185 D1
Marguerite Ave. Kirk 79 E3
Marguerite Dr. Kirk 79 E3
Marguerite Gdns. Kirk 79 E3
Marguerite Gdns. Udd 141 D1
Marguerite Gr. Kirk 79 E3
Marguerite Pl. Ayr 239 E2
Marguerite Pl. M of C 58 A3
Marian Dr. Holy 143 E1
Marigold Ave. Mother 163 F4
Marigold Sq. Ayr 239 D2
Marigold Way. Car 201 F4
Marina Rd. Pres 236 A4
Marine Cres. Glasg 116 C3
Marine Dr. Shew 224 A3
Marine Gdns. Glasg 116 C3
Marine View Ct. Troon 229 E1
Mariner Ave. Falk 41 D3
Mariner Dr. Falk 41 D3
Mariner Gdns. Falk 41 E3
Mariner Rd. Falk 41 E3
Mariner St. Falk 41 D3
Mariscat Rd. Glasg 116 C1
Marjory Dr. Pais 114 A4
Marjory Rd. Ren 94 A1
Market Cl. Kils 60 B4
Market End. Lan 215 D2
Market Pl. Car 187 F1
Market Pl. Kil 89 E4
Market Pl. Kils 60 B4
Market Pl. Tan 141 E4
Market Rd. Car 187 F1
Market Rd. Kirk 80 A4
Market Rd. Tan 141 E4
Market Sq. Kils 60 B4
Market St. Aird 123 D4
Market St. Kils 60 B4
Market St. Tan 141 E4
Markethill Rd. E Kil 159 F2
Markethill Rd. E Kil 159 F3
Markethill Roundabout. E Kil 159 F2
Markinch Rd. P Glasg 68 C3
Marlborough Ave. Glasg 95 F2
Marlborough Dr. Stir 2 B2
Marlborough La N. Glasg 95 F2
Marlborough La S. Glasg 95 F2
Marlborough Pk. E Kil 180 A4
Marldon La. Glasg 95 F2
Marlepark. Ayr 239 D2
Marley Way. M of C 58 A3
Marlfield Gdns. Hat 142 A4
Marloch Ave. P Glasg 69 D3
Marlow St. Glasg 116 C3
Marlow Terr. Glasg 116 C2
Marmion Ave. Helen 25 D4
Marmion Cres. Mother 142 B1
Marmion Dr. Kirk 79 F4
Marmion Pl. Cumb 82 C4
Marmion Rd. Cumb 82 C4
Marmion Rd. Pais 132 C4
Marmion St. Falk 42 A4
Marne St. Glasg 118 A4
Marnoch Dr. Glen 101 E3
Marnoch Way. Muir 80 C1
Marnock Terr. Pais 114 A1
Marr Dr. Troon 229 E2
Marr's Wynd. Lan 215 E3
Marress Rd. Irvine 219 D2
Marress Roundabout. Irvine 219 D1
Marrswood Gn. Ham 162 A2
Marrwood Ave. Kirk 80 A3
Mars Rd. Gour 44 B1
Marschal Ct. Bann 7 E2
Marshall Gr. Ham 162 A2
Marshall La. Wish 165 D2
Marshall St. Coat 121 F2
Marshall St. Lark 185 D1
Marshall St. Wish 164 C1
Marshall's La. Pais 113 F2
Marshill. All 10 A3
Marsmount Rd. Pres 233 F1
Mart St. Glasg 117 E3
Martha St. Glasg 117 E4
Martin Ave. Bonh 28 A4
Martin Ave. Irvine 219 E3
Martin Cres. Glasg 120 B3
Martin Ct. Ham 162 B2
Martin Pl. Holy 143 E2
Martin Sq. Salt 206 A1
Martin St. Coat 122 B4
Martin St. Glasg 117 F2
Martinside. E Kil 180 C3
Martlet Dr. John 131 E4
Martyn St. Aird 122 C3
Martyrs Pl. Bish 98 A4
Marwick St. Glasg 118 A4
Mary Dr. Hat 141 F2
Mary Love Pl. Salt 206 A1
Mary Rae Rd. Hat 141 F2
Mary Sq. Coat 120 C3
Mary St. Green 45 E2
Mary St. Ham 162 B1
Mary St. John 112 A2
Mary St. Laur 42 C2
Mary St. P Glasg 47 D1
Mary St. Pais 113 F1
Mary Stevenson Dr. All 10 A4
Mary Young Pl. Newt M 157 F3
Maryborough Ave. Pres 236 A3
Maryborough Rd. Pres 236 A3
Maryfield Pl. Ayr 236 A2
Maryfield Pl. Falk 41 D2
Maryfield Rd. Ayr 236 A2
Maryhill Rd. Bear 76 A1
Maryhill Rd. Glasg 96 B3
Maryknowe Rd. Holy 143 E1
Maryland Dr. Glasg 115 F3
Maryland Gdns. Glasg 115 F3
Maryland Rd. Dumb 50 B3
Marypark Rd. Lang 70 A4
Maryston St. Glasg 98 B1
Maryville Ave. Glasg 136 B1
Maryville View. Tan 120 B1
Marywood Sq. Glasg 116 C1
Mashock Path. Car 201 D1
Mason La. Mother 163 F3
Mason St. Lark 185 E1
Mason St. Mother 163 F3
Masonfield Ave. Cumb 61 E1
Masonhill Pl. Ayr 239 E3
Masonhill Rd. Ayr 239 E3
Masterton St. Glasg 97 E2
Mather Terr. Laur 42 C2
Matherton Ave. Newt M 157 D3
Matheson Wlk. Bonh 27 F4
Mathew Smith Ave. Kilmk 227 F3
Mathie Cres. Gour 44 C3
Mathieson Rd. Glasg 118 B1
Mathieson St. Pais 114 A3
Matilda Rd. Glasg 116 C2
Matthew McWhirter Pl. Lark 185 D2
Matthew Pl. Kilw 207 F3
Mauchline Ave. Kirk 59 D
Mauchline Ct. Ham 161 E
Mauchline Ct. Kirk 59 D
Mauchline. E Kil 160 C2
Mauchline La. Gour 44 C2
Mauchline Rd. Hurl 228 C3
Mauchline St. Glasg 117 D2
Mauchline Terr. Gour 44 C2
Maukinfauld Ct. Glasg 118 B2
Maukinfauld Rd. Glasg 118 C2
Mauldslie Dr. Law 187 D3
Mauldslie Pl. Ash 199 F4
Mauldslie Rd. Car 187 D
Mauldslie Rd. Law 186 C
Mauldslie St. Coat 122 A3
Mauldslie St. Glasg 118 A2
Mauldslie St. Hat 142 A2
Maule Dr. Glasg 96 A1
Maunsheugh Rd. Fen 213 D2
Maurice Ave. Bann 7 E2
Mavis Bank. Bish 97 F4
Mavis Bank. Udd 161 E4
Mavis Rd. Green 45 D2
Mavisbank Ave. Shi 66 B3
Mavisbank Gdns. Glasg 116 C
Mavisbank Gdns. Hat 142 A
Mavisbank Rd. Glasg 116 B
Mavisbank St. Aird 122 C
Mavisbank St. New 166 B
Mavisbank Terr. John 111 F
Mavisbank Terr. Pais 113 F
Mavor Ave. E Kil 160 A
Mavor Roundabout. E Kil 159 F
Maxholm Rd. Kilmk 227 F
Maxton Ave. Barr 134 A
Maxton Cres. Alva 5 E
Maxton Cres. Wish 165 E
Maxton Terr. Glasg 138 C
Maxton Terr. Gour 44 C
Maxwell Ave. Bear 75 F
Maxwell Ave. Glasg 116 C
Maxwell Ave. Glasg 120 A
Maxwell Cres. Udd 161 E
Maxwell Ct. Beith 171 D
Maxwell Ct. Kilmk 223 E
Maxwell Dr. Ersk 72 C
Maxwell Dr. Glasg 116 B
Maxwell Dr. Glasg 120 A
Maxwell Gdns. Glasg 116 B
Maxwell Gdns. Hurl 228 C
Maxwell Gn. Irvine 220 A
Maxwell Gr. Glasg 116 B
Maxwell Oval. Glasg 116 C
Maxwell Path. Lark 185 E
Maxwell Pl. Coat 121 F
Maxwell Pl. Glasg 117 D
Maxwell Pl. Kils 36 B
Maxwell Pl. Steven 206 C
Maxwell Pl. Stir 7 D
Maxwell Rd. Bishop 72 A
Maxwell Rd. Glasg 117 D
Maxwell St. Clyde 73 F
Maxwell St. Glasg 117 E
Maxwell St. Glasg 117 E
Maxwell St. Glasg 120 A
Maxwell St. P Glasg 47 F

Maxwell St. Pais	113	F3
Maxwell Terr. Glasg	116	C2
Maxwellton Ave. E Kil	160	A2
Maxwellton Pl. E Kil	160	A2
Maxwellton Rd. E Kil	160	B2
Maxwellton Rd. P Glasg	68	C3
Maxwellton Rd. Pais	113	D2
Maxwellton St. Pais	113	E2
Maxwellton Rd. Glasg	98	B1
Maxwood Pl. Irvine	220	A3
May Gdns. Ham	162	B3
May Rd. Pais	133	F4
May St. Ham	162	B3
May Terr. Glasg	136	B2
May Terr. Glasg	137	D4
Maybank La. Glasg	117	D1
Maybank St. Glasg	117	D1
Mayberry Cres. Glasg	119	E3
Mayberry Gdns. Glasg	119	E3
Mayberry Gr. Glasg	119	E3
Mayberry Pl. Udd	161	E4
Maybole Cres. Newt M	157	D2
Maybole Gdns. Ham	161	E1
Maybole Gr. Newt M	157	D2
Maybole Pl. Coat	122	C2
Maybole Rd. Ayr	239	D2
Maybole Rd. P Glasg	68	C3
Mayfield Ave. Clarks	134	C3
Mayfield Ave. Hurl	228	C3
Mayfield Cres. How	130	C3
Mayfield Cres. Steven	206	B1
Mayfield Ct. How	130	C3
Mayfield Dr. How	130	C3
Mayfield Dr. Steven	206	B1
Mayfield Dr. Bank	39	D2
Mayfield Dr. How	130	C3
Mayfield Mews. Falk	41	F2
Mayfield Pl. Car	202	A4
Mayfield Pl. Salt	217	D4
Mayfield Rd. Ham	161	F2
Mayfield Rd. Salt	217	D4
Mayfield Rd. Salt	217	D4
Mayfield St. Glasg	96	C3
Mayfield St. Stir	7	D2
Mayne Ave. B of A	2	A3
Mayville St. Steven	206	B1
Mc Donald Ave. John	111	F1
Mc Laurin Cres. John	111	F1
Mc Lelland Dr. Plains	104	A1
Mc Phail St. Green	46	B2
McAdam Ct. Pres	236	B3
McAlister Rd. Alex	27	F3
McAlley Ct. B of A	1	C4
McAllister Ave. Aird	123	E4
McAllister Ct. Kilmar	227	F4
McAlpine St. Glasg	117	D4
McAlpine St. Wish	165	D1
McArdle Ave. Mother	163	E4
McArthur Pk Kirk	79	E4
McArthur St. Glasg	136	B4
McAslin Ct. Glasg	117	F4
McAslin St. Glasg	117	F4
McAuslan Pl. Helen	16	C1
McCall's Ave. Ayr	236	A1
McCallum Ave. Glasg	139	D4
McCallum Cres. Gour	44	C4
McCallum Ct. E Kil	159	D2
McCallum Gdns. Hat	141	F1
McCallum Gr. E Kil	159	D2
McCallum Pl. E Kil	159	D2
McCallum Rd. Lark	185	D1
McCASH Pl. Kirk	79	E4
McClue Ave. Ren	94	B2
McClue Rd. Ren	94	B2
McClurg Ct. Mother	163	F3
McColgan Pl. Ayr	236	B2
McColl Ave. Alex	27	E3
McColl Pl. Alex	27	E3
McConnell Rd. Loch	129	D1
McCormack Gdns. Holy	143	F2
McCracken Ave. Ren	94	A1
McCracken Dr. Tan	141	E4
McCreery St. Clyde	94	B4
McCulloch Ave. Tan	141	E3
McCulloch La. Alex	27	E4
McCulloch St. Glasg	116	C2
McDonald Cres. Clyde	94	B4
McDonald Dr. Irvine	219	D3
McDonald Pl. Holy	143	D3
McDonald Pl. Neil	154	C4
McDowall Ave. Aird	205	E1
McDowall Pl. Aird	205	E1
McEwan Gdns. E Kil	159	D2
McEwans Way. Stone	198	B1
McFarlane Rd. Bonh	28	A4
McFarlane St. Glasg	117	F3
McFarlane St. Pais	113	F3
McGavin Ave. Kilw	208	A2
McGavin Way. Kilw	207	E2
McGhee St. Clyde	74	A2
McGibney Dr. Irvine	219	E1
McGillivary Ave. Salt	205	F1
McGown Pl. Ham	162	A3
McGown St. Pais	113	D3
McGregor Ave. Aird	123	E4

McGregor Ave. Bonh	28	A4
McGregor Ave. Ren	94	A1
McGregor Ave. Steven	206	B1
McGregor Dr. Dumb	50	B2
Mcgregor Path. Glen	101	E3
McGregor Rd. Cumb	61	F1
McGregor St. Clyde	94	B4
McGregor St. Glasg	115	F3
McGregor St. Mother	164	B2
McGrigor Rd. Miln	54	C2
McGrigor Rd. Stir	7	D2
McHardy Cres. Beith	171	F2
McInnes Ct. Wish	165	D2
McInnes Pl. Wish	186	A4
McIntosh Ct. Bonh	28	A4
McIntosh Ct. Glasg	117	F4
McIntosh Quadrant. Hat	141	F1
McIntosh Way. Mother	163	E3
McIntyre Pl. Pais	113	F1
McIntyre Terr. Glasg	139	D3
McIsaac Rd. Salt	217	D4
McIver St. Glasg	139	F3
McKay Cres. John	112	A1
McKay Gr. Hat	141	F3
McKay Pl. E Kil	159	D2
McKechnie St. Glasg	116	A4
McKellar Ave. Aird	205	E1
McKenna Dr. Aird	122	C4
McKenzie Ave. Clyde	74	A2
McKenzie Dr. Bonh	19	F1
McKenzie St. Pais	113	E3
McKenzie's Cl. Lan	215	D2
McKerrell St. Pais	114	A3
McKillop Pl. Salt	205	F1
McKim Wlk. Alex	49	E4
McKinlay Ave. Bonh	20	A1
McKinlay Cres. Al	10	B3
McKinlay Cres. Irvine	219	D1
Mckinnon Pl. Salt	206	A1
McKnight Ave. Fen	213	F2
McLachlan Ave. Stir	7	D1
McLachlan St. Lar	23	E1
McLaren Ave. Ren	94	B1
Mclaren Ct. Glasg	136	A1
McLaren Ct. Lar	23	E1
McLaren Gr. E Kil	159	D2
Mclaren Pl. Glasg	136	C1
McLaren Ave. Stir	7	D2
McLaren Cres. Bonh	19	F1
McLean Dr. Hat	141	F1
McLean Dr. Irvine	225	E4
Mclean Gdns. Stone	198	C1
McLean Pl. Pais	113	E4
McLean St. Ayr	236	B1
McLees La. Mother	163	E4
McLelland Dr. Kirk	227	F4
McLennan St. Glasg	137	D4
McLeod Rd. Dumb	50	B2
McLeod St. Green	46	B2
McLuckie Pl. Kilw	207	E2
McLuckie Pk. Kilw	207	E2
McMillan Cres. Beith	171	D4
McMillan Dr. Ard	205	D2
McMillan Pl. Shew	224	C3
McMillan Rd. Wish	164	B1
McMillan Way. Law	186	C1
McNair St. Glasg	119	D3
McNaught Pl. Alex	27	E1
McNaught Pl. Kilm	222	A4
McNay Cres. Salt	206	A1
McNeil Ave. Clyde	74	C1
McNeil Pl. Wish	186	B4
McNeil St. Glasg	117	E4
McNeill Ave. Pres	233	E1
McPhail St. Glasg	117	F2
McPhater St. Glasg	97	D1
McPherson Cres. Chap	123	F1
McPherson Dr. Gour	44	B4
McPherson Dr. Udd	141	D2
McPherson La. Alex	27	E4
McPherson St. Hat	142	A2
McShannon Gr. Hat	142	A2
McVean Pl. Bank	39	D2
Meadow Ave. Irvine	219	E2
Meadow Ave. Udd	161	E3
Meadow Ct. Car	188	A4
Meadow Ct. Dumb	49	F3
Meadow La. N Sau	5	D1
Meadow La. Ren	94	B3
Meadow La. Udd	141	D1
Meadow Path. Chap	123	E3
Meadow Pl. Alva	5	D3
Meadow Pk. Ayr	239	D3
Meadow Pl. Stir	2	B1
Meadow Rd. Dumb	50	A2
Meadow Rd. Glasg	96	A1
Meadow Rd. Kilnc	202	A2
Meadow Rd. Mother	164	B1
Meadow St. Coat	122	A2
Meadow St. Falk	42	C2
Meadow View. Cumb	62	B2
Meadow View. Plains	104	A1
Meadow View. Newt M	156	B3
Meadowbank La. Pres	236	A4
Meadowbank La. Udd	140	C3
Meadowbank Pl. Newt M	156	B3

Meadowbank St. Dumb	49	F2
Meadowburn Ave. Kirk	79	F3
Meadowburn Ave. Newt M	156	B3
Meadowburn. Bish	78	A2
Meadowburn Rd. Wish	165	E2
Meadowfield Pl. New	166	B3
Meadowfoot Rd. W Kil	190	B2
Meadowforth Rd. Stir	7	E4
Meadowhead Ave. Muir	80	C1
Meadowhead Ave. Shew	224	C2
Meadowhead Rd. Mother	164	B2
Meadowhead Rd. Plains	103	F1
Meadowhead.		
Roundabout. Shew	224	C1
Meadowhill. Newt M	156	B3
Meadowhill St. Lark	185	D2
Meadowland Rd. B of A	2	A3
Meadowpark Dr. Ayr	239	D3
Meadowpark St. Glasg	118	A4
Meadows Ave. Lark	185	D2
Meadows The. Hous	91	F1
Meadows The. Kilw	207	E2
Meadowside Ave. John	112	B1
Meadowside. Beith	171	D4
Meadowside Gdns. Aird	123	E4
Meadowside. Ham	183	D3
Meadowside. Hurl	228	C4
Meadowside Pl. Aird	123	E4
Meadowside Rd. Kils	59	F3
Meadowside St. Glasg	96	A1
Meadowside St. Ren	94	B3
Meadowside. W Kil	190	B3
Meadowwell St. Glasg	119	D3
Meadside Ave. Kilbar	111	D2
Meadside Rd. Kilbar	111	D2
Mealkirk St. Dunt	74	B4
Mearns Ct. Ham	183	F4
Mearns Rd. Mother	163	E4
Mearns Rd. Newt M	156	B4
Mearns St. Green	45	F2
Mearns St. Green	45	F3
Mearns Way. Bish	78	B1
Mearnscroft Gdns. Newt M	156	C2
Mearnscroft Rd. Newt M	156	C2
Medine Ave. Beith	150	A1
Medine Ct. Beith	150	A1
Medlar Rd. Cumb	62	B1
Medrox Gdns. Cumb	81	F3
Medwin Ct. E Kil	179	F4
Medwin Gdns. E Kil	179	F4
Medwin St. Glasg	139	F3
Medwyn Pl. All	9	F3
Medwyn St. Glasg	95	E2
Medwyn St. Glasg	95	F1
Meek Pl. Glasg	139	D4
Meeks Rd. Falk	42	A3
Meetinghouse La. Pais	113	F3
Megan St. Glasg	117	F2
Meikle Ave. Ren	94	B1
Meikle Bin Brae. Lennox	57	F4
Meikle Cres. Gree	103	E4
Meikle Cres. Ham	183	E4
Meikle Ct. Stew	195	F1
Meikle Drumgray Rd. Gree	103	F4
Meikle Earnock Rd. Ham	183	D4
Meikle Kirk Rd. Ayr	239	D1
Meikle Rd. Coat	101	E1
Meikleham St. Kilb	126	A1
Meikleham St. Kirk	58	C1
Meikleriggs Dr. Pais	133	D1
Meiklem St. Hat	142	B3
Meiklerig Cres. Glasg	115	E1
Meiklerigs Dr. Pais	113	E4
Meiklewood Ave. Pres	233	E1
Meiklewood Gdns. Glasg	115	E3
Meiklewood Rd. Kilmk	222	C3
Melbourne Ave. Clyde	73	E3
Melbourne Ave. E Kil	180	B4
Melbourne Ct. Glasg	136	B2
Melbourne Gr. E Kil	180	A4
Melbourne Rd. Salt	216	C4
Melbourne St. Glasg	117	F3
Melbourne Terr. Salt	216	C4
Meldon Pl. Glasg	115	E3
Meldrum Gdns. Glasg	116	B1
Meldrum Mains. Glenm	102	C2
Meldrum St. Clyde	94	B4
Melford Ave. Glasg	136	B1
Melford Ave. Kirk	79	D2
Melford Ave. Shot	147	D2
Melford Gdns. John	111	E1
Melford Rd. Hat	141	F4
Melford Way. Pais	114	A4
Melfort Ave. Clyde	74	B1
Melfort Ave. Glasg	116	A2
Melfort Dr. Stir	7	D2
Melfort Path. New	165	F4
Melfort Quadrant. Holy	143	E2
Melfort Rd. Ham	161	F1
Mellerstain Dr. Glasg	94	C3
Mellock Gdns. Falk	41	F1
Melness Pl. Glasg	115	E4
Melrose Ave. Chap	123	E1
Melrose Ave. Coat	120	C3
Melrose Ave. Glasg	135	D4
Melrose Ave. Holy	143	D3
Melrose Ave. Lin	112	A3
Melrose Ave. Pais	113	D1
Melrose Cres. Wish	165	D3

Melrose Ct. Glasg	138	A4
Melrose Gdns. Glasg	96	C2
Melrose Gdns. Tan	120	C1
Melrose Gdns. Twe	59	F2
Melrose Pl. Coat	121	F4
Melrose Pl. Falk	42	A2
Melrose Pl. Lark	185	D1
Melrose Pl. Udd	140	B1
Melrose Rd. Cumb	62	B2
Melrose Rd. Glasg	68	C4
Melrose St. Glasg	97	D1
Melrose St. Ham	162	A3
Melrose Terr. E Kil	159	F2
Melrose Terr. Ham	162	A3
Melvaig Pl. Glasg	96	B3
Melvick Pl. Glasg	115	E4
Melville Ct. Glasg	117	E3
Melville Dr. Mother	163	F3
Melville Gdns. Bish	78	A1
Melville Pk. E Kil	160	A2
Melville Pl. B of A	2	A4
Melville Pl. Car	187	F1
Melville St. Falk	42	A3
Melville St. Lark	185	D1
Melville Terr. Stir	7	D3
Melvinhall Rd. Lan	215	D3
Memel St. Glasg	97	F3
Memus Ave. Glasg	136	A1
Menock Rd. Glasg	137	E3
Mennock La. Troon	229	F3
Mennock St. Cle	144	B1
Menock Rd. Glasg	137	E3
Menstrie Rd. Men	4	A3
Menteith Ave. Bish	78	A1
Menteith Ct. All	10	B3
Menteith Dr. Glasg	138	B1
Menteith Gdns. Bear	75	E4
Menteith Loan. Holy	143	D3
Menteith Pl. Glasg	138	B1
Menteith Rd. Mother	163	F4
Menzies Dr. Glasg	98	A3
Menzies Dr. Stir	2	C1
Menzies Pl. Glasg	98	A3
Menzies Rd. Glasg	98	A3
Merchant La. Glasg	117	E3
Merchants Ct. Kilbar	111	D2
Merchiston Ave. Falk	42	A4
Merchiston Ave. Lin	111	F3
Merchiston Gdns. Falk	42	A4
Merchiston Rd. Falk	42	A3
Merchiston St. Glasg	118	C4
Merchiston Terr. Falk	42	A4
Mercury La. Gour	44	B2
Meredith Dr. Stir	23	F2
Merino Rd. Green	45	F2
Merkins Ave. Dumb	50	A3
Merkland Ct. Glasg	96	A1
Merkland Ct. Kirk	79	D3
Merkland Dr. Kirk	79	D3
Merkland Dr. Falk	80	A4
Merkland Pl. Kirk	59	D1
Merkland St. Glasg	96	A1
Merkland Rd. Coat	101	E1
Merksworth Ave. Dairy	191	E4
Merksworth Way. Pais	113	F4
Merlewood Rd. W Kil	190	A2
Merlin Ave. Green	45	D3
Merlin Ave. Hat	142	A4
Merlin La. Green	45	D3
Merlin Way. Pais	114	A4
Merlinford Ave. Ren	94	C2
Merlinford Cres. Ren	94	C2
Merlinford Way. Ren	94	C2
Merrick Ave. Salt	233	D1
Merrick Ave. Troon	229	F2
Merrick Ct. Aird	103	D1
Merrick Gdns. Bear	75	E4
Merrick Gdns. Glasg	116	B3
Merrick Quadrant. Salt	183	F2
Merrick Pl. Irvine	220	A1
Merrick St. Sym	231	E2
Merrick Dr. Kilmk	228	A2
Merrick Terr. Tan	141	D3
Merrick View. Stew	195	F1
Merry Way. Glasg	138	A2
Merry St. Holy	143	D1
Merry St. Mother	163	F4
Merrytoun Ave. Glasg	136	B2
Merrycrest Ave. Glasg	136	B2
Merrycroft Ave. Glasg	135	B2
Merryflats. Twe	59	F2
Merrygreen Pl. Stew	195	F1
Merryland Ct. Glasg	116	B4
Merryland Pl. Glasg	116	B4
Merryland St. Glasg	116	A4
Merrylee Ave. P Glasg	68	C4
Merrylee Cres. Glasg	136	B3
Merrylee Pk. Glasg	136	B2
Merrylee Park Mews. Glasg	136	B3
Merrylee Rd. Glasg	136	C3
Merrylee Rd. Udd	161	E4
Merryston Ct. Coat	121	F3

Merrystone St. Coat	121	F4
Merryton Ave. Glasg	75	D2
Merryton Ave. Glasg	136	B2
Merryton Pl. Glasg	75	D2
Merryton Rd. Lark	184	C3
Merryton Rd. Mother	164	B1
Merryton St. Lark	184	C3
Merryvale Ave. Glasg	136	B2
Merryvale Pl. Glasg	136	B3
Merryvale Rd. Irvine	219	E1
Merryvale		
Roundabout. Irvine	219	E1
Merton Dr. Glasg	115	D3
Merville Cres. Cali	66	C3
Merville Terr. Cali	66	C3
Meryon Gdns. Glasg	119	E1
Meryon Rd. Glasg	119	E2
Metcalfe Pl. Shew	224	C3
Methil Rd. P Glasg	68	C3
Methil St. Glasg	95	E2
Methlan Pk. Dumb	49	E1
Methuen Rd. Ren	93	F1
Methuen Rd. Ren	114	A4
Methven Ave. Bear	76	A3
Methven Ave. Kilmk	227	F2
Methven Pl. E Kil	159	E1
Methven Pl. Kilmk	227	F2
Methven Rd. Newt M	157	D4
Methven St. Clyde	73	F2
Methven St. Glasg	118	B2
Metropole La. Glasg	117	E3
Mews La. Ayr	238	C4
Mews La. Green	45	E4
Mews La. Klimk	227	F4
Mews La. Pais	113	F4
Mharie Pl. Bonh	27	F1
Michael		
McParland Dr. Lennox	78	A4
Michael Terr. Chap	123	F1
Micklehouse Oval. Glasg	120	A3
Micklehouse Pl. Glasg	120	A3
Micklehouse Rd. Glasg	120	A3
Micklehouse Wynd. Glasg	120	A3
Mid Ave. P Glasg	68	C4
Mid Barrwood Rd. Kils	60	C4
Mid Carbarns. Wish	164	B1
Mid Dykes Rd. Salt	205	F1
Mid Pk. E Kil	180	C4
Mid Rd. Beith	150	A1
Mid Rd. Cumb	82	C3
Mid Rd. Eagle	178	B3
Mid Rig. Irvine	220	A2
Mid-Loan St. Car	201	F2
Mid-Wharf St. Glasg	97	E1
Midas Pl. Holy	142	C3
Midcroft Ave. Glasg	137	F3
Midcroft. Bish	77	F2
Middle Pk. Pais	113	E1
Middle Ward St. Dunt	74	B4
Middlefield. E Kil	180	C3
Middlefield Rd. Falk	42	B3
Middlehouse Ct. Car	187	E1
Middlemass Ct. Falk	42	A3
Middlemass Dr. Kilmk	228	A4
Middlemuir Ave. Kirk	79	E3
Middlemuir Rd. Kirk	79	E3
Middlemuir Rd. Stir	7	E3
Middlepart. Salt	206	A1
Middlepart. Steven	206	B1
Middlepenny Pl. Lang	70	A4
Middlepenny Rd. Lang	70	A4
Middlerigg Rd. Cumb	61	F1
Middleton Ave. Glasg	116	C3
Middleton Cres. Pais	113	D3
Middleton Dr. Helen	25	C4
Middleton Dr. Mili	55	E1
Middleton Pk. Irvine	220	A2
Middleton Rd. Lin	112	B3
Middleton Rd. Pais	113	D3
Middleton St. Alex	27	E3
Middleton St. Glasg	116	B3
Middleton. Men	4	A3
Middleton Pk. Irvine	220	A2
Middleton Rd. Irvine	220	A2
Midland Dr. Glasg	137	D4
Midland St. Glasg	117	D3
Midlem Dr. Glasg	115	E3
Midlem Oval. Glasg	115	E3
Midlock St. Glasg	116	B3
Midlothian Dr. Glasg	136	B1
Midthorn Cres. Falk	42	C3
Midton Ave. Pres	236	A4
Midton Ave. Pres	233	E4
Midton Pl. Hour	44	A2
Midton Rd. How	131	D3
Midton Rd. Kilmk	227	F1
Midton Rd. Pres	236	B4
Midton St. Glasg	97	F2
Midton. Men	3	F3
Migvie Pl. Glasg	96	B3
Milford. E Kil	180	A4
Milford St. Glasg	119	D4
Milgarholm Ave. Irvine	219	D2
Milgarholm		
Roundabout. Irvine	219	E1
Mill Ave. Kilmk	222	A3
Mill Brae. Ayr	239	D4
Mill Brae. B of W	110	B4
Mill Brae Ct. Coat	121	E3

Mill Cres. Glasg 117 F2
Mill Cres. Irvine 219 F2
Mill Cres. Lennox 57 E1
Mill Ct. Glasg 138 A4
Mill Ct. Ham 162 B1
Mill Ct. Kilmk 228 A4
Mill Gr. Ham 162 B1
Mill Hill. Cam 6 B3
Mill Loan. Aird 123 D4
Mill of Gryffe Rd. B of W 110 B4
Mill Pk. Dalry 191 E4
Mill Pk. Ham 162 B1
Mill Pl. Lin 112 A3
Mill Rd. Aird 103 D1
Mill Rd. All 10 A3
Mill Rd. Cam 6 B3
Mill Rd. Car 187 F1
Mill Rd. Card 26 A1
Mill Rd. Cle 145 F1
Mill Rd. Clyde 94 B4
Mill Rd. East 127 F3
Mill Rd. Glasg 139 E3
Mill Rd. Gree 63 F3
Mill Rd. Ham 162 B1
Mill Rd. Irvine 219 F1
Mill Rd. Kilb 149 D1
Mill Rd. Kils 37 E2
Mill Rd. Kils 59 F4
Mill Rd. Mother 163 F4
Mill Rd. New 166 C3
Mill Rd. Sten 24 A2
Mill Rd. Udd 141 D1
Mill Rig. E Kil 180 B2
Mill Rise. Kirk 79 E2
Mill St. All 10 A3
Mill St. Ayr 239 D4
Mill St. Cald 104 C3
Mill St. Glasg 117 F2
Mill St. Glasg 138 A3
Mill St. Green 45 F2
Mill St. Kilmk 227 F4
Mill St. Pais 113 F2
Mill St. Stone 198 C1
Mill Way. Kirk 80 A4
Mill Wynd. Ayr 238 C4
Millands Ave. Udd 140 B1
Millar Pl. Bon 40 A2
Millar Pl. Stir 2 B1
Millar St. Coat 217 D4
Millar St. Green 46 A1
Millar St. Pais 113 F3
Millar St. Stone 198 C1
Millar Terr. Glasg 118 A1
Millarbank St. Glasg 97 F2
Millars Pl. Kirk 79 E2
Millars Wynd. N Sau 5 E1
Millarston Ave. Pais 113 D2
Millarston Dr. Pais 113 D2
Millbank Ave. Hat 142 B2
Millbank Rd. P Glasg 68 B4
Millbank Rd. Wish 164 C1
Millbeg Cres. Glasg 119 F3
Millbeg Pl. Glasg 119 F3
Millbrae Ave. Muir 100 B4
Millbrae Cres. Clyde 94 B4
Millbrae Cres. Glasg 136 C4
Millbrae Ct. Glasg 136 C4
Millbrae Gdns. Glasg 136 C4
Millbrae Rd. Glasg 136 C4
Millbrix Ave. Glasg 95 D3
Millbrook. E Kil 159 D1
Millbrook Pl. Men 3 F3
Millburn Ave. Clyde 94 C4
Millburn Ave. Glasg 138 A3
Millburn Ave. Ran 94 C2
Millburn Cres. Dumb 50 A2
Millburn Ct. E Kil 179 F4
Millburn Dr. Kil 89 D4
Millburn Dr. Ren 94 C2
Millburn Gdns. E Kil 179 F4
Millburn La. Lark 185 E1
Millburn Rd. Alex 27 E2
Millburn Rd. Ash 186 A1
Millburn Rd. Dumb 50 A2
Millburn Rd. P Glasg 68 B4
Millburn Rd. Ren 94 B2
Millburn St. Falk 42 B3
Millburn St. Glasg 98 A1
Millburn St. Lennox 57 F4
Millburn St. Mother 163 F4
Millburn Terr. Irvine 220 A3
Millburn Way. E Kil 179 F4
Millburn Way. Ren 94 C2
Millcroft Rd. Cumb 62 A1
Millcroft Rd. Cumb 62 A1
Millcroft Rd. Glenm 82 C2
Millcroft Rd. Glenm 83 D2
Milldown Pl. Irvine 220 B1
Miller Ct. Dumb 50 A2
Miller Field Pl. Ham 162 C1
Miller Pl. Air 14 C2
Miller Pl. Ard 205 D2
Miller Pl. East 127 F3
Miller Rd. Ayr 238 C4
Miller Rd. Bonh 27 F4
Miller St. Car 188 A1

Miller St. Clyde 74 A1
Miller St. Coat 122 A3
Miller St. Dumb 50 A2
Miller St. East 127 F3
Miller St. Glasg 117 E4
Miller St. Ham 162 C2
Miller St. John 112 A2
Miller St. Lark 185 D2
Miller St. Wish 165 D2
Miller's Pl. Aird 123 D4
Millerfield Pl. Glasg 118 A2
Millerfield Rd. Glasg 118 A2
Millerslea Gdns. Helen 16 C1
Millersneuk Ave. Klrk 79 E2
Millersneuk Cres. Stepps 99 D3
Millersneuk Rd. Klrk 79 E2
Millerston St. Glasg 118 A3
Millfield Ave. Ersk 72 C1
Millfield Ave. Mother 163 F4
Millfield Cres. Ersk 73 D1
Millfield Dr. Ersk 73 D1
Millfield Gdns. Ersk 72 C1
Millfield Hill. Ersk 72 C1
Millfield La. Ersk 72 C1
Millfield Meadows. Ersk 72 C1
Millfield Pl. Ersk 72 C1
Millfield View. Ersk 72 C1
Millfield Wlk. Ersk 73 D1
Millfield Wynd. Ersk 72 C1
Millflats St. Falk 24 A1
Millford Dr. Lin 112 A3
Millgary La. Glasg 96 C2
Millgate Ave. Udd 140 C4
Millgate Ct. Udd 140 C4
Millgate Rd. Ham 162 B1
Millglen Pl. Ard 205 E2
Millhall Rd. Eagle 179 E2
Millhall Rd. Stir 7 E3
Millheugh Brae. Lark 184 C1
Millheugh. Lark 184 C1
Millheugh Pl. Udd 161 E3
Millheugh Rd. Stone 198 C3
Millhill Ave. Kilm 222 B4
Millhill Terr. Kilmk 222 C2
Millholm Rd. Glasg 137 D2
Millhouse Cres. Glasg 96 B4
Millhouse Dr. Glasg 96 B4
Millichen Rd. Glasg 76 C3
Millig St. Helen 16 B2
Milliken Dr. Kilbar 111 E1
Milliken Park Rd. John 111 E1
Milliken Rd. Kilbar 111 E1
Millport Ave. Glasg 137 E4
Millport Rd. P Glasg 68 C3
Millroad Dr. Glasg 117 F3
Millroad Gdns. Glasg 117 F3
Millroad St. Glasg 117 F3
Millrock Ct. Troon 229 E2
Millstream Cres. Cald 105 D2
Millview. Barr 134 B2
Millview Pl. Glasg 135 D2
Millview Terr. Neil 154 B4
Millwood St. Glasg 136 C4
Millbank Ave. Udd 118 A4
Milncroft Pl. Glasg 99 D1
Milncroft Rd. Glasg 99 D1
Milndavie Cres. Strath 31 E2
Milndavie Rd. Strath 31 E1
Milnepark Rd. Bann 11 F4
Milner La. Glasg 95 F3
Milner Rd. Glasg 95 F3
Milngavie Rd. Bear 75 F2
Milngavie Rd. Bear 75 F4
Milngavie Rd. Strath 31 E1
Milnpark Gdns. Glasg 116 C3
Milnpark St. Glasg 116 C3
Milnwood Dr. Hat 142 B2
Milnwood Dr. Mother 142 B2
Milovaig Ave. Glasg 76 B1
Milovaig St. Glasg 76 B1
Milrig Rd. Glasg 138 A4
Milton Ave. Glasg 138 C3
Milton Ave. Kilmk 223 E3
Milton Brae. Dumb 50 C1
Milton Brae. Stir 7 D1
Milton Cl. Duni 21 E2
Milton Cres. Bann 7 E1
Milton Cres. Irvine 220 B1
Milton Ct. Dumb 50 C1
Milton Ct. Irvine 220 B1
Milton Douglas Rd. Dunt 74 A1
Milton Dr. Bish 97 F4
Milton Dr. Kilmk 223 E3
Milton Eas. Bonh 27 F3
Milton Gdns. Bann 7 D1
Milton Gdns. Tan 140 C4
Milton Hill. Dumb 50 C1
Milton Mains Rd. Clyde 74 A1
Milton Pk. Ayr 239 D2
Milton Pk. Kilb 149 D1
Milton Pl. Duni 21 E2
Milton Quadrant. Kilb 149 D2
Milton Rd. Bann 7 E1
Milton Rd. Car 201 E4

Milton Rd. E Kil 159 D1
Milton Rd. Hurl 223 F1
Milton Rd. Irvine 220 B1
Milton Rd. Kilb 149 D2
Milton Rd. Kilmk 228 B4
Milton Rd. Kirk 58 B1
Milton Rd. Lennox 57 F4
Milton Rd. P Glasg 68 C3
Milton Row. Duni 21 F2
Milton St. Aird 123 D4
Milton St. Car 187 F1
Milton St. Glasg 97 E1
Milton St. Ham 162 A2
Milton St. Mother 163 F4
Milton Terr. Bann 7 D1
Milton Terr. Ham 162 A3
Milton View. Cross 226 C3
Milverton Ave. Bear 75 E3
Milverton Rd. Glasg 136 A1
Mimosa Rd. B of W 110 B4
Minard Rd. Glasg 116 C1
Minard Rd. P Glasg 68 C4
Minard Rd. Shot 146 B3
Minard Way. Tan 141 D4
Minch Way. Aird 123 E3
Mincher Cres. Mother 163 F2
Mine Rd. B of A 2 A4
Minella Gdns. Hat 142 A4
Minerva La. Gour 44 B2
Minerva St. Glasg 116 C4
Minerva Terr. Gour 44 B2
Minerva Way. Glasg 116 C4
Mingarry La. Glasg 96 C2
Mingarry St. Glasg 96 C2
Mingulay Cres. Glasg 97 E4
Mingulay Pl. Bish 97 F4
Mingulay St. Glasg 97 E4
Minmoir Rd. Glasg 134 C4
Minister Wik. Coat 120 C3
Minstrel Rd. Glasg 75 E1
Minthill Pl. East 127 E3
Minto Ave. Glasg 138 B2
Minto Cres. Glasg 115 F3
Minto Ct. Alva 5 D3
Minto Dr. Glasg 75 E1
Minto Pk. Wish 165 E3
Minto St. Glasg 115 F3
Minto St. Green 45 E2
Minto St. Glasg 97 D3
Mirren Dr. Dunt 73 F4
Mirren's Shore. P Glasg 47 E1
Mirrlees Dr. Glasg 96 B2
Mirrlees La. Glasg 96 B2
Misk Knowes. Steven 217 F3
Mission La. Falk 42 A2
Mitchell Ave. Glasg 139 F3
Mitchell Ave. Ren 94 A1
Mitchell Ct. Kilmk 228 A4
Mitchell Dr. Card 48 A3
Mitchell Dr. Glasg 138 A3
Mitchell Dr. Miln 55 E1
Mitchell Hill Rd. Glasg 137 F1
Mitchell La. Glasg 117 D4
Mitchell Pl. Falk 41 F1
Mitchell Pl. Salt 205 F1
Mitchell Rd. Cumb 62 A2
Mitchell St. Aird 122 C4
Mitchell St. Beith 150 B1
Mitchell St. Coat 121 E3
Mitchell St. Glasg 117 D4
Mitchell St. Green 46 C1
Mitchell Way. Alex 27 F1
Mitchison Rd. Cumb 62 A2
Mitre Ct. Glasg 95 F2
Mitre La. Glasg 95 F3
Mitre La W. Glasg 95 E2
Mitre Rd. Glasg 95 F2
Moat Ave. Glasg 95 E3
Mochrum Ct. Pres 236 B3
Mochrum Rd. Glasg 136 C3
Modan Rd. Stir 7 D2
Moffat Ave. Sten 24 B2
Moffat Ct. E Kil 179 F4
Moffat Gdns. E Kil 179 F4
Moffat Pl. Coat 122 C2
Moffat Pl. E Kil 179 F4
Moffat Pl. Udd 140 B1
Moffat Rd. Aird 123 F4
Moffat St. Glasg 117 E2
Moffat St. Green 46 B2
Moffat View. Plains 104 A2
Moffathill. Chap 124 A3
Mogarth Ave. Pais 132 C4
Moidart Ave. Ren 94 A2
Moidart Cres. Glasg 115 F3
Moidart Ct. Barr 134 A2
Moidart Gdns. Kirk 80 A4
Moidart Gdns. Newt M 156 C3
Moidart Pl. Glasg 115 F3
Moidart Rd. Glasg 115 F3
Moidart Rd. P Glasg 68 C4
Moir St. All 10 A4
Moir St. Glasg 117 F3
Molendinar St. Glasg 117 F3
Molendinar Terr. Neil 154 B3
Mollanbowie Rd. Bonh 19 F1
Mollins Ct. Cumb 81 E3

Mollins Rd. Cumb 81 E3
Mollinsburn Rd. Glenm 81 F1
Mollinsburn Rd. Glenm 102 B3
Mollinsburn St. Glasg 97 F2
Mollison Ave. East 127 F3
Monach Gdns. Irvine 225 D4
Monach Rd. Glasg 119 E4
Monach Rd. P Glasg 69 D4
Monaebrook Pl. Helen 25 C4
Monar Dr. Glasg 97 D2
Monar Pl. Glasg 97 D2
Monar Way. New 165 F3
Monart Pl. Glasg 96 C2
Moncks Rd. Falk 42 B2
Moncreiff Gdns. Klrk 79 E3
Moncreiff Ave. Klrk 79 E3
Moncrieff St. Pais 113 F3
Moncrieffe Rd. Chap 123 E2
Moness Dr. Glasg 115 F2
Moneiburgh Cres. Kils 36 C1
Monieburgh Rd. Kils 36 C1
Monikie Gdns. Bish 78 B1
Monkcastle Dr. Glasg 139 D3
Monkland Ave. Klrk 79 E3
Monkland La. Coat 121 F2
Monkland St. Aird 123 D4
Monkland Terr. Glen 101 E3
Monkland View. Calder 123 D1
Monkland View Cres. Coat 121 D3
Monkland View. Tan 121 D1
Monklands. Troon 229 F4
Monkreddan Cres. Kilw 207 E3
Monks La. Car 201 F2
Monks Rd. Aird 123 E2
Monksbridge Ave. Glasg 75 F1
Monkscourt Ave. Aird 122 C4
Monkscroft Ave. Glasg 96 A1
Monkscroft Ct. Glasg 96 A1
Monkscroft Gdns. Glasg 96 A1
Monkton Ct. Pres 233 E1
Monkton Dr. Glasg 75 E1
Monkton Gdns. Newt M 157 D2
Monkton Pl. P Glasg 68 B4
Monkton Rd. Pres 233 E1
Monkton Rd. Pres 233 E1
Monktonhall Pl. Troon 233 D4
Monkwood Pl. Ayr 239 D1
Monmouth Ave. Glasg 96 A3
Monreith Ave. Bear 75 E1
Monreith Rd E. Glasg 137 D3
Monreith Rd. Glasg 136 C3
Monroe Dr. Tan 120 C1
Monroe Pl. Tan 120 C1
Montague La. Glasg 96 A2
Montague St. Glasg 96 C1
Montclair Pl. Lin 112 A3
Monteith Dr. Glasg 158 A4
Monteith Gdns. Glasg 157 F4
Monteith Pl. Glasg 117 F3
Monteith Pl. Udd 161 F4
Monteith Row. Glasg 117 F3
Monteith Wlk. Shot 146 C3
Montfode Ct. Ard 205 E2
Montfode Dr. Ard 205 D2
Montford Ave. Glasg 137 D4
Montford Ave. Ruth 137 F4
Montfort Pl. Falk 42 A2
Montgomerie Cres. Salt 216 C4
Montgomerie Pier Rd. Ard 205 D1
Montgomerie Rd. Pres 233 D1
Montgomerie Rd. Salt 216 C4
Montgomerie St. Ard 205 D1
Montgomerie St. P Glasg 47 E1
Montgomerie Terr. Ayr 235 F1
Montgomery Ave. Coat 121 E4
Montgomery Ave. Pais 114 A4
Montgomery Cres. Wish 185 E4
Montgomery Dr. Eagle 178 C2
Montgomery Dr. Kilb 149 D1
Montgomery Dr. Kilbar 111 D2
Montgomery Pl. E Kil 159 F1
Montgomery Pl. Kilmk 222 C1
Montgomery Pl. Lark 185 D1
Montgomery Rd. Pais 114 A4
Montgomery Sq. Eagle 178 C2
Montgomery St. E Kil 159 F1
Montgomery St. Falk 42 C3
Montgomery St. Glasg 139 F3
Montgomery St. Irvine 219 D1
Montgomery St. Kilmk 222 C1
Montgomery St. Lark 185 D1
Montgomery Terr. M of C 58 B3
Montgomery Way. Stir 2 C2
Montgomeryfield. Irvine 225 D4
Montgreenan View. Kilw 207 F2
Montraive St. Glasg 118 B1

Montrave St. Glasg 115 E2
Montreal Pk. E Kil 159 E1
Montrose Ave. Glasg 119 D3
Montrose Ave. Glasg 119 E1
Montrose Ave. P Glasg 68 C3
Montrose Dr. Bear 75 F4
Montrose Gdns. Bla 140 B3
Montrose Gdns. Miln 55 D2
Montrose Gdns. Udd 140 B3
Montrose Rd. Lin 112 A3
Montrose Rd. Pais 132 C4
Montrose St. Clyde 74 B1
Montrose St. Glasg 117 E4
Montrose St. Mother 142 C2
Montrose Terr. B of W 110 B4
Montrose Terr. Bish 98 B1
Monument Cres. Pres 233 F1
Monument Rd. Ayr 238 C2
Monymusk Gdns. Bish 78 B1
Monymusk Pl. Glasg 74 C3
Moodie Ct. Kilmk 227 F3
Moodiesburn St. Glasg 98 C1
Moor Park Cres. Pres 236 B3
Moor Park Pl. Pres 236 B3
Moor Pk. Pres 236 B2
Moor Pl. Pres 236 B2
Moor Rd. Eagle 178 B2
Moor Rd. Lan 202 C1
Moor Rd. Miln 55 D1
Moor Rd. Pres 236 B3
Moor Rd. Strath 31 E1
Moorburn Ave. Glasg 136 B1
Moorburn Pl. Lin 111 F3
Moorcroft Rd. Newt M 156 B2
Moore Dr. Bear 75 F2
Moore Dr. Helen 25 D4
Moore Gdns. Ham 183 F4
Moore St. Glasg 117 F3
Moore St. Holy 143 D2
Moorfield Ave. Kilmk 227 E3
Moorfield Ave. P Glasg 68 B4
Moorfield Ind Est. Cross 227 D4
Moorfield La. Gour 44 B4
Moorfield Rd. Glasg 226 B3
Moorfield Rd. Gour 44 B4
Moorfield Rd. Pres 236 B4
Moorfield Rd. Udd 161 E3
Moorfield
  Roundabout. Cross 227 D4
Moorfoot Ave. Glasg 136 A1
Moorfoot Ave. Pais 113 E1
Moorfoot. Bish 78 B1
Moorfoot Dr. Gour 44 B3
Moorfoot Dr. Wish 164 C2
Moorfoot Path. Pais 133 E4
Moorfoot Pl. Irvine 220 A2
Moorfoot St. Glasg 118 C3
Moorfoot Way. Bear 75 E4
Moorfoot Way. Irvine 220 A2
Moorhill Rd. Newt M 156 B2
Moorhouse Ave. Glasg 94 C3
Moorhouse Ave. Pais 113 D1
Moorhouse St. Barr 134 B1
Moorpark Ave. Muir 100 B4
Moorpark Dr. Pais 217 E4
Moorpark Pl. Steven 217 E4
Moorpark Rd E. Steven 217 F4
Moorpark Rd W. Steven 217 E4
Moorpark Sq. Ren 94 A1
Moorside St. Car 188 A1
Morag Ave. Udd 140 B1
Moraine Ave. Glasg 95 D3
Moraine Cres. Glasg 75 D1
Moraine Dr. Glasg 75 D1
Moraine Dr. Newt M 157 E4
Moraine Pl. Glasg 75 D1
Morar Ave. Clyde 74 A2
Morar Ave. Card 102 C1
Morar Cres. Bear 77 E3
Morar Cres. Bish 72 B1
Morar Cres. Clyde 74 A2
Morar Cres. Coat 101 E1
Morar Ct. Clyde 74 A2
Morar Ct. Cumb 82 A4
Morar Ct. Ham 162 A1
Morar Dr. Bear 76 A2
Morar Dr. Clyde 74 A2
Morar Dr. Cumb 82 A4
Morar Dr. Falk 24 C2
Morar Dr. Lin 112 A3
Morar Dr. Pais 113 D1
Morar Dr. Ruth 137 F2
Morar Pl. E Kil 159 F2
Morar Pl. Irvine 219 E3
Morar Pl. Newt M 156 B4
Morar Pl. Ren 94 A2
Morar Rd. Clyde 74 A2
Morar Rd. P Glasg 68 C4
Morar Rd. Wish 165 D1
Morar St. Wish 165 D1
Morar Terr. Glasg 138 B2
Morar Terr. Udd 141 E4
Morar Way. Holy 143 D2
Morar Way. Shot 147 D2
Moravia Ave. Udd 141 D2

Moray Ave. Aird 123 D3
Moray Dr. Glasg 157 F4
Moray Dr. Lennox 57 D1
Moray Gate. Udd 140 C2
Moray Gdns. Cumb 61 F3
Moray Gdns. Glasg 157 F4
Moray Pl. Bish 78 B1
Moray Pl. Glasg 116 C1
Moray Pl. Kirk 59 D1
Moray Pl. Lin 112 A3
Moray Pl. Muir 100 B4
Moray Pl. Udd 161 E3
Moray Quadrant. Hat 142 A3
Moray Rd. P Glasg 47 E1
Moray Way. Holy 143 D3
Mordaunt St. Glasg 118 A2
Moredun Cres. Glasg 119 E4
Moredun Rd. Pais 113 D1
Moredun St. Glasg 119 E4
Morefield Rd. Glasg 115 E4
Morgan Ave. Aird 123 D3
Morgan Mews. Glasg 117 D2
Morgan St. Ham 162 B1
Morgan St. Lark 184 C2
Morina Gdns. Glasg 135 E2
Morion Rd. Glasg 95 E4
Moriston Ct. New 165 F3
Morland. E Kil 160 B2
Morley Cres. Stir 7 D2
Morley St. Glasg 137 D4
Morna La. Glasg 95 F1
Mornay Way. Shot 146 B2
Morningside Rd. New 166 B2
Morningside St. Glasg 118 C4
Morrin Path. Glasg 97 F2
Morrin St. Glasg 97 F2
Morris Cres. Hurl 228 C3
Morris Cres. Udd 161 E4
Morris La. Kilmk 223 D1
Morris

Moodie Ave. Steven 217 F4
Morris Rd. Pres 233 E1
Morris St. Green 46 B2
Morris St. Ham 162 B1
Morris St. Lark 185 E1
Morris Terr. Stir 7 D4
Morrison Ave. Kilmk 160 B2
Morrishall Dr. Beith 171 D4
Morrison Ave. Bon 39 F3
Morrison Ave. Steven 206 C1
Morrison Dr. Bann 7 E1
Morrison Dr. Lennox 57 F4
Morrison Gdns. Ayr 239 D3
Morton Pl. Kilmk 222 C1
Morton Rd. Ayr 239 D3
Morton St. Glasg 211 E4
Morton St. Mother 163 F4
Morven Ave. Bish 78 B1
Morven Ave. Kilmk 222 C2
Morven Cres. Pais 133 E4
Morven Ave. Udd 140 B1
Morven Cres. Troon 229 E2
Morven Ct. Aird 103 D1
Morven Ct. Falk 42 B1
Morven Dr. Lin 112 A3
Morven Dr. Newt M 157 E4
Morven Rd. Stone 229 E2
Morven Gdns. Tan 140 C4
Morven La. Udd 140 B1
Morven Rd. Bear 75 F3
Morven Rd. Glasg 138 C2
Morven St. Coat 122 A4
Morven St. Glasg 115 F3
Morven Way. Udd 141 D2
Morville Cres. Kilw 207 F3
Mosesfield St. Glasg 97 F3
Moss Ave. Cald 105 D3
Moss Ave. Lin 112 A3
Moss Dr. Barr 134 A3
Moss Dr. Inch 93 D4
Moss Dr. Shew 224 C3
Moss Heights Ave. Glasg .. 115 E3
Moss Knowe. Cumb 62 B1
Moss Path. Glasg 119 F2
Moss Rd. Aird 123 D3
Moss Rd. Auld 180 B2
Moss Rd. B of W 110 C4
Moss Rd. Coat 25 E3
Moss Rd. Cumb 62 C2
Moss Rd. Fall 8 B2
Moss Rd. Glasg 115 E4
Moss Rd. Kil 89 E4
Moss Rd. Kil 79 D3
Moss Rd. Kirk 60 A4
Moss Rd. Lin 112 B4
Moss Rd. Muir 100 B4
Moss Rd. P Glasg 68 C4

Moss Rd. Wish 165 F2
Moss Side Ave. Aird 122 C4
Moss St. Pais 113 F3
Moss-Side Ave. Car 187 E1
Moss-Side Rd. Glasg 116 C1
Mossacre Rd. Wish 165 F2
Mossband La. Shot 146 C3
Mossbank Ave. Glasg 96 C2
Mossbank Cres. Holy 143 F2
Mossbank Dr. Glasg 98 C2
Mossbank. E Kil 179 F4
Mossbank. Pres 236 C4
Mossbank Rd. Wish 165 E2
Mossbank. Udd 161 E3
Mossbell Rd. Hat 141 F3
Mossblown St. Lark 184 C2
Mossburn Ave. Bonh 19 F1
Mossburn Ave. East 127 E3
Mossburn Rd. Wish 165 E2
Mossburn St. Wish 165 E1
Mosscastle Rd. Glasg 99 E1
Mosscastle Rd. Slam 86 A4
Mossdale Ct. Hat 142 B3
Mossdale. E Kil 159 E2
Mossdale Gdns. Ham 161 F1
Mossend Ave. Glasg 16 C1
Mossend La. Glasg 119 E4
Mossend Pl. Helen 16 C1
Mossend St. Glasg 119 E4
Mossgiel Ave. Cowie 12 B4
Mossgiel Ave. Glasg 138 A3
Mossgiel Ave. Stir 2 A1
Mossgiel Ave. Troon 229 F2
Mossgiel Cres. Newt M 157 F3
Mossgiel Dr. Clyde 74 B2
Mossgiel Dr. Irvine 219 E2
Mossgiel Gdns. Kirk 56 C1
Mossgiel Gdns. Tan 140 C4
Mossgiel La. Lark 185 E1
Mossgiel Pl. Ayr 239 D3
Mossgiel Pl. Steven 206 C2
Mossgiel Rd. Ayr 239 D3
Mossgiel Rd. Cumb 62 A1
Mossgiel Rd. Glasg 136 B3
Mossgiel Rd. Glasg 136 B4
Mossgiel Rd. Salt 200 A2
Mossgiel St. Falk 41 D3
Mossgiel Terr. Udd 140 B1
Mossgiel Way. Holy 143 D2
Mosshall Gr. Holy 143 E4
Mosshall Rd. Holy 143 E4
Mosshall Rd. Holy 143 F2
Mosshead Rd. Bear 76 A4
Mosshead Rd. Kilmk 228 A2
Mosshill Rd. Hat 142 A4
Mosside Rd. Kilmk 222 C2
Mosside. P Glasg 68 B2
Mossland Dr. Wish 165 E2
Mossland Rd. Glasg 114 C4
Mosslands Rd. Pais 113 F4
Mosslingal. E Kil 180 C3
Mossmulloch. E Kil 180 C3
Mossneuk Ave. E Kil 179 F4
Mossneuk Cres. Wish 165 F2
Mossneuk Dr. Pais 133 E4
Mossneuk Dr. Wish 165 E2
Mossneuk Pk. Wish 165 E2
Mossneuk Rd. E Kil 180 A4
Mossneuk St. Coat 121 F2
Mosspark Ave. Glasg 115 F2
Mosspark Ave. Miln 55 D2
Mosspark Bvd. Glasg 115 F2
Mosspark Dr. Glasg 115 F2
Mosspark La. Glasg 115 F2
Mosspark Oval. Glasg 115 F2
Mosspark Rd. Coat 121 F2
Mosspark Rd. Miln 55 D2
Mosspark Sq. Glasg 115 F2
Mossvale Cres. Glasg 99 E1
Mossvale La. Pais 113 F4
Mossvale Path. Glasg 99 E2
Mossvale Rd. Glasg 99 E1
Mossvale Sq. Glasg 99 E1
Mossvale Sq. Pais 113 E3
Mossvale St. Pais 113 E4
Mossvale Terr. Muir 81 D2
Mossvale Way. Glasg 99 E1
Mossvale Wlk. Glasg 99 E1
Mossview Cres. Aird 123 D3
Mossview La. Glasg 115 D3
Mossview Quadrant. Glasg 115 E3
Mossview Rd. Stepps 99 F3
Mossywood Ct. Cumb 81 F4
Mossywood Pl. Cumb 81 F4
Mossywood Rd. Cumb 81 F4
Mote Hill. Ham 162 C3
Mote View. Cross 221 E1
Motehill Rd. Pais 114 A4
Motherwell Rd. Chap 144 A3
Motherwell Rd. Ham 163 D2

Motherwell Rd. Hat 142 A2
Motherwell Rd. Holy 143 E1
Motherwell St. Aird 123 E4
Moulin Cir. Glasg 115 D2
Moulin Pl. Glasg 115 D2
Moulin Rd. Glasg 115 D2
Moulin Terr. Glasg 115 D2
Mount Annan Dr. Glasg 137 D4
Mount Ave. Kilmk 227 E3
Mount Ave. Sym 231 E2
Mount Cameron Dr. N. E Kil 181 D4
Mount Cameron Dr. S. E Kil 181 D4
Mount Charles Cres. Ayr .. 238 B1
Mount Harriet Ave. Stepps .. 99 F3
Mount Harriet Dr. Stepps .. 99 F3
Mount Hope. B of A 2 B4
Mount Oliphant. Cowie 12 B4
Mount Oliphant Cres. Ayr . 239 D3
Mount Oliphant Pl. Ayr 239 D3
Mount Pleasant Cres. M of C .. 58 A3
Mount Pleasant Dr. O Kill ... 73 D3
Mount Pleasant St. Green ... 45 F2
Mount St. Glasg 96 C2
Mount Stewart St. Car 187 F1
Mount Stuart St. Glasg 136 C4
Mount The. Ayr 239 D2
Mount Vernon Ave. Coat .. 121 F4
Mount Vernon Ave. Glasg . 119 F2
Mount View. Irvine 220 B1
Mount William. N Sau 5 F1
Mountainblue St. Glasg 118 A3
Mountblow Rd. Clyde 73 E3
Mountgarrie Rd. Glasg 115 E4
Mounthenrick. E Kil 180 C3
Mournian Way. Ham 162 B1
Mousebank La. Lan 214 C2
Mousebank Rd. Lan 214 C3
Mousemill Rd. Lan 214 B3
Mowbray Ave. Muir 100 C3
Mowbray Ct. Bann 7 E2
Mowbray. E Kil 160 B2
Moy Path. New 165 F3
Moyne Rd. Glasg 115 D1
Muckcroft Rd. Muir 80 A2
Mudale Ct. Falk 42 B1
Mugdock Rd. Miln 55 D2
Muir Cl. Stew 195 E1
Muir Cres. Alex 27 E4
Muir Ct. Glasg 135 F4
Muir Dr. Irvine 219 F4
Muir Dr. Steven 217 E4
Muir Dr. Troon 229 E3
Muir Rd. Dumb 50 B3
Muir St. Alex 27 E4
Muir St. Bish 78 A1
Muir St. Coat 121 F4
Muir St. Ham 162 C2
Muir St. Lar 23 E1
Muir St. Lark 185 D3
Muir St. Law 186 C3
Muir St. Mother 163 E4
Muir St. Ren 94 B2
Muir St. Udd 161 E3
Muir Terr. Pais 114 A4
Muiralehouse Rd. Bann 11 F4
Muirbank Ave. Glasg 137 F4
Muirbank Gdns. Glasg 137 F4
Muirbrae Rd. Glasg 138 A2
Muirbrae Way. Glasg 138 A2
Muirburn Ave. Glasg 136 C3
Muirburn Pl. Beith 150 A3
Muirburn Rd. Glasg 198 A1
Muircroft Dr. Cle 144 A1
Muirdrum Ave. Glasg 115 E2
Muirdyke Ave. Sten 24 B2
Muirdyke Rd. Coat 121 E4
Muirdyke Rd. Glasg 102 A3
Muirdykes Ave. Glasg 115 D3
Muirdykes Cres. Pais 113 D3
Muirdykes Rd. Glasg 115 D3
Muirdykes Rd. Pais 113 D3
Muiredge
and Jersey Rd. Cle 145 D1
Muiredge
and Jersey Rd. Sals 145 E4
Muiredge Ct. Udd 140 C3
Muiredge Terr. Glasg 120 A2
Muirend Ave. Glasg 136 C3
Muirend Rd. Card 48 A4
Muirend Rd. Glasg 136 C3
Muirend Rd. Kilmk 222 C3
Muirend St. Stir 7 D3
Muirend St. Kilb 149 D1
Muirfield Cres. Glasg 76 C1
Muirfield Ct. Glasg 136 C3
Muirfield Meadows. Udd .. 140 C1
Muirfield Pl. Kilw 207 E2
Muirfield Rd. Cumb 62 A3
Muirfield Rd. Lar 23 F1
Muirhall Pl. Lar 23 E2
Muirhall Rd. Lar 23 E2
Muirhall Terr. Lar 125 D1
Muirhead Cotts. Kirk 80 A4
Muirhead Dr. Holy 143 F2
Muirhead Dr. Lin 112 A3

Muirhead Gdns. Glasg 120 B2
Muirhead Gdns. Sals 125 D1
Muirhead Pl. East 127 E2
Muirhead Pl. Sten 23 F2
Muirhead Rd. Sten 23 F2
Muirhead St. Kirk 79 E4
Muirhead St. Loch 129 E1
Muirhead Terr. Mother 163 F2
Muirhead Way. Bish 78 B1
Muirhead-Braehead
Interchange. Cumb 62 A2
Muirhill Ave. Glasg 136 C3
Muirhill Cres. Glasg 95 D4
Muirhouse Ave. Mother ... 164 A2
Muirhouse Ave. New 166 A3
Muirhouse Dr. Mother 164 B1
Muirhouse La. E Kil 180 C4
Muirhouse Pk. Bear 75 E4
Muirhouse Rd. Mother 164 A1
Muirhouse St. Glasg 117 D2
Muirkirk Dr. Glasg 95 F4
Muirkirk Dr. Ham 161 E1
Muirlee Rd. Car 188 A1
Muirlees Cres. Miln 54 C1
Muirmadkin Rd. Hat 142 A3
Muirmaillen Ave. Cle 144 B1
Muirpark Ave. Ren 94 B1
Muirpark Dr. Bish 98 A4
Muirpark Dr. Shi 66 B3
Muirpark Gdns. Men 4 C2
Muirpark Rd. Beith 150 A1
Muirpark St. Glasg 96 A1
Muirshiel Ave. Glasg 135 E3
Muirshiel Cres. Glasg 135 E3
Muirside Ave. Glasg 120 A2
Muirside Ave. Glasg 119 F2
Muirside Ave. Kirk 80 A4
Muirside Ct. Kilw 207 E1
Muirside Pl. Kilw 207 E1
Muirside Dr. New 165 F3
Muirside Rd. Glasg 120 A2
Muirside Rd. Kilw 207 E1
Muirside Rd. Pais 113 D4
Muirside Rd. Tull 4 B2
Muirside St. Glasg 120 A2
Muirskeith Cres. Glasg 137 D3
Muirskeith Pl. Glasg 136 C3
Muirskeith Rd. Glasg 136 C3
Muirton. Dr. Bish 77 F2
Muirton Rd. Fal 7 F3
Muiryfauld Dr. Glasg 118 C3
Muiryhall St. Coat 122 A4
Muiryhall St E. Coat 122 B4
Mulben Cres. Glasg 134 C4
Mulben Pl. Glasg 134 C4
Mulben Terr. Glasg 134 C4
Mulberry Dr. E Kil 180 B3
Mulberry Rd. Glasg 136 B3
Mulberry Rd. Tan 140 B1
Mulberry Way. E Kil 180 B3
Muldron Terr. Shot 147 D1
Mulgrew Ave. Salt 206 A1
Mull. Aird 123 E3
Mull Ave. Pais 133 F4
Mull Ave. Ren 94 B1
Mull Cres. Irvine 220 A1
Mull Ct. All 10 A3
Mull Ct. Irvine 220 A1
Mull. E Kil 181 E4
Mull Pl. Irvine 220 A1
Mull Quadrant. Wish 165 F3
Mull St. Glasg 98 A1
Mull Terr. Irvine 220 A1
Mullardoch St. Glasg 76 B1
Mulvey Cres. Aird 122 C4
Mungalend. Falk 42 A4
Mungalhead Rd. Falk 42 A4
Mungo Pk. E Kil 180 B4
Mungo Pl. Tan 121 D1
Munlochy Rd. Glasg 115 E4
Munnoch Cres. Ard 205 D3
Munro Ave. Kilmk 222 B1
Munro Ave. Stir 2 A1
Munro Ct. Dunt 73 F3
Munro Dr. E Helen 16 C2
Munro Dr. Kilb 170 A4
Munro Dr. M of C 58 A3
Munro D W. Helen 16 B2
Munro Gdns. Laur 42 C2
Munro La. Glasg 95 F3
Munro Pl. All 9 F3
Munro Pl. E Kil 160 A2
Munro Pl. Glasg 95 F3
Munro Pl. Kilmk 222 C1
Munro Pl. Salt 200 B2
Munro St. Alex 27 F3
Munro St. Green 45 D2
Munro St. Sten 23 F3
Munro Wk. Salt 206 A1
Murano St. Glasg 96 C2
Murchie Dr. Pres 236 B3
Murchison Dr. E Kil 180 A4

Murchison Rd. Hous 91 E1
Murchland Ave. Fen 213 D2
Murchland Way. Irvine 219 E2
Murdieston St. Green 45 E2
Murdoch Cres. Steven 217 E4
Murdoch Dr. Miln 76 B4
Murdoch Pl. Holy 142 C2
Murdoch Pl. Shew 224 C3
Murdoch Rd. E Kil 180 C4
Murdoch Sq. Hat 142 B4
Murdoch's Lone. Ayr 238 C1
Murdostoun Cres. East 127 E3
Murdostoun Gdns. Wish .. 165 E3
Murdostoun Terr. Cle 144 C1
Murdostoun View. New ... 165 F3
Mure Ave. Kilmk 223 D3
Mure Pl. Uplaw 153 D2
Muriel La. Barr 134 B2
Muriel St. Barr 134 B2
Murnin Ct. Stir 7 F2
Murnin Rd. Bon 40 A2
Murray Ave. Kils 60 B4
Murray Ave. Salt 205 F1
Murray Dr. Stone 198 C1
Murray Gdns. M of C 58 B3
Murray Pl. Barr 75 D4
Murray Path. Udd 140 C3
Murray Pl. Ayr 236 B2
Murray Pl. Barr 134 B2
Murray Pl. Camb 6 B3
Murray Pl. Dumb 50 B2
Murray Pl. Gour 44 C3
Murray Pl. Kilmk 223 E1
Murray Pl. Tan 7 D4
Murray Pl. Tan 141 F4
Murray Rd. Law 186 C2
Murray Rd. The. E Kil 180 C4
Murray Rd. Udd 141 D2
Murray

Roundabout The. E Kil . 180 C4
Murray Sq. The. E Kil 180 C4
Murray St. Ayr 236 B1
Murray St. Green 45 E3
Murray St. Pais 113 E3
Murray St. Ren 94 B2
Murray Terr. Mother 163 D4
Murrayfield. Bish 78 A2
Murrayfield Dr. Bear 75 F1
Murrayfield Dr. Glasg 7 E1
Murrayfield St. Glasg 118 C4
Murrayfield Terr. Bann 7 E1
Murrayhill. E Kil 180 B4
Murrayshall Rd. Stir 7 D2
Murrayside. Stone 198 B1
Murrin Ave. Bish 78 B1
Murroch Ave. Dumb 50 B3
Murroch Cres. Bonh 28 A1
Murroes Rd. Glasg 115 E4
Musgrove Pl. E Kil 180 B4
Muslin St. Glasg 117 F2
Muttonhole Rd. Ham 182 C4
Muttonhole Rd. Quart 183 D2
Mybster Pl. Glasg 115 E4
Myers Cres. Udd 141 D3
Mylne Pl. Sten 24 A1
Myothill Rd. Bank 39 E4
Myres Rd. Glasg 135 E4
Myreside Pl. Glasg 118 B3
Myreside St. Glasg 118 C3
Myreton Ave. Kil 89 E4
Myreton Dr. Bann 11 F4
Myreton. N Sau 4 A3
Myrie Gdns. Bish 78 A1
Myroch Pl. Glasg 100 B1
Myrtle Ave. Kirk 79 E3
Myrtle Bank. Beith 171 D4
Myrtle Dr. Holy 143 D3
Myrtle Dr. Mother 164 B2
Myrtle Hill La. Glasg 137 E4
Myrtle La. Lark 185 E1
Myrtle Pk. Glasg 137 E4
Myrtle Pl. Glasg 137 E4
Myrtle Rd. Clyde 73 E2
Myrtle Rd. Tan 141 D4
Myrtle Sq. Bish 98 A4
Myrtle St. Udd 140 B1
Myrtle View Rd. Glasg 137 E4
Myrtle Wlk. Glasg 138 C3
Myvot Ave. Cumb 82 A3
Myvot Rd. Cumb 82 A3

Nailer Rd. Falk 41 F3
Nailer Rd. Stir 7 D1
Nairn Ave. Hat 142 A3
Nairn Ave. Udd 141 F4
Nairn Cres. Aird 123 D3
Nairn Cres. Stew 195 E1
Nairn Ct. Kilw 207 D2
Nairn Dr. Gour 44 B3
Nairn Pl. Clyde 73 F2
Nairn Pl. E Kil 160 B2
Nairn Quadrant. Wish 165 D3
Nairn Rd. Gour 44 B2
Nairn St. Clyde 73 F2
Nairn St. Glasg 96 B1

Nairn St. Lark 184 C1
Nairn St. Udd 161 E3
Nairn Way. Cumb 62 A3
Nairnside Rd. Glasg 98 B4
Naismith Ct. Stone 198 C1
Naismith St. Glasg 97 D2
Naismith Wlk. Hat 142 B4
Nansen St. Glasg 97 D2
Napier Ave. Card 48 A4
Napier Cres. Dumb 49 E2
Napier Cres. Falk 42 A4
Napier Ct. Card 48 A4
Napier Ct. Clyde 73 E3
Napier Ct. Cumb 62 B4
Napier Dr. Glasg 116 A4
Napier Gdns. Lin 112 B3
Napier Hill. E Kil 180 C4
Napier La. E Kil 180 C4
Napier Pl. Clyde 73 E3
Napier Pl. Cumb 62 B4
Napier Pl. Falk 42 A4
Napier Pl. Glasg 116 A4
Napier Rd. Cumb 62 B4
Napier Rd. Glasg 116 A4
Napier Rd. Glasg 116 A4
Napier Sq. Hat 142 B4
Napier St. Clyde 94 B4
Napier St. Glasg 97 D2
Napier St. John 111 F2
Napier St. Lin 112 B3
Napier Terr. Glasg 116 A4
Napier Way. Cumb 62 B4
Napiershall La. Glasg 96 C1
Napiershall Pl. Glasg 96 C1
Napiershall St. Glasg 96 C1
Napierston Rd. Bonh 27 F3
Naproch Pl. Newt M 157 E3
Naseby Ave. Glasg 95 F2
Naseby La. Glasg 95 F2
Nasmyth Ave. Bear 75 D4
Nasmyth Rd. Glasg 115 D4
Nasmyth Rd N. Glasg 115 D4
Nasmyth Rd S. Glasg 115 D4
Nassau Pl. E Kil 159 D1
Naver Ct. Shot 147 D2
Navar Pl. Pais 114 A1
Naver St. Glasg 98 C1
Navy Way. Ros 15 D2
Naylor La. Aird 123 D4
Naysmyth Bank. E Kil 180 C4
Nebit The. Alva 4 C3
Needle Grn. Card 187 F1
Neidpath Ave. Coat 122 A2
Neidpath Dr. Sten 23 F2
Neidpath Pl. Coat 122 A2
Neidpath Pl. Coat 122 A2
Neidpath Rd. Car 187 F2
Neidpath Rd E. Newt M 157 D3
Neidpath Rd W. Newt M 157 D3
Neil Ave. Irvine 219 E3
Neil St. Green 45 D2
Neil St. Ren 94 B3
Neilsland Dr. Ham 183 E4
Neilsland Dr. Mother 163 D3
Neilsland Oval. Glasg 115 E1
Neilsland Rd. Ham 183 E4
Neilsland Sq. Glasg 115 E1
Neilsland Sq. Ham 162 B1
Neilsland St. Ham 162 B1
Neilson St. Falk 42 A2
Neilson St. Rat 142 A3
Neilston Ave. Glasg 135 E3
Neilston Pl. Kils 36 A1
Neilston Rd. Neil 154 C4
Neilston Rd. Pais 113 F1
Neilston Rd. Uplaw 153 D2
Neilvaig Dr. Glasg 138 B2
Nelson Ct. Glasg 121 F2
Nelson Cres. Mother 164 A2
Nelson Mandela Pl. Glasg .. 117 E4
Nelson Pl. Ayr 236 A1
Nelson Pl. Glasg 120 A2
Nelson Pl. Helen 17 D1
Nelson Pl. Stir 7 E3
Nelson Rd. Gour 44 C3
Nelson St. Glasg 117 D3
Nelson St. Glasg 120 A2
Nelson St. Green 45 F3
Nelson St. Kilmk 227 F4
Nelson Terr. E Kil 181 D4
Nephmair Moor Rd. Car 201 E1
Nemphlar Moor Rd. Lan 214 A4
Nemphlar Rd. Lan 214 A4
Nemphlar Hill. Lan 214 A4
Neptune St. Glasg 116 A4
Neptune Way. Holy 142 D3
Nerston Rd. E Kil 159 F3
Ness Ave. John 131 E4
Ness Dr. E Kil 160 A1
Ness Dr. Udd 140 C1
Ness Gdns. Bish 78 A1
Ness Gdns. Lark 199 D4
Ness Pl. Troon 229 F3
Ness Rd. Green 45 E3
Ness Rd. Ren 94 A2
Ness St. Glasg 98 C1
Ness St. Wish 186 A4

Ness Terr. Ham 162 A1
Ness Way. Holy 143 D3
Nethan Ave. Wish 164 B1
Nethan Gate. Ham 162 B2
Nethan Glen. Cro 201 D1
Nethan Path. Lark 199 D4
Nethan St. Glasg 116 A4
Nethan St. Mother 142 B1
Nethanfoot Brig Rd. Cro 201 D1
Nether
  Auldhouse Rd. Glasg 136 B3
Netherbank Rd. Wish 164 B1
Netherblane. Strath 75 D2
Netherburg Ave. Dumb 50 A2
Netherbog Rd. Dumb 50 A2
Netherburn Ave. Glasg 136 C1
Netherburn Ave. Hous 111 F4
Netherburn Gdns. Hous 111 F4
Netherburn Rd. Ash 200 A4
Netherby Dr. Glasg 116 B2
Netherby Pl. Air 14 B2
Nethercairn Pl. Newt M 157 E3
Nethercairn Rd. Glasg 136 B2
Nethercliffe Ave. Glasg 136 C1
Nethercraigs Dr. Pais 133 E4
Nethercraigs Rd. Pais 133 D4
Nethercroy Rd. Kils 60 C3
Netherdale Cres. Wish 164 B1
Netherdale Dr. Glasg 114 C2
Netherdale. Newt M 157 D3
Netherdale Rd. Wish 164 C1
Netherfield St. Glasg 118 B3
Netherfield The. Alva 4 C3
Netherhall Rd. Wish 164 B1
Netherhill Ave. Glasg 137 D1
Netherhill Cotts. Pais 114 A4
Netherhill Rd. Muir 80 C1
Netherhill Rd. Pais 114 A4
Netherhill Way. Pais 114 A4
Netherhouse Ave. Coat 121 F2
Netherhouse Ave. Kirk 79 F2
Netherhouse Pl. Glasg 120 C4
Netherhouse Rd. Glasg 120 C4
Netherland Rd. Bear 211 F4
Netherlee Cres. Dairy 169 D1
Netherlee Rd. Glasg 137 D2
Nethermains Rd. Den 21 E1
Nethermains Rd. Milt 57 F1
Nethermains Rd. Miln 78 A4
Nethermir Rd. W Kil 190 B2
Netherpark Ave. Glasg 137 D1
Netherplace Cres. Glasg 135 D4
Netherplace Cres. Newt M .. 156 B2
Netherplace Rd. Glasg 135 D4
Netherplace Rd. Newt M 156 A2
Netherton Ave. P Glasg 69 D4
Netherton Ct. Glasg 137 F1
Netherton Ct. Newt M 157 D3
Netherton Dr. Barr 134 C1
Netherton Oval. Lennox 57 D4
Netherton Oval. Lennox 33 D1
Netherton Rd. E Kil 180 A2
Netherton Rd. E Kil 180 B4
Netherton Rd. Glasg 95 F4
Netherton Rd. Newt M 156 C2
Netherton Rd. Wish 164 C1
Netherton St. East 127 E3
Netherton St. Glasg 95 F4
Netherton St. Wish 164 C1
Nethervale Ave. Glasg 137 D1
Netherview Rd. Glasg 137 D1
Netherway. Glasg 136 C1
Netherwood Ave. Cumb 81 F4
Netherwood Ct. Cumb 82 A4
Netherwood Ct. Cumb 62 A1
Netherwood Pl. Cumb 81 F4
Netherwood Rd. Cumb 81 F4
Netherwood Rd. Mother 164 B2
Netherwood Way. Cumb 82 A4
Nethy Way. Ren 94 C1
Neucks The. Slam 97 D3
Neuk Ave. Hous 91 E1
Neuk Ave. Muir 100 B4
Neuk Cres. Hous 91 E1
Neuk The. Mother 164 C2
Neuk Way. Glasg 139 E4
Neukfoot La. Uplaw 153 D2
Nevan Rd. Troon 229 F3
Neville. E Kil 160 B2
Nevis Ave. Ham 162 A1
Nevis Cres. All 10 A4
Nevis Ct. Barr 134 B1
Nevis Dr. Lennox 57 D1
Nevis Pl. Falk 42 B1
Nevis Pl. Kilmk 228 A2
Nevis Pl. Shot 147 D2
Nevis Rd. Bear 75 D4
Nevis Rd. Glasg 136 A3
Nevis Rd. Ren 94 A1
Nevis Way. Irvine 93 F1
Nevis Way. Irvine 220 A2
Newark St. Lark 185 D1
New Ashtree St. Mother 164 C2
New Ave. How 130 C3
New Bridge St. Ayr 235 F1
New Buildings. Lan 215 D1

New City Rd. Glasg 97 D1
New City Row. Strath 31 D2
New Cross. Ham 162 C2
New Dock La. Green 46 A3
New Edinburgh Rd. Tan 141 E3
New England Rd. Sall 206 A1
New Hallglen Rd. Falk 42 B1
New Inchinnan Rd. Pais 113 F4
New Kirk Rd. Bear 75 F3
New La. Calder 123 D2
New Lairdsland Rd. Kirk 79 E4
New Lanark Rd. Lan 214 C1
New Line Rd. Bann 11 D4
New Luce Dr. Glasg 119 E2
New Mill Rd. Kilmk 228 A4
New Park St. Ham 162 B3
New Plymouth. E Kil 180 A4
New Rd. Ayr 235 F1
New Rd. Bann 7 D1
New Rd. Glasg 139 F2
New Sneddon St. Pais 113 F3
New St. B of A 1 C4
New St. Beith 171 D4
New St. Dalry 191 E4
New St. Durt 74 A3
New St. Irvine 219 D1
New St. Kilbar 111 D2
New St. Kilmk 227 F3
New St. Loch 129 E1
New St. Pais 113 F2
New St. Slam 86 A4
New St. Steven 217 E4
New St. Stew 195 E1
New St. Stone 198 C1
New St. Udd 161 E4
New Stevenston Rd. Holy 143 E4
New View Cres. Hat 142 A2
New View Dr. Hat 142 A2
New View Pl. Hat 142 A2
New Wynd. Glasg 117 E3
Newall Rd. Pais 113 F4
Neward Ave. Pres 236 B3
Newark Ave. Green 45 E4
Newark Dr. Glasg 116 C2
Newark Dr. Glasg 116 C2
Newark Dr. Glasg 133 E4
Newark Dr. Wish 165 E3
Newark Pl. Glasg 119 E2
Newark Pl. Wish 165 E3
Newark St. Green 45 E4
Newark St. P Glasg 47 E1
Newark Terr. Pres 236 B3
Newarthill Rd. Holy 143 E1
Newbarns St. Car 187 F2
Newbattle Ave. Calder 123 D1
Newbattle Ct. Glasg 119 D1
Newbattle Gdns. Glasg 119 D1
Newbattle Pl. Glasg 119 D1
Newbattle Rd. Glasg 119 D1
Newbiggin Cres. Tull 4 B1
Newbold Ave. Bish 97 F4
Newburgh. Ersk 73 D2
Newburgh St. Glasg 136 B4
Newcastleton Dr. Glasg 76 C1
Newcroft Dr. Glasg 137 E3
Newdyke Ave. Kirk 79 F4
Newdyke Rd. Kirk 79 F4
Newdykes Farm Rd. Pres ... 233 E1
Newdykes Rd. Pres 233 E1
Newfield Cres. Ham 162 A2
Newfield Pl. Dund 225 F1
Newfield La. Udd 141 D3
Newfield Pl. Glasg 225 F1
Newfield Pl. Glasg 135 F1
Newfield Pl. Glasg 137 F4
Newfield Pl. Irvine 220 A3
Newfield Rd. Stone 198 C1
Newfield Sq. Glasg 135 D3
Newhall St. Glasg 117 F2
Newhaven Rd. Glasg 119 D4
Newhaven St. Glasg 119 D3
Newhills Rd. Glasg 119 F4
Newhouse Dr. Falk 41 F1
Newhouse Dr. Kilb 169 F4
Newhouse
  Interchange. Shew 224 C3
Newhouse. Stir 7 D3
Newhouse Way. Irvine 220 A3
Newhousemill Rd. E Kil 181 E4
Newhousemill Rd. Ham 182 A4
Newhouses Rd. Brox 61 D2
Newhut Rd. Mother 142 B1
Newington St. Glasg 118 A3
Newlands Dr. Kilmk 228 C3
Newlands Dr. Udd 141 D2
Newlands Gdns. John 112 B1
Newlands Pl. E Kil 159 F1
Newlands Pl. Kilmk 222 C1
Newlands Rd. E Kil 159 F1
Newlands Rd. E Kil 179 F3
Newlands Rd. E Kil 180 A4
Newlands Rd. Glasg 136 C3
Newlands St. Coat 121 F3
Newlands St. Lan 122 A2
Newlands St. Lan 215 E2
Newlands Terr. Car 187 F1
Newlands Terr. M of C 58 B3

Newlandsfield Rd. Glasg 136 B4
Newlandsmuir Rd. E Kil 180 A3
Newmains Ave. Inch 93 D3
Newmains Rd. Ren 94 B1
Newmarket. Bann 7 F1
Newmarket St. Ayr 238 C4
Newmarket St. Falk 42 A3
Newmill
  and Canthill Rd. Shot 145 F1
Newmill Gdns. Shot 145 F2
Newmill Rd. Dunlop 195 E4
Newmill Rd. Glasg 98 B3
Newmill-Canthill Rd. Shot .. 146 A1
Newmills. Tull 4 A2
Newmoor
  Interchange. Irvine 219 F1
Newmoor Rd. Pais 114 C2
Newpark Cres. Glasg 139 D4
Newpark Cres. Stir 7 D1
Newpark Rd. Stir 7 D1
Newrose Ave. Hat 142 B4
Newshot Dr. Ersk 73 E1
Newstead Gdns. Glasg 76 C1
Newton Brae. Glasg 139 F3
Newton Brae. Udd 140 A3
Newton Dr. John 112 C2
Newton Dr. Newt M 156 C2
Newton Gr. Newt M 156 C2
Newton of Barr. Loch 129 E1
Newton Park Ct. Ayr 236 A1
Newton Pl. Glasg 96 C1
Newton Rd. Bishop 92 C2
Newton Rd. Kirk 79 F2
Newton St. Coat 121 F2
Newton St. Green 45 E3
Newton St. Kilb 149 D1
Newton St. Pais 113 E2
Newton St. Pais 113 E2
Newton Terr. Green 45 E3
Newton Terr. John 112 C2
Newton Terrace La. Glasg .. 116 C4
Newton Trad Est. Ayr 236 A1
Newton Way. Pais 114 A4
Newton Wlk. Kilmk 228 A4
Newtongrange Ave. Glasg . 119 D1
Newtongrange
  Gdns. Glasg 119 D2
Newtonhead. Irvine 220 A3
Newtonlea Ave. Newt M ... 156 C2
Newtonshaw. N Sau 5 E1
Newtown St. Kils 60 B4
Newtyle Pl. Bish 78 B1
Newtyle Pl. Pais 114 B2
Nicholas St. Glasg 117 E4
Nicholson St. Glasg 117 D3
Nicklaus Way. Holy 143 F4
Nicol St. Aird 103 E1
Nicol St. Green 45 E2
Nicolson Ct. Stepps 99 F3
Nicolson St. Green 45 F3
Niddrie Rd. Glasg 117 D1
Niddrie Sq. Glasg 116 C1
Niddry St. Pais 113 F3
Nigel Gdns. Glasg 116 B1
Nigel St. Mother 163 E3
Nigg Pl. Glasg 120 A4
Nightingale Pl. John 131 E3
Nikitas Ave. Lark 199 D4
Nile Ct. Ayr 238 C4
Nile St. Green 45 F2
Nimmo Dr. Glasg 115 F4
Nimmo Pl. Car 187 F2
Nimmo Pl. Wish 165 E4
Nimmo St. Green 45 E2
Nineyard St. Salt 216 C4
Ninian Ave. Hous 111 E4
Ninian Rd. Aird 123 E3
Ninian's Rise. Kirk 79 F4
Ninian's Terr. Kilw 207 F1
Nisbet Dr. Den 21 E1
Nisbet Dr. Pres 236 B3
Nisbet St. Glasg 118 B3
Nisbet Pl. Chap 123 F1
Nisbet St. Chap 143 F1
Nith Ave. Pais 112 C1
Nith Dr. Ham 183 D4
Nith Dr. Ren 94 C1
Nith La. New 165 D3
Nith Path. Cle 144 A1
Nith Pl. Dund 225 F1
Nith Pl. John 131 E4
Nith Pl. Kilmk 228 A3
Nith Quadrant. Holy 143 E2
Nith St. Glasg 98 B1
Nithsdale Cres. Bear 75 D3
Nithsdale Cross. Glasg 116 B2
Nithsdale Dr. Glasg 116 C1
Nithsdale. E Kil 160 B2
Nithsdale Pl. Glasg 116 C2
Nithsdale Rd. Glasg 116 A2
Nithsdale Rd. Glasg 116 A2
Nithsdale St. Glasg 116 C2
Nithsdale St. Shot 146 C2
Nitshill Rd. Glasg 135 D3

Nitshill Rd. Glasg 135 E2
Niven Ct. Kilmk 223 E2
Niven St. Glasg 96 B3
Noble Rd. Hat 142 A3
Nobles Pl. Hat 141 F2
Nobles View. Hat 141 F2
Nobleston. Bonh 27 F1
Noldrum Ave. Glasg 139 E4
Noldrum Gdns. Glasg 139 E4
Noltmire Rd. Ayr 236 B2
Noran Cres. Troon 229 F3
Norbreck Dr. Glasg 136 B2
Norby Rd. Glasg 95 F2
Noremac Way. Hat 141 F4
Norfield Dr. Glasg 137 E4
Norfolk Cres. Bish 77 F2
Norfolk Ct. Glasg 117 D3
Norfolk House. E Kil 159 F1
Norfolk Rd. Gour 44 C2
Norfolk St. Glasg 117 D3
Norham St. Glasg 116 C1
Norman Cres. Irvine 219 D3
Norman St. Glasg 117 F1
Norse La N. Glasg 95 E2
Norse La S. Glasg 95 E2
Norse Rd. Glasg 95 E2
North and South Rd. Cle ... 144 C1
North Ave. Car 187 E1
North Ave. Clyde 74 A1
North Ave. Glasg 96 B4
North Ave. Holy 143 D1
North Bank Pl. Clyde 94 B4
North Bank St. Clyde 94 B4
North Barr Ave. Ersk 73 D1
North Barr. Ersk 73 D1
North Berwick Ave. Cumb ... 61 F3
North Berwick Cres. E Kil .. 180 A3
North Biggar Rd. Aird 123 D4
North Birbiston Rd. Lennox .. 57 F4
North Bridge St. Aird 122 C4
North British Rd. Udd 140 C2
North Bute St. Coat 122 A2
North Calder Dr. Aird 123 E3
North Calder Pl. Tan 121 E1
North Campbell Ave. Miln ... 54 C1
North Canal Bank. Glasg 97 E1
North Canal Bank St. Glasg . 97 E1
North Carbrain Rd. Cumb ... 61 F1
North Castle St. All 10 A3
North Claremont La. Miln ... 55 D1
North Claremont St. Glasg .. 96 C1
North Corsebar Rd. Pais 113 E1
North Court La. Glasg 117 E4
North Crescent Ave. Ard ... 205 F2
North Crescent Rd. Ard 205 D2
North Croft St. Pais 113 F3
North Ct. Glasg 117 E4
North Dean Park Ave. Udd .. 141 D1
North Douglas St. Clyde 94 B4
North Dr. Kilb 170 A4
North Dr. Lin 112 A3
North Dr. Troon 229 F2
North Dryburgh Rd. Wish .. 165 D3
North Dumgoyne Ave. Miln . 54 C2
North Elgin Pl. Clyde 94 B4
North Elgin St. Clyde 94 B4
North Erskine Pk. Bear 75 E3
North Faulds Rd. Lan 215 F3
North Frederick St. Glasg .. 117 E4
North Gardner St. Glasg 96 A2
North
  Gargieston Rd. Kilmk ... 227 E3
North Gower St. Glasg 116 B3
North Grange Rd. Bear 75 F3
North Hamilton Pl. Kilmk .. 222 C1
North Hamilton St. Kilmk .. 222 C1
North Hanover St. Glasg 117 E4
North Harbour St. Ayr 235 F1
North
  Iverton Park Rd. John .. 112 A2
North Kilmeny Cres. Wish .. 165 E3
North La. Lin 112 B3
North Lodge Ave. Mother .. 163 F2
North Lodge Rd. Ren 94 A2
North Main St. Alex 27 E3
North Main St. Sten 24 B2
North Moraine La. Glasg 75 E1
North Neuk. Troon 229 F4
North Orchard St. Mother .. 163 E3
North Park Ave. Ayr 236 A2
North Park Ave. Glasg 135 F2
North Portland St. Glasg ... 117 E4
North Rd. Coat 122 A1
North Rd. Dumb 42 A4
North Rd. John 111 F1
North Rd. W Kil 190 B3
North Shore Rd. Troon 229 F2
North Shore Rd. Troon 229 F2
North Sq. Coat 121 F4
North St. Alex 27 F3
North St. All 10 A3
North St. Falk 42 A2
North St. Glasg 116 C4
North St. Green 45 E4
North St. Hous 91 D2

North St. Lark

Pappert. Bonh

North St. Lark 185 D2
North St. Mother 163 F4
North St. Stir 113 F3
North St. Pais 2 B1
North Vennel. Irvine 220 A2
North Vennel. Lan 215 D2
North View. Bear 75 E1
North View Rd. B of W 110 C3
North Wallace St. Glasg 97 E1
North Wood Rd. Tull 4 B1
North Woodside Rd. Glasg ... 96 C2
Northacre. Kilw 207 F3
Northall Quadrant. Holy 143 D1
Northampton Dr. Glasg 96 A3
Northampton La. Glasg 96 A3
Northbank Ave. Glasg 139 E3
Northbank Ave. Klrk 79 E4
Northbank Rd. Klrk 79 D4
Northbank St. Glasg 139 E3
Northbrae Pl. Glasg 95 D3
Northburn Ave. Aird 103 D1
Northburn Rd. Aird 103 D1
Northburn Rd. Aird 102 B1
Northburn St. Plains 104 A1
Northcraig Rd. Kilmk 223 D2
Northcroft Rd. Muir 80 C1
Northdoon Pl. Ayr 238 B2
Northend. Carn 6 A3
Northfield Ave. Ayr 236 A2
Northfield Ave. P Glasg 68 C4
Northfield Ave. Shot 147 D1
Northfield Dr. Bonh 27 F3
Northfield E Kil 179 F4
Northfield Pl. Ayr 236 A2
Northfield Rd. Bonh 28 A3
Northfield Rd. Duni 21 E2
Northfield St. Kils 36 A1
Northfield St. Mother 163 F4
Northgate Quadrant. Glasg .. 98 B3
Northgate Rd. Glasg 98 B4
Northinch Ct. Glasg 95 E1
Northinch St. Glasg 95 E1
Northland Dr. Glasg 95 E3
Northland La. Glasg 95 E3
Northmuir Dr. Wish 165 E2
Northmuir Rd. Glasg 75 D2
Northpark St. Glasg 96 C2
Northumberland St. Glasg ... 96 C2
Northway. Udd 140 B1
Northwood Dr. New 166 A3
Norton St. Alva 5 D4
Norval St. Glasg 96 A1
Norwood Ave. Ayr 96 A3
Norwood Ave. All 9 F4
Norwood Ave. Bon 40 A4
Norwood Ave. Klrk 79 D4
Norwood Cres. All 9 F4
Norwood Dr. Glasg 136 A1
Norwood Gr. All 9 F4
Norwood Pk. Bear 75 F2
Norwood Pl. Bon 40 A4
Norwood Terr. Tan 141 D4
Norwood Ave. Glasg 96 A3
Nottingham La. Glasg 96 A3
Nottingham La. Glasg 96 A3
Novar Dr. Glasg 96 A2
Novar Gdns. Bish 77 F1
Novar St. Ham 162 B1
Nuneaton St. Glasg 118 A2
Nurseries Rd. Glasg 119 F3
Nursery Ave. Ersk 72 C2
Nursery Ave. Kilmk 228 A4
Nursery Ave. Pres 235 D2
Nursery Buildings. Lan 215 D1
Nursery Ct. Car 187 F2
Nursery Dr. Aird 200 A4
Nursery Gr. Kil 69 E1
Nursery La. Glasg 117 D1
Nursery La. Kil 69 E1
Nursery Pl. Ayr 205 E1
Nursery Pl. Udd 161 E3
Nursery Rd. Ayr 239 D3
Nursery Rd. Falk 41 F2
Nursery Rd. Glasg 117 D2
Nursery St. Helen 226 C3
Nursery St. Kilmk 227 F4
Nutberry Ct. Glasg 117 D1

O'Connor Ct. Salt 216 C4
O'Hare. Bonh 28 A2
O'Neil Ave. Bish 98 A4
O'Wood Ave. Holy 143 D3
Oak Ave. E Kil 180 A3
Oak Ave. Glasg 120 A2
Oak Cres. Plea 12 B2
Oak Dr. Fall 8 B2
Oak Dr. Glasg 139 E2
Oak Dr. Klrk 79 D3
Oak Dr. Lar 23 E1
Oak Fern Dr. E Kil 159 E2
Oak Fern Gr. E Kil 159 E2
Oak Lea. Ham 162 C2
Oak Path. Holy 143 D3
Oak Pk. Bish 78 A1
Oak Pk. Mother 163 E2
Oak Pl. Coat 122 A3
Oak Pl. E Kil 180 A3
Oak Pl. Kilmk 227 E4

Oak Pl. Tan 141 E4
Oak Rd. Ard 205 E2
Oak Rd. Clyde 73 F3
Oak Rd. Cumb 62 C2
Oak Rd. Pais 114 A1
Oak St. Stir 1 C1
Oakbank Ave. Wish 164 C1
Oakbank Dr. Barr 155 F4
Oakbank Ind Est. Glasg ... 97 D2
Oakbank P Glasg 68 C4
Oakbank St. Aird 123 E4
Oakburn Ave. Milt 54 C1
Oakburn Cres. Miln 54 C1
Oakdene Ave. Bell 142 A4
Oakdene Ave. Tan 141 D4
Oakdene Cres. Holy 143 E2
Oakfield Ave. Glasg 96 C1
Oakfield Dr. Mother 163 F3
Oakfield La. Glasg 96 C1
Oakfield Rd. Mother 163 F3
Oakhill Ave. Glasg 119 F2
Oakland Dr. Steven 206 C1
Oaklands Ave. Irvine 219 E2
Oaklea Cres. Udd 161 E4
Oakleigh Dr. Green 46 C4
Oakley Dr. Glasg 136 C2
Oakley Terr. Glasg 117 F4
Oaks The. Glasg 137 D2
Oaks The. John 111 F1
Oakshaw Brae. Pais 113 E3
Oakshaw St E. Pais 113 F3
Oakshaw St W. Pais 113 E3
Oakshawhead. Pais 113 E3
Oakside Pl. Ham 183 E4
Oakview Quadrant. Hat 141 F2
Oakwood Ave. Ayr 236 C1
Oakwood Ave. Pais 113 D1
Oakwood Dr. Beith 171 D4
Oakwood Dr. Newt M 156 C2
Oates Gdns. Mother 164 A2
Oatfield St. Glasg 98 C2
Oban Dr. Glasg 96 C2
Oban La. Glasg 96 C2
Oban Terr. Gour 44 C2
Oberon. Al 9 F4
Obiston Gdns. Glasg 119 D3
Observatory La. Glasg 96 B2
Observatory Rd. Glasg 96 B2
Ochil Cres. Stir 2 A1
Ochil Ct. Irvine 220 A2
Ochil Ct. Tull 4 B2
Ochil Dr. Barr 134 B1
Ochil Dr. Pais 133 F4
Ochil Dr. Sten 23 F2
Ochil Pl. Glasg 119 D2
Ochil Pl. Kilmk 228 A2
Ochil Rd. Alva 5 E3
Ochil Rd. Bear 75 D4
Ochil Rd. Bish 78 B1
Ochil Rd. Men 4 A1
Ochil Rd. Ren 94 A1
Ochil Rd. Stir 2 B2
Ochil St. All 10 A4
Ochil St. Tull 4 B2
Ochil St. Glasg 119 D2
Ochil St. Tull 4 A2
Ochil St. Wish 164 C2
Ochil View. Den 39 E4
Ochil View. Stir 2 C4
Ochil View. Tan 141 D4
Ochilmount. Bann 7 F1
Ochiltree Ave. Glasg 95 F4
Ochiltree Dr. Ham 161 F1
Ochiltree Terr. Falk 41 D3
Ochilview. Alva 5 D4
Ochilview. Cowie 12 C3
Ochville Terr. Fish 5 E2
Octavia Terr. Green 45 E4
Odense Ct. E Kil 180 C3
Ogilface Cres. Blac 107 E1
Ogilvie Ct. Aird 123 F4
Ogilvie Pl. B of A 2 A2
Ogilvie Pl. Glasg 118 B2
Ogilvie Pl. Kilmk 223 E1
Ogilvie Rd. Stir 7 D1
Ogilvie St. Glasg 118 B2
Old Aisle Rd. Klrk 79 F4
Old Auchans View. Dund ... 225 F1
Old Avon Rd. Ham 163 D1
Old Belladyke Rd. Lar 23 D2
Old Biggar Rd. Gree 83 D1
Old Bore Rd. Aird 123 F4
Old Bothwell Rd. Udd 162 A4
Old Bridge
  of Weir Rd. B of W 90 C1
Old Bridge
  of Weir Rd. Hous 91 D1
Old Bridge Rd. Ayr 236 C2
Old Bridge St. All 10 A3
Old Bridge St. Pais 235 F1
Old Bridgend. Car 187 F1
Old Castle Rd. Glasg 137 D3
Old Church Gdns. Coat 121 D3
Old Coach Rd. E Kil 159 F2
Old Cotts. Pais 134 B4
Old Cross. Aird 123 D4
Old Cross. Ham 162 C2
Old Dalmarnock Rd. Glasg . 117 F2

Old Dalnottar Rd. O Kill . 73 E3
Old Denny Rd. Lar 23 D2
Old Drove Rd. Carn 6 B3
Old Dumbarton Rd. Glasg .. 96 B1
Old Eastfield St. East ... 127 E3
Old Edinburgh Rd. Tan 140 C4
Old Edinburgh Rd. Tan 141 D4
Old Edinburgh Rd. Tan 141 D4
Old Farm Rd. Ayr 236 B2
Old Gartloch Rd. Muir 100 C3
Old Glasgow Rd. Cumb 62 A2
Old Glasgow Rd. Stew 195 F1
Old Glasgow Rd. Udd 140 B4
Old Glasgow Rd. Udd 140 C3
Old Govan Rd. Ren 94 B3
Old Greenock Rd. Bishop .. 71 E3
Old Greenock Rd. Ersk 72 C1
Old Greenock Rd. Lang 70 B3
Old Hillfoot Rd. Ayr 239 D3
Old Inns Interchange. Cumb 62 B3
Old Irvine Rd. Kilmk 227 F4
Old Lanark Rd. Car 202 A4
Old Lanark Rd. Kilnc 202 A2
Old Lanark Rd. Lan 202 C1
Old Largs Rd. Green 45 F1
Old Loans Rd. Troon 230 A2
Old Luss Rd. Alex 19 D1
Old Luss Rd. Helen 16 C1
Old Luss Rd. Helen 16 C4
Old Manse Rd. Glasg 119 E3
Old Manse Rd. Wish 164 C1
Old Military Rd. Gart 20 C4
Old Mill Rd. Alla 146 A1
Old Mill Rd. Dunt 74 A3
Old Mill Rd. E Kil 159 F1
Old Mill Rd. Glasg 139 E3
Old Mill Rd. Kilmk 228 A4
Old Mill Rd. Udd 140 C3
Old Mill Rd. Udd 141 D1
Old Mill View. Kils 60 C2
Old Mill Wk. Bonh 27 F4
Old Monkland Rd. Coat 121 F2
Old Mugdock Rd. Strath ... 31 E1
Old Playfield Rd. E Kil .. 158 B4
Old Quarry Rd. Cumb 81 E3
Old Quarry Rd. Steven 217 E4
Old Raise Rd. Salt 206 A1
Old Rd. John 112 B2
Old Redding Rd. Laur 42 C2
Old Renfrew Rd. Glasg 95 D1
Old Rome Way. Cross 226 C3
Old Rutherglen Rd. Glasg . 117 E2
Old School Ct. Tull 4 A1
Old Schoolhouse La. Hous . 91 D2
Old Shettleston Rd. Glasg 118 C3
Old Sneddon St. Pais 113 F3
Old St. Dunt 73 F3
Old St. Kilmk 227 F3
Old Stable Row. Coat 122 A4
Old Town. Bann 7 E1
Old Union St. Aird 123 D4
Old Willowyard Rd. Beith . 171 D4
Old Wishaw Rd. Car 187 F2
Old Wishaw Rd. Law 187 D3
Old Wood Rd. Glasg 120 A2
Old Woodwynd Rd. Kilw 207 F2
Old Wynd. Glasg 117 E3
Oldbarhills Ind Est. Pais 134 B4
Oldhall Dr. Kil 69 E1
Oldhall Rd. Pais 114 B3
Oldhall Roundabout. Shew . 224 C3
Oilard Ave. Udd 141 D2
Oliphant Cres. Newt M 157 F3
Oliphant Cres. Pais 132 C4
Oliphant Dr. Kilmk 228 B4
Oliphant Oval. Pais 132 C4
Olive Bank. Tan 121 E1
Olive Ct. Holy 143 D3
Olive Rd. Kilmk 227 E4
Olive St. Glasg 98 B2
Oliver Rd. Falk 42 B2
Olympia Arcade. E Kil 180 C4
Olympia Ct. E Kil 180 C4
Olympia St. Glasg 117 F3
Olympia The. E Kil 180 C4
Olympia Way. E Kil 159 F1
Omoa Rd. Cle 144 C1
Onich Pl. Shot 147 D2
Onslow Dr. Glasg 118 A4
Onslow. E Kil 180 B4
Onslow Rd. Clyde 74 B1
Onslow Sq. Glasg 118 A4
Ontario Pk. E Kil 159 F2
Ontario Pl. E Kil 159 D1
Onthank Dr. Kilmk 222 C1
Onyx St. Bell 142 A2
Open Shore. Green 46 A3
Oran Gate. Glasg 96 C2
Oran Gdns. Glasg 96 C2
Oran Pl. Glasg 96 C2
Oran St. Glasg 96 C2
Orangefield Dr. Pres 233 E1
Orangefield La. Green 45 E3
Orangefield Ind Est. Pres 233 E1
Orangefield La. Green 45 E3
Orbiston Ct. Mother 164 A3
Orbiston Dr. Dunt 74 B4

Orbiston Dr. Hat 142 B2
Orbiston Pl. Dunt 74 B4
Orbiston Rd. Bell 141 F2
Orbiston Rd. Hat 142 A1
Orbiston Sq. Hat 141 F2
Orbiston St. Mother 163 F3
Orcades Dr. Glasg 137 D2
Orchard Ave. Ayr 239 D3
Orchard Ave. Udd 141 D1
Orchard Brae. Kirk 79 F2
Orchard Ct. Glasg 136 A2
Orchard Ct. Glasg 139 D3
Orchard Dr. Glasg 136 A2
Orchard Dr. Glasg 137 F4
Orchard Dr. Udd 161 E4
Orchard Field. Klrk 79 F2
Orchard Gate. Lark 185 D1
Orchard Gn. E Kil 160 A2
Orchard Gr. Glasg 136 A2
Orchard Gr. Kil 69 F1
Orchard Park Ave. Glasg .. 136 A2
Orchard Pk. Glasg 136 B2
Orchard Pl. Ayr 239 D3
Orchard Pl. Glasg 139 D3
Orchard Pl. Ham 162 C2
Orchard Pl. Kilw 207 F2
Orchard Pl. Klw 207 F2
Orchard St. Car 187 F1
Orchard St. Falk 41 F2
Orchard St. Glasg 119 F2
Orchard St. Green 46 A2
Orchard St. Ham 162 C2
Orchard St. Kilmk 222 C1
Orchard St. Mother 163 E4
Orchard St. Pais 113 F2
Orchard St. Ren 94 B2
Orchard St. W Kil 190 B3
Orchard St. Wish 186 A3
Orchard Way. E Kil 4 A1
Orchard View Dr. Lan 214 A2
Orchardcroft. Stir 7 D4
Orchardton Rd. Cumb 81 E4
Orchy Ave. Glasg 136 C1
Orchy Cres. Aird 123 E2
Orchy Cres. Bear 75 E1
Orchy Cres. Pais 112 C1
Orchy Ct. Clyde 74 B3
Orchy Dr. Glasg 136 C1
Orchy Gdns. Glasg 136 C1
Orchy St. Glasg 137 D3
Orchy Terr. E Kil 160 A1
Orefield Pl. E Kil 159 F2
Oregon Pl. Glasg 117 E2
Orion Pl. Holy 142 C3
Orion Way. Car 187 E1
Orion Way. Glasg 139 D3
Orkney Ct. All 10 A3
Orkney Pl. Falk 42 A1
Orkney Pl. Glasg 116 A4
Orkney Quadrant. Wish 166 A4
Orkney St. Glasg 116 A4
Orlando. E Kil 160 B3
Orleans Ave. Glasg 95 F2
Orleans La. Glasg 95 F2
Ormiston Ave. Glasg 95 D2
Ormiston Dr. Ham 183 E4
Ormiston La. Glasg 95 E2
Ormiston La N. Glasg 95 E2
Ormiston La S. Glasg 95 E2
Ormonde Ave. Glasg 136 C2
Ormonde Cres. Glasg 136 C2
Ormonde Ct. Glasg 136 C2
Ormonde Dr. Glasg 136 C2
Ornsay St. Glasg 97 F4
Oronsay Ave. P Glasg 69 D3
Oronsay Cres. Bear 76 A2
Orr St. Glasg 113 F3
Orr St. Glasg 117 F3
Orr St. Pais 113 F3
Orr Terr. East 127 E2
Orr Terr. Neil 154 B3
Orton St. Glasg 116 A3
Osborne Cres. Thorn 158 A2
Osborne Gdns. Falk 41 F2
Osborne St. Clyde 74 A2
Osborne St. Falk 41 F2
Osborne St. Glasg 117 E3
Oslie View. Stew 195 F1
Osprey Dr. Kilmk 228 B4
Osprey Dr. Tan 141 D4
Osprey Rd. Green 45 D2
Ossian Ave. Glasg 114 C3
Ossian Rd. Glasg 136 C3
Oswald Ct. Ayr 236 A2
Oswald Dr. Pres 235 E2
Oswald Gdns. Car 201 F2
Oswald La. Ayr 235 F1
Oswald Pl. Ayr 236 A3
Oswald Rd. Ayr 236 A2
Oswald St. Falk 42 A3
Oswald St. Glasg 117 D4
Oswald Wlk. Miln 76 B4
Otago La. Glasg 96 C1
Otago La N. Glasg 96 C1

Otago Pk. E Kil 159 D1
Otago St. Glasg 96 C1
Othello. E Kil 160 A3
Ottawa Cres. Clyde 73 E2
Otterburn Ave. Kilmk 223 D3
Otterburn Dr. Glasg 136 B1
Otterswick Pl. Glasg 99 E1
Ottoline Dr. Troon 229 F1
Oudenarde Ct. Car 188 A1
Outdale Ave. Pres 236 C4
Oval The. Glasg 136 C1
Oval The. Glen 101 E3
Overburn Ave. Glasg 74 C3
Overbrae Pl. Glasg 74 C3
Overburn Ave. Dumb 49 F3
Overburn Cres. Dumb 49 F3
Overburn Terr. Dumb 50 A3
Overdale Ave. Glasg 136 C4
Overdale Cres. Pres 236 C4
Overdale Gdns. Glasg 136 C4
Overdale Pl. Wish 186 B3
Overdale St. Glasg 136 C4
Overjohnstone Dr. Mother . 164 B2
Overlea Ave. Glasg 138 B3
Overlee Rd. Newt M 157 F4
Overmills Cres. Ayr 239 E4
Overmills Rd. Ayr 239 E4
Overnewton Pl. Glasg 116 B4
Overnewton Sq. Glasg 96 B1
Overnewton St. Glasg 96 B1
Overton Cres. Den 21 E1
Overton Cres. John 112 A2
Overton Cres. John 45 E2
Overton Cres. W Kil 190 B3
Overton Ct. W Kil 190 B3
Overton Dr. W Kil 190 B3
Overton Gdns. Kil 69 F1
Overton Gr. Kil 69 F1
Overton Pl. Irvine 220 A3
Overton Rd. Alex 27 E2
Overton Rd. Glasg 200 B3
Overton Rd. Glasg 139 E2
Overton Rd. John 112 A1
Overton St. Alex 27 F3
Overton St. Glasg 139 E2
Overtoun Ave. Dumb 50 A2
Overtoun Dr. Clyde 73 F2
Overtoun Dr. Glasg 138 A4
Overtoun Rd. Clyde 73 F2
Overtown Ave. Glasg 135 D3
Overtown Ct. New 165 F1
Overtown Rd. Wish 165 F1
Overtown St. Glasg 118 A3
Overwood Dr. Dumb 50 A2
Overwood Dr. Glasg 137 E3
Overwood Gr. Dumb 50 A2
Owen Ave. E Kil 180 B4
Owen Kelly Pl. Salt 205 F1
Owen Pk. E Kil 180 B4
Owen St. Mother 163 E4
Owendale Ave. Hat 142 A4
Oxford Ave. Gour 45 D3
Oxford Dr. Lin 112 A3
Oxford La. Glasg 117 D3
Oxford Rd. Gour 44 B2
Oxford Rd. Ren 94 B2
Oxford St. Coat 121 F3
Oxford St. Glasg 117 D3
Oxford St. Klrk 79 E4
Oxgang Pl. Klrk 79 F3
Oxhill Pl. Dumb 49 E2
Oxhill Rd. Dumb 49 E2
Oxton Dr. Glasg 115 D3

Pacemuir La. Kil 89 D3
Pacemuir Rd. Kil 89 E4
Paddock St. Coat 122 B2
Paddock The. Irvine 220 B3
Paddock The. Thorn 158 A3
Paddockholm
  North Ind Est. Kilb 149 D1
Paddockholm Rd. Kilb 149 D1
Paddockholm
  South Ind Est. Kilb 149 D1
Padulf Pl. Kilb 149 D1
Paidmyre Cres. Newt M 156 B2
Paidmyre Gdns. Newt M 156 B2
Paidmyre Rd. Newt M 156 B2
Paisley Rd. Barr 134 A2
Paisley Rd. Glasg 116 C3
Paisley Rd. Ren 94 B1
Paisley Rd W. Glasg 115 E2
Paisley St. Ard 205 E1
Palacecraig St. Coat 122 A2
Palacecraig St. Coat 96 D4
Palermo St. Glasg 97 F2
Palladium Pl. Glasg 95 E2
Palm Pl. Tan 121 E1
Palm Pl. Tan 75 E1
Palmer Ave. Glasg 75 E1
Palmerston. E Kil 180 A4
Palmerston Pl. Glasg 116 B4
Palmerston Pl. John 131 E4
Pandora Way. Tan 141 D4
Pankhurst Pl. E Kil 159 F1
Panmure St. Glasg 97 D3
Panrock Ct. Troon 229 F2
Pantonville Rd. W Kil 190 B2
Papermill Rd. Green 46 C3
Pappert. Bonh 28 A2

Pardovan Pl. Falk 41 F3
Paris Ave. Den 21 F1
Park Ave. Bank 39 F3
Park Ave. Barr 134 A1
Park Ave. Bath 150 A1
Park Ave. Bish 78 A2
Park Ave. Both 19 F1
Park Ave. Car 83 E4
Park Ave. Dumb 50 A2
Park Ave. Glasg 96 C1
Park Ave. Gour 45 D4
Park Ave. Holy 143 D3
Park Ave. John 112 B1
Park Ave. Kilw 207 E2
Park Ave. Kirk 79 E4
Park Ave. Lar 23 E1
Park Ave. Laur 42 C2
Park Ave. Miln 55 D1
Park Ave. Pais 113 E1
Park Ave. Pres 236 A4
Park Ave. Stir 7 D3
Park Ave. Twe 59 F2
Park Bank. Ersk 73 D1
Park Brae. Ersk 93 E4
Park Burn Ct. Ham 162 A3
Park Cir. Ayr 238 C4
Park Cir. Car 187 F2
Park Circus. Glasg 96 C1
Park Circus La. Ayr 238 C4
Park Circus La. Glasg 96 C1
Park Circus Pl. Glasg 96 C1
Park Cres. Aird 122 C4
Park Cres. Bann 7 E1
Park Cres. Bear 75 E3
Park Cres. Bish 78 A1
Park Cres. Dumb 49 F3
Park Cres. Eagle 178 B2
Park Cres. Inch 93 E4
Park Cres. Lennox 57 E1
Park Cres. N Sau 5 E1
Park Cres. Sten 24 A1
Park Cres. Stew 211 E4
Park Cres. Udd 161 E3
Park Ct. Beith 79 E4
Park Ct. Bish 78 A2
Park Ct. Clyde 73 F2
Park Ct. Glasg 136 A2
Park Ct. Mother 163 E3
Park Dr. Barn 7 E1
Park Dr. Ersk 93 D4
Park Dr. Ersk 93 E4
Park Dr. Glasg 138 A4
Park Dr. Ham 163 E1
Park Dr. Hat 142 A2
Park Dr. Lan 214 C2
Park Dr. Lar 23 E1
Park Dr. New 166 A3
Park Dr. Thorn 158 B2
Park Gardens La. Glasg 96 C1
Park Gate. Ersk 93 D4
Park Gate. Glasg 96 C1
Park Gate Pl. Hat 141 F3
Park Gdns. Bann 7 E1
Park Gdns. Glasg 96 C1
Park Gdns. Kilbar 111 D2
Park Glade. Ersk 93 D4
Park Gn. Ersk 93 D4
Park Gr. Card 48 A4
Park Gr. Ersk 93 E4
Park Hill. Ersk 73 D1
Park La. Aird 205 E2
Park La. Car 187 F1
Park La. Glasg 117 F3
Park La. Kils 60 B4
Park La. Kilw 207 E3
Park La. Stir 7 D4
Park Lea. Cald 105 D2
Park Moor. Ersk 93 D4
Park Pl. All 10 B4
Park Pl. Hat 141 E4
Park Pl. Irvine 219 D3
Park Pl. John 111 F1
Park Pl. Lan 214 C2
Park Pl. Stir 6 C3
Park Pl. Strath 31 D2
Park Pl. Thorn 158 B2
Park Quadrant. Glasg 96 C1
Park Quadrant. Wish 164 C1
Park Rd. Aird 205 E1
Park Rd. B of W 90 B1
Park Rd. Bish 78 A2
Park Rd. Blac 107 F2
Park Rd. Calder 123 D2
Park Rd. Clyde 73 F2
Park Rd. Coat 121 D3
Park Rd. Falk 24 A1
Park Rd. Glasg 96 C1
Park Rd. Glasg 136 B1
Park Rd. Glasg 139 E4
Park Rd. Ham 162 B2
Park Rd. Hat 142 A2
Park Rd. Holy 143 D1
Park Rd. Inch 111 F1
Park Rd. John 111 F1
Park Rd. Kil 89 E4
Park Rd. Men 4 B3

Park Rd. Miln 55 D1
Park Rd. Muir 100 B4
Park Rd. Pais 113 E1
Park Rd. Salt 216 C4
Park Rd. Shot 146 B3
Park Ridge. Ersk 93 E4
Park St. Aird 122 C4
Park St. Alex 27 E3
Park St. Alva 5 D4
Park St. Bon 40 B2
Park St. Car 59 D2
Park St. Cle 144 A2
Park St. Coat 122 A4
Park St. Cowie 12 C4
Park St. Dumb 50 A2
Park St. Falk 42 A3
Park St. Holy 143 D2
Park St. Kilmk 222 C1
Park St. Kirk 80 A4
Park St. Mother 163 F3
Park St S. Glasg 96 C1
Park Terr. Ayr 238 C4
Park Terr. Card 48 A4
Park Terr. E Kil 159 F1
Park Terr. Glasg 96 C1
Park Terr. Gour 44 C4
Park Terr. Stir 7 D3
Park Terr. Tull 4 A1
Park
    Terrace East La. Glasg 96 C1
Park Terrace La. Glasg 96 C1
Park Top. Ersk 73 E1
Park View. Aird 205 E2
Park View. Cald 105 D3
Park View. Kilb 149 D1
Park View. Kilbar 111 D2
Park View. Lark 185 D2
Park View. Pais 113 E1
Park Way. Cumb 62 A2
Park Winding. Ersk 93 E4
Park Wood. Ersk 73 E1
Parkandarroch Cres. Car .. 188 A1
Parkburn Ave. Kirk 79 E4
Parkburn Rd. Kils 36 B1
Parkdyke. Stir 6 C3
Parkend Ave. Salt 217 D4
Parkend Cres. Shi 66 B3
Parkend Gdns. Salt 217 D4
Parkend Rd. Salt 217 D4
Parker Pl. Kils 60 B4
Parker Pl. Lark 185 D2
Parkfield. E Kil 180 C3
Parkfoot Ct. Falk 42 A3
Parkgate. Alva 4 C3
Parkgrove Ave. Glasg 136 B2
Parkgrove Terr. Glasg 96 C1
Parkgrove
    Terrace La. Glasg 96 C1
Parkhall Rd. Clyde 73 F2
Parkhall St. E Kil 159 F1
Parkhall Terr. Clyde 73 F3
Parkhead Ave. Kilw 207 F2
Parkhead Cross. Glasg 118 C3
Parkhead Ct N Sau 10 B4
Parkhead Ct. N Sau 10 B4
Parkhead La. Aird 123 D4
Parkhead Rd. Falk 42 A1
Parkhead Rd N Sau 10 B4
Parkhead St. Aird 123 D4
Parkhead St. Mother 163 F3
Parkhill Ave. Cross 226 C4
Parkhill Ave. P Glasg 69 D4
Parkhill Dr. Dalry 191 E4
Parkhill Dr. Glasg 138 A4
Parkhill Dr. Loch 129 E2
Parkhill Rd. Glasg 136 B4
Parkholm La. Glasg 116 C3
Parkhouse Dr. Kilb 149 D1
Parkhouse Gdns. Salt 205 E1
Parkhouse Rd. Ard 205 E1
Parkhouse Rd. Glasg 135 D2
Parkhouse St. Ayr 238 C4
Parkinch. Ersk 93 E4
Parklands Rd. Glasg 136 C2
Parklea. Bish 57 E3
Parklee Dr. E Kil 158 C4
Parkneuk Rd. Glasg 136 B2
Parkneuk Rd. Ham 161 D1
Parkneuk St. Mother 163 E4
Parkneuk Way. Lark 185 D2
Parks View. Ham 183 E3
Parksail Dr. Ersk 93 E4
Parksail. Ersk 93 E4
Parkside Ct. Plea 12 B2
Parkside Rd. Shot 146 B2
Parkthorn View. Dund 225 F1
Parkvale Ave. Ersk 93 E4
Parkvale Cres. Ersk 93 F4
Parkvale Dr. Ersk 93 E4
Parkvale Gdns. Ersk 93 E4
Parkvale Pl. Ersk 93 E4
Parkvale Way. Ersk 93 E4
Parkview Ave. Falk 41 F1
Parkview Ave. Kirk 79 E4
Parkview. Ayr 238 C1
Parkview Cres. New 166 A2
Parkview Ct. Kirk 79 E4

Parkview Dr. Coat 121 F4
Parkview Dr. Stepps 99 F3
Parkville Dr. Ham 161 F3
Parkville Rd. Hat 142 B4
Parkway. All 10 A4
Parkway. Ct. Coat 121 F3
Parkway. Ersk 93 D4
Parkway Pl. Coat 121 F3
Parnell St. Aird 122 C3
Parnie St. Glasg 117 E3
Parry Terr. E Kil 159 D1
Parsonage Row. Glasg 117 E4
Parsonage Sq. Glasg 117 E3
Parterre. Irvine 219 D1
Partick Bridge St. Glasg 96 B1
Partick St. Coat 122 B3
Partickhill Ave. Glasg 96 A2
Partickhill Ct. Glasg 96 A2
Partickhill Rd. Glasg 96 A1
Partridge Rd. Green 45 D3
Patchy Pk. Lark 199 D4
Paterson Ave. Irvine 219 F3
Paterson Cres. Irvine 219 E3
Paterson Dr. Helen 16 A1
Paterson Dr. Shi 66 B3
Paterson St. B of A 2 A3
Paterson St. Glasg 117 D3
Paterson St. Mother 163 F4
Paterson Terr. E Kil 180 B4
Path The. Bann 7 E1
Pather St. Wish 165 D1
Pathfoot Ave. B of A 2 B4
Pathfoot Dr. B of A 2 A4
Pathfoot. Kilw 207 F2
Pathfoot Rd. B of A 2 B3
Pathfoot View. Kilw 207 F2
Pathhead Gdns. Glasg 98 C3
Pathhead Rd. E Kil 158 B4
Patna Ct. Ham 161 F1
Patna St. Glasg 118 A2
Paton St. All 10 A3
Paton St. Glasg 118 A4
Paton St. Green 45 E3
Patrick Ave. Steven 206 B1
Patrick Dr. Shi 66 C4
Patrick St. Green 45 F3
Patrick St. Pais 113 F2
Patterson Dr. Law 187 D3
Patterton Dr. Barr 134 B1
Patterton St. Clyde 74 C2
Paul Dr. Air 119 E3
Pavilion Pl. Salt 205 E1
Pavilion View. All 9 F4
Paxstones Cres. East 127 F3
Paxstone Dr. East 127 F3
Payne St. Glasg 97 D4
Peace Ave. Kil 89 F1
Peace Ave. Kilmk 222 B1
Peacock Ave. Pais 112 C1
Peacock Cross. Ham 162 B2
Peacock Dr. Ham 162 A2
Peacock Dr. Pais 112 C1
Peacock Loan. Car 187 F2
Pearce La. Glasg 116 A4
Pearce St. Glasg 116 A4
Pearl St. Hat 142 A2
Pearson Dr. Ren 94 B2
Pearson Pl. Bank 39 E3
Pearson Pl. Lin 112 A3
Peat Pl. Glasg 135 D3
Peat Rd. B of W 110 B3
Peat Rd. Glasg 135 D3
Peat Rd. Green 45 E2
Peathill Ave. Muir 100 A4
Peathill Rd. Bon 40 A3
Peathill St. Glasg 97 D1
Peatland Quadrant. Kilmk . 228 A2
Peatland Rd. Kilmk 228 A2
Pebbles Dr. Ayr 138 B4
Peden Ave. Dalry 191 D4
Peden Pl. Irvine 219 E1
Peden St. East 127 E3
Pedmyre La. E Kil 158 B4
Peebles Path. Coat 122 B3
Peebles St. Ayr 235 F1
Peel Brae. Kirk 63 F1
Peel Ct. Glasg 139 D3
Peel Glen Rd. Bear 75 D3
Peel Glen Rd. Glasg 75 D2
Peel La. Glasg 96 A1
Peel Park Pl. E Kil 158 C1
Peel Pl. Coat 121 D2
Peel Pl. Udd 141 D2
Peel Rd. Thorn 158 A1
Peel St. Glasg 96 A1
Peel St. Card 48 A4
Peel St. Glasg 96 A1
Pegasus Ave. Car 187 F1
Pegasus Rd. Holy 142 C3
Peggiesmill Pl. Ayr 239 D3
Peggiesmill Rd. Ayr 239 D3
Peile St. Green 45 E3
Peiter Pl. Udd 161 E4
Peistream Ave. Stir 7 D2

Pemberton Valley. Ayr 239 D1
Pembroke. E Kil 160 B2
Pembroke Rd. Gour 44 B2
Pembroke St. Glasg 116 C4
Pembroke St. Lar 23 E2
Penbreck Ct. Irvine 220 A3
Pencaitland Dr. Glasg 119 D2
Pencaitland Gr. Glasg 119 D2
Pencaitland Pl. Glasg 76 C1
Pendeen Cres. Glasg 119 F3
Pendeen Pl. Glasg 119 F3
Pendeen Rd. Glasg 119 F3
Pendicle Cres. Bear 75 E2
Pendicle Rd. Bear 75 E2
Pendreich Way. Stir 2 A2
Penfold Cres. E Kil 180 B4
Penilee Rd. Glasg 114 C3
Penilee Rd. Glasg 114 C3
Penilee Terr. Glasg 114 C3
Peninver Dr. Glasg 115 F4
Penman Ave. Glasg 137 F4
Pennan. Ersk 73 D2
Pennan Pl. Glasg 95 D3
Penneld Rd. Glasg 114 C3
Penniecroft Ave. Dumb 50 B3
Pennyburn Rd. Kilw 207 E1
Pennyfern Dr. Green 45 D2
Pennyfern Rd. Green 45 D2
Pennyroyal Ct. E Kil 159 E2
Pennyvenie Way. Irvine .. 220 A3
Penrith Ave. Glasg 136 B1
Penrith Dr. Glasg 96 A3
Penrith Pl. E Kil 179 F3
Penryn Gdns. Glasg 119 E4
Penston Rd. Glasg 119 E4
Pentland Ave. Lin 112 A3
Pentland Ave. P Glasg 68 C3
Pentland Cres. Pais 133 E4
Pentland Ct. Aird 103 D1
Pentland Ct. Barr 134 B1
Pentland Ct. Barr 134 B1
Pentland Dr. Barr 134 B1
Pentland Dr. Bish 78 B1
Pentland Dr. Pres 236 B3
Pentland Dr. Ren 114 A4
Pentland Pl. Bear 75 D4
Pentland Pl. Irvine 220 A2
Pentland Rd. Glasg 136 B3
Pentland Rd. Kilmk 228 A2
Pentland Rd. Wish 164 C2
Penzance Way. Muir 80 C1
Peockland Gdns. John 112 A2
Peockland Pl. John 112 A2
Peploe Dr. E Kil 160 B3
Perceton
    Roundabout. Irvine 220 B3
Percelon Row. Irvine 220 B3
Percy Dr. Glasg 136 B1
Percy Rd. Ren 94 A1
Percy St. Glasg 116 B3
Percy St. Lark 185 D2
Perran Gdns. Muir 80 C1
Perray Ave. Dumb 49 D3
Perth Ave. Aird 123 D2
Perth Cres. Clyde 73 E3
Perth St. Glasg 116 C3
Peter Coats Building. Pais . 113 F2
Peter D.Stirling Rd. Kirk 58 B1
Peters Ave. Bonh 20 A1
Petersburn Pl. Aird 123 E3
Petersburn Rd. Aird 123 E3
Petershill Dr. Glasg 98 B2
Petershill Pl. Glasg 98 A2
Petershill Rd. Glasg 98 A2
Peterson Dr. Clyde 94 C4
Peterson Gdns. Clyde 94 C4
Petition Pl. Udd 141 D3
Pettigrew St. Glasg 119 D3
Peveril Ave. Glasg 116 B1
Peveril Ave. Glasg 138 B3
Peveril Ct. Glasg 138 B3
Pharonhill St. Glasg 118 B3
Philip Dr. Lar 23 E1
Philip Murray Rd. Tan 141 E4
Philip Sq. Ayr 236 A1
Philip St. Falk 42 A4
Philipshill Rd. E Kil 158 C2
Phoenix Cres. Tan 141 F4
Phoenix Pl. Holy 143 D2
Phoenix Pl. John 112 B2
Phoenix Retail Park. Lin .. 112 C3
Piccadilly St. Glasg 116 C4
Picken St. Kilmk 227 F3
Pickerstonhill. Holy 143 F2
Picketlaw Dr. E Kil 158 B4
Picketlaw Farm Rd. E Kil .. 158 B4
Pier Rd. Alex 19 E1
Pier Rd. Rhu 15 F2
Piershill St. Glasg 118 C4
Pierland Pl. Irvine 220 A3
Pikeman Rd. Glasg 95 E4
Pilmuir Ave. Glasg 136 C2
Pilrig St. Glasg 118 C4
Pilton Rd. Glasg 75 D2
Pine Brae. Ayr 239 E3
Pine Cl. Cumb 62 C2
Pine Cres. Cumb 62 C2

Pine Cres. E Kil 180 A3
Pine Cres. John 112 A1
Pine Ct. Coat 121 F2
Pine Ct. Cumb 62 C2
Pine Ct. E Kil 180 B3
Pine Gr. All 10 B3
Pine Gr. Calder 123 D1
Pine Gr. Cumb 62 C2
Pine Gr. Holy 143 D3
Pine Gr. Tan 141 D4
Pine House. Pres 236 A3
Pine Lawn. Wish 165 E3
Pine Pk. Ham 162 C1
Pine Pl. Cumb 62 C2
Pine Pl. Glasg 117 E2
Pine Rd. Clyde 73 E2
Pine Rd. Cumb 62 C2
Pine Rd. Dumb 49 F2
Pine Rd. Kilmk 227 E4
Pine St. Aird 123 E4
Pine St. Green 45 F2
Pine St. Lennox 57 F2
Pine St. Pais 114 A1
Pine Wlk. Lar 23 E1
Pinelands. Bish 78 A3
Pines The. Glasg 137 D2
Pinewood Ave. Kirk 79 D3
Pinewood Ct. Dumb 50 B3
Pinewood Ct. Kirk 79 D3
Pinewood Pl. Kirk 79 D3
Pinkerton Ave. Glasg 137 F4
Pinkston Dr. Glasg 97 F1
Pinkston Rd. Glasg 97 F1
Pinmore. Kilw 207 F2
Pinmore Pl. Glasg 134 C3
Pinmore St. Glasg 134 C3
Pinwherry Pl. Udd 141 D2
Piper Ave. House 111 E4
Piper Rd. Aird 123 E3
Piper Rd. Hous 111 E4
Piperhill. Ayr 239 D1
Pirleyhill Dr. Shi 66 B3
Pirnhall Rd. Bann 42 A1
Pirnhall Rd. Barn 111 D4
Pirnhall Rd. Bann 11 D4
Pirnie Pl. Kils 60 B4
Pirnmill Ave. Mother 163 F4
Pirnmill Ave. Helen 16 C1
Pirnmill Rd. Salt 205 F1
Pit Rd. Hat 141 F3
Pit Rd. Kirk 80 A4
Pitcairn Cres. E Kil 179 F4
Pitcairn Gr. E Kil 180 A4
Pitcairn Pl. E Kil 179 F4
Pitcairn St. Glasg 119 E3
Pitcairn Terr. Ham 162 A2
Pitcaple Dr. Glasg 136 A3
Pitlalm Rd. Fish 5 F2
Pitlochry Dr. Glasg 115 E2
Pittochry Dr. Lark 185 E1
Pitmedden Rd. Bish 78 B1
Pitmilly Rd. Glasg 75 F2
Pitreavie Ct. Ham 183 D4
Pitreavie Pl. Glasg 99 E2
Pitt St. Glasg 117 D4
Pitt Terr. Stir 7 D3
Place Of Bonhill. Alex 27 E2
Place View. Kilbar 149 D1
Pladda Ave. Irvine 220 A1
Pladda Ave. P Glasg 69 D4
Pladda Cres. Irvine 220 A1
Pladda Ct. Irvine 220 A1
Pladda Dr. Pres 236 B3
Pladda Rd. Ren 94 B1
Pladda St. Salt 205 F1
Pladda St. Mother 163 D4
Pladda Terr. Irvine 220 A1
Pladda Way. Helen 16 C1
Pladda Wynd. Irvine 220 A1
Plaintrees Ct. Pais 113 F1
Plan View. Kilb 149 D2
Plane Pl. Tan 121 E1
Planetree Pl. John 112 A1
Planetree Rd. Clyde 74 A3
Plant St. Glasg 118 B3
Plantation Ave. Holy 143 D3
Plantation
    Park Gdns. Glasg 116 B3
Plantation Sq. Glasg 116 C3
Plateau Dr. Troon 229 F4
Platthorn Dr. E Kil 159 F1
Platthorn Rd. E Kil 159 F1
Playfair St. Glasg 118 A2
Playingfield Cres. Cross .. 221 F1
Playingfield Rd. Cross 221 F1
Plaza The. E Kil 159 F1
Pleaknowe Cres. Muir 80 C1
Pleamuir Pl. Cumb 61 E1
Pleasance Ct. Falk 42 A2
Pleasance. Falk 42 A2
Pleasance La. Glasg 136 A3
Pleasance Rd. Falk 42 A2
Pleasance Sq. Falk 42 A2
Pleasance St. Glasg 136 B4
Pleasantside Ave. P Glasg . 69 D4
Plotcock Rd. Quart 198 B4

Plotcock Rd. Stone 198 B4
Plover Dr. E Kil 180 A3
Plover Pl. John 213 D2
Plusgarten Loan. New 165 F4
Plymouth Ave. Gour 44 C3
Poet's View. Kirk 79 F4
Poindfauld Terr. Dumb 50 A2
Pointhouse Rd. Glasg 116 B4
Pokely Pl. Stew 195 F1
Polbae Cres. Eagle 178 C3
Poles Rd. Fen 213 D2
Polkemmet Dr. Hart 127 F3
Polkemmet La. Hart 127 F3
Polkemmet Rd. Hart 127 F3
Pollick Ave. Uplaw 153 D2
Pollick Farm La. Dunlop 153 D2
Pollok Ave. Eagle 178 C3
Pollok Ave. Ham 162 A2
Pollok Cres. Kilw 207 F1
Pollok Rd. Bear 76 A2
Pollok Rd. Newt M 156 B2
Pollok St. Hat 142 B3
Pollok St. Mother 163 F4
Pollock Ave. Glasg 136 A4
Pollok Dr. Bish 77 F1
Pollok La. E Kil 160 A2
Pollok Pl. E Kil 160 A2
Pollokshaws Rd. Glasg 116 C1
Pollokshaws Rd. Glasg 117 D2
Polmadie Ave. Glasg 117 E1
Polmadie Rd. Glasg 117 E1
Polmadie St. Glasg 117 E1
Polmaise Ave. 7 D2
Polmaise Cres. Fall 8 B3
Polmaise Ct. Stir 7 D2
Polmaise Rd. Cam 6 C2
Polmaise Rd. Stir 6 C3
Polnoon Ave. Glasg 95 D3
Polnoon Dr. Eagle 178 C3
Polnoon St. Eagle 178 B2
Polo Ave. Troon 229 F1
Polo Gdns. Troon 229 F1
Polson Dr. John 111 F1
Polsons Cres. Pais 113 E1
Polwarth La. Glasg 96 A2
Polwarth St. Glasg 96 A2
Pomona Pl. Ham 161 F1
Pompee Rd. N Sau 5 F1
Poplar Ave. Bishop 72 A1
Poplar Ave. Glasg 94 B4
Poplar Ave. Newt M 156 C2
Poplar Ave. John 112 A1
Poplar Cres. Bishop 72 A1
Poplar Ct. Coat 121 F2
Poplar Dr. Clyde 73 F3
Poplar Dr. Kirk 79 D3
Poplar Dr. M of C 58 B3
Poplar Gdns. E Kil 180 B3
Poplar Pl. Gour 44 B3
Poplar Pl. Holy 143 D2
Poplar Pl. Tan 141 E4
Poplar Pl. Udd 140 B1
Poplar Rd. Dumb 49 F2
Poplar St. Aird 123 E4
Poplar St. Green 46 C1
Poplar Way. Ayr 239 E3
Poplars. The. Bear 75 E4
Poplars The. Tull 4 A1
Poplin St. Glasg 118 A2
Porchester St. Glasg 99 E1
Port Dundas Ind Est. Glasg 97 E1
Port Dundas Pl. Glasg 117 D4
Port Dundas Rd. Glasg 97 E1
Port Glasgow Rd. Green 46 C2
Port Glasgow Rd. Kil 69 D1
Port St. Glasg 116 C4
Port St. Stir 7 D3
Portal Rd. Glasg 95 E4
Portdownie. Falk 41 E3
Portencross Rd. W Kil 190 B3
Porter St. Glasg 116 B3
Porterfield Rd. Kil 89 F4
Porterfield Rd. Ren 94 A2
Porters La. Chap 123 E1
Porters Well. Udd 140 C3
Portessie. Ersk 73 D1
Porthlethen. Ersk 73 D1
Portland Ave. Irvine 224 A4
Portland Brae. Hurl 228 C3
Portland Ct. Hurl 228 C3
Portland Pk. Ham 162 C1
Portland Pl. Ham 162 C1
Portland Pl. Irvine 224 A4
Portland Pl. Kilma 227 F4
Portland Pl. Lan 215 D2
Portland Pl. Steven 217 E4
Portland Rd. Irvine 224 A4
Portland Rd. Kilmk 227 F4
Portland Rd. Pais 114 A2
Portland
  Roundabout. Irvine 219 D1
Portland Sq. Ham 162 C1
Portland St. Coat 122 A4
Portland St. Green 45 F3
Portland St. Troon 229 E2
Portland Terr. Troon 229 D1
Portland Wynd. Lark 185 D2
Portman St. Glasg 116 C3

Portmark Ave. Ayr 238 B1
Portmarnock Dr. Glasg 96 C4
Porton Pl. Bishop 72 A2
Portpatrick Pl. O Kil 72 C4
Portreath Rd. Muir 80 C2
Portree Terr. Gour 44 C2
Portsmouth Dr. Gour 44 C3
Portsoy Ave. Glasg 94 C4
Portsoy. Ersk 73 D1
Portsoy Pl. Glasg 94 C4
Portugal St. Glasg 117 D3
Portwell. Ham 162 C2
Possil Cross. Glasg 97 E2
Possil Rd. Glasg 97 D2
Postgate. Ham 162 C2
Posthill. N Sau 5 E1
Potassels Rd. Muir 100 B4
Potrail Pl. Ham 162 A2
Potter Cl. Glasg 118 C2
Potter Gr. Glasg 118 C2
Potter Pl. Glasg 118 C2
Potter Pl. Gran 24 C2
Potter St. Glasg 118 C2
Potterhill Ave. Pais 133 F4
Potterhill Rd. Glasg 115 D1
Potters Wynd. Lan 215 E3
Pottery Pl. Kilmk 222 C1
Pottery St. Green 46 C2
Pottis Rd. Bann 7 F4
Potts Way. Mother 142 B1
Powbrae Rd. Udd 140 B4
Powburn Cres. Udd 140 B4
Powfoot St. Glasg 118 B3
Powforth Cl. Lark 184 C2
Powgree Cres. Beith 171 E3
Powmill Rd. Pres 233 E1
Powrie St. Glasg 99 E2
Prentice Rd. Mother 163 E3
President Kennedy Dr. Plea 12 B2
Preston Pl. Glasg 117 D1
Preston Pl. Gour 44 B4
Preston St. Glasg 117 D1
Prestonfield Ave. Kilw 207 D2
Prestonfield. Miln 54 C1
Prestwick Pl. Newt M 157 D2
Prestwick Rd. Ayr 236 A2
Prestwick St. Glasg 135 D3
Pretoria Rd. Lar 23 D1
Priestfield St. Udd 161 E3
Priesthill Ave. Glasg 135 E3
Priesthill Cres. Glasg 135 E3
Priesthill Rd. Glasg 135 E3
Priestknowe
  Roundabout. E Kil 159 F1
Prieston Rd. B of W 110 B4
Primrose Ave. Hat 142 A4
Primrose Ave. Lark 199 D4
Primrose Cres. Mother 163 F3
Primrose Ct. Glasg 95 E2
Primrose Pk. Ayr 239 E2
Primrose Pl. Udd 141 D3
Primrose Pl. Cumb 82 A3
Primrose Pl. Kilmk 222 B1
Primrose Pl. Salt 206 A1
Primrose St. Tan 141 E4
Primrose St. Alt 10 A4
Primrose St. Bon 40 A3
Primrose St. Glasg 95 E2
Primrose Way. Car 201 F4
Prince Albert Rd. Glasg 96 B2
Prince Albert Terr. Helen 16 B1
Prince Edward St. Glasg 117 D1
Prince of
  Wales Gdns. Glasg 96 B4
Prince Pl. New 166 A3
Prince's Gdns. Glasg 96 A2
Prince's Pl. Glasg 96 B2
Prince's Terr. Glasg 96 B2
Princes Ct. Ayr 236 A1
Princes Gate. Glasg 138 A4
Princes Gate. Udd 140 C2
Princes Mall. E Kil 159 F1
Princes Pk. Ersk 72 C2
Princes Pl. Ard 205 D1
Princes Sq. Barr 134 B2
Princes Sq. E Kil 159 F1
Princes
  Square Shop Ctr. Glasg 117 E4
Princes St. Ard 205 D1
Princes St. Cald 105 D3
Princes St. Call 66 C3
Princes St E. Helen 16 C1
Princes St. Falk 42 A3
Princes St. Glasg 138 A4
Princes St. Green 45 F3
Princes St. Kilmk 227 F4
Princes St. Mother 163 F4
Princes St. Pres 47 E1
Princes St. Salt 216 B4
Princes St. Stir 7 D4
Princess
  Anne Quadrant. Holy 142 C3
Princess Cres. Pais 114 A3
Princess Ct. Helen 16 C1
Princess Ct. Kilmk 228 A2
Princess Dr. Coat 121 D3
Princess Rd. Holy 142 C3
Princess Sq. New 165 F3

Princess St. Bon 40 A3
Princess Way. Ros 15 D2
Printers Land. Thorn 158 A3
Priory Ave. Pais 114 A4
Priory Dr. Udd 140 B4
Priory Gate. Wish 186 A4
Priory Pl. Cumb 60 C1
Priory Pl. Glasg 95 E4
Priory Rd. Glasg 95 E4
Priory St. Udd 161 E4
Priory Terr. Wish 164 B1
Procession Rd. Pais 133 E3
Professors' Sq. Glasg 96 B1
Progress Dr. Cald 105 D3
Promenade. Ayr 236 A2
Prosen St. Glasg 118 C2
Prospect Ave. Glasg 138 C3
Prospect Ave. Udd 140 C4
Prospect Ct. Ham 161 E3
Prospect Dr. Ash 199 F4
Prospect Rd. Cumb 61 E3
Prospect Rd. Glasg 136 B4
Prospect St. Falk 41 F3
Prospecthill Cir. Glasg 117 E1
Prospecthill Cres. Glasg 137 F4
Prospecthill Dr. Glasg 137 E4
Prospecthill Pl. Glasg 137 F4
Prospecthill Pl. Green 45 F2
Prospecthill Rd. Falk 42 A1
Prospecthill Rd. Glasg 137 E4
Prospecthill Rd. Salt 206 A1
Prospecthill Sq. Glasg 137 E4
Prospecthill St. Green 45 F2
Provand
  Victoria Gate. Glasg 96 E3
Provan Hall Cres. Glasg 120 A2
Provanhill St. Glasg 97 F1
Provanmill Rd. Glasg 98 C1
Provost Cl. John 111 F2
Provost Gate. Lark 185 D2
Provost
  Hunter Ave. Alva 5 E4
Pullar Ave. B of A 2 A3
Pullar Ct. B of A 2 A3
Pundeavon Ave. Kilb 149 D2
Purdie. E Kil 160 B3
Purdie St. Ham 162 A3
Purdon St. Glasg 96 A1
Putyan Ave. Dalry 191 D4
Pyatshaw Rd. Lark 185 D1

Quadrant Rd. Glasg 136 C3
Quadrant The. Glasg 157 F4
Quail Rd. Ayr 236 A2
Quakerfield. Bann 7 F1
Quarrelton Rd. John 111 F1
Quarrier St. Green 46 B2
Quarrolhall Cres. Stew 24 A2
Quarry Ave. Glasg 139 F2
Quarry Dr. Kil 69 E1
Quarry Dr. Kirk 79 F4
Quarry Knowe. Bann 11 F4
Quarry Knowe. Dumb 49 E3
Quarry Knowe Pl. Hat 141 F2
Quarry Knowe. Rhu 15 F3
Quarry La. Dumb 49 E3
Quarry La. Eagle 178 B2
Quarry La. Lennox 33 E1
Quarry Pk. E Kil 180 C4
Quarry Pl. Dumb 49 E3
Quarry Pl. Glasg 138 C3
Quarry Pl. Ham 162 A4
Quarry Pl. N Sau 10 B4
Quarry Pl. Shot 146 B3
Quarry Rd. Aird 103 D1
Quarry Rd. Barr 134 A2
Quarry Rd. Cam 6 B3
Quarry Rd. E Kil 180 B3
Quarry Rd. Irvine 219 E2
Quarry Rd. Lark 185 D1
Quarry Rd. P Glasg 68 C4
Quarry Rd. Pais 113 F3
Quarry Rd. Shot 146 B3
Quarry St. Coat 122 B4
Quarry St. Ham 162 C2
Quarry St. Holy 143 D2
Quarry St. John 111 F1
Quarry St. Lark 185 D1
Quarry St. Shot 146 B3
Quarry St. Wish 165 D2
Quarrybank. Kilbar 111 E1
Quarrybrae Ave. Newt M 157 E4
Quarrybrae Gdns. Tan 141 E3
Quarrybrae St. Glasg 118 C3
Quarryknowe. Glasg 137 F4
Quarryknowe. Lan 215 D2
Quarryknowe St. Dunt 74 C4
Quarryknowe St. Glasg 118 C3
Quarryside St. Glenm 102 C2
Quarrywood Ave. Glasg 98 B2
Quarrywood Rd. Glasg 98 B2
Quay Pend. Dumb 49 F2
Quay Rd. Glasg 118 A1
Quay Road N. Glasg 118 A1
Quay St. Dumb 49 F2
Quay St. Salt 216 C4
Quebec Dr. E Kil 159 E1
Quebec Gr. E Kil 159 E1
Quebec Wynd. Glasg 139 D2

Queen
  Elizabeth Ave. Glasg 114 C4
Queen Elizabeth Ct. Mother 163 E4
Queen Elizabeth Sq. Glasg 117 E2
Queen Margaret Dr. Glasg .. 96 C2
Queen Mary Ave. Clyde 74 B1
Queen Mary Ave. Glasg 117 D1
Queen Mary St. Glasg 118 A2
Queen Pl. Irvine 219 E3
Queen Sq. Glasg 116 C1
Queen St. Alt 10 A4
Queen St. Alva 5 D4
Queen St. Ayr 236 A1
Queen St. Bann 7 E1
Queen St. Falk 42 B3
Queen St. Falk 8 B2
Queen St. Glasg 117 E4
Queen St. Glasg 138 A4
Queen St. Ham 162 A3
Queen St. Helen 16 B2
Queen St. Kilmk 227 F4
Queen St. Kilw 208 A2
Queen St. Kirk 79 E4
Queen St. Mother 163 F4
Queen St. New 165 F3
Queen St. P Glasg 47 E1
Queen St. Pais 113 F2
Queen St. Ren 94 B2
Queen St. Stir 7 D4
Queen St. Stone 198 C1
Queen Victoria Dr. Glasg 95 E2
Queen
  Victoria Gate. Glasg 95 E3
Queen Victoria St. Aird 122 C4
Queen's Ave. B of A 2 A3
Queen's Ave. Glasg 139 D3
Queen's Court. Helen 25 C4
Queen's Cres. Car 188 A1
Queen's Cres. Chap 123 E1
Queen's Cres. Falk 41 F3
Queen's Cres. Glasg 97 D1
Queen's Cres. B of A 1 C3
Queen's Ct. Miln 76 A4
Queen's Dr. Alex 27 E2
Queen's Dr. Ard 205 E2
Queen's Dr. Cumb 61 F3
Queen's Dr. Glasg 117 D1
Queen's Dr. Kilmk 228 A3
Queen's Dr. Lar 23 E1
Queen's Dr La. Glasg 117 D1
Queen's Gdns. Glasg 96 B2
Queen's La. B of A 2 A4
Queen's Park Ave. Glasg .. 117 D1
Queen's Pl. Glasg 96 B2
Queen's Pl. Kilw 208 A2
Queen's Quadrant. Ayr 236 A1
Queen's Rd. John 112 B1
Queen's Rd. Stir 2 A1
Queen's St. Call 66 C3
Queen's St. Cle 144 A1
Queen's Terr. Ayr 238 C4
Queen's Terrace La. Ayr 238 C4
Queens Cres. Hat 141 F2
Queens Cres. Holy 142 C2
Queens Dr. Bishop 72 B2
Queens Dr. Dunl 21 F2
Queens Dr. Falk 41 E3
Queens Dr. Ham 183 E3
Queens Point. Rhu 15 E3
Queens Terr. Pres 233 D1
Queens Way. Alex 27 E2
Queens Way. Lennox 78 A4
Queensbank Ave. Muir 100 C4
Queensberry Ave. Bear 75 F4
Queensberry Ave. Newt M .. 157 F4
Queensborough
  Gdns. Glasg 96 A2
Queensby Ave. Glasg 120 A3
Queensby Dr. Glasg 120 A3
Queensby Pl. Glasg 120 B3
Queensby Rd. Glasg 120 B3
Queensdale Ave. Lark 199 D4
Queensdale Rd. Lark 199 D4
Queensferry St. Glasg 117 F1
Queenshaugh Dr. Stir 2 C1
Queensland Ct. Glasg 115 E3
Queensland Dr. Glasg 115 E3
Queensland Gdns. Glasg .. 115 E3
Queensland La E. Glasg 115 E3
Queensland La W. Glasg .. 115 E3
Queenslie St. Glasg 98 B1
Queensway. E Kil 159 E4
Queensway. Gour 44 B3
Queenzieburn Ind Est. Kils .. 60 A4
Quendale Dr. Glasg 118 C2
Quentin St. Glasg 116 C1
Quinton Gdns. Glasg 120 A3

Raasay Cres. Aird 123 F3
Raasay Dr. Pais 133 E4
Raasay Gdns. Newt M 156 C3
Raasay Pl. Glasg 97 E4

Raasay St. Glasg 97 E4
Racecourse Rd. Ayr 238 C2
Racecourse View. Ayr 238 C3
Racecourse View. Ham 162 C3
Rachan St. Glasg 100 B1
Radnor St. Clyde 74 A1
Rae St. Sten 23 E2
Raeberry St. Glasg 96 C2
Raebog Cres. Aird 102 C1
Raebog Rd. Glenm 102 C2
Raeburn Ave. E Kil 160 A3
Raeburn Cres. Ham 161 F2
Raeburn Pl. E Kil 160 A2
Raeburn Wlk. Hat 142 A4
Raes Rd. Car 201 D4
Raeside Ave. Newt M 156 B2
Raeswood Dr. Glasg 114 C2
Raeswood Pl. Glasg 135 D4
Raeswood Rd. Glasg 114 C2
Raewell Cres. Hat 141 F2
Rafford St. Glasg 116 A4
Raggithill Ave. Moss 237 F3
Raglan St. Bonh 27 F2
Raglan St. Glasg 97 D1
Raglan Street La. Bonh 27 F2
Railway Rd. Aird 122 B4
Raise St. Salt 216 C4
Raith Ave. Glasg 137 E2
Raith Ave. Pres 236 C4
Raith Dr. Hat 142 A2
Raith Dr. Cumb 82 B2
Raith Rd. Fen 213 D2
Raith Terr. Pres 236 C4
Raithburn Ave. Glasg 137 E2
Raithburn Ave. Kilmk 222 C2
Raithburn Rd. Glasg 137 E2
Raithhill. Ayr 239 D1
Raleigh Ct. Falk 41 F3
Ralston Ave. Glasg 114 C2
Ralston Ct. Glasg 114 C2
Ralston Dr. Hurl 228 B4
Ralston Path. Glasg 114 C2
Ralston Pl. Glasg 114 C2
Ralston Rd. Barr 134 B1
Ralston Rd. Bear 75 F3
Ralston St. Aird 122 C4
Ralston St. Pais 113 F1
Ralstonyards Rd. Hurl 228 C4
Ramage Rd. Car 188 A1
Ramillies Ct. Car 188 A1
Ramoth. Lan 214 B2
Rampart Ave. Glasg 95 D3
Ramsay Ave. John 111 F1
Ramsay Ct. Newt M 157 F4
Ramsay Ave. Laur 42 C2
Ramsay Cres. Kilbar 111 D1
Ramsay Ct. Newt M 156 C2
Ramsay Hill. E Kil 160 A2
Ramsay Pl. Coat 121 F3
Ramsay Pl. John 111 F1
Ramsay Pl. Stir 2 A1
Ramsay St. Clyde 73 F2
Ramsey Tullis Ave. Tull 4 B1
Ramsey Tullis Dr. Tull 4 B1
Ramsey Wynd. Hat 142 A4
Ramstane Pl. Irvine 220 B3
Ranald Gdns. Glasg 139 E3
Randolph Ave. Glasg 137 D1
Randolph Cres. Bann 7 E1
Randolph Ct. Stir 7 D3
Randolph Dr. Glasg 136 C1
Randolph Gdns. Den 21 E1
Randolph La. Glasg 95 F2
Randolph Pl. Bann 7 E1
Randolph Rd. Glasg 95 F2
Randolph Rd. Glasg 96 A2
Randolph Rd. Stir 7 D3
Randolph Terr. Stir 7 D2
Randyford Rd. Falk 42 C3
Randyford St. Falk 42 C3
Ranfurly Ct. B of W 110 B4
Ranfurly Pl. B of W 110 C3
Ranfurly Rd. B of W 110 C3
Ranfurly Rd. Glasg 114 C3
Range Ave. Mother 164 B2
Range Pl. Ham 162 C1
Range Rd. Mother 164 A2
Rangehouse Rd. E Kil 160 A2
Ranken Dr. Irvine 219 E2
Rankin Cres. Gree 83 F1
Rankin Ct. Kilmk 223 D3
Rankin Pl. Newt M 156 B3
Rankin Rd. Wish 165 F2
Rankin St. Car 187 F2
Rankin St. Green 45 E2
Rankine Pl. John 111 F2
Rankine St. John 111 F2
Rannoch Ave. Bish 78 A1
Rannoch Ave. Coat 101 E1
Rannoch Ave. Ham 162 A1
Rannoch Ave. Newt M 156 C3
Rannoch Ct. Cumb 62 A3
Rannoch Ct. Ham 161 F3
Rannoch Dr. Bear 76 A2

Rannoch Dr. Cumb 82 A3
Rannoch Dr. Kirk 59 D1
Rannoch Dr. Ren 94 B2
Rannoch Dr. Wish 165 D1
Rannoch Gdns. Bish 78 B1
Rannoch Gn. E Kil 159 F2
Rannoch Pl. Irvine 219 D4
Rannoch Pl. Irvine 219 E3
Rannoch Pl. Pais 114 A2
Rannoch Pl. Shi 66 C4
Rannoch Pl. Sten 146 C3
Rannoch Pl. Sten 23 F2
Rannoch Rd. Aird 102 C1
Rannoch Rd. John 131 F4
Rannoch Rd. Kil 89 E4
Rannoch Rd. Tan 120 C1
Rannoch St. Glasg 137 D3
Rannoch Terr. Lark 185 E1
Rannoch Way. Udd 141 D2
Rannock La. Muir 81 D1
Raploch Ave. Glasg 95 D2
Raploch Cres. Dunt 74 B4
Raploch La. Glasg 95 D2
Raploch Rd. Lark 184 C2
Raploch Rd. Stir 1 A4
Raploch St. Lark 184 C2
Rashieburn. Ersk 73 D1
Rashieglen. Ersk 73 D1
Rashiehill. Ersk 73 D1
Rashiehill Rd. Slam 46 A4
Rashielee Ave. Ersk 73 D1
Rashielee Rd. Ersk 73 D1
Rashiewood. Ersk 73 D1
Rashley Sq. Ard 205 E2
Rathlin Ave. Kirk 227 F2
Rathlin House. Pres 236 A3
Rathlin St. Glasg 116 A4
Rathlin Terr. Dumb 49 E3
Ratho Dr. Glasg 97 F2
Ratho Pk. Ham 183 D4
Ratho St. Green 46 B2
Rattray. Ersk 73 D2
Rattray St. Glasg 118 C2
Ravel Row. Glasg 118 B3
Ravelston Rd. Bear 75 F1
Ravelston St. Glasg 118 C3
Raven Rd. Green 45 D3
Ravens Ct. Bish 97 F4
Ravenscliffe Dr. Glasg 136 A2
Ravenscourt. Thorn 158 B3
Ravenscraig Ave. Pais 113 E1
Ravenscraig Ct. Hat 142 A3
Ravenscraig Dr. Glasg 135 E3
Ravenscraig Rd. Stew 211 E4
Ravenscraig Terr. Glasg 135 E3
Ravenshall Rd. Glasg 136 B4
Ravenshill Dr. Cle 144 B1
Ravenstone Dr. Glasg 136 B1
Ravenswood Ave. Pais 132 C4
Ravenswood Dr. Glasg 136 B1
Ravenswood Rd. Glasg 120 B3
Rawyards Ave. Aird 103 D1
Raymond Pl. E Kil 159 E1
Rayne Pl. Glasg 75 D2
Ream Ave. Aird 123 F3
Reay Ave. Card 48 A4
Recawr Pk. Ayr 239 D2
Red Bridge Ct. Coat 122 A4
Red Cross House. Irvine 219 E1
Red Deer Rd. E Kil 180 B4
Red Fox Dr. Bonh 27 F4
Red Gables Sq. Ard 205 D2
Red Rd. Card 25 F2
Red Rd. Glasg 98 A2
Red Road Ct. Glasg 98 A2
Red Row. Alex 27 E1
Redan St. Glasg 117 F3
Redbrae Rd. Kirk 79 F4
Redburn Ave. Glasg 157 D4
Redburn. Bonh 28 A1
Redburn
Caravan Pk. Irvine 219 D4
Redburn Ct. Cumb 62 C3
Redburn Ind Est. Irvine 219 E4
Redburn Pl. Cumb 62 C3
Redburn Pl. Irvine 219 D4
Redburn Rd. Blac 107 D1
Redburn Rd. Cumb 62 C3
Redburn
Roundabout. Irvine 219 D4
Redcastle Sq. Glasg 99 E1
Redcliffe Dr. E Kil 180 A4
Redclyffe Gdns. Helen 16 B2
Reddance Terr. Dalry 191 D2
Reddans Pk. Stew 195 E1
Redding Ave. Kilmk 222 C2
Redding Rd. Laur 42 C2
Rederech Cres. Ham 161 F1
Redford St. Glasg 118 B4
Redgate Pl. Glasg 95 D2
Redgauntlet Rd. Helen 25 C4
Redgrave. E Kil 160 B3
Redhaws Rd. Shot 147 D2
Redhill Rd. Cumb 61 E2
Redhills View. Lennox 57 F4
Redholme. Lark 185 D1
Redhouse La. Car 187 F2
Redhurst Cres. Pais 133 E4

Redhurst La. Pais 133 E4
Redhurst Way. Pais 133 E4
Redlands La. Glasg 96 B2
Redlands Rd. Glasg 96 B2
Redlands Rd. Tull 4 A2
Redlands Terr. Glasg 96 B2
Redlands Terrace La. Glasg 96 B2
Redlawood Pl. Glasg 140 A3
Redlawood Rd. Glasg 140 A3
Redmire Cres. Alla 167 D4
Redmoss Rd. Dunt 73 F4
Redmoss Rd. M of C 58 A3
Redmoss St. Glasg 97 D3
Rednock St. Glasg 97 E2
Redpath Dr. Glasg 115 E3
Redpath Dr. Sten 24 A2
Redstone Ave. Kilw 208 A2
Redwell Pl. All 9 F4
Redwing Gdns. Wish 165 D1
Redwood Ave. E Kil 158 C1
Redwood Cres. Bishop 72 B2
Redwood Cres. E Kil 158 C1
Redwood Cres. Tan 141 E4
Redwood Ct. E Kil 179 F4
Redwood Ct. Kil 158 C1
Redwood Dr. E Kil 158 C1
Redwood Dr. Glasg 98 A2
Redwood Pl. E Kil 158 C1
Redwood Pl. Kirk 79 D3
Redwood Pl. Tan 141 E4
Redwood Rd. Cumb 62 B2
Redwood Rd. Holy 143 D3
Reedlands Dr. Den 39 E4
Reedloch Dr. Troon 229 F4
Reek St. Beith 171 F4
Reelick Ave. Clyde 94 C4
Reelick Quadrant. Clyde 94 C4
Reema Rd. Hat 142 A3
Reen Pl. Udd 141 D2
Reform St. Beith 150 A1
Regal Ct. Dalry 191 E4
Regency Way. Ham 163 D1
Regent Moray St. Glasg 96 B1
Regent Park Sq. Glasg 116 C1
Regent Pl. Clyde 73 F2
Regent Sq. Kirk 79 E2
Regent St. Clyde 73 F2
Regent St. Green 45 F2
Regent St. Kirk 79 E2
Regent St. Pais 114 A3
Regents Gate. Udd 140 B2
Register Ave. Hat 142 A2
Register Rd. Kils 60 C4
Regwood St. Glasg 136 B4
Reid Ave. Bear 76 A3
Reid Ave. Lin 112 A3
Reid Gr. Mother 164 A2
Reid Pl. Glasg 117 F2
Reid St. Aird 103 D1
Reid St. Coat 122 A4
Reid St. Glasg 117 F2
Reid St. Glasg 138 A4
Reid St. Ham 161 F3
Reid St. Salt 125 D1
Reid's Ave. Steven 206 B1
Reidvale St. Glasg 118 A3
Reilly Rd. Bon 40 A4
Reilly Rd. Hous 91 E4
Reith Dr. E Kil 180 B4
Remus Pl. Holy 142 C3
Renfield La. Glasg 117 D4
Renfield St. Glasg 117 D4
Renfield St. Ren 94 B2
Renfrew Ct. Glasg 117 E4
Renfrew La. Glasg 117 D4
Renfrew Rd. Glasg 95 D1
Renfrew Rd. Pais 113 F4
Rennie Ct. Coat 121 E2
Rennie St. Glasg 117 D4
Rennie Pl. E Kil 159 D2
Rennie Rd. Salt 216 C4
Rennie Rd. Kils 36 A1
Rennie St. Falk 42 A2
Rennie St. Kilmk 228 A4
Renshaw Dr. Glasg 115 D3
Renshaw Rd. Bishop 72 A2
Renshaw Rd. John 112 B1
Renton Rd. Alex 49 E3
Renton Rd. Dumb 49 E3
Renton Rd. Green 46 B1
Renton St. Glasg 97 E1
Renwick Pl. Lan 215 E3
Renwick Way. Pres 236 B3
Resipol Rd. Stepps 99 F3
Reston Dr. Glasg 115 D3
Reuther Ave. Glasg 138 A4
Revoch Dr. Glasg 95 D3
Reynolds Path. Wish 165 E1
Rhannan Rd. Glasg 137 D3
Rhannan Terr. Glasg 137 D3
Rhindhouse Pl. Glasg 120 B3
Rhindhouse Rd. Glasg 120 B3
Rhindmuir Ave. Glasg 120 B3
Rhindmuir Cres. Glasg 120 B3
Rhindmuir Ct. Glasg 120 B3
Rhindmuir Dr. Glasg 120 B3

Rhindmuir Gdns. Glasg 120 B3
Rhindmuir Gr. Glasg 120 B3
Rhindmuir Path. Glasg 120 B3
Rhindmuir Rd. Glasg 120 B3
Rhindmuir Rd. Glasg 120 B3
Rhindmuir View. Glasg 120 B3
Rhindmuir Wynd. Glasg 120 B3
Rhinds St. Coat 121 E2
Rhindsdale Cres. Glasg 120 B3
Rhodders Gr. Alva 5 D4
Rhu Quad. Wish 186 B3
Rhu Rd. Lower. Helen 16 A1
Rhu Rd. Lower. Ros 15 F1
Rhu Road Higher. Helen 16 A2
Rhu-Ellen Ct. Rhu 15 E2
Rhyber Ave. Lan 215 D3
Rhymer St. Glasg 97 F1
Rhymie Rd. Glasg 119 E2
Rhymiebank. Stone 198 B1
Rhynie Dr. Glasg 116 A3
Riach Gdns. Mother 142 B1
Ribblesdale. E Kil 159 E2
Riccarton. E Kil 180 A4
Riccarton Rd. Hurl 228 B3
Riccarton St. Glasg 117 E1
Riccartsbar Ave. Pais 113 E2
Richard Pl. Troon 229 E2
Richardland Pl. Kilmk 228 A4
Richardland Rd. Kilmk 227 F4
Richardson Ave. Hurl 228 C3
Richie Ave. Card 48 A4
Richmond Ave. Newt M 157 F4
Richmond Ct. Glasg 138 B4
Richmond Dr. Bish 78 A2
Richmond Dr. Glasg 138 B4
Richmond Dr. Glasg 138 C3
Richmond Dr. Lin 112 A4
Richmond Gdns. Muir 100 A4
Richmond Gr. Glasg 138 B4
Richmond Pl. Glasg 138 B4
Richmond St. Clyde 74 B1
Richmond St. Glasg 117 E4
Richmond Terr. Dund 225 F1
Riddell St. Clyde 74 B2
Riddell St. Coat 122 B4
Riddon Ave. Clyde 94 C4
Riddon Pl. Clyde 94 C4
Riddrie Cres. Glasg 118 C4
Riddrie Knowes. Glasg 118 C4
Riddrievale Ct. Glasg 98 C1
Riddrievale St. Glasg 98 C1
Ridgepark Dr. Lan 215 D4
Ried Ct. Hurl 228 C4
Rig St. Stew 211 E4
Rigby St. Glasg 118 C3
Rigfoot. Irvine 220 A3
Rigghead. Stew 211 E4
Riggs The. Miln 55 D2
Riggs The. Pres 233 E1
Riggs The. Steven 206 B1
Riggside Rd. Glasg 99 E1
Righead Gate. E Kil 159 F1
Righead Roundabout. E Kil 159 E1
Rigland Way. Ren 94 B2
Riglaw Pl. Glasg 95 D4
Rigmuir Rd. Glasg 115 E3
Rimmon Cres. Shot 146 C3
Rimsdale St. Glasg 118 A3
Ring Rd. All 10 A4
Ringford St. Glasg 97 F2
Ripon Dr. Glasg 96 A3
Risk St. Clyde 73 F2
Risk St. Dumb 49 E3
Ristol Rd. Glasg 95 D3
Ritchie Cres. John 112 B2
Ritchie Pl. Kilmk 223 E1
Ritchie Pl. Newt M 156 B2
Ritchie St. Glasg 117 D2
Ritchie St. Mother 164 B2
Ritchie St. W Kil 190 B3
Ritchie's Ct. Lan 215 D2
River Pl. Kilb 149 D1
River Rd. Glasg 139 D4
River St. Ayr 235 F1
River St. Ayr 24 A1
River Terr. Ayr 235 F1
River View. Cree. Card 48 A4
River Wlk. Kilw 207 F1
Riverbank Dr. Hat 142 B2
Riverbank St. Glasg 136 B4
Riverbank St. Glasg 136 B4
Riverdale Gdns. Ham 162 C1
Riverford Rd. Glasg 118 B1
Riverford Rd. Glasg 136 B4
Riversdale La. Glasg 95 D2
Riverside. Bonh 27 F4
Riverside Dr. Stir 2 B2
Riverside Gdns. Newt M 157 F3
Riverside. Hous 91 E1
Riverside La. Dumb 49 F2
Riverside. Miln 55 D1
Riverside Pk. Glasg 137 D1
Riverside Pl. Ayr 239 D4
Riverside Pl. Glasg 139 F3

Riverside Rd. Eagle 178 C4
Riverside Rd. Glasg 136 C4
Riverside Rd. Green 46 A2
Riverside Rd. Irvine 220 B1
Riverside Rd. Kilb 149 D1
Riverside Rd. Lan 214 B2
Riverside Rd. Lark 185 D2
Riverside Rd. Stew 211 F4
Riverside Way. All 10 A2
Riverside Way. Shew 224 C4
Riverview Dr. Glasg 117 D3
Riverview Gdns. Glasg 117 D3
Riverview Pl. Glasg 117 D3
Roaden Ave. Pais 132 C4
Roaden Rd. Pais 132 C4
Roadhead. How 150 C4
Roadside. Cumb 62 A3
Roadside Pl. Gree 103 E4
Robb Terr. Kirk 80 A3
Robert Bruce Ct. Lar 23 D1
Robert Burns Ave. Clyde 74 B2
Robert Burns Ave. Holy 143 F2
Robert Burns Ct. Beith 150 A1
Robert
Burns Quadrant. Hat 141 F3
Robert Creighton Pl. Kilmk 222 C1
Robert Dick Ct. Tull 4 B1
Robert Kinmond Ave. Tull 4 B1
Robert Knox Ave. Tull 4 B1
Robert Noble Pl. Kilmk 222 B1
Robert Smillie Cres. Lark 185 D1
Robert St. Chap 123 F2
Robert St. Glasg 116 A4
Robert St. P Glasg 47 F1
Robert St. Shot 146 C2
Robert
Templeton Dr. Glasg 139 D3
Robert W Service Ct. Kilw 207 F1
Robertland Rigg. Stew 195 F1
Robertland Sq. Stew 211 F4
Roberton Ave. Glasg 116 B1
Roberton St. Chap 123 F2
Roberts St. Wish 165 D2
Robertson Ave. Bon 40 A3
Robertson Ave. Glasg 236 B1
Robertson Cres. Neil 154 B4
Robertson Cres. Salt 217 D4
Robertson Dr. E Kil 160 A1
Robertson Dr. Hat 142 A2
Robertson La. Glasg 117 D4
Robertson Pl. Kilmk 228 A4
Robertson St. Aird 122 C4
Robertson St. Alva 5 D4
Robertson St. Barr 134 A1
Robertson St. Glasg 117 D4
Robertson St. Ham 161 F3
Robertson Terr. Glasg 120 B3
Robin Rd. Green 45 D3
Robin Way. Glasg 139 E4
Robroyston Ave. Glasg 98 C2
Robroyston Rd. Bish 78 C1
Robroyston Rd. Glasg 98 B2
Robroyston Rd. Glasg 98 C3
Robroyston St. Stepps 79 D2
Robshill Ct. Newt M 156 B2
Robslee Ave. Ayr 238 C3
Robslee Cres. Glasg 136 A2
Robslee Dr. Glasg 136 A2
Robslee Rd. Glasg 136 A2
Robson Gr. Glasg 117 D2
Rochdale Pl. Kirk 79 E4
Roche Way. Dalry 191 E4
Rochsoles Dr. Aird 103 D1
Rochsolloch
Farm Cotts. Aird 122 C4
Rochsolloch Rd. Aird 122 B3
Rock Dr. Kilbar 111 D1
Rock St. Glasg 97 D2
Rockall Dr. Glasg 137 E2
Rockbank Pl. Dunt 74 B3
Rockbank Pl. Glasg 118 A3
Rockbank St. Glasg 118 A3
Rockburn Cres. Hat 142 A4
Rockburn Dr. Newt M 157 E4
Rockcliffe St. Glasg 117 F2
Rockfield Pl. Glasg 98 B3
Rockfield Rd. Glasg 98 B3
Rockhampton Ave. E Kil 180 A4
Rockmount Ave. Barr 134 B1
Rockmount Ave. Glasg 136 A2
Rockpark Ct. Salt 217 D4
Rockrose Pk. Ayr 239 D2
Rockwell Ave. Pais 133 E4
Rodding The. Lan 215 D3
Roddinghead Rd. Newt M 157 D3
Rodger Ave. Newt M 156 B3
Rodger Dr. Glasg 138 A3
Rodger Pl. Glasg 138 A3
Rodil Ave. Glasg 137 E2
Rodney Pl. Helen 17 D1
Rodney Rd. Gour 44 C3
Rodney St. Glasg 97 D1
Roebank Dr. Barr 134 B1
Roebank Rd. Beith 150 B1
Roebank St. Glasg 118 A4

Roffey Park Rd. Pais 114 B3
Rogart St. Glasg 117 F3
Rogerfield Rd. Glasg 120 B4
Rogers Ct. Stone 198 B1
Rokeby La. Glasg 96 C2
Roland Cres. Newt M 156 C2
Roman Ave. Bear 75 F3
Roman Ave. Glasg 75 F3
Roman Cres. O Kil 72 C4
Roman Ct. Bear 75 F3
Roman Ct. Lan 215 F4
Roman Dr. Bear 75 F3
Roman Dr. Falk 41 E3
Roman Hill Rd. Dunt 74 A4
Roman Pl. Hat 141 F2
Roman Rd. Ayr 239 E3
Roman Rd. Bear 75 F3
Roman Rd. Bon 40 A2
Roman Rd. Dunt 74 A3
Roman Rd. Kirk 79 D4
Roman Rd. Mother 163 F4
Roman Way. Tan 141 E3
Romney Ave. Glasg 137 E3
Rona Ave. P Glasg 69 D4
Rona Pl. Kilmk 223 D3
Rona St. Glasg 98 A1
Rona Terr. Glasg 138 C2
Ronades Rd. Falk 42 A4
Ronald Cres. Lar 23 D1
Ronald Pl. Stir 7 D4
Ronaldsay Ct. Irvine 225 D4
Ronaldsay Dr. Bish 78 B1
Ronaldsay Pl. Cumb 82 B4
Ronaldsay St. Glasg 97 E4
Ronaldshaw Pk. Ayr 238 C3
Ronay St. Glasg 97 E4
Ronay St. Wish 165 F3
Rook Rd. Green 45 D3
Rooksdell Ave. Pais 113 E1
Ropework La. Glasg 117 E3
Rorison Pl. Ash 185 F1
Rose Pl. Salt 206 A1
Rose Cres. Gour 44 B3
Rose Cres. Ham 161 F2
Rose Dale. Bish 98 A4
Rose Knowe Rd. Glasg 137 E4
Rose Mount Ct. Aird 123 E4
Rose St. All 4 C4
Rose St. Bon 40 A3
Rose St. Cumb 82 A3
Rose St. Glasg 97 D1
Rose St. Green 45 E2
Rose St. Kirk 79 E4
Rose St. Mother 164 A3
Rose Terr. Den 21 E1
Rose Terr. Sten 23 F2
Rosebank Ave. Falk 41 F3
Rosebank Ave. Kirk 79 F4
Rosebank Ave. Udd 140 C1
Rosebank Cres. Ayr 238 C3
Rosebank Dr. Glasg 139 E2
Rosebank Dr. Udd 140 C1
Rosebank Gdns. Irvine 219 F4
Rosebank La. Udd 141 D2
Rosebank. N Sau 5 E1
Rosebank Pl. Falk 41 F3
Rosebank Pl. Ham 162 A2
Rosebank Pl. Kilmk 222 C1
Rosebank Rd. Hat 142 A4
Rosebank Rd. Wish 186 B3
Rosebank St. Aird 123 F4
Rosebank Terr. Coat 121 D2
Rosebank Terr. Kil 89 E4
Rosebery Pk. Ayr 239 D1
Roseberry La. Chap 123 F2
Roseberry Rd. Ham 162 A2
Roseberry Rd. Chap 123 F2
Rosebery Pl. Stir 117 F1
Rosebery Pl. Stir 2 B1
Rosedale Ave. Pais 132 B4
Rosedale Dr. Glasg 120 A2
Rosedale. E Kil 159 E2
Rosedale Gdns. Glasg 96 B4
Rosedale Gdns. Lennox 16 C1
Rosedale St. Lan 214 C1
Rosedene Terr. Hat 142 A3
Rosefield Gdns. Udd 140 C4
Rosegreen Cres. Hat 142 A4
Rosehall Ind Est. Coat 122 A2
Rosehall Ind Rd. Coat 122 A2
Rosehall Rd. Hat 141 F3
Rosehall Rd. Sten 23 F2
Rosehall Terr. Falk 42 A2
Rosehall Terr. Wish 164 C1
Rosehill Dr. Cumb 62 C3
Rosehill Rd. Lennox 78 B4
Rosehill Rd. Lennox 78 B4
Rosemount. Cumb 61 F3
Rosemount Dr. Troon 229 E4

281

Rosemount Gdns. Pres Saline St. Coat

Rosemount Gdns. Pres 236 B3
Rosemount. Kilw 207 E1
Rosemount La. B of W 110 A3
Rosemount La. Lark 185 E1
Rosemount Meadows. Udd 140 C1
Rosemount Pl. Gour 44 A3
Rosemount St. Glasg 97 F1
Rosendale Way. Udd 161 F4
Roseneath Dr. Helen 16 A1
Roseneath St. Green 45 E4
Rosenheath Gate. E Kil 159 E1
Rosepark Ave. Tan 141 E3
Rosepark Cotts. Coat 121 F2
Rosevale Cres. Ham 162 A1
Rosevale Cres. Hat 142 B2
Rosevale Rd. Bear 75 F2
Rosevale St. Glasg 96 A1
Rosewood Ave. Hat 142 A4
Rosewood Ave. Pais 113 D1
Rosewood Path. Hat 141 F3
Rosewood St. Glasg 95 F4
Roslea Dr. Glasg 118 A4
Roslin Ct. Kil 89 E4
Roslin St. Green 45 F3
Roslin Tower. Glasg 138 C2
Roslyn Dr. Coat 120 C3
Rosneath Rd. P Glasg 68 B4
Rosneath Rd. Ros 15 D1
Rosneath St. Glasg 116 A4
Ross Ave. Kirk 79 F4
Ross Ave. Ren 94 A1
Ross Cres. Falk 41 E3
Ross Cres. Mother 163 E3
Ross Ct. Stir 7 D2
Ross Dr. Aird 122 C2
Ross Dr. Mother 163 E3
Ross Dr. Tan 121 E1
Ross Gdns. Mother 163 E3
Ross Hall Pl. Ren 94 B2
Ross Pl. Glasg 138 B2
Ross Rd. Salt 205 F1
Ross St. Ayr 236 B1
Ross St. Coat 122 A4
Ross St. Glasg 117 E3
Ross St. Pais 114 A2
Ross Terr. Ham 163 E1
Rossbank Rd. P Glasg 47 D1
Rossendale Ct. Glasg 136 B4
Rossendale Rd. Glasg 136 B4
Rosshall Ave. Pais 114 B2
Rosshill Ave. Glasg 114 C3
Rosshill Rd. Glasg 114 C3
Rossie Cres. Bish 98 B4
Rossland Cres. Bishop 72 A2
Rossland Pl. Bishop 72 B1
Rosslea Dr. Glasg 136 B1
Rosslyn Ave. E Kil 160 A2
Rosslyn Ave. Glasg 138 B4
Rosslyn Ct. Ham 162 A2
Rosslyn Pl. Ayr 236 A2
Rosslyn Rd. Ash 199 F4
Rosslyn Rd. Bear 75 D3
Rosslyn Terr. Glasg 96 B2
Rostan Rd. Glasg 136 B3
Rosyth Rd. Glasg 117 F1
Rosyth St. Glasg 117 F1
Rotherwick Dr. Pais 114 C2
Rotherwood Ave. Glasg 75 E1
Rotherwood Ave. Glasg 75 F1
Rotherwood Ave. Pais 132 C4
Rotherwood La. Glasg 75 E1
Rotherwood Pl. Glasg 95 E4
Rotherwood Way. Pais 132 C4
Rothes Dr. Glasg 96 B4
Rothes Pl. Glasg 76 B1
Rothesay Cres. Coat 122 A2
Rothesay Pl. Coat 122 A2
Rothesay Pl. E Kil 159 F1
Rothesay Pl. Kilmk 222 C2
Rothesay Rd. Gour 44 C2
Rothesay St. E Kil 180 C4
Rottenrow E. Glasg 117 E4
Rottenrow. Glasg 117 E4
Rottenrow. Glasg 117 F4
Roughburn Rd. B of A 2 A3
Roughcraig St. Aird 103 D1
Roughlands Cres. Sten 24 A2
Roughlands Dr. Sten 24 A2
Roughlea Pl. Troon 229 F3
Roughrigg Rd. Chap 124 B3
Rouken Glen Rd. Glasg 136 A1
Roukenburn St. Glasg 135 F2
Round Riding Rd. Dumb 50 A2
Roundel The. Falk 42 B4
Roundel The. Wish 165 E1
Roundelwood. N Sau 5 D1
Roundhill Dr. John 112 C2
Roundknowe Rd. Glasg 120 B1
Rowallan Cres. Pres 236 B4
Rowallan Dr. Bann 11 F4
Rowallan Dr. Kilmk 223 D2
Rowallan Gdns. Glasg 96 A2
Rowallan. Kilw 207 E1
Rowallan La. Glasg 96 A2
Rowallan La. Newt M 157 F4
Rowallan Rd. Glasg 135 F1
Rowallan St. Helen 16 A2
Rowallan Terr. Stepps 99 D2
Rowallen Dr. Bann 11 F4
Rowan Ave. M of C 58 B3
Rowan Ave. Ren 94 B2
Rowan Cres. Ayr 239 E3
Rowan Cres. Falk 41 D2
Rowan Cres. Kirk 79 E3
Rowan Ct. Bann 7 F1
Rowan Ct. Wish 164 B1
Rowan Dr. Bank 38 C1
Rowan Dr. Bear 76 A4
Rowan Dr. Clyde 73 F2
Rowan Dr. Dumb 49 D2
Rowan Gate. Pais 113 F1
Rowan Gdns. Glasg 116 A2
Rowan House. Pres 236 A3
Rowan La. Holy 143 D1
Rowan Pl. Beith 171 E4
Rowan Pl. Coat 121 F2
Rowan Pl. Glasg 139 E3
Rowan Pl. Kilmk 227 E4
Rowan Pl. Troon 229 E2
Rowan Pl. Udd 161 E4
Rowan Rd. Cumb 62 B2
Rowan Rd. Glasg 116 A2
Rowan Rd. Lin 111 F4
Rowan Rise. Ham 162 C1
Rowan St. Beith 171 E4
Rowan St. Green 45 E3
Rowan St. Pais 113 F1
Rowan St. Wish 165 D3
Rowan Terr. Irvine 219 E2
Rowanbank Pl. Aird 122 B4
Rowanbank Rd. Pres 236 C4
Rowand Ave. Glasg 136 B2
Rowandale Ave. Glasg 120 A2
Rowanden Ave. Hat 142 A3
Rowanhill Pl. Kilmk 227 E4
Rowanlea Ave. Pais 132 C4
Rowanlea Dr. Glasg 136 B2
Rowanlea. Plains 103 F2
Rowanpark Dr. Barr 134 A3
Rowans Gdns. Udd 141 D2
Rowans The. Bish 77 F1
Rowans The. N Sau 5 E1
Rowanside Terr. Ard 205 E2
Rowantree Ave. Glasg 138 A3
Rowantree Ave. Holy 143 E4
Rowantree Ave. Tan 141 E4
Rowantree Gdns. Glasg 138 A3
Rowantree Gdns. Irvine 220 A3
Rowantree Pl. John 111 F1
Rowantree Pl. Lark 185 E1
Rowantree Pl. Lennox 57 F4
Rowantree Rd. John 112 A1
Rowantree Terr. Holy 143 D3
Rowantree Terr. Lennox 57 F4
Rowantreehill Rd. Kil 89 F4
Rowena Ave. Glasg 75 E1
Rowmore Quays. Rhu 15 F2
Roxburgh Ave. Green 45 F2
Roxburgh Dr. Bear 75 F4
Roxburgh Dr. Coat 122 B2
Roxburgh Pk. E Kil 159 F1
Roxburgh Pl. Sten 23 F2
Roxburgh Pl. Udd 161 E4
Roxburgh Rd. Hurl 228 C3
Roxburgh Rd. Pais 132 B4
Roxburgh St. Glasg 96 B2
Roxburgh St. Green 45 F2
Roxburgh St. Green 45 F3
Roxburgh Way. Green 45 F2
Roy St. Glasg 97 E2
Roy Young Ave. Bonh 28 A4
Royal Cres. Glasg 116 C4
Royal Dr. Ham 163 D1
Royal Exchange Ct. Glasg 117 E4
Royal Exchange Sq. Glasg 117 E4
Royal Gdns. Stir 7 D4
Royal Inch Terr. Ren 94 B3
Royal St. Gour 44 C4
Royal Terr. Glasg 96 C1
Royal Terr. Wish 165 E4
Royal Terrace La. Glasg 96 C1
Royellen Ave. Ham 161 F1
Royston Rd. Glasg 98 B2
Royston Sq. Glasg 97 F1
Roystonhill. Glasg 97 F1
Rozelle Ave. Glasg 75 D2
Rozelle Terr. Ayr 239 D1
Rubie Cres. Irvine 219 E1
Rubislaw Dr. Bear 75 F2
Ruby St. Glasg 118 A2
Ruchazie Pl. Glasg 118 C4
Ruchazie Rd. Glasg 118 C4
Ruchill Pl. Glasg 96 C3
Ruchill St. Glasg 96 C3
Rue End St. Green 46 A2
Ruel St. Glasg 137 D4
Ruffiees Ave. Barr 134 B2
Rugby Ave. Glasg 95 D4
Rugby Cres. Kilmk 227 E4
Rugby Rd. Kilmk 227 E4
Rulley View. Duni 21 E2
Rullion Pl. Glasg 118 C4
Rumford St. Glasg 117 F2
Rumlie The. Slam 86 A3
Runciman Pl. E Kil 160 A2
Rundell Dr. M of C 58 B3
Rupert St. Glasg 96 C1
Rushyhill St. Glasg 98 A2
Ruskie Rd. Stir 2 A2
Ruskin La. Glasg 96 C2
Ruskin Pl. Glasg 96 C2
Ruskin Pl. Kils 60 B4
Ruskin Sq. Bish 78 A1
Ruskin Terr. Glasg 96 C2
Russel St. Falk 42 A3
Russell Colt St. Coat 122 A4
Russell Ct. Kilmk 223 E2
Russell Dr. Alex 27 E4
Russell Dr. Ayr 236 A1
Russell Dr. Bear 75 F3
Russell Dr. Dalry 191 E4
Russell Gdns. Newt M 156 B2
Russell Gdns. Tan 141 D4
Russell La. Wish 165 D1
Russell Pl. E Kil 180 B4
Russell Pl. Lin 111 F3
Russell Pl. Thorn 158 A3
Russell Rd. Dunt 73 F4
Russell Rd. Lan 215 D3
Russell St. Ayr 236 A1
Russell St. Chap 123 F1
Russell St. Ham 161 F3
Russell St. Hat 142 B3
Russell St. John 112 A2
Russell St. Pais 113 E4
Russell St. Wish 165 D1
Rutherford Ave. Bear 75 D4
Rutherford Ave. Kirk 80 A3
Rutherford Ct. B of A 2 A4
Rutherford Ct. Clyde 74 A1
Rutherford La. E Kil 180 C4
Rutherford Sq. E Kil 180 C4
Rutherglen Rd. Glasg 117 F1
Ruthven Ave. Glasg 136 B1
Ruthven La. Glasg 96 B2
Ruthven La. Glen 101 E3
Ruthven Pl. Bish 98 B4
Ruthven Pl. Troon 229 F2
Ruthven St. Glasg 96 B2
Rutland Cres. Glasg 116 C3
Rutland Pl. Glasg 116 C3
Ryan Rd. Bish 78 A1
Ryan Way. Glasg 138 B2
Ryat Dr. Newt M 156 B3
Ryat Gn. Newt M 156 B3
Ryatt Linn. Ersk 72 C1
Rydal Gr. E Kil 179 F3
Rydal Pl. E Kil 179 F3
Ryde Rd. Wish 165 E2
Ryden Mains Rd. Glenm 102 B2
Rye Cres. Glasg 98 A3
Rye Rd. Glasg 98 B3
Rye Way. Pais 112 C1
Ryebank Rd. Glasg 98 B3
Ryecroft Dr. Glasg 120 A3
Ryedale Pl. Glasg 75 D2
Ryefield Ave. Coat 121 E4
Ryefield Ave. John 111 E1
Ryefield Pl. John 111 E1
Ryefield Rd. Glasg 98 A3
Ryehill Pl. Glasg 98 B3
Ryehill Rd. Glasg 98 B2
Ryemount Rd. Glasg 98 B3
Ryeside Pl. Dalry 169 E1
Ryeside Rd. Glasg 98 A2
Rylands Dr. Glasg 119 E2
Rylands Gdns. Glasg 119 F2
Rylands. Pres 236 B3
Rylees Cres. Glasg 114 C3
Rylees Pl. Glasg 114 C3
Rylees Rd. Glasg 114 C3
Rysland Ave. Newt M 156 C3
Rysland Cres. Newt M 156 C3
Rysland Dr. Fen 213 D2
Ryvra Rd. Glasg 95 E3
Sachelcourt Ave. Bishop 72 A1
Sackville Ave. Glasg 95 F3
Sackville La. Glasg 95 F3
Saddell Rd. Glasg 75 D2
Saffronhall Cres. Ham 162 B2
Saffronhall La. Ham 162 B2
Sainford Cres. Falk 24 A1
St Abb's Dr. Pais 113 D1
St Andrew St. Green 46 A2
St Andrew's Ave. Bish 77 F1
St Andrew's Ave. Pres 236 B3
St Andrew's Brae. Dumb 50 A3
St Andrew's Cres. Dumb 50 A3
St Andrew's Cres. Pais 113 E4
St Andrew's Cross. Glasg 117 D2
St Andrew's Ct. Lar 23 D2
St Andrew's Dr. Air 14 A4
St Andrew's Dr. Glasg 116 B2
St Andrew's Dr. Ham 161 E2
St Andrew's Dr. Inch 113 E4
St Andrew's Dr W. Inch 93 E1
St Andrew's Gdns. Aird 123 D4
St Andrew's Gdns. Dalry 191 D3
St Andrew's Pl. Steven 206 C1
St Andrew's Rd. Ard 205 E2
St Andrew's Rd. Glasg 116 C2
St Andrew's Rd. Ren 94 B1
St Andrew's Sq. Glasg 117 E3
St Andrew's St. Ayr 239 D4
St Andrew's St. Glasg 117 E3
St Andrew's St. Kilmk 227 F4
St Andrew's Wlk. Kilmk 227 F4
St Andrews Ave. Udd 141 D1
St Andrews Cres. Glasg 116 C2
St Andrews Ct. E Kil 180 B3
St Andrews Ct. Holy 143 D3
St Andrews Dr. B of W 110 B3
St Andrews Dr. Cumb 62 A3
St Andrews Dr. Gour 44 A3
St Andrews Gate. Hat 141 F3
St Andrews La. Alex 27 F2
St Andrews La. Gour 44 A3
St Andrews Path. Lark 185 E1
St Andrews Pl. Beith 171 D4
St Andrews Pl. Falk 42 A2
St Andrews Pl. Kils 36 B1
St Andrews St. Holy 143 D3
St Andrews Wynd. Helen 16 C2
St Ann's Dr. Glasg 136 B1
St Anne's Cres. Bann 7 F1
St Barchan's Rd. Kilbar 111 D1
St Blane's Dr. Glasg 137 F3
St Boswell's Cres. Pais 113 D1
St Boswells Dr. Coat 122 B2
St Brennans Ct. Kilb 170 A4
St Bride's Ave. Tan 141 E4
St Bride's Dr. W Kil 190 B3
St Bride's Pl. Irvine 219 E3
St Bride's Rd. Glasg 136 B3
St Bride's Rd. W Kil 190 B3
St Brides Way. Udd 141 D2
St Bryde St. E Kil 159 F1
St Catherine's Rd. Glasg 136 B1
St Catherines Cres. Shot 146 C3
St Clair Ave. Glasg 136 B2
St Clair Terr. Troon 229 D1
St Columba Dr. Kirk 79 F4
St Columba Pl. Steven 206 C1
St Crispin's Pl. Falk 42 A2
St Cuthbert's Cres. Pres 236 B3
St Cuthbert's Rd. Pres 236 B3
St Cyrus Gdns. Bish 78 B1
St Cyrus Rd. Bish 78 B1
St David's Ct. Lar 23 D1
St David's Pl. Lark 185 D2
St Davids Dr. Aird 123 E2
St Denis Way. Coat 121 F4
St Edmunds Gr. Miln 55 D2
St Enoch Ave. Tan 141 E4
St Enoch Pl. Glasg 117 D4
St Enoch Shopping Ctr. Glasg 117 E3
St Enoch Sq. Glasg 117 D3
St Fillans Dr. Hous 91 D1
St Fillans Rd. Stepps 99 E3
St Flanan Rd. Twe 59 E1
St George's Cross. Glasg 97 D1
St George's Ct. Lar 23 D1
St George's Pl. Glasg 97 D1
St George's Rd. Ayr 236 A2
St George's Rd. Glasg 97 D1
St Germains. Bear 75 F2
St Giles Pk. Ham 162 A1
St Giles Sq. Falk 41 D3
St Giles Way. Falk 41 D3
St Giles Way. Ham 162 A1
St Helena Cres. Dunt 74 B3
St Inan Ave. Irvine 219 F2
St Inan's Dr. Beith 150 B1
St Ives Rd. Muir 80 C2
St James Ave. Pais 113 D4
St James Ct. Coat 121 F2
St James' Orch. Stir 2 B1
St James' Pl. Steven 206 C1
St James Rd. Glasg 117 E4
St James' St. Pais 113 F3
St James Terr. Kil 89 E4
St James Way. Coat 121 F2
St Joan's Cres. Kilw 207 F1
St John St. Ayr 235 F1
St John St. Coat 122 A4
St John St. Pres 236 B4
St John St. Stir 7 D4
St John's Ave. Falk 42 B3
St John's Ct. Glasg 116 C2
St John's Gate. Den 21 E1
St John's Gdns. Den 21 E1
St John's Gr. Den 21 E1
St John's Pl. Steven 206 C1
St John's Quadrant. Glasg 116 C2
St John's Rd. Glasg 116 C2
St John's Rd. Gour 44 C4
St Kenneth Dr. Glasg 115 F4
St Kentigerns Rd. Lan 215 D3
St Kilda Bank. Irvine 220 A1
St Kilda Ct. Irvine 220 A1
St Kilda Pl. Irvine 220 A1
St Kilda Way. Wish 165 F3
St Laurence Cres. Slam 86 A3
St Lawrence Pk. E Kil 159 E1
St Lawrence Pl. Salt 206 A1
St Lawrence St. Green 46 A2
St Leonard St. Lan 215 D3
St Leonard's Dr. Glasg 136 B2
St Leonard's Rd. Ayr 239 D3
St Leonard's Rd. Lan 215 D2
St Leonards Rd. E Kil 160 B1
St Leonards Wlk. Coat 122 B2
St Luke's Ave. Car 201 F4
St Machan's Way. Lennox 33 E1
St Machars Rd. B of W 110 C4
St Margaret Ave. Dalry 191 D4
St Margaret's Ave. Kils 37 F2
St Margaret's Dr. Wish 164 C1
St Margaret's Pl. Glasg 117 E3
St Margaret's Rd. Ard 205 E2
St Mark Gdns. Glasg 118 C3
St Mark St. Glasg 118 C3
St Marnock Pl. Kilmk 227 F4
St Marnock St. Glasg 118 A3
St Marnock St. Kilmk 227 F4
St Mary's Cres. Barr 134 B1
St Mary's Ct. Wish 165 D1
St Mary's La. Glasg 117 D4
St Mary's Pl. Salt 205 F1
St Mary's Rd. Bish 77 F1
St Mary's Rd. Hat 141 F3
St Mary's Way. Dumb 49 F2
St Mary's Wynd. Stir 7 D4
St Marys Gdns. Barr 134 B1
St Maur's Cres. Kilmk 222 C2
St Maur's Pl. Kilmk 222 C2
St Maurice's Roundabout. Cumb 61 D1
St Maurs Gdns. Kilm 222 B4
St Medan's Pl. Salt 205 F1
St Meddans Cres. Troon 229 E2
St Meddans Ct. Troon 229 E1
St Meddans St. Troon 229 E1
St Michael Dr. Helen 16 C1
St Michael Rd. Wish 164 B1
St Mirren St. Pais 113 F2
St Mirren's Rd. Kils 60 C4
St Modan's Way. Ros 15 D2
St Modans Ct. Falk 42 A2
St Monach's Pl. Steven 206 C1
St Monance St. Glasg 97 F3
St Mungo Ave. Glasg 117 E4
St Mungo Ct. B of W 110 C4
St Mungo Pl. Glasg 117 E4
St Mungo Pl. Ham 161 E2
St Mungo St. Bish 97 F4
St Mungo's. Lan 215 D2
St Mungo's Rd. Cumb 61 F1
St Nicholas Rd. Lan 215 D3
St Nicholas Rd. Pres 236 A4
St Ninian St. Glasg 117 E3
St Ninian's Cres. Pais 113 F1
St Ninian's Dr. Ard 205 E2
St Ninian's. Lan 215 D3
St Ninian's Pl. Ham 161 F2
St Ninian's Rd. Ham 161 F2
St Ninian's Rd. Pres 236 A4
St Ninians Pl. Stone 198 C1
St Ninians Rd. Pais 113 F1
St Ninians Rd. Stir 6 C3
St Ninians Rd. Stir 7 D3
St Palladius Terr. Dalry 191 E4
St Patrick's Ct. Lan 214 C2
St Patrick's Rd. Lan 214 C2
St Peter's La. Glasg 117 D4
St Peter's Path. Glasg 97 D1
St Peter's St. Glasg 97 D1
St Phillans Ave. Ayr 239 D3
St Quivox Rd. Pres 236 B4
St Rhonans La. Alex 27 F2
St Rollox Brae. Glasg 97 F1
St Ronan's Dr. Glasg 136 B4
St Ronan's Dr. Ham 183 E4
St Ronans Dr. Glasg 138 B3
St Serf's Pl. Tull 4 A2
St Serf's Rd. Tull 4 A2
St Serf's Wlk. Alva 4 C3
St Stephen's Cres. Glasg 138 C2
St Stephen's Pl. Steven 206 C1
St Stephens Ave. Glasg 138 B2
St Teiling. Lan 215 D3
St Thomas's Pl. Stir 6 C3
St Thomas's Well. Stir 6 B4
St Valery Dr. Stir 7 D2
St Vigeans Ave. Newt M 156 B2
St Vincent Cres. Ayr 239 D1
St Vincent Cres. Glasg 116 C4
St Vincent Crescent La. Glasg 116 C4
St Vincent La. Glasg 117 D4
St Vincent Pl. E Kil 180 A4
St Vincent Pl. Glasg 117 E4
St Vincent Pl. Lan 215 D2
St Vincent Pl. Mother 163 F4
St Vincent St. Glasg 116 C4
St Vincent St. Glasg 117 D4
St Vincent Terr. Glasg 116 C4
St Winifred's Way. Wish 165 D2
St Winning's La. Kilw 207 E2
St Winning's Rd. Kilw 207 E2
St Winning's Rd. Kilw 207 F2
St Winning's Well. Kilw 207 E2
St Winnoc Rd. Loch 129 E2
Salamanca St. Glasg 118 B3
Salen Loan. Shot 147 D2
Salen St. Glasg 115 F3
Saline St. Coat 122 B3

Salisbury Ave. Hurl 228 C3
Salisbury Cres. Mother 163 D4
Salisbury, E Kil 160 B2
Salisbury Pl. Clyde 73 E3
Salisbury Pl. Pres 236 B4
Salisbury St. Glasg 117 D2
Salkeld St. Glasg 117 D3
Salmon Dr. Falk 41 F1
Salmon St. Green 45 F3
Salmona St. Glasg 97 D2
Saltaire Ave. Udd 141 D3
Saltcoats Rd. Salt 217 D4
Saltcoats Rd. Steven 217 E4
Satherland Rd. Barr 134 C2
Saltfield La. Ayr 235 F1
Saltire Cres. Lark 185 E1
Saltmarket. Glasg 117 E3
Saltmarket Pl. Glasg 117 E3
Saltoun La. Glasg 96 B2
Saltoun St. Glasg 96 B2
Saltpans Rd. Ayr 235 F2
Salvia St. Glasg 138 C3
Samson Ave. Kilm 228 A4
Sanda Pl. Kilmk 223 D3
Sanda Pl. Salt 205 F1
Sanda St. Glasg 96 C2
Sandaig Rd. Glasg 119 F3
Sandale Path. Udd 161 E3
Sandalwood Ave. E Kil 159 E2
Sandbank Ave. Glasg 96 B4
Sandbank Cres. Bonh 27 F3
Sandbank Cres. Glasg 96 B3
Sandbank Dr. Glasg 96 B4
Sandbank Terr. Glasg 96 B4
Sandbed La. Kilmk 227 F4
Sandbed St. Kilmk 227 F4
Sandend. Ersk 73 D2
Sandend Rd. Glasg 135 D4
Sanderling Pl. John 131 E3
Sanderling Rd. Pais 113 F3
Sanderson Ave. Udd 219 D1
Sanderson Ave. Tan 141 E3
Sandfield Ave. Miln 55 D2
Sandfield Rd. Pres 236 B4
Sandfield St. Glasg 96 C3
Sandford Gdns. Glasg 120 A3
Sandgate Ave. Glasg 119 E2
Sandgate. Ayr 238 C4
Sandhaven Pl. Glasg 135 D4
Sandhaven Rd. Glasg 135 D4
Sandhill Gdns. Troon 229 F2
Sandholes Rd. Kilbar 111 E3
Sandholes St. Pais 113 E2
Sandholm Pl. Glasg 94 C3
Sandholm Terr. Glasg 94 C3
Sandlefield Rd. Glasg 117 E2
Sandielands Ave. Hart 93 E4
Sandlands Cres. Mother .. 163 D3
Sandlands St. Glasg 119 E3
Sandlands. Troon 229 E1
Sandmill St. Glasg 98 A1
Sandpiper Dr. E Kil 180 A3
Sandpiper Pl. E Kil 180 A3
Sandpiper Rd. Loch 129 E1
Sandra Rd. Bish 78 B1
Sandray Ave. P Glasg 69 D4
Sandringham Ave. Newt M 157 D3
Sandringham Ct. Newt M . 157 D3
Sandringham Dr. John 112 A1
Sandringham La. Glasg 96 B2
Sandringham Terr. Green .. 45 F4
Sandwood Cres. Glasg 115 D3
Sandwood Rd. Glasg 115 D3
Sandy Ct. W Kil 190 B2
Sandy Rd. Carl 187 F1
Sandy Rd. Glasg 96 A1
Sandy Rd. Irvine 219 D3
Sandy Rd. Ren 94 B1
Sandy Rd. W Kil 190 B2
Sandyfaulds Sq. Glasg 117 E2
Sandyfaulds St. Glasg 117 E2
Sandyford Ave. Holy 143 E4
Sandyford Pl. Glasg 116 C4
Sandyford Pl. Holy 143 E4
Sandyford Place La. Glasg 116 C4
Sandyford Rd. Holy 143 E4
Sandyford Rd. Pres 236 A4
Sandyford Rd. Ren 114 A4
Sandyhill Ave. Shot 147 D2
Sandyhill Terr. Coy 239 F3
Sandyhills Cres. Glasg 119 D2
Sandyhills Dr. Glasg 119 D2
Sandyhills Gr. Glasg 119 D1
Sandyhills Pl. Glasg 119 D2
Sandyhills Rd. Glasg 119 D2
Sandyknowes Rd. Cumb .. 83 D4
Sandylands Cres. Mother . 163 E3
Sandylands Prom. Salt 205 D2
Sandyvale Pl. Shot 147 D2
Sannox Dr. Mother 143 D4
Sannox Dr. Salt 206 A1
Sannox Gdns. Glasg 118 A4
Sannox Pl. Ayr 236 B1
Sannox Pl. Helen 16 C2
Sannox Rd. Kilmk 222 B1
Sannox View. Ayr 236 C1

Sanquhar Ave. Pres 236 B4
Sanquhar Gdns. Udd 140 A1
Sapphire Rd. Hat 142 A2
Saracen Head Rd. Glasg .. 117 F3
Saracen St. Glasg 97 E2
Sardinia La. Glasg 96 B2
Sark Dr. Troon 229 F3
Saskatoon Pl. E Kil 159 D1
Saucel Hill Terr. Pais 113 F2
Saucel Pl. Pais 113 F2
Sauchie Ct. Bann 7 F1
Sauchiehall La. Glasg 117 D4
Sauchiehall St. Glasg 117 D4
Sauchiesmoor Rd. Car 202 A4
Saugh Ave. Uplaw 173 E4
Saughs Ave. Glasg 98 C3
Saughs Dr. Glasg 98 C3
Saughs Gate. Glasg 98 C3
Saughs Pl. Glasg 98 C3
Saughs Rd. Glasg 98 C3
Saughs Rd. Glasg 99 D3
Saughs Rd. Stepps 99 D3
Saughton St. Glasg 118 C4
Saughtree Ave. Salt 205 F1
Saunders Ct. Barr 134 A2
Saunterne Rd. Pres 233 E1
Savoy Ct. Ayr 238 C4
Savoy Pk. Ayr 238 C4
Savoy St. Glasg 117 F2
Sawers Ave. Den 21 E1
Sawmill Rd. Glasg 95 F1
Sawmillfield St. Glasg 97 D1
Saxon Rd. Glasg 96 B1
Scadlock Rd. Pais 113 D3
Scalpay. E Kil 160 B1
Scalpay Pl. Glasg 99 F2
Scalpay Pl. Kilmk 223 D3
Scalpay St. Glasg 99 F2
Scamadale Rd. Gree 84 B2
Scapa St. Glasg 96 C4
Scaraway Dr. Glasg 97 E4
Scaraway Pl. Glasg 97 E4
Scaraway St. Glasg 97 E4
Scaraway Terr. Glasg 97 E4
Scarba Dr. Glasg 136 A3
Scarba Quadrant. Wish ... 164 C1
Scarffe Ave. Lin 111 F3
Scargie Rd. Kilmk 227 F2
Scarhill Ave. Aird 122 C3
Scarhill La. Aird 123 D3
Scarhill St. Cle 144 A1
Scarhill St. Coat 121 F2
Scarlemuir. Lan 214 C3
Scarlow St. P Glasg 47 E1
Scarrel Dr. Glasg 138 A2
Scarrel Rd. Glasg 138 A2
Scarrel Terr. Glasg 138 A2
Scaur O' Doon Rd. Ayr ... 238 B2
Schaw Ct. Bear 75 F3
Schaw Ct. N Sau 5 E1
Schaw Dr. Bear 75 F3
Schaw Rd. Pais 114 A3
Schawpark Ave. N Sau 5 E1
Schiltron Way. Bann 7 E2
Scholar's Gate. E Kil 180 B3
School Ave. Glasg 140 C3
School La. Alla 167 D4
School La. Car 187 F1
School La. Dumb 49 E2
School La. Irvine 219 D1
School La. Lennox 57 E4
School La. M of C 58 B3
School La. Men 4 A4
School Quadrant. Aird 102 C1
School Rd. Glasg 114 C3
School Rd. Kilb 149 D1
School Rd. Lennox 57 F1
School Rd. New 166 A2
School Rd. Newt M 156 B2
School Rd. Rhu 15 E3
School Rd. Sals 125 E2
School Rd. Stepps 99 F3
School Rd. Tull 4 A1
School St. Chap 123 E1
School St. Coat 122 A2
School St. Ham 162 B1
School St. Shot 146 C2
School Wk. Stem 23 E3
School Wynd. Kilb 149 D1
School Wynd. Pais 113 F3
Schoolhouse La. Udd 161 E3
Schoolwell St. Steven 206 B1
Scioncroft Ave. Glasg 138 B4
Sclandersburn Rd. Den ... 39 E4
Scone Pl. E Kil 159 E2
Scone St. Glasg 97 D2
Sconser St. Glasg 76 C1
Scorton Gdns. Glasg 119 F2
Scotia Cres. Lark 185 D1
Scotia Gdns. Ham 183 E4
Scotia Pl. Falk 42 B3
Scotia St. Mother 163 E3
Scotland Dr. Glasg 116 C3
Scotland St W. Glasg 116 C3
Scotsblair Ave. Kirk 79 E4
Scotsburn Rd. Glasg 98 B2
Scotstoun Rd. Cowie 12 C4

Scotstoun St. Glasg 95 E2
Scott Ave. John 131 F4
Scott Ave. M of C 58 B3
Scott Ave. O Kil 72 B4
Scott Cres. All 10 A3
Scott Cres. Cumb 82 B4
Scott Cres. Kilmk 227 F4
Scott Cres. Troon 229 F2
Scott Ct. Helen 16 B1
Scott Dr. Bear 75 E3
Scott Dr. Cumb 82 B4
Scott Gr. Ham 162 B1
Scott Hill. E Kil 160 A2
Scott House. Cumb 62 A2
Scott Pl. Hat 142 A4
Scott Pl. Salt 205 F1
Scott Pl. Troon 229 E3
Scott Rd. Glasg 114 C4
Scott Rd. Irvine 219 E1
Scott Rd. Kilmk 227 F4
Scott St. Bonh 27 F2
Scott St. Clyde 73 F2
Scott St. Glasg 97 D1
Scott St. Glasg 120 A2
Scott St. Green 46 A2
Scott St. Ham 162 B1
Scott St. Lark 185 D1
Scott St. Mother 163 F4
Scott St. Stir 2 A1
Scott's Pl. Aird 123 D4
Seabank Rd. Ayr 235 F1
Seabank St. Salt 217 D4
Seabegs Cres. Bon 40 A2
Seabegs Pl. Bon 39 F2
Seabegs Rd. Bon 39 F2
Seafar Rd. Cumb 61 F1
Seafield Ave. Bear 75 F4
Seafield Cottage La. Green 45 E4
Seafield Cres. Ayr 238 C3
Seafield Cres. Cumb 60 C1
Seafield Ct. Aird 205 D2
Seafield Ct. Falk 41 F1
Seafield Dr. Ayr 238 B3
Seafield Dr. Glasg 138 B2
Seafield Pl. Irvine 220 A1
Seaford St. Kilmk 227 F4
Seaforth Cres. Ayr 236 A3
Seaforth Cres. Barr 134 A2
Seaforth La. Muir 81 D1
Seaforth Pl. Hat 141 F2
Seaforth Pl. Stir 2 A1
Seaforth Rd. Ayr 236 A2
Seaforth Rd. Clyde 74 A1
Seaforth Rd. Falk 24 B1
Seaforth Rd N. Glasg 115 D4
Seaforth Rd S. Glasg 115 D4
Seagate. Irvine 219 D2
Seagate. Pres 233 E1
Seamill Path. Glasg 134 C3
Seamill St. Glasg 134 C3
Seamore St. Glasg 97 D1
Seath Ave. Aird 122 C4
Seath Ave. Lang 70 B3
Seath Rd. Glasg 114 B3
Seath St. Glasg 117 E1
Seaton Pl. Falk 42 B2
Seaton Terr. Ham 162 A2
Seaton Terr. Irvine 219 E3
Seaview Ave. Salt 216 C4
Seaview Terr. Troon 230 A2
Seaward La. Glasg 116 C3
Seaward St. Glasg 116 C3
Second Ave. Bear 76 A2
Second Ave. Bonh 27 F3
Second Ave. Clyde 74 A2
Second Ave. Dumb 50 B1
Second Ave. Glasg 137 D3
Second Ave. Irvine 224 B4
Second Ave. Ren 94 B1
Second Ave. Stepps 99 F1
Second Ave. Steven 99 D2
Second Ave. Tan 120 C1
Second Gdns. Glasg 116 A2
Second Rd. Ham 161 F3
Second St. Tan 140 C4
Seedhill. Pais 113 F2
Seedhill Rd. Pais 114 A2
Seggielea La. Glasg 95 E3
Seggielea Rd. Glasg 95 E3
Segton Ave. Kilw 207 E2
Seil Dr. Glasg 137 E2
Selborne Pl. Glasg 95 F3
Selborne Place La. Glasg . 95 F3
Selborne Rd. Glasg 95 F3
Selbourne Ave. Coat 122 A2
Selby Gdns. Glasg 119 E3
Selby Pl. Coat 101 E1
Selby St. Coat 101 E1
Selkirk Ave. Glasg 115 E2
Selkirk Ave. Pais 133 D4
Selkirk Dr. Glasg 138 B4
Selkirk Pl. E Kil 160 B2
Selkirk Pl. Ham 162 B1
Selkirk Rd. P Glasg 68 B4
Selkirk St. Ham 162 B1

Selkirk St. Udd 161 E4
Selkirk St. Wish 165 E3
Selkirk Way. Coat 122 C2
Selkirk Way. Hat 142 A4
Sella Rd. Bon 39 F2
Selvieland Rd. Glasg 114 C3
Semphill Gdns. E Kil 160 A1
Sempie St. Ham 161 F2
Sempill Ave. Ersk 72 C1
Semple Ave. Bishop 72 A3
Semple Ave. Loch 129 E2
Semple Pl. Lin 112 A4
Semple Rd. Pres 236 B3
Semple View. How 130 C3
Senga Cres. Hat 142 A4
Seres Rd. Newt M 157 F2
Sergeant Law Rd. Pais ... 132 C2
Sergeant Law Rd. Uplaw . 132 D3
Sergeant Law Rd. Uplaw . 153 D4
Seright Cres. Hurl 228 B4
Seright Sq. Hurl 228 B4
Serpentine Wk. Green 46 B2
Sersley Dr. Kilb 148 C1
Service St. Lennox 33 E1
Seton Dr. Stir 7 E2
Seton La. Ayr 205 E1
Seton St. Ayr 205 E1
Seton Terr. Glasg 117 F4
Settle Gdns. Glasg 119 D2
Seven Sisters. Kirk 79 F3
Seventh Ave. Tan 140 C4
Seventh Rd. Ham 183 E4
Severn Rd. E Kil 179 F4
Seymour Ave. Kilw 207 F1
Seymour Gn. E Kil 180 A4
Seyton Ave. Glasg 136 B3
Seyton La. E Kil 159 F2
Shaftesbury St. All 10 A4
Shaftesbury St. Glasg 116 C4
Shafton Pl. Glasg 95 F4
Shafton Rd. Glasg 95 F4
Shaftsbury Ave. Clyde ... 73 F1
Shaftsbury Cres. Holy ... 143 E2
Shakespeare Ave. Clyde . 73 F2
Shakespeare St. Glasg ... 96 C3
Shalloch Pk. Ayr 238 B1
Shalloch Pl. Irvine 220 A1
Shamrock Dr. Glasg 238 A2
Shamrock St. Kirk 79 E4
Shand La. Car 187 F2
Shand St. Wish 165 E1
Shandon Brae. Bonh 27 F4
Shandon Cres. Bonh 27 F4
Shandon Cres. Hat 142 A4
Shandon Pl. Green 46 B1
Shandon Terr. Ham 161 F2
Shandwick St. Glasg 120 A4
Shankland La. Green 46 C1
Shankland Rd. Green 46 C1
Shanks Ave. Barr 134 B3
Shanks Ave. Den 39 F4
Shanks Cres. John 111 F1
Shanks Ct. Kilmk 222 C1
Shanks St. Aird 123 D4
Shanks St. Glasg 96 C3
Shannon Dr. Falk 41 F2
Shannon St. Glasg 97 D3
Shapinsay St. Glasg 97 E4
Sharon St. Dalry 191 D4
Sharp Ave. Coat 121 E2
Sharp St. Gour 44 C4
Sharp St. Mother 163 D4
Sharpe Ave. Irvine 220 B1
Sharphill Ind Est. Salt ... 206 A2
Shavian Terr. Kilw 207 F1
Shavin Brae. Ayr 239 E3
Shaw Ave. Bishop 72 B2
Shaw Ct. Ersk 72 B4
Shaw Pl. Dalry 191 D4
Shaw Pl. Green 45 F3
Shaw Pl. Lin 112 A3
Shaw Rd. Miln 76 A4
Shaw Rd. Newt M 156 C2
Shaw St. Glasg 116 A4
Shaw St. Salt 206 A1
Shawbank Pl. Kilmk 228 A4
Shawbridge St. Glasg 136 B4
Shawburn Cres. Ham 162 A2
Shawburn St. Ham 162 A2
Shawfarm Ct. Pres 233 E1
Shawfarm Gdns. Pres 233 E1
Shawfield Dr. Glasg 117 F1
Shawfield Rd. Glasg 117 F2
Shawhead Ave. Coat 122 A2
Shawhead Cotts. Coat ... 122 A2
Shawhill Cres. Newt M .. 156 C2
Shawhill Rd. Glasg 136 B4
Shawholm Cres. Glasg ... 136 A4
Shawlands Cross. Glasg .. 136 C4
Shawlands Sq. Glasg 136 B4
Shawmoss Rd. Glasg 116 B1
Shawpark St. Glasg 96 C3
Shawrigg Rd. Lark 185 E1

Shaws Rd. Lark 199 E4
Shawstonfoot Rd. Cle 145 D1
Shawwood Cres. Newt M . 156 C2
Shearer Dr. Ham 183 E4
Shearer Quadrant. Bonh . 28 A4
Sheddens Pl. Glasg 118 C3
Sheena Dr. Bonh 27 F1
Sheepburn Rd. Udd 140 C4
Sheila St. Glasg 98 C2
Sheildhill. E Kil 180 C4
Shelling Hill. Ham 162 C2
Sheldaig Rd. Glasg 97 D4
Sheldrake Pl. John 131 E3
Shelbridge Way. Aird 205 E1
Shelley Ct. Glasg 96 A3
Shelley Dr. Clyde 74 A3
Shelley Dr. Udd 141 D1
Shelley Rd. Glasg 96 A3
Sheils Rd. Kirk 58 C1
Sherbrooke Ave. Glasg .. 116 B2
Sherbrooke Dr. Glasg 116 B2
Sherbrooke Pl. E Kil 159 E1
Sherbrooke Pl. Glasg 116 B2
Sherburn Gdns. Glasg ... 119 F2
Sherdale Ave. Chap 123 E1
Sheriff Park Ave. Glasg .. 138 A4
Sheriffmuir Rd. B of A ... 2 B4
Sheriffmuirlands. Stir 2 B2
Sheriff La. Sten 23 F2
Sherry Dr. Ham 162 A1
Sherwood Ave. Pais 114 A3
Sherwood Ave. Udd 141 D3
Sherwood Dr. Glasg 136 A2
Sherwood Pl. Glasg 75 C2
Sherwood Rd. Hurl 228 C3
Sherwood Rd. Pres 236 C4
Shetland Ct. All 10 A3
Shetland Dr. Glasg 137 E2
Shettleston Rd. Glasg 119 D3
Shettleston

Sheddings. Glasg 118 C3
Shewalton Dr. Shew 225 E3
Shewalton Rd. Shew 224 B3
Shewalton Rd. Shew 225 D3
Shiel Ave. E Kil 159 F2
Shiel Ct. Barr 134 A3
Shiel Gdns. Falk 24 B1
Shiel Gdns. Shot 147 D2
Shiel Hill. Ayr 239 D2
Shiel Pl. Aird 122 B3
Shiel Pl. E Kil 159 F2
Shiel Pl. Irvine 219 E3
Shiel Rd. Bish 78 A1
Shiel Terr. New 165 F3
Shielbridge Gdns. Glasg . 76 C3
Shieldaig Dr. Glasg 138 A2
Shieldburn Rd. Glasg 115 E4
Shieldhall Gdns. Glasg ... 115 D4
Shieldhall Rd. Glasg 115 D4
Shieldhill Rd. Car 201 F4
Shields Dr. Mother 164 B2
Shields Loan. Lan 214 C3
Shields Rd. Auld 180 A2
Shields Rd. Glasg 116 C2
Shields Rd. Mother 164 B2
Shielhope Ct. Irvine 220 A2
Shieling Pk. Ayr 238 C4
Shilford Ave. Glasg 95 D3
Shilford Rd. Uplaw 132 B1
Shillay St. Glasg 99 F2
Shillaw Dr. Pres 236 B3
Shillaw Pl. Pres 236 B3
Shillinghill. All 10 A3
Shillingworth Pl. B of W . 110 B3
Shilton Dr. Glasg 135 D3
Shilton La. Ersk 72 C2
Shinwell Ave. Clyde 74 B1
Shipbank La. Glasg 117 E3
Shiphaugh Pl. Stir 2 B2
Shira Terr. E Kil 160 A3
Shire Way. All 9 F3
Shirley Quadrant. Mother 163 E2
Shirley's Ct. Lan 215 D2
Shirra's Brae Rd. Stir ... 7 F2
Shirrel Ave. Hat 142 A4
Shirrel Rd. Holy 143 D2
Shirva Lea. Twe 59 F2
Shiskine Dr. Glasg 96 B4
Shiskine Dr. Kilmk 222 C2
Shiskine Pl. Glasg 96 B4
Shiskine Pl. Helen 16 C1
Shiskine St. Glasg 96 B4
Sholto Cres. Tan 141 E4
Shore Rd. Air 92 D1
Shore Rd. Steven 217 E4
Shore Rd. Troon 229 D3
Shore St. Glasg 118 A1
Shore St. Gour 44 C4
Shore. The. All 10 A3
Shortlees Cres. Kilmk 227 F1
Shortlees Rd. Kilmk 227 F1
Shortridge St. Glasg 96 C3
Shortroods Ave. Pais 113 F4
Shortroods Cres. Pais 113 F4
Shortroods Rd. Pais 113 F4
Shotts Rd. Sals 126 C1

Shotts St. Glasg 119 E4
Shottsburn St. Sals 126 A2
Shottskirk Rd. Shot 146 B3
Shuna Pl. Glasg 96 C3
Shuna Pl. Newt M 156 A3
Shuna St. Glasg 96 C3
Shuttle St. Glasg 117 E4
Shuttle St. Kilbar 111 D2
Shuttle St. Kils 60 B4
Shuttle St. Pais 113 F2
Sidehead Rd. East 127 F3
Sidehead Rd. Stone 198 C1
Sidland Rd. Glasg 98 B3
Sidlaw Ave. Barr 134 B1
Sidlaw Ave. Ham 161 F1
Sidlaw Ave. P Glasg 68 C3
Sidlaw Dr. Wish 164 C2
Sidlaw Foot. Irvine 220 B1
Sidlaw Pl. Kilmk 228 A2
Sidlaw Rd. Bear 75 D4
Sidney St. Salt 216 C4
Sielga Pl. Glasg 120 A4
Siemens Pl. Glasg 98 A1
Siemens St. Glasg 98 A1
Sievewright St. Glasg 118 B1
Sighthill Loan. Lark 185 D2
Sighthill Terr. Sals 125 D1
Sikeside Pl. Coat 122 B3
Sikeside St. Coat 122 B3
Silk St. Pais 113 F3
Silkin Ave. Clyde 74 B1
Sillars Meadow. Irvine ... 219 F1
Silvan Pl. Thorn 158 A3
Silver Firs. Holy 143 E2
Silverburn Dr. Quarl 183 F2
Silverburn Cres. Holy 143 E2
Silverburn St. Glasg 118 C4
Silverdale Cres. Lan 214 C2
Silverdale. E Kil 159 E2
Silverdale Gr. Lan 214 C2
Silverdale St. Glasg 118 B2
Silverdale Terr. Plains ... 103 F2
Silverfir St. Glasg 117 E2
Silvergrove St. Glasg 117 F3
Silvermuir Ave. Lan 215 F4
Silverton Ave. Dumb 50 A2
Silvertonhill Ave. Ham ... 162 C1
Silvertonhill La. Ham 50 A2
Silvertonhill Pl. Ham 183 E4
Silverwells Cres. Udd 141 D1
Silverwells. Udd 141 D1
Silverwood Ct. Udd 141 D1
Silverwood Rd. Hurl 228 B4
Sim St. Stew 211 E4
Simons Cres. Kilmk 227 F2
Simons Cres. Ren 94 B3
Simpson Ct. Clyde 74 A1
Simpson Ct. Udd 140 C3
Simpson Dr. E Kil 180 B4
Simpson Pl. E Kil 180 B4
Simpson Pl. Kilmk 227 F2
Simpson Quadrant. Bonh .. 28 A4
Simpson St. Cross 222 A1
Simpson St. Falk 41 F3
Simpson St. Glasg 96 C2
Simpson Way. Hat 142 B4
Simshill Rd. Glasg 137 E2
Simson Ave. W Kil 190 C2
Sinclair Ave. Bear 75 F3
Sinclair Cres. Den 21 E1
Sinclair Ct. Bann 7 F1
Sinclair Dr. Kilmk 223 E2
Sinclair Dr. Coat 121 E4
Sinclair Dr. Fall 8 B2
Sinclair Dr. Glasg 136 C4
Sinclair Dr. Helen 16 C2
Sinclair Gdns. Bish 98 A4
Sinclair Gr. Hat 141 F1
Sinclair La. Helen 16 C2
Sinclair Pk. E Kil 180 C4
Sinclair Pl. E Kil 180 C4
Sinclair St. Clyde 94 B2
Sinclair St. Green 48 B2
Sinclair St. Helen 16 B1
Sinclair St. Miln 55 D1
Sinclair St. Steven 206 B3
Singer Rd. Clyde 73 F2
Singer Rd. E Kil 181 D3
Singer St. Clyde 74 A2
Sir Michael Pl. Green 45 F3
Sir Michael Pl. Pais 113 E2
Sir Michael St. Green 45 F3
Sixth Ave. Ren 94 B1
Sixth St. Tan 120 C1
Skaethorn Rd. Glasg 96 A4
Skaethorn Rd. Glasg 96 B4
Skaithmuir Ave. Sten 24 A2
Skaithmuir Cres. Sten 24 A2
Skara Wik. New 165 F4
Skaterigg Dr. Glasg 95 F3
Skaterigg Gdns. Glasg 95 F3
Skaterigg La. Glasg 95 F3
Skelbo Pl. Glasg 100 B3
Skellyton Cres. Lark 185 D1
Skelmorlie Pl. Kilw 207 E2
Skelmorlie Pl. Sten 23 F2
Skene Rd. Glasg 116 A3

Skene Rd. Kilmk 223 E2
Skene St. Bon 40 A3
Skene Gr. E Kil 179 F3
Skermieland Rd. Fen 213 D2
Skerray Quadrant. Glasg ... 97 E4
Skerray St. Glasg 97 E4
Skerryvore Pl. Glasg 119 D4
Skerryvore Rd. Glasg 119 D4
Skibo La. Glasg 135 F2
Skipness Ave. Car 200 A4
Skipness Dr. Glasg 115 E4
Skirsa Ct. Glasg 97 D4
Skirsa Pl. Glasg 96 C4
Skirsa Sq. Glasg 97 D4
Skirsa St. Glasg 96 C4
Skirving St. Glasg 136 C4
Skovlunde Way. E Kil 180 C3
Skye Ave. Ren 94 B1
Skye Cres. Clyde 73 E3
Skye Cres. Gour 44 C3
Skye Cres. Pais 133 E4
Skye Ct. Irvine 225 D4
Skye Ct. Cumb 82 B4
Skye Dr. Clyde 73 E3
Skye Dr. Cumb 82 B4
Skye. E Kil 160 B1
Skye Gdns. Bear 75 D3
Skye Pl. Cumb 82 B4
Skye Quadrant. Wish 165 F3
Skye Rd. Cumb 82 B4
Skye Rd. Glasg 138 B2
Skye Rd. P Glasg 69 D3
Skye Rd. Pres 233 F1
Skye St. Green 45 E2
Skyeside Rd. Aird 122 C2
Skythorn Way. Falk 41 F1
Slaemuir Ave. P Glasg 68 C3
Slakiewood Ave. Muir 100 C4
Slamannan Rd. Avon 87 F3
Slamannan Rd. Falk 42 A1
Slamannan Rd. Slam 86 A1
Slatefield Ct. Glasg 118 A3
Slatefield. Lennox 57 E4
Slatefield St. Glasg 118 A3
Sleaford Ave. Mother 163 E2
Slenavon Ave. Glasg 137 E1
Slessor Dr. E Kil 180 C4
Slioch Sq. Holy 143 E2
Sloan Ave. Irvine 219 E1
Sloan Pl. Ayr 236 B1
Sloan St. Ayr 236 B1
Sloy St. Glasg 97 E2
Sloy St. Wish 165 D1
Small Cres. Udd 161 E4
Smeaton Ave. Lennox 78 A4
Smeaton St. Glasg 96 C3
Smiddy Ct. Kilw 207 F2
Smiddy Ct. Lan 215 D2
Smillie Pl. Kilmk 227 E3
Smillie St. Green 46 C1
Smith Ave. Beith 170 B3
Smith Ave. Irvine 219 E2
Smith Ave. Wish 186 A4
Smith Cres. Bonh 27 F4
Smith Cres. Dunt 74 A3
Smith Cres. Kilw 207 F1
Smith Dr. San 217 D4
Smith Pl. Den 21 E1
Smith Quadrant. Coat 122 B4
Smith St. Ayr 239 D4
Smith St. Falk 42 A4
Smith St. Glasg 95 F1
Smith St. Green 45 F3
Smith St. Pres 236 B4
Smith Terr. Glasg 118 A1
Smith's La. Pais 113 F3
Smithfield Loan. All 9 F3
Smithhills St. Pais 113 F3
Smithston Cotts. Green 46 C2
Smithstone Cres. Kils 60 C3
Smithstone Ct. Irvine 219 F3
Smithstone Terr. Kilw 207 D4
Smithstone Way. Irvine .. 219 F3
Smithview. Wish 186 B4
Smithy Brae. Kil 89 E4
Smithy Ct. Card 48 A4
Smithy Rd. Card 48 A4
Smithycroft. Ham 163 D1
Smithycroft Rd. Glasg 98 C1
Smithyends. Cumb 62 A3
Smollett Rd. Dumb 50 A2
Smollett St. Alex 27 E3
Smuggler's Way. Rhu 15 E3
Smugglers Brig Rd. Cro .. 201 D1
Smyllum Pk. Lan 215 E2
Smyllum Rd. Lan 215 E2
Snaefell Ave. Glasg 138 B2
Snaefell Cres. Glasg 138 B2
Sneddon Ave. Wish 165 E1
Sneddon St. Ham 161 F3
Sneddon Terr. Ham 161 F3
Snowdon Pl. Glasg 117 E2
Snowdon St. Glasg 117 E2
Snowdon Place La. Stir 7 D3
Snowdon St. Glasg 117 E2
Snowdon Terr. W Kil 190 A3
Snowdrop Sq. Ayr 239 D2

Snuff Mill Rd. Glasg 137 D3
Society St. Glasg 118 A3
Solar Ct. Lark 199 D4
Sollas Pl. Clyde 94 C4
Solway Ave. Ham 183 D4
Solway Bank 39 E4
Solway Pl. Kilmk 228 A2
Solway Pl. Muir 80 B1
Solway Pl. Troon 229 F3
Solway Rd. Bish 78 B1
Solway St. Glasg 117 F1
Somerford Rd. Bear 75 F1
Somerled Ave. Ren 94 A1
Somerset Ave. Ham 162 A2
Somerset Pl. Glasg 96 C1
Somerset
   Place Meuse. Glasg 96 C1
Somerset Rd. Ayr 236 A1
Somervell St. Glasg 138 C3
Somerville Ct. Beith 150 A1
Somerville Dr. E Kil 180 C4
Somerville Dr. Glasg 137 D4
Somerville La. E Kil 180 C4
Somerville Pl. Helen 25 C4
Somerville Terr. E Kil ... 180 C4
Sommerville Dr. Steven .. 217 F3
Sophia Cres. Irvine 219 D3
Sorbie Dr. Stone 198 C1
Sorbie Rd. Ard 205 F2
Sorbie Rd. Salt 205 F1
Sorby St. Glasg 118 B3
Sorley St. Glasg 95 F1
Som St. Glasg 118 A2
Sorrel Dr. Ayr 239 E2
Soulflar Dr. Den 21 E1
Souls St. Kilmk 223 D1
Sourlie Roundabout. Irvine 219 F3
Sourlie Terr. Irvine 219 F3
Souter Dr. Kilmk 228 B4
Souter Pl. Ayr 239 D3
Southerhouse Path. Coat . 121 F3
Southerhouse Rd. Coat ... 121 F3
South Annandale St. Glasg 117 D1
South Approach Rd. Air ... 24 C4
South Ave. Car 187 F1
South Ave. Clyde 74 A3
South Ave. Ham 161 F3
South Ave. Pais 133 F4
South Ave. Ren 94 B2
South Bank St. Clyde 94 B4
South Bantaskine Dr. Falk . 42 A4
South Bantaskine Rd. Falk . 42 A4
South Barrwood Rd. Kils ... 60 C4
South Beach Espl. Troon . 229 E1
South Beach La. Troon ... 229 E1
South Beach Rd. Ayr 235 F1
South Beach Rd. Salt 205 E1
South Beach. Troon 229 E1
South Biggar Rd. Aird ... 123 D4
South Brae. Lennox 57 E4
South Bridge St. Aird ... 122 C4
South Broomage Ave. Lar .. 23 E1
South Burn Rd. Aird 122 B4
South Campbell St. Pais . 113 F2
South Carbrain Rd. Cumb . 62 A1
South Chester St. Glasg . 119 D3
South Church Pl. Bonh 27 F4
South Circular Rd. Coat . 122 A3
South Claremont La. Miln . 55 D1
South
   Commonhead Ave. Aird 103 D4
South Crescent Rd. Salt . 205 E1
South Crosshill Rd. Bish . 78 A1
South Dean Park Ave. Udd 141 D1
South Dean Rd. Kilmk ... 223 D1
South Douglas St. Clyde .. 94 B4
South Dr. Kilb 170 A4
South Dr. Lin 112 A3
South Dr. Troon 229 F2
South Dumbreck Rd. Kils . 60 A4
South Elgin Pl. Clyde 94 B4
South Elgin St. Clyde 94 B4
South Erskine Pk. Bear 75 E3
South Exchange Ct. Glasg 117 E4
South Frederick St. Glasg 117 E4
South Gargieston Dr. Kilmk 227 E3
South Glassford St. Miln .. 55 D1
South Green Dr. Air 14 C2
South Hamilton Pl. Kilmk 227 F4
South Hamilton St. Kilmk 227 F4
South Hirst Rd. Sals 126 B2
South Isle Rd. Ard 205 E3
South Kilruskin Rd. W Kil 190 B2
South Loan. Muir 100 B4
South Lodge Ct. Ayr 239 D3
South Mains Cotts. Hous .. 91 F1
South Mains Rd. Miln 54 C1
South Medrox St. Glen ... 101 E4
South Melville La. Falk 42 A3
South Moraine La. Glasg . 95 F3
South Mound. Hous 91 D1
South Muirhead Rd. Cumb . 62 A1
South Neuk. Kilb 170 A4
South
   Newmoor Ave. Irvine .. 219 F1
South Nimmo St. Aird ... 123 D4
South Park Dr. Pais 113 F1
South Park Rd. Ham 162 B1

South Pl. Hat 141 F2
South Pleasance Ave. Falk . 42 A2
South Portland St. Glasg . 117 D3
South Rd. P Glasg 68 C4
South Rd. Thorn 158 A3
South Rd. W Kil 190 B2
South Robertson St. Aird . 122 C4
South Scott St. Glasg 120 A2
South St. Camb 9 D2
South St. Glasg 95 E2
South St. Green 45 E3
South St. Hous 91 D1
South St. Inch 93 D2
South St. Stir 2 B1
South Vennel. Irvine 220 A2
South Vennel. Lan 215 D2
South Vesalius St. Glasg . 119 D3
South View. Clyde 73 F2
South View. Lar 141 F2
South View. Udd 140 B1
South Woodside Rd. Glasg . 96 C1
South Woodside Rd. Glasg . 96 A3
Southampton Dr. Glasg 96 A3
Southampton La. Glasg 96 A3
Southbank Dr. Kirk 79 E4
Southbank Rd. Kirk 79 E4
Southbank St. Glasg 118 B3
Southbar Ave. Glasg 95 D4
Southbar Rd. Inch 93 D4
Southbrae Ave. B of W ... 110 A4
Southbrae Dr. Glasg 95 E2
Southbrae La. Glasg 95 F3
Southburn Rd. Strath 31 E2
Southcroft. Alva 4 C3
Southcroft Rd. Glasg 117 F1
Southcroft St. Glasg 94 C3
Southdeen Ave. Glasg 75 D2
Southdeen Rd. Glasg 75 D2
Southend Pl. Hat 141 F2
Southend Rd. Dunt 74 A3
Southern Ave. Glasg 137 E3
Southerness Dr. Cumb 62 A3
Southesk Ave. Bish 77 F2
Southesk Gdns. Bish 77 F2
Southfield Ave. P Glasg ... 68 C4
Southfield Ave. Pais 133 F2
Southfield. Coat 122 B3
Southfield Cres. Coat 122 B3
Southfield Cres. Glasg ... 135 E4
Southfield Cres. Stir 7 D3
Southfield Dr. Slamn 86 A3
Southfield Pk. Ayr 239 D3
Southfield Pl. Cumb 61 E1
Southfield Rd. Shot 147 E4
Southgate. E Kil 159 F1
Southgate. Miln 55 D1
Southhill Ave. Glasg 138 B4
Southhook Rd. Cross 221 F2
Southhook Rd. Kilmk 222 B1
Southinch Ave. Clyde 94 C3
Southinch La. Clyde 94 C3
Southlea Ave. Glasg 136 A2
Southloch Gdns. Glasg 97 F2
Southloch St. Glasg 97 F2
Southmuir Pl. Glasg 96 B3
Southook Row. Irvine 220 A3
Southpark Ave. Glasg 96 C1
Southpark Ave. Pres 236 A4
Southpark La. Glasg 96 C1
Southpark Rd. Ayr 238 C3
Southpark Terr. Glasg 96 C1
Southview. Ave. Newt M . 157 F3
Southview. Bear 75 E3
Southview Cres. B of W 90 B1
Southview. Dr. Strath 31 D2
Southview. Pl. Muir 100 C3
Southview. Rd. Strath 31 D2
Southview. Terr. Bish 97 F4
Southward Way. Troon ... 229 E2
Southwood Rd. Glasg 114 C3
Southwood Dr. Glasg 137 E3
Southwood Rd. Troon 233 D3
Soutra Pl. Glasg 119 D4
Spairdrum Rd. Glenm 82 C2
Spairdrum Rd. Glenm 83 D2
Spalehall Dr. Holy 143 F2
Spallander Rd. Troon 229 E3
Spancer Gdns. Kilmk 228 B4
Spateston Rd. John 131 E4
Spean Ave. E Kil 160 A1
Spean St. Glasg 137 D3
Speedwell Sq. Ayr 239 D2
Speir's Dr. Lin 112 B4
Speirs Rd. Bear 76 A2
Speirshall Cl. Glasg 94 C3
Speirshall Terr. Glasg 94 C3
Spence St. Bon 40 A3
Spence St. Glasg 96 B4
Spencer Dr. Pais 132 C4
Spencer St. Clyde 74 A2
Spencer St. Glasg 95 F4
Spencerfield Gdns. Ham . 162 C2

Spey Ave. Kilmk 228 A3
Spey Ave. Pais 112 C1
Spey Ct. Glasg 123 E3
Spey Ct. New 165 F3
Spey Ct. Stir 7 E3
Spey Dr. Ren 94 C1
Spey Gdns. Ham 183 D4
Spey Gr. E Kil 179 F4
Spey Pl. John 131 E4
Spey Rd. Bear 75 E1
Spey Rd. Pres 233 E1
Spey Rd. Troon 229 F2
Spey St. Glasg 118 A3
Spey Terr. E Kil 179 F4
Spey Wik. Holy 143 D3
Spey Wynd. Lark 199 D4
Speyburn Pl. Irvine 219 F3
Spiers Gr. Glasg 135 F2
Spiers Pl. Beith 171 D4
Spiers Rd. Hous 91 D1
Spiers Rd. John 112 A2
Spiers Rd. Loch 129 D2
Spiers Wharf. Glasg 97 D1
Spiersbridge Ave. Glasg . 135 F2
Spiersbridge La. Glasg ... 135 F2
Spiersbridge La. Glasg ... 135 F2
Spiersbridge Rd. Glasg .. 135 F2
Spiersbridge Terr. Glasg . 135 F2
Spiersland Way. Beith 171 F4
Spindlehow Rd. Tan 141 D4
Spindlehowe Rd. Udd 140 C3
Spindleside Rd. Cle 144 B1
Spinkhill. Laur 42 C1
Spinners Gdns. Pais 113 D2
Spinners La. Dunt 74 A4
Spinningdale. Stone 198 B1
Spital Rd. Stone 198 C1
Spittal Hill. B of A 2 B2
Spittal Rd. Glasg 137 F3
Spittal St. Stir 7 D2
Spoutmouth. Glasg 117 E3
Sprig Way. East 127 F3
Spring La. Cad 104 C2
Springbank Gdns. Falk 42 B3
Springbank Rd. Pais 113 E4
Springbank Rd. Shot 146 B3
Springbank Rd. Stir 7 E3
Springbank St. Glasg 97 D2
Springbank Terr. Pais ... 113 E4
Springboig Ave. Glasg ... 119 E3
Springboig Rd. Glasg 119 E3
Springburn Pl. E Kil 159 D2
Springburn Rd. Glasg 97 F2
Springburn Way. Glasg ... 97 F2
Springcroft Ave. Glasg .. 120 B3
Springcroft Gdns. Glasg . 120 B3
Springcroft Rd. Glasg ... 120 A4
Springfield Ave. Bish 98 A4
Springfield Ave. Pais 114 A2
Springfield Ave. Pres 236 B4
Springfield Ave. Udd 140 C3
Springfield Cres. Bish 98 A4
Springfield Cres. Car 201 F4
Springfield Cres. Udd ... 140 C3
Springfield Dr. Glasg 137 F3
Springfield Dr. Barr 134 C1
Springfield. Dr. Falk 41 F3
Springfield Sq. Bish 98 A4
Springfield Woods. John . 112 A1
Springhead Rd. Alla 167 D4
Springhill
   and Leadloch Rd. Shot . 147 F1
Springhill Ave. Aird 123 D4
Springhill Ave. Coat 121 E2
Springhill Ave. Cross 226 C4
Springhill Ave. Kilmk ... 227 F4
Springhill Pl. Coat 121 E2
Springhill Pl. Kilmk 227 F4
Springhill Rd. Barr 134 A1
Springhill Rd. Glasg 120 A3
Springhill Rd. Newt M ... 157 F4
Springhill Rd. P Glasg 47 E1
Springhill Rd. Shot 147 D2
Springhill Terr. Spring .. 220 C1
Springkell Ave. Glasg ... 116 B2
Springkell Dr. Glasg 116 A1
Springkell Gate. Glasg .. 116 A1
Springkell Gdns. Glasg . 116 B1
Springkell St. Green 46 A2

Springkerse Rd. Stir 7 E3
Springside Pl. Glasg 75 D2
Springside Terr. Spring 220 C1
Springvale. W Kil 190 C4
Springvale Pk. Ayr 238 C3
Springvale Pl. Salt 216 C4
Springvale Rd. Ayr 238 C3
Springvale St. Salt 216 C4
Springvale Terr. Glasg 97 F2
Springwell Cres. Ham 161 F4
Springwell Pl. Stew 195 F1
Springwells Ave. Aird 123 E4
Springwells Cres. Aird 123 E4
Springwood Ave. Stir 6 C3
Springwood Dr. Kil 69 E1
Sprotwell Terr. N Sau 5 E1
Spruce Ave. Green 46 A2
Spruce Ave. Ham 162 C1
Spruce Ave. John 112 A1
Spruce Ave. Udd 161 E4
Spruce Ct. Coat 121 F2
Spruce Ct. Ham 162 C1
Spruce Dr. Kirk 79 D3
Spruce House. Pres 236 A3
Spruce Pk. Ayr 239 E3
Spruce Rd. Cumb 62 B2
Spruce Rd. Tan 221 E1
Spruce St. Glasg 97 E3
Spruce Way. Holy 143 D2
Sprucebank Ave. Lang 70 B4
Spy's La. Rhu 15 F2
Spynie Pl. Bish 78 B1
Synie Way. New 165 F3
Square The. Fall 8 B2
Squire St. Glasg 95 F1
Stable Pl. Miln 54 C2
Stable Rd. Shot 147 D3
Stable Wynd. Troon 230 A2
Stables The. Strath 55 D3
Staffa Ave. P Glasg 69 D4
Staffa Ave. Ren 94 B1
Staffa Ct. Irvine 225 D4
Staffa Dr. Aird 123 F4
Staffa Dr. Kirk 80 A1
Staffa Dr. Pais 133 F4
Staffa. E Kil 181 E4
Staffa Pl. Falk 42 A1
Staffa Rd. Glasg 138 C2
Staffa St. Glasg 118 A4
Staffa St. Gour 44 C3
Staffin St. Glasg 76 B1
Staffin Rd. Troon 229 F3
Staffin St. Glasg 76 C1
Stafflar Dr. Kilmk 227 F2
Stafford Cres. Gour 44 C2
Stafford Rd. Gour 44 C2
Stafford St. Glasg 97 E1
Stafford St. Ham 141 F2
Stafford St. Helen 16 B1
Stafford St. Kilmk 222 C1
Stafford St W. Helen 16 B1
Stathdway S. Gour 44 C2
Stag St. Glasg 116 A4
Staigbraes Pl. Aird 102 C1
Stairlie Cres. W Kil 190 B3
Stalker St. Mother 164 B2
Stamford St. Glasg 118 A3
Stamperland Ave. Glasg 157 F4
Stamperland Cres. Glasg 157 F4
Stamperland Dr. Glasg 157 F4
Stamperland Gdns. Glasg 157 F4
Stamperland Hill. Glasg 157 F4
Stanalane St. Glasg 135 F2
Standalane. Kilm 222 B3
Standalane. Stew 211 E4
Standburn Rd. Glasg 98 B3
Stane Rd. P Glasg 68 C4
Stane Rd. Shot 147 D1
Staneacre Pk. Ham 162 C2
Stanecastle Dr. Irvine 219 F3
Stanecastle Gate. Irvine 219 F3
Stanecastle
   Interchange. Irvine 219 F2
Stanecastle Rd. Irvine 219 F2
Stanecraigs Pl. New 165 F3
Stanefield Dr. Holy 143 F2
Stanely Cres. Pais 133 D4
Stanely Ct. Pais 133 D4
Stanely Dr. Pais 113 E1
Stanely Rd. Pais 113 E1
Stanford St. Clyde 74 B1
Stanhope Dr. Glasg 138 B3
Stanhope Pl. Wish 186 A4
Stanistone Rd. Car 188 A1
Stanley Ave. Ard 205 E2
Stanley Ave. Pais 113 D1
Stanley Dr. Ard 205 E2
Stanley Dr. B of A 2 A4
Stanley Dr. Bish 78 A1
Stanley Dr. Hat 142 A3
Stanley Dr. Kilbar 111 E3
Stanley La. Kilbar 111 E3
Stanley Pk. Aird 123 D4
Stanley Pl. Salt 205 F1
Stanley Pl. Udd 140 B1
Stanley Rd. Ard 205 E2

Stanley Rd. Salt 216 C4
Stanley St. Glasg 116 C3
Stanley St. Ham 161 F2
Stanley Street La. Glasg 116 C3
Stanmore Ave. Lan 215 D3
Stanmore Cres. Lan 215 E3
Stanmore Rd. Glasg 137 D4
Stanmore Rd. Lan 215 E3
Stanners La. Green 46 A2
Stannis St. Plains 104 A1
Stanton Ave. All 9 F3
Stark Ave. Dunt 73 F3
Stark Ave. Falk 41 E3
Starling Way. Tan 141 F4
Starryshaw Rd. Shot 146 C3
Starrystile St. Glasg 119 D4
Station Ave. Green 46 A2
Station Ave. How 130 C3
Station Brae. Neil 154 B4
Station Bridge. Ayr 239 D4
Station Cres. Ren 94 C2
Station Dr. Hurl 228 B3
Station Dr. Pres 233 E1
Station Dr. Spring 221 D2
Station Pl. Law 187 D3
Station Rd. Aird 123 F4
Station Rd. Ash 200 B2
Station Rd. Ayr 239 D4
Station Rd. B of A 1 C4
Station Rd. Bann 7 F1
Station Rd. Bear 75 E2
Station Rd. Bish 77 D4
Station Rd. Bishop 72 A1
Station Rd. Blac 107 E1
Station Rd. Calct 104 C2
Station Rd. Camb 4 A1
Station Rd. Car 187 F1
Station Rd. Cle 144 A1
Station Rd. Cowie 12 A3
Station Rd. Dumb 49 F2
Station Rd. Dunlop 195 D4
Station Rd. Glasg 96 B4
Station Rd. Glasg 120 B2
Station Rd. Glasg 136 B2
Station Rd. Gour 44 C4
Station Rd. Ham 162 C2
Station Rd. Helen 23 D3
Station Rd. Holy 143 D2
Station Rd. How 130 C3
Station Rd. Kilbar 111 D1
Station Rd. Kils 36 B1
Station Rd. Lang 70 B3
Station Rd. Lark 185 D2
Station Rd. Law 187 D3
Station Rd. Lennox 57 E4
Station Rd. Miln 55 E1
Station Rd. Muir 100 B3
Station Rd. Neil 154 B4
Station Rd. O Kill 73 D3
Station Rd. P Glasg 47 E1
Station Rd. Pais 113 D2
Station Rd. Plains 104 A1
Station Rd. Pres 233 E1
Station Rd. Pres 233 E2
Station Rd. Ren 94 C2
Station Rd. Rhu 15 F3
Station Rd. Shot 146 C2
Station Rd. Siam 86 A3
Station Rd. Spring 220 C1
Station Rd. Stepps 99 D3
Station Rd. Steven 217 E4
Station Rd. Str 7 D4
Station Rd. Strath 31 D2
Station Rd. Thorn 158 A3
Station Rd. Tull 4 A1
Station Rd. Udd 140 C1
Station Rd. Udd 140 C3
Station Rd. Udd 141 D1
Station Rd. Wish 165 D1
Station Rise. Loch 129 E1
Station Row. Shew 225 F3
Station Row. Siam 86 A3
Station St. Alex 27 E1
Station Way. Udd 140 C3
Steading The. Wish 165 D3
Steadman Pl. Irvine 225 D4
Steel Ave. Glasg 137 E3
Steel St. Gour 44 C4
Steel St. Wish 165 D1
Steele Cres. Bonh 28 A4
Steele Wlk. Bonh 28 A4
Steeple St. Kilbar 111 D2
Steeple St. Kilbar 111 D2
Steeples View. Troon 229 F4
Stein Sq. Bann 7 F1
Stenhouse Ave. Muir 100 B4
Stenton Cres. Wish 164 B1
Stenton Cres. Wish 164 B1
Stenton Pl. Wish 164 B1
Stepends Rd. Chap 124 B4
Stepends Rd. Plains 104 B4
Stepford Pl. Glasg 119 F4
Stepford Rd. Glasg 120 A4
Stephen Cres. Glasg 119 F3
Stephenson Pl. E Kil 180 B4

Stephenson Sq. E Kil 180 B4
Stephenson St. Glasg 114 C4
Stephenson Terr. E Kil 180 B4
Stepps Rd. Glasg 119 E4
Stepps Rd. Stepps 79 F1
Steps Pl. Irvine 219 E3
Steps St. Sten 23 F2
Steuart Rd. B of A 1 C4
Steven St. Alex 27 F3
Stevenson Ct. B of A 2 A3
Stevenson Pl. Hat 142 A4
Stevenson St. Car 187 F1
Stevenson St. Clyde 73 F2
Stevenson St. Glasg 117 F3
Stevenson St. Kilmk 222 B1
Stevenson St. Pais 113 F2
Stevenston Ct. Holy 143 D2
Stevenston Ind Est. Steven ... 217 F4
Stevenston Rd. Kilw 207 E2
Stevenston St. Holy 143 D2
Stewart Ave. Newt M 156 C3
Stewart Ave. Ren 94 A1
Stewart Ave. Udd 161 E4
Stewart Cres. New 166 A4
Stewart Ct. Barr 134 B2
Stewart Ct. Glasg 138 B4
Stewart Dr. Coat 121 D3
Stewart Dr. Dunt 74 A3
Stewart Dr. Irvine 219 E2
Stewart Dr. Newt M 157 F4
Stewart Gr. East 127 F3
Stewart Quadrant. Holy 143 D3
Stewart Rd. Ayr 236 B2
Stewart Rd. Falk 42 B3
Stewart Rd. Pais 133 F4
Stewart Sq. Steven 217 F4
Stewart St. Barr 134 B2
Stewart St. Bon 39 F3
Stewart St. Cam 6 B3
Stewart St. Car 187 F1
Stewart St. Clyde 73 F2
Stewart St. Coat 122 A4
Stewart St. Glasg 97 D1
Stewart St. Ham 162 A1
Stewart St. Hat 142 A3
Stewart St. Miln 55 D1
Stewartfield Cres. E Kil 159 E2
Stewartfield Dr. E Kil 159 E2
Stewartfield Rd. E Kil 159 E2
Stewartfield Way. E Kil 159 E2
Stewartgill Pl. Ash 185 F1
Stewarton Dr. Glasg 138 C3
Stewarton Rd. Dunlop 195 D4
Stewarton Rd. Fen 213 D2
Stewarton Rd. Glasg 155 F1
Stewarton St. Wish 165 E1
Stewarton Terr. Wish 165 E1
Stewartville St. Glasg 96 A1
Stinchar Rd. Pres 233 E1
Stirling Ave. Bear 75 F1
Stirling Ave. E Kil 180 A4
Stirling Ave. Kilmk 222 B1
Stirling Cres. Kilmk 222 B1
Stirling Dr. Bear 75 E3
Stirling Dr. Bish 77 F2
Stirling Dr. Gour 43 F3
Stirling Dr. Ham 161 F2
Stirling Dr. John 111 E1
Stirling Dr. Lin 112 A3
Stirling Gdns. Bish 77 F2
Stirling Pl. Lennox 57 F4
Stirling Rd. Aird 103 D1
Stirling Rd. All 9 F4
Stirling Rd. Alva 5 D4
Stirling Rd. Bonh 20 A1
Stirling Rd. Bonh 27 F1
Stirling Rd. Car 187 F2
Stirling Rd. Chap 123 E2
Stirling Rd. Cumb 83 D2
Stirling Rd. Dumb 50 C4
Stirling Rd. Falk 41 E4
Stirling Rd. Fall 8 B2
Stirling Rd. Glasg 117 E4
Stirling Rd. Kils 60 C4
Stirling Rd. Lar 23 D1
Stirling Rd. Lar 22 C3
Stirling Rd. Tor 22 C3
Stirling Rd. Tull 4 A2
Stirling St. Aird 123 D4
Stirling St. Alex 27 E1
Stirling St. Alva 5 D4
Stirling St. Coat 121 E2
Stirling St. Cumb 62 A2
Stirling St. Den 21 F1
Stirling St. Duni 21 E2
Stirling St. Mother 164 A2
Stirling Way. Glasg 120 A2
Stirling Way. Ren 94 B1
Stirlingauld Pl. Glasg 117 D3
Stirrat St. Glasg 96 B3
Stirrat St. Pais 113 E4
Stobbs Cres. Kilw 207 F1
Stobbs Terr. Kilw 207 F1

Stobcross Rd. Glasg 116 B4
Stobcross St. Coat 122 A3
Stobcross St. Glasg 116 C4
Stobhill Cotts. Glasg 98 A4
Stobhill Rd. Bish 97 F4
Stobo Ct. E Kil 160 B2
Stobo. E Kil 160 B2
Stobo St. Wish 165 E3
Stobs Dr. Barr 134 A2
Stobs Pl. Glasg 100 B1
Stock Ave. Pais 113 F2
Stock St. Pais 113 F1
Stockbridge Cres. Kilb 149 D2
Stockholm Cres. Pais 113 F2
Stockiemuir Ave. Bear 75 F4
Stockiemuir Ct. Bear 75 F4
Stockiemuir Rd. Bear 75 E4
Stockiemuir Rd. Miln 54 B1
Stocks Rd. Cle 144 C1
Stockwell Pl. Glasg 117 E3
Stockwell St. Glasg 117 E3
Stoddard Sq. John 112 B2
Stonebyres Ct. Ham 162 A2
Stonecraig Rd. Wish 165 E1
Stonecrop Pl. Ayr 239 E2
Stoneyke Cres. Car 188 A2
Stonedyke Rd. Car 188 A2
Stonefield Ave. Glasg 96 B3
Stonefield Ave. Pais 113 F1
Stonefield Cres. Newt M 157 E4
Stonefield Cres. Pais 113 D1
Stonefield Cres. Udd 161 E3
Stonefield Dr. Pais 113 F1
Stonefield Gdns. Car 188 A2
Stonefield Gdns. Pais 113 F1
Stonefield Green. Pais 113 F1
Stonefield Park Gdns. Udd ... 141 D2
Stonefield Pk. Ayr 238 B1
Stonefield Pl. Pais 133 F4
Stonefield Pl. Udd 161 E3
Stonefield Rd. Udd 161 E3
Stonehall Ave. Ham 162 A1
Stonehaven Rd. Gour 44 C2
Stonelaw Dr. Glasg 138 A3
Stonelaw Rd. Glasg 138 A3
Stonelaw Towers. Glasg 138 B3
Stoneleigh Pl. Green 45 E4
Stoneleigh Rd. Green 45 E4
Stoneside Dr. Glasg 136 A3
Stoneside Sq. Glasg 136 A3
Stoney Brae. Pais 113 F3
Stonewetts Cotts. Muir 80 C1
Stoneyetts Rd. Muir 80 C1
Stoneyholm Rd. Kilb 149 D1
Stoneymeadow Rd. E Kil 160 B3
Stoneymollan Rd. Card 26 A3
Stoneywood Pk. Duni 21 D1
Stonyflat Ave. Dumb 50 A3
Stonyflat Rd. Dumb 50 A3
Stonyhill Ave. Kilmk 227 F2
Stonyhurst St. Glasg 97 D2
Stonyhurst St. Glasg 97 E2
Stonylee Rd. Cumb 62 A1
Stoopshill Cres. Beith 191 F4
Storie St. Pais 113 F2
Stormlyand Way. Barr 134 B1
Stornoway Cres. Wish 165 F3
Stornoway St. Glasg 97 E4
Stow Brae. Pais 113 F2
Stow Pl. Pais 113 F2
Strachan St. Falk 41 F2
Strachan St. Hat 142 A2
Strachur St. Glasg 97 D3
Straehouse Wynd. Car 188 A1
Strain Cres. Aird 123 D3
Straiton Dr. Ham 161 E1
Straiton St. Glasg 118 C4
Strand. Beith 191 E4
Strand St. Kilmk 222 C1
Strandhead. Stew 211 E4
Strang Pr. Pres 236 B3
Strang's Pl. Cali 66 C3
Stranka Ave. Pais 113 E2
Stranraer Dr. Glasg 75 F1
Stratford. E Kil 160 B3
Stratford St. Glasg 96 C3
Strath Carron. Law 187 D3
Strath Dearn. Law 187 D3
Strath Elgin. Law 187 D3
Strath Halladale. Law 187 D3
Strath Nairn. Law 187 D3
Strath Naver. Law 187 D3
Strathallan Ct. B of A 2 A3
Strathallan Gdns. Kirk 79 E4
Strathallan Rd. B of A 2 A3
Strathallon Pl. Glasg 138 B2
Strathaven Rd. E Kil 181 D4
Strathaven Rd. Eagle 178 C2
Strathaven Rd. Ham 183 D4
Strathaven Rd. Stone 198 C1
Strathavon Cres. Aird 103 D1
Strathay Pl. Ayr 239 D4
Strathblane Cres. Aird 103 D2
Strathblane Rd. Lennox 55 E2
Strathblane Rd. Miln 55 E2
Strathbran St. Glasg 118 B2
Strathcairn Cres. Aird 103 D2

Strathcarron Pl. Glasg 96 B3
Strathcarron Rd. Pais 114 A1
Strathcarron Rd. Ard 205 E2
Strathclyde Ct. Helen 16 A2
Strathclyde Dr. Glasg 138 A3
Strathclyde Path. Udd 140 C3
Strathclyde Pl. Helen 16 A4
Strathclyde Rd. Dumb 50 A3
Strathclyde Rd. Mother 163 D3
Strathclyde St. Glasg 118 A1
Strathclyde Vew. Udd 161 E4
Strathclyde Way. Hat 142 B4
Strathclyde Way. Hat 142 B4
Strathcona Dr. Glasg 96 A4
Strathcona Gdns. Glasg 96 A4
Strathcona La. E Kil 180 C4
Strathcona Pl. E Kil 180 C4
Strathcona Pl. Glasg 138 B2
Strathcona St. Glasg 96 A4
Strathdearn Gr. Stir 2 A2
Strathdee Ave. Dunt 74 A3
Strathdee Rd. Glasg 136 C1
Strathdon Ave. Glasg 136 C1
Strathdon Ave. Pais 113 E1
Strathdon Dr. Glasg 136 C1
Strathdon Pl. Ayr 238 B1
Strathearn Rd. Kirk 59 D1
Strathearn Rd. Newt M 157 F3
Strathendrick Dr. Glasg 136 C2
Strathfillan Rd. E Kil 159 E1
Strathkelvin Ave. Bish 97 F4
Strathlachlan Ave. Car 188 A1
Strathleven Dr. Bonh 27 F1
Strathleven Pl. Dumb 49 F2
Strathmiglo Pl. Sten 23 F2
Strathmore Ave. Pais 114 B2
Strathmore Ave. Udd 140 B1
Strathmore Cres. Aird 103 D1
Strathmore Gdns. Glasg 97 D4
Strathmore Pk. Helen 16 A2
Strathmore Pl. Ham 162 C2
Strathmurgo Cres. Aird 102 C1
Strathord Pl. Muir 81 D2
Strathord St. Glasg 119 D2
Strathpeffer Cres. Aird 103 D1
Strathspey Cres. Aird 103 D2
Strathtay Ave. Glasg 157 F4
Strathtummel Cres. Aird 103 D2
Strathview Gr. Glasg 136 C1
Strathview Pk. Glasg 136 C1
Strathview Rd. Hat 141 F2
Strathy Pl. Glasg 96 B3
Strathy Pl. Kilmk 222 C3
Strathyre Gdns. Bear 76 B3
Strathyre Gdns. Glenm 102 C3
Strathyre Gdns. Miln 81 D2
Strathyre Rd. Ham 161 F3
Strathyre St. Glasg 136 C1
Stratton Dr. Glasg 136 A1
Strauss Ave. Clyde 74 C1
Stravaig Path. Pais 133 D4
Stravaig Wlk. Pais 133 D4
Stravanan Rd. Glasg 137 E1
Stravanan St. Glasg 137 E1
Stravenhouse Rd. Law 186 C2
Strawberry Field Rd. Hous ... 91 D1
Strawberrybank Rd. Kilmk ... 223 D1
Strawhill Rd. Newt M 157 F3
Strenabey Ave. Glasg 138 B2
Stripehead. All 10 A3
Striven Cres. Wish 165 D1
Striven Dr. Falk 24 B1
Striven Gdns. Glasg 96 C2
Striven Terr. Ham 162 A1
Stroma Ave. P Glasg 69 D4
Stroma Ct. Irvine 225 E4
Stroma St. Glasg 98 A1
Stromness St. Glasg 117 D2
Strone Cres. Green 46 A2
Strone Gdns. Kils 60 A4
Strone Path. Glen 101 E3
Strone Rd. Glasg 119 D4
Stronend St. Glasg 97 D3
Stronsay Ct. Irvine 225 D4
Stronsay Pl. Bish 78 B1
Stronsay Pl. Kilmk 223 D3
Stronsay St. Glasg 98 A1
Stronsay Way. Irvine 220 A1
Stronvar Dr. Glasg 96 A2
Strood Rd. E Kil 180 B3
Strowan Cres. Glasg 119 D2
Strowan St. Glasg 119 D2
Strowan's Rd. Dumb 50 B2
Strowan's Well Rd. Dumb 50 B2
Struan Ave. Glasg 136 B2
Struan Gdns. Glasg 137 D2
Struan Rd. Glasg 137 D3
Strudee Howe. Alva 5 D4
Strude Mill. Alva 5 D4
Strude St. Alva 5 D4
Struie St. Glasg 118 C4
Struma Dr. Newt M 157 E4
Struther St. Lark 199 D4
Struther & Swinhill Rd. Lark .. 199 E3
Struther & Swinhill Rd. Lark .. 199 D3
Struthers Ave. Hurl 228 B4
Struthers Cres. E Kil 160 A2

Struthers Pl. Troon 229 F4
Stuart Ave. Glasg 138 A3
Stuart Ct. O Kil 73 D3
Stuart Dr. Bish 97 F4
Stuart Dr. Lan 215 D3
Stuart Dr. Lark 185 E1
Stuart Pl. Dund 225 F1
Stuart Quadrant. Wish 164 C1
Stuart Rd. Bishop 72 A2
Stuart Rd. Dumb 50 B2
Stuart St. E Kil 159 F1
Stuart St. O Kil 73 D3
Stuarton Pk. E Kil 159 F1
Stuckieckie Rd. Helen 17 D1
Sturrock St. Kilmk 227 F4
Succoth St. Glasg 95 F4
Sudbury Cres. E Kil 159 D1
Suffolk Rd. Gour 44 C2
Suffolk St. Glasg 117 E3
Suffolk St. Helen 16 B1
Sugworth Ave. Glasg 120 A3
Sumburgh St. Glasg 119 D4
Summer St. Glasg 117 F3
Summerfiel Cotts. Glasg 95 F1
Summerfield Rd. Cumb 82 A3
Summerfield St. Glasg 118 A2
Summerford. Falk 41 E2
Summerford Gdns. Falk 41 E2
Summerford Rd. Falk 41 E2
Summerhill and
  Garngibbock Rd. Glen 82 B2
Summerhill Ave. Lark 185 D1
Summerhill Rd. Glasg 75 D2
Summerhill Rd. Newt M 157 F2
Summerhill Way. Hat 141 F2
Summerlea Rd. Glasg 135 F2
Summerlea Rd. W Kil 190 A2
Summerlee Cotts. Coat 121 F4
Summerlee Rd. Lark 184 C3
Summerlee Rd. Mother 164 B2
Summerlee St. Coat 121 F4
Summerlee St. Glasg 119 E4
Summertown Rd. Glasg 116 A4
Suna Path. Shot 147 D2
Sunart Ave. Ren 94 A2
Sunart Ct. Ham 162 A1
Sunart Rd. Bish 78 B1
Sunart Rd. Bish 78 B1
Sunart St. Wish 165 D1
Sunbury Ave. Newt M 157 E4
Sundale Ave. Newt M 157 E3
Sunderland Ave. Dumb 49 E2
Sunderland Ct. Kilb 170 A4
Sundrum Pl. Kilw 207 E1
Sunflower Gdns. Mother 163 F4
Sunningdale Ave. Ayr 239 D2
Sunningdale Ave. Newt M 156 C3
Sunningdale Dr. B of W 110 B3
Sunningdale Rd. Glasg 96 C4
Sunningdale Sq. Kilw 207 E2
Sunningdale Wynd. Udd 140 C2
Sunnybank Gr. Newt M 157 E3
Sunnybank St. Glasg 118 A2
Sunnydale Dr. Blac 107 F2
Sunnydale Rd. Blac 107 F2
Sunnyhill. Twe 59 F2
Sunnylaw Dr. Pais 113 D1
Sunnylaw Pl. Falk 41 F2
Sunnylaw Rd. B of A 2 A4
Sunnylaw Way. M of C 27 A3
Sunnyside Ave. Udd 140 C3
Sunnyside Ave. P Glasg 69 D4
Sunnyside Ct. All 10 A4
Sunnyside Cres. Holy 143 D3
Sunnyside Ct. All 10 A4
Sunnyside Dr. Coat 121 D3
Sunnyside Dr. Glasg 75 D1
Sunnyside Dr. Glasg 75 D1
Sunnyside. Kilm 222 A4
Sunnyside Pl. Barr 134 A1
Sunnyside Pl. Glasg 75 D1
Sunnyside Pl. Holy 143 D3
Sunnyside Rd. All 10 B4
Sunnyside Rd. Cle 165 D4
Sunnyside Rd. Coat 122 A4
Sunnyside Rd. Falk 41 F3
Sunnyside Rd. Kilmk 227 F1
Sunnyside Rd. Lan 214 B3
Sunnyside Rd. Pais 113 E1
Sunnyside Rd. Quart 184 B2
Sunnyside Sq E. Kilmk 227 F1
Sunnyside Sq W. Kilmk 227 F1
Sunnyside St. Falk 41 F3
Sunnyside. Stir 7 D2
Sunnyside Terr. Holy 143 D3
Surrey La. Glasg 117 D2
Surrey St. Glasg 117 D2
Susannah St. Alex 27 F3
Sussex St. Glasg 116 C3
Sutcliffe Rd. Glasg 95 F4
Sutherland Ave. All 10 B4
Sutherland Ave. Bear 75 F4
Sutherland Ave. Glasg 116 B2

Sutherland Ave. Stir 2 B1
Sutherland Dr. Aird 122 C3
Sutherland Dr. Den 39 E4
Sutherland Dr. Dumb 50 B2
Sutherland Dr. Glasg 136 B1
Sutherland Dr. Kilmk 223 E1
Sutherland La. Glasg 96 B1
Sutherland Pl. Hat 141 F1
Sutherland Rd. Clyde 74 A1
Sutherland Rd. Green 45 D2
Sutherland St. Helen 16 A1
Sutherland St. Pais 113 E3
Sutherland St. Udd 161 E3
Sutherland Way. E Kil 160 B2
Sutton Ct. Kilw 207 D2
Sutton Pk Cres. Sten 23 F2
Sutton Pl. Falk 42 B3
Swaledale. E Kil 159 E2
Swallow Rd. Dunt 74 B4
Swan Pl. John 131 E4
Swan St. Clyde 73 F2
Swan St. Glasg 97 E1
Swanson Rd. Alex 27 E4
Swanston St. Glasg 118 A1
Sween Ave. Glasg 137 D2
Sween Dr. Ham 162 A1
Sween Path. Hat 142 B2
Sweethill Terr. Coat 122 B2
Sweethill Wlk. Hat 142 B2
Sweethope Gdns. Udd 141 D1
Sweethope Pl. Udd 141 D2
Swift Bank. Ham 161 F1
Swift Pl. E Kil 179 F3
Swift Pl. John 131 E4
Swindon St. Clyde 73 E2
Swinhill Rd. Ash 199 E3
Swinstie Rd. Cle 165 E4
Swinstie View. Cle 144 B1
Swinton Ave. Glasg 120 B3
Swinton Cres. Coat 121 D2
Swinton Cres. Glasg 120 B3
Swinton Dr. Glasg 115 D3
Swinton Gdns. Glasg 120 B3
Swinton Path. Glasg 120 B3
Swinton Pl. Glasg 115 D3
Swinton Rd. Glasg 120 B3
Swinton View. Glasg 120 B3
Swisscot Ave. Ham 183 D4
Swisscot Wlk. Ham 183 D4
Switchback Rd. Bear 75 F1
Sword St. Aird 122 C4
Sword St. Glasg 117 F3
Sword's Way. Falk 24 A1
Swordale Pl. Glasg 120 A4
Sycamore Ave. Beith 150 A1
Sycamore Ave. John 112 A1
Sycamore Ave. Kirk 79 E3
Sycamore Ave. Tan 141 E4
Sycamore Cres. Aird 123 E3
Sycamore Cres. Ayr 239 E3
Sycamore Cres. E Kil 180 B3
Sycamore Ct. Beith 150 A1
Sycamore Ct. E Kil 180 B3
Sycamore Dr. Aird 123 E3
Sycamore Dr. Clyde 74 A2
Sycamore Dr. Ham 162 C2
Sycamore Gr. Udd 161 E4
Sycamore Pl. E Kil 180 B3
Sycamore Pl. Gour 44 B3
Sycamore Pl. Holy 143 E2
Sycamore Way. Cambus 6 C3
Sycamore Way. E Kil 158 B4
Sycamore Way. M of C 58 B3
Sycamores The. Tull 4 A1
Sydenham La. Glasg 96 B2
Sydenham Rd. Glasg 96 B2
Sydes Brae. Ham 161 D2
Sydney Dr. E Kil 180 B4
Sydney Pl. E Kil 180 B4
Sydney St. Clyde 73 E2
Sydney St. Glasg 117 F3
Sykehead Ave. Hat 142 A3
Sykes Terr. Neil 154 C4
Sykeside Rd. Aird 122 C2
Sylvania Way. Clyde 74 A1
Sylvania Way S. Clyde 74 A1
Symington Dr. Clyde 74 A1
Symington Pl. Shaw 224 C4
Symington Pl. Sten 24 A2
Symington Rd N. Sym 231 E2
Symington Rd S. Sym 231 E2
Symington Sq. E Kil 180 C4
Syms La. Ayr 236 A1
Syriam Pl. Glasg 97 F2
Syriam St. Glasg 97 F3

Tabard Pl. Glasg 95 E4
Tabard Rd. Glasg 95 E4
Tabernacle La. Glasg 139 D3
Tabernacle St. Glasg 139 D3
Taggart Rd. Kils 60 C2
Taig Rd. Kirk 80 A4
Tait Ave. Barr 91 B2
Tait Dr. Lar 41 E4
Takmadoon Rd. Kils 36 C2
Talbot Dr. Glasg 95 D3
Talbot. E Kil 160 B2

Talbot Pl. Glasg 95 D3
Talbot Rd. Bonh 28 A4
Talbot Terr. Glasg 95 D3
Talbot Terr. Tan 140 C4
Talisman Ave. Dumb 49 E2
Talisman Cres. Helen 25 C4
Talisman Cres. Mother 142 B1
Talisman Rd. Glasg 95 E3
Talisman Rd. Pais 132 C4
Talisman Wlk. Salt 206 A1
Talla Rd. Glasg 115 D3
Tallant Ave. Glasg 75 D2
Tallant Terr. Glasg 75 E2
Tam O'Shanter Dr. Cowie 12 B4
Tam's Brig. Ayr 236 A2
Tamar Dr. E Kil 179 F3
Tamarack Cres. Tan 141 E4
Tambowie Ave. Miln 54 C1
Tambowie Cres. Miln 54 C1
Tambowie St. Glasg 95 F4
Tamfourhill Ave. Falk 41 E2
Tamfourhill Rd. Falk 41 E2
Tammy Dale's Rd. Kilw 207 F2
Tamshill St. Glasg 96 C4
Tanar Ave. Ren 94 C1
Tanar Way. Ren 94 C1
Tandlehill Rd. Kilbar 111 D1
Tanera Ave. Glasg 137 E2
Tanfield Pl. Glasg 119 E4
Tanfield St. Glasg 119 E4
Tankerland Rd. Glasg 137 D3
Tanna Dr. Glasg 115 F2
Tannadice Ave. Glasg 115 E2
Tannahill Cres. John 111 F1
Tannahill Dr. E Kil 160 B2
Tannahill Rd. Glasg 136 C3
Tannahill Rd. Pais 113 D3
Tannahill Terr. Pais 113 D3
Tanners Rd. Falk 42 A2
Tannery La. Stir 2 A1
Tannoch Dr. Cumb 82 C4
Tannoch Dr. Miln 55 D2
Tannoch Pl. Cumb 82 C4
Tannoch Rd. Uplaw 153 D2
Tannock St. Glasg 97 D2
Tannock St. Miln 55 D1
Tantallon Ave. Gour 43 F3
Tantallon Ct. Car 187 F2
Tantallon Dr. Coat 101 E1
Tantallon Dr. Pais 113 D1
Tantallon Pk. E Kil 159 E1
Tantallon Rd. Glasg 120 A2
Tantallon Rd. Glasg 136 C4
Tantallon Rd. Udd 141 D2
Tantera Ct. Falk 42 A1
Tanziekneww Ave. Glasg 139 D2
Tanziekneww Dr. Glasg 139 D2
Tanziekneww Pl. Glasg 139 D2
Tanziekneww Rd. Glasg 139 D2
Tappoch Pl. Lar 23 D2
Taransay St. Glasg 116 A4
Tarbert Ave. Udd 140 B1
Tarbert Ave. W Kil 190 C3
Tarbert Ave. Wish 165 D1
Tarbert Pl. Car 188 A1
Tarbet St. Gour 44 C4
Tarbolton Dr. Clyde 74 B2
Tarbolton. E Kil 160 B2
Tarbolton Path. Lark 184 C2
Tarbolton Rd. Cumb 82 A2
Tarbolton Rd. Glasg 136 B3
Tarbolton Rd. Pres 233 F2
Tarbolton St. Sym 231 F3
Tarbolton St. Clyde 74 B2
Tarbrax Path. Shot 147 D2
Tarbrax Way. Ham 162 A2
Tarduff Pl. Dunt 21 D1
Tarff Ave. Eagle 178 C3
Tarfside Ave. Glasg 115 E2
Tarfside Gdns. Glasg 115 F2
Tarfside Oval. Glasg 115 E2
Target Rd. Aird 123 D3
Tarland St. Glasg 115 F3
Tarras Dr. Ren 94 C1
Tarras Pl. Glasg 139 E3
Tarryholme Dr. Irvine 219 E1
Tasker St. Green 45 E3
Tasman Dr. E Kil 180 A4
Tasmania Quadrant. Wish 165 F2
Tassie Pl. E Kil 180 A4
Tassie St. Glasg 136 B4
Tattershall Rd. Glasg 99 E1
Tavistock Dr. Glasg 136 B3
Tay Ave. Pais 112 C1
Tay Ave. Ren 94 C2
Tay Cres. Bish 78 A1
Tay Cres. Glasg 98 C1
Tay Ct. All 10 B3
Tay Ct. E Kil 179 F4
Tay Gdns. Ham 183 D4
Tay Gr. E Kil 179 F4
Tay Loan. Holy 143 D3
Tay Pl. Dumb 50 A4
Tay Pl. E Kil 179 F4
Tay Pl. John 131 E4

Tay Pl. Kilmk 228 A3
Tay Pl. Lark 199 D4
Tay St. Coat 101 E1
Tay St. Falk 24 B1
Tay St. Green 45 D3
Tay Terr. E Kil 179 F4
Taybank Dr. Ayr 239 D2
Tayinloan Dr. Car 202 A4
Taylor Ave. Holy 143 E1
Taylor Ave. Kilbar 110 C2
Taylor Pl. Glasg 117 E4
Taylor St. Alex 27 E4
Taylor St. Ayr 235 F1
Taylor St. Clyde 94 B4
Taylor St. Glasg 117 E4
Taylor's Rd. Lar 23 E1
Taymouth Dr. Gour 43 F3
Taymouth St. Glasg 119 D2
Taynish Dr. Glasg 137 D3
Tayside. Aird 102 C1
Teak Pl. Tan 121 E1
Teal Cres. E Kil 179 F3
Teal Ct. Tan 141 F4
Tealing Ave. Glasg 115 E2
Tealing Cres. Glasg 115 E2
Teasel Ave. Glasg 135 D2
Teawell Rd. Newt M 156 B3
Teesdale. E Kil 159 E2
Teign Gr. E Kil 179 F3
Teith Ave. Ren 94 C1
Teith Dr. Bear 75 E2
Teith Pl. Glasg 139 E3
Teith Pl. Kilmk 228 A3
Teith St. Glasg 98 C1
Telegraph Rd. Cald 105 D4
Telephone La. Glasg 96 B1
Telford Ct. Bann 7 F3
Telford Ct. Clyde 74 A1
Telford Pl. Cumb 83 D4
Telford Pl. Irvine 219 F1
Telford Rd. Cumb 83 D4
Telford Rd. E Kil 180 C4
Telford Sq. Falk 41 F3
Telford St. Hat 142 A3
Teme Pl. E Kil 179 F4
Templand Cres. Dalry 191 E4
Templand Rd. Dalry 191 E4
Templar Ave. Glasg 75 E1
Temple Denny Rd. Den 21 E1
Temple Gdns. Glasg 95 F4
Temple Rd. Glasg 96 A4
Templehill. Troon 229 D2
Templeland Rd. Glasg 115 E1
Templerigg Ct. Pres 233 E1
Templerigg St. Pres 233 E1
Templeton Bsns Ctr. Glasg 117 F3
Templeton Cres. Pres 236 B4
Templeton Gdns. Pres 236 B4
Templeton St. Glasg 117 F3
Ten Acres. N Sau 5 D1
Tennant
  Complex The. E Kil 159 D1
Tennant Rd. Pais 113 D3
Tennant St. Ren 94 B2
Tennant St. Ren 122 A3
Tennyson Dr. Glasg 118 C2
Tern Pl. John 131 E4
Terrace Rd. Green 46 A2
Terregles Ave. Glasg 116 B1
Terregles Cres. Glasg 116 B1
Terregles Dr. Glasg 116 B1
Teviot Ave. Bish 78 A2
Teviot Ave. Pais 132 C4
Teviot Cres. Bear 75 E1
Teviot Dr. Bishop 72 B1
Teviot Pl. Glasg 139 F3
Teviot Rd. P Glasg 68 C3
Teviot Sq. Cumb 82 A2
Teviot St. Coat 101 E1
Teviot St. Falk 41 F2
Teviot St. Glasg 116 A3
Teviot Terr. John 131 E4
Teviot Way. Udd 161 E4
Teviotdale. Newt M 157 E3
Tewkesbury Rd. E Kil 160 B2
Thane Rd. Glasg 95 E3
Thanes Gate. Udd 140 C3
Thankerton Ave. Holy 142 C3
Thankerton Rd. Lark 185 D1
Tharsis St. Glasg 97 F1
Thimble St. Alex 27 E4
Third Ave. Bonh 27 F3
Third Ave. Dumb 50 B1
Third Ave. Glasg 139 D4
Third Ave. Irvine 224 A4
Third Ave. Ren 94 B3
Third Ave. Stepps 79 E1

Third Ave. Stepps 99 E3
Third Gdns. Glasg 116 A2
Third Rd. Ham 183 F1
Third St. Tan 140 C4
Thirdpart Cres. Clyde 94 C4
Thirdpart Pl. Kilmk 227 E4
Thirlmere. E Kil 179 F3
Thistle Ave. Dunt 21 E2
Thistle Bank. Kirk 79 E2
Thistle Cres. Lark 185 D1
Thistle Gdns. Holy 143 D2
Thistle Pl. E Kil 159 E2
Thistle Quadrant. Aird 103 D1
Thistle Rd. Holy 143 D2
Thistle St. Aird 103 D1
Thistle St. All 10 B3
Thistle St. Cle 144 B1
Thistle St. Falk 42 B3
Thistle St. Glasg 117 D2
Thistle St. Glasg 117 E3
Thistle St. Klrk 79 E2
Thistle St. Pais 113 E1
Thistle Terr. Steven 206 C1
Thistle Wlk. Ayr 239 D2
Thistleneuk. O Kil 73 D4
Thom St. Green 45 F2
Thomas Campbell St. Salt 217 D4
Thomas Muir Ave. Bish 98 A4
Thomas Muir La. Green 46 C1
Thomas Muir St. Green 46 C1
Thomas St. Alex 27 F2
Thomas St. Pais 113 D2
Thompson Ave. Klrk 79 F4
Thompson Pl. Clyde 74 B3
Thompson Pl. Stam 86 A2
Thompson St. Glasg 118 A3
Thompson St. Ren 94 B1
Thompson's Cl. Lan 215 D2
Thomson Ave. John 111 F2
Thomson Ave. Wish 164 B1
Thomson Dr. Aird 122 C3
Thomson Dr. Bear 75 F3
Thomson Dr. Tan 141 E3
Thomson Gr. Glasg 139 D4
Thomson Pl. Cam 85 D3
Thomson St. Ayr 236 B1
Thomson St. Car 187 F1
Thomson St. Glasg 111 F1
Thomson St. Kilmk 222 C1
Thomson Terr. Stew 211 E4
Thorn Ave. Thorn 158 B2
Thorn Brae. John 112 A2
Thorn Ct. John 112 A1
Thorn Dr. Bear 75 F3
Thorn Dr. Glasg 138 B2
Thorn Rd. Bear 75 E3
Thorn Rd. Hat 142 A3
Thorn Terr. Kilmk 223 D2
Thornbank St. Glasg 116 B4
Thornbridge Ave. Glasg 120 A3
Thornbridge Ave. Glasg 120 A3
Thornbridge Gdns. Falk 42 C2
Thornbridge Rd. Glasg 120 A3
Thornbridge Rd. Falk 42 C2
Thornbridge Sq. Falk 42 C3
Thorncliffe Gdns. Glasg 116 C1
Thorncroft Dr. Glasg 137 E2
Thorndale. Bonh 39 D1
Thorndean Ave. Hat 142 A2
Thorndean Cres. Hat 142 A2
Thornden La. Glasg 95 D2
Thornden. Ave. Holy 143 E1
Thorndene Ct. Falk 41 F1
Thorndene. John 112 A2
Thorndyke. E Kil 160 B3
Thorne Rd. All 4 C1
Thornhill Ave. John 112 A1
Thornhill Ct. Kilw 207 D2
Thornhill Dr. John 112 A1
Thornhill Gdns. John 112 A2
Thornhill. John 112 A2
Thornhill La. Udd 141 E1
Thornhill Path. Glasg 118 B3
Thornhill Pl. Glasg 118 B3
Thornhill Rd. Ham 161 F2
Thornhill Way. Coat 122 B2
Thornhouse Ave. Irvine 219 E1
Thorniecroft Dr. Cumb 82 B3
Thorniecroft Pl. Cumb 82 B3
Thornielee. E Kil 160 A1
Thorniewood Gdns. Tan 141 D4
Thorniewood Rd. Tan 140 C4
Thornlea Dr. Glasg 136 C1
Thornlea St. Car 202 A4
Thornley Ave. Glasg 95 D3
Thornlie Gill. Wish 165 D1
Thornliebank Rd. Glasg 135 F1
Thornliebank Rd. Glasg 136 C1
Thornly Park Ave. Pais 133 F4
Thornly Park Dr. Pais 133 F4
Thornly Park Gdns. Pais 113 F1
Thornly Park Rd. Pais 133 F4
Thornside Rd. John 112 A2

Thornton Ave. Bon 40 A3
Thornton Ave. Cross 221 F1
Thornton La. Glasg 96 C4
Thornton Pl. Ham 183 E3
Thornton Rd. Thorn 158 B1
Thornton St. Coat 101 E1
Thornton St. Glasg 96 C4
Thorntree Ave. Beith 150 B1
Thorntree Ave. Ham 161 F3
Thorntree Way. Udd 141 D2
Thornwood Ave. Ayr 236 C1
Thornwood Ave. Glasg 96 A1
Thornwood Ave. Klrk 79 D3
Thornwood Cres. Glasg 95 F2
Thornwood Dr. B of W 110 A4
Thornwood Dr. Glasg 95 F1
Thornwood Dr. Glasg 96 A2
Thornwood Dr. Irvine 219 E1
Thornwood Dr. Pais 113 D1
Thornwood Gdns. Glasg 96 A1
Thornwood Pl. Glasg 95 F2
Thornwood Quadrant. Glasg 95 F2
Thornwood Rd. Glasg 95 F1
Thornwood Terr. Glasg 95 F1
Thornyburn Dr. Glasg 120 B2
Thornyburn Pl. Glasg 120 B2
Thornyflat Dr. Ayr 236 C1
Thornyflat Rd. Ayr 236 C1
Thornyflat St. Ayr 236 C1
Thornyflat Wish 165 E2
Thrashbush Cres. Wish 165 E2
Thrashbush Rd. Wish 165 E2
Threave Ct. Car 187 F2
Three Rivers Wlk. E Kil 180 A4
Three Stanes
    Roundabout. Shew 224 B3
Threepwood Rd. Beith 150 C1
Threestonehill Ave. Glasg ... 119 E3
Threshold. E Kil 160 A1
Threshold Pk. E Kil 160 A1
Triplee Rd. B of W 110 D4
Thrums Ave. Bish 78 B1
Thrums. E Kil 160 B3
Thrums Gdns. Bish 78 B1
Thrush Pl. John 131 C4
Thrushbush La. Aird 103 D1
Thrushbush Quadrant. Aird ... 103 D1
Thrushbush Rd. Aird 103 D1
Thrushcraig Cres. Pais 113 F1
Thurso St. Glasg 96 B1
Thurston Rd. Glasg 115 D3
Tibbermore Rd. Glasg 96 A2
Tig Rd. Ayr 236 A2
Tighnasheen Way. Udd 140 B1
Till St. Wish 165 D3
Tillanburn Rd. Holy 143 F2
Tillet Oval. Pais 113 E4
Tillie St. Glasg 96 C2
Tillicairn Dr. Glasg 99 E1
Tillycairn Rd. Glasg 99 E1
Till Rd. New 165 E4
Till Rd. Pres 233 E2
Tilt St. Glasg 98 C1
Timmons Pl. Den 21 E1
Timmons Terr. Chap 123 E1
Tinker's La. Mother 163 E3
Tinkel Gdns. Muir 80 C2
Tinto Ave. Klrk 228 A2
Tinto Cres. Wish 165 E1
Tinto Dr. Barr 134 B1
Tinto Rd. Aird 123 D3
Tinto Rd. Bear 75 E3
Tinto Rd. Bish 78 B1
Tinto Rd. Glasg 136 B3
Tinto St. Wish 165 E1
Tinto View. Ham 183 F4
Tinto Way. Cle 144 A1
Tintock Dr. Kirk 58 C4
Tintock Rd. Kirk 59 D1
Tinwald Path. Glasg 115 D3
Tiree Ave. P Glasg 69 D4
Tiree Ave. Pais 133 E4
Tiree Ave. Ren 94 B1
Tiree Cres. New 165 F3
Tiree Ct. Cumb 82 B4
Tiree Ct. Irvine 225 D4
Tiree Dr. Cumb 82 B4
Tiree. E Kil 181 E4
Tiree Gdns. Bear 75 D3
Tiree Gdns. Glenm 102 C3
Tiree Pl. Falk 42 A1
Tiree Pl. Newt M 156 A3
Tiree Pl. Old 93 D3
Tiree Rd. Cumb 82 B4
Tiree St. Glasg 98 B1
Tirry Ave. Ren 94 C1
Tirry Way. Ren 94 C1
Titania. All 10 A4
Titchfield Rd. Troon 229 D1
Titchfield St. Kilmk 227 F2
Titchfield Way. Irvine 220 A3
Titwood Dr. Kilmk 222 C2
Titwood Rd. Glasg 116 B1
Titwood Rd. Newt M 156 C1
Tiverton Ave. Glasg 119 E2
Tivoli Ct. E Kil 160 D2
Tobago Pl. E Kil 159 D1
Tobago Pl. Glasg 117 F3
Tobago St. Glasg 117 F3

Tobago St. Green 45 F3
Tobermory Rd. Glasg 138 B2
Tobour Dr. Pais 133 F4
Todd St. Glasg 118 B4
Todhill Ave. Kilmk 222 C2
Todhills. E Kil 180 C4
Todholm Cres. Pais 114 A1
Todholm Rd. Pais 114 A1
Todholm Terr. Pais 114 A1
Todrig Dr. Kilmk 227 F2
Tofthill Ave. Bish 77 F1
Tofthill Gdns. Bish 77 F1
Tofts Cres. Dairy 191 E4
Tofts. Dairy 191 E4
Togo Pl. Green 45 F2
Tolbooth St. Falk 42 A2
Toll La. Glasg 116 C3
Tolbooth St. Mother 163 F3
Toll St. Mother 163 F3
Toll Wynd. Ham 183 E4
Tollbrae Ave. Aird 123 D4
Tollcross Rd. Glasg 118 C2
Tollerton Dr. Irvine 219 E2
Tollhouse Gdns. Hat 142 B2
Tollhouse Way. Irvine 220 A3
Tollpark Cres. New 166 A3
Tollpark Pl. Cumb 62 C4
Tollpark Rd. Cumb 62 C4
Tolsta St. Glasg 76 C1
Tom-A-Mhoit. Ros 15 D2
Tomtain Brae. Cumb 81 F4
Tomtain Ct. Cumb 81 F4
Toner Gdns. Wish 186 A4
Tontine Cres. Alex 49 E4
Tontine La. Glasg 117 E3
Tontine Pk. Alex 49 E4
Tontine Pl. Glasg 136 C2
Topaz Terr. Hat 142 A2
Tophill Entry. Falk 41 F3
Topperisfield. Kilbar 111 E1
Torbeg House. Pres 236 A3
Torbothie Rd. Shot 147 D2
Torbreck St. Glasg 115 F3
Torbrex Farm Rd. Stir 7 D2
Torbrex La. Stir 7 D3
Torbrex Rd. Stir 7 D3
Torburn Ave. Glasg 136 A2
Torburn Ave. Plea 12 B2
Tordene Path. Cumb 61 F2
Torgyle St. Glasg 76 B1
Tormeadow Rd. Newt M 156 B2
Tormore St. Glasg 115 E3
Tormusk Dr. Glasg 138 A2
Tormusk Rd. Glasg 138 A2
Tormes St. Glasg 96 B1
Torogay Pl. Bish 97 F4
Torogay St. Glasg 97 E4
Torogay Terr. Glasg 97 E4
Toronto Way. Glasg 139 E4
Torphin Cres. Glasg 119 D4
Torr Ave. Kil 89 F1
Torr Cres. Rhu 15 F3
Torr La. Rhu 89 F1
Torr Rd. B of W 110 A4
Torr Rd. Bish 78 B1
Torr St. Glasg 97 E2
Torran Rd. Glasg 119 F4
Torrance Ave. Aird 123 E4
Torrance Rd. E Kil 159 F1
Torrance Rd. Green 46 A1
Torrance Rd. Lennox 78 A4
Torrance St. Glasg 97 E2
Torranyard Terr. Ham 161 F1
Torriden Pl. Coat 121 F3
Torriden St. Coat 121 F3
Torridon Ave. Falk 24 B1
Torridon Ave. Glasg 116 A2
Torridon Ave. Holy 143 E2
Torridon Ct. All 10 B3
Torridon Gdns. Bear 75 F4
Torridon Gdns. Newt M 157 D2
Torrin Loan. Shot 147 D2
Torrin Rd. Glasg 76 B1
Torrinch Dr. Bonh 49 E1
Torrington Ave. Glasg 157 D4
Torrington Cres. Glasg 119 E2
Torrisdale Pl. Coat 121 F4
Torrisdale St. Coat 121 F4
Torrisdale St. Glasg 117 D1
Torry Dr. Alva 4 C4
Torryburn Rd. Glasg 98 B2
Torwood Ave. Lar 23 D1
Torwood Brae. Ham 161 F1
Torwood La. Muir 81 D1
Torwoodhill Pl. Rhu 15 F2
Torwoodhill Rd. Rhu 15 F2
Toryglen Rd. Glasg 137 F4
Toryglen St. Glasg 117 F1
Touch Rd. Cam 6 A3
Touchhill Cres. Plea 12 B2
Touchhill Rd. Kilmk 222 C2
Townhead Terr. Ham 161 E4
Touward Ct. Udd 161 E4
Toward Rd. Glasg 119 E4
Tower Ave. Barr 134 B2

Tower Cres. Ren 94 A1
Tower Dr. Gour 44 B3
Tower Dr. Ren 94 A1
Tower Pl. Clack 10 C3
Tower Pl. Helen 16 B1
Tower Pl. John 112 A1
Tower Pl. Miln 55 D1
Tower Rd. Bish 56 C2
Tower Rd. Cumb 83 D3
Tower Rd. John 111 F1
Tower Rd. Lennox 56 C2
Tower St. All 10 A4
Tower St. Glasg 116 C3
Tower Terr. Pais 113 E2
Tower View. N Sau 5 F1
Towerhill Ave. Kilm 222 B3
Towerhill Rd. Glasg 75 E1
Towerlands
    Farm Rd. Irvine 220 A2
Towerlands Gate. Irvine 220 A1
Towerlands
    Interchange. Irvine 219 F2
Towerlands Rd. Irvine 220 B1
Towerlands Rd. Spring 220 C1
Towers Ct. Falk 42 A3
Towers Pl. Aird 123 F4
Towers Pl. Stir 2 B2
Towers Rd. Aird 123 F4
Towerside Cres. Glasg 115 D1
Towerside Rd. Glasg 115 D1
Towie Pl. Glasg 96 B3
Towie Pl. Udd 140 C3
Town House St. Den 21 F1
Townend. Kilm 222 B4
Townend La. Dalry 191 E4
Townend Rd. Dumb 50 A3
Townend Rd. Kilmk 227 F2
Townend St. Dalry 191 E4
Townend Terr. Sym 231 E2
Townhead. Irvine 220 B1
Townhead Dr. Holy 143 F2
Townhead. Irvine 219 E1
Townhead. Kilb 149 D1
Townhead. Kilm 222 B4
Townhead. Kilw 207 E2
Townhead. Kirk 79 F4
Townhead Pl. Tart 141 D4
Townhead Rd. Coat 101 E1
Townhead Rd. Helen 17 D1
Townhead Rd. Newt M 156 B2
Townhead Rd. Salt 217 D4
Townhead St. Beith 171 D4
Townhead St. Ham 162 C2
Townhead St. Steven 206 B1
Townhead St. Stone 198 C1
Townhead Terr. Pais 113 E2
Townhill Rd. Ham 161 F2
Townhill Terr. Ham 161 F2
Townholm. Kilmk 223 D1
Townsend Rd. New 166 A4
Townsend St. Glasg 97 E1
Tradeston St. Glasg 117 D3
Trafalgar St. Clyde 73 F1
Trafalgar St. Glasg 117 F2
Trafalgar St. Green 45 F2
Trainard Ave. Glasg 118 C2
Tramore Cres. Pres 236 B4
Tranent Pl. Cle 144 B1
Tranent Pl. Glasg 118 C4
Traquair Ave. Pais 132 C4
Traquair Ave. Wish 165 E3
Traquair Dr. Glasg 115 D3
Traquair Wynd. Udd 161 E4
Treebank Cres. Ayr 239 E3
Treeburn Ave. Glasg 136 A2
Tweed Cres. Glasg 98 C1
Tree Park Ave. Barr 134 A2
Treesbank. Kilw 207 E1
Treesbank Rd. Kilmk 223 D3
Trefoil Ave. Glasg 116 B1
Trefoil Pl. Ayr 239 E2
Trelawney Terr. Steven 217 F3
Trent Pl. E Kil 179 F3
Trent St. Coat 101 E1
Tresta Rd. Glasg 98 B2
Triboch St. Lark 184 C2
Trident Way. Ren 94 B1
Trinidad Grn. E Kil 159 D1
Trinity Ave. Glasg 115 E2
Trinity Cres. Beith 150 B1
Trinity Dr. Dalry 191 E3
Trinity Dr. Glasg 139 E2
Trinity Way. Lark 185 E1
Trinley Rd. Glasg 75 E1
Trinity Rd. Holy 143 E2
Tron Ct. Tull 4 A1
Trondra Path. Glasg 119 F4
Trondra Pl. Glasg 119 F4
Trongate. Glasg 117 E3
Trongate. Stone 198 C1
Tron Ave. E Kil 160 B3
Tron Ct. E Kil 180 A3
Tron Dr. B of W 110 B4
Troon Pl. Newt M 157 D2
Troon Rd. Troon 230 A2

Troon St. Glasg 118 A2
Trossachs Ave. Holy 143 D3
Trossachs Ct. Glasg 97 D2
Trossachs Rd. Glasg 138 B1
Trossachs St. Glasg 97 D2
Troubridge Ave. Kilbar 111 D1
Troubridge Cres. Kilbar 111 D1
Trows Rd. Wish 186 A3
Truce Rd. Glasg 95 D4
Truro Ave. Muir 80 C2
Tryfield Pl. Ayr 236 A1
Tryst Rd. Cumb 61 F1
Tryst Rd. Cumb 62 A1
Tryst Rd. Sten 23 E2
Tryst Way. Sten 23 E2
Tudhope Cres. Alex 27 E4
Tudor La S. Glasg 95 F2
Tudor Rd. Glasg 95 F2
Tudor St. Glasg 118 C1
Tullallan Pl. E Kil 181 D4
Tullallan Terr. Sten 24 A2
Tullibody Rd. All 9 F4
Tullibody Rd. Tull 4 C1
Tullichewan Cres. Alex 27 E4
Tullichewan Dr. Alex 27 E4
Tullichewan Rd. Alex 27 F4
Tulligarth Pk. All 10 A4
Tullis Ct. Glasg 117 F2
Tulloch Gdns. Mother 164 A2
Tulloch Rd. Shot 147 D2
Tulloch St. Glasg 137 D3
Tulloch-Ard Pl. Glasg 138 B2
Tullymet Rd. Ham 183 E4
Tummel Dr. Aird 102 C1
Tummel Gn. E Kil 159 F2
Tummel Pl. Sten 23 F2
Tummel St. Glasg 98 C1
Tummel Way. Pais 112 C1
Tunnel St. Glasg 116 C4
Tuphall Rd. Ham 162 B1
Turnberry Ave. Glasg 96 A2
Turnberry Ave. Gour 44 A3
Turnberry Cres. Aird 22 A3
Turnberry Ct. B of W 207 D2
Turnberry Ct. B of W 110 B3
Turnberry Dr. Glasg 137 F3
Turnberry Dr. Ham 161 E1
Turnberry Dr. Kilmk 227 F2
Turnberry Dr. Newt M 157 D3
Turnberry Gdns. Chap 123 F1
Turnberry Gdns. Cumb 61 F3
Turnberry Pl. E Kil 180 A3
Turnberry Pl. Glasg 137 F2
Turnberry Rd. Glasg 96 A2
Turnberry Wynd. Udd 140 C1
Turnbull Ave. Alex 27 E2
Turnbull Cres. Alex 27 E2
Turnbull St. Glasg 117 E3
Turner Pl. Kilmk 223 D2
Turner Rd. Glasg 97 F1
Turner Rd. Pais 113 F4
Turner St. Coat 121 F3
Turnhill Ave. Inch 93 D4
Turnhill Cres. Inch 93 D4
Turnhill Dr. Inch 93 D4
Turnhill Gdns. Inch 93 D4
Turningshaw Rd. Hous 91 F3
Turnlaw. E Kil 180 B2
Turnlaw Rd. Glasg 139 D1
Turnlaw St. Glasg 117 F3
Turquoise Terr. Hat 142 A2
Turret Cres. Glasg 95 E4
Turret Ct. All 10 B3
Turret Rd. Glasg 95 E4
Turriff St. Glasg 117 D2
Twain Ave. Sten 24 A2
Tweed Ave. Pais 112 C1
Tweed Cres. Glasg 98 C1
Tweed Cres. Kilmk 228 A3
Tweed Cres. Ren 94 C1
Tweed Cres. Wish 165 E3
Tweed Dr. Aird 123 E3
Tweed Dr. Bear 75 E2
Tweed La. Holy 143 E2
Tweed Pl. John 131 E4
Tweed St. Ayr 236 A2
Tweed St. E Kil 179 F4
Tweed St. Green 45 D3
Tweed St. Lark 185 D1
Tweedmuir Pl. Coat 122 B2
Tweedmuir. Bish 78 B1
Tweedsmuir Cres. Bear 75 F4
Tweedsmuir Pk. Ham 183 E2
Tweedsmuir Rd. Glasg 116 A3
Tweedvale Ave. Clyde 94 C3
Tweedvale Pl. Clyde 94 C3
Tweedsmuir Rd. Pais 114 A2
Tweedvale St. Glasg 100 B1
Tylney Rd. Pais 114 B2
Tyndrum Rd. Bear 76 A3
Tyndrum St. Glasg 97 E1
Tyne Pl. E Kil 179 F4
Tynecastle Cres. Glasg 119 D4
Tynecastle Path. Glasg 119 D4
Tynecastle Pl. Glasg 119 D4
Tynecastle St. Glasg 119 D4
Tynron Ct. Ham 161 F1
Tynwald Ave. Glasg 138 B2

U.P. La. Kils 60 B4
U.P. Rd. Kils 60 B4
Uddingston Rd. Udd 141 D2
Uddingston Rd. Udd 141 D2
Udston Terr. Ham 161 F3
Uig Pl. Glasg 119 F3
Uist Ave. P Glasg 69 D4
Uist Cres. Stepps 99 F2
Uist Dr. Kirk 80 A4
Uist St. Glasg 115 F4
Uist Ave. Wish 165 F3
Ulg Way. Shot 147 D2
Ullswater. E Kil 179 F3
Ulundi Rd. John 111 F1
Ulva St. Glasg 95 F2
Umberly Rd. Kilmk 227 F2
Underbank Cotts. Cam 6 B3
Underwood. Kilw 207 E3
Underwood La. Pais 113 E3
Underwood Pl. Kilmk 227 F2
Underwood Rd. Glasg 138 B3
Underwood Rd. Pais 113 E3
Underwood Rd. Pres 236 B4
Underwood St. Glasg 136 C3
Union Ave. Ayr 236 C4
Union Ave. Ayr 238 C4
Union Ave. Glasg 136 C3
Union Pl. Glasg 117 D4
Union Pl. Lar 23 D1
Union Rd. B of A 2 A3
Union St. All 10 A3
Union St. B of A 187 F1
Union St. Car 187 F1
Union St. Falk 42 A4
Union St. Glasg 117 D4
Union St. Green 45 F3
Union St. Holy 143 D2
Union St. Kirk 79 E4
Union St. Lark 185 D2
Union St. Pais 113 F1
Union St. Salt 216 C4
Union St. Shot 146 B3
Union St. Sten 23 E2
Union St. Stir 2 A1
Union St. Stone 198 C1
Union St. Troon 229 D2
Union Stone at La. Bonh 27 E2
Unitas Cres. Car 187 F1
Unitas Rd. Hat 142 B3
Unity Pk. Shot 146 B2
Unity Pl. Glasg 97 D1
Universal Rd. Gran 42 C4
University Ave. Glasg 96 B1
University Gdns. Glasg 96 B1
University Pl. Glasg 96 B1
University Rd W. B of A 2 A3
Unsted Pl. Pais 114 A2
Unthank Rd. Hat 142 B3
Uphall Pl. Glasg 118 C4
Upland La. Glasg 95 E2
Upland Rd. Glasg 95 E2
Uplawmoor Rd. Neil 154 A3
Uplawmoor Rd. Uplaw 153 F2
Upper Adelaide St. Helen 16 C1
Upper Arthur St. Alex 27 E2
Upper Bourtree Ct. Glasg ... 138 B2
Upper Bourtree Dr. Glasg ... 138 B2
Upper Bridge St. Alex 27 E2
Upper Bridge St. Stir 1 C1
Upper Cartsburn St. Green .. 46 A2
Upper Castlehill. Stir 7 D4
Upper Colquhoun St. Helen ... 16 B2
Upper Craigs. Stir 7 D4
Upper Crofts. Ayr 238 C1
Upper Glenburn Rd. Bear 75 E3
Upper Glenfinlas St. Helen .. 16 C1
Upper Hall Rd. Rhu 15 E3
Upper Loaning. Ayr 238 C1
Upper Mill St. Aird 123 D4
Upper Newmarket St. Falk ... 42 A3
Upper Smollett St. Alex 27 E2
Upper
    Stoneymollan Rd. Alex 27 E4
Upper
    Sutherland Cres. Helen ... 16 A2
Upper Sutherland St. Helen .. 16 A2
Upper Torwoodhill Rd. Rhu .. 15 F2
Ure Cres. Bon 40 A3
Urquhart Cres. Ren 94 B1
Urquhart Dr. E Kil 160 A2
Urquhart Gr. Gour 43 F3
Urquhart Pl. Helen 16 A2
Urquhart Rd. Kilmk 223 E1
Urrdale Rd. Glasg 116 A3
Usmore Pl. Glasg 119 F3

Vaila Pl. Glasg 97 D4
Vaila St. Glasg 96 C4
Vale of Ieven Ind Est. Bonh . 27 F2
Vale Pl. Bon 40 A3
Valentine Cres. Tan 141 D4
Valetta Pl. Clyde 73 E2
Valeview. Lar 23 E1
Valeview Terr. Dumb 50 A3

Valeview Terr. Glasg

Wellhall Ct. Ham

Valeview Terr. Glasg 137 D4
Vallantine Cres. Tan 141 D4
Vallay St. Glasg 97 E4
Valley Ct. Ham 162 B1
Valley View. Glasg 139 E3
Valleybank. Kils 37 E2
Valleyfield Dr. Cumb 60 C1
Valleyfield. E Kil 159 E1
Valleyfield. M of C 58 A3
Valleyfield Pl. Stir 7 E3
Valleyfield St. Glasg 97 F2
Valleyview Dr. Falk 42 A4
Vancouver Ct. E Kil 159 D1
Vancouver Dr. E Kil 159 D1
Vancouver La. Glasg 95 E2
Vancouver Pl. Clyde 73 E2
Vancouver Rd. Glasg 95 E2
Vanguard St. Clyde 74 B1
Vanguard Way. Ren 94 B1
Vanguard Way. Newt M 157 E4
Varna La. Glasg 95 F2
Varna Rd. Glasg 95 F2
Vamsdorf Way. Aird 123 F3
Vasart Pl. Glasg 96 C2
Vaults La. Kilw 207 F2
Veir Terr. Dumb 49 F2
Veitch Pl. Lennox 57 E4
Veitches Ct. Dunt 74 A3
Vennachar St. Shot 146 C3
Vennacher Rd. Ren 94 A2
Vennard St. Dalry 191 D4
Vennard Gdns. Glasg 116 C1
Vennel La. Stew 211 F4
Vennel St. Stew 211 F4
Vennel The. Den 21 F1
Vennel Ave. Glasg 117 E4
Vermont St. Glasg 116 C3
Vermont Dr. Glasg 116 C3
Vernon Bank. E Kil 159 F2
Vernon Dr. Lin 112 A3
Vernon Pl. Dund 225 F1
Vernon St. Salt 216 C4
Verona Ave. Glasg 95 E2
Verona La. Glasg 95 E2
Vesalius St. Glasg 119 D3
Viaduct Circ. Kilw 207 F3
Viaduct Rd. Newt M 157 F4
Vicar St. Falk 42 A3
Vicarfield St. Glasg 116 A4
Vicariand Pl. Glasg 139 D2
Vicariand Rd. Glasg 139 D3
Vicars Rd. Stone 198 C1
Vicars Wlk. Glasg 139 D2
Vickers St. Mother 163 D4
Victor St. Plains 104 A1
Victoria Ave. Car 187 F1
Victoria Cir. Glasg 96 B2
Victoria Cres. Aird 122 C3
Victoria Cres. Irvine 219 E1
Victoria Cres. Kils 60 A4
Victoria Cres. Mother 164 B2
Victoria Cres. Newt M 157 F4
Victoria Crescent La. Glasg . 96 B2
Victoria Crescent Pl. Glasg . 96 B2
Victoria Crescent Rd. Glasg 96 B2
Victoria Cross. Glasg 117 D1
Victoria Dr. E. Ren 94 B1
Victoria Dr. Troon 229 E1
Victoria Dr. W. Ren 94 A2
Victoria Gdns. Aird 122 C4
Victoria Gdns. Barr 134 A2
Victoria Gdns. Kil 69 E1
Victoria Gdns. Pais 113 E1
Victoria Park Cnr. Glasg 95 E3
Victoria Park Dr N. Glasg ... 95 F2
Victoria Park Dr S. Glasg ... 95 E2
Victoria Park Gdns N. Glasg 95 E2
Victoria Park Gdns S. Glasg 95 E2
Victoria Park La N. Glasg ... 95 E2
Victoria Park La S. Glasg ... 95 E2
Victoria Park St. Glasg 95 E2
Victoria Pk. Ayr 238 C3
Victoria Pk. Kils 60 A4
Victoria Pl. Aird 122 C3
Victoria Pl. Glasg 138 A4
Victoria Pl. Hat 141 F2
Victoria Pl. Kils 60 B4
Victoria Pl. Miln 55 D1
Victoria Pl. Stir 7 D4
Victoria Quadrant. Holy 142 C3
Victoria Rd. Barr 134 A2
Victoria Rd. Cumb 61 E3
Victoria Rd. East 127 F3
Victoria Rd. Falk 42 B3
Victoria Rd. Glasg 117 D2
Victoria Rd. Glasg 138 A3
Victoria Rd. Gour 44 B4
Victoria Rd. Helen 16 C1
Victoria Rd. Kilbar 111 D3
Victoria Rd. Kils 79 E2
Victoria Rd. Pais 113 E1
Victoria Rd. Salt 217 D4
Victoria Rd. Stepps 99 E3
Victoria Rd. Stir 7 D4
Victoria Roundabout. Irvine 219 D1
Victoria Sq. Stir 7 D4
Victoria St. Alex 27 F2
Victoria St. All 10 A4

Victoria St. Ayr 236 A1
Victoria St. Dumb 50 A2
Victoria St. East 127 F3
Victoria St. Glasg 138 A4
Victoria St. Lark 185 D2
Victoria St. New 166 A2
Victoria St. Udd 161 E4
Victoria St. Tun. Cumb 61 E3
Victoria Terr. Men 4 A4
Victoria Way. Stew 195 F1
Victory Dr. Kilbar 111 D2
Victory Way. Glasg 120 A2
Viewbank Ave. Calder 123 D1
Viewbank. Glasg 136 A2
Viewbank St. Glen 101 F3
Viewfield. Aird 122 C4
Viewfield Ave. Bish 97 F4
Viewfield Ave. Glasg 119 F3
Viewfield Ave. Kirk 79 E3
Viewfield Ave. Loch 129 D1
Viewfield Ave. M of C 58 A3
Viewfield Ave. Udd 140 C1
Viewfield Dr. Alva 4 C3
Viewfield Dr. Bish 97 F4
Viewfield Dr. Glasg 119 F3
Viewfield La. Glasg 96 C1
Viewfield Rd. Ayr 236 A1
Viewfield Rd. Bank 38 B2
Viewfield Rd. Bish 97 F4
Viewfield Rd. Coat 121 E2
Viewfield Rd. Hat 141 F2
Viewfield St. East 127 F3
Viewfield St. Stir 7 D4
Viewmount Dr. Glasg 96 B4
Viewpark Ave. Glasg 118 A4
Viewpark Ct. Glasg 138 B3
Viewpark Dr. Glasg 138 A3
Viewpark. Miln 55 D1
Viewpark Pl. Mother 163 E3
Viewpark Rd. Mother 163 E3
Viewpark
Shopping Ctr. Tan 141 E3
Viewpoint Pl. Glasg 97 F3
Viewpoint Rd. Glasg 97 F3
Viking Cres. Hous 111 E4
Viking Rd. Aird 123 D3
Viking Terr. E Kil 180 C3
Viking Way. Ren 94 B1
Villa Bank. Den 21 F1
Villafield Ave. Bish 78 A2
Villafield Dr. Bish 78 A2
Villafield Loan. Bish 78 A2
Village Gdns. Udd 140 C1
Village Rd. Glasg 139 F2
Vine Park Ave. Newt M 222 A4
Vine Park Dr. Kilm 222 A4
Vine St. Glasg 96 A1
Vinebugh Ave. Irvine 219 E2
Vineburgh Ct. Irvine 219 D2
Vinicombe La. Glasg 96 B2
Vinicombe St. Glasg 96 B2
Vintner St. Glasg 97 E1
Viola Pl. Lennox 78 B4
Violet Gdns. Car 201 F4
Violet Pl. Holy 143 D3
Violet St. Pais 114 A2
Virginia Ct. Glasg 117 E4
Virginia Gdns. Aird 236 A1
Virginia Gdns. Miln 76 B4
Virginia Pl. Glasg 117 E4
Virginia St. Green 46 A2
Viscount Ave. Ren 94 B1
Vivian Ave. Miln 54 C1
Voil Dr. Glasg 137 D2
Voil Rd. Stir 2 A2
Vorlich Ct. Barr 134 B1
Vorlich Dr. Shi 86 C4
Vorlich Gdns. Bear 75 E4
Vorlich Pl. Kilmk 228 A2
Vorlich Pl. Stir 2 A2
Vorlich Wynd. Holy 143 E2
Vrackie Pl. Kilmk 228 A2
Vulcan St. Glasg 97 F2
Vulcan St. Mother 163 F4

W Lodge Gdns. All 9 F4
Waddell Ave. Glenm 102 B2
Waddell Ct. Glasg 117 E3
Waddell St. Kilmk 222 C2
Waddell St. Aird 103 D1
Waddell St. Glasg 117 E2
Waddell St. Stan 29 E4
Waggon Rd. Ayr 235 F1
Waggon Rd. Falk 42 A4
Waid Ave. Newt M 156 B3
Waldemar Rd. Glasg 95 E4
Walden Rd. Hurl 226 C3
Walker Dr. Glasg 95 F4
Walk The. All 10 A3
Walker Ave. Kilmk 228 A4
Walker Ave. Troon 229 E3
Walker Ct. Glasg 96 A1
Walker Dr. John 112 B1
Walker Path. Tan 141 D4
Walker Rd. Ayr 236 A1

Walker St. Glasg 96 A1
Walker St. Green 45 E3
Walker St. Kilb 149 D1
Walker St. Pais 113 E2
Walkerburn Dr. Wish 165 E3
Walkerburn Rd. Glasg 115 D2
Walkinshaw Cres. Pais 113 D3
Walkinshaw Rd. Inch 93 E2
Walkinshaw St. Glasg 118 A2
Walkinshaw St. John 112 A2
Wall Gdns. Falk 41 E3
Wall St. Falk 41 E3
Wallace Ave. Bishop 72 A2
Wallace Ave. Dund 225 F1
Wallace Ave. John 112 B1
Wallace Ave. Steven 206 B1
Wallace Ave. Troon 229 E3
Wallace Cres. Den 21 E1
Wallace Cres. Plea 12 B2
Wallace Ct. Pres 236 B4
Wallace Dr. Stir 2 A1
Wallace Dr. Lark 185 E1
Wallace Gdns. Lennox 57 D1
Wallace Gdns. Stir 2 B2
Wallace Pl. Cam 6 B3
Wallace Pl. Falk 42 B3
Wallace Pl. Falk 8 B2
Wallace Pl. Green 45 F3
Wallace Pl. Ham 163 D1
Wallace Pl. Udd 140 C1
Wallace Rd. Holy 143 E2
Wallace Rd. Irvine 219 E2
Wallace Rd. Ren 94 A1
Wallace St. All 10 B4
Wallace St. Bann 7 F1
Wallace St. Clyde 74 A1
Wallace St. Coat 122 A3
Wallace St. Dumb 50 A2
Wallace St. Falk 42 B3
Wallace St. Glasg 117 D3
Wallace St. Glasg 138 A4
Wallace St. Green 45 E2
Wallace St. Kirk 227 F4
Wallace St. Mother 163 E4
Wallace St. P Glasg 47 F1
Wallace St. Pais 113 F3
Wallace St. Plains 104 A1
Wallace St. Stir 2 A1
Wallace View. Kilmk ... 227 F3
Wallace View. Tull 4 B2
Wallace Way. Lan 215 E2
Wallacefield Rd. Kilmk . 227 F2
Wallacehill Rd. Kilmk .. 227 F2
Wallacewell Cres. Glasg 98 A3
Wallacewell Pl. Glasg .. 98 A3
Wallacewell
Quadrant. Glasg 98 B3
Wallacewell Rd. Glasg . 98 B3
Wallbrae Rd. Cumb 83 D4
Wallneuk Rd. Pais 113 F3
Walls St. Glasg 117 E4
Wallstale Rd. Stir 7 D2
Walmer Cres. Glasg ... 116 B3
Walnut Cres. Glasg ... 97 E3
Walnut Cres. John 112 A1
Walnut Dr. Kils 79 D3
Walnut Pl. Glasg 97 E3
Walnut Pl. Tan 121 E1
Walnut Rd. Glasg 97 E3
Walnut Rd. Kilmk 227 E4
Walpole Pl. John 131 E4
Walter St. Glasg 118 B4
Walter St. Wish 165 E2
Walton Ave. Newt M .. 156 B3
Walton St. Barr 134 B2
Walton St. Glasg 136 C4
Wamba Ave. Glasg 95 F4
Wamphray Pl. E Kil ... 179 E4
Wandilla Ave. Clyde .. 74 B1
Ward St. All 10 A3
Warden Rd. Glasg 95 E4
Wardend Rd. Lennox .. 57 D1
Wardhill Rd. Glasg 98 A3
Wardhouse Rd. Pais ... 133 E4
Wardie Pl. Glasg 119 F4
Wardie Rd. Glasg 120 A4
Wardlaw Ave. Glasg .. 138 A4
Wardlaw Cres. E Kil .. 181 D4
Wardlaw Dr. Glasg ... 94 B4
Wardlaw Rd. Bear 75 F1
Wardlaw Rd. Fen 223 F3
Wardneuk Dr. Kilmk . 223 D2
Wardneuk. Pres 236 B3
Wardpark Ct. Cumb .. 62 B3
Wardpark Pl. Cumb .. 62 B3
Wardpark Rd. Cumb .. 62 B3
Wardrop Pl. E Kil 159 F2
Wardrop St. Beith ... 171 E4
Wardrop St. Glasg ... 95 F4
Wardrop St. Pais 113 F2
Wardrop Terr. Beith . 171 E4
Wards Cres. Coat 121 F3
Wards Pl. Kilmk 227 F4
Ware Rd. Glasg 120 A4
Warilda Ave. Clyde .. 74 B1
Warlock Dr. B of W .. 90 B1

Warlock Rd. Hous 90 B2
Warly Dr. Dund 225 F1
Warly Pl. Dund 225 F1
Warner St. Steven 217 E4
Warnock Cres. Hat 142 A2
Warnock Rd. Newt M .. 156 B4
Warnock St. Glasg 117 F4
Warren Rd. Ham 183 E4
Warren St. Glasg 117 D1
Warren Wlk. Lennox ... 57 F4
Warriston Cres. Glasg . 118 C4
Warriston Pl. Glasg ... 119 D4
Warriston St. Glasg ... 118 C4
Warriston Way. Glasg . 138 B2
Warrix Ave. Irvine 219 E1
Warrix Gdns. Troon ... 232 C4
Warrix Interchange. Irvine 219 F1
Warroch St. Glasg 116 C4
Warwick. E Kil 160 B2
Warwick Gr. Ham 161 F3
Warwick Hill. Irvine .. 220 A3
Warwick Rd. Gour 44 C2
Warwickhill Rd. Kilmk 222 B1
Washington Rd. Kirk .. 79 D4
Washington Rd. Pais .. 113 F4
Washington St. Glasg . 117 D4
Watchmeal Cres. Dunt 74 B4
Water La. Kilmk 227 F4
Water Rd. Barr 134 B2
Water Row. Glasg 116 A4
Water St. P Glasg 47 E1
Waterbank Rd. E Kil .. 158 B3
Watercut Rd. Irvine .. 218 C4
Watercut Rd. Kilw 219 D4
Waterfoot Ave. Glasg 135 E4
Waterfoot Rd. Newt M 157 E2
Waterfoot Terr. Glasg 135 E4
Waterford Rd. Glasg . 136 A2
Waterlands Gdns. Car 188 A2
Waterlands Pl. Law .. 187 D2
Waterloo Dr. Lan 215 D3
Waterloo Gdns. Kirk . 58 B1
Waterloo La. Glasg .. 117 D4
Waterloo Rd. Lan 215 D3
Waterloo Rd. Pres ... 236 A3
Waterloo St. Glasg .. 117 D4
Watermill Ave. Kirk .. 79 E2
Waterslaugh Dr. Cle . 144 A1
Watersedge Ct. Rhu .. 15 E2
Waterside Ave. Newt M 156 B2
Waterside Ct. Kilmk .. 227 F4
Waterside Dr. Newt M 156 B2
Waterside Gdns. E Kil 158 B4
Waterside Gdns. Ham 162 C1
Waterside. Irvine 219 D2
Waterside Rd. E Kil .. 158 B4
Waterside Rd. Kilw .. 207 F2
Waterside Rd. Kirk .. 79 F4
Waterside Rd. Thorn . 158 B3
Waterside St. Glasg . 117 E2
Waterside St. Kilmk . 227 F4
Watersay St. Fen 213 D1
Waterston Way. Loch 129 E2
Waterytetts Dr. Kil .. 69 E1
Watling Ave. Falk 41 E3
Watling Dr. Falk 41 E3
Watling Gdns. Falk .. 41 E3
Watling Pl. E Kil 159 D1
Watling St. Falk 41 E3
Watling St. Mother .. 142 B1
Watling St. Tan 140 C4
Watson Ave. Glasg .. 136 A4
Watson Ave. Lin 112 A3
Watson Ave. Steven . 199 D2
Watson Cres. Kils ... 60 C4
Watson Pl. Bank 39 E2
Watson Pl. Udd 161 D4
Watson St. Falk 42 A3
Watson St. Glasg ... 117 E3
Watson St. Kilmk .. 228 A4
Watson St. Lan 184 C2
Watson St. Mother . 163 F3
Watson St. Udd 140 C3
Watson St. Udd 161 E4
Watson Terr. Irvine 219 E1
Watsonville Pk. Mother 163 F3
Watstone Rd. Stone 199 D1
Watt Cres. Hat 142 A4
Watt Cres. Falk 41 F3
Watt La. B of W 110 C4
Watt Low Ave. Glasg 137 F3
Watt Pl. Green 46 A3
Watt Pl. Miln 54 C2
Watt Rd. B of W ... 110 B4
Watt Rd. Glasg 115 D4
Watt St. Aird 103 E1
Watt St. Glasg 116 C4
Watt St. Green 45 F3
Watt St. Steven ... 206 A1
Wattfield Rd. Ayr .. 238 C3
Waukglen Ave. Glasg 135 D1
Waukglen Cres. Glasg 135 E1
Waukglen Dr. Glasg 135 D1
Waukglen Gdns. Glasg 135 D1
Waukglen Path. Glasg 135 D2
Waukglen Pl. Glasg . 135 D2
Waukglen Rd. Glasg 135 D2
Waukglenmill Rd. Dunt 55 D2
Waukmill Rd. Kilmk . 228 A4

Waulkmill Ave. Barr ... 134 B2
Waulkmill Pl. Kilmk ... 228 A4
Waulkmill St. Glasg ... 135 F2
Waverley Ave. Helen .. 25 D4
Waverley Ave. Kilmk .. 222 B1
Waverley Cres. Bon ... 40 A2
Waverley Cres. Cumb . 82 B4
Waverley Cres. Ham .. 161 F2
Waverley Cres. Kirk .. 79 E4
Waverley Cres. Lan .. 215 E2
Waverley Cres. Stir ... 2 B1
Waverley Ct. Helen ... 16 B1
Waverley Ct. Udd 141 D1
Waverley Dr. Aird 103 D1
Waverley Dr. Glasg .. 138 B4
Waverley Dr. Wish ... 165 D2
Waverley. E Kil 160 B2
Waverley Gdns. Glasg 116 C1
Waverley Gdns. John 112 B1
Waverley Pl. Salt 205 F1
Waverley Rd. Pale ... 132 C4
Waverley St. Coat .. 102 A1
Waverley St. Falk ... 42 A4
Waverley St. Glasg .. 116 C1
Waverley St. Green .. 45 E2
Waverley St. Ham ... 161 F2
Waverley St. Lark .. 199 D4
Waverley Terr. Dumb 49 D2
Waverley Terr. Tan .. 23 E1
Waverley Terr. Udd .. 161 E3
Waverley Way. Pais . 132 C4
Weardale La. Glasg . 119 E4
Weardale St. Glasg . 119 E4
Weaver Ave. Newt M 156 B4
Weaver Cres. Aird .. 123 D3
Weaver La. Kilbar ... 111 E2
Weaver Pl. E Kil 179 F4
Weaver Row. Stir ... 7 D2
Weaver St. Ayr 235 F1
Weaver St. Glasg ... 117 E4
Weaver Terr. Pais .. 114 A2
Weavers Ave. Pais .. 113 D2
Weavers Rd. Pais ... 113 D2
Weavers Way. Stone 198 C1
Weavers Wlk. Lan .. 215 D1
Webster Ave. Sten .. 23 E1
Webster Groves. Wish 165 E3
Webster St. Clyde .. 94 C4
Webster St. Glasg .. 118 A2
Wedderlea Dr. Glasg 115 D3
Wee Cl. Beith 171 D4
Wee Row. Falk 42 A3
Wee Sunnyside Rd. Quart 184 A1
Weensmoor Rd. Glasg 134 C2
Weeple Dr. Lin 112 A3
Weighhouse Cl. Pais 113 F2
Weighhouse Rd. Car 187 E2
Weir Ave. Barr 134 B1
Weir Ave. Pres 233 E1
Weir Dr. Fall 8 B2
Weir Pl. Kilb 149 D1
Weir Pl. Kilw 146 C2
Weir Rd. Ard 205 E2
Weir Rd. Ayr 235 F2
Weir St. Coat 122 A4
Weir St. Falk 42 B3
Weir St. Green 46 A3
Weir St. Pais 113 F3
Weir St. Stir 1 C1
Weirston Rd. Kilw . 208 A2
Weirwood Ave. Glasg 120 A3
Weirwood Gdns. Glasg 119 F2
Welbeck Cres. Troon 229 D1
Welbeck Ct. Troon .. 229 D1
Welbeck Mews. Troon 229 D1
Welbeck Rd. Glasg . 135 D2
Welbeck St. Green .. 45 E4
Welbeck St. Kilmk . 222 C2
Welton Pl. Kils 60 C2
Welfare Ave. Glasg . 139 E2
Well Gn. Glasg 136 B4
Well La. Lennox 57 E4
Well Rd. B of A 2 A4
Well Rd. Kilbar 111 D2
Well Rd. Lan 215 D2
Well St. Pais 113 E3
Well St. W Kil 190 B3
Welland Pl. E Kil ... 179 F4
Wellbank Gdns. W Kil 190 B3
Wellbank Pl. Udd ... 140 C3
Wellbrae. Lark 185 D1
Wellbrae Rd. Ham .. 162 A1
Wellbrae. Stone ... 198 C1
Wellbrae Terr. Muir 80 C1
Wellcroft Pl. Glasg 117 D2
Wellcroft Rd. Ham . 161 F2
Wellcroft Terr. Ham 161 F2
Wellesley Cres. E Kil 179 F4
Wellesley Dr. E Kil . 179 F4
Wellfield Ave. Glasg 136 A2
Wellfield St. Glasg . 97 F2
Wellgate Dr. B of A . 2 B4
Wellgate. Lan 215 D2
Wellgate St. Lark .. 185 D2
Wellgatehead. Lan . 215 D2
Wellgreen. Stir 7 D3
Wellhall Ct. Ham .. 162 A2

288
Wellhall Rd. Ham
William St. P Glasg

Wellhall Rd. Ham ... 162 A2
Wellhead Ct. Lan ... 215 D2
Wellhouse Cres. Glasg ... 119 F4
Wellhouse Rd. Glasg ... 119 F4
Wellington Ave. Hurl ... 228 B4
Wellington. E Kil ... 180 A4
Wellington La. Ayr ... 238 C4
Wellington La. Glasg ... 117 D4
Wellington Pl. Clyde ... 73 E2
Wellington Pl. Coat ... 121 E3
Wellington Pl. Kilmk ... 222 C1
Wellington Pl. Wish ... 186 B4
Wellington Rd. Bish ... 78 A2
Wellington Sq. Ayr ... 238 C4
Wellington St. Aird ... 103 D1
Wellington St. Glasg ... 117 D4
Wellington St. Green ... 45 F2
Wellington St. Kilmk ... 222 C1
Wellington St. Mother ... 164 B3
Wellington St. Pais ... 113 E3
Wellington St. Pres ... 236 A3
Wellington Terr. Lan ... 214 C3
Wellington Way. Green ... 45 F2
Wellington Way. Ren ... 94 B1
Wellknowe Ave. Thorn ... 158 B1
Wellknowe Pl. Thorn ... 158 B2
Wellknowe Rd. Thorn ... 158 B2
Wellmeadow Cl. Newt M ... 156 B3
Wellmeadow Gn. Newt M .. 156 B3
Wellmeadow Rd. Glasg ... 136 A3
Wellmeadow St. Pais ... 113 E2
Wellmeadow Way. Newt M 156 B3
Wellpark Ave. Kilmk ... 228 B4
Wellpark. Ayr ... 238 C1
Wellpark Bldgs. Green ... 46 A2
Wellpark Cres. Stir ... 6 C2
Wellpark Ct. Kilmk ... 228 B4
Wellpark Gr. Kilmk ... 228 B4
Wellpark La. Salt ... 216 C4
Wellpark Pl. Kilmk ... 228 B4
Wellpark Rd. Bank ... 38 B1
Wellpark Rd. Mother ... 163 E3
Wellpark Rd. Salt ... 216 C4
Wellpark St. Glasg ... 117 F4
Wellpark Terr. Bon ... 40 A3
Wellpark Terr. Neil ... 154 B3
Wells St. Clyde ... 73 F2
Wellshot Dr. Glasg ... 138 C3
Wellshot Rd. Glasg ... 118 C2
Wellside Ave. Aird ... 103 D1
Wellside Dr. Glasg ... 139 E2
Wellside La. Aird ... 103 D1
Wellside Pl. Falk ... 42 A3
Wellside Quadrant. Aird ... 103 D1
Wellsquarry Rd. E Kil ... 159 E3
Wellview Dr. Mother ... 163 E3
Wellwood Ave. Lan ... 215 D3
Wellwood. Kilw ... 207 E1
Wellwynd. Aird ... 122 C4
Wellyard La. Gour ... 44 B2
Wellyard Way. Gour ... 44 B1
Wellyard Wynd. Gour ... 44 B1
Welsh Dr. Ham ... 183 E4
Welsh Dr. Udd ... 161 E3
Welsh Gdns. B of A ... 2 A4
Welsh Pl. Salt ... 205 F1
Wemyss Ave. Newt M ... 156 B4
Wemyss Bay St. Green ... 45 F2
Wemyss Dr. Cumb ... 60 C1
Wendur Way. Pais ... 113 E4
Wenlock Rd. Pais ... 113 F1
Wensleydale. E Kil ... 159 E2
Wentworth Dr. Glasg ... 76 C1
Wentworth Sq. Kilw ... 207 E2
Wesley St. Aird ... 122 C4
West Abercromby St. Helen 16 B2
West Academy St. Wish ... 164 C2
West Ave. Car ... 187 F1
West Ave. Ham ... 161 F3
West Ave. Holy ... 143 D1
West Ave. Plains ... 104 A2
West Ave. Ren ... 94 B2
West Ave. Stepps ... 99 E3
West Ave. Tan ... 141 E3
West
Balgrochan Rd. Lennox .. 57 D1
West Barmoss Ave. P Glasg 68 C4
West Benhar Rd. East ... 127 D2
West Blackhall St. Green ... 45 F3
West Boreland Rd. Den ... 21 E1
West Bowhouse Way. Irvine220 A3
West Bowhouse
Workshops. Irvine ... 220 A3
West Brae. Pais ... 113 E2
West Bridge St. Falk ... 42 A3
West Bridgend. Dumb ... 49 F2
West Buchanan Pl. Pais ... 113 E2
West Burn Rd. Stew ... 195 F1
West Burn St. Green ... 45 F3
West Burnside St. Kils ... 60 B4
West Campbell St. Glasg ... 117 D4
West Campbell St. Pais ... 113 D2
West Canal St. Coat ... 121 F4
West Carmuirs Loan. Bon ... 40 C3
West Chapelton Ave. Bear .. 75 F2
West Chapelton Cres. Bear . 75 F2
West Chapelton Dr. Bear ... 75 F2
West Chapelton La. Bear ... 75 F2
West Clyde St. Helen ... 16 B1
West Clyde St. Lark ... 185 D1
West Coats Rd. Glasg ... 138 C3
West Cres. Troon ... 229 F2
West Ct. Clyde ... 73 F2
West Dhuhill Dr. Helen ... 16 B2
West Doura Ave. Salt ... 205 F1
West Doura Way. Kilw ... 207 E2
West Dr. Aird ... 123 F3
West Dr. Lar ... 23 E1
West End. Dalry ... 191 D4
West End Dr. Hat ... 141 F2
West End Gdns. All ... 10 A3
West End Pl. Hat ... 141 F2
West Fairholm St. Lark ... 184 C3
West Faulds Rd. Lan ... 215 F3
West Fullarton St. Kilmk ... 222 C1
West Gate. Wish ... 165 E2
West George La. Glasg ... 117 D4
West George St. Coat ... 122 A4
West George St. Glasg ... 117 D4
West George St. Kilmk ... 222 C1
West Glebe Terr. Ham ... 162 B1
West Glen Gdns. Kil ... 69 F1
West Glen Rd. Kil ... 69 F1
West Glen Rd. Lang ... 70 A1
West Gr. Troon ... 229 F2
West Graham St. Glasg ... 97 D1
West Greenhill Pl. Glasg ... 116 C4
West Hamilton St. Mother .. 163 F3
West High St. Kirk ... 58 B1
West James St. Alva ... 5 D3
West Johnstone St. Alva ... 5 D3
West Kilbride Rd. Dalry ... 191 D4
West King St. Helen ... 16 A1
West Kirk St. Aird ... 122 C4
West Kirklands Pl. Dalry ... 191 D4
West La. Pais ... 113 D2
West Langlands St. Kilmk .. 222 C1
West Lennox Dr. Helen ... 16 B2
West Link Rd. B of A ... 2 B3
West Lodge Rd. Ren ... 94 A2
West Main St. East ... 127 F3
West Mains Rd. E Kil ... 159 E1
West Mains Rd. Gran ... 42 C4
West Montrose St. Helen ... 16 B1
West Murrayfield. Bann ... 7 E1
West Nemphlar Rd. Lan ... 214 B3
West Netherton St. Kilmk ... 227 F4
West Nile St. Glasg ... 117 E4
West Park Cres. Kilm ... 222 A4
West Park Dr. Kilm ... 222 A4
West Pl. New ... 166 A3
West Port. Lan ... 214 C2
West Portland St. Troon ... 229 D1
West Porton Pl. Bishop ... 71 F2
West Prince's La. Glasg ... 96 C1
West Prince's St. Glasg ... 96 C1
West Princes St. Helen ... 16 B1
West Quay. P Glasg ... 47 E1
West Rd. Irvine ... 219 D2
West Rd. Kilbar ... 111 D2
West Rd. Lennox ... 57 D1
West Rd. P Glasg ... 68 C4
West Regent La. Glasg ... 117 D4
West Regent St. Glasg ... 117 D4
West Rossdhu Dr. Helen ... 16 B2
West Row. Strath ... 31 D2
West Sanquhar Rd. Ayr ... 236 A2
West Scott Terr. Ham ... 162 B1
West Shaw St. Green ... 45 F3
West Shaw St. Kilmk ... 227 F3
West St. Clyde ... 94 C4
West St. Glasg ... 117 D3
West St. Pais ... 113 E2
West Stewart St. Green ... 45 F3
West Stewart St. Ham ... 162 B2
West Stirling St. Alva ... 4 C4
West Thomson St. Clyde ... 74 A2
West Thornlie St. Wish ... 165 D1
West Vennel. All ... 10 A3
West View. Dunlop ... 195 D4
West View. Fen ... 213 F2
West Wellbrae Cres. Ham . 183 D4
West Whitby St. Glasg ... 118 B2
West
Woodside Ave. P Glasg .. 68 C3
West Woodstock St. Kilmk . 227 F4
Westbank Ct. Glasg ... 96 C1
Westbank La. Glasg ... 96 C1
Westbank Quadrant. Glasg . 96 C1
Westborne Gdns. Helen ... 16 B1
Westbourn Bldgs. Green ... 45 F3
Westbourne Ave. Pres ... 236 B4
Westbourne Cres. Bear ... 75 E3
Westbourne Dr. Bear ... 75 E3
Westbourne
Gardens La. Glasg ... 96 B2
Westbourne Gdns N. Glasg . 96 B2
Westbourne Gdns. Pres ... 236 B4
Westbourne Gdns S. Glasg . 96 B2
Westbourne Gdns W. Glasg 96 B2
Westbourne Rd. Glasg ... 96 A2
Westbourne
Terrace La N. Glasg ... 96 B2
Westbourne
Terrace La S. Glasg ... 96 A2
Westbrae Dr. Glasg ... 95 F2
Westbrae Rd. Newt M ... 156 C3
Westburn Ave. Falk ... 41 F2
Westburn Ave. Glasg ... 139 E3
Westburn Ave. Pais ... 113 D3
Westburn Cres. Dunt ... 74 A4
Westburn Cres. Glasg ... 137 F4
Westburn Farm Rd. Glasg . 139 D3
Westburn Rd. Glasg ... 139 E3
Westburn Rd. Glasg ... 140 A3
Westburn Way. Pais ... 113 D3
Westcliff. Dumb ... 49 D2
Westclyffe St. Glasg ... 116 C1
Westcott Pl. Lan ... 215 E3
Westcraigs Pk. Blac ... 107 E2
Westcraigs Rd. Blac ... 107 E2
Westcraigs Rd. East ... 127 F3
Westend. Bear ... 76 A1
Westend Ct. Law ... 186 C2
Westend Park St. Glasg ... 96 C1
Wester Carriagehill. Pais ... 113 F1
Wester Cleddens Rd. Bish ... 78 B1
Wester Common Dr. Glasg .. 97 D2
Wester Common Rd. Glasg . 97 D2
Wester
Mavisbank Ave. Aird ... 122 C4
Wester Moffat Ave. Aird ... 123 F4
Wester Moffat Cres. Aird ... 123 F4
Wester Myvot Rd. Glen ... 82 A2
Wester Rd. Glasg ... 119 E2
Westerburn St. Glasg ... 118 C3
Westercraigs. Glasg ... 117 F4
Westerdale. E Kil ... 159 E2
Westerfield Rd. E Kil ... 158 B2
Westerglen Rd. Falk ... 42 A1
Westergreens Ave. Kirk ... 79 E3
Westerhill Rd. Bish ... 78 B2
Westerhouse Ct. Car ... 187 E1
Westerhouse Rd. Glasg ... 120 A4
Westerkirk Dr. Glasg ... 76 C1
Westerlands Dr. Stir ... 7 D3
Westerlea Ct. B of A ... 2 A3
Westerlea Dr. B of A ... 2 A3
Westermains Ave. Kirk ... 79 D4
Western Ave. Falk ... 42 A3
Western Ave. Glasg ... 137 F4
Western Cres. Kilb ... 170 A4
Western Isles Rd. Clyde ... 73 E3
Western Rd. Glasg ... 138 C2
Western Rd. Kilmk ... 223 D2
Westerton Ave. Glasg ... 95 F4
Westerton Ave. Lark ... 185 D1
Westerton Ave. Thorn ... 158 A3
Westerton. Cowie ... 12 B4
Westerton Dr. B of A ... 2 A4
Westerton La. Thorn ... 158 A3
Westerton. Lennox ... 57 F4
Westerton Terr. Sten ... 24 B2
Westfield Ave. Glasg ... 137 F4
Westfield Cres. Bear ... 75 F1
Westfield Dr. Bear ... 75 F1
Westfield Dr. Cumb ... 81 F4
Westfield Dr. Glasg ... 115 D3
Westfield Dr. Green ... 45 E4
Westfield Dr. Kil ... 89 D4
Westfield. Dumb ... 49 E2
Westfield. Kilb ... 170 A4
Westfield Pl. Den ... 21 F1
Westfield Rd. Ayr ... 238 C3
Westfield Rd. Cumb ... 81 F4
Westfield Rd. Glasg ... 136 A2
Westfield Rd. Holy ... 143 E4
Westfield Rd. Kils ... 36 A1
Westfield Rd. P Glasg ... 68 C4
Westfield St. Falk ... 42 C3
Westfields. Bish ... 77 F2
Westgarth Pl. E Kil ... 159 D2
Westgate Way. Hat ... 141 F2
Westhouse Ave. Glasg ... 137 F4
Westhouse Gdns. Glasg ... 137 F4
Westland Dr. Glasg ... 95 E2
Westlands Gdns. Pais ... 113 E1
Westlea Pl. Aird ... 123 D3
Westminster Pl. Sten ... 23 F2
Westminster Terr. Glasg ... 116 C4
Westmoor Cres. Kilmk ... 227 E4
Westmoreland St. Glasg ... 117 D1
Westmorland Rd. Gour ... 44 C2
Westmuir Pl. Glasg ... 137 F4
Westmuir St. Glasg ... 118 B3
Weston Pl. Pres ... 236 B3
Weston Terr. W Kil ... 190 B3
Westpark Ct. Steven ... 217 E4
Westpark Dr. Pais ... 113 D3
Westport. E Kil ... 159 D1
Westport St. Kils ... 60 B4
Westray Ave. Newt M ... 156 B4
Westray Ave. P Glasg ... 69 D3
Westray Cir. Glasg ... 97 E3
Westray Ct. Cumb ... 82 C4
Westray Pl. Bish ... 78 B1
Westray Pl. Glasg ... 97 E4
Westray Rd. Cumb ... 82 C4
Westray Sq. Glasg ... 97 E4
Westray St. Glasg ... 97 E4
Westray Terr. Falk ... 42 B1
Westray Wynd. New ... 165 F3
Westside Gdns. Glasg ... 96 B1
Westview Cres. Tull ... 4 B1
Westward Way. Troon ... 229 F4
Westwood Ave. Ayr ... 236 C1
Westwood Ave. Glasg ... 136 A2
Westwood Cres. Ayr ... 236 C1
Westwood Cres. Ham ... 162 B1
Westwood Dr. Cle ... 144 C1
Westwood Gdns. Pais ... 113 D3
Westwood Hill. E Kil ... 180 A4
Westwood Quadrant. Clyde . 74 B1
Westwood Rd. E Kil ... 180 A4
Westwood Rd. Glasg ... 136 A3
Westwood Rd. New ... 166 A3
Westwood Sq. E Kil ... 180 A4
Weymouth Cres. Gour ... 44 C3
Weymouth Dr. Glasg ... 96 A3
Whamflet Ave. Glasg ... 120 B4
Wharry Rd. Alva ... 4 C4
Whatriggs Rd. Kilmk ... 228 A2
Wheatfield Rd. Ayr ... 238 C4
Wheatfield Rd. Bear ... 75 E1
Wheatholm Cres. Aird ... 103 D1
Wheatholm St. Aird ... 103 D1
Wheatland Ave. Udd ... 161 E4
Wheatland Dr. Lan ... 214 C3
Wheatlandhead Ct. Udd ... 161 E4
Wheatlands Ave. Bon ... 40 A3
Wheatlands Dr. Kilbar ... 111 D2
Wheatlands
Farm Rd. Kilbar ... 111 D2
Wheatlandside. Lan ... 214 C3
Wheatley Cres. Kils ... 60 B4
Wheatley Rd. Salt ... 206 A1
Wheatley Rd. Steven ... 206 C1
Wheatpark Rd. Lan ... 214 C2
Whifflet Ct. Coat ... 122 A3
Whifflet St. Coat ... 122 A2
Whin Ave. Barr ... 134 A2
Whin Hill. E Kil ... 160 A2
Whin Hill Rd. Ayr ... 239 D1
Whin Loan. Kils ... 59 E4
Whin Pl. E Kil ... 160 A3
Whin St. Clyde ... 74 A2
Whinfell Dr. E Kil ... 180 A3
Whinfell Gdns. E Kil ... 180 A3
Whinfield Ave. Pres ... 236 B3
Whinfield Rd. Glasg ... 135 D2
Whinfield Rd. Pres ... 236 A3
Whinhall Ave. Aird ... 102 C1
Whinhall Rd. Aird ... 102 C1
Whinhill Rd. Glasg ... 115 D2
Whinhill Rd. Green ... 46 A2
Whinhill Rd. Pais ... 114 A1
Whinknowe. Ash ... 199 F4
Whinney Gr. Wish ... 165 F2
Whinnie Knowe. Lark ... 184 C1
Whinpark Ave. Hat ... 141 F2
Whinriggs. Stone ... 198 B1
Whins Rd. All ... 10 B4
Whins Rd. Glasg ... 116 B1
Whins Rd. Stir ... 7 D1
Whins Rd. Troon ... 229 F4
Whinwell Rd. Stir ... 2 A1
Whirlie Dr. Hous ... 111 D4
Whirlie Rd. Hous ... 91 D1
Whirlies
Roundabout The. E Kil . 160 A2
Whirlow Gdns. Glasg ... 120 A3
Whirlow Rd. Glasg ... 120 A3
Whistleberry Cres. Ham ... 162 A4
Whistleberry Dr. Ham ... 162 A4
Whistleberry Rd. Ham ... 162 A4
Whistlefield Ct. Bear ... 75 F2
Whitacres Path. Glasg ... 135 D2
Whitacres Rd. Glasg ... 135 D2
Whitburn St. Glasg ... 118 C4
White Ave. Dumb ... 50 A2
White Cart Rd. Pais ... 113 F4
White Craig Rd. Ard ... 205 E2
White St. Ayr ... 236 A2
White St. Clyde ... 94 B4
White St. Glasg ... 96 B1
Whiteadder Pl. E Kil ... 179 E4
Whitecraigs Pl. Glasg ... 96 C4
Whitecrook St. Clyde ... 74 B1
Whitefield Ave. Glasg ... 139 D2
Whitefield Rd. Glasg ... 116 B3
Whitefield Terr. Lennox ... 33 E1
Whiteford Ave. Dumb ... 50 B3
Whiteford Cres. Dumb ... 50 B3
Whiteford Ct. Ham ... 183 E3
Whiteford Pl. Dumb ... 50 B3
Whiteford Rd. Pais ... 114 A1
Whiteford View. Ayr ... 239 E4
Whitegates Pl. Falk ... 41 E2
Whitehall Ave. Pres ... 236 B4
Whitehall St. Glasg ... 116 C4
Whitehaugh Ave. Pais ... 114 A3
Whitehaugh Cres. Glasg ... 135 D2
Whitehaugh Dr. Pais ... 114 A3
Whitehaugh Rd. Glasg ... 135 D2
Whitehill Ave. Aird ... 103 D1
Whitehill Ave. Cumb ... 61 E1
Whitehill Ave. Kirk ... 58 C1
Whitehill Ave. Stepps ... 99 E3
Whitehill Cres. Car ... 187 F2
Whitehill Cres. Dunt ... 74 C4
Whitehill Cres. Kirk ... 58 C1
Whitehill Cres. Lan ... 214 C2
Whitehill Farm Rd. Stepps ... 99 E3
Whitehill Gdns. Glasg ... 118 A4
Whitehill Pl. Stir ... 7 D3
Whitehill Rd. Bear ... 75 E2
Whitehill Rd. Ham ... 162 A3
Whitehill St. Glasg ... 118 A4
Whitehill Street La. Glasg .. 118 A4
Whitehill Terr. Lan ... 214 C2
Whitehills Dr. E Kil ... 180 C4
Whitehills. Ersk ... 73 D1
Whitehills Pl. E Kil ... 180 C4
Whitehills Terr. E Kil ... 180 C4
Whitehirst Park Rd. Kilw ... 207 D2
Whitehope Green. Irvine ... 220 A2
Whitehorse Wlk. E Kil ... 180 A4
Whitehouse Rd. Stir ... 7 E4
Whitehurst. Bear ... 75 E3
Whitekirk Pl. Glasg ... 75 D1
Whitelaw Ave. Glen ... 101 F3
Whitelaw Cres. Hat ... 142 B2
Whitelaw St. Blac ... 107 E1
Whitelaw St. Glasg ... 96 B4
Whitelaw Terr. Twe ... 59 F2
Whitelea Ave. Kil ... 89 E4
Whitelea Cres. Kil ... 89 E4
Whitelea Rd. Kil ... 89 E4
Whitelee Cres. Newt M ... 156 A3
Whitelee. E Kil ... 180 B3
Whitelee Gate. Newt M ... 156 A3
Whitelees Rd. Cumb ... 62 C3
Whitelees Rd. Green ... 46 C1
Whitelees Rd. Lan ... 203 F1
Whitelees Rd. Lan ... 215 E2
Whiteloans. Udd ... 141 D2
Whitemoss Ave. E Kil ... 159 F1
Whitemoss Ave. Glasg ... 136 C2
Whitemoss Gr. E Kil ... 160 A1
Whitemoss
Roundabout. E Kil ... 160 A1
Whitepond Ave. Hat ... 141 F2
Whites' Loan. Lan ... 215 E3
Whitesbridge Ave. Pais ... 113 D3
Whitesbridge Cl. Pais ... 113 D3
Whiteshaw Ave. Car ... 187 E1
Whiteshaw Dr. Car ... 187 E1
Whiteshaw Rd. Law ... 187 D2
Whiteside Rd. Pres ... 236 B4
Whiteside Terr. Pres ... 236 B4
Whitestone Ave. Cumb ... 61 D1
Whitevale St. Glasg ... 118 A4
Whitewisp Ct. Irvine ... 220 A2
Whitfield Dr. Ayr ... 236 B2
Whithope Rd. Glasg ... 134 C2
Whithope Terr. Glasg ... 134 C2
Whithorn Cres. Muir ... 80 C2
Whitlawburn Ave. Glasg ... 138 C2
Whitlawburn Rd. Glasg ... 138 C2
Whitlawburn Terr. Glasg ... 138 C2
Whitlees Cres. Ard ... 205 E2
Whitlees Ct. Ard ... 205 F2
Whitletts Ct. Ayr ... 236 C1
Whitletts Rd. Ayr ... 236 B1
Whitriggs Rd. Glasg ... 134 C2
Whitslade St. Glasg ... 100 A1
Whitsun Dale. E Kil ... 159 E2
Whittagreen Ave. Holy ... 143 E2
Whittagreen Cres. Holy ... 143 E1
Whittagreen Ct. Holy ... 143 E2
Whittingehame Dr. Glasg ... 96 A3
Whittingehame La. Glasg ... 95 F3
Whittington St. Coat ... 122 A3
Whittle Pl. Irvine ... 219 F1
Whittle Rd. Ayr ... 236 B2
Whittlemuir Ave. Glasg ... 136 C2
Whitton Dr. Glasg ... 136 C2
Whitton St. Glasg ... 96 B4
Whitworth Dr. Clyde ... 74 A1
Whitworth St. Glasg ... 97 D3
Whyte Ave. Glasg ... 138 C3
Whyte Ave. Irvine ... 219 E1
Whyte Cnr. Dumb ... 50 C1
Whyte St. East ... 127 F3
Wick Ave. Aird ... 122 C2
Wickets The. Pais ... 114 A2
Wickham Ave. Newt M ... 156 B3
Wide Cl. Lan ... 215 D2
Wigton Ave. Newt M ... 156 B4
Wigtoun Pl. Cumb ... 62 A2
Wildcat Rd. W Kil ... 190 A2
Wilderness The. Air ... 14 B2
Wildman Rd. Wish ... 187 D4
Wilfred Ave. Glasg ... 95 E4
Wilkie Cres. Lark ... 185 D1
Wilkie Loan. Hat ... 142 A4
Wilkie Rd. Udd ... 141 D3
William Booth Pl. Stir ... 7 D2
William Dr. Ham ... 183 E4
William Mann Dr. Newt M ... 156 B2
William St. Coat ... 122 A3
William St. Dunt ... 74 A3
William St. Glasg ... 116 C4
William St. Green ... 46 A3
William St. Ham ... 162 A3
William St. Helen ... 16 B1
William St. John ... 111 F2
William St. Kilmk ... 222 C1
William St. Kils ... 60 B4
William St. P Glasg ... 47 D1

William St. Pais 113 E2
Williamfield Ave. Stir 7 D2
Williamfield Gr. Irvine 219 D2
Williamfield Pk. Irvine 219 D2
Williamsburgh Terr. Pais ... 114 A3
Williamson Ave. Dumb 50 A2
Williamson Ave. Falk 24 A1
Williamson Dr. Helen 16 C1
Williamson Pl. Falk 42 B4
Williamson Pl. John 112 A1
Williamson St. Clyde 74 A2
Williamson St. Falk 42 A2
Williamwood Dr. Glasg 138 C1
Williamwood Pk. Glasg 136 C1
Willie Mair's Brae. Kilmk .. 223 D1
Willie Ross Pl. Kilmk 223 E2
Willison's La. P Glasg 47 E1
Willock St. Kilmk 227 F3
Willockston Rd. Troon 229 D3
Willoughby Dr. Glasg 95 F3
Willoughby La. Glasg 95 F3
Willow Ave. Bish 98 A4
Willow Ave. John 112 B1
Willow Ave. Kirk 79 E3
Willow Cres. Coat 122 A2
Willow Ct. E Kil 180 A3
Willow Dr. Aird 123 E4
Willow Dr. Bank 38 C1
Willow Dr. John 112 A1
Willow Dr. M of C 58 D3
Willow Gdns. Irvine 219 F3
Willow Gr. Holy 143 D3
Willow La. Glasg 119 D1
Willow La. Troon 229 E2
Willow Pk. Ayr 239 E2
Willow Pl. John 112 A1
Willow Pl. Tan 141 E4
Willow Rd. Kilmk 227 E4
Willow St. Glasg 95 F4
Willow Way. Ham 162 C1
Willowbank Cres. Glasg 96 C1
Willowbank Gdns. Klrk 79 E4
Willowbank. Lark 185 D3
Willowburn St. Glasg 96 C1
Willowburn Rd. Beith 170 C4
Willowdale Cres. Glasg 120 A2
Willowdale Gdns. Glasg 120 A2
Willowford Rd. Glasg 135 D2
Willows The. E Kil 158 C4
Willows The. Tull 4 A1
Willowyard Rd. Beith 170 C4
Wills Rd. Ayr 236 B1
Wilmot Dr. Wish 165 E4
Wilmot Rd. Glasg 95 E3
Wilsgait St. Cle 144 B2
Wilson Ave. Den 21 E1
Wilson Ave. Irvine 219 D2
Wilson Ave. Lin 112 A3
Wilson Ave. Troon 230 A1
Wilson Dr. Bann 7 E3
Wilson Dr. Falk 41 E3
Wilson Gdns. Falk 41 E3
Wilson Pl. Bon 40 A2
Wilson Pl. Dund 225 F1
Wilson Pl. E Kil 160 A2
Wilson Pl. Newt M 156 B2
Wilson Rd. Alla 167 D4
Wilson St. Aird 122 C4
Wilson St. Alex 27 F3
Wilson St. Ayr 236 A1
Wilson St. Beith 150 B1
Wilson St. Coat 122 B4
Wilson St. Glasg 117 E4
Wilson St. Ham 162 A3
Wilson St. Lark 185 D1
Wilson St. Mother 163 F4
Wilson St. P Glasg 47 E1
Wilson St. Pais 113 E2
Wilson St. Ren 94 B2
Wilton Crescent La. Glasg . 96 C2
Wilton Dr. Glasg 96 C2
Wilton Rd. Car 202 A4
Wilton St. Coat 101 E1
Wilton St. Glasg 96 C2
Wiltonburn Path. Glasg 135 D2
Wiltonburn Rd. Glasg 135 D2
Wilverton Rd. Glasg 95 F4
Winburne Cres. Ham 162 B2
Winchester Ave. Den 21 F2
Winchester Dr. Glasg 96 A3
Windelstraw Ct. Irvine 220 A2
Windermere E Kil 179 F3
Windhill Cres. Glasg 136 A3
Windhill Pl. Glasg 136 A3
Windhill Rd. Glasg 136 A3
Windlaw Ct. Glasg 137 E1
Windlaw Gdns. Glasg 136 C2
Windlaw Park Gdns. Glasg .. 136 C2
Windlaw Rd. E Kil 158 B4
Windlaw Rd. Glasg 137 E1
Windlaw Rd. Ham 162 B2

Windmill St. Salt 216 C4
Windmillhill St. Mother 163 F3
Windrow Terr. Wish 165 E4
Windsor Ave. Falk 41 F2
Windsor Ave. Newt M 156 C3
Windsor Cres. Clyde 74 A2
Windsor Cres. John 112 A1
Windsor Cres. Pais 114 A3
Windsor St. Car 187 F1
Windsor Dr. Duni 21 E2
Windsor Dr. Falk 41 F2
Windsor Dr. Glenm 102 C2
Windsor Gdns. All 9 F4
Windsor Gdns. Falk 41 F2
Windsor Gdns. Ham 162 A3
Windsor Path. Lark 185 E1
Windsor Pl. Shot 146 C3
Windsor Pl. Stir 7 D4
Windsor St. Men 3 F3
Windsor St. Shot 146 C3
Windsor Terr. Glasg 97 D1
Windsor Wk. Tan 141 D4
Windward Pk. Ayr 239 D1
Windward Rd. E Kil 159 D1
Windy Yetts. Twe 59 F2
Windyedge
and Hareshaw Rd. Chap 144 B2
Windyedge Cres. Glasg 95 E3
Windyedge Pl. Glasg 95 E3
Windyhill Pk. Eagle 157 F1
Windyridge. Ham 162 C1
Windyridge Pl. Udd 161 E4
Winehouse Yett. Dund 225 F1
Winfield Ave. Glasg 138 C4
Wingate Ave. Dalry 191 D4
Wingate Cres. E Kil 160 B2
Wingate Dr. E Kil 160 B2
Wingate Pk. E Kil 160 B2
Wingate St. Wish 165 D2
Wingfaulds Ave. Dalry 191 D4
Wingfield Gdns. Udd 141 D1
Winifred St. Glasg 98 B2
Winning Ct. Udd 140 C1
Winning Quadrant. Mother .. 164 B2
Winning Row. Glasg 118 B3
Winnipeg Dr. E Kil 180 A4
Winstanley Wynd. Kilw 207 E3
Winston Ave. Pres 236 B4
Winston Cres. Lennox 57 D2
Winston Rd. Helen 17 D1
Wintergreen Dr. E Kil 159 E2
Winton Ave. Eagle 178 C2
Winton Ave. Glasg 136 B1
Winton Ave. Kilw 207 E2
Winton Cir. Salt 216 C4
Winton Cres. Udd 161 E4
Winton Dr. Glasg 96 B3
Winton Gdns. Tan 141 D4
Winton La. Ard 205 E1
Winton La. Glasg 96 B3
Winton Pk. E Kil 159 D1
Winton Pl. Ard 205 E1
Winton Rd. Irvine 219 E3
Winton St. Salt 216 C4
Wirran Pl. Clyde 94 C4
Wishart Ave. Dunt 74 B4
Wishart Dr. Stir 7 E2
Wishart St. Glasg 117 E4
Wishaw High Rd. Cle 165 E4
Wishaw Low Rd. Cle 165 D4
Wishaw Rd. Wish 186 C4
Wishawhill St. Wish 164 C2
Wisner Ct. Glasg 138 C3
Wisteria La. Car 201 F4
Wiston St. Glasg 139 F3
Witch Rd. Kilmk 222 C1
Witches Linn. Ard 205 D2
Witchill Pl. Kilmk 222 C1
Witchknowe Ave. Kilmk 227 F2
Witchknowe Ct. Kilmk 227 F3
Witchknowe Rd. Kilmk 227 F3
Witchwood Ct. Coat 101 E1
Woddrop St. Glasg 118 A1
Wolcott Dr. Udd 161 D4
Wolfe Ave. Newt M 156 B4
Wolfe Rd. Falk 42 B2
Wolseley St. Glasg 117 E2
Wood Aven Dr. E Kil 159 E2
Wood Avens. Tull 4 A1
Wood Cres. Falk 207 F2
Wood Cres. Mother 142 B1
Wood Farm Rd. Glasg 136 A1
Wood Gr. Irvine 220 B1
Wood La. Bish 98 B4
Wood Pk. Ayr 239 D2
Wood Pl. Strath 31 D2
Wood Quadrant. Clyde 94 C4
Wood Rd. Troon 229 D1

Wood St. Aird 103 E1
Wood St. Coat 121 F4
Wood St. Glasg 118 A4
Wood St. Green 45 E4
Wood St. Kilw 207 F2
Wood St. Mother 163 F4
Wood St. Pais 114 A2
Wood View. Holy 143 D3
Woodbank Cres. John 111 F1
Woodbank Cres. Newt M 157 F3
Woodbank Ct. Alex 27 E4
Woodbank Gdns. Alex 27 E4
Woodbank Rd. Cross 221 F1
Woodburn Ave. Aird 122 C3
Woodburn Ave. Bonh 28 A4
Woodburn Ave. Kilw 207 F2
Woodburn Ave. Udd 161 F4
Woodburn Cres. Bon 39 F2
Woodburn Dr. All 9 F4
Woodburn Gdns. Falk 42 C3
Woodburn Pl. Hous 111 F4
Woodburn Rd. Beith 171 E4
Woodburn Rd. Falk 42 B3
Woodburn Rd. Glasg 136 B3
Woodburn Rd. Holy 143 E4
Woodburn St. Falk 42 C3
Woodburn St. Mother 163 F4
Woodburn Terr. Lark 185 E1
Woodburn Way. Alva 5 D3
Woodburn Way. Cumb 61 E1
Woodburn Way. Miln 55 D1
Woodcroft Ave. Glasg 95 F2
Woodvale. Mother 163 E2
Woodend Ct. Glasg 119 F1
Woodend Dr. Glasg 95 F3
Woodend Dr. Pais 114 B2
Woodend Gdns. Glasg 119 E1
Woodend La. Glasg 95 F3
Woodend Oval. Coy 209 F4
Woodend Pl. John 112 A1
Woodend Rd. Ayr 239 D1
Woodend Rd. Car 188 A1
Woodend Rd. Glasg 119 F1
Woodend Rd. Glasg 120 A1
Woodend St. Helen 16 A1
Woodfield Ave. Ayr 236 A3
Woodfield Ave. Bish 98 A4
Woodfield Cres. Ayr 236 A2
Woodfield Dr. Aird 103 E1
Woodfield Rd. Ayr 236 A2
Woodfield. Tan 141 E3
Woodfoot Pl. Glasg 135 D2
Woodfoot Quadrant. Glasg ... 135 D2
Woodfoot Rd. Glasg 135 D2
Woodhall Ave. Calder 123 D1
Woodhall Ave. Coat 121 F2
Woodhall Ave. Ham 162 A2
Woodhall Ave. Holy 142 C3
Woodhall
Cottage Rd. Calder . 123 E1
Woodhall Mill Rd. Calder . 123 D1
Woodhall Pl. Coat 121 F2
Woodhall Rd. Calder 123 D1
Woodhall Rd. Car 201 E1
Woodhall Rd. New 165 F2
Woodhall St. Chap 123 E1
Woodhall St. Glasg 118 A1
Woodhall Terr. P Glasg 69 D4
Woodhead Ave. Cumb 81 F4
Woodhead Ave. Klrk 79 E4
Woodhead Ave. Udd 161 D2
Woodhead Cres. Ham 183 D4
Woodhead Cres. Tan 140 C4
Woodhead Ct. Cumb 81 F4
Woodhead Gdns. Ham 162 A4
Woodhead Gr. Cumb 81 F4
Woodhead Pl. Cumb 81 F4
Woodhead Rd. Glasg 135 D3
Woodhead Rd. Muir 100 A3
Woodhead Terr. Muir 100 A4
Woodhead View. Cumb 81 F4
Woodhill Cres. Irvine 220 A3
Woodhill Gr. Bish 98 B4
Woodhill Pl. Kilm 222 A3
Woodhill Rd. Blac 107 D2
Woodhill Rd. Glasg 98 B4
Woodhill Rd. Kilm 222 A3
Woodholm Ave. Glasg 137 D3
Woodhouse St. Thorn 158 A3
Woodhouse St. Glasg 95 F4
Woodilee Cotts. Kirk 79 F4
Woodilee Rd. Holy 143 F2
Woodilee Rd. Kirk 79 F3
Woodland Ave. Aird 123 E4
Woodland Ave. Klrk 79 D4
Woodland Cres. Eagle 178 B3
Woodland Cres. Glasg 139 E2
Woodland Gdns. E Kil 158 B4
Woodland Gdns. Ham 162 C1

Woodland Pl. Ard 205 E2
Woodland Terr. Lark 185 E1
Woodland Way. Cumb 62 A2
Woodland Way. Den 39 E4
Woodlands Ave. Irvine 219 E2
Woodlands Ave. Law 187 D3
Woodlands Ave. Muir 100 C3
Woodlands Ave. Udd 141 D2
Woodlands Ave. Ayr 239 D2
Woodlands Cres. Falk 42 A2
Woodlands Cres. Glasg 135 C2
Woodlands Cres. Udd 141 D2
Woodlands Ct. Alex 27 E4
Woodlands Dr. Glasg 135 F1
Woodlands Dr. Coat 101 E3
Woodlands Dr. Holy 142 C3
Woodlands Dr. Mother 163 E3
Woodlands Gate. Glasg 96 C1
Woodlands Gate. Glasg 135 F2
Woodlands Gr. Kilmk 223 D2
Woodlands Pk. Glasg 135 F2
Woodlands Pl. Kilmk 223 D2
Woodlands Rd. Glasg 96 C1
Woodlands Rd. Holy 143 D3
Woodlands Rd. Mother 163 F2
Woodlands St. Miln 55 D1
Woodlands St. Mother 163 F2
Woodlands St. Pres 236 A4
Woodlands Terr. Glasg 96 C1
Woodlands Terr. Udd 141 D2
Woodlands. The. Hat 142 B2
Woodlea Ave. Aird 123 E2
Woodlea Cres. Cross 221 F1
Woodlea Dr. Glasg 136 B2
Woodlea Dr. Ham 183 E4
Woodlea Pk. N Sau 10 A4
Woodlea Pl. Ayr 239 D1
Woodlinn Ave. Glasg 137 D3
Woodmill Dr. Lennox 57 E1
Woodmill Gdns. Cumb 82 C4
Woodmill Pl. Ayr 236 B4
Woodneuk La. Muir 100 C3
Woodneuk Rd. Glasg 135 D3
Woodneuk Rd. Muir 100 C3
Woodneuk St. Chap 123 E1
Woodneuk Terr. Muir 100 C3
Woodrow Ave. Holy 143 D1
Woodrow Ave. Kil 69 E1
Woodrow Cir. Glasg 116 B2
Woodrow Pl. Glasg 116 B2
Woodrow Rd. Glasg 116 B2
Woods La. Ren 94 B2
Woodside Ave. B of W 90 B1
Woodside Ave. Glasg 136 A2
Woodside Ave. Ham 162 C4
Woodside Ave. Kilmk 227 E3
Woodside Ave. Kils 60 C4
Woodside Ave. Klrk 79 E3
Woodside Cres. Barr 134 B1
Woodside Cres. Bonh 27 F3
Woodside Cres. Glasg 96 C1
Woodside Cres. Newt M 166 A3
Woodside Cres. Pais 113 E2
Woodside Dr. Cam 6 B3
Woodside Dr. Calder 123 D1
Woodside Dr. Newt M 157 F3
Woodside Gdns. Coat 121 E2
Woodside Gdns. E Kil 158 B4
Woodside Gr. Kilmk 227 E3
Woodside La. Kilbar 111 E3
Woodside Pl. Dunlop 195 F4
Woodside Pl. Falk 8 B2
Woodside Pl. Glasg 96 C1
Woodside Pl. Tull 4 A1
Woodside Place La. Glasg . 96 C1
Woodside Rd. All 4 C3
Woodside Rd. Beith 150 A1
Woodside Rd. Cald 106 A2
Woodside Rd. E Kil 158 B4
Woodside Rd. Kilbar 111 E3
Woodside St. Chap 123 E1
Woodside St. Coat 121 E2
Woodside St. Holy 143 E2
Woodside Terr. Clack 10 C2
Woodside Terr. Glasg 96 C1
Woodside Terrace La. Glasg 96 C1
Woodside Wlk. Ham 162 C1
Woodstock Ave. Glasg 116 B1
Woodstock Ave. Kirk 79 F4
Woodstock Dr. Wish 165 E4
Woodstock Pl. Kilmk 222 C1

Woodstock Rd. Green 45 E2
Woodstock Rd. Lan 215 D2
Woodstock St. Kilmk 227 F4
Woodstock Way. Pais 132 C4
Woodstone Ct. Rhu 15 F2
Woodvale Ave. Aird 123 E3
Woodvale Ave. Bear 76 A1
Woodvale Dr. Pais 113 D3
Woodview Dr. Aird 123 D3
Woodview Dr. Hat 142 B4
Woodview La. Aird 123 D3
Woodview Rd. Lark 199 D4
Woodview. Tan 141 E4
Woodview Terr. Ham 161 E2
Woodville Pk. Glasg 116 A3
Woodville St. Glasg 116 A3
Woodwynd. Kilw 207 F2
Woodyard Rd. Dumb 49 F2
Woolyett Pk. Thorn 157 F3
Wooer St. Falk 42 A2
Wordsworth Way. Udd 141 D2
Works Ave. Glasg 139 F3
Workshops. Coat 122 A3
Worsley Cres. Newt M 156 B4
Wotherspoon Dr. Beith 150 A1
Wraes Ave. Barr 134 B2
Wraes View. Barr 133 F1
Wraisland Cres. Bishop 71 F2
Wrangholm Cres. Holy 143 D2
Wrangholm Dr. Holy 143 D2
Wren Ct. Tan 141 F4
Wren Pl. John 131 E4
Wren Rd. Green 45 D2
Wright Ave. Barr 134 A1
Wright St. Falk 42 A3
Wright St. Ren 94 A1
Wright Way. Holy 143 D2
Wrightfield Pl. Ayr 238 C1
Wrightlands Cres. Inch 93 F4
Wyburn Pl. Ayr 236 A2
Wye Cres. Coat 101 E1
Wykeham Pl. Glasg 95 E3
Wykeham Rd. Glasg 95 E3
Wylie Ave. Alex 27 E2
Wylie Ave. Newt M 156 B4
Wylie. E Kil 160 B3
Wylie St. Ham 162 B1
Wylie Rd. Salt 217 D4
Wynd Beatson. Tarr 121 D1
Wynd The. Alva 5 D4
Wynd The. Cumb 62 A3
Wyndford Dr. Glasg 96 B3
Wyndford Pl. Glasg 96 B3
Wyndford Rd. Cumb 62 B4
Wyndford Rd. Glasg 96 B3
Wyndford Terr. Tan 141 D4
Wyndham St. Glasg 96 B2
Wynyard Gn. E Kil 180 A4
Wyper Pl. Glasg 118 A3
Wyvis Ave. Glasg 75 F1
Wyvis Ave. Bear 75 E4
Wyvis Cres. Glasg 94 C4
Wyvis Gdns. Kilmk 228 A2
Wyvis Pl. Glasg 94 C4
Wyvis Pl. Irvine 220 A2
Wyvis Pl. Shot 147 D2
Wyvis Quadrant. Glasg 94 C4
Wyvis Rd. Kilmk 228 A2

Yair Dr. Glasg 115 D3
Yardley Pl. Falk 24 A1
Yardside Rd. Kilm 222 A4
Yarrow Cres. Bishop 72 B1
Yarrow Ct. Glasg 139 E2
Yarrow Gardens La. Glasg . 96 C2
Yarrow Gdns. Glasg 96 C2
Yarrow Pk. E Kil 160 A1
Yarrow Rd. Bish 78 A2
Yarrow Rd. Glasg 137 F4
Yarrow Way. Udd 141 F4
Yate St. Glasg 118 A3
Yerton Brae. W Kil 190 B2
Yetholm Terr. Ham 161 F2
Yett Rd. Holy 143 E2
Yetts Ave. Kil 69 E1
Yetts Cres. Kirk 79 F4
Yetts Hole Rd. Glen 102 A3
Yetts The. Cam 6 B3
Yew Dr. Glasg 98 A2
Yew Pl. John 111 F1
Yew Tree Cres. Ham 162 A2
Yieldshields Rd. Car 189 D2
Yoker Ferry Rd. Glasg 94 C3
Yoker Mill Gdns. Clyde 94 C4
Yoker Mill Rd. Clyde 94 C4
Yokerburn Terr. Clyde 94 B4
Yonderton Pl. W Kil 190 B2
York Dr. Falk 42 B3
York Dr. Glasg 138 B3
York La. Ayr 235 F1
York St. Clyde 94 B1
York St. Falk 42 A3
York St. Glasg 117 D4
York St. Wish 165 D1

York Street La. Ayr

o|s Ordnance Survey

STREET ATLASES

The Ordnance Survey Street Atlases provide unique and definitive mapping of entire counties

Street Atlases available

- **Berkshire**
- Bristol and Avon
- Buckinghamshire
- Cardiff, Swansea and Glamorgan
- Cheshire
- Derbyshire
- **Durham**
- Edinburgh

- East Essex
- West Essex
- Glasgow
- **Greater Manchester**
- North Hampshire
- South Hampshire
- **Hertfordshire**
- East Kent
- West Kent
- **Lancashire**

- Merseyside
- Nottinghamshire
- Oxfordshire
- Staffordshire
- **Surrey**
- East Sussex
- West Sussex
- **Tyne and Wear**
- Warwickshire
- **South Yorkshire**
- **West Yorkshire**

The Street Atlases are revised and updated on a regular basis and new titles are added to the series. Each title is available in three formats and as from 1996 the atlases are being produced in colour. All the atlases contain Ordnance Survey mapping.

The series is available from all good bookshops or by mail order direct from the publisher. However, the order form on the following pages may not reflect the complete range of titles available so it is advisable to check by telephone before placing your order.

Payment can be made in the following ways:

By phone *Phone your order through on our special Credit Card Hotline on 01733 371999 (Fax: 01733 370585). Speak to our customer service team during office hours (9am to 5pm) or leave a message on the answering machine, quoting your full credit card number plus expiry date and your full name and address.*

By post *Simply fill out the order form (you may photocopy it) and send it to: Reed Books Direct, 43 Stapledon Road, Orton Southgate, Peterborough PE2 6TD.*

Ordnance Survey **STREET ATLASES ORDER FORM**

NEW COLOUR EDITIONS

	HARDBACK	SPIRAL	POCKET	£ Total
	Quantity @ £10.99 each	Quantity @ £8.99 each	Quantity @ £4.99 each	
BERKSHIRE	0 540 06170 0	0 540 06172 7	0 540 06173 5	➤
	Quantity @ £10.99 each	Quantity @ £8.99 each	Quantity @ £3.99 each	£ Total
MERSEYSIDE	0 540 06480 7	0 540 06481 5	0 540 06482 3	➤
	Quantity @ £12.99 each	Quantity @ £8.99 each	Quantity @ £4.99 each	£ Total
SURREY	0 540 06435 1	0 540 06436 X	0 540 06438 6	➤
	Quantity @ £12.99 each	Quantity @ £9.99 each	Quantity @ £4.99 each	£ Total
DURHAM	0 540 06365 7	0 540 06366 5	0 540 06367 3	➤
GREATER MANCHESTER	0 540 06485 8	0 540 06486 6	0 540 06487 4	➤
HERTFORDSHIRE	0 540 06174 3	0 540 06175 1	0 540 06176 X	➤
TYNE AND WEAR	0 540 06370 3	0 540 06371 1	0 540 06372 X	➤
SOUTH YORKSHIRE	0 540 06330 4	0 540 06331 2	0 540 06332 0	➤
WEST YORKSHIRE	0 540 06329 0	0 540 06327 4	0 540 06328 2	➤
	Quantity @ £14.99 each	Quantity @ £9.99 each	Quantity @ £4.99 each	£ Total
LANCASHIRE	0 540 06440 8	0 540 06441 6	0 540 06443 2	➤

BLACK AND WHITE EDITIONS

	HARDBACK	SOFTBACK	POCKET	£ Total
	Quantity @ £12.99 each	Quantity @ £9.99 each	Quantity @ £4.99 each	
BRISTOL AND AVON	0 540 06140 9	0 540 06141 7	0 540 06142 5	➤
CARDIFF	0 540 06186 7	0 540 06187 5	0 540 06207 3	➤
CHESHIRE	0 540 06143 3	0 540 06144 1	0 540 06145 X	➤
DERBYSHIRE	0 540 06137 9	0 540 06138 7	0 540 06139 5	➤
EDINBURGH	0 540 06180 8	0 540 06181 6	0 540 06182 4	➤
GLASGOW	0 540 06183 2	0 540 06184 0	0 540 06185 9	➤
STAFFORDSHIRE	0 540 06134 4	0 540 06135 2	0 540 06136 0	➤

OS Ordnance Survey STREET ATLASES ORDER FORM

BLACK AND WHITE EDITIONS

	HARDBACK Quantity @ £12.99 each	SOFTBACK Quantity @ £8.99 each	POCKET Quantity @ £4.99 each	£ Total
EAST ESSEX	0 540 05848 3	0 540 05866 1	0 540 05850 5	➤
WEST ESSEX	0 540 05849 1	0 540 05867 X	0 540 05851 3	➤
NORTH HAMPSHIRE	0 540 05852 1	0 540 05853 X	0 540 05854 8	➤
SOUTH HAMPSHIRE	0 540 05855 6	0 540 05856 4	0 540 05857 2	➤
EAST KENT	0 540 06026 7	0 540 06027 5	0 540 06028 3	➤
NOTTINGHAMSHIRE	0 540 05858 0	0 540 05859 9	0 540 05860 2	➤
OXFORDSHIRE	0 540 05986 2	0 540 05987 0	0 540 05988 9	➤
EAST SUSSEX	0 540 05875 0	0 540 05874 2	0 540 05873 4	➤
	Quantity @ £12.99 each	Quantity @ £9.99 each	Quantity @ £4.99 each	£ Total
BUCKINGHAMSHIRE	0 540 05989 7	0 540 05990 0	0 540 05991 9	➤
WEST KENT	0 540 06029 1	0 540 06031 3	0 540 06030 5	➤
WEST SUSSEX	0 540 05876 9	0 540 05877 7	0 540 05878 5	➤

BLACK AND WHITE EDITIONS

	HARDBACK Quantity @ £10.99 each	SOFTBACK Quantity @ £8.99 each	POCKET Quantity @ £4.99 each	£ Total
WARWICKSHIRE	0 540 05642 1	—	—	➤

Name...

Address...

....

....Postcode

◆ Free postage and packing

◆ All available titles will normally be dispatched within 5 working days of receipt of order but please allow up to 28 days for delivery

☐ Please tick this box if you do not wish your name to be used by other carefully selected organisations that may wish to send you information about other products and services

Registered Office: Michelin House, 81 Fulham Road, London SW3 6RB.
Registered in England number: 1974080

I enclose a cheque / postal order, for a **total** of ☐
made payable to *Reed Book Services*, or please debit my

☐ Access ☐ American Express ☐ Visa

account by ☐

Account no ☐☐☐☐ ☐☐☐☐ ☐☐☐☐ ☐☐☐☐
Expiry date ☐☐ ☐☐

Signature...

Post to:
Reed Books Direct, 43 Stapledon Road, Orton Southgate, Peterborough PE2 6TD